The Minor League Milwaukee Brewers, 1859–1952

The Minor League Milwaukee Brewers, 1859–1952

Brian A. Podoll

McFarland & Company, Inc., Publishers
Jefferson, North Carolina, and London

LIBRARY OF CONGRESS CATALOGUING-IN-PUBLICATION DATA

Podoll, Brian A.
    The minor league Milwaukee Brewers, 1859–1952 /
Brian A. Podoll.
        p.   cm.
    Includes bibliographical references and index.

    ISBN-13: 978-0-7864-1455-0
    (softcover : 50# alkaline paper) ∞

    1. Minor league baseball — Wisconsin — Milwaukee — History.
2. Milwaukee Brewers (Baseball team) — History.   I. Title.
GV863.W5P63   2003
796.357'64'0977595 — dc21   2003014384

British Library cataloguing data are available

©2003 Brian A. Podoll. All rights reserved

*No part of this book may be reproduced or transmitted in any form
or by any means, electronic or mechanical, including photocopying
or recording, or by any information storage and retrieval system,
without permission in writing from the publisher.*

Manufactured in the United States of America

Cover image: Milwaukee's first A.A. pennant winners,
with goat mascot, 1913 (Milwaukee Public Library)

McFarland & Company, Inc., Publishers
   Box 611, Jefferson, North Carolina 28640
      www.mcfarlandpub.com

Contents

Acknowledgments	vi
Preface	1
1. From the Mists of the Ancients	3
2. Northwestern by Western	30
3. That Mack Daddy Vibe (or When Irish Eyes Are Winning)	65
4. Last Team Standing	101
5. The Lady Is a Champ	147
6. Borchert's Orchard	189
7. Framed in Black	226
8. Pennants 3, World War II	264
9. From Curtain Call to Wrecking Ball	312
Appendix A: Notes from a Conversation with Bud Selig	337
Appendix B: Milwaukee Baseball Statistics	340
Notes	345
Bibliography	355
Index	357

Acknowledgments

In memory of my late Grandpa, Frank Podoll, and late Dad, Orville Podoll, neither of whom were city men, but for whom good old country hardball was the only real sport. The day ground was broken for Miller Park in Milwaukee was the day my old man was laid to rest in his native Adams County, Wisconsin.

In memory of my late Ma, Dorothy (Fries) Podoll, who wasn't a real baseball fan, but those minor league Milwaukee Brewers represented the good, safe, and still heavily German Milwaukee where she grew up.

May Bud Selig find the same passion to save the Montreals and Minnesotas of the baseball world and may his heir figure out a way to revive the old Brewer tradition of no more than three straight losing seasons. Mr. Selig was kind enough to share some memories for a postscript to this book (Appendix A).

As for the practical thanks in the production of this book, the folks at the Portage (Wisconsin) Public Library, Dawn Foster and her staff of Amy Bedessem, Michelle Hartley, Karen Kappenman, Sheril Lannoye, and Loretta Spychalla, were of great help in keeping the Milwaukee newspaper microfilms via the State Historical Society of Wisconsin in Madison coming and their reader/printer functioning!

Likewise to the ladies at the Ethel Everhard Library in Westfield, Wisconsin, Bridget Donohue, Penny Tolbert, and Amy Beaver: thank you for keeping the library comfortable for research! And I offer a nod to Darryl Brock and authors Bill Ryczek, Marshall Wright, and James Riley.

Additional thanks go to the staff at the Milwaukee Public Library for the access to their outstanding photograph collection, to photograph department intern Amy L. Miles and research associate Russell Wolinsky at the National Baseball Hall of Fame and Museum in Cooperstown, N.Y., and Sarah Johnson at *The Milwaukee Journal Sentinel*.

Preface

Outside Milwaukee's palatial new retractable-roofed Miller Park stand statues of two of the city's baseball heroes, Hank Aaron and Robin Yount. While these two gentlemen actually played on the same ball club, in reality, they represent the two generations of major league baseball with which most Wisconsinites can still identify. The National League Milwaukee Braves of the 1950s–1960s were a phenomenal aberration in the city's overall baseball cosmic continuum. The modern Milwaukee Brewers were actually closer to their roots when they spent their first 29 seasons in the American League.

There was greater familiarity about the rivalries with American League clubs in Minnesota, Kansas City, and Detroit — all cities the minor league Brewers traveled to — than any that awaited the big league Brewers in the National League's Central Division. Baseball has existed in Milwaukee for 143 years. The current generations still wistful over the Eddie Mathews and Warren Spahns, Paul Molitors and Cecil Coopers of the last half-century will learn from this book that their heroes are but a microcosm of a city once a baseball talent hotbed.

The Minor League Milwaukee Brewers pays tribute to all levels of the city's professional baseball before that fateful 1953 day when Lou Perini's Boston Braves hit Beertown. The "Brewers" name was constant from 1894 to 1952. The old "Schnits" even had a black boy mascot, "Snowball." From heroes like Rufus King, the man who brought baseball to Milwaukee, Abner Dalrymple, Cal Broughton, Clark Griffith, Harry Clark, and Buzz Clarkson, to Connie Mack and Connie "Iron Woman" Wisniewski, Unser Choe Hauser and Al Unser, everyone, even Jim Thorpe, gets their Milwaukee props. As 1944 Brewer manager Casey Stengel said, "You could look it up!"

The year 2002 marks the 100th and 50th anniversaries of the Milwaukee Brewers' run in the old Triple-A American Association, with 5 pennants in their last 10 years. As Bob Krause may have played on his organ at Borchert Field, "Roll Out the Barrel!"

1
From the Mists of the Ancients

At least a couple, modern generations of Milwaukeeans have grown up as Yankee-haters. We're talking *New York Yankees* baseball, particularly of the George Steinbrenner variety. Even back in 1957, when the Milwaukee Braves defeated the Mickey Mantle-led Yanks in that season's World Series, comments by New York players made "Bushville's" victory that much sweeter.[1]

Those who have gnashed their teeth at the arrogance of a Reggie Jackson or the sexual misdeeds of a Luis Polonia and Mark Whiten, may foment a belch of consternation at the notion that it was honest-to-goodness Yankees who brought the future National Pastime to Wisconsin's "Gathering Place at the Waters."

Milwaukee, that confluence of the Menomonee, Kinnickinnic, and Milwaukee Rivers at Lake Michigan's shore, may well have once seen its earliest Native Americans play some form of baggataway. That sport, which evolved into the modern game of lacrosse — from which the Wisconsin city La Crosse gets its name[2] — was the game of choice amongst the Potawatomi and other local Algonquian tribal peoples.

Baseball may have been the pioneer of the major American sports, but in early Milwaukee, nearly a handful of sporting organizations predated the burgeoning "National Pastime." Among Scotch immigrants, the Milwaukee Curling Club was formed as a traditional means of whiling away the winter.

The "Cream City's" locale on the Great Lake gave natural rise to the Milwaukee Yacht Club and in this era, the Milwaukee Gun Club also came to be. Most prominent, since the city's population grew to be of 60 percent German immigrants by the 1850s, was the Milwaukee *Turnverein* — the Turners, or gymnastics society.[3] The latter organization would go onto national and even international acclaim by the 1880s.

Suffice it to say there was a vibrant pursuit of athletic endeavors, already during the city's first couple decades. Arising from the frontier trading outpost communities of Juneautown, Kilbourntown, and Walker's Point by 1837, "Milwaukee" became chartered as a city in 1846, two years prior to Wisconsin statehood.[4]

For those of us devoted to Our Great Game, 1846 was also the seminal year of baseball's development. Tossing the 1839 Abner Doubleday "legend" properly out the window, June of 1846 was when the New York Nine took to the Elysian Fields at Hoboken, New Jersey, and thoroughly pasted the New York Knickerbocker Base Ball Club 23–1 on a diamond laid out and umpired over by Alexander Cartwright.[5]

In these days of cable sports channel up-to-the-minute sports tickers and instantaneous news flashes, ponder for a moment just how slow society was back at that time.

Supposedly as early as 1836, a primitive form of baseball was staged in Milwaukee,[6] but as bat-and-ball games go, either cricket, or some form of rounders, town ball, or stool ball may have been enjoyed by young kids.

With migratory Yankees pushing westward, and European immigrants following in their stead, leisure time was at a premium. As early as 1856, a Milwaukee club defeated another from Chicago at cricket,[7] but again, that was *10 years* after the Knickerbockers codified their rules. In this regard, they were the baseball equivalent of their brethren in England, the Marylebone All-Cricket Club.

We are prone, nowadays, at least in sporting terms, to measure decades by the dominant teams of their times. Consider this: It took fully *13 years*, from the time of the Knickerbockers' founding for the game of baseball, under those "National Rules," to reach the "northwestern" outpost of 20,000 called Milwaukee.

For the uninitiated, the explanation for constant references to "Cream City," or future, ball clubs nicknamed "Creams" had absolutely nothing to do with Milwaukee being the largest city in "America's Dairyland." The moniker arose from the many buildings in the city made of that colored brick.[8] The ability to produce bricks of that hue derived from the silt at the bottom of the Menomonee River.

Fortunately, no one ever suggested calling Milwaukee's NBA basketball team the "Bricks," nor to anyone's knowledge did any of the city's earliest practitioners of baseball wave brickbats!

That "base ball" reached the Cream City at all was due in large part to the diligence of New York City–born Rufus King. The grandson of a namesake United States senator and son of the president of Columbia University, *this* Rufus King entered West Point Military Academy at the age of *15* in 1829. As an adult, he would cut his editorial teeth at Albany, New York. That capital city region, around the triumvirate of Albany, Schenectady, and Lansingburgh (Troy) would become one of the early hotbeds for baseball beyond the boundaries of New York City.

In 1845, Rufus King's hankering to move west led him to heed Solomon Juneau's call to take the editorial reins of the *Milwaukee Sentinel* newspaper.[9] The Easterner wasted no time in personifying the role of gentlemanly civic activist. In carrying on that tradition of his forebears, Rufus may have been *King*, but he could not get elected mayor of his adopted city in 1848. Still, in 1859, the then 45-year-old King supplemented his editorial duties by serving as Milwaukee's superintendent of schools.

King and associates from the city's business and professional ranks curiously chose November 30th of that same year to stake out the first of three "base ball" contests in wintry weather. To simply tell locals now that these contests took place at the State Fair Grounds would distort the notion of what that actually meant.

Those grounds, where Abraham Lincoln had delivered a memorable address the year previous,[10] were on old Spring Street (Wisconsin Avenue) hill. Today, it is part of Marquette University's campus.

Much like those Knickerbockers, who cavorted the Elysian Fields, these "base ball" games were the gentlemanly pursuit of middle-aged, mature men. Even though the sport was on the cusp of professionalism, with *wunderkind* fastball pitcher James Creighton[11] supposedly accepting under-the-table pay from the Brooklyn Excelsiors in 1860, baseball was not yet the do-or-die domain of bread-winning young athletes.

Subscriptions to Rufus King's *Milwaukee Sentinel* ran $7.00 for one year, $3.50 for six months, or $1.75 for three months. By comparison, the current, *individual* Sunday edition of the *Milwaukee Journal Sentinel* is $1.75! Sprinkled throughout the news of the day were dispatches of author Washington Irving's death, the chancellor of the state university addressing a gathering of the Teachers' Institute at Spring Street Congregational Church, and ads by the Fox and Wisconsin Improvement Company, offering thousands of acres of choice farm lands!

Overwhelming coverage of all else was the "Black Friday" of December 2, 1859, in Virginia. That state's Governor Wise and U.S. President James Buchanan would be on hand to witness the martyrdom, at a hangman's noose, of abolitionist John Brown.

To insure that no northern reporters would be permitted to record the parting words of the man nicknamed "Ossawatomie," 2,500 state and federal troops were on guard. We don't know if the late Curt Flood would have agreed with this assessment, but the article concluded:

"The bell that tolls for the departing spirit of John Brown will ring the knell of AFRICAN SLAVERY!!."

In a socially charged atmosphere, where the embers of impending civil war were aswirl from Kansas to Virginia, some well-to-do guys in Milwaukee decided the time was right to try playing some ball.

Talk about flying blind! There were no baseball precepts, beyond read-

Lithograph of Rufus King circa 1860. Photograph courtesy of Milwaukee Public Library Local History Collection.

ing the rules, for King and his court to go on. No frame of reference, nothing for the mind's eye. One hundred years before the Milwaukee Braves would lose the National League pennant playoff game to the Los Angeles Dodgers, one hundred years before your writer was born, they had no Hank Aarons or Robin Younts to emulate.

Remember, outside of maybe military training, this may have been the first rudimentary athletic undertaking for any of these civic stalwarts. They had no gloves and used bats of their own gnarly making. They pitched underhanded from 45 feet away.[12]

Whereas any modern batting order might have a fast guy leading off, followed by a fine bunter, social initiative may have dictated Milwaukee's baseball infancy. Whether Rufus King and banker John L. Hathaway were those "fast" leadoff men or even their lineups' best hitters, remains uncertain. What was clear was that to the organizers went the top spot.

They were complete novices, playing in climate conditions that would cancel even the most important World Series 7th game. Nothing would deter Milwaukee's local Yankees from racking up scores that frightfully compare to the modern Brewers' current pitching staff!

Since it took the better part of the 19th Century to perfect any level of fielding teamwork, it's safe to say that Milwaukee's introductory course on diamond competition was something other than 14-karat. What was described in Thursday morning's *Sentinel* of December 1, 1859, as a "very spirited impromptu match" was so impromptu that there were only "six on a side."

With addresses from the city directory, the result[13]:

	1st innings	2nd do.	3rd do.	Total.
*J(ohn) L. HATHAWAY [broker with Charles O. Belden at State Bank Bldg.] home at Jackson and corner of Oneida	0	2	3	5
*F.J. BOSWORTH [H. Bosworth & Sons, wholesale druggists 139 E. Water] home on corner of Division and Milwaukee	4	0	0	4

	1st innings	2nd do.	3rd do.	Total.
*C. STEELE	4	0	3	7
[Atkins, Steele, & White] home 172 Van Buren				
*F. CLARKE	3	2	3	8
[A.F. Clarke, money broker 14 Young's Block] home Prospect near Division				
*L. SEXTON	3	2	3	8
Lester H. Sexton, [Sexton Bros. & Co., dry goods 143 & 145 E. Water] home corner of Marshall & Biddle				
*H. SANDS	1	1	3	5
corner Lyon and Marshall				
*F.J. HILL	1	2	0	3
[H. & J.F. Hill, E. Water, Yellow Warehouse] produce & commercial forwarding boards Hotel Wettstein				
	16	9	15	40

	1st innings	2nd do.	3rd do.	Total.
*R(ufus) KING	2	2	3	7
[editor Daily Sentinel & Supt. of Schools] home 109 Mason				
*Cap. COATE	3	0	3	6
*(William) H. BARCLAY	1	2	0	3
[commercial office Northern Transit Company] boards Newhall House				
*J(edd) P.C. COTTRILL	2(sic)	1	1	5(sic)
Butler, Buttrick, & Cottrill home, corner Oneida and Marshall				
*C(hester) B. ALLEN	2	2	3	7
book-keeper, J.W. Ledyard boards Mann, between Wisconsin and Mason				
*J.(W.) LEDYARD	2	1	3	6
grocer, 161 E. Water home, Wisconsin, between Van Buren and Cass				
*F.H(oratio?) HILL	1	0	1	2
[H. & J.F. Hill] home, corner of Jefferson and Mason				
	13	8	14	35

Unfortunately, no indication was given as to who played which position, or whether there were any extra-base hits, errors, strikeouts, or the like. In showing the winning Hathaway side here first, only runs give us any clue as to the nature of the play. Reality says this game probably resembled a bad match up in a slow-pitch softball beer league.

In the duel between leadoff captains, King appeared to have the better of Hathaway, outscoring him seven runs to five. That advantage did not translate into victory for King's side. With no real measuring stick, as to the quality of their play, the participants' enthusiasm left them hoping for "fair weather" and a rematch that next afternoon. Nearly two weeks later, "fine winter weather" brought this report on Monday, December 12, 1859:

"Friday and Saturday were fine samples of our December weather. The air though cool, was bland, the sunshine brilliant, and everybody abroad enjoying the exhilarating atmosphere. Saturday afternoon, the river was alive with *skates* [emphasis mine] and the Base Ball Club had a spirited game on the Fair Grounds."

It took three weeks for word to reach from Connecticut that a schoolmaster won a verdict for pulling a pupil's hair four years earlier. It took a mere three days for the *Sentinel* to relay the results of the "vigorous" game of "base ball under the national rules," the prior Saturday afternoon. And it occurred only about a mile down the street!

This time, with nine to a side and six innings, the results were still the same. Hathaway was one of three, amongst his charges, to lead the way with five runs in a 33–23 triumph. The Tuesday morning *Sentinel* of December 13, 1859, listed this score from Saturday, December 10th:

King	1	0	0	0		1–2	Hathaway	1	1	1	1	0	1–5
Sexton	1	1	0	0		1–3	Allen		1	0	1	1	1–4
Barclay	1	1	1	1		0–4	Clark	1	1	1	1	1	0–5
Hewitt	1	0	0	1		1–3	Beck		0	1	0	1	1–3
Granberry| 0	0	1	1		1–3	Bagnall		1	0	1	0	0–2
Fitch	1	0	1	1		1–4	[Coate?]	1	1	1	1	0	1–5
Hempsted			0	1		0–1	Gardner			1	1	1	0–3
Ledyard				1		1–2	Steele		0	1	1		1–3
Chandler				1		0–1	Bosworth		0	1	1		1–3
						23							33

In the case of these expanded, actual "nines," it appears that Chauncey P. Hewitt, a clerk at G.P. Hewitt & Sons hardware and stoves, who lived 154 Van Buren, joined the fray for King's side. Likewise did G.L. Granberry, a boarder at Newhall House, and music store proprietor H.N. Hempsted. His store was a couple doors down from the Hewitt concern at 173 E. Water, but he also boarded at Newhall.[14]

The Newhall House must've been the hangout for baseball enthusiasts, as it also supplied one addition for Hathaway's nine. Benjamin Bagnall, of the lumber concerns Bagnall & Company & A. Warren Phelps at Clybourn and the corner of W. Water was that man. Howard C. Gardner was a bookkeeper, who resided at 312 Jackson. It is unknown whether he swung a nightstick at the plate, but "Beck" was Chief of Police William Beck, his home at 437 Jefferson.

Nearly all these men lived in what would now be Milwaukee's Downtown near East Side. Today, that area is exclusively a commercial district.

Four days after that score was printed amongst ads informing buyers of the new "Yankee Fire Kindler" to "strike for your firesides and your homes," and Hartford, Connecticut's Aetna Insurance Company proclaiming "cash capital $1,000,000" were nuggets such as these:

"PERSONAL — It gave us pleasure to meet in the city, yesterday the portly form and good-natured countenance of Judge Hoen of Madison. The Judge wears the ermine of the county of 'old Dane' as gracefully and worthily as his best friends anticipated he would."

"TELEGRAPH! The Hanging of 3 Negroes at Charleston, S.C. was witnessed by 1,600 persons." A swimming school for women opened in Paris.

"PARADOX — When is a man most down in the world? When he is hard up."

The last of Milwaukee's three pioneer baseball games was announced in the Saturday morning edition of the *Sentinel* December 17, 1859. Players were requested to be on the State Fair ground at "one o'clock punctually." Rufus King and John L. Hathaway each had eleven men in their parties now as J.W. Ledyard and J.B. Lathrop were to serve as umpires.

Hathaway added G.C. Stevens (who didn't play), Norman J. Emmons of Emmons, Van Dyke, & Hamilton law firm, who lived at the southwest corner of Astor and Oneida, and a J.C. Cruise. If debating with umpires would require legal assistance, King was not to be outdone! He stacked his deck with lawyer A.C. May, who resided at the southeast corner of Cass and Oneida, fellow barrister David B. Ogden of Ogden, Brown, & Ogden at 1 & 2 Albany Bldg. (corner of Main and Michigan). David boarded at the corner of Astor and Division. Representing the furniture ware business was G.K. Kimball of Noyes, Flertzheim, & Company at 218 & 220 E. Water, though his home was on Marshall, between Knapp and Ogden.

Strange, that David Ogden should be a mere boarder, yet a street already bore his name.

The "well-contested match" came off as scheduled, but as was cited in the December 20th paper of that Tuesday morn, "The weather was blustering and patches of snow on the ground made it slippery and rather too damp for sharp play." This box score revealed even less than the first two, but Ledyard was the ump, and five innings were played to a side:

J.L. Hathaway	5	R. King	[1?]
C.B. Allen	3	G.L. Granberry	3
J.P.C. Cottrill	6	H.C. Gardiner	4
F.D. Clark	3	A.C. May	5
F.J. Bosworth	6	Capt. Coote	4
W. Beck	7	D.B. Ogden	3
N.J. Emmons	5	W. Barclay	5
H.S. Hempsted	5	Jas. Sexton	4
C. Steele	0	J.K. Kimball	4
Geo. Rockwell	4		
	44		33

Like George Steinbrenner and Ted Turner today, "He who has the gold makes the rules." Well, Police Chief Beck may have wielded the biggest stick in this final contest, but in banker John L. Hathaway's case, he who had the gold also scored the runs!

Local historian Harry H. Anderson, in quoting this same game summary for the summer 1983 wrote, "The last of these pioneer contests ... established the tradition of Milwaukee's indifference to cold weather baseball."[15] Well for the players, maybe. No mention was ever made of spectators at these games, though there had to be at least the strong likelihood of some curious onlookers. If there were, their ghosts will be dancing a celebratory dance atop Miller Park's new roof. As Mr. Anderson cited from another column of that same day, "a furious snowstorm" prevailed by 11 P.M.

Rufus King's reward for introducing "base ball" to the Cream City was to see his side defeated. His thirst for competitive baseball did not end on that cold December day.

Wising up to what time of year the sport was really meant to be played, King and his cohorts put their enthusiasm into the formation of the Milwaukee Base Ball Club, for the spring of 1860. In an irony of titles, King ascended as president that early April.[16]

By the end of that month, King's *Sentinel* carried headlines about the "Terrible Scenes at Rome on Garibaldi's Birthday — Outrages on American Citizens" and trumpeted on its editorial masthead:

> Presidential Election!
> THE GREAT CAMPAIGN
> IS AT HAND!!
> Let Every Republican Prepare
> for the Conflict!!
> Circulate Truth among the People!!

If you think the line between journalism and commerce get blurred today, well not only did King's paper run regularly paid advertisements (e.g., the one column ad for Spalding's Prepared Glue produced by Henry C. Spalding & Company of New York, not Al Spalding of later baseball renown), but an item titled "Schiedam Gin" would tell of the arrival of said product from Rotterdam, to J.W. Ledyard's store. Nothing like greasing the umpire with a little free publicity!

By April 20 and 21, 1860, the Milwaukee Base Ball Club was organizing its membership and scheduling matches to encourage "the public, and ladies especially" to attend. The more things change, the more they stay the same.

More telling of the social disparities of the time was this dispatch from the *Chicago Record:* "SOME TIME SINCE, a Roman Catholic girl stole a lot of silver spoons from a Protestant preacher in whose family she was a servant.

The priest having found the thief, determined to have the spoons sent back, and then ensued a correspondence something like the following-

'To the Protestant preacher — I send your spoons back. If your servant girl had been a Protestant you would never have got them again.' yours catholic priest. 'To the Catholic Priest — I thank you for the spoons. If the girl had been a Protestant she never would have stolen them.' Yours, PROTESTANT PREACHER.[17]

The Milwaukee Base Ball Club practiced the game under the "New York rules" of the Knickerbockers, a team that had attained such popularity across the Northeast. Besides the aforementioned underhand delivery from 45 feet, pitchers were not allowed any jerking motion. Candy Cummings had not yet arrived to develop the curve. Brooklyn's Excelsior hero James Creighton may have faced the damnation of both the priest and the preacher, because he fudged all of that with his velocity and sleightest of hand.[18] Though pitchers stood that close, the offensive counter-measure was that bats could be any length, but their diameter could be no more than three-and-a-half inches. Just try and determine the "sweet spot" on one of the unwieldy, knotted, and lathe-marred "wagon tongues" of the time! The weights and sizes of these bats could support birlers from the Wisconsin northwoods! Another rule, that lasted over another 20 years, was that the batsman could call for a high or low pitch, depending upon the preference of his ability.[19]

This method of baseball evolution, coupled with the calamitous task of barehanded fielding, made double-digit scoring by both sides a commonality. If batboys had been in use back then, "Timber!" might have been their rallying cry just to avoid decimation.

Throughout the spring of 1860, there were regular newspaper notices for base ball practices and games, wherein the members were to meet at the corner of Main and Wisconsin and be "conveyed by Davis' omnibus" to the Spring Street Hill grounds, ten minutes prior. Rufus King even used the bully pulpit of his print to chastise a challenge from the Janesville (Wisc.) Base Ball Club.

Apparently, that outfit must've played something more akin to the old town ball rules because the Milwaukees, who had doted upon themselves strictly intramural activities, played by the "new code."[20] The Janesvilles' "good old fashioned game" was in Milwaukee's estimation, a "miserable one," not of the lively, manly, and attractive form calculated to develop skill or excite interest. With two large clubs "in full blast" and more coming, the best Milwaukee would offer is a compromise of rules to Janesville.

This was 1860 mind you, and already statements were appearing that said, "it is sufficient to know that Americans are too highly strung." Maybe it came from watching intramural scores like 33 to 27, or 27 to 26? Maybe it was from smoking "segars"? Maybe it was John L. Hathaway's ad, that was not just for "Real Estate, Money," but that said he was a "Collection Agency," too? If J.W. Ledyard's Schiedam Gin wasn't enough to sooth the populace's senses, maybe

June 13th word that he was in New York and "kindly forwarded for the use of our Milwaukee Base Ball Club, six bats and twelve balls, made in New York, according to the National Association of Base Ball Clubs" would.[21]

Being the good sport that he was, Rufus King didn't let just baseball dominate his pages. In fact, on June 20th, he ran this:

> CRICKET — We hear that a lively game of Cricket was played at LATTON'S, on the Janesville Plank Road, last Saturday afternoon. Why do not our Englishmen and others in our city, who are fond of this manly game, get up a Cricket Club? We used to have a capital one here; and gave our Chicago neighbors several good beating with it.

Whether this served as any impetus or not, by August 6, 1860, a special meeting of the Milwaukee Base Ball Club was called at C.B. Allen's on Main Street "to set upon the challenge" of the Chicago Base Ball Club. Attendance must not have been very good, or deliberation was indeed deep, because the meeting notice was repeated the next day.

Rufus King was nothing if not competitive. Not content to just field all comers on the baseball grounds, he also took on his competitors in the press. August 8th's *Sentinel* demonstrated thusly:

> THE WISCONSIN is publishing a highly interesting and long-winded batch of nonsense which is entitled *Shambuzzywuzzy*.— Whether the editor of that paper intends to try himself at a higher order of literature, or is only amusing himself during the hot weather, we know not. If the readers of *The Wisconsin* can stand it, we ought to.

The larger events, that would consume the entire nation, devoured friendly rivalries of all stripes, and the existence of that first Milwaukee BaseBall Club was among the casualties. The November 1860 election of Abraham Lincoln to the presidency ignited Confederate guns at Fort Sumter, South Carolina. Rufus King had originally supported close friend Senator William Seward for the republican nomination, but once Lincoln earned the call, King was unabashed in his support of "Honest Abe." Before baseball fans could ever remember Fleet Walker, celebrate Jackie Robinson, or enjoy the likes of Buck O'Neill and Hank Aaron, the United States would have to endure this first and bloodiest phase of social regurgitation.

America's Civil War would dry up any real baseball activity in Milwaukee. However, by the spring of 1861, a surprising number of the city's baseball pioneers volunteered to receive their military baptism with drills on the old Fair Grounds baseball field.[22] That Spring Street site was re-christened Camp Scott, and some of Milwaukee's citizen-soldiers marched on to serve in Wisconsin's famous Iron Brigade. In fact, their first commanding officer was none other than Brigadier General Rufus King.[23] King had been in personally poor finances, and once William Seward became Lincoln's secretary of state, King was to be appointed minister to the Papal States at Rome. Like everything else, the war led to incredible twists of fate, not the least of which would be Rufus King crossing paths with none other than Abner Doubleday. Yes, that Abner Doubleday! In a conference debate of generals in Virginia, King had to decide whether to move his brigade from Centreville onto Manassas. Of the three other generals on the scene, Doubleday was said to be "sullen and silent" offering no insight as to what course of action to take. The subject of baseball was not an icebreaker in this situation.[24] Since the sport's inception, baseball's popularity has increased during wartime. Unlike the imperial Japanese of World War II, who loved the game, but were forced to de-Americanize its terminology, Confederate soldiers couldn't resist its allure after deriding it as some Yankee conspiratorial concoction.

Within one year after the War Between the States ended, organized baseball players under the aegis of the National Association, grew in representation from over 100 clubs in 1866 to nearly 240 in 1867. Its preeminence as "The National Pastime" was truly taking off.[25]

Amongst the Wisconsin affiliates of the National Association was the Cream City Base Ball Club of Milwaukee. Henry H. West, whose name still lives on as the office supplies firm of H.H. West in the metro area, served as the first president. This Cream City nine was organized in October 1865: and in Midwest regional competition, it rose to an amateur standing of the upper echelon.[26]

Unlike Rufus King's middle-aged pursuers of recreational activity, the new club boasted young men of a more athletic incline in their late teens and early twenties. That ability served them well in inter-city contests.

A return to normality allowed the Camp Scott site of the old Fair Grounds to be revitalized by the Cream City club. After two seasons there, the nine chose in 1867 to relocate near the lakefront. Meat packer and hotelier John Plankinton advanced the financial support to remake another former Civil War site, known as Camp Reno or Camp Sigel, into an enclosed field. It was in Plankinton's interest to promote this development. As owner of the city's only horse-drawn streetcar line, it ran to the vicinity of the Prospect Avenue field.[27]

Baseball business was so good by 1868 that the gate receipts repaid Plankinton's advance. Baseball has been the historical, economic model for all major American team sports, and Plankinton's venture with the Cream City club was no exception. The concessionaire's contract for 1870 required him to erect the team's clubhouse and acceptably maintain the grounds. In return, Plankinton held an exclusive right to sell refreshments at the games.[28]

The Cream City nine laid no bricks, by any means, on the diamond either. By February, 1868, the Grain Exchange proudly displayed the Milwaukee club's trophies and awards from 1866 and 1867. This success came at the expense of other Wisconsin clubs and its tournaments at Chicago and Rockford, Illinois. Madison, Janesville, and Beloit could put up their best, but it was to no avail. The Milwaukees would lose only one game in intrastate play during that period.

A home field advantage certainly didn't serve the Cream City against one of baseball's early marquee road shows. Anchored in the pitcher's box by future Hall of Famer Al Spalding, the Forest City team of Rockford rocked Milwaukee 24–10 at the Prospect Avenue grounds. The equalizer came at Rockford later that season with the Cream City squeezing out a 14–13 victory. This "wonderfully small score at the time" placed Milwaukee third in a ten-team tournament.[29]

The line between amateur and professional status of players was rapidly eroding in this post-Civil War boom. No one as yet had the audacity to outfit an entirely professional ensemble. Players like Dickey Pearce of the Brooklyn Atlantics, who invented the bunt and at 5'3" put the "short" into refining shortstop play, second baseman Al Reach of the Philadelphia Athletics, or Jewish outfielder/lefty second baseman Lip Pike, "the Iron Batter" and Mickey Mantle of his era, all thrust the veneer of indecency off the concept of play for pay.[30]

Under the table remuneration, or stashing away stars into bogus, off-field jobs, was giving way to the allure of garnering large, paying crowds on the road. Eastern clubs, like National of Washington and those same Atlantics, cashed in.

Milwaukee's Cream City nine established their credentials against the best of the Midwestern amateurs, but when the *Milwaukee Sentinel* devoted part of their Saturday, June 20th front page to biographical sketches of their newly-arrived competitors, "the Atlantic Nine," the days of innocence were over. The Brooklyn club was a mostly pro contingent that had dominated the sport throughout most of the 1860s. Besides Dickey Pearce, a model hitter whose "fiery temperament" detracted little from his greatness, the Atlantics' lineup was dotted with standouts like pioneer switch-hitting catcher/3rd baseman Bob "Death to Flying Things" Ferguson, "Old Reliable" lefty-hitting 1st baseman Joe Start, pitcher/outfielder George "the Charmer" Zettlein, and last, but certainly not least, a future Milwaukee manager, outfielder Jack Chapman.

Anticipation for this 1868 duel was such that the *Sentinel* carried a June 17th dispatch under "THE NATIONAL GAME" of the Atlantics' 18–15 defeat by the Niagaras of Buffalo. Under the classified advertising of "amusements," admission prices for the great contest at the Cream City Grounds were 25 cents, or 50 cents for carriages. The Tuesday morning *Sentinel* of June 23, 1868, gave this remarkable, inning-by-inning recount, from the previous day's game:

ATLANTICS VS. CREAM CITY
The Great Match at Camp Reno

A more glorious day than yesterday could scarcely have been chosen for the playing of a match at the national game. The sun had been showering its sultry rays on the hot streets since noon, but as the time approached for the beginning of the contest clouds began to rise in the sky, and at three o'clock the sun was partially obscured with great banks of vapor, throwing shadows which covered the grounds at intervals throughout the playing.

The Atlantics were received with enthusiasm as they stepped from their carriages, and little time was lost before the game began, the Cream City going to bat precisely at three o'clock.

[Lineups for both clubs were given here.]

All seemed in perfect condition for the combat, the pure lake breezes acted like wine in its exhilerating influence on the athletes; and yet there appeared to be a little nervousness among our boys — a consciousness that they were going into a fight with the odds against them, and when the Cream City went out without having made a run, the hope of winning had certainly grown no stronger, and the Atlantics made six consecutive runs, from Pearce to Ferguson inclusive, before MacDonald was out on a foul, and Zettlein and Pearce on flies, leaving Pratt on the 3rd base when his side went out, and the Cream City went to bat...

SECOND INNINGS

Here Clarence Smith took the bat, and sent the ball flying among the carriages, while he made a run which assured his return home. His successors were not so fortunate, and no other run was made by our club. Smith, of the Atlantics, sent out a fly, which was finely caught by Sweet, and Start got home — The only run made by the Atlantics. This result was cheering to the Cream City, who had now recovered confidence, and Sweet took the bat at the...

THIRD INNINGS

Wood was gradually getting around when Larkin sent the ball whizzing out of reach securing three runs for the Cream City. The Atlantics made two runs during this innings.

FOURTH INNINGS

The Cream City here made the score of a cypher, Wells going out on a foul, and Sweet and Wood on flies. Start went out on the Atlantics, to begin with, Larkin took a fly finely from Pratt, and Zettlein finished their business after they had got seven runs.

FIFTH INNINGS

In this innings the Cream City made two runs and the Atlantics five.

SIXTH INNINGS

Crane took a fly handsomely from Wells, and Sweet, having been forced from the first base by a bat of Woods, the two latter were out, and the Cream City retired to field without having made a run. The Atlantics now began to show their peculiar mettle, and made eleven runs, in the course of which Norris took two beautiful and difficult flies, eliciting enthusiastic cheers from the audience.

SEVENTH INNINGS

Runs were made by Norris, Smith, and McFayden, and on going to field, Hooley and Wells exchanged positions. The Atlantics made six runs, before resigning the bat.

EIGHTH INNINGS

Goose egg for the Cream City. Atlantics made twenty-four, including a home-run by Chapman, with so much fine play as makes it impractical to particularize.

NINTH INNINGS

... a score of four for the (sic) Cream City and five for the Atlantics, giving the game to the latter by 67 to 13.

After the game was over a throwing match came off between the contending clubs for a purse of $23, Redlington's throw of 336 feet being the best. Messrs. Chapman's and Smith's throws were respectively 319 feet 9 inches and 310 feet.

We have omitted mention of much fine playing from want of space, and the account of the game here given will undoubtedly seem meager to its admirers. The Cream City have done about all they expected to do, and are rather jubilant than otherwise over their defeat, for which there is no reason to the contrary. The Atlantics are professionals who make base ball their whole business and study from one year to another. The Cream City Club is composed of amateurs who spend only the leisure they can borrow from their business to indulge in this recreation. As amateurs they play well, and it is not desirable that men who have capacities for more effective work in life should devote themselves entirely to the one object of manipulating a ball and bat. We have all every reason to be satisfied.

The following is the score: [addresses again via city directory]

CREAM CITY	O	R	ATLANTICS	O	R
(J.H.) Wood, 1.b	5	1	(Dickey) Pearce, s.s.	5	5
(Martin, jr.) Larkin, c.f.	2	2	(Charlie) Smith, 3.b	6	5
lawyer room 16 library bldg.			(Joe) Start, 1.b.	2	8
Wisconsin, n.e. cor Main,			(Jack) Chapman, l.f.	5	6
res. 417 Spring			(Fred) Crane, 2.b.	3	8
(George) Redlington, c.	4	1	(Dan) McDonald, c.?f.	0	11
railroad clerk or conductor,			(Bob) Ferguson, c.	1	10
res. 443 Jefferson			(Al) Pratt, p.	2	7
(Charles S.) Norris, l.f.	3	1			
clerk, G.D. Norris & Company,			(George) Zettlein, r.f.	3	7
shipchandlers & sailmakers —				27	67
19 & 21 Erie,bds. 566 Van Buren					
(Clarence) Smith, p.	0	4			
clerk, Munn & Layton cattleyard,					
bds. n.s. Hinman near Clermont					
(Archie) McFayden, s.s.	2	2			
clerk, bds. 218 Grove-later					
doorkeeper, Chamber of Commerce					
(1 of 4 in city) Hooley, 3.b.	3	1			
(E.C.) Wells, r.f.	5	0			
gunsmith, res. 421 Sycamore					
(1 of 3 in city) Sweet, 2.b	3	1			
	27(13)				

INNINGS   1 2 3 4 5 6 7 8 9
Cream City 0 1 3 0 2 0 3 0 4–13
Atlantics   6 1 2 7 5 11 6 24 5–67

PASSED BALLS, Cream City 11, Atlantics 7; CALLED BALLS, Cream City 21, Atlantics 8; PASSED ON CALLED BALLS, Atlantics 3; FLY CATCHES, Cream City 13, Atlantics 12; TIME OF GAME 3½ hours; UMPIRE, M. Treadway, President of Capital City Base Ball Club, Madison; SCORERS, Messrs. Allen and Delaney

So, when subjected to the pummeling by 1867's nominal "National Champions," Milwaukee's pecksniffian attitude towards professional ne'er-do-wells reads like so much hard cheese. Bob Ferguson may have been "Death to Flying Things," by virtue of his soft hands afield, but with his ten runs, the box score revealed just how deadly the switch-hitter could be with the bat and on the basepaths, too.

The verbatim reproduction of this game's coverage is just a treasure chest of sports writing in its infancy. It's surprising to see the term "goose egg" already employed, and note the premium placed upon the ability to catch fly balls, bare-handed. It was a testimony to the growing vitality of baseball that reportage of this match-up dominated the heart of the Milwaukee newspaper's front page. No endorsements, no pre-game shows, no flashy scoreboard intros (no scoreboard for that matter), and yet, the greatness of the Atlantics was lost on no one. Just how far they were, behind the curve, would be demonstrated yet again, to the Cream City.

If the summer of 1868 wasn't exactly the "Summer of Love" of a century later, or even Victorian lust, it certainly had its other diversions. Like the visiting exhibition of three-year-old Sophie Cantz, "the Baby Woman," whose pristine, adult features made her "the most startling curiosity in the annals of time." Perhaps of greater sporting import to local Teutonic patrons, who were also enjoying a "Saengerfest" (singers' festival), would be "entertainment by members of the Milwaukee Gymnasium under direction of Mr. George Brosius" at the Music Hall. Brosius would be the Turnverein's equivalent of Connie Mack—50 years of tutorial leadership.[31]

No sooner were the Cream City able to lick the wounds from their Atlantic shellacking, another Eastern club saw them as a baseball piñata. On Thursday, July 9, 1868, the Milwaukee club received a letter from the "famous Union club of Morrisania, N.Y., the present champions of the United States."

The Unions had ventured from their home, a part of the Bronx near where Yankee Stadium now stands, for a "tour of the West." The challenge went to the Cream City for an August 7th date in Milwaukee and onto Madison the next day, for a match with the Capital Citys.

"It is conceded that the Unions play the finest game of any club in the country, and the Cream City is now going to work in earnest to produce a nine who can and will play together."[32]

To that end, the Milwaukee club challenged Ripon and Janesville for tune-ups, something the July 11th *Sentinel* was "glad to hear that the Cream City is waking up to its business and taking energetic measures for practice, and though we print elsewhere, the challenge from the 'hunkidori', we have to confess that we do not, at all, agree with the sarcastic implications contained therein."

That last bit of folderol was understood only by A.C. Botkin, then editor of the *Sentinel*. General Rufus King had not only been long-departed as the Cream City's voice in print, he served in the war and already returned back to America from a five-year stint as the U.S. minister to the Papal States in Rome. Badgered by an underling as a favorite appointee of close friend Secretary of State William Seward, King earned praise for the extradition of John Surratt. The latter had vanished into the Vatican Guard after his complicity in President Abraham Lincoln's assassination. But for a brief visit back to Milwaukee, the good general was now living his twilight out in Elizabeth, New Jersey.[33]

Without wandering too far astray here, the name "Rufus King" posed a puzzle in constructing this research. In his excellent McFarland book, *When Johnny Came Sliding Home*, author William J. Ryczek lists a "Rufus King" as the centerfielder for the 1868 Cincinnati Red Stockings. Stephen D. Guschov's equally fine McFarland publication on that Porkopolis nine, said King is even mentioned in the team song.

As much as Milwaukee's Rufus King was a baseball enthusiast, he would've been age 54 at the time and was serving as deputy collector of customs for the Port of New York. His poor health, deriving from his wartime experience, had left him nearly an invalid. He would resign his customs post a year later,[34] but it's safe to conclude that he was not the Red Stockings' outfielder.

However, he did have a first cousin in the Rhineland City who bore his same name. This man was as much a fixture in the development of Cincinnati as the general was to Milwaukee, and equally revered in its social circles. But, again, if he had the legs of a centerfielder, he was doing so at the age of 51! One thing is certain, the Cincinnati Rufus King had no offspring, no "junior" playing for the Reds, as it were.[35]

The Cream City amateurs were pursuing the ultimate feather for their collective cap before the Union match. The "goldball" for the state championship was now on the line against Madison's Capital City nine. Why "goldball" was one word, but "base ball" remained two, is anybody's guess.

Botkin's *Sentinel* had no mercy upon the anonymous correspondent, who was flushed out on July 30th. The complainant bemoaned the lack of rousing welcome that the 1867 Cream City goldball triumph produced ... no escort, no speeches, or the like. The paper slyly credited the club for being more manly "than this childish wail would imply," but if they weren't up to holding the honor, "they had much better resign it to some other club."

The Milwaukee players chose to vent this questioning of their virility upon the visiting Capital Citys. Among those vying for the goldball on behalf of the Madison side was catcher John Nichols and leftfielder James Nichols. Whether either or both of these men were related to Hall of Fame pitcher Charles "Kid" Nichols, Madison-born himself, is unclear.

The baseball food chain was such that a July 31st dispatch out of Cleveland noted that the visiting Unions of Morrisania axed the home Forest City club, 25–2.

This made for an uneasy anticipation amongst the Cream City, but even more so for the Madison nine.

The "first match" for the goldball showcased the "pluck and endurance" of the Milwaukee side. The "fine audience" at the Camp Reno grounds, now rechristened "Cream City Park," included visitors from as far away as "St. Louis and other Southern cities."

This August 1st engagement was a mismatch of the same degree that Morrisania had lying in wait. The Cream City showed an aggressiveness on the basepaths that would make recent Brewer manager and former base thief extraordinaire Davey Lopes proud. The stolen base was a newfangled development for the game, having been dared by Philadelphia's Ned Cuthbert.[36] Cream City's leadoff man, first baseman J.H. Wood stole a couple bases, and catcher George Redlington and centerfielder Martin Larkin, jr. also contributed one each. Thanks to a homerun by pitcher Clarence Smith, "who had sent the ball far enough away to have walked, if he wished," Milwaukee had built a 17–2 lead by the fourth inning (the plural was no longer being used).

But for some "magnificent fly catches, which elicited the wildest applause from all who witnessed them," from Capitals' centerfielder Thorpe, Milwaukee pretty much had their way with their neighbors from 80 miles to the west. The 41–15 assault was led by Wood's eight tallies, as well as a stumbling fly catch on his knees, which "created much enthusiasm." Second baseman Charles S. Norris shone in the field, and from his number nine spot in the order, added six scores. Shortstop Archie McFayden's five runs were supplemented by playing well at his position. The Cream City already had a 27–14 lead when they erupted for 14 more runs in the ninth. If another match was played, it is unclear when, but this performance clearly secured the goldball for Milwaukee. This three hour-and-ten minute affair was umpired by yet another Nichols, Mr. A.N. Nichols of the Forest City Club in Rockford.

The minutiae of hubbub about everyday Milwaukee included references to the "Caledonian Games" of Scotch prowess, a visiting troupe of "Ethiopian Minstrels," the invention of "Burnham's Milwaukee Brick Machine," and the proud announcement that the city now had 18 letter carriers. Lurking further inside the newspaper's pages was yet another dispatch from Cleveland, this dated August 2nd: "The Union Club of Morrisania played a match game of base ball with the Railway Unions of this place to-day, which resulted in favor of the former by a score of 43 to 8."

The coming of the Unions did not generate quite the same palpitations nor the lofty front page bios that the Atlantics did, yet a recitation of their eight westward victories gave some premonition of what was to come. In fact, the *Sentinel* observed that this game did not create the level of interest that the Capital City match-up had. The Unions were indeed "the champions of the United States," but the nature of their claim was somewhat different than the outright dominance previously shown by the Atlantics. Because of a competitive structure that gave more weight to the number of series won against top-flight opposition, rather than an outright won-loss record, the Unions won the title.

By the time that August 7th clash would take place, the city's popular skating rink was hosting a *Sommernachtfest* by the Musical Society, a Turners' Convention met at Monroe, Wisconsin, and a certain Civil War hero/1868 presidential candidate was being sized up under this headline:

> GRANT AND THE ISRAELITES
> Views of Our Intelligent Hebrews

An August 4th dispatch from Troy, New York, cited that "4,000 were on the ground" of Rensselaer Park to see the Unions of Lansingburgh subdue Mutual of New York, 22–12. The "National Game" was becoming a staple of summertime news.

Morrisania's Unions did not boast as famous a lineup as the Brooklyn Atlantics, but the core of their success was rooted in three players. Charley Pabor was perhaps the game's first left-handed pitcher of note and bore a nickname that was the curious equal to the Atlantics' Bob Ferguson. Pabor was a light-hearted eccentric, with a chicken-eating superstition of an early-day Wade Boggs, and as such he was "the Old Woman in the Red Cap." His long-time battery mate was his diametric opposite in disposition, but the gnarly "Old Man," catcher Dave Birdsall, somehow made this combo mesh.

Another player of note was rightfielder Esteban "Steve" Bellan, who was the first Cuban to enter the ranks of American professional baseball. It would be great to see that tradition someday renewed, but only after Fidel Castro meets his Maker, someone the former refuses to acknowledge. The Unions' 1868 tour also featured Hall of Fame superstar shortstop George Wright.

Wright's ability to throw ambidextrously from his position and his superlative slugging ability were only part of his repertoire. Like English-born Al Reach in Philly and Illinois' Al Spalding, George Wright's acumen allowed him to eventually also prosper in the sporting goods business.[37]

The August 7th exhibition was affected by very dusty, windy conditions. The paper quoted one Unions' member remark that he "had played ball before, but never in a hurricane." Fielding with dust-encrusted eyes, under a blazing sun caused muffs by both sides. Again, the same tack as with the Atlantics blowout was taken (i.e., the local non-professionals trying their best against the national champions). This match did not precipitate the same inning-by-inning review that did. Despite having George Wright in the heart of the Unions' order, it was Charley Pabor who ruled. Wright garnered nary an individual mention.

> Both the batting and pitching of Pabor were such as to disconcert any player with the least symptoms of nerves, his left hand doing more than yeoman's service in

both branches of business. Indeed the glories of the rest of the nine fade away in comparison with his perplexing pitching, his stealing bases, and his two home runs, with time enough left once to have got around a second time.

Though his nickname is never applied in the article, few things can be worse than being whipped by "the Old Woman in the Red Cap!"

The Cream City boys' lone highlight consisted of catcher Redlington and 2nd baseman Clark running down Morrisania's Henry Austin in a pickle between third and home. "The thing was very neatly performed, and drew forth a tremendous round of applause." Centerfielder Martin Larkin, Jr. distinguished with "two or three fine fly catches" as well.

Goodwill between the clubs was toasted in print, the Unions facing opposition "worthy of their steel," and the Cream City praising their antagonists as fair, gentlemanly, and skillful. The same could not be said for some elements of the audience, which was determined to be the largest of the season. Disappointed, the paper reported, "We should have been still more gratified if the youngsters who made it their business to shriek out orders after the captains of the nines, had been gently removed from the grounds."

Cream City pitcher Clarence Smith was not the equal of Morrisania's Pabor in terms of producing runs, but each was the member of his respective sides not to be put out, a feat repeated by Smith from the Atlantics game.

The score is as follows:

CREAM CITY	O	R	L	F	UNIONS	O	R	L	F
Wood, 1.b.	5	1	0	0	(John) Goldie, 1.b.	4	4	0	1
McFayden, s.s.	3	3	0	2	(Henry) Austin, c.f.	3	5	0	1
Redlington, c.	1	3	1	1	(Al) Martin, 2.b.	5	3	0	0
Clark, 2.b.	4	1	0	0	(Charley) Pabor, p.	0	8	0	0
Larkin, c.f.	4	0	1	2	(George) Wright, s.s.	2	5	1	1
(Wm. H.) Dodsworth, master of transportation, Amer. Exp. Company boards Unoin Depot Hotel	3	2	0	0	(Dave) Birdsall, c.	3	5	0	3
					(Ed) Shelly, 3.b.	3	4	1	0
					(George) Smith, l.f.	4	4	0	1
					(Steve) Bellan, r.f.	3	5	0	0
Smith, p.	0	3	2	1					
Welles, l.f.	3	2	0	2					
Norris, 2.b.	4	1	0	0					
	27	16				27	43		

Innings
Cream City 2 2 0 0 2 2 3 3 2–16
Unions   3 2 3 5 4 2 11 7 6–43

Out on Bases, Cream City 11, Unions 10
Struck out, Cream City 2, Unions 0
Umpire–Mr. Job Tabor, of Endeavor Base Ball Club, of New York

Missed Fly Catches, Cream City 3, Unions 3
Wild Throws, Cream City 4, Unions 3
Passed Balls, Cream City 11, Unions 10
Out on Fouls, Cream City 8, Unions 8
Homeruns, Cream City 0, Unions 2
Time of game–Three hours
Scorers–Messrs. Allen and Lash

Many of the statistics, save for the final score, would point to a relatively

The 1868 Cream City Baseball Club, which lost to the Brooklyn Atlantics and Unions of Morrisania, N.Y., but were Wisconsin amateur champions. *Back row:* Archie McFayden SS, E.C. Wells LF, Martin Larkin, Jr. CF; W.H. Dodsworth RF, Clarence Smith P, George L. Red(l)ington Capt./C. *Front row:* J.H. Wood 1B, F.A. Smith 3B, Charles S. Norris 2B. A mural of this photograph is now on a Miller Park luxury box concourse wall. Milwaukee Public Library's Historic Photograph Collection.

even game. The difference seemed to be clearly Pabor, who switched from being a lefty-throwing 2nd baseman with Morrisania in 1865 to taking the pitcher's box the next year. The nucleus of their triumphant 1868 campaign evaporated under the Unions' desire to remain a strictly amateur operation. George Wright would return to Milwaukee the next summer as the highest paid member of his brother Harry's all-professional Cincinnati Red Stockings. Morrisania's foundation, the Pabor and Birdsall battery, went adrift for 1869, until reuniting the next season.[38]

As an all-amateur, local team, the Cream City had no such worries. In fact, despite the sobering losses to semi-pro visitors, mid-April of 1869 heralded a season "unsurpassed in interest. The national game seems to have as strong a hold on our people as cricket does upon the English."

The next line could apply to the city, now: "We hope our citizens will wake up to the conviction that it is a necessity to have a first class club here like the C.C., and lend their aid in maintaining its high standard and name."[39]

At the Kirby House on that Thursday evening of April 15, 1869, the Cream City's officialdom was elected: M.A. Boardman as president, pitcher Clarence Smith as vice-president, and F.A. Smith as secretary and treasurer. These three were joined on the "Board of Managers" by outfielder E.C. Wells and 1st baseman James Wood. Retained as scorer was R. Allen, Jr.

The club's benevolence extended to both the clergy, who would be allowed free use of the grounds and materials, and to other clubs that could obtain the practice use of the grounds for a seasonal fee of ten dollars.[40]

On Monday, July 26, 1869, the champion club of Wisconsin, this same Cream City nine, would receive its greatest challenge ever. Those professional Cincinnati Red Stockings wanted a game at Milwaukee that Friday and made arrangements to stay at the Plankinton House. The "C.C.'s" could only hope that a few days of practice would wring a "creditable score" against the Rhineland City juggernaut.

Acknowledging that they were up against it, a 500-member organization that laid out over $20,000 for its own suburban grounds with a capacity for 4,000, not to mention its $9,500 pay roll, Milwaukee could offer little more than its hospitality. Despite the *gemuetlichkeit* of a visit to the National Military Asylum at Wood (now the VA Hospital) and other points of interest, the Porkopolis pros were not as reciprocally courteous on the diamond. On a red hot July 30th afternoon, Red Stocking pitcher Asa Brainard would sizzle the most. The alcohol-propelled Brainard, who was both nicknamed "Count" and for whom the term "ace" was coined, led the three-hour massacre.[41]

Harry Wright's ensemble ran rampant, scoring in every inning. It was as if they brought the Ohio River with them, such was the flood of scoring. Fifteen runs. Sixteen runs. Nineteen runs. The latter outburst occurred in the sixth inning when nineteen straight strikers of this crimson-hosed tide reached base before anyone could be put out. Brainard, in the slugging pitcher tradition carried on by the likes of Monte Ward, George Van Haltren, Smoky Joe Wood, Lefty O'Doul, and someone named Babe Ruth, single-handedly outscored Milwaukee. Scoring ten runs on rapping eleven hits, the Count even nailed down his own pitching win with a couple stolen bases. In slaying all opposition during their cross-country tour, the 85–7 onslaught heaped upon their Cream City hosts was among the most lopsided Red Stockings victories of all.

For the 3,000 Milwaukeeans who witnessed this invincibility, exposure to this far higher caliber of predominantly eastern skill superceded the humiliation dealt to the locals. The *Milwaukee Sentinel* could not even bring itself to print the box score, only a victims list of Porkopolis' march into history. The batsmanship of Cincinnati's shortstop George Wright, rightfielder Cal McVey and 1st baseman Charlie Gould were singled out, the latter two as "Western" players.

The Cincinnatians may have left the C.C.'s in a shambles, riding the steamer *Manitowoc* back down to Chicago for a next day match with Rockford, but things could've been worse. Milwaukee may have felt like the German comedian Heinsdorf. Under an item headline "NOT DEAD," the article said, "He is recovering." Maybe he was just Andy Kaufman, before Andy Kaufman?

Adding insult to injury, a group of Milwaukee policemen were "diligently practicing" as a baseball nine, with an eye towards challenging the Cream City Club. As the newspaper said, "Keep the ball moving."

Even though the Red Stocking slaughter was so one-sided, another baseball tradition grew out of it, even at this early stage. Longing for the "good old days" was already in effect by the mid-1880s when overhand pitching with a dead ball came to be. In the face of fewer base hits, lower scores, and less excitement for the "cranks," as fans who suffered from baseball "krankheit" (sickness) were then called, one Milwaukee player reminisced about that gross defeat to Cincinnati.[42]

Publicly, he lamented for a return to yesteryear, when four straight homeruns by the Porkopolitans would whip Milwaukeeans into a sustained frenzy. Sadly, modern baseball economics have created a similar scenario for the Major League Milwaukee Brewers. The current Reds are just as capable of four homers in a row, but is the paying clientele as receptive?

Once the Red Stockings broke the mold for all-out professionalism, the Cream Citys remained on the sidelines. Creation of baseball's first major league, the National Association, went through its five-year parade of coping with unreliable schedules. "Revolvers," players jumping contracts in mid-season, and "hippodromers," the scourge of those throwing games for wagering, all without Milwaukee's participation, negatively affected the team.

The pressure for professional quality play grew to the point that the Cream City club finally dissolved in 1876. As an organization, the National Association was run by its players. In effect, it was an asylum run by the inmates. That Milwaukee wasn't in that milieu, which collapsed under its own weight, was probably to its benefit. Under the machinations of Chicago's William Hulbert, the association gave way to the owner-controlled National League.[43] That also occurred in the United States' centennial year of 1876.

Perhaps equally fitting with the Cream City's demise came the sad news that General Rufus King died that October 13th. In the *Sentinel's* page 4 obituary/tribute to him no mention was made of his original deliverance of the national game to Milwaukee. His more substantial civic contributions were myriad and immense, but not even a later biographer recognized his enhancement of the city's sporting scene.[44] "King is dead! Long live King!"

The good general, whose editorial writing style was remembered as "Addisonian in its purity and elegance," was laid to rest with his father and grandfather, in the old yard of Grace Church at Jamaica, Long Island, New York.

With Rufus King dead, the last vestiges of gentlemanly, amateur baseball, as he presided over its practitioners in the Cream City, also died. That world view of the National Pastime, where "base ball clubs" flourished in places like Irvington or Elizabeth, New Jersey was no longer. The Morrisanias, Keokuks, and Rockfords went awash under the wave of tight-fisted, big-city elitism by National League teams.

Remnants from the Cream City Club's dissolution latched onto Milwaukee's new preeminent team, the West End Club. They played their home games by the outer limits of Wells Street. Still competing against primarily amateur and semi-pro nines from southeastern Wisconsin and the upper Midwest, the occasional visiting professional club also mixed into their record.

September 1876 gave the first real hint that Milwaukee may have finally been jumping onto the professional bandwagon. The last few games of that American Centennial season noted that five of the West Ends, three being local, were being paid to play. Foremost among them were John Carbine and 1st baseman Cherokee Fisher, both of whom had National Association experience. In the course of vanquishing foes like the Janesville Mutuals (20–4, 24–2), Liberty of Chicago (25–1), or even Chicago's own West Ends (28–7), Carbine emerged as the second leading hitter (.290, 1.60 hits per game) and Fisher the leading fielder ("errors to chances, .09," or a .910 average).[45]

Of their 23 wins and 8 defeats, two losses came at the hands of the visiting "San Franciscos" in July (4–8, 3–12). The pinnacle of the West Ends' commitment towards eventually sponsoring a fully pro team came late in the season. The National League's first pennant-winners, the Chicago White Stockings, agreed to an exhibition encounter. It took ten innings, before Milwaukee ultimately succumbed 10–7, but through the first nine stanzas, the West Ends' Harry Chandler successfully dueled from the pitcher's box with Chicago manager Al Spalding.

The right-handed Chandler possessed an effective curve ball, but when it came down to cases, Spalding hadn't won more League games (42) than Milwaukee had played for nothing. A vast improvement over the lambasting by the Cincinnati Reds of seven years before, one local paper opined that Milwaukee was prepared to "sustain a first-class professional club."[46]

After years of local amateur clubs mimicking the nicknames of the leading sides of the day (e.g., the Atlantics, Eckfords, Mutuals, or Athletics; much like Little Leaguers copy their favorite major league teams today), the West Ends waded deeper into the larger pool of talent. To that end only two or three homegrown locals would wear the Gothic "W.E." on their chests. The 1877 roster featured six former National Association players, as well as two outstanding prospects, with no major league experience.

Of the latter, young catcher Charlie Bennett would go on to have a stellar 15-year career; and moreover, would have the field of the future American League Detroit Tigers named after him. Over half his career was in Tigertown, but the honor was bestowed when he tragically lost both of his legs in a railroad accident. He was among the better defensive backstops of his time.

The second prospect would enjoy a recurring relationship with Milwaukee. Abner Dalrymple, baseball's real Abner D., hailed from Warren, Illinois, just over the Wisconsin border.[47]

A truly potent, lefty hitter, outfielder Dalrymple would later star with the Chicago White Stockings and even lead the National League in homers one season. The pitcher's box, for this newly reconstituted West End team, was the domain of local curveball hero Harry Chandler and National Association vet Sam Weaver, a later major league star.

A better aggregation of players brought with it, the rigors of a stronger schedule. Nearly all comers from the professional, semi-pro, college, and amateur ranks were open to challenge by the West Ends. Top-flight pro teams often peppered their travels with exhibitions as a means of fulfilling payroll requirements.

This custom would benefit the Milwaukees of 1877, both at the admission gate and in a fourth-place in the League Alliance.[48] Loosely organized in affiliation with the National League, it was formed as a hedge against any potential upstart major league. Milwaukee's West Ends fared well under this irregular schedule, posting a 19–13 won-loss mark. Although the schedule was often dictated by convenience or necessity, the club's successful krank support warranted its first major league entry onto the National League's 1878 roll call.

"The League," as it was most simply referred to, had just endured its first serious gambling scandal. Driven by the weakness of four Louisville players (Jim Devlin, George Hall, Al Nichols, and Bill Craver), who polluted the brilliance of the 1877 pennant race, they were seduced by game fixing wagerers. The league's integrity and survival were threatened.

The four malcontents would be the first ever banished by the fledgling "senior circuit." The credibility of the league's clubs was reflected in its damaged financial ledgers. Boston's Red Caps, led by the legitimately most valuable player (had such an award existed) Deacon White, Al Spalding's Chicago White Stockings and the Cincinnati Red Stockings were permitted to remain in the league, that was now reorganized with only six teams. The newcomers were the Providence Grays, the Indianapolis Blues, and the Milwaukee Grays.[49]

The title of editor-in-chief at the *Milwaukee Sentinel* seemed to bear with it the mantle of baseball advocacy. Carrying the tradition of the late Rufus King a step farther, John L. Kaine, the new league club's president, would hire former Brooklyn Atlantic outfielder Jack Chapman (remember his homer against Cream City?) as his field manager.

The man who would pilot "Chapman's Grays" brought both his playing experience and his endurance in managing the ill-fated Louisville debacle. Held in regard throughout the baseball community, Chapman would forge his Grays from five of the West Ends' best, including both Dalrymple and Bennett, and an extensive recruiting effort. The result looked to have the makings of a competitive team, if not an outstanding one.

Kaine knew full well that if his venture were to succeed, his league club would need an appropriate showcase for its talents. He made certain that the landscaping and enclosure of the Milwaukee Baseball Grounds were ready for opening day in early May. The erection of the grandstand for the park was between Clybourn and Michigan and Tenth and Eleventh Streets. Today, motorists and pedestrians alike would know that as somewhere beneath Marquette Interchange of the freeway system.

Resplendent in their "handsome" gray uniforms with black trim, and a Gothic style "M" emblazoned upon their chests, Chapman's Milwaukees opened the 1878 National League season with a portent of things to come. They would be swept at Cincinnati and lose two of three at Indianapolis.

The lone victory at the Hoosier capital came on May 9th, when Sam Weaver underhandedly hurled the 2–1 win. It would be one of a very precious few highlights for this team. Weaver was the primary hurler in these days of perhaps a single change pitcher, but beyond his Milwaukee experience, he would prove capable of winning 26 games, two consecutive seasons, in the majors.

For the Grays' home opener, Weaver scattered six hits to thwart Cincinnati, 8–5. The encouragement generated before those 1,500 kranks would be short-lived, however.[50]

There is little doubt that Chapman could only grimace at what would transpire the rest of the way. The core of the team's on-field misfortune was its hands of stone. Or something akin to lobster mitts. Whatever the problem, Chapman's Grays were plagued by a display of fielding more reminiscent of the original King-Hathaway rivalry.

Milwaukee didn't just finish dead last in the standings, but the Grays led the league in errors, turned the fewest double plays, and their fielding average was 30 points behind the next worse team!

Compounding these dire straits were the injuries to their catching tandem, Charlie Bennett and Bill Holbert. Bennett became crippled by a sore throwing arm after only the first week of play. His throws could barely reach second base after that. Holbert, who'd enjoy a 12-year major league stint and wed the daughter of a Milwaukee policeman, fared no better. Catching back then should have earned hazard pay, for the use of masks was not standard, chest protectors about six years away, and mitts non-existent.[51]

The price for that lack of evolution was a split finger on Holbert's throwing hand, the result of a foul tip. The square-jawed Chapman had every reason to turn to jelly, as both his starting backstop and his replacement were now rendered nearly useless. The Brooklynite manager made telegraph lines across the country sizzle in a desperate attempt to fill this most fundamental of defensive needs.

Grays' president John L. Kaine attributed Weaver's pitching ineffectiveness to the catching woes. Chapman was forced to substitute hardy but incapable outfielders or infielders to bear the backstop burden. So that these teammates could handle his pitches, Weaver would have to tone down his fastball and curve. Either he would be pounded by the opposition or the lapses of his non-catchers would spell doom.

Weaver pitched well enough to rank fourth in ERA (1.95), gave up the fewest walks and second-fewest hits per nine innings, but the atrocious defense accounted for his 12–31 record.[52] The replacements to the replacement could handle replacement pitcher Mike Golden more easily, but so did opposing batters. Golden was something less than his name — a paltry 3–13.

At the time, passed balls were counted as errors, so far too often, the Grays were deluged with 11-error games. Bennett's and Holbert's absences were lamented as the source of a disastrous season. Winning one out of every four games was wearing on Milwaukee's paying clientele.

With Weaver in the box, Milwaukee's Grays won their last home game on September 16th and the bragging rights to being grayer than Providence's Grays, 4–3. For those 300 brave souls in attendance, who weathered through one huge gray area of 1878, one thing was confirmed in black and white: Milwaukee's 15–45 finish was just awful.

The lone bright bat in this travesty was leftfielder Abner Dalrymple. The Illinoisan spoiled the rod in his assault on the National League batting title to the tune of a .356 average. Originally, Dalrymple was recognized as the rightful batting champion. But, unlike most current, revisionist history, which weighs in subjectively on matters out of the context of their time, some of baseball's steps can be retraced through the cold, hard numbers of scorebooks. Ol' Abner would suffer when such an exercise was applied to his moment in the sun. Later historians would credit Providence centerfielder Paul Hines as 1878's king of swing.[53]

Such were the financial straits of the Grays. They were in danger of folding as early as June. Kaine unloaded the ballclub onto William P. Rogers by July 2nd. What Rogers bought himself was a team that was careening into a 15-game losing streak, even with the return of Charlie Bennett. No longer burdened by his financial interests in the Grays, Kaine stopped publishing accounts of their games in his *Sentinel*. The paper did print the final scores, at least![54]

The battering the Grays endured wasn't limited to the diamond. By August 31st, the players staged a mini-strike after having not been paid. Despite caving in to play that day's scheduled contest versus Indianapolis, the players still had to wait several more days for their paychecks.

At December's annual National League confab, three Milwaukee players, infielder Johnny Peters, outfielder/pitcher Mike Golden, and utility man Joe Ellick, filed formal charges of non-payment against the team.

Rogers' response was that Peters' amount was in dispute and there was a receipt to prove payment to Golden. Confronted with this brew-ha-ha from Brew City, the heavy hand of the league came down with this ultimatum: Pay your debts in twenty days, including those to the players, and withdraw honorably from The League.

Rogers took this decision, by leaving the meeting and attending an opera. The *Sentinel's* take was that "the Milwaukeeans were bounced from the League at the Cleveland meeting yesterday. The Chicago crowd were too much for them." Be that as it may have been, Rogers dissolved the Grays within a few weeks. As the *Sentinel* lamented, "If they could keep their expenses as low as their scores..."[55]

In those first twenty years since what Rufus King had wrought upon the Cream City, both baseball and Milwaukee had now seemed turned inside out. The seed planted by that "Damn Yankee" had not dried up completely, but would require an ever-vigilant resuscitation, even to this day. And to this day, on Milwaukee's near North Side, stands Rufus King High School.

Oh, sure, it would be easy to say it was named after him for his stature as the city's first superintendent of schools, his civic leadership through editing the newspaper, or even his accomplishments as soldier and statesman. But, you know what? It would really be preferable to think that he was honored for being the man who first brought baseball to Milwaukee!

2
Northwestern by Western

Milwaukee and Wisconsin were in what was considered the United States' "Old Northwest," the former British territory annexed after the American Revolution. Appellations of that frontier imagery, despite Oregon and California having already joined the Union by 1850, still persist today: Northwestern University in suburban Chicago, or "the Quiet Company," long known as Northwestern Mutual Life Insurance (now Financial Services), right in Milwaukee.[1] The author's late Grandpa Podoll not only caught for a couple semi-pro clubs, the barnstorming Nebraska Indians and more local Kilbourn (Wisconsin Dells) Independents ca. 1910, but he also attended an auto school, Milwaukee's Northwestern Motor Institute, in 1913.[2]

The five-year interim between 1878–1883 left Milwaukee void of any professional baseball, though local amateur games could draw crowds up to 2,000. Translating that interest back into a professional venture, in an age when blacks, Indians, Norwegians, Crackers, and even a newspaper's own readers were taunted and lampooned, was another matter.[3]

Wisconsin's only contribution to the major leagues by 1883 had been Watertown's Pete Norton and his hitless at-bat with the 1871 Washington Olympics.[4] That's why Al Spalding's signing of 6'-7" Milwaukee catcher named Henry Graham as a reserve for his Chicago White Stockings locked in so many lines of type. Homerism aside, he never saw the light of day on a National League diamond.[5]

The Northwestern had been the premier minor league of 1883. The pennant-winning Toledo Blue Stockings took their black catcher, Fleet Walker, to the major American Association for 1884. Any obituaries for the shaky loop seemed premature when both Milwaukee and it received an 1883 Christmas present.

The impetus for remedying Milwaukee's state as the only city of its size in the Union without professional baseball came not from a local man. Rockford's James F. McKee was guaranteed the job of field manager, in return for canvassing local subscribers necessary to the joint stock company of $10,000.

The team's hierarchy, elected at the Plankinton Hotel on December 28th, put up a cool $5,000 on the spot.[6] Shares were divided at $125 a pop.

Consider that some 15 years earlier, Cincinnati's absolutely peerless, first all-professional payroll was $9,500. Now, just to outfit a minor league club in Milwaukee required more up front.

That hierarchy, which won Milwaukee's admission into the Northwestern League on January 9, 1884; consisted of: President John C. Iversen (Scandinavian?), mirror emporium proprietor and art dealer; Vice-President Louis Auer, politician and financier; Secretary George F. Ziegler, Jr.; confectioner; and Corresponding Secretary Harry D. Quin, a stationery supplier whose name would resonate into Milwaukee's turn-of-the-century baseball future.[7]

Renewing their league memberships were the Michigan outposts of Bay City, Grand Rapids, and Saginaw, as well as Fort Wayne and Peoria. Despite its clout as the circuit's largest city, Milwaukee would be outpoliticked on scheduling matters by the seven other additions: Evansville, Minneapolis, Muskegon, Quincy (Ill.), St. Paul, Stillwater (Minn.), and Terre Haute. A 25¢ admission charge compared favorably to the National League's 50¢.

James McKee relied heavily upon his knowledge of talent south of the state line in bringing 21 men "under engagement" to start the new Cream Citys' campaign. The new Wright Street Grounds, bounded by West Clarke, North 11th, North 12th, and West Wright Streets would be home.[8]

One prescient admirer of the Milwaukees would wish them *bon voyage* by composing the following anagram for the March 10, 1884, *Milwaukee Sentinel:*

> May all your hits three bases be
> In every inning, two or three
> Let your fielders miss no fly
> While grounders by no chance get by
> All your throws be straight as shots
> Unless your pitcher's curves so hot
> Knock out your opposition all
> Every pool give your first ball
> Exact the pennant, too, next fall

Another hallmark of March 10th was McKee's signing of the man who would be his most valuable position player, catcher Cal Broughton. The pride of Magnolia, Wisconsin, would rise from that Janesville-area hotbed to catch in the bigs for portions of four seasons, the first Wisconsinite to really impact the majors.

Janesville's Tom Morrissey, whose 3rd baseman–brother John had a "cup of coffee" up with Buffalo and Detroit, would also man the hot corner for the '84 Cream Citys. Tom Morrissey would become a first base fixture for Milwaukee throughout the 1880s.[9]

This would be the first year that strictly overhand pitching was allowed. Lefty Ohioan Ed Cushman would utilize it to terrifying effect, whiffing a dozen St. Paul batsmen on six hits for Milwaukee's 13–1 home opening triumph.[10]

The initial promise of the nine, also known as the "Grays," evaporated after the first couple weeks. Cushman's 3-inning ineffectiveness culminated in a 25–4 torrent of runs that cascaded like the very Grand Rapids itself.[11]

McKee's Cream Citys lurched into mid-June with a 15–18 record, good for sixth place. President Iversen's pledge to pump in new talent flew right in the face of Henry Lucas and his upstart major Union Association's drain of Northwestern and Eastern League players. Milwaukee's wagering kranks fumed over a 5–10 road trip and withdrew their pool from the next home stand.[12]

Their Northwestern rivals flailed about for economic survival, but the Irishman McKee was rather Scotch with the Cream City checkbook. His frugality in turning $1,800 to the black from a month-long road trip would not be rewarded. Officials of the floundering club announced his resignation on June 26th. He was paid through the stipulation of his November 1st contract, but in a move only McKee himself could love, club hierarchy saved money by promoting team Captain/2nd baseman Tom Loftus to be their skipper.

This St. Louis native was a century ahead of Wisconsin Democrat majority leader Tom Loftus, a Madison-area state speaker who lost the state's gubernatorial election, but was later appointed by President Bill Clinton as ambassador to his ancestral Norway. Were the two related?[13]

The managerial change managed to shake the Cream Citys out of their doldrums. Ed Cushman opened a home stand with a 3–1 tagging of Quincy. The press observed that "an unusually large number of ladies were present" among the 1,500 attendees, and they "appeared to take as fully deep an interest in the sport as their male companions."[14]

Things jelled, both on the field and at the gate, by mid-July. The club, now over .500, averaged over 2,000 kranks per game in a weekend series with Saginaw.[15]

August heat wilted a full one-third of the Northwestern League under financial stress. Early that month, Fort Wayne and Stillwater pulled the plug, and a weeek later, Terre Haute and Peoria folded their tents. Not even the latter's 38–25, .603 record could save them. The Milwaukees staved off such ruin.[16]

That first stage of collapse left the Milwaukees awarded with the Northwestern League championship. The survivors fared no better, under a revised schedule, when Loftus' 11–3 crew clinched that title, too. In total, Milwaukee's Northwestern record was 41–30, .577.

Henry Lucas negotiated with Loftus to have Milwaukee join the Union Association. They would be replacing the Eastern League's dominant Wilmington (Del.) Quicksteps, who had already replaced the defunct Keystone of

Philadelphia charter team.[17] The Cream Citys would find the pastures of the U.A. greener.

Ed Cushman would especially thrive. He followed up his September 27th, 3–0 shutout debut against National of Washington by going one better the next day. These Nationals had a floating roster with very much of a local D.C. amateur imprint, but they were only one of two Union charter clubs to turn a profit. Goose eggs abounded in Cushman's 5–0 no-hitter! He was undefeated in four games.[18]

Milwaukee's wood bore little potency, so it would rely upon its arms. Cal Broughton hit a sound .308 versus Union pitching and Vermonter Henry Porter chipped in .275 as a pitcher/outfielder. Porter's 3–3 record at the points accounted for 75 percent of Milwaukee's losses, however. Al (Cod) Myers rapped a tidy .326 from his 2nd base spot in these dozen Union games. The folding of the Northwestern Quincy nine delivered to Milwaukee not only one of baseball's great, curious nicknames, but also one of the best lefty pitchers of the 1880s. Charles Busted Baldwin came from tiny Oramel in western New York to remain a fine 1–1, 2.65 ERA in Milwaukee's Union memory.[19]

In return for his standout performance, the spiffy gent who never smoke, drank, nor cussed couldn't earn a nickname like his other Baldwin contemporaries, Clarence the "Kid" or Mark as "Fido." Charley's middle name could have kept any tormentors on edge, but he would have to be known as "Lady" Baldwin. Not since the days of another Charley, that Pabor character from the old Unions of Morrisania, who was "the Old Woman in the Red Cap," could a nickname raise an eyebrow or two! Remember, Pabor was a lefty, too. Baldwin's ladylike .222 mirrored the team's overall .223 U.A. batting. Oh, but for the modern Brewers to have a quality southpaw now.[20]

That made it all the more unusual that a club's two best pitchers served from the left wing, but that was precisely what the Cream City B.C. had in Cushman and Baldwin.

The convoluted nature of the Union Association's standings gave Milwaukee the second best winning percentage, but their dozen game schedule left them 35½ games behind Henry Lucas and his own gargantuan St. Louis Maroons.[21]

Milwaukee was so aroused by its flirtation with this third major league challenger that an estimated 4,000 kranks cheered on the October 12th season finale, a 5–2 victory over the Baltimore Monumentals.[22]

Exuberance for Milwaukee's major league future would vanish as quickly as Lucas could pack his Union bags and cave in to the National League. His fortune would evaporate, too. Later in life, he took a job as a railroad ticket manager.[23]

That short, major ride kept the embers of professional baseball smoldering for Milwaukee's baseball kranks. The Hot Stove League was thoroughly stoked by the epoch of the baseball wars of 1884.

The shakeout, from the Union Association's dissolution, made for a scramble in the pursuit of marginal talent between the two remaining major leagues and the new rise of regional, state, and even provincial minor leagues. No fewer than the Eastern League, [Eastern] New England League, Southern New England League (which wouldn't finish 1885), New York State League, a three-team Colorado League, and even the Canadian (or Ontario) League comprised of five clubs from that province all joined the first Western League[24] for 1885.

On March 31st of that year, Manager Tom Loftus represented the Milwaukees at a St. Louis confab that gave birth to this "Western League." Minneapolis, Keokuk (Iowa), and Omaha all vied for the sixth slot, with the Nebraska city getting the nod. Kansas City joined the Toledos and Clevelands, thus Milwaukee would open the season April 18th at the Indianapolis Hoosiers. Milwaukee practiced at the old 10th Street Grounds.

Baseball received modest challenges in the sports pages from lacrosse and roller polo. Manager Bill Watkins of the National League Detroits was opposed to polo as a form of keeping baseball players in shape. He believed in gymnasium practice for preliminary work.[25]

Milwaukee's new baseball aggregation had no such compunction about tuning up with exhibitions against higher competition. Trotting out a lineup deep with Union Association experience, the Milwaukee nine lost a pair of early April weekend exhibitions against Charlie Comiskey's potent American Association St. Louis Brown Stockings.[26]

Thanks to the hospitality of their Mound City hosts, Milwaukee was even allowed to use multi-talented Browns' Shortstop Yank Robinson, to bat sixth in the Cream City order. Tom Forster, a 2nd baseman with prior experience in both majors, at Detroit and Pittsburgh, would weigh in as an 1880s fixture as Milwaukee's leadoff man.

Unlike today's game, it was still possible to see a pitcher bat as high as second in the order. In this Milwaukee club's case, it was lefty Dick Burns. Coming off an outstanding season as the second pitcher for the U.A. Cincinnati Outlaw Reds, the Holyoke, Massachusetts man also played 44 games in the outfield and even a couple at short for that club. He led that third major league with 12 triples and finished third in slugging to go with a .306 BA and 4 homers. Other than Milwaukee's Ed Cushman, Dick Burns was the only Union pitcher to throw a no-no. He did so at Kansas City on August 26, 1884, a 3–1 gem.[27]

Though Burns did not rank in the top of any Union pitching category, he prevailed in the new overhand era well enough to forge a 23–15 record, with a fine 2.46 ERA, in nearly 330 innings. All these fine credentials meant nothing to the Brown Stockings, who swept the exhibitions, 4–2 and 6–1. The latter April 5th Sunday loss fell squarely upon the shoulders and "poor catching" of 6'-6", 220-pound Milwaukee native Anton Falch. He also brought up the bottom of the batting order.

Another of three returnees from 1884 was leftfielder Steve Behel, who batted third. Cleanup duties went to right fielder "Stooping Jack" Gorman, a St. Louisan, who was mostly a 1st baseman in stints with the Browns and Pittsburgh's Alleghenys, besides the previous year's KC Unions. Vagabond giant, 6'-2", 223-pound Jumbo Schoeneck, who rode the Union ride with Chicago, Pittsburgh, and Baltimore in 1884, hit fifth behind Gorman and held down first base.

If this lineup sounds like "They Might Be Giants," well, representing the opposite end of the measuring stick was 3rd baseman Trick McSorley. Another St. Louis resident, at 5'-4", 142 lbs. Milwaukee's seventh batter bounced between the 1884 Fleet Walker Toledo club and both of the Mound City's major clubs over three years.

As the Cream City hadn't ironed out its problems at short, McSorley hit between the loaned Robinson and center fielder/pitching returnee Lady Baldwin. For all the promise that this 1885 Milwaukee Western League club held, again with an unusual tandem of lefty pitchers, it was not to be fulfilled. Fallout from player disloyalty, in the form of shortstop Tom (a.k.a. "Pete") Sexton and catcher Kid Baldwin, reflected the nagging instability that even a "national agreement" would not cure.[28]

Sexton took his act to Omaha's Omahogs and a correspondent suggested to Loftus that, if the Baltimore Monumentals' Dick Phelan was blacklisted, he should negotiate with Art Whitney from the last year's Saginaws and Alleghenys. Corresponding with Milwaukee management several months prior, "He was offered the courthouse, the Plankinton House, but he desired the Exposition Building thrown in, and local management ceased bidding for his services."[29] The hope was to keep Tom Forster at second.

This particular Art Whitney filled out an 11-year major league career, predominantly as a 3rd baseman, and in the strange life cycles of baseball, 40 years later saw another Whitney star at third for the Phillies. "Pinky" Whitney was a fine-hitting native of San Antonio, whose given name was also Arthur. The original came from Massachusetts.[30]

The "name game" wasn't separated by just generations either, but even amongst potential teammates. Despite Sexton's departure, the most severe bile towards desertion was reserved for catcher Kid Baldwin. Every other player seemed to be called a "Kid" back then, but when Baldwin fled with Milwaukee's $300 contractual advance to the majors' greener pastures of American Association Cincinnati, he betrothed the possibility to form a "Baldwin-Baldwin" battery with the "Lady."[31]

Cincinnati's manager, O.P. "Ollie" Caylor, was singularly raked over the coals by April 5, 1885's *Sentinel*. "The newspaper said that Caylor, as a person who has done more to bring odium and discredit upon the baseball profession than any other man, was allowed a voice in the deliberations of the (National Agreement) Arbitration committee." It went on to say that

Clarence "Kid" Baldwin, the catcher who took Milwaukee's money and ran in 1885. National Baseball Library & Archive Photograph Collection.

"there is no longer occasion for surprise that justice and honesty were disregarded."

Milwaukee's president John C. Iversen reacted to the Kid's desertion thusly, "I'm about sick of the baseball business. The player seems to have no sense of honor, while most of the professional managers are absolutely dishonest. It's about time that honest men left the baseball business to the disreputable sharks who are fast destroying it."

Milwaukee's management would seek a U.S. court injunction to prevent Kid Baldwin from playing anywhere but the Cream City. How Iversen's words still seem to resonate through the echoes of 117 years. How fast it has been destroyed.

Cream City manager Tom Loftus vented his spleen to a *St. Louis Globe-Democrat* reporter: "I guess the Cincinnati club will have to pay me the $300 advanced to 'Kid' Baldwin, and I don't know but I am better off than if he couldn't play and I couldn't get my $300. But I don't see what authority the Arbitration committee has to let him sign right away. I think there must be a mistake about that."

Notorious St. Louis Browns' owner Chris Von der Ahe, who was a bystander, chimed in, "They can't do that, they must wait ten days."

"They can do as they like," remarked a ballplayer, who overheard the conversation. The *Globe-Democrat* also took note of the St. Louis imprint upon the Milwaukee ballclub, by way of Gorman, Loftus, and McSorley who was greeted by "hundreds of friends" during the Cream City exhibitions there.

In making their case against Kid Baldwin, Milwaukee officials awaited replies from the various leagues. For his part, Baldwin was reported to have paid $100 to the Quincy team to have them present a petition on his behalf.

While this sort of internecine warfare consumed baseball, the rest of the world turned. Reports of 5,000 men killed in a bloody encounter in Afghanistan fueled rumors from Russia to London to Berlin; Turkey opposed the Mahdi's Islamic uprising in the Soudan; and dispatches from Winnipeg told of "Northwestern Indians Determined Upon Rebellion." Former Milwaukee Mayor-cum-Wisconsin governor George W. Peck, who penned "Peck's Bad Boy," pre-empted any effort by America's new reformist president Grover Cleveland to be made Milwaukee postmaster. Peck's plea was somewhat "in the same vein as Bill Nye's (not "the Science Guy!") famous resignation at Laramie." Former President U.S. Grant's health was failing.[32]

The Western League of 1885 demonstrated that not only was the nation ill-prepared to support three major leagues the past season, but newly-burgeoning cities in the Midwest still were not ready for top-level minor league baseball either.

The Milwaukees won their April 18th opener at Indianapolis, 3–1, but in the economic debacle that was the Western League, the Hoosiers would give way to a Detroit franchise. Likewise, the Omahogs were replaced by Keokuk, Iowa's "Keokuks." Kansas City's Cowboys, the Forest City club representing Cleveland, and those holy Toledos would all survive the short duration with Milwaukee.[33]

As *The Sentinel* noted, "Keokuk admitted into alliance with the Western League and may soon be here during the season. Thornberg, of this city and [Cooperstown, N.Y.-bred John "Bud"] Fowler, the favorite colored player of last year's Stillwater club, are members of the Keokuk team."

The league proved to be such a failure that it didn't even warrant mention in the 1886 *Spalding's Official Baseball Guide*.

America's festering sores between capital and labor would burst in 1886, like the balloons flown by the Army's "aeronauts." Milwaukee's *Sentinel*, which never spared its boiling ink on even dandies or bumpkins, made no secret of its right-to-work stance against "red socialism."

Rink polo and curling gave way to the $1,000 deposits mounted by Duluth, Eau Claire, Minneapolis, and Milwaukee to form another Northwestern League in February 1886. One Ted Sullivan, born on the "auld sod" of County Clare, Ireland, and the man credited with shortening the term fanatics to "fans," led the Milwaukee effort. With major league experience from the KC Unions of 1884, he would pilot the new club. Oshkosh was finally added by Easter to balance out a six-club schedule that seemed carved in sand.

Sullivan seemed to be held by the local press in fine regard, but the slow search for talent hadn't quite reached as far as Cuba, where "a prominent railroad there offered a purse of $3,000 for the leading nines to play for." Sullivan had a hand in drawing up the league schedule, and with the appointment of local stationer and baseball goods dealer H(arry) D. Quin, both firmed up Milwaukee's primacy over the league.[34]

Sullivan's fully assembled Milwaukees would not begin to pursue the 1886 pennant until May 8th. Practice skirmishes versus the likes of Racine College and a visit to clubs of the Western League made up the spring. The Milwaukees lost their first exhibition at St. Joe, Mo., 5–2, despite 10 strikeouts by young pitcher Harper.[35]

And despite alleged favoritism by the umpire, Sullivan's charges took their second and last game at Omaha before 5,000 people on Sunday, April 18th. Backstop Holmes caught "no less than eight foul tips off the bat." Sullivan's own contractual sleight of hand conjured up a quartet of St. Joe's four crack batters, including Milwaukeean Pat Sullivan. The four eluded the law in Missouri. They were being pursued with an injunction.[36]

The Monday morning, April 19th *Sentinel* sports page opened with a scene only from this era:

> The baseball season of 1886 has begun. The fact was painfully evident when three ragged little urchins with soiled faces and still dirtier hands climbed the stairs leading to the editorial rooms of the Sentinel.
>
> 'Is de sportin' editor in?' queried the largest and grimiest urchin of the group.
>
> The speaker was directed to the desk of the person he was seeking, and approaching that individual the little fellow yelled in the most approved baseball tones:
>
> 'Soy, mister, der Young Picketts beat der American Eagles 'safternoon twenty-three to t'irteen. Put it in der paper, will yer?'
>
> The miniature Buck Ewing was assured that the important information would be given to the world and shouldering their bats, the dust-stained exponents of the national game took their departure.

Maybe Ted Sullivan should have hired their little hands, because with labor disputes rampant throughout the nation, the paper also prophesized that "THE NEXT ORGANIZATION TO GO ON STRIKE WILL BE THE BASEBALL CLUBS."

Neo-arctic weather haunted Milwaukee's Wright Street Grounds through Easter Sunday, but by May Day, a water-logged gathering of 300 watched Racine's collegians commit 32 errors to Milwaukee's 14. The 17–3 Milwaukee win incredibly took only 2-hours and 20-minutes! The 8-hour workday was foremost in the national debate, so time-efficient baseball seemed a natural by-product.[37]

Weaknesses on Ted Sullivan's ballclub were enunciated by one of Milwaukee's strong amateur nines, the Maple Leafs. After 1,000 witnessed a lefty curve artist named Cusick baffle the so-called professionals, 4–3, at the May 2nd Wright Street affair, Ted Sullivan added him to his payroll.[38]

Past favorites had moved on. Dickie Burns was in Rochester, Lady Baldwin moved up to the Milwaukee wagerers' National League favorites, the Detroit Wolverines. Only 2nd base/leadoff man Capt. Tom Sexton, was one known commodity. The Milwaukee club's management could only reward each member of the fairer sex, who would attend Thursday games, with "handsome souvenirs."[39]

Nationally, there were "eight fully-equipped baseball associations now in existence, employing over 700 players, whose salaries aggregate $800,000." Another $100,000 could be added by the 300 players in numerous state and local leagues. "Pounding the pigskin," not the traditionally thought horsehide, was now an extensive undertaking. And Milwaukee's hired Hessians were probably overpaid.[40]

Three days before the Milwaukees' home opener, "pestiferous Socialists" waved a red flag at the bulls of the state militia. One of the city's darkest days of violent agitation ended when Lincoln Avenue, in Bay View, flowed with the blood of six dead or dying Polish rioters.[41]

The only flag that mattered to the skilled baseball laborers of the Northwestern League was a championship flag. Eau Claire's "ball-tossers from the lumber district" included future Milwaukee manager Pongo Joe Cantillon in right field. They rolled into the May 8th Milwaukee opener, eager to avenge a 14-4 sawdusting at Oshkosh.

A stalwart crowd of 500 braved threatening weather to watch the visitors unmercifully trounce Milwaukee, 12-8. Cusick earned the starting pitching nod, but the only dividend he paid was homering out of the third spot in the order.[42]

Porous defense, ham-fisted even by the rough standards in converting from bare-handed play to rudimentary, fingerless gloves was the recurring theme in undoing Ted Sullivan's team.

A shivering 800 true believers saw Milwaukee-born catcher Pat Sullivan's 8 passed balls in the next day's 12-5 drubbing by Eau Claire. Captain Sexton, the Rock Islander of Milwaukee's Union run, set a terrible example from the opener, with 6 errors at second.[43]

The Milwaukees would be thumped at Oshkosh, 14-5, where the home club's right fielder happened to be the game's first deaf mute, William "Dummy" Hoy. The road show would have to roll on to Eau Claire, where the keystone switch of Sexton and Dougherty on May 12th finally notched Cusick and Milwaukee their first triumph, 9-2.

Coverage of the Northwestern League was as sporadic as its spread-out schedule. Major league clubs had played 90-100 games by late August, the loop only 60. The same lousy weather that had launched the 1886 campaign still dogged the dog days of summer.

Rain put its kibosh on the Saturday, August 28th home game, where only 200 people would see two balls pitched.[44] Lowly Minneapolis sent out Bill Sowders, who was considered the best pitcher in the Northwestern League, while the locals had One-Arm Daily in the box. Daily's left arm was stumped at the elbow, but the man who mesmerized Florida coloreds with his fielding prowess in 1884 and was a two-time 20-game winner in the bigs now washed out as well.[45]

Milwaukee would take to the road until September 11th when all postponed games would be redux. The notion arose that Milwaukee might fill a void in the major American Association for 1887, but "Plan B," as envisioned by Tom Loftus, Nin Alexander of St. Joe, and Ted Sullivan was for a new

Western association. Six cities that allowed Sunday baseball — Chicago, Indianapolis, Kansas City, St. Joseph, and St. Louis, and Milwaukee — would make a circuit "entirely independent" of either major league.[46]

That hope needed to be sustained, for 1886 was dwindling away in sullen mediocrity. In the type of supplemental road exhibitions common to the era, Manager Sullivan even pitched at Leroy, Minnesota on September 2nd, where he led a 19–6 demolition of the home club.[47]

His overhaul of the Milwaukees, throughout the season, turned them into effective spoilers in the pennant race. Lew Say, a U.A. alum at second, and catcher Tug Arundel were among the reinforcements; the latter caught Daily's 2–0 September 11th shutout at St. Paul in 1-hour, 40-minutes. "Had Milwaukee started the season with its present nine it would undoubtedly be first in the race."[48]

Once back home, Ted Sullivan's bush antics would warrant a forfeit to Duluth from the league secretary, Milwaukeean H.D. (Harry) Quin. The Duluths were a denied a 3 o'clock admittance to the Monday, September 20th game in question after Sullivan "turned the hose on the grounds and flooded the diamond as far as possible."[49] Quin's ultimatum threatened Milwaukee's expulsion from the league.

The *Sentinel* correspondent despaired that the same should have been done with an earlier contest in Duluth, but now minced no words in condemning Sullivan's "utter incompetency."

Eau Claire wailed at being jobbed by Umpire McIver in an 11–2 loss at Oshkosh, but blasted St. Paul, 21–7, on September 30th. That same day, Minneapolis surrendered at Duluth after 7 innings, down 9–4. Duluth's home field advantage was snow squalls.[50]

The season was declared over on October 3rd, with the following standings:

	GP	W	L		GP	W	L
Duluth	78	45	33	St. Paul	80	38	42
Eau Claire	79	43	36	MILWAUKEE	75(?)	35	42
Oshkosh	77	39	38	Minneapolis	78	35	43

Three forfeits, including one to Minneapolis, sent Milwaukee "at the foot of the list" the next day.[51] Sullivan's crew washed out so poorly that they arranged an October 10th Sunday benefit game against the local Bay Views. Hometown boy Tommy Nagle was back from Eau Claire, native Pat Sullivan moved to first, and even Steve Behel came from the A.A. New York Metropolitans for left field. Bay View called upon ringer Gus Krock to pitch.[52]

If the short-lived Ted Sullivan era in Milwaukee ended with his being asked to kiss the blarney stone, it was only because it was being hurled at his Irish-born mug!

Thanks to the arrival of Jim Hart, 1887 would be everything 1886 wasn't for Milwaukee and the reorganized and expanded Northwestern League. Hart had been a sub-.500 leader of the American Association Louisville Colonels the past two seasons, but the influx of Falls City players would be a real step up.[53]

Hart was, in fact, one of three incorporators of the newly reconstituted club, along with L.A. Hansen and H. Deifert. The Pennsylvanian Hart filed articles of association on Saturday, April 16, 1887. The capital stock of $25,000 was divided into 250 shares.[54]

Around the horn, Hart brought back Milwaukee favorites big Tom Morrissey at first, Tommy Forster at second, and Cal Broughton. "Pooh Bah" Williams, a 24-year-old sprinter from Bellaire, Ohio, took over left field. He came from the Maple Leaves of Guelph, Ontario.[55] Versatility arrived from Louisville in the form of Joe "the Socker" Strauss and 31-year-old Leech Maskrey. One of that city's Reccius brothers played second.[56]

Whereas Hart had a fine mix of major league experience at the positions, he would be completely reliant upon youth in the pitcher's box. With five arms under his tutelage, he also may have had one of the largest staffs of the day. Just as Ted Sullivan had Pat Sullivan playing under him, Jim Hart would have a pitcher named Hart, too.

Jim Hart went to great lengths to erase the bad taste left by Sullivan. Wright Street Grounds were furnished with new benches to replace old chairs and expand capacity, and the city's finest would be admitted to all games during the season, merely by flashing their badges.[57] Admission was 25¢, with the grandstand requiring "25¢ extra."

The goodwill generated 2,000-3,000 spectators to see the nattily attired Milwaukees first exhibition win over the Chicago Whitings on Sunday, April 17, 1887. A handful of White Stockings were among the 40-50 contingent from the Windy City. A fundamental rule change, wherein a batter no longer had to call for a high or low pitch, allowed the Milwaukees to pound the "Swedish Wonder," Charlie Hallstrom of Jönköping.[58]

Hallstrom would have the last laugh by autumn with his Oshkosh teammates. The morning newspaper rang in the return of the heroes of the ballfield, but questioned the lack of exercise by spectators, at least that beyond exercising their lungs by yelling at the umpire.[59]

Joe Strauss' third base coaching, "though amusing, [was] a trifle copious," in a 7-6 exhibition over Kalamazoo on Wednesday, April 20th. The locals took advantage of future big league manager Al Buckenberger's 3 miscues, but maybe Strauss was trying to be the Cream Citys' answer to the St. Louis Browns' Arlie Latham.[60]

Jim Hart scored a major coup when those National League Champion Chicago White Stockings agreed to a Tuesday, April 26th exhibition. Spalding and Anson's nine demanded a large guarantee, hence the 50¢ admission charge.[61]

Hart accomplished this, remarkably, from the distance of California, where he courted speedy southpaw pitching outfielder George Van Haltren. As huge an addition as the Oaklander would've been to Milwaukee's prospects, it was fool's gold to think he could be induced east. At least if your city wasn't named Chicago, with whom he ultimately signed.[62]

Much like the Detroit Wolverines were welcomed in their St. Paul exhibition visit, Chicago's White Stockings also had a "cold and benumbing" reception in Milwaukee. For the 2,000 witnesses, it was the local boys' 11 errors that proved to be their own worst enemy — that and utter domination by future Hall of Fame pitcher John Clarkson.

The 8–6 final was deceptive because the temperamental Yankee craftsman from Massachusetts toyed with the Milwaukees, allowing only one hit up to the eighth inning. He showed mercy in the final innings by merely tossing balls to the plate. The grateful home team managed 5 more hits and that, combined with Chicago's 4 miscues, provided all of Milwaukee's scoring. Clarkson kept the ball on the ground — so saith his one putout, 10 assists.

Dizzied by their 1-hour, 50-minute encounter with greatness, Jim Hart was left to wonder whether the weather would ever become decent enough for his son to appear as his club's mascot. "Among the pictures of the Milwaukee team displayed in several windows through the town is a cute one of Manager Hart's little boy."

The Northwestern League secretary, Milwaukee's own Harry D. Quin, issued printed circulars, detailing the circuit's adopted rules, regulations, umpires, and scores. Tickets were also available at his East Water Street bookstore or at Phil Lederer's cigar store at 105 Grand Avenue (now Wisconsin Avenue). Advance purchases were recommended to avoid the rush to the park.

At the Saturday April 30th home opener for the Northwestern League pennant, Jim Hart "arranged for the hitching of teams (meaning horses) in a vacant lot on Wright Street just opposite the entrance to the grounds."[63] The patrons were accommodated that way, but despite the Milwaukees' mammoth 16–6 victory over Eau Claire, most of the crowd did not find favor with the "wordy coaching" practiced by the players. The majority preferred a "quieter style of coaching." Hart's men walked 13 times and stole as many bases. Right fielder Leech Maskrey also nailed two men before they could reach first.

Milwaukee and Eau Claire bolted out of the gate in diametrically polar directions. The Cream City won "six straights," while Manager Lucas' hapless "up north" nine would start 0–11.

Milwaukee fell to third place before regaining the league lead on Memorial Day. Thanks to Joe Strauss, visiting Oshkosh was sent a half-game back by a 6–2 margin[64]

The visiting delegation "dropped their boodle," when their pitcher, local Bay View man Gus Krock, was dropped like a ton of bricks by his own catcher. Strauss had reached first base on a 5th inning single. When he "was off for second like a shot," catcher Ed Gastfield's lightning throw struck Krock's noggin square. Laid out on the grass "as if ready to die," he shook the cobwebs for a few minutes to vigorously go on and finish with 10 strikeouts. Strauss usurped the once and final lead with two 7th inning steals, scoring on Broughton's sacrifice fly (not yet counted in those days). "The wildest enthusiasm" gave Strauss an "immense ovation." Baseball was again front-page news. Of course, the other 3/4 of the page was ads.

Whether the following was a mere perpetration of imagery by a *Sentinel* writer or simply baseball lore making the rounds, it doesn't matter, it is classic: "Small boy (outside of baseball grounds)—How many's on de groun's, Jimmy? Jim-Jimmy (cooling his eye at a knothole)—'Bout four tousand. Small boy—Cops un all? Jimmy—No includin' cops 'bout fi'tousand."[65]

Maybe those were just the umpire's escorts?

Milwaukee pitchers Shenkel and Smith tossed the league's first two shutouts, back-to-back, Thursday, June 23rd, and Saturday, June 25th. A diminutive (5'-6", 130 lbs.) Louisville lefthander, the boyish 23-year-old Shenkel duped Eau Claire's Lumbermen league laggards on a 4-hit, 5–0 masterpiece. It was achieved in a mere 97 minutes![66] Morrissey went 4-for-5.

Smith, the 22-year-old amateur success, was a 5'-10", 190-pound "lightning pitcher... of great strength." Broughton was the one catcher capable of handling his speedy delivery when he joined Shenkel on the goose-egg bandwagon with a 7-zip defeat of Des Moines.[67] Pitching for "the Hawkeye men" was Peek-A-Boo Veach, who allowed at least one hit to every Milwaukee man. Smith's 4-hit pitching clinic took only 88 minutes!

On such Saturdays, ladies were welcome at the Wright Street Park for free if accompanied by a gentleman, but Sundays were no free lunch for anybody, period. The *Sentinel* took the occasion of their 50th anniversary (June 27th) to give a rare, specific attendance figure (3,090). League standings seemed an afterthought.

If highlight reels had existed, Maskrey's left-handed snatch of a liner to right in that game, "probably the most brilliant play of the year," may well have qualified for an "ESPY!" Incredibly, ol' Leech had only one hitless game in Milwaukee's 36 to date.

Oshkosh's Gus Krock was to duel Milwaukee's Smith on July 3rd in a 17-inning struggle of legendary proportions.[68] In the last dozen frames, Oshkosh could only muster 3 hits off Smith. Morrissey's grounder, between third and short, allowed Forster to amble in for the lead. "The crowd rose as one man...[emitted] the most frantic shouts of joy." The noise from 2,000 throats "could be heard blocks away." Big Smith whiffed Dummy Hoy to end it, the crowd in the palm of his throwing hand.

The road was as unkind to Jim Hart's Milwaukees through July as the toll of league became to Secretary Harry D. Quin. Milwaukee's H. P. Alsted received a box of three eggs on July 20th from a friend in Des Moines. Each egg contained the score of a sweep in Iowa.⁶⁹ Nothing was mentioned of those seven won by Milwaukee.

Quin's resignation led to the unanimous selection of Al Spalding's confidant Sam Morton as his replacement. The 30-year-old Morton had served the post before in 1880 and 1884. Quin was not done as Milwaukee's staunchest baseball advocate, however.

Milwaukee limped into a critical July 21st series with St. Paul, full of lame pitching arms and minus iron catcher Cal Broughton. St. Paul had won all four prior match-ups, but Milwaukee's 40–20 record kept the locals one win up in the ledger. That changed when unsaintly Bill Sowders hurled for St. Paul.⁷⁰

The season's largest weekday crowd of 2,000 collectively gasped at a rerun of the beaning that he last administered to Forster. This time, Strauss was the unfortunate one to shrug off the skullthuggery to the side of the head. Sowders added insult to injury when his ground rule double set up Plover, Wisconsin's Walt Wilmot's slow grounder to score the winning run.

Another 2,000 turned out to see Milwaukee retaliate the next day, thanks to St. Paul third sacker Elmer Cleveland's trio of costly miscues.⁷¹ The 5–2 final wasn't art. A hilariously concocted conspiracy of St. Paul lulling the locals into false security was worth the read alone! Two loud loyalists, a man with a tin horn and a stout young man in the grand stand, were among the record-eclipsing 3,500 celebrants to see pitcher Varney Anderson fend off their Gopher State challengers for the second time in three tries, 9–8. Milwaukee was now up 2½ games.

A "novice" supplied a special take on the game for the morning paper. The game's ethics were questioned: lack of sympathy for the injured, the baleful influence of gambling. Baseball could retain its public benefit if it remained a healthy diversion "in this hurried money-getting age," not a dissipation. So went this 1887 sermon.

Milwaukee was now a city at the forefront of both office innovation, as a convention of business educators displayed, and the Northwestern League. But, in a page that just as easily could be gleaned from 1994, not 1887, indignant citizens were called upon to rail against the foul water quality of the Milwaukee River.⁷² Nothing's perfect.

Tom Morrissey overcame the laughable humiliation of scrambling unnecessarily to score on all fours in an August 1st, 7–3 win over Duluth.⁷³ A "hideous" stunted dwarf in a "ridiculous dime museum plug hat" gazed an evil spell from Oshkosh's bench to put the whammy upon Milwaukee when it hosted an 11–2 showdown loss in mid-August.⁷⁴

America's lovely young first lady drew headlines with "MRS. CLEVELAND GOES BATHING" when the Milwaukees faced another form of dwarf: Legendary Davy Force, the 38-year-old shortstop of major league seasons past. At 5'-4" "Tom Thumb" made his debut for Des Moines in their sharply fielded 2–1 loss at Milwaukee.⁷⁵

One week later, Jim Hart's men would pulverize LaCrosse with 4 homeruns over the Wright Street Grounds' centerfield fence.[76] Cal Broughton did it twice, ably abetted by Socker Joe Strauss and shortstop Roussey. As much as Milwaukee's pennant hopes remained aloft, coverage was spotty until deep into September. The league had a "pretty" race going.

The statement "the Flour City Men Play Like A Lot Of Amateurs" explained Milwaukee's 15–5 drubbing of Minneapolis on the 18th. Oshkosh was pulling out all the stops in its mad dash for the flag.[77] So much so that they were later accused of still paying the appropriately-named pitcher Con Murphy, while shipping him to Minneapolis for a late series against Milwaukee.

Jim Hart trotted out some significant help of his own: Jumbo McGinnis, all 5'-10", 197 pounds of him; smooth center fielder Lou Sylvester, and returning prodigal son Ed Cushman. All were American Association castoffs. All were vital to the stretch run.[78]

Cushman, at ease with his old batterymate Broughton, subdued St. Paul, 4–3, before 2,000.[79] The Milwaukees last 16 games were to be on the road, but favorably against second division clubs, save St. Paul. The Milwaukees' assistant manager, George Bailey, would not find a wonderful life there, thanks to partisan umpiring. Flour City finagling about the shade of the sky bred a Minneapolis forfeit.[80]

A rescheduled game at Milwaukee made the Eau Claires their final October 11th whipping boy, 9–3. The bitter home nine went after Mississippian Dug Crothers with "blood in their eye," for a 7-run 9th. The paltry frozen attendance of 400 (including 30 ladies) knew it was over.

	Wins	Losses	Percent		Wins	Losses	Percent
Oshkosh	76	41	.649	Minneapolis	53	65	.449
MILWAUKEE	78	43	.644	LaCrosse	45	77	.369
Des Moines	73	45	.619	Duluth	40	76	.345
St. Paul	75	48	.610	Eau Claire	39	84	.317

Oshkosh owner E. P. Sawyer was taken to task for its expenditures of $20,000 over and above receipts and his desire for additional Duluth games, if so to insure the flag.[81] The Sawdust City and St. Paul faced printed vitriol for trying to manipulate umpires. Sawyer's lavishness brought sarcasm that the pennant should be made of a rare and elaborate material. Still, the four first division teams made an absolutely splendid race of it.

Jim Hart could only hang his bowler on the unlikely contingency that the league's board of directors would agree with his protest on the alleged Murphy payola scheme. Otherwise, before Tom Forster and Leech Maskrey departed for California winter playing engagements, a few of the ballclub's friends threw them a banquet.

Other admirers would later be encouraged to contribute similar testimonials, but by banquet's end, a gentleman presented Joe Strauss with a handsome gold medal. It represented a bat and a ball, with a diamond inlaid at its center.

"Several have done lots of good work." That 1887 season was a medal winner, indeed.

If it was fitting that a man named Sawyer buzzsawed his way to the Northwestern League pennant, it was equally appropriate that the brief gratification of the Oshkosh glory would be swept away like so much sawdust.

Sawyer's robber baron excesses and the smaller Northwestern cities like Duluth, Eau Claire, and LaCrosse were cast away for the larger markets of the 1888 Western Association. Oshkosh would not see any professional baseball for another three seasons, yet their best amateurs would challenge Milwaukee.[82]

Manager Jim Hart's retooled Milwaukees would now be facing the likes of Chicago, Des Moines, Kansas City, Minneapolis, Omaha, St. Louis, and St. Paul. It wasn't evident in the *Sentinel's* coverage, but 1888 was supposed to be the first season that a Milwaukee baseball club was actually called the "Brewers." Items of the actual brewing industry beyond Milwaukee made its pages: Pittsburg's (sic) non-intoxicating drink called "swankey" still had 2½ percent alcohol and wouldn't circumvent the local license law. New York's Central Labor Union called for a boycott on "pool beer," which would affect five breweries there.[83]

The Milwaukee baseball club now had the benefit of playing in the new and larger Athletic Park. It was over "100 feet broader and considerably more than that longer" than the old Wright Street Grounds. It was a $40,000 facility, in the days when managers still flipped a coin for the first at bat. Any ball hit over the fence would be an uncommon entitlement to a home run.[84] Travel time from the corner of Grand Avenue and West Water Streets were comparable. The horse car company guaranteed arrival in 25 minutes, but the return trip, nearly the same as the old park, could be easily made in 20 minutes.

Jim Hart used his old Louisville Colonels's American Association stomping grounds to measure his club's spring progress.[85] Only four of his 1887 contenders were in the batting order to face erratic southpaw Toad Ramsey: leadoff/shortstop Tom Forster, Joe "the Socker" Strauss was at third and batting third, right fielder Leech Maskrey, and Mills behind the plate. Shenkel suffered a reversal of errors by each club, an 8–5 exhibition opener for the Falls City. Both pitchers went the distance in Eclipse Park.

Among their western rivals, St. Paul would have to do without its ace, Cyclone Jim Duryea, because he was "pretty badly broken up." Kansas City owner Ed Menges liberally rewarded his upstarts' 4–2 victory over their American Association neighboring Cowboys.[86] The exhibition drew 6,000 and pitcher John McCarty received an extra $50, each other member, $25.

A couple familiar names were with the St. Louis Whites' entry. Former Milwaukee manager Tom Loftus was at the helm in his hometown and signed recently released catcher Tug Arundel from the National League Indianapolis Hoosiers.[87]

It was at the Saturday, April 28th opener in St. Louis that Whites' pitcher Harry Staley would be promoted to the Browns after sterilizing Milwaukee.[88] "May Day" might as well have been the distress call on May 1st when the Mound City's 5-run twelfth salted an 8–3 win. Future Hall of Famer "Eagle Eye" Jake Beckley, from up the Mississippi River at Hannibal, Missouri, manned first base for St. Louis.

Hart's lefthanders, Shenkel and Cusick, struggled in that series, but as news of this 1888 edition of Milwaukee's nine traveled slowly, fortunes were reversed. The St. Louis Whites turned white, tumbling into last place by late June. Milwaukee, meanwhile, built themselves a fine 21–17 mark, only 3½ games off of league-leading St. Paul's pace, and a ½ game up on KC.[89]

Milwaukee took particular relish in making "mince-meat" of Chicago pitcher Frank Dwyer for the second consecutive game. New center fielder Jimmy McAleer joined the hit parade that made Dwyer "feel as if he had been through a grist mill. And churned in a washing machine." Long came in from left to his relief, but a combined 21 hits gave Milwaukee the Sunday, June 24th win by a 17–7 final.[90]

Dwyer was actually promoted from these Maroons to the White Stockings, where he went 4–1. McAleer's debut, after a $500 purchase from Memphis, was 4-for-6 at the plate and a show in center, too. The Youngstown, Ohio man would go on to be the only one to represent Cleveland in three different major leagues.[91]

The downfall of the St. Louis Whites could be attributed to owner Chris Von der Ahe's "tricky behavior" after mocking the schedule with Des Moines and having a fire sale of his roster. W.C. Bryan's Sioux City nine, backed by a $10,000 bond, was welcomed in their stead.[92]

Ridding the circuit of Von der Ahe may have been music to everyone's ears, so much so that a letter writer to *The Sentinel* suggested that it be played at Athletic Park during games. As much as the paper agreed with it as a "good scheme," musical interludes weren't about to happen.

By July 4th, Jim Hart relieved pitcher John Quincy Adams Struck of his lambasting in the sports pages by sending him to the Bloomington club of the Inter-State League. In return, Hart paid $1,000 for that club and league's best pitcher, who averaged over 12 strikeouts per game. He was first identified as "Griffin." He was Clark Griffith. And he was needed.[93]

A Wednesday sweep at Minneapolis on Independence Day dropped Milwaukee to 19–22, 10 games behind St. Paul. In fact, Cal Broughton now caught for the Flour City.[94] Two days later, Milwaukee shook those inferiors in a peculiar game, where the "punk" variety dead balls hadn't been countersigned by Secretary Morton. Minneapolis 3rd baseman Patsy Tebeau accepted 15 of an incredible 17 chances (2 putouts, 13 assists, 2 errors), and Tom Forster was fined $20 for refusing to sit on the players' bench. He asserted that he had a right to stand behind the line in front of it. Umpire Brennan, a lightning rod for constant altercations, nearly called the game, a 4–1 final.

Zephyrs wreaked havoc about the circuit. For their Western baptism, Sioux City was blown away twice by a rainy gale at Des Moines and a Chicago game at St. Paul was canceled because part of the fence around the wet grounds was blown down.[95] The shaky Maroons were also for sale.

Back at Milwaukee's Athletic Park, the July game prior to Friday the 13th was called a 10-inning tie due to "cold weather." Friday the 13th was another matter. The indifferent Clark Griffith fared so meekly against the visiting Chicago Maroons that many surmised he was pitching for his release to the mutually interested St. Louis Browns.[96] Still, in this July contest, steam heaters were being suggested for the grand stand, even though it was thought even the steam would freeze. The loss dropped Milwaukee to sixth, behind the Maroons.

Hart tinkered with his batting order, moving McAleer to leadoff, flip-flopping Morrissey and Forster, Strauss and 1st baseman Fuller. What showed promise at first led to a shutout by Kansas City's future Hall of Famer Kid Nichols on July 30th. The proceeds of that game were given to the Priests of Pallas organization.[97] Milwaukee's prayer was unanswered. They had a 32–34 fifth place mark, still a half-game behind those KC Blues.

After having been attended to by a Dr. Pepper and a Dr. Lincoln, the remains of Civil War hero General Phil Sheridan were now in Washington on August 10th. The remainder of Milwaukee's season, never advancing beyond fifth place, was pretty much D.O.A. also.[98]

There were some highlights. Shenkel's 4-hit, 11-inning win versus Minneapolis, when he scored the winning run on that same Friday, August 10th, was noteworthy. There was the encouraging vigor of four young signees and a deal that brought shortstop Joe Walsh and pitcher George Winkleman from Minneapolis.[99]

The bottom line though was that Western Association salaries were too high, overall, and for Milwaukee, a payroll that was now $5,000 higher, produced worse results. Hart claimed it was more than he ever paid out in his American Association days.[100]

Ed Cushman was now drawing his paycheck from Des Moines, but "Cush" was falling out of favor in Milwaukee. He snubbed a Milwaukee crowd for the second or third time in mid-August, which was to the Milwaukees' benefit until they blew the game on pitcher Stephens' walks.[101]

Then there was Sioux City manager Bryan's refusal to play the second game of a doubleheader on August 17th at Milwaukee, under Umpire Cusick. Claiming biased robbery, the real motive was thought to be that Bryan didn't want to subject his pitcher Seibel to a beating.[102] The cornhusker Captain Davy Force was thought to be in on the one-game game plan, but in apologizing to refund-seekers, Jim Hart alluded to the nearby Bryan as a "monkey."

Future Hall of Fame manager Frank Selee ended speculation about his Omaha club leaving the Western Association for the American Association. He added that he thought his friend Hart made a mistake in not advocating Oshkosh's retention to their circuit.[103]

An ad ran for "GUNS, RIFLES, REVOLVERS — and — AMMUNITION/ Fishing tackle, base ball and tennis goods" at A. W. Friese, 395 Broadway. August Friese would become the sporting editor of *The Sentinel*.[104]

Hart tinkered further with his lineup, making 35-year-old 1st baseman Bill Hawes his leadoff man. Bobby Lowe, the future Boston Beaneater, who would be the first major leaguer to ever clout 4 homers in an 1894 game, was one of Milwaukee's few constants out in left. He overcame a fractured collarbone to finish the year.[105]

Hart's Friday August 24th trial in the pitching box for his Fremont, Ohio find, Wilson, went all awry. The wild man hit four Kansas City batters, and actually broke the arm of their 2nd baseman, Joe (Old Hoss) Ardner, just above the wrist.[106] A physician responded to Captain Jimmy Manning's plea to the grandstand, driving Ardner to the city, where his arm was set. A distraught Wilson was tattooed by KC bats for base hits. Their 1st baseman, Jumbo Ed Cartwright, nearly branded Wilson personally after taking a hot curve to the side. His "equipoise" overcame his disgust and he dropped his bat on the trip to first.

Wilson renewed himself by winning the first half of a Wednesday, September 5th twin dip at Des Moines. Milwaukee was the first club to reach the century mark in the schedule, though instability would do in Davenport, which replaced Minneapolis.[107]

Like Ed Cushman, old hero Cal Broughton also came in for criticism when he rolled into town for a Friday, September 14th tie with St. Paul. The 11-inning, 4-all assault was marked by Broughton's brash mouth, Bill Sowders' 17 strikeouts for St. Paul, and another ex-Milwaukeean's dirty work.[108] John Pickett's knockdown of Bill Hawes at first put the latter out of commission for 5 minutes. The butting nearly caused a hemorrhage in his upper left breast.

League Secretary Sam Morton likewise seemed to be abusing Milwaukee's record as his inefficient record keeping lopped off 4 wins. Unreliable standings and the club's own uneven play left the 5th place Milwaukees at least 20 games behind Des Moines, though they snatched a late season win over the Hawkeyes. Clark Griffith won the final Sunday, October 7th home effort over Omaha, 6–5, even though his teammates managed only 3 hits. Pleasant weather made for one of the finer turnouts of 2,500. Griffith finished 17–12 for the year.[109]

Jim Hart licked his financial losses and Harry Quin made the returning battery of future Cooperstown enshrinee Griffith and catcher W.C. Crossley the fundament of the revamped 1889 squad. Hart signed to manage the Boston Nationals.[110] Quin fought with Rochester to secure the services of one of the

Catches W.C. Crossley, as he appeared in the Monday, April 1, 1889, *Milwaukee Sentinel.*

game's grand old players to manage and captain his nine. Rochester was eager for an exhibition afterwards.

"Uncle Ezra" Sutton's career predated the first professional league, the National Association, but the Palmyra, N.Y. native was amongst the consistently good 3rd basemen of the 19th century. Superb in his Boston Red Stockings days of the 1870s, he remained a lock at the hot corner in the Hub until his first try at leadership in Milwaukee.[111]

No one could question Sutton's credentials as a gentleman and player, but early on, nagging doubts lingered about his ability to inspire teamwork. Sutton was going on 39, slipping himself into the lineup in center and at second, but mostly at short.

Tom Morrissey came back to 1st base for a third go-round against the newly renamed Western League competition. The league added Denver and St. Joseph this time.[112]

Clark Griffith effectively relieved Shenkel in a chilly April 6th exhibition at Louisville, forcing the Colonels to an 8–8 tie.[113] Bobby Lowe was one of the only other returnees in a lineup that now saw right fielder Tom Poorman in the leadoff spot, Gus Alberts at third and cleanup, and Billy Klusman at 2nd. Sutton was already on the lookout for new pitching material, when his Milwaukees dropped a 9–4 exhibition to the sick and injured National League Hoosiers at Indianapolis.[114] Shortstop Joe Herr would relieve Shenkel in this 90-minute loss on Friday, April 12th.

Harry Quin paid the St. Louis Browns' Chris Von der Ahe $1,000 for Julie Freeman, who was supposedly in demand by a half-dozen other teams. Freeman had given up only 20 hits in 4 games against three National Leagues clubs.[115] In Milwaukee's Saturday April 20, 1889 Western Association opener at St. Joseph, the new twirler was reached for 22 hits, going the distance in a 19–7 debacle.[116] Freeman's new catcher, George McVey, went down, injured. Davy Force was now a Western umpire, one whose "rank" decisions were under fire a month later.

By May 20th, the headline read, "THEIR LONG SUIT — The Milwaukees Are The Champion Losers." That 12–9 loss to a St. Paul team that now had Pickett and Hawes as teammates put Sutton's boys at 4–17, 3½ games behind 7th place Des Moines. A big crowd gave "Old Reliable" Cal Broughton, now St. Paul's left fielder, kind ripples of applause and Joe Herr, now at second, exercised his lungs as the home first base coach.[117] "Uncle" Ezra's scoring contribution came on his "gentle little sacrifice tip" to right fielder Fred Carroll, which scored Morrissey after his 2-run "drei-sacker." Angry hail made the white-clad Milwaukees ready for the wake.

Sutton was a "general favorite here as a player," but by July 1st, his qualifications to captain the nine were rendered nil. The Milwaukees were still entrenched in last place. Sutton remained second in the batting order for the time being under the new captaincy of George Shoch. The new shortstop brought 4 years of Washington National League experience with him.[118]

Sam Morton's oversight of the Western Association was also under siege. St. Paul, Minneapolis, Sioux City, and Omaha stood by him, while Milwaukee, Denver, Des Moines, and St. Joseph sought his ouster. Umpiring assignments were at the roots of complaints against him.[119]

Shoch should've heeded the advice of Sheboygan Falls dairy farmer A.X. Hyatt, who fed rutabagas to his cows at just the right time for optimum milk output. Shoch could only put himself into the cleanup spot in another 7–6 relapse against Des Moines. Leech Maskrey was now the leadoff man for them and Jimmy Macullar was their lefty-throwing shortstop.[120]

Uncle Ezra was splitting time between second and mostly center now, and while his base running was still heady, his patrol of the deep garden may have hastened his retirement.

George Washington Davies of Portage, Wisconsin, and right-handed American Association journeyman Ed Knouff were two pitchers brought in to give the club hope of digging its way out. They would have to labor mightily just to reach 20 games under .500.

At the beginning of the season, an Omaha crank offered $3 to members of his home team for every home run. The league leaders responded by calling upon him 38 times by mid-July. Sioux City's directors were desperate to unload their .500 team.[121]

Shoch administered a shock treatment by August 1st in the form of $50 fines. One who tried to escape the consequences was newly traded infielder Kirby, who took up third for visiting Denver. Ed (Baldy) Silch came over to patrol center for Milwaukee. Denver manager Dave Rowe compensated Kirby the $50 just to seal the deal. No tears were shed for the loss of the grandstanding Kirby. Uncle Ezra settled back in at second.[122]

Silch contributed a couple hits in that July 31st 16–6 romp over Denver, while Kirby went 1-for-4, with an error for Denver. Milwaukee still lagged 4½ games behind 7th place Des Moines. A coup to bounce Sam Morton, led by Harry Quin, failed by mid-August. Milwaukee's new Exposition Building was opening to great fanfare.[123]

Alexander, a pitcher released earlier by Des Moines, would absorb a terrible humiliation at Sioux City on that same Tuesday, August 20th. The Corn

Huskers crushed Milwaukee, 20–2, in 2-hours, 3 minutes and the newcomer went the distance. Moreover, Sutton was hit on the arm by a Billy Crowell pitch and badly injured. Lowe took over at second.[124]

At home, a "naval battle" staged in Milwaukee Bay attracted 100,000 from all over the region. On Thursday, August 28th, another couple thousand watched Milwaukee errors kick away a 7-run seventh inning to St. Paul.[125]

Captain Shoch's troops did a remarkable turnabout through September, though Sutton, still called the manager, has his joy tempered by the loss of his pocketbook. He was willing to let anyone who found it keep its $44. He just wanted his valuable papers returned.[126]

The Milwaukees crawled over Des Moines by August 20th, reversing that 4½ game difference. In one month, their 15–9 run would lift them to 51–60 and now chasing Sioux City for 4th place. Speculation was already rumbling that Milwaukee might replace Cincinnati in the American Association since Porkopolis had abolished Sunday ball.[127]

At a minimum, the Western Association looked likely to return and for those baseball cranks who needed amusement during winter evenings, a card-and-chip baseball board game reached Milwaukee. It was developed by ex-newspaperman F.W. Norstrand of New York.[128]

Billy Earle, "the Little Globetrotter," would answer the call from those Cincinnati Americans as a catching utility man to fill in the rest of the way for Shoch and Sutton. Clark Griffith even played left field, but it was Shoch's defense that sent St. Joe packing, 9–2, on September 19th. The Milwaukees' run on Sioux City took a ludicrous turn when Umpire Drescher was absent from the Tuesday, September 24th match-up at Athletic Park. Shoch suggested that a double umpire system be tried, which would allow Sioux City pitcher Bill Burdick and Ezra Sutton to call the game. The Iowans wouldn't have it.[129]

It was either Burdick or no game. It might as well have been that as Burdick brazenly stole the game, allowing his teammate Bradley, running between second and third to kick a batted ball away from Shoch. Milwaukee's captain withdrew his men from the field. At the urging of his fellow players, in the heat of a 10-minute argument, Burdick forfeited the game, 9–0, to his own Sioux City team! Downtown people spoke of lynching him at his hotel.

Four days later, Captain Shoch's circus leap to stop a liner towards center field "about twenty-five feet above the earth" was just one way his club vented upon front-running Omaha.[130] Earle, Mills, Alberts, and Silch all contributed 3 hits in the 19–7 win. It was suggested that club directors keep an eye on visiting manager Billy Harrington, known for his 1887 work at LaCrosse and past two pennant-winners at Lima and Canton, Ohio.

At 5 o'clock Sunday afternoon, September 29th "Mr. (Elmer) Cleveland, formerly of Washington, now of Omaha," closed the curtain on 1889 with a high fly to Silch in center. Some 3,000 saw the 15–6, 6–1 sweep of the top rung Nebraska team.[131] Prizes were awarded to Shoch for his 3 steals, and to

Earle and Alberts for 4 hits each, all to lead the twinbill. A base-running contest between Alberts, Omaha's Walsh, and Milwaukee left fielder/backup backstop Mills was won by the latter in 14 3/4 seconds.

All the fun and frivolity capped a fierce 8–3 finish for the Sutton-Shoch side:

	Won	Lost	Percent		Won	Lost	Percent
Omaha	83	37	.692	MILWAUKEE	59	63	.484
St. Paul	75	47	.615	Denver	61	70	.421
Minneapolis	65	56	.537	St. Joseph	41	65	.385
Sioux City	60	60	.500	Des Moines	41	76	.350

The team that started awfully at 4–17 went 55–46 the rest of the way. Had they sustained that .545 pace out of the chute, third place may have been possible. Incredibly, the end of the raucous 1880s would blow up in the Brotherhood War, which would suck up more talent between three major leagues.[132] Milwaukee would return most of its team for 1890.

Charlie Cushman, a 40-year-old New York City man, who would spend the rest of his life in Milwaukee, was named to manage the Cream City club. He was a National League umpire and in three years of managing Toronto in the International Association won the 1887 bunting.[133]

Even the April 6th intrasquad game between the "Never-been-beaten-club" and "Star players" had the 500 cranks on the bleaching boards howling with joy at Cushman's "hummers." His little rulebook for his players included stiff fines for violating "excessive indulgence of spirituous liquors."[134] Those guilty paid $25 on the first offense, $50 for number two, $100 for a third strike, and anything beyond that would be punished by suspension for the season's balance.

Gus Alberts at third was now being compared to the less reliable "zwei-sacker" Strauss, only "Herr Albert's beautiful Irish brogue" was lampooned. And slick 2nd baseman Welch was a "daisy."

Cushman's charges crept out to a slow 4–6 beginning, but battered St. Paul at home on Tuesday April 29th, much the same way they had dealt the local amateur Phoenix a 51–3 practice trouncing.[135] The 16–5 walkaway was rife with scattershot errors by the Apostles. Cal Broughton, back behind the plate, was responsible for three of the even dozen. In the third inning, the miscues "came so thick and fast that even the boys who occupied the private seats in the trees outside became disgusted and went of[f] to play on the hay stacks nearby."[136]

"Cream City Air Was Too Much For The Men From The Centennial State" when Milwaukee sent poor Dave Rowe's first place Denver team to defeat, 10–5, on May 15th. Another prodigal son was now back in left field for Milwaukee. Good old Abner Dalrymple, the lone hero from the sorry 1878

Clark Griffith, the future Hall of Famer, who was Milwaukee's pitching ace in 1888 to 1890. National Baseball Library & Archive Photograph Collection.

National League Grays, launched two triples from the No. 2 slot. The top five teams were clustered within a half-game of Denver.[137]

One "NIGHT MAN" advocated in a *Sentinel* letter that if Manager Cushman would up the starting times of his games from 3:45 to 2:30 or 3:00, he could increase his gate intake. The writer knew of 50 to 75 night men who would attend if they'd get home in time for work.[138] Fifty years later, Bill Veeck would cater to just such people.

Milwaukee went a full game up on Minneapolis, for first, by keeping Des Moines "as busy as census takers" on July 1st. This quintiplied contest had 5 Des Moines errors and only 5 hits off of Clark Griffith, for a 4–2 fair and square outcome.[139] This time, a player from each team substituted for a sick and travel weary Umpire Hoover.

Dalrymple was now in the cleanup spot and Bob Pettit now in center. Pettit was a bone of contention earlier in the spring when National League president Nick Young, chairman of the National Board of Arbitration, dragged his feet in securing Pettit's services from New Haven. Milwaukee's $250 annual payment to the board for protecting its interests seemed in vain.[140] A more famous Bob Pettit would play basketball for Milwaukee 65 years later.[141]

Cushman trotted out a fixed lineup that went about every win like a day at the office. In fact, his "Brewers" won 9 to 5 at Omaha on September 18th. They were two full games behind first place Kansas City and 1½ games up on Minneapolis. Veteran Bill Krieg solidified the back-stop work. John Thornton and Renwick pitched in yeoman fashion, but Clark Griffith finished with 25 triumphs.[142]

At Denver, the Brewers waltzed a hoodoo war dance around the homeboys, who committed 10 errors before 1,000 disgusted partisans. The Wednesday, September 24th final added up to 10–6, despite Denver homers from center fielder Jim Curtis and pitcher Edgar McNabb.[143]

The close of the 1890 season was fraught with questions about the fallout of the Players League and Milwaukee's future in the American Association. Harry Quin was invited by A.A. president Zack Phelp to attend a reorganization meeting for the next year, but Quin decided to wait out propositions from other parties. The A.A. was being overwhelmed by franchise offers going for thousands of dollars and it wasn't going around offering proposals.[144]

A tale of two managers was told in Denver's Dave (Eli) Rowe and Jim Hart, who was up to Milwaukee from Chicago in late September. The bullheaded Rowe refused to make up two postponed games with Milwaukee, despite the Brewers' willingness to waive the $100 gate guarantee. Rowe was so intent upon seeing the Minneapolis Millers (as they were now called) wrest second from Milwaukee that he was willing to forego $200 to see that end.[145] Rumors of Rowe leaving his Denver "rowdies" to join one of Al Spalding's Chicago enterprises would be met with a good riddance.

Hart, on the other hand, saw Milwaukee friends tear up his return ticket, obliging him to miss his 4 o'clock train back to Chicago. He was just back from England "where he met with great success in introducing America's national game to the Johnnies Bull."[146]

Rowe's Denver club was still among those on precipitous financial ground. Des Moines did collapse in favor of Lincoln to finish out 1890, and Sioux City and St. Paul were on the verge of ruin. Omaha was like Denver, a money loser. Any salary limit schemes that had been tried were invariably broken.[147]

The Brewers could only wonder what a strong third pitcher may have done for their pennant chances as they took the final two games at pennant-winning KC. The Sunday, September 28th "razzle dazzle" slugfest of errors drew 6,000. Griffith won, 15–8. Local ministers debated whether "Christ is a myth" in the secularization of Wisconsin's public schools, while the Blues had God on their side.[148] The Brewers were outbatted, 9–6, but graciously raised Kansas City's clinched pennant with three hearty cheers. The Blues and their fans reciprocated:

	Won	Lost	Percent		Won	Lost	Percent
Kansas City	80	39	.672	Sioux City	58	64	.462
MILWAUKEE	78	41	.649	Omaha	51	69	.425
Minneapolis	76	46	.621	Lincoln	48	72	.399
Denver	60	58	.509	St. Paul	36	90	.296

(Minneapolis supposedly claimed second, with their last win over Sioux City.)

Charlie Cushman refused to kick about the Brewers falling short, but did say that he thought that the combination of players subbing as umpires and his own sick and lame didn't help. Griffith's final outing was under the high fever of malaria. Cush took the blame in Renwick's absence of training at fielding his position better.[149]

The "new men" pitched well enough to fool "Old Anse" and his Chicago Colts. Cap Anson's National Leaguers won 40 of their last 46 regular games before being stymied 8–1 in an October 1st exhibition at Athletic Park. Lefty Renwick even scored on Tom Poorman's triple after singling. Poorman went 2-for-2 when the game was called in the sixth due to rain and dark. Anson, a 22-year veteran of the game, went hitless but even caught the last couple frames.[150]

The 1891 season, in some ways, mirrored Milwaukee's 1884 experience. Optimism reigned that, now with a "thorough business man," L.C. Krauthoff, as presidential secretary of the Western Association, the loop would be stronger than ever and a party to the National Agreement.[151]

Milwaukee was bolstered behind the scenes by its stock company, as was Denver. Dave Rowe wasn't gone from the league but was firing up the Lincoln entry. Charlie Cushman would have to make his pennant dash without Clark Griffith, who accepted $750 more than the $1,500 the Brewers offered. Griff would finally be united with Chris Von der Ahe's St. Louis Browns. Had Griffith not departed so abruptly, Milwaukee may have tacked on another $200-$300.[152]

Charlie Cushman considered a Milwaukee tradition in replacing his ace. Ted Sullivan managed Pat Sullivan; Jim Hart managed a pitching namesake. Cushman's directors thought of Ed Cushman, who was out in Pennsylvania. History would not repeat this time. George Davies, practicing with the university team at Madison, would be tried again.[153]

Manager Cushman was uniquely adept at securing the men he wanted. Only Jesse Burkett, a future Hall of Famer who joined another western club, was his 1891 exception.

Here was Cushman's nucleus in 1890 numbers:

	BA	R	SH	SB	FA
Left fielder Abner Dalrymple	.328	116	16	79	.875
Captain/Shortstop George Shoch	.294	123	20	37	.909
3rd Baseman Gus Alberts	.248	93	16	38	.885

Californian Sam Dungan signed on as a backup catcher/outfielder. He would later be "terrible Sammy" to Western League hurlers throughout the 90s.

Eddie Burke took over as leadoff man in center field. Cushman began the year with the vocal W.J. Campion replacing Morrissey at first and his Toronto alum John Grim at second. This would not hold. Another '89 Toronto man, via the Phillies, right-hander Tom Vickery came off a 24–22 year in the National League. More compensation for the loss of Griffith came from Fred Smith, known to Milwaukeeans for his pitching with Des Moines in '88. He brought a 19–13 ledger from the 1890 American Association Toledo Maumees. Phillies vet Pop Schriver was pegged to catch before bolting to Chicago.[154]

It was Smith who took the ball in a 4–1 loss at Omaha on Friday, April 17th. Burke and Pettit won popular favor from the 1,500 Nebraskans for their

2 — *Northwestern by Western* 57

Composite of the Milwaukee Team, as they appeared in the Sunday, April 5, 1891, *Milwaukee Sentinel.*

fabulous outfield play, but it was home hurler Dad Clark who had the last word. He held Milwaukee to a mere Dalrymple single. Omaha's leadoff man was future Milwaukee player/manager Larry Twitchell, who shone out in center.[155]

Cushman's club was representing a Milwaukee that was still steadily growing in population between 204,000–225,000 despite the effect of strikes and the migratory work attraction connected to Chicago's Columbia Exposition.[156]

A July 4th split with the Sioux City Indians drew Athletic Park's largest doubleheader crowd ever. A blushing "ex-captain" Shoch was surprised with the gift of a "very handsome watch charm." So overcome to speak, Shoch could only tip his hat and "proceeded to make one of the shortest base hits ever seen on the diamond."[157] Umpire Gaffney rapped him on the shoulder in his first at-bat of the afternoon game seen by 4,700 to make the presentation.

When 2,100 showed up for the morning game, Tom Vickery fended off an Indian uprising, watching his 8–1 lead get whittled away to an 8–7 final. Sioux City looked a little like the ghost of Milwaukee past, with Morrissey, Strauss, and Earle in their order. Vickery added a double and triple to his cause, but walked 5 and whiffed 7.

Shoch's limelight gave way to the abandonment of Davies by his defense. Dungan and Campion bungled the Indians into a two-run 7th to seal the lead. Among Davies' own two hits was a double.

The combined 6,800 saw their Milwaukees (38–27) stalemated into 2nd place, 3½ games behind Omaha. The Milwaukees flip-flopped their bench on the diamond, too, from left to right side, as is common now.

Cushman denied he was on the verge of releasing Campion when Tom Vickery's limber lightning rod of an arm "possessed the power of a Corliss engine" on August 1st. Dignitaries like ex-congressman Van Schaick, "little Van" in the white plug hat, and Police Chief Janssen marveled at Vickery's magnificent 2-hitter, which he bestowed upon the Lincoln club.[158]

Only a base on balls, a hit, and a sacrifice fly denied him a 90-minute shutout, at 5–1. Janssen exclaimed to fellow patron George Porth, "By Jove, George, we'll have to find an office for that pitcher." It would have to be in the high rent district because Milwaukee made first place its own, stretching a 7½ game lead over Omaha.

Howard (Slim Jim) Earl, a 6'-2", 180-pound right fielder from Ezra Sutton's hometown of Palmyra, N.Y., now batted third for Milwaukee and was in for the duration. Here were the Western Association standings at Sunday, August 16, 1891:

	Won	Lost	Percent		Won	Lost	Percent
MILWAUKEE	59	37	.615	Kansas City	48	47	.505
Omaha	46	38	.548	Lincoln	44	47	.484
Minneapolis	52	45	.536	Denver	38	55	.409
Sioux City	48	46	.511	Duluth	39	59	.398

The Minneapolis club refused to come to Milwaukee amid the growing likelihood that President H.E. Gillette's team was going into the American Association.[159] When it was clear that Louisville stockholders had pooled enough resources to retain their franchise, the only question was whether Milwaukee could merge with Cincinnati over Chris Von der Ahe's rather big head.

The fate of the Western Association itself was now in doubt, with acting president E.A. Krauthoff calling a special meeting at the West Hotel in Minneapolis. He believed the season could be completed with six clubs.[160]

The Milwaukee-Cincinnati merger meant that the Cream City would inherit the latter's place in the A.A. standings, its schedule and debts. A combine of the best talent, maybe including aging superstar King Kelly, was now at Cushman's disposal.

Well, the King hightailed it to Boston, but Milwaukee upgraded its few weaknesses with handsome Jack Carney at first, Jimmy Canavan at second, and Farmer Vaughn to mostly catch. Lefty Frank Killen and Cincy's Frank Dwyer (remember him?) made the rotation with Davies.[161]

Von der Ahe had owned 3/4 of the Cincinnati stock, but his syndicate made Edward Penau a figurehead president. The bombastic German acquiesced when he claimed he was ending the Western Association threat to the A.A. by welcoming Milwaukee.[162] Kelly's field management of the Porkers couldn't have been a more *bon vivant* contrast to Cushman's sober efficiency. Von der Ahe vowed he'd be back at Porkopolis.

Cushman had forfeited Milwaukee's final Western game, a 4–1 lead over Sioux City, when Gillette called him off the field to announce the move on August 15th. Cushman then took his team off the field and two days later, Gillette's group paid $12,000 for its major league privilege.[163]

Cushman's Milwaukees opened their brief American stint, with George Davies beating Von der Ahe's 2nd place Browns and Jack Stivetts, 7–2. They staggered, winning only 5 of their first 15 games, all on the road. Home again on September 7th, they annihilated the last place Washington Statesmen, 30–3, and went on to win 17 of their last 22.

Umpire Bob "Death to Flying Things" Ferguson made his first Milwaukee visit in 23 years, since the Brooklyn Atlantics' 1868 tour, to hold forth over the largest crowd in Milwaukee history on September 20th. That Sunday's 7,500 broke the previous Sabbath's record of 6,751 for a Philadelphia Athletics doubleheader.[164]

Stretch ropes were necessary to keep people off the diamond and the pennant waving Boston Reds were on the docket. Chaotic clusters of chairs in the upstairs boxes forced some of "the mass of humanity" into standing or improvising with dirty boards and ginger ale cases. There was gross mismanagement of this overflow from the outset, some two hours before game time. Milwaukee outdrew the other American games that day.

Oh, and the game, itself? Well, the glamorous Reds had a couple future

One Brewer owner's business, as it was advertised in the Tuesday, April 12, 1892, *Milwaukee Sentinel*.

Hall of Famers, 1st baseman Big Dan Brouthers and right fielder Hugh Duffy. Duffy would become quite familiar with Milwaukee later on. Errors made for a 3-run Boston fifth and Charlie Buffinton withstood any modest Milwaukee comeback. The home team's Howard Earl went 3-for-4, with the game's only homer. Earl was tagged out on a mistaken gambol to second, but Ferguson upheld Dalrymple's final Milwaukee run in the eighth. Ferguson lived up to his "King of Umpires" philosophy.

A five-minute delay occurred in the fourth when a photographer asked the sweating Reds to cease operations so he could take a statue-like shot of them in the field. Such was the major league awe to strike Milwaukee.

For their combined efforts, between the Rhineland City and the German-Athens of America, Canavan ranked fourth in the A.A. with his double-digit homer total and Dwyer had 19 total wins. The only A.A. appearance for both George Shoch and old Abner Dalrymple equaled their team-leading .315 and .311, respectively.[165]

Gillette thought he had found Milwaukee's major league answer in the excitement over the American Association. He even went so far as to entice budding star shortstop Bad Bill Dahlen from Chicago for a fast $3,500. Just as Henry Lucas and the Union Association had done to the Cream City seven years before, Von der Ahe and the dissolving A.A. would repeat.[166]

Four American franchises, the Baltimore Orioles, Louisville Colonels, Washington's renamed Senators, and Von der Ahe's Browns, would be absorbed by the National League. The garrulous German was left in charge of buying out the Western clubs. Columbus became the sixth team consolidated and Von der Ahe rendered Milwaukee irrelevant.[167]

Gillette would make a stand at a joint major league meeting at Indianapolis. The merger/disbandment plan had already been conceived as Milwaukee joined the A.A., so his demand for $20,000 was without a leg to stand on. His price wilted down to $13,000 and he finally settled at $6,000. Milwaukee would not see major league baseball for another decade.[168]

Gillette would fade to the background after being drowned by "the Beer and Whisky League." Jimmy Williams would be credited as the club president, who kept Cushman and his remnants intact, to try another Western League for 1892. John C. Iversen fudged on resigning the presidency, thinking his own business would suffer for it. Iversen hung on, but by the April 16th Opening Day at Indianapolis, Williams was in charge.[169]

Charlie Cushman's tune-ups in Louisville were punishing. Williams was providing material that, if not destined for winning a pennant, was hustling. Near freezing temperatures on April 10th made the turnstile count of 2,534 shiver, but because of Umpire Diller and four critical errors Milwaukee was defeated, 10–3. The next day rematch was even worse, 16–6, with pitcher Alex Ferson's wildness dictating the story. He was hit as badly as Harry Burrell.[170]

That Milwaukee's pitching staff looked like a gristmill made sense. The city overtook St. Louis to become the nation's second "Flour City" to Minneapolis. The Chamber of Commerce also beat the drum that Milwaukee was acknowledged as the leading barley market in the country, too. That, and a new battery might get you a competitive ball club.[171]

Cushman's cold-suffering team of charley horses learned another exhibition lesson, 9–4, at Columbus on April 12th. Seven errors, including one by Ferson himself, did him in.[172] Former Milwaukee southpaw Fritz Clausen held his old mates to 4 hits, two of those by Hamburg. Their Ohio hosts kept up the winless road march with an 11–5 thumping.[173]

Abner Dalrymple applied again to President Williams and Manager Cushman and again pondered Ed Cushman, who did desire to join the Western League.[174]

It would take the actual Western League opener at Indianapolis, on Saturday April 16th, for Milwaukee to finally win its first game.[175] Billy Harrington, once the object of Milwaukee's eye, was now the Hoosiers' skipper. A festive atmosphere, renewed by the lusty lungs of 2,400 brought President Benjamin Harrison's hometown back into the baseball fold after three years.

One would think the death of the American Association would have spread out a higher caliber of talent to trickle down to the minors. One would think. The lineup brewed by Charlie Cushman was a far cry from that which had just flirted with the majors. Howard Earl, now at first, and backup catcher Bill Krieg were the only returning Brewers.

"The Hon. Lawrence Twitchell" was now in on the scorecard as the left fielder, batting third. He was on the backside of some fine major league experience. Likewise for leadoff shortstop Chippy McGarr. The name "Ward" at second would sound impressive if it were future Hall of Famer Monte Ward. The reality was that the second Brewer in the order was none other than Piggy

Ward. Fred Lake was a Nova Scotian catcher with 5 games of Boston National exposure. Henry now grazed out in center. Charlie was the port of Hamburg out in right from his hometown 1890 Louisvilles. Fred Roat, the 3rd baseman from Oregon, Illinois (not Illinois, Oregon), also saw 1890 duty with the Pittsburg Pirates.[176]

"Colonel" Alex Ferson was a Philly man with a full .500 season for N.L. Washington in 1889. The right-hander was joined by Vermonter Harry Burrell, who went 5–2 for the '91 Browns. Wild Bill Widner was a late spring addition, who claimed a 20-loss year for the Columbus Americans in 1889 in his 4-season major resume.[177]

Cushman lobbied Williams to acquire pitching outfield reserve Smiling Al Maul and catching outfield reserve John Berger, both from Pittsburg. It was no go. His roster was relatively young and marginal. Only faith in his acumen would prevail.[178]

Alex Ferson fashioned an effective 6-hit, 5–4 win in the Hoosier sendoff. Teamwork was reflected on Larry Twitchell's relay from deep center to Henry to Roat at third. Wilie O'Brien, "fat as a prize pig," pelted the pill "chasing toward third with the speed of a drunken man in a fog." Roat blocked the bag as O'Brien puffed "like a porpoise." Anyone faster had a home run.

The Hoosiers' captain was Moxie Hengle, a onetime Union Association 2nd baseman. His double play partner, shortstop Billy Clingman, would later gain familiarity in Milwaukee. Another man with a future, Ohio governor William McKinley, threw out the first ball at the Western Association opener at Columbus.

These weren't your father's Brewers, but all the spring training woes that befell them melted away with a 6–0 start. Wicked liners flew through the Apostles' halos at St. Paul, where Henry and Widner's 3 hits apiece punctuated the 14–4 excommunication, not to mention 7 miscues served by the hosts.[179]

The heady start ended on Saturday April 30th as Kansas City doled out the 8–3 Blues. The 2,000 spectators overlooked a dusty gale to enjoy Gus Alberts' left field homer against his ex-team. KC at 7–3, now nipped at the Brewers' heels. Fred Lake hit a rare Milwaukee homer.[180]

Tom Vickery returned to Athletic Park in Omaha spangles on Sunday May 15th and pelted his mentor, Charlie Cushman, with goose eggs. Omaha president Ralph Stout's twinkling baby blues were among the 3,000 pairs of eyes in the audience.[181] Visiting Chicago president, good old Jim bless his Hart, wondered from the press box how Anson allowed "such a light as this to be hidden under a minor league bushel."

Harry Burrell matched Vickery in allowing only 7 hits as a 2–0 loser, but it was Fred Roat's triumvirate of "uselessly rheumatic" throws that were "no better than a left-handed woman with a cramp" that did it. Vickery committed only his own error for Dave Rowe's crowd. Rowe, playing first himself, scored the second run.

This loss, coupled with host Columbus' 4–1 victory over Minneapolis, put the Ohio club ahead of the 11–4 Brewers, to top the Western leader board.

Unbeknownst to the participants, the Brewers' Monday May 30th split at Minneapolis would close an era of Midwestern minor league baseball, especially for Milwaukee.[182] An uncharacteristic two errors from Twitchell in left, another by Henry's split duty between third and center, and an even dozen left on base equaled a 7–5 Miller "W." The afternoon gallop gave the Millers 4 runs in the first, but a 5-run Milwaukee seventh put the 10–8 decision out of reach. Henry went 3-for-5 with a homer; Krieg hit two home runs.

This circuit died on Memorial Day, strangely enough. The final 1892 ledger read:

	Played	*Won*	*Lost*	*Percent*		*Played*	*Won*	*Lost*	*Percent*
Columbus	32	24	8	.750	Omaha	26	12	14	.462
MILWAUKEE	26	17	9	.654	Minneapolis	24	9	15	.375
Toledo	25	14	11	.560	Fort Wayne	24	8	16	.333
Kansas City	26	12	14	.462	Indianapolis	19	3	16	.157

For the third consecutive season, albeit this abbreviated one, Charlie Cushman had a Milwaukee baseball club near the top of the heap. And if you look closely at the Western alignment, you'll see that only Louisville and St. Paul are missing, among the later Brewer rivals for the first half of the 20th Century.

The year 1893 was both a breakwater and a watershed for the National Pastime and Milwaukee's history in it. The bank panic and national depression of that year would seem the logical culprits as to why no "western" baseball took flight. That should have been the spike in "the Gay 90s," back when that term had an innocent connotation.

The Sunday morning *Milwaukee Sentinel* of April 15, 1893, said that local investors just weren't stirred by a recent stab at the National League's Louisville franchise. They did not blame the state of the economy, however. They attributed the disinterest in watching professional baseball to the health craze of bicycling.

There is no byline to this item, but blame is given to the antic behavior, the "faking" in all pro sports, that bred a suspicious public. "Baseball will never become extinct, but it is safe to say that it will never again reach any greater degree of popularity except in amateur form." Only until the game returned to its roots, so went the surmise, where local young men defeat those of a rival city for its own glory, could it overcome its "precarious" state.

A 12-team Southern League was under way, but the volume of patronage raised doubts about its future. Herman Cleaver was accepting a challenge via *The Sentinel*, of a Reinhold Schott to wrestle for $50 a side for the state championship.

Oh, life went on, Thomas Edison unveiled his "kinetograph," essentially his motion picture invention, in Chicago.

Gus Alberts even returned to Milwaukee to draw up a schedule for the amateur city league. He would play 3rd base and wear the gray uniform of the Laurels "with blue trimmings and white stockings." A J. Langsdorf caught for South Milwaukee. A league would later bear his surname.

On May 13, 1893, Milwaukee street sporting goods dealer A.W. Friese legally pursued an attachment to the receipts of the Chicago Colts for nearly $700. This was without warning to Messrs. Anson and Hart, but it was to recoup the 1891 signing of Bill Dahlen.[183] Friese was secretary and treasurer of the Milwaukee Baseball Club at the time. On Bill's signed contract, Friese advanced him $500, though Dahlen was still under a 5-year agreement with Chicago. Milwaukee demands for Dahlen's services, much less returning the advance, were ignored. The collapsed Milwaukee club owed Friese $350, which he settled up in carrying the claim against Dahlen and winning a Chicago court case. Garnisheeing Dahlen's salary was futile, as Hart claimed he was overdrawn and owed nothing. Hence Friese's authorization for his attorney.

This legal maneuver had a local precedent. Abner Dalrymple was indebted to Denver upon his return to Milwaukee. His Rocky Mountain creditors attached to Milwaukee's receipts at Minneapolis and claims had to be repaid.

Would a gilt-edged era end with Bad Bill having a guilt edge?

3

That Mack Daddy Vibe
(or, When Irish Eyes Are Winning)

The rebound from the national economic depression would be seized upon by one Cincinnati sportswriter named Byron Bancroft "Ban" Johnson. The National League was now entrenched as a 12-team monopoly over the major league landscape after the fallout from the Players League uprising and collapse of the American Association.

It was Johnson's own fallout with Cincinnati Reds' owner John T. Brush that led the scribe to the helm of a resurrected Western League.[1] Why Johnson allowed Brush to remain his nemesis as owner of the Western Indianapolis franchise remains unclear. Milwaukee was again the 900-pound gorilla of this circuit, its population of 250,000 only remotely approached by Detroit's 215,000. Detroit, Indianapolis, Kansas City, and Toledo had all flexed past major league aspirations with Milwaukee.[2] Under Johnson's tight-fisted guidance, all but smaller Toledo now had an opportunity to flourish.

Although Minneapolis was larger than Indy or KC, it never tested the major league waters. It would be a bulwark franchise in the Western League. Two cities, Grand Rapids and Sioux City, remained under 100,000 population. "The expenses of running the league are also in the lowest notch and President Johnson will see that they are kept there."[3] That early credo allowed this Western League to survive as firmly as touring Prussian strongman Eugen Sandow.

In 1894, Milwaukee was clearly America's "Beer City," both in terms of output and prestige. Captain Frederick Pabst had successfully outmaneuvered St. Louis' Adolphus Busch, in capturing the "America's Best" blue ribbon for his brew at the 1893 Columbian Exposition.[4] In this backdrop, it made sense for Milwaukee's new Western League baseball club to be christened the "Brewers."[5] The nickname would serve the Cream City for 59 consecutive seasons.

Club secretary Phil Lederer and returning field manager Charlie Cushman saw to it that these new Brewers were sartorially resplendent, particularly on the road. Cushman "properly" cast his vote for the Republican ticket, while awaiting the uniforms' arrival to their Cincinnati Dennison Hotel spring training headquarters on April 5th. The threads came via Chicago.[6]

The home uniforms were white, with black caps, stockings, belts, and trim, plus, when cold enough, black cardigan jackets. The road duds were "as pretty as could be gotten up." The shirts, knickerbockers, and caps were all a chocolate gray. The stockings, belts, and cardigan jackets were maroon, as were two small bands around the caps and "Milwaukee" across the chest. Also worn on those gray shirts would be a fluttering little blue ribbon. This wasn't proof of team members belonging to an abstinence society, but that they represented the city that made the best beer in the world. That was thanks to Pabst's achievement. Manager Cushman said the canvas sack full of bats, that accompanied the uniforms, were "charged to their capacity with base hits."[7]

The game had changed since Milwaukee last had a team. The pitcher's slab was moved back to 60'-6" and with only a couple days practice under those maroon belts, Cushman's nine split against the National League's Cincinnati Reds and Cleveland Spiders. The offensive explosion to come, from the rule change, would be huge.[8]

Milwaukee's regular season would prove to be the baseball equivalent of the human sacrifices then still being performed by the tribal Tchuktchi people in Siberia. Sacrifices were now officially being acknowledged, without a time at bat. The baseball bunt variety, that is.[9]

New enthusiasm abounded for baseball in the West and the Brewers would open with a Wednesday April 25th visit to Kansas City. The Blues would remain their designated rivals for nearly six decades. Led by the Artillery band in carriages from the Metropolis Hotel, the clubs squared off before 2,000 at Exposition Park. (Why weren't they the "Kansas City Expos?")

Milwaukee's starting pitcher, Charlie Hastings, was turned into so much "hasty pudding" in the 12–3 barrage. The Brewers' lone saving grace, only 3 errors in 50 total chances, reflected the generally marked improvement of fielding throughout baseball.[10] Most runs were now earned.

Bicycle racing was now the rage and if the Western League pennant race were an allegory, Milwaukee was running it on square tires. Of course, cricket season was opening in May. Perhaps the Brewers could turn to "Hood's Sarsaparilla Cures," as endorsed by Joseph E. Zuber of Red Oak, Iowa. One of his Hawkeye namesakes would pitch for Milwaukee 45 years later.[11]

Cold weather by Decoration Day made the Indianapolis crowd of 800 comparable to National League figures. Old Abner Dalrymple now led off for the Hoosiers, going 3-for-4, but he was no match for Milwaukee's 13–4 table turning. Brewer shortstop Bob Langsford (born Robert Hugo Lankswert) went 5-for-6, but rightfielder/Captain Pat Luby's cleanup homer was the longest ever on the grounds. Billy Clingman, the 3rd baseman of a managerial future, added 2 homers.[12]

Milwaukee's 6th place stragglers were already 8 games behind little Sioux

City's Huskers and could only hope that having the fewest games played could make up the difference. The July 4th split at Grand Rapids offered no solace. They eked out a 10–9 opener over the Rustlers, while 2,000 "hooted and hissed" at Umpire Sheridan "all through the game in a way no other umpire has ever been treated in this city."[13] Milwaukee 1st baseman George "Scoops" Carey hit safely and Luby knocked a ball over the clubhouse, 40 feet inside the 235-foot post. Sheridan called what should have been a ground rule double a homer. Carey drove home new 2nd baseman Shorty Howe with the winning run. The Brewers went to pieces like amateurs in the afternoon as 3,000 saw them commit 6 errors and George Stephens allow 20 hits in the duration of a 16–8 loss.

Ban Johnson, in the Sunday, April 1, 1894, *Milwaukee Sentinel.*

The last place look up to the Detroit Creams triggered personnel movement. Captain Luby went to the Minneapolis Millers, only to get racked on the slab for 22 hits on behalf of Manager John Barnes' stormers. That return spelled a 16–7 feast on July 22nd for host Milwaukee.[14]

The Brewers still couldn't escape dead last on August 10th, even though a dozen new bats from Michigan timber beat the visiting Sioux league leaders like a tom-tom, 13–4. Carey, old shortstop Gus Klopf, and new leadoff man Bill Goodenough all hit 11-for-16. Good enough.[15]

Charlie Cushman reported the detailed maladies of a Brewer handful to club president Henry Killilea by late August. At least Cush wasn't banished to an aunt in Chicago like May Kaatz, a teenage Jewess who dared to marry the Christian John Schultz.[16] The Brewers escaped with an undermanned 15–11 escapade at Minneapolis, featuring a Larry Twitchell home run.

It was when Twitchell assumed the club captaincy that Milwaukee made a late September parry at respectability. The complete right hander had a fine career back with the strong National League Detroit Wolverines of the mid-1880s. He both pitched and played the outfield there. He split his time between left field and 2nd base now.[17]

The Brewers proved the only Western League club incapable of even .400 ball, yet they drew an outstanding 5,000 to a September 2nd split with Toledo's Swamp Angels.[18] A club that had gone through four shortstops through the season played out the string in an otherwise funereal atmosphere.

Even a 10-game win streak, that was snapped by Indianapolis at Athletic Park on September 10th, couldn't ease the overall pain. George Carey's 4th inning solo homer in that loss had plenty to spare: "That would have made about six singles if it had been broken up and distributed about the grounds."[19]

Slip in an exhibition 6–6 tie with Brooklyn's National League Bridegroom aggregation and you have a last place finish worthy of 20 games behind Sioux City. George Shoch, the 35-year-old former favorite at short, pined for another job with the locals, while speculation swirled about a possible transfer of the National League Louisville Colonels to Milwaukee.[20]

The idea that combined rosters of cellar-dwellers Louisville and Milwaukee still couldn't create anything better than a 6th place N.L. club was anathema to *The Sentinel*: "Milwaukee will never again tolerate a team that makes a poor showing, and to impose a National league team on a city that would not be up amongst the fighting clubs would be suicide."

Louisville "hoodoo" manager Bald Billy Barnie, a moneymaker for his stockholders at every career stop, nonetheless drew a wary eye from the Milwaukee press. He was equated "in these hard Democratic times" with President Grover Cleveland's "sensational array of mistakes."

Milwaukee had spent $5,000 over any other Western team, going through 50 players and extravagant, first class expenses. They broke even when nearly every other club made money.[21]

The Brewers' strong 1894 finish cut Captain Twitchell as a winning figure. Not only did the Louisville idea fall apart, but Larry was promoted to manager for 1895. Sioux City's pennant-winning Huskers were considering a move to or merger with Cincinnati, but would ultimately become the St. Paul Saints. A flag in the Western League's smallest city only guaranteed its worst attendance. Thus, the Millers' rival was born.[22]

The news was littered with lovers' murder/suicides, interracial infatuation, the "wooly-faced girl" at Wonderland, a failed income tax attempt, and speculation about "Jack the Ripper." In March, 1895, well wishes rained upon Germany's 80-year-old "Iron Chancellor," Prince Otto von Bismarck. Just plain rain at Milwaukee's new Lloyd Street Ball Park drove Twitchell's first arrivals to condition themselves at Bader's bowling alley.[23]

After nearly a full month of exercise, Twitchell's intrasquad game drew 5,000 on April 28th. The Regulars withstood the Colts, 2–1, but the youngsters were bolstered by a few vets: Klopf at third and George Rettger in center, batting cleanup. Rettger then changed sides in mid-battle, relieving Kirtley Baker on the slab. Even boss man Twitchell was hit by a pitch, but it was Al McCauley, the "gray-haired guardian of the base Carey left behind," who stole the show. He clouted a pair of home runs.[24]

"Pop" was a lampoon target, after the initial regular season sweep by Minneapolis. "Twitchell's men stood about as though they were making mental calculations of how long it would take [the Irishman] to run a mile if it took him twenty minutes to from first to second."[25]

Last place was made even more bitterly cold by the May 14th weather in a 4–1 loss to Kansas City. Ex-Brewer Charlie Hastings' 3-hitter made it so cold "that everybody who saw the game should have been arrested for being in attendance." One fur coat-wearer in the right field bleachers even wrapped his feet with a buffalo robe from his buggy.[26]

Captain Larry's Brewers cured themselves with a Memorial Day rout to sweep St. Paul. He went 3-for-5 himself in pouncing upon the "crippled, discouraged, and disgruntled" visitors. The Apostles' Pepper was peppered for 27 hits in a 25–7 clinic. Left fielder Jim Long, center fielder William "Buck" Weaver (4-for-6, not the Black Sox man), and pitcher Kirtley Baker (5-for-6) all homered. "The St. Paul fielders ran until their heated breath came in fitful gusts and the Brewers sprinted around the bases until they left a path deep cut in the rust-colored earth."[27]

Milwaukee's 4th place tie with the Toledo Swamp Angels left them 8 games in back of Indianapolis. Brewer bats now had a reputation, but St. Paul's ill fortune would not remain.

Twitchell's experiment with moving Gus Klopf out to right and playing himself at third drew criticism about the captain's throws to first. That he had no experience wasn't weighed, but *The Sentinel* pooh-poohed the strategy, including having Weaver behind the plate, as everyone would be better off where they started.[28] Pitching lifted them to .500 by June 30th.

Captain Larry kept his Brewers on an even keel deep into August. An 11-inning, 5–4 win at Detroit featured three 2-baggers from the cleanup manager. Kirtley Baker puzzled the now-named "Tigers" on 5 hits. A mere 800 watched George Nicol now patrol center on this Milwaukee August 24th. In 5th place and 15½ games behind Indy, the Brewers chased Minneapolis.[29]

One of baseball's greatest nicknames, the Terre Haute Hottentots, supplanted Toledo by July. In a Sunday, September 1st visit, the Hottentots overcame a Gussie Klopf homer in the 7th inning, but the Bay View native's two crucial errors in right field paved the way for Terre Haute's 6–5 redemption.[30]

The Western League magnates saw no humor in the misbegotten Toledo/Hottentot ownership of Denny Long. Columbus, Ohio, "a good lively baseball town," was sure to replace them. Milwaukee's Mr. Killilea joined KC's Jim Manning, the Grand Rapids president George E. Ellis, St. Paul manager Charlie Comiskey, and his good friend, league president Ban Johnson, all at a secret Chicago Great Northern Hotel meeting to oust Long. Omaha had a chance to "break in."[31]

Twitchell's Brewers slipped away through September. They dropped to 8 games below .500, before a Saturday, September 14th display of "old time village common ball."[32] The Hoosiers outhit Milwaukee 21–16, but 4 errors by the league-leaders led to a 17–15 Brewers margin. Thanks to their 9-run 7th inning, Milwaukee held a 17–8 lead going into the ninth. George Rettger went the 2-hour, 10-minute distance and leadoff George Nicol tripled and homered. Indy's 7-run outburst made a close call, but they kept a 13–4 season advantage over Milwaukee.

Double-digits were the order of that September 14th: Detroit lost at St. Paul 10–8, host Kansas City upended Grand Rapids 15–7, and host Minneapolis thwarted Terre Haute 16–13.

The terrific slugging continued into the final Detroit series battle for 5th place. The late season arrival of Fred (Dutch) Hartman at 3rd base was like "giving a cup of spring water to a man dying of thirst."[33] His season-long services may have meant an even higher placement.

Both starters were knocked out of the box, in the 17–12 Brewer triumph on September 20th. The Portage, Wisconsin battery of 16-year-old pitcher Claude Elliott and catcher LaFleur let their hometown amateurs get lambasted by Wausau, 8–1, just so Elliott could be relived by George Stephens in the third inning here. George Nicol robbed old Al McCauley, now with Detroit, of a 6th inning home run. Buck Weaver's clincher-setting homer capped a 5-for-6 day.[34]

Despite a slow, 6th place finish, President Killilea claimed the most successful financial season — a profit of $10,000 — in Milwaukee baseball history. Had the team remained in the race after Indianapolis ended a 9-game win streak on July 29th, another $5,000 was anticipated.[35]

Miller secretary Tom Murphy conferred with club presidents Vanderbeck of Detroit and the Brewers' Killilea at Milwaukee's Republican House on the way to a September 26th W.L. meeting at Chicago. He fended off a syndicate of Minneapolis businessmen to retain his club.[36]

By then, Brewer players had dispersed to their homes: Twitchell, the native Clevelander, went to Columbus; Patrick Bolan, who was likely to be out of a catching job, went back to Memphis; the Portage battery returned home; George Rettger went to Cleveland; George Stephens went to Romeo, Michigan; Kirtley Baker went to Lawrenceburg, Indiana; the ailing 1st Baseman Bob Stafford, back to Greensborough (sic), N.C.; Billy Niles and Taylor, who would switch between second and short the next year, both went to Covington, Kentucky; George Nicol went to Barry, Illinois; and Dutch Hartman went to Rockford.[37]

Buck Weaver was to link back up with Twitchell, Rettger, Niles, Nicol, and 2nd baseman Sharpe, who came from his Bonaparte, Iowa home. All were to go from Denver by club secretary Engel to represent Oakland in the California winter league.

Maybe the Brewers' profitability saved Twitchell's managerial position, but his versatility brought a certain "ginger and pep" to the ballclub. He would seek out another twirler for '96.

The California experience did nothing for "Wallace" Taylor's waistline if the next spring 16–2 exercise over City League amateurs was any indicator. Any word of his playing for a month in Cincinnati beforehand had to be rumor because his portliness excited comment. With his flaming red undershirt, Wally now "looked for all the world like the typical foreman of the gas house." His resemblance to stout Alderman Ramsey had cigars wagered as to his identity![38]

Just so those amateurs had a half a chance on that April 12th, they were given a 4-out handicap. Twitchell was loudly cheered himself, but his recruits found quick favor. Foremost among those arrivals was a fast, little catcher named Kid "Spear" (Speer), who threw faultlessly to the bases and his triple to left center would be the game's longest hit.

The next day, "Harry Wright Day" was observed in Cincinnati, with what may have been the original Old-Timers Games. The first would be played between picked survivors of the 1860s and the second would be between the Reds of 1882 and the present league outfit. Veteran baseball writer Henry Chadwick was also to be a guest of honor.[39]

Unidentified Milwaukee player of the 1890s. Milwaukee Public Library Historical Photograph Collection.

Tradition held for many offerings of flowers, but only a bouquet was presented to Twitchell on Opening Day, Wednesday, April 22, 1896. If the cold didn't wilt the flowers, the outcome may have. Charlie Comiskey's St. Paul Apostles pulled off a triple play to spite the mayor and 3,000 of his fellow burghers.[40] Dutch Hartman, batting ahead of Twitchell in the order, hit a hard liner to Voiceless Tim O'Rourke, who converted the trifecta with John Pickett.

Umpire Sandy McDermott, normally held in high regard by this front-page account, was "as unmoved by reason as a woman" even with Ban Johnson there. It was left to Pebbly Jack Glasscock, a near-Hall of Fame shortstop who now held down first for the Apostles, to decide the outcome. The Old Battle Ax launched a sweeping Kirtley Baker out-curve to the fence for what should have been a home run. He stopped at second when the winning run scored in the 10th.

Born-Irishman Tony Mullane, the ambidextrous "Apollo of the Box," finished that win for the Apostles, another 1880s hero battling Father Time. A fitting ad for Waltham Watches adorned that sports page.

The Brewers were further stymied by the Millers' "Willie Bill" Hutchinson at the end of their opening home stand. Not fast enough for National League company in the eyes of aspiring thespian "Emperor Anson" in Chicago, Hutch's speed made "like a long flash of light in the night." In his 4-hit, 8–2 decision, Dutch Hartman had half of Milwaukee's hits.[41]

Honest-to-goodness brewers were waging a lobbying fight in Washington, D.C. against "adulterated" beer — anything made from grains besides barley, malts, and hops.[42] General strikes plagued the city of Milwaukee. After a particularly poor Tuesday, May 5th loss to Kansas City, the 500 "tried and true cranks," who rode what few buses were available, loudly defamed Twitchell and his players. Their walkout was something of a strike itself.

Perhaps the Western League umpire did likewise, since his whereabouts was unknown for this contest. Kirtley Baker and Blues' catcher Johnny Kling were "exceptionally good for players" filling in. The league was chastised for not policing its umps better. Brewer leadoff man Nicol's homer was one of only 3 hits off sandlot amateur Bevis from the banks of the Kaw.

Twitchell's Brewers overcame a slew of poor fielding judgement to climb over .500 by June 1st. His pitching protege, Kid Nonnemacher, was presented with a watch and flower horseshoe at that Memorial Day game against his hometown Columbus Senators.[43] A dropped fly by future Brewer manager Pongo Joe Cantillon in right initiated Twitchell's homecoming for a 2-run Milwaukee first. It was Kid Speer's third hit of the game that won it, however, 7–6.

A month later, *The Sentinel* went so far as to lament on its July 6th editorial page, "It appears a hopeless task trying to reform the Milwaukee baseball club. It either had no form to begin with or else it is irretrievably lost."

That criticism jolted Twitchell to step aside as manager but remain batting cleanup in right field. Bob Glenalvin, an Indianapolis native born Robert J. Dowling, brought a couple years of Chicago N.L. exposure to play second, bat sixth, and take over the managerial reins.[44]

Maybe it was the karma of a humungous Baptist Young People's Union convention in Milwaukee for that weekend, but Glenalvin's Brewers romped over the Indianapolis league-leaders, 10–1. That Tuesday, July 14th hoot meant four straight before a small crowd of enthusiasts. Lanky Bob Stafford's 3-run triple off Wee Willie Damman set the tone for much wailing and teeth gnashing back in Indy where the game was reproduced on a stage. Glenalvin was a '95 Hoosier.

Larry Twitchell's 1½ seasons led Milwaukee absolutely nowhere. Still mired in 6th place, he left the Brewers entirely for St. Paul by mid-August.[45]

Glenalvin's noodling with the lineup made no better progress, especially his rescue of wild pitcher George Borchers from the ash heap. As a Miller, Borchers had walked 9 Apostles on Independence Day, allowing 14 runs all in one inning. Glenalvin tested him again on August 18th.

Twitchell took revenge upon the wildman. St. Paul's new center fielder bat fifth in that order, contributing 3 hits and a sacrifice. Borchers allowed 26 hits and an even dozen walks in a God-awful 29–6 bombardment of Milwaukee that took only 2-hours, 10-minutes.[46] What was Glenalvin thinking? The travesty left his club 50–57, in 6th place.

Other Western League games, like the Columbus Buckeyes' 7 unearned runs to the Grand Rapids Yellowjackets' six, were carried as line scores. Like the Brewers, N.L. results came in full boxes.

The Brewers' September drift followed past precedents. A high, botched Dutch Hartman throw from third over Bob Stafford's head at first handed a game to the Hoosiers. Such abominable fielding ruined the home closeout and prompted a challenge from Manager Hansell of the Quins, the premier City League amateur nine. Hansell remarked that the pros would be "puddin" for his team after watching Wally Taylor's 3 errors in the first two stanzas versus Detroit. Glenalvin accepted the challenge, even after Buck Weaver, Stafford, and he all "played horse with the ball."[47] Ban Johnson was branded a "Jonah" by Weaver for attending the season's bookend losses. Hansell's challenge offered 60 percent of the receipts to the winner. He was to pitch.

The *Sentinel* gossip column defended the home club from foreign snipes, The *Kansas City World* urged that umpire Parisian Bob Caruthers, a once-great pitcher with the St. Louis Brown Stockings, be escorted and booted from their grounds "by a man wearing hobnailed shoes."[48] They also claimed that the Brewers' leadoff center fielder, Bob McHale, was being "knocked by Milwaukee fans."

The local newspaper thought the treatment for Parisian Bob was "a nice thing to advocate in the Missouri town where lynchings are common as afternoon pink teas in Milwaukee." Moreover, they upheld McHale as one of the Brewers' "most popular players."

Glenalvin had to be on *The Sentinel's* good side, for while a Pittsburg exchange claimed Brewers patrons were as sore with his management as Detroit

Milwaukee's City League champion Otto Bros. ballclub, who beat the Brewers in 1896. Milwaukee Public Library Historical Photograph Collection.

had been and that he was worse than Twitchell, the morning press protested that he had "greatly improved the teamwork" of the team. The 29-game, 6th place finish behind pennant winning Minneapolis offered ammo to be sure.

With nothing to show for three Western League seasons, Milwaukee dispelled the idea that the largest market often ruled the roost. A thorough housecleaning was in order.

Ban Johnson's circuit was now by far the pre-eminent minor operation in the land. President Killilea summoned a fellow Irishman, recently retired from the bench of the Pittsburg Pirates to rescue his unfermented Milwaukee Brewers.

Part ownership of the ballclub was another enticement for one Cornelius Alexander McGillicuddy, better known by the simplified baseball monicker of Connie Mack.[49] The long, lean former shoe factory worker had forged an 11-year playing career as a light-hitting, but stalwart defensive catcher. He hailed from East Brookfield, Massachusetts, spending his first four seasons with the National League's Washington Statesmen in the late 1880s.

Mack enjoyed his best full season on the field, when he bolted to Deacon White's Buffalo Bisons in the ill-fated Players League rebellion of 1890. In the aftermath of its demise, he literally caught on with the Pirates back in the N.L. At 6'-1", 170-pounds, he would be tagged "the Tall Tactician" when he assumed the Pittsburg managerial post in 1894.

Following Al Buckenberger's footsteps, his 12-10 finish that year couldn't lift the Pirates out of seventh place, but insured a .500 finish overall. Mack made himself essentially his third string catcher in '95 and '96 and a 71–61, .535 finish could again do no better than 7th. The Brewers were taking on a man who at least knew how to win, even though his lesser 66–63, .512 mark of 1896 lifted Pittsburg all the way up to sixth in the standings.

Much like Bill Veeck would do some 45 years later with the Brewers, Connie Mack made Milwaukee his proving grounds, his personal laboratory. The 1897 season would be one of much upheaval for the Western League as a whole, not just Milwaukee. As Mack reinvented his new team, the final shakedown was that Columbus and the Brewers were finally good enough to advance into the first division, while Minneapolis and Kansas City slipped badly.[50]

Grand Rapids identified itself with a fourth nickname in four years. The Rustlers, Gold Bugs, and Yellowjackets now gave way to simply the "Bobs." The league's last small market disbanded after a disastrous 1897 when "nine animated corpses," who were frighteningly outclassed, with players who "couldn't move faster than an ice wagon with one wheel gone."[51] Throwing in the towel, they were the only club in Ban Johnson's Western League to ever lose 100 games in a season (35–100, .250). They finished exactly 63 games behind the pennant-winning Indianapolis Hoosiers. The cruise director for this Titanic over the Grand Rapids was none other than Bob Glenalvin.

Kansas City no longer had Bob Caruthers' umpiring to kick about. He hired on with the smaller pastures of Tom Hickey's Western Association.[52]

Only three regulars would survive Connie Mack's overhaul of the Brewers: George Nicol, Buck Weaver (who had no chances at first in a spring exhibition), and Kid Speer. On Tuesday, April 20, 1897, Mack invited the Page Fence Giants, the colored aggregation that played ironically out of the town of Adrian Michigan, that racist Cap Anson was named for.[53]

Chattering teeth and blue noses held the turnout at Lloyd Street Grounds to a meager 300. The Page nine were coming off a loss at Peoria, but there was some consensus that, if not for his pigment, southpaw pitcher George Wilson would be a star in the National League. Page Fence was formed and captained by shortstop Grant "Home Run" Johnson, whose career would extend into the first two decades of the 20th Century. They also had light-complexioned Charlie Grant, famous as John McGraw's ruse to smuggle "Chief Tokahoma" onto 1901's Baltimore Orioles.[54]

Before facing the colored Giants, Mack tuned up against a Sheboygan club, from which he claimed catcher John Raih for 1898, but heavy snowfall prevented a game with the Matthews. Yet another "Kid," Milwaukee's own Ed Lewee (or Leewe), became Mack's fixture at short. A pair of Irishmen competed at second, Tom Daly and one of Cleveland's 5 ball-playing brothers, Tom Delahanty. One year St. Louis vet Bert Myers upheld the traditional German at third. Mack follower Joe Wright took his lefty bat out to left and Irv Waldron in right would be the era's leadoff lock.

The Page Fence Giants' Wilson kept the Brewers guessing through the first 4 innings, but then the "colored boy" went unsteady, walking four and hitting two batsmen in 8 innings. He earned everyone's respect, but suffered through a 5th inning bludgeon that consisted of Wright's homer and a Myers triple, Delahanty and Nicol doubles, plus a couple singles that all added up to 5 runs. Nicol also pilfered a couple sacks in his 4-for-4 day.[55]

Amongst returning pitchers Fred Barnes, George Rettger, and Bert Jones, each going 3 frames, only Rettger was seriously touched for 3 runs in the fifth. Johnson and Grant were the only Page Fencemen to hit for extra bases, each doubling. Defensively, Lewee accepted six difficult assists at short and "Speer stopped four darkey baserunners who attempted to steal second." The 9–4 Brewer win took two hours as they subdued an eighth inning threat with 3 men on. It was the first known appearance by a black baseball team in Milwaukee.

Daly turned an ankle in a final exhibition against the University of Wisconsin varsity nine. Mack postulated in a dispatch, circulated by *The Cincinnati Commercial-Tribune,* that ballplayers would never again try and form a union. He spoke firsthand in light of the 1890 Brotherhood disaster. "The only dissatisfied men are the ones who did not play good ball last year and are being cut this season."[56]

Of course, much like other former players-turned-owners, namely Al Spalding and Charlie Comiskey, Mack would go on to demonstrate some penurious ways with the Philadelphia A's.

The Thursday, April 22nd home opener warranted front-page coverage. And again, everyone was confounded by the club's inability to win a lid-lifter.[57] For the first time, an exact crowd of 3,163 was announced. After Killilea and Mack scouted ominous skies from the elevated vantage point of the Republican House roof, the weather brightened favorably.

The parade of the teams from the St. Charles Hotel to the grounds led to bleachers that were filled an hour before game time, a "record" weekday crowd. Zeitz's military band welcomed the visiting gray and black Minneapolis Millers, defending league champions. The locals shone in bright new white and blue uniforms.

Everything was grand, except for the 8–6 final. Three miscues by Bert Myers at third, another by Joe Wright in left, and two misjudged flies by Lippert in right compounded the inability to overcome Miller starter Pat Carney at crucial times. The debut was spoiled, but among its curious coincidences was that Bud Lally patrolled leftfield for Minneapolis, but he would die in Milwaukee 36 years later. The game's umpire was also a Lally and his decision to allow the Millers' Wisconsinite Walt Wilmot to score from second, as teammate Cassidy "mixed up" with Buck Weaver at first, was of a dubious nature.

The Millers' cleanup hitter was right fielder "Doggy" Miller, another 13 year majors vet, like German-born 3rd baseman Willie Kuehne. Future Cleveland shortstop Neal Ball led off for them. A 7th-inning rally by the Brewers couldn't separate the wheat from the chaff.

The inauspicious debut to the Mack era was further disrupted by the white stuff, the wet stuff, and early injuries.[58] Still, it wasn't to be the same old same old.

The Milwaukee Brewers finally found enough synchronization to post the organization's first winning season. Their 85–51, .626 record merited their first appearance in the first division, a mere half-game behind St. Paul and 14½ behind the bunting-snatchers from Indianapolis. They would also turn "a handsome profit."[59]

The Hoosiers attempted an ill-conceived Cup playoff with the runner-up Columbus Senators. The anti-climactic disaster, modeled after the National League's Temple Cup, was abandoned before either side could win 4 games.[60]

Cornelius Alexander McGillicuddy — Connie Mack — "The Tall Tactitian" and future Hall of Famer, who taught the Western League Brewers how to win. National Baseball Library & Archive Photograph Collection.

Even in an age when the Philadelphia Phillies could have an entire outfield of .400 hitters, the assault on the Western League batting crown by outfielder Sam Dungan of terminally-5th place Detroit was no less astounding. He finished at a .455 clip.[61]

Connie Mack had now raised the bar for Milwaukee. Expectations at the single-decked Lloyd Street Ball Park would be genuinely higher for 1898. No longer would fans look over its billboarded center field fence, dangerously propped by wooden supports, for divine inspiration. The Cross Lutheran Church steeple rose above the wooden grandstand that went less than 10 rows deep. It was shorter than the open bleachers on each side, but there was a short incline to the very short right field fence there.[62]

That anticipation was tempered only by the reality that President William McKinley was about to lead the United States into war with Spain. "Remember the Maine" reverberated across the country after that ship was exploded in Cuba.[63] On the local political front, the industrial suburb of South Milwaukee pitted Populist-Prohibitionist-Democrat Samuel R. Wallace for mayor against the re-election of Republican nominee George C. Bush.[64]

Joys Bros. which advertised awnings, tents, and the like, would decades later still be known as Laacke and Joys. "Basket ball" in its infancy, saw the Milwaukee Athletic Club defeat Co. A by a "decisive" 14 to 9 score.[65] Schlitz brewery was building a $25,000 bowling alley.

In the Western League, the Omaha Babes replaced the crestfallen Grand Rapids franchise and George Decker was orphaning Chicago's N.L. Orphans to manage there.[66]

Success for Connie Mack also bred holdouts. He worked out with 14-year major league veteran Adonis Terry, a 4-time 20-game winner. Terry would become one of Milwaukee's most prominent bowling proprietors, but for now, he formed a "midget battery" with Mack. Kid Speer and George Nicol also engaged in March limbering at Milwaukee Park, as Lloyd Street was also called.[67] George Rettger, Bill Reidy, Bert Myers, and George Shoch all refused to ink up.

Ads touting rail travel to California's winter paradise or Alaska's Klondike gold rush were juxtaposed with the death of a man who went no further west than Chicago for his fortune. Edward Carqueville, "said to be the oldest lithographer in the West," was a direct descendant of Martin Luther. Milwaukee's special summer carnival honored Wisconsin's 50th anniversary and *The Sentinel* even printed a special history of "Deutsch-Wisconsin" in the German *Fraktur* text.[68]

Ban Johnson enforced a salary limit upon his Western League, despite kicking from the Indianapolis champs about salary cuts. They flouted their affairs with John Brush's Cincinnatis. Connie Mack likewise tolerated no monkeying around, threatening to send Myers to the lesser Western Association just to deny his release to Washington.

Mack still had the returning swift Irv Waldron, the "best rungetter in the league," if not Nicol. And his third base dilemma opened the job to Kid Lewee, who signed from the helm of a Cincinnati tinsmith shop. Fred Barnes was a possibility for the Kid's job at short, joining the dotted line from Lincoln, Nebraska. Barnes prepped there for a post-baseball career as an electrical engineer. Lewee led Eastern League third sackers 2 years earlier and Mack was a 1st base idea himself. Joe Cantillon, who would manage the Brewers in a few years, was now conditioning himself in Milwaukee to be a Western League umpire. "Pongo Joe" was from Janesville, Wisconsin.

Quin Blank Book & Stationery Co. on 427 East Water Street was now advertising as the Northwestern Agents for Reach's Celebrated Sporting Goods, including their "Special Wagon Tongue Bats."[69]

Adonis Terry and Charley Cushman were among the well wishers to see eight Brewers off to their Louisville training site. Cush warned auburn-haired southpaw Adolphus Vollendorf, "If you don't beat out Elliott when Milwaukee plays against Detroit, I will never speak to you again or recommend another player to a baseball club."[70]

President Killilea was as cryptic towards ballplayers: "There are really only

Some 1898 Brewers, as they appeared in the *Milwaukee Sentinel.*

two periods in their existence, when they growl over their salaries — when they enter the game and lack experience, and when they become so old that they have outlived their usefulness."[71]

St. Paul manager Charlie Comiskey said that mechanics play ball from the neck down, while artists play from the crowns of their heads to the soles of their feet. Any artists for Milwaukee were facing cold and shoe-top deep mud at Louisville, but they tried for a 4-game exhibition series with the now-St. Louis Cardinals by April 9th.[72]

On April 8th, Assistant District Attorney Bell prepared an opinion that Republican George O. Bush was legally elected mayor of South Milwaukee, and by that, the city council backed off from trying to abuse the Election Board's returns to count him out. Sound familiar?[73]

Bert Myers was condemned to reserve limbo when the Brewers fell for the opening count at Columbus on April 21st. Upholding this time-honored custom, an 8–2 tally, was erstwhile pitcher Fred Barnes at 3rd base. Officially charged with only one error, his "judgement was as yellow as a canary's feathers."[74] Only 1,000 there heard an actual gong to inaugurate the season.

The May 2nd return engagement of Tom Loftus' Senators in Milwaukee left "soup for Columbus, joy for [Brewer] fans, and a heavy load removed from Matt Killilea's mind."[75] Matt was Henry's brother and they were among the nearly 400 witnesses to brave unfavorable climes. "Hi Hi" Seligman may have had a worthy rooting successor in "Cheer Up!" Scheftels. He conducted an "anvil chorus" upon Senators' 1st baseman George "White Wings" Tebeau quite artistically.

The Brewers walloped Columbus, 10–5, on a muddy diamond, but Fred Barnes was yet a fright afield. George Nicol was tossed by Umpire Manassau, so Fred switched from his hot corner afflictions to promptly misjudging a ball to deep center. Old George Shoch took up at third.

A mid-May convention of police chiefs in Milwaukee's Pfister Hotel revealed the Western depredations of Butch Cassidy's outlaw gang, robbers who paralleled the James family. The U.S. invasion of Cuba was imminent and the red-hot bat of Detroit's Sam Dungan arrived in the Beer City.[76] The Tiger outfielder wielded a 4-for-4 day in front of 5,500; but the Brewers boiled lefty Noodles Hahn with a 9–1 cannonade. Even Milwaukee pitcher Jack Taylor went 3-for-4. George Nicol roamed center for the Brewers. "Nicholl" did likewise for Detroit.

Whatever patriotic fervor the war with Spain was eliciting, it surely fell flat on the Friday, May 28th visit by the Kansas City Blues.[77] The game was played for the benefit of the Soldiers' Monument fund, but a crowd of less than 1,000 raised a piddly $167.38. Even city officials, baseball stockholders, and press reps left their free pasteboards behind to patronize the box office.

A committee of a Mrs. Ely's ladies handled the intake, but with $30,000 necessary, other fund raisers at an authors' carnival and a special vaudeville matinee at the Alhambra Theater had to be radically more bountiful.

Connie Mack's crew did their part by hammering KC, 12–3. The Blues were kept "on a leather-hunting expedition they will not forget until the blue expanse of Lake Michigan separates them from the Cream City." It also finally put the Brewers over .500 (16–15), but still in 5th place, a game behind the club from the Kaw. John Raih finally tested the mask and "windpad," too.

Mack, himself, even grandstanded at first, to allow one Badger on in a

Connie Mack dreams of winning the pennant in the Thursday, August 18, 1898, *Milwaukee Sentinel*.

June 2nd exhibition 11–2 joust over the U.W. at Madison. Old Adonis Terry's pitches just whistled past the collegians, who mustered only four hits. Mack took his crippled road show back to the league wars.[78] Between Shoch's index finger, Weaver's strained muscles, and a witch hazel-less Nicol, the club was again wanting at third and left.

The dog days of August were anything but. Mack, craving the pennant, foresaw a fast finish. The appellation applied to the Brewer skip by *The Minneapolis Times* was "Conrad McGillicuddy," but that notwithstanding, the phenomenal pitching of George Rettger and Jack Taylor fostered the surge. Taylor was likely to be sold to Chicago for the next year and Mack sent for Vollendorf to report back from the New Havens when he was done in the East. Shoch settled in at third base.[79]

Milwaukee's Bahn Frei (Path Free) Turner Hall wasn't faring as well. The gymnastic facility was auctioned off for $1 to the P. Schoenhofen Brewery of

Chicago.[80] Jack Taylor turned the visiting St. Joes (nee Omaha) inside out, with a 2–0 whitewash on August 17th. William Reidy followed that with a 4-hit, 6–1 win over St. Paul before 2,000; he added 2 hits that August 19th.

Milwaukee was now a half-game behind top-rung Kansas City. It was the Brewers' finest run since topping the old Western Association in 1891 before going major to the old A.A. With an 11–4 season edge over St. Paul, what did their *Globe* think of Brewer wood-chopping now?[81]

Rettger nearly shut out Minnesota's capital nine on Sunday, August 21st. Only a wild throw by catcher Broadway Aleck Smith, secured by Mack from Brooklyn until Speer regained health, kept 5,500 delighted fans from seeing goose eggs.[82] The 6–2 final still wasn't enough to overtake KC. Brooklyn's magnate Charles Ebbets was in town seeking the services of 2nd base/Captain Tom Daly and the Ohio "Brakeman" Jack Taylor for 1899.

Taylor must have succumbed to the pressure of Ebbets' interest, for the next day, he was as "ragged as a tramp's coat" and as "costly ... as an Easter bonnet" in an 8–4 loss to the Saints.[83] Daly likewise wilted with the willow at RBI opportunities.

Clarence "Ginger" Beaumont, from just down the road south of Milwaukee, a native of Rochester in Racine County, arrived just in time to vault the Brewers into a first place tie with the Blues. In the straight-up confrontation with Kansas City, the young left fielder from Waupun dazzled 2,000 onlookers with his sensational shag of Hal O'Hagan's low line drive to prevent a score. Before Jupiter Pluvius rendered the five-inning, 55-minute battle finis, with a torrential deluge, Beaumont added to his heroics with a 2-run homer off Dale Gear.[84]

Umpire Sheridan called the game at 5–3 and the youngster was the object of roaring, hat-throwing joy. It took three more days, but on Friday, August 26th, Mack's Brewers finally sat alone atop the Western League! The celebration garnered front-page coverage.[85] Reidy's 2–0 shutout of Minneapolis put the locals two full games ahead of both Indianapolis, who moved percentage points up on the Blues.

The Millers' McNeely held Milwaukee to 6 hits himself, but Weaver crossed the rubber on a bungled double play and Nicol's speed forced another wild throw to set up his score on Beaumont's sacrifice fly. Again, the RBI hero! These exhilarating nine innings took a mere 65 minutes!

The *Sentinel's* August 29th editorial page screamed, "AND NOW STAY THERE, CONNIE ... Connie Mack's troops have the true war spirit and are fighting hard."

Even though the Brewers took two of the next three from the Millers, they fell a percentage point behind Indy. Over the din of local crowing, Manager Franklin of Eastern League Buffalo offered $2,000 that three of his circuit's clubs could beat three Western League sides. Mack and Minneapolis' Walt Wilmot were skeptical of the bluff.[86]

Beaumont was the hero again, saving a rubber match over Columbus when his feint to go home drew a wild throw from third by the Brewer bench. His winning score was witnessed by his father, who drove (by buggy, it's assumed) the 33 miles up from Rochester.[87]

The excitement, commensurate with maintaining the league lead, drew modest weekday crowds in the 1,200–1,800 range. Beaumont continued his wicked ways with Columbus pitching, adding a 4-for-4 notch to his belt. Alex Smith's 13-game help ended with his rejoining the Trolley Dodgers in Chicago.[88]

The final doubleheader against Detroit drew an incredible 8,500 spectators. The Sunday, September 4th revelers wallowed in Adonis Terry's 6-hit, 6–2 victory in game one and Captain Daly's 3-for-4 day snared him as many runs as the Tigers. Game two was called after the Detroit half of the 7th, so both teams could catch their trains.[89] Lefty McDonald notched a 6–1 seal on first place in his first local outing. Beaumont sat out the twinbill with injured fingers.

Clarence "Ginger" Beaumont, the Rochester, Wisconsin, outfielder who stole the 1898 Brewers show. National Baseball Library & Archive Photograph Collection.

It was timely that Cornell University professor Burt G. Wilder, M.D., a "Brainologist," was soliciting bequests of brain matter from educated persons in Milwaukee.[90] The mania caused by the Brewers would have made for great study!

Alas, when Mack's Milwaukees hit the road for the final stretch, the hold upon first sailed away, just like Captain J.C. Iversen's (remember him?) yacht, *Frances*. A three-game sweep at Indianapolis catapulted the Hoosiers into first.[91]

Here was the *Sentinel's* editorial assessment: "The Milwaukee Baseball club lost no time in disabusing the public of the idea that it had any serious intentions on the pennant."[92] Of course, they faltered without their ramrod, Beaumont, who rejoined them by going hitless in a 4–3 exhibition win against his old Waupun mates. Mack even caught Charles McDonald there.[93]

Ban Johnson arrived in Milwaukee in mid-month to consider which among Buffalo, Toronto, Denver, or Chicago might replace weak sisters

Columbus and St. Joseph. St. Joe's rough ride through the Western League ended mercifully with a rescheduled 6–1 loss at Milwaukee on Monday, September 19th. A mere 500 saw a sloppy 8 errors between both sides but the Brewers cinched third place at 82–57, .590. They finished 6½ games behind KC, 1½ up on St. Paul.[94] Reidy won only his ninth versus 19 defeats.

Kansas City's Cowboys seized the pennant from Indy on the last game of the season. Manager Jimmy Manning was carried aloft among 8,000 frenzied celebrants.[95]

To editorial disdain, the Brewers sold their leading regular hitter (.295), 2nd base/Captain Tom Daly to Brooklyn for $800 and Jack Taylor's 28–15 record to President Jim Hart (remember him?) of Chicago for another $2,000. For Daly, Milwaukee would receive keystone man Bill Hallman from the Trolley Dodgers. Taylor was expected to pitch against the Baltimore Orioles that week.[96]

For the first time, *The Sentinel* published the club's statistics in some detail. In Daly, they were also losing their leading doubles (24) and sacrifice (20) hitter. His 9 homers were runner-up to 1st base-

Ginger Beaumont, when he still shagged flies for the 1910 pennant-winning Chicago Cubs, at the end of his career. National Baseball Library & Archive Photograph Collection.

man Bob Stafford. Daly also tied Waldron for the team lead in stolen bases, with 48. Ginger Beaumont's dash with destiny meant .354. He'd start 12 big league years at Pittsburg.

Adonis Terry was stellar, posting the best pitching percentage, .786 (11–3), while swinging a .306 bat. Fielding was still relative to the era, but Lewee had 62 miscues at short, Daly 56 at the keystone.[97] Still, Mr. Mack had found a winning formula, bolstered by George Rettger's 25–15 pitching.

That wonderful exasperation crafted by Connie Mack in 1898 receded to a sideswipe of harsh reality to end the century. That penchant for squandering such accrued goodwill would be a pattern throughout his managerial career.

Still, the spring of 1899 brought out the verse in *The Colorado Springs Gazette*[98]:

> The Baseball Season
>
> Get out the club and paddle suit
> Produce the whirling sphere
> For there is no denying it
> The baseball season's near
>
> Get colors gay and horns of tin
> Both relics from last year
> Witch hazel, too — and rub it in
> The baseball season's near
>
> Come, grease the lungs and thorax
> That yelling may be clear
> This statement is no hoax-
> The baseball season's near
>
> Just keep your eye on April set
> The day will soon be here,—
> The boys here now sent forth the word
> The first ball game is near
>
> Awaken from your lethargy
> The time is almost here
> When we must lose our apathy
> The baseball season's near
>
> Soon we will hear the crazy shout
> That echoes far and near
> And tells us that beyond a doubt
> The baseball season's near
>
> The lads up at the college
> Will cross Chicago's tracks
> And impart some baseball knowledge
> To the Windy City cracks
>
> So get the rooters ready
> Soon to bleachers we'll adhere
> Young woman, tell your "steady"
> That the baseball season's here.

Prior to the Western League banquet held at Milwaukee's Republican House on March 22nd, the 1899 schedule gave Milwaukee 10 Sunday home games and Columbus here on Memorial Day. Connie Mack's men would be in Kansas City on July 4th and Columbus on Labor Day.[99] The total number of games would be scaled back to 126 also.

Matt Killilea hosted the dinner and Mack and treasurer Fred Gross joined in the toasts. Buffalo's Franklin was now a welcome member and tribute was paid to the unexpected passing of Marcus P. Hayne of Minneapolis. A veritable "love feast, hatchets were buried and good fellowship marked the closing

Base Ball Uniforms
MADE TO ORDER
Special Low Prices Made If Ordered Before March 25

We Furnish Everything in the

SPORTING LINE
AT REDUCED RATES

Send for Catalogue and Price List.

QUIN BLANK BOOK & STATIONERY CO.
Northwestern Agents Reach's Celebrated Sporting Goods.

Complete from $3.00 up **427 East Water Street** - - **Milwaukee**

Harry Quin's business, as advertised in the March 23, 1899, *Milwaukee Sentinel*.

hours of the social season of the league." Killilea arrived late from Madison to preside over it.

Mack used spring training to weirdly toy with calling his club "the Milwaukee Giants," given that he supposedly had the biggest men in the league.[100] He even trotted out new uniforms, now with dark blue trim, to mark the occasion. By the time regulation play began, they were back to the "Brewers" in the sports pages.

Maybe if he had read the "Carnival Edition" of *The Sentinel*, which touted that Milwaukee had more insurance companies than any other western city, he would have christened them the "Insurers," "Actuaries," "Quotes," or maybe "Premiums." Des Moines and Omaha would probably have something to say about the city's claim as the "Western Insurance Center."[101] The Kansas City Blues would be in during that late June Carnival week.

It was actually calculated that, at opposite ends of the Western League, Buffalo would rack up the most mileage, 10,164; and Kansas City, 9,000. The Brewers were a middling 9,170.[102]

If baseball wasn't "the Best Spring Tonic," then Dr. Williams advertised that his "Pink Pills for Pale People" were. At least they did "not act on the bowels!" America's war to liberate Cuba, "Porto Rico," and the Philippines from Spanish domination was pressing on well. The "Superior Quality" of Blatz Bock Beer was out by April Fool's Day.[103]

This time, Killilea and Mack had all their charges agreed to terms, except Shoch, who was expected to see only utility duty. An April 5th *Sentinel* editorial waxed, "The Milwaukee baseball team will take a short term course with the athletic class of Wisconsin university next week which ought to qualify Connie Mack's men to enter Professor [Amos Alonzo] Stagg's amateur prize tournament for professional athletes."[104]

Snow still engulfed Milwaukee's baseball park, hence Mack's plan to go to Madison. It wasn't until Tuesday, April 11th that his "Giants" finally tested new Bill Hallman at cleanup, just as the "Mutt and Jeff" battery of 6'-6" Cy Swaim and pudgy little Kid Speer. They outdid the Badger varsity in that initial scrimmage, 13–10. While these two teams toiled before joshing students, legislators, and "street gamins" (as opposed to Peter Gammons), a local Milwaukee product, Eddie Bach, pitched up a storm for Georgetown University.¹⁰⁵ In allowing 9 hits to the albeit woeful Washington Senators, Bach forced a 3–3 tie. The Senators were in their last National League season.

Other members of Connie Mack's 1899 Brewers, as they appeared in the Sunday morning April 16th *Milwaukee Sentinel*. Bert Husting later became a U.S. district attorney in Milwaukee.

Mack had to scrounge up some City League players to flush out a couple intrasquad contests, while playing first for the "Colts" himself. They also whipped Stagg's varsity Chicago Maroons, 18–6. Also crushed were Jefferson (Wisc.) with Columbus lefty hope Ed Heimerl, 22–3.

Across the Atlantic, Finns petitioned against the Russification of their land by Tsar Nicholas II's empire. This defense of Finnish nationalism would lay the seeds for a form of baseball to be played there some two decades later.¹⁰⁶

When the Minneapolis Millers opened the 1899 championship race at Milwaukee on Thursday April 27th, Ban Johnson threatened to fine the batsman if he tried to swing at his ceremonial first pitch.¹⁰⁷ The 2,500 attendees couldn't officially enjoy Milwaukee's 2–0, 4-inning lead when "Jupiter Pluvius placed a quietus on King Baseball." Players from both teams were entertained at the Academy that evening, however, by the Thanhouser-Hatch company. And they watched from boxes specially decorated with baseball paraphernalia, too.

Mack's Brewers slowly climbed to the promised land of a first place tie with St. Paul by June 7th. Along the way, they crushed the Saints in Minnesota, 16–4, on May 11th. Irv Waldron went 4-for-4 and Kid Speer's 3-for-4 led the way.¹⁰⁸

MILWAUKEE BASEBALL NINE TO-DAY.

SPEER, Catcher.　　　　HART, Pitcher.　　　　SHOCH, Short Stop.
STAFFORD, First Base.　HALIMAN, Capt. & 2d Base.　GRAY, Third Base.
BARNES, Left Field.　　NICOL, Center Field.　　WALDRON, Right Field.

Opening Day lineup, in the Thursday, April 27, 1899, *Milwaukee Sentinel*.

Only 300 were there, but St. Paul still had Bob Glenalvin at second and batting third, plus the "Bald Eagle," Frank Isbell, playing first. He would later reach World Series heights as Chicago's "Hitless Wonder" White Sox 2nd baseman.

A May 21st loss at Detroit had many among the 6,000 resorting to the sunnier warmth of the center field fence where the bitter cold wind was blocked.[109] Crowded foul lines retarded outfielders' movement, but enforcing ground rule doubles wasn't much needed. Tiger righty John Cronin held Milwaukee to only five hits.

Connie Mack changed course, steering his team away from off-day exhibitions and focusing on batting practice instead. He decided his players benefited more from the respite. Mack received a "glad hand" when the Brewers first entered Buffalo in memory of his Brotherhood days as the Bisons' mainstay backstop.[110]

Milwaukee Club's Long and Short Battery. Monday, April 17, 1899, *Milwaukee Sentinel*.

That city's own *Courier* was hard on their current 7th place incarnate:

> Rub-a-dub-dub, nine dubs in a club
> And who do you think were there?
> A bad bunch of fielders and weak wattle wielders
> And all went up in the air.

A disastrous Brewer road trip ended on June 13th, with a 4–2 travail on Bumpus Jones' 5-hitter at Columbus.[111] Kid Lewee was released by the Senators and expected to be offered another trial. Mack didn't worry about his team's dogged batting slump, but .500 meant 6th place.

The record continued to deteriorate, and fresh bodies were hired. Jim Viox (pronounced "Vicks") came from KC to handle 2nd base. Canadian Bunk Congalton, a lefty bat from Guelph, Ontario, took over the number 3 slot in the order, as well as center field.[112]

St. Paul's *Pioneer-Press* said that when Congalton was good, "he was very, very good, but when he is bad he is awful." This was some 30 years before Mae West, but judging fly balls over his head was his Achilles' heel.[113] Revived Brewer bats had the final say, disgracing the Saints' Chauncey Fisher in an 11–6 drubbing up there.

Mack's 1899 Brewers season unraveled to the point of dropping their final home double bill to last place Buffalo.[114] Rettger and Reidy still pitched effectively, but an atrocious defensive letdown by Weaver, Waldron, and Gray led to the latter's benching for game two. Only Viox now shone at short and added a game two homer. Sixth place was kept from KC and the Bisons.

The final split at Indianapolis left the Brewers a thoroughly disappointing 20½ games behind the perennial Hoosier pennant-winners. The influence of Cincinnati's John T. Brush over Indianapolis clouded the league and Grand Rapids finished the season for failed Columbus.[115]

President Ban Johnson feared for his Western League to turn the new century. His grave consideration was that the National Pastime was losing its hold upon the public. Charlie Comiskey and Tom Loftus were among all the circuit's managers to concur that "baseball was in decadence."

Connie Mack could only sign up a 20-year-old Chicago shortstop named Edward Holly, who caught his eye during a July 7th visit to the Manistees in Michigan.[116] Those he sent packing could be rode out of town on the surreys, buggies, or phaetons sold at John Dorsch & Son at Wells and Second Streets. Those being dealt in the Hot Stove League could buy their Buck's Steel Range at F.W. Schneck & Co. House Furnishers at 255–259 Third Street.

Irv Waldron led the 1899 Brewers in batting (.335), runs (100), triples (9), and stolen bases (42). Bob Stafford led with 8 homers, but his anemic .219 would lead to a younger replacement. Rettger, Reidy, and Fond du Lac, Wisconsin's Bert (Pete) Husting, all pitched winning ball, but Billy Hart's 6–14 was the millstone. Gray's 44 errors at third remained a vexation.[117]

Detroit's Sam Dungan won four Western League batting titles, but moved onto Kansas City. He would never seriously impact the major league level.

Ban Johnson's response to "decadence in baseball" in one sense fueled it all the more. For 1900, his "Western League" would no longer be regional in scope. It crept eastward and into larger markets, although at this turn of the century juncture, his new "American League" would not yet claim major status. It was organized at the 1611 Grand Avenue home of Henry Killilea.[118]

Johnson's good friend, Charlie Comiskey, relocated his St. Paul Saints to revive the original Chicago White Stockings nickname. They trained at the University of Illinois at Champaign. The 1899 Cleveland Spiders were bled dry by syndicate ownership in St. Louis and crashed to the worst record in major league history (20–134). Abandoned by the National League contraction of four franchises, Cleveland's Spiders were reorganized from transplanted Grand Rapids by Kilgoyle Summers. He was assisted by Connie Mack.

American League magnates pondered replacing Minneapolis with N.L. orphan Louisville, but Johnson would not stand for it.[119]

America's Dairyland, the State of Wisconsin, would wage war upon oleomargarine by taxation, the same way the National Pastime's magnates were about to battle one another.[120]

Milwaukee became one such battleground. A laconic Harry Quin was confronted about the National League's desire to lease his Athletic Park. The senior circuit's counter to Ban Johnson was to form a minor American Association headed by Robert Young, son of N.L. President Nick Young. Quin would only admit that he was working for a better brand of ball in Milwaukee. His associate, Milwaukee's 4th Ward alderman and merchant tailor Charles Shelton Havenor also downplayed their efforts. Havenor's links to the street railway lobby led to *The Sentinel* opposing his re-election. He won anyway.[121]

Ban Johnson saw the proposed association, which included the abolished N.L. cities of Baltimore, Cleveland, Louisville, and Washington, plus Chicago, New York, Philadelphia, and St. Louis as just a bluff.

Adonis Terry hadn't applied to *any* league, but left the door open to umpiring, should an opportunity present itself. The sound of falling bowling pins was his real calling.[122]

The world by April Fool's Day 1900 saw Londoners naming their babies after Boer War heroes. U.S. Senator W.N. Roach of North Dakota endorsed "Peruna, The Catarrh Cure" in print. Phil R. Miller's Unique New Musical Comedy-Travesty, "The Hottest Coon in Dixie," played at Milwaukee's Bijou Theater with the original "Clorindy" Chorus of 18 Colored Singers. If they shopped at The Hub's children's clothing department, they could receive a free, full-sized mandolin, banjo or violin, with every $10 purchase.[123]

Milwaukee's Athletic Club faced Fond du Lac's traveling Co. E team for potentially the state basketball championship and a chance to stake a claim at the national title.[124]

The *Buffalo Express* baseball writer saw Connie Mack's Brewers as a "racy" team.[125] That was apropos because Mayor David S. Rose's wide-open welcome mat to "gamblers, pugilists, and prostitutes" turned staid Milwaukee into a racy town. Hizzoner was also under scrutiny for casting his lot with the "street car gang."[126]

For the first time, Connie Mack trained his Brewers at southern Indiana's resort town of Richmond. He had filled his quota of ball-tossers by inking former Philly George Wheeler to join Willie Reidy, George Rettger, Pete Dowling, Tully Sparks, and Charles McDonald. Bert Husting weighed the renewal of his Brewer ties at the University of Wisconsin in Madison.[127]

Big Bill Clark wafted the ball over the race track fence at Richmond and Fred Barnes awaited a train ticket to fulfill his Indianapolis offer. In Milwaukee, Harry Quin bought out his St. Louis partner, R.O. McGuire, for sole control of his home ballpark. Quin went ahead towards "resuscitation of the New American Association of baseball clubs."[128]

Before the gentlemanly Brewers pulled up stakes from their "mecca of hospitality," the witty 3rd baseman of the champion Colored Columbia Giants asked Clark to direct his hits elsewhere after nearly being out in the hospital.[129] Milwaukee disposed of Springfield, then lost a 10-inning exhibition before 1,800 at Dayton before heading home for opening day.

With that looming on the horizon, Mayor Rose banned baseball poolrooms, but allowed one to continue for horse races.[130] Charlie Comiskey's desire to transfer the opening series from his weather-beaten grounds in Chicago up to Milwaukee left him cooling at Killilea's heels. The Brewers president spent Easter at his Winneconne, Wisconsin home, "knowing that there he would be able to pay his respects to the American hen without undue doubts as to the integrity of the crop, so the popular rival of Hart was compelled to wait." Truth was, neither city's diamond was in good condition.[131]

Captain/3rd baseman Jimmy Burke would be the first Milwaukee Brewer to ever have his actual photograph published in *The Sentinel*, Saturday, April 21, 1900. In the report of an intrasquad game won 5–4 by the Regulars, even Mack himself still only warranted a sketch![132]

The price of horseflesh in Milwaukee wasn't about to be affected by the 13 "autos" now in use in the city. Demand for the "steedless carriages" was rising. Their silent running reminded one of the "darkey" view of electric street cars in Philadelphia: "Dem Yankees is great folks, first dey 'mancipates de black man, now dey gone 'mancipates de mule."[133]

Just like that, the nattily gray Brewers with blue stockings were also off and running. It took 10 innings to upend their counterparts in white stockings to win the first American League game ever played in Chicago.[134] The 5–4 contest was played before 4,500 on Saturday, April 21st. On molasses-slow, rain-sogged old Wanderers Cricket Grounds, Pete Dowling sealed fate by striking out his German-born opposite number, John Katoll and Herm McFarland. When deaf mute Dummy Hoy fouled out that stranded Frank Isbell and catcher Peanuts Joe Sugden.

Milwaukee's swarthy 2nd baseman Dave Fultz got on with a safety. He advanced on Norwegian John Anderson's hit to right and then scored the game-winner on shortstop Wid Conroy's sacrifice fly to deep right. Chicago spread five errors to Milwaukee's none.

Chicago must have felt like the "Underdrawers Sag" ad for Racine Union Suits, "the Acme of Comfort." Comiskey's last laugh had 12,000 click his turnstiles for the Sunday rematch, a 5–3 Brewer loss. That was larger than any crowd in Western League history.[135]

The *Sentinel* remarked "as usual the Milwaukee baseball team commences the season with a pennant-winning pace." The home-and-home opener brought the White Stockings up to Milwaukee, where 4,000 showed.[136] The

Brewers took first place with a 3-run second and likewise seventh, for a 6–2 final. Old Fred "Dutch" Hartman's triple for Chicago won his share of applause. George Wheeler avenged his game two Chicago loss by allowing only 4 hits in 90 minutes. When Wee Willie Clark opened the 6th inning scoring, he was "wagging his stumps in a manner what would have done credit to a sprinter." Clark was a 5-year National League veteran.

To see the Brewers repeat the feat the next day, only 2,400 came. Sunday, April 29th, however, the number of fans broke not only Milwaukee attendance records, but exceeded the opening Chicago crowd.[137] Over 12,000 saw the Brewers fall into a first-place tie with 5–3 Cleveland and infielder Frank Isbell flexed his right wing to pitch Chicago within a half-game off the pace.

Milwaukee congressman Theobald Otjen advocated repealing war taxes on beer and tobacco in Washington, now that the Spaniards were well in hand. It wasn't another vice, but the Brewers scored on a Buffalo Hooker, named Ed, to the tune of 6–2 on May 15th. Milwaukee bunted their way to victory before 600 Buffaloans.[138]

At home, Mack's men split the Millers on May 30th, but 6,000 saw the 11-inning morning win and only 600 stuck around for the afternoon loss. Indianapolis built its lead, but Cleveland directly usurped the crippled Brewers' hold on second in early June, thanks to umpire Pongo Joe Cantillon's "hoodoo."[139]

Independence Day at Kansas City liberated the Brewers back into second over Indy, but the fourth straight win left them two behind the White Stockings. Sam Dungan's solo homer was the only damage in game one off Bert Husting, but 4-for-4 from Buttermilk Tommy Dowd insured the afternoon 10–2 score.[140]

Milwaukee staved off the visiting Hoosiers in a crucial mid-July series, but the Sunday July 29th debut of Rube Waddell pulled in 6,000 local loyalists.[141] His 2-hit shutout of Cleveland had small boys waiting afterwards outside the team's dressing room. Ancient Lou Bierbauer was now at second for Milwaukee. His German surname translated as "beer farmer or peasant." Center field fill-in Fred Ketcham went 3-for-3, but they still chased Indy from third place.

Pittsburgh catcher Chief Zimmer defied Connie Mack's prediction about players' unions when he was elected president of the major league Ball Players Protective Association[142] in New York. That metropolis had nothing on industrial Milwaukee. The 1900 U.S. Census revealed that Beertown grew more, proportionately, than any other large city in the nation. Now at 285,315 its 39.54 percent growth of the last decade surely surpassed Louisville's 27 percent or 10 percent in Cincinnati. Even the Chicago press congratulated Milwaukee![143]

The even more critical mid-August home-and-away series with Chicago all but scuttled the Brewers' pennant hopes. Two losses and a tie at home and a twinbill whitewash to start in Chicago left it up to Waddell to be the stopper.

Not only was he the August 11th stopper, but the eccentric lefty went all 22 innings to sweep a doubleheader! The "king pin threw crooked ones all around the White Legs" for 17 grueling innings. Only after Irv Waldron got on by a 1st base error and scored via a 3-bagger by that cleanup Son of Norway John Anderson could the elated Waddell do a handspring.[144]

The hero Rube "started in to pitch another seventeen if need be," and fellow southpaw Ed Doheny matched game two's 1-hitter. The 10,000 fans got their money's worth, but the walking Bill Hallman had home plate passage, after advancing on Anderson's grounder and "Indian" Ed Abbaticchio's hit. The 2nd baseman obtained from the Millers a few weeks earlier was really baseball's pioneer of Italian descent. After 5 innings, darkness halted the game.[145]

This salvage of the series still left the Brewers at 57–50 in fourth and a half-game behind even Detroit now. Waddell nearly shut out the Tigers on August 27th, too, but was stopped by his own wild throw to catch Dick Harley napping at third. Rube cruised, 9–1, in front of 2,000 in Michigan.[146]

Charlie Comiskey and Jim Hart of the N.L. Orphans agreed that a proposed post-season series between the two Windy City teams couldn't be pulled off. Connie Mack was recruited to guide a squad of American Leaguers on a Pacific Coast barnstorm. The all-stars included Buffalo center fielder Jake Gettman, a German born in the colony of Frank, Russia.[147]

Big Rube nearly had his ankle broken by a vicious Socks Seybold low liner at Indy on August 31st. The Brewers had slid back past the Hoosier "Indians" (as they were now sometimes called) for runner-up status to Chicago.[148] Mack protested that darkness shortened game two after Umpire Manassau called it. A difference may have been Waddell's wild throw on the Seybold play, which knitted 2 more bases for Socks. Manassau preserved the 3–2 Indy lead after five.

Only Hallman would go hitless in the 22-hit, 13–5 revenge the next day after Manassau canceled that first game due to unfit field conditions. The 45-minute wait of drainage and sprinkled sawdust were all the Mackmen needed.[149]

Waddell's 10–3 Milwaukee adventure ended when Pittsburgh asked for his return and Chief Zimmer came to claim his daft batterymate. In what was essentially a trade/loan of suspended twirlers, Pete Husting returned from the Pirates.[150] That was only after he shut out a team of Homestead steel workers, 9–0, striking out 6 on 6 hits and contributing a couple knocks, including a double. With Harry Smith ill, Dave Diggins couldn't hold the Rube's Brewer offerings.

Umpires and Hoosiers were more and more a combustible mix by season's end. Right fielder George Hogriever, long a Western League vet, was escorted from Umpire Sheridan by a Milwaukee policeman after carping over being struck out by George Rettger.[151] Manager Bill Watkins did nothing to check his recalcitrant baby, who tried to fudge his way back by claiming the need to retrieve his glove. He should have mellowed out at Milwaukee's *Jahrmarkt* bash.

Connie Mack's club could not overtake the White Stockings in the remaining handful of games and attendance reflected it. The Hogriever act was caught by 1,500 and the home wrap-up loss to Cleveland drew a meager 400.[152]

Mack's Brewers and Comiskey's White Stockings should have been sufficient rivals, but further rumblings of an "American Association" had a growing Milwaukee imprint. Gus Koch and Joe O'Brien were joining Quin and Havenor in exploring the venture. O'Brien was to manage one of the richest clubs or be league secretary.[153]

Koch, once a suitor for the Detroit Tigers, had enough capital to set up shop in Philadelphia. Havenor was aiming to be the proprietor in Chicago. Quin was thought to be not as well heeled as these two, but as sole owner in Milwaukee, he'd have the advantage of his own ballpark.

The touch of an "angel," Quin's multi-millionaire acquaintance Senator Clark of Montana would lurk behind the ongoing drama. The only acknowledgement by the participants, other than it would be a "sure go," was that a $5,000 deposit had to be anteed up "before business will be talked with it at all."

The *Sentinel* weighed in with an unusual column, praising Ban Johnson, Killilea, and especially Mack. It echoed the fans' lament that heavy-hitting John Anderson "ought to be twins," but sharply pointed out how the local angle of the association movement pressured the Brewers into a better performance. In the uncertain political climate of the game, at least Milwaukee would not fall dead like Minneapolis.[154]

That last Tuesday, September 18th loss to Cleveland possessed a number of unique qualities, not the least of which was that the awkward visiting twirler, Ruest, outdid Rettger.[155] The next spring, Ruest looked like he was just off the boat, "a Hans newly fit for fair." John Anderson, the switch-hitting "Terrible Swede" from Sasbourg, Norway, was off to see his wife and baby at Worcester, Massachusetts. Ed Abbaticchio, or "Abbey" in the box score, filled in at first.

And for the first time, few bleacher occupants would recognize the manager. Connie Mack dressed for his last Brewers game in his "street clothes." He'd do so for the next 50 years.

The machinations of the association project, which flip-flopped between American or National as its tag, proceeded while Mack barnstormed his boys through Sheboygan, Oshkosh, Chicago, and a Delevan series with the colored Columbia Giants.[156] It was by then that Willie Reidy, who had reversed his 1900 fortune to 19–8, signed on to join Rube Waddell at Pittsburgh. Waddell was now battling the likes of Cy Young in the National League.

"Tower of strength" Anderson and utility Dave Fultz, another pair of Brewers to be actually pictured in the paper, were claimed by Brooklyn despite the dispute of Matt Killilea. When put to Fultz as to whom he really belonged, he replied with a laugh, "I will give it up, but I suppose there was some arrangement whereby Brooklyn could have me again if they wanted me." The loss of both gentlemen was a regret.[157]

Harry Quin, now with Charles W. Clark — son of the ex-Montana senator — as his partner, claimed to have a prominent National Leaguer verbally lined up to manage.[158] He denied any amalgamation rumor with Ban Johnson. Henry Killilea would join brother Matt and Fred C. Gross to deny any sale of the Brewers, who profited about $8,000.

Milwaukee, now America's 14th largest city, ahead of pre-auto Detroit, would be in the eye of the maelstrom in the evolving baseball wars. Matt Killilea feared no competition. Fans could not foresee supporting two teams. The morning paper speculated, "In time, a majority of the Milwaukee alderman may become baseball magnates and hold valuable franchises of their own to give away."[159]

Adonis Terry, the old pitcher/erstwhile umpire for one, would go bowling. He formed "Terry's Shirtwaists" to compete in the fingerball league at his new alley. Attorney Henry J. Killilea helped defend a south side butcher to beat a murderous intent rap. Everyone could "Prolong Life and Fool Father Time by Drinking Miller's the BEST Milwaukee Beer." The butcher's name just happened to be Michael Jordan.[160]

A prominent National Leaguer would come to manage in Milwaukee for 1901, but he would not be in Harry Quin's employ. Ban Johnson escalated baseball's tensions by declaring his American League to now be of major rank. In so doing, he further infiltrated the East, casting away Buffalo, Indianapolis, Kansas City, and Minneapolis for Baltimore, Boston, Philadelphia, and Washington.[161] Magnate Charles Somers already financed Cleveland and Chicago in the American League. His money helped propel undertakings in Boston and Philadelphia. The Hub City club even paid homage to him by calling themselves the Somersets, but the brotherly love of part ownership enticed Connie Mack to leave Milwaukee and manage the revived Philadelphia Athletics name. Ben Shibe, a sporting goods partner of English-born baseball pioneer Al Reach bought into the Athletics, but that now pitted him against Reach's own Phillies.[162]

War was on and the Killileas brought future Hall of Fame center fielder Hugh Duffy to pilot the Brewers. As one of the "Heavenly Twins" of the Boston Beaneaters, Duffy knew pennant-winning ways. His generally fruitless managerial career would face a calamitous start here.[163]

Contract-jumping and player raids would permeate the next three seasons, so while certain Milwaukee favorites were retained, like John Anderson, Wid Conroy at short, Jimmy Burke, Bill Hallman and Irv Waldron; plus hurlers like Reidy, Husting, Sparks, and Dowling; the overall play in the American League elevated to such a degree that the Brewers were now clearly overmatched.[164]

The Milwaukee quartet — Quin, Havenor, Koch, and O'Brien — still pursued the elusive American Association and even brought Walt Wilmot in as their supposed manager. A rental issue for a Philadelphia club, foisted upon it by Colonel John J. Rogers, was credited with smashing the proposed organization.[165]

Western promoters were deciding between Detroit, Grand Rapids, or Milwaukee to join Columbus, Dayton, Ft. Wayne, Indianapolis, Louisville, and Mansfield (Ohio) to reconstitute an American Association. President Patrick T. Powers, who oversaw the minor leagues' interest towards a National Agreement, was willing to protect Bill Watkins' players and territorial rights at Indianapolis, but wouldn't do likewise for Toledo's Interstate League magnate, Charles Strobel. His Kansas City squabble meant any "American Association" would have to wait another season.[166]

The legal union of players to teams and teams to leagues was a battlefield with which Milwaukee Attorney William F. Green, representing the "Afro-American league," could identify. He lobbied in Madison against restrictions on inter-racial weddings.[167]

Hugh Duffy would ultimately put his Brewers through their spring paces again at Richmond, Indiana. Secretary Fred Gross would receive some irksome print that while no magnate was a more regular attendee at American League meetings, none took a less active part than him. Duffy reformulated his catching corps and until then even borrowed an opposition backstop for one trial encounter.[168]

Duffy wasn't even familiar with all the men recommended to him by Mack and other league magnates. He moved his charges to St. Louis for an additional two weeks of polish. Much ado was made of the 2-year deal signed by Beaver Dam right-hander, Emerson "Pink" Hawley, a 9-year National League veteran. The fashionable Pink came off an 18–18 year with the New York Giants, so he received about the same $3,000 from Milwaukee. There was the delusional idea that the Brewers now had the A.L.'s strongest arms.[169]

Billy Gilbert took over the middle bag and future Brewer interim manager Bill Friel was the Brewers' "extra." Ban Johnson could trumpet his league's ascendancy and the Brewers' prospects 'til hell won't have it, but the reality was that Comiskey, Mack, et al left Milwaukee in the dust. Comiskey even siphoned mound ace and ex-Brewer Clark Griffith from the cross-town Orphans just to hedge his bets. The new White Stockings manager even observed that Milwaukee lush Virgil (Ned) Garvin was the rare defensive-style pitcher capable of success.[170]

William Carley and Ike Christiansen of Milwaukee were rummaging up two city clubs to compete in a Wisconsin State League against Appleton, Kaukauna, Oshkosh, Wausau, and a pick from Fond du Lac, Green Bay, Menasha, and Stevens Point. The two men would schedule their home games at Lloyd Street on Sundays when the American Leaguers were away.[171]

Duffy's 14 Brewers were in "high feather" for the Tuesday, April 23rd opener at Detroit. Pitcher Tully Sparks, Friel, and eventual first-string catcher Billy Maloney were left home for additional prep. A downpour sent home 7,000 disappointed fans in Michigan.[172]

Brewers to Detroit—You just wait till my *"Pitchers"* get to *"Working."*

Cad Brand, *The Sentinel*, Monday, April 29, 1901.

The sports page headline, after the Thursday retry, would sum up the season: "BREWERS ARE VANQUISHED." Hawley, Dowling, and Husting were easy marks for the Tigers, but an overflow of 9,000 at Bennett Field saw an incredible 14–13 slugfest marred by 11 errors between the 35 hits. Bennett Field had been named after onetime Milwaukee catcher Charlie Bennett, a Detroit favorite who lost his legs in a tragic accident.[173] That last of Pop Dillon's 4 doubles, a ground rule special into the leftfield hordes, capped a 10-run comeback in the ninth. Dillon rode the shoulders of six men, awash in a throng of shouting thousands "until he begged to be put down."

The American League was off to a popular start, outdrawing its National rivals in the openers by 9,000. It would take six tries before Duffy's boys could snap their "hoodoo" at Cleveland. A couple hit batsmen by the Blues' Ed Scott and four singles, topped by Joe Connors' pinch-hit for Garvin, salted the 8–6 difference in the sixth. Pete Dowling, who would be sold to Cleveland the next month, nailed down the victory.[174] The Brewers limped home in last, 2–6, though ex-Georgetown backstop Maloney was a bright 2-for-3, 3-run spot in the second Cleveland tilt.

Duffy's third base coaching and "gingering" up of the team in the field still found favor by the ruinous 11–3 home opening loss to Chicago. To compound their inadequacy, English-born Hall of Fame umpire Tom Connolly, who was recommended to the American League by Connie Mack, sent three Brewers (including Burke and Maloney) to the bench. John (Buckshot) Skopec, an "olive-skinned Bohemian" from the Interstate League, walked 5 Brewers, but checked them on 6 hits. The organized band of bell-rattlers and horn-blowers were quieted. Friday, May 3, 1901, would be a day to live in misery.[175]

Gross could only offer free Tuesdays and Fridays to feminine devotees as any sort of salve to the growing ignominy.[176]

Duffy would be tossed by Connolly in a 14–1 spanking at Chicago on Thursday, May 16th. The club may have reached its pinnacle in the standings, sixth at 8–12. Garvin, the "elongated gyrator," was well on his way to joining Bill Reidy as a 20-game loser. Perhaps they could have turned to "Doc" Truss, the middleman for Milwaukee's "colored theatrical folk," before their big show was completely drained of all its color. They could have done little worse than recruit Charles "Chic" Anderson, the Caucasian legless bootblack, who polished leather at the corner of Grand and West Water.[177] Even the Sentinels rematched with Chicago's crack colored Unions team.

By mid-June, the Milwaukee Brewers never left last place again. President Matt Killilea could only admire Boston's American grounds and equipment. Their pitching down the dumper, it was suggested that the Brewers follow the lead of a Kokomo manager, who gave his players unlimited leave and absence after a 34–4 bruising. Only Duffy's faith remained a roseate hue.[178]

The Brewers could do no better than chase "despised" Cleveland the rest of the way. At least "Honest John" Anderson provided some July 4th second game fireworks for 2,800 fans. He made good on his 10th inning threat to Detroit southpaw Ed Siever: "Put one over and I'll hit it a mile." Anderson's swing at the waist-high bullet sent it bounding into left for Maloney to score the 8–7 clincher.[179]

Henry J. Killilea was reassuring local patrons as late as August 1st that the franchise was a fixture. He was losing money, but outdrawing a winning Baltimore Orioles club that was expected to move to New York. Cleveland was being targeted for the old Von der Ahe grounds at St. Louis. Duffy still seemed to be a popular idol to Brewers loyalists.[180]

Later that month, Washington manager Jimmy Manning was the first to foretell of the Brewers' doom, but he thought Baltimore would remain and Pittsburgh would be the other selection to relocate. Duffy sought locally bred reinforcements after a soggy August 15th loss at Philly, a 6–4 decision to Mack's Athletics.[181] Davy (Kangaroo) Jones, the Welsh outfielder from Cambria, Wisconsin, came up from Rockford. He swung a weak .173 in 14 Brewer appearances, but went on to a productive 10-year major league career. That same Three-I League club provided right-hander Claude Elliott, now more seasoned and almost Jones' neighbor. Known as "Chaucer" or Old Pardee, the Pardeeville man would not yet take the points for Milwaukee.[182]

The entire nation would be stunned by the assassination of President William McKinley on Friday, September 6th at Buffalo's Pan-American Exposition.[183] He was seriously wounded by a Detroit anarchist of Polish descent named Leon Czolgosz, whose surname translated into "creeping" or "snake." McKinley would not die until a week later, at 2:15 a.m., Saturday, September 14th.

The fallen commander-in-chief ebbed much like the rest of the Brewers' season. Washington's baseball Nationals shared their grief on Saturday, September 7th, slaughtering home Milwaukee's Sparks and Husting 20–8 in only 7 innings. Duffy's whereabouts was unknown, still desperately on a futile hunt for talent. Manawa, Wisconsin's Ed Bruyette was a utility addition of little consequence. All Duffy dug up for his dog team was New Haven shortstop George Bone.[184]

Ban Johnson still hadn't tipped his hand to Henry Killilea when both men met with *Boston Globe* sportswriter-cum-New England League president Tim Murnane. The Milwaukee session was to enlist the American League as a mentor to the minor circuit. That Murnane was one of Johnson's biggest boosters in ink didn't hurt either.[185]

"William Blockhead Gilbert" and his "Dumb Play" handed Chicago the first game of the final home series. Milwaukee's own General Arthur MacArthur, the recent Philippine campaign hero in line to command the nation's military forces, certainly wasn't about to stop back from Chicago to see any of this. The raw, cold, and cloudy Friday that McKinley lay at death's door, some 1,200 watched the Brewers split with the pennant-winning White Stockings.[186]

Milwaukeean shortstop George McBride, hired from the State League Milwaukee Sentinels' 3rd base outpost, batted second behind left fielder and former Indy malcontent George Hogriever in those contests. Wid Conroy deserted for N.L. Chicago and Hawley to Kaukauna.

Duffy's Brewers staggered through a terrible 2–12 road finish, though they beat John Katoll at Chicago. He had tragically lost his wife and daughter at the end of the last year. Milwaukee had a final 4–0 shutout hurled at them by Iron Man Wiley Piatt.[187] Duffy remained in limbo.

Not even the black cartoon caricatures of the Gold Dust Twins could clean up Killilea's mess. Despite the money he lost, he was still in denial as Johnson shifted the franchise to St. Louis. The Thursday, September 12th announcement made clear that raiding the rival Cardinals would create a strong new Browns club for 1902 at the Mound City's Grand Avenue Grounds.[188]

Western League President "Theodore" (Thomas) J. Hickey looked at dropping Colorado Springs, Denver, and Des Moines in favor of Indianapolis, Louisville, Milwaukee, and maybe even Chicago. The Killileas, rumored to favor making the majors into a trust, wanted no part of any minor operation and went duck hunting at Winneconne.[189] The minors appealed for protection.

Despite that the city was the birthplace of the American League, the Dead Ball Era meant the A.L. was dead in Milwaukee for another 69 years.

4
Last Team Standing

Baseball is nothing if not a game of redemption. For Hugh Duffy, his angel of redemption arrived in Milwaukee at the end of March 1902. Duffy could have packed up his managerial failure, but still productive .308 batting average, and went back home to the East.

But, no, his "financial angel," W.T. Van Brunt, would be the wellspring from which not just Duffy's proposed Milwaukee team, but the entire Western League would be financed.[1] It was amazing that Van Brunt, who could base a club in his hometown of St. Joseph — perhaps the circuit's smallest market — had the wherewithal as a street railway king to boost the venture.

And boost it, he did. Kansas City joined Milwaukee as a battlefield between the American Association and the Western League. In the majors, Boston, Chicago, New York, Philadelphia, and St. Louis would all try to support two professional baseball clubs. That struggle would endure for the next five decades. Only America's Beer City and Missouri's famous cowtown would wage this test at the minor league level.[2]

Besides the two aforementioned Missouri cities, Van Brunt lined up Denver and Colorado Springs from the outer reaches. Des Moines, Omaha, and Peoria made the Western League's final cut. Meat packer Fred Gross, fresh from his American League try as the Brewers' secretary, was Van Brunt's front man in soliciting the Milwaukee effort. Rudolf Giljohann rejected being the local angel.[3]

Just as the National and American Leagues tore at one another, the war of words and bitter contract jumping grew between what were at this stage two ephemeral minor entities. Western League president Jim Whitfield was "in bad odor" and deserved to be blacklisted in the eyes of *Sentinel* sporting editor A.W. Friese, who knew a thing or two about ill-gotten contracts.[4] The war with Tom Hickey's American Association had other consequences from abusing the reserve rule. The raids by A.A. Louisville's "White Wings" Tebeau had the trickle down effect of nearly breaking the Eastern League.[5]

Wild rumors across the baseball spectrum, like the persisting St. Louis

Cardinals move to Milwaukee, major league clubs switching leagues, and the like percolated through the spring.[6] W.F. Steinel of Milwaukee was heading up a Wisconsin State Baseball League, that would again include an entry from the big city.[7]

Harry Quin and Charles Havenor set about to transform the Troop A military barracks, a campgrounds at 8th and Chambers, back into what was once Athletic Park. Stables had to be torn down and construction changes would occupy two months as their Brewers opened on the A.A.'s eastern swing. Quin's establishment was also supplying uniforms to the Kansas City Blues, Louisville Colonels, and Toledo Mud Hens.[8]

The Brewers' ownership duo, with the monetary blessing of young Charley Clark out in Montana, enlisted the shortstop of the '01 Washington Americans, Billy Clingman, to manage their team.[9] Havenor was already challenging Gross to a pre-season series between the competing local clubs. Clark held a half-interest in the refurbished Athletic Park. Buck Enright, a Chicago, Milwaukee, and St. Paul Railroad employee hired by Hickey as an A.A. umpire, supervised the building of the players' quarters, drainage, and diamond layout there.[10]

The *Sentinel's* Friese seemed to clearly side with the Brewers' efforts but would be judicious in his actual game coverage of both teams. He held a high personal regard for Duffy, but thought him incapable as a manager. It was from the playing skipper's old nickname "Angel Child" that Friese's headlines would dub the Western club as "Duffy's Angels."

In the 1860s-1870s, disloyal players were "revolvers."[11] The rancor surrounding contract jumping revealed players' callous disregard for any integrity whatsoever. The odium besieged Clingman's Brewers. An advance of $100 was all it took for outfielder Charlie Jones to jump to the Denver Westerns. Byron McKibben, the St. Joseph manager, couldn't pry the two "Kids," Leewe and Speer, who trained at Milwaukee's Barnickel gym. Leewe was set for the A.A.'s KC Blues and Speer to catch for the Brewers. The extra $50 a month wasn't enough.[12]

English-born catcher Al Shaw, the man who hit the first American League homer for Detroit in 1900, deserted with Quin's advance for Buffalo. Addie Joss, the brilliant Juneau, Wisconsin hurler with a Hall of Fame future, was so addled that he signed with Toledo, Brooklyn, and Cleveland simultaneously. Cleveland ultimately won the claim. Pitcher Pete Dowling took "French leave for California after securing all the advance money the Milwaukee magnates would trust him with."[13]

The game's disrepute was such that Tom Hickey characterized his Western rivals, Van Brunt and syndicate partner Tom Burns, brother of a Colorado Springs mine owner, as a "stripling organization." The pair figured to be exacting revenge upon Hickey for his usurpation of Western markets Kansas City, Minneapolis, and St. Paul in his new American Association.[14]

Clingman's Brewers began training in Cincinnati on April 1st. One local boy, who was at the heart of direct tug-of-war with Duffy, was 3rd baseman George McBride of the Sentinels. He had the late trial with the '01 Brewers and signed with Clingman. He would go on to be one of the best major league "all field, no hit" shortstops of the next decade.[15]

Milwaukee's baseball interests were now clearly divided when both clubs opened the regular season with road losses.[16] Clingmans' faulty defensive alignments and the yanking of starter Claude Elliott for cold southpaw Nick Altrock were blamed for the 5–4 defeat to the Hoosiers at Indianapolis. Chilling wind and poor streetcar access kept the welcome to 3,500 people.

In Omaha, the Angels' slovenly fielding and weak bats led to an 11–4 burial by Rourke's prohibitive Western League favorites. Starter Hen Fricken hit 3 batters and Canadian Jim Cockman had a couple hits that couldn't compensate for his blundering trifecta at third.

Cockman's brilliant 2nd base stops in the Angels' home opener on Friday, May 2nd, made for a warm welcome. Since they arrived with a 2–5 last place mark, only 700 were at Lloyd Street.[17] Omaha was again the nemesis, with Alloway's 2–0 whitewash over Fricken. Little Pete Burg, the 5'-1", 150-pound replacement at third, had been released to Duffy by the sympathetic Nebraska club. Burg loomed "out in the gloom like a lighthouse in a fog."

The winners' base running was as "yellow as the cover of a dime novel," but the Angels' teamwork was as absent as "a five dollar tithe in a poor box."

Henry Killilea was now the principal stockholder of the successful Boston Americans and in the small fraternity that is baseball, he sent Wisconsinite Pete Husting, who pitched for him in Milwaukee, to Philly's Connie Mack, who managed for him in Milwaukee.[18]

Clingman's Brewers were not to open at Quin's new Athletic Park until Friday, May 23rd, but the "liberal ministrations of Jupiter Pluvius" rendered the environs a quagmire.[19] Clingman was in search of new infielders, as his 9–15 club equaled the sixth place showing of Duffy's 8–15 aggregate. Clingman wanted to move Sam Dungan, now a Brewer, from first to the outer garden.[20]

Friese made things even more confusing by calling Duffy's men the "Brewers" in a Kansas City loss to the "Blue Stockings."[21] Big Milwaukee Shortstop Frank Gatins did homer, though. Clingman's Brewers were then beat at KC on June 1st by the A.A. Blues, while Cockman's 11th inning catch saved the Angels' 10–9 win at the Colorado Springs Millionaires. Still, Duffy's team tumbled back to last, at 10–21.

Saturday, June 14th was a rare instance of both teams going head-to-head for the Milwaukee patron's coin. Walt Wilmot's Minneapolis Millers made the debut of Brewer pitcher Harry Cook a harsh 9–5 one before 500 at Athletic Park. Black clouds were figurative and literal for the Angels' fatal 6th inning at Lloyd Street.[22] Kansas City delivered the 5–1 blow to the chin, but only 250 showed up. And there was a gunboat crisis in "Hayti?"

July 4th marked the independence of Duffy's Angels from the Brewers. A sweep of Denver, the first game being a belligerent forfeit, gave the 4,500 at home a third place club, now 31-26. The Brewers languished in sixth, and Quin would maybe protest the umpiring of the second loss at Kansas City.[23]

Both teams rode outstanding pitching performances to road victories on Tuesday, July 15th. Sam McMakin paralyzed the Millers on a 4-hitter up north, but Cy Swormstedt shutout the Des Moines Midgets of the old Australian undertaker, Uncle Joe Quinn.[24]

Another 500 at Athletic Park would see McMakin's 9th-inning fumble give a Brewers loss to the Hoosiers. Clingman's crew now climbed to 40-46 by August 1st, but was mired in sixth.[25] Duffy and nine of his corps actually took in that game on an off day. It was so, due to a train delay of the Kansas City "contract-jumpers."

The Angels fell to fourth, two games behind that KC contingent at midmonth. In a weird play, Omaha's Pears distracted Swormstedt, on a slow roller, with mutual laughter.[26] Swormstedt forgot to throw him out and Pears loped to first, bat in hand.

Both Milwaukee clubs would lose doubleheaders at Kansas City on August 31st. What was noticeably different was the support along the Kaw River.[27] Dale Gear's A.A. Blues drew 4,500 to sweep the Brewers and Kid Nichols' Western Blue Stockings/Sox had 2,300 to drop the now first place Angels. Nichols was the Madison, Wisconsin-born pitcher bound for the Hall of Fame. Big Jack Thornton, a one-time hurler, relieved Swormstedt on the slab for Duffy from his 1st base outpost in Game Two.

Pioneers of an even older Milwaukee sports tradition were reuniting. The last two members of the German gymnastics society, the *Turnverein Milwaukee*, would recall that 1849 was the year their first building was erected. That was four years before their actual incorporation. At least the Turners weren't the Concatenated Order of Hoo Hoo, an Osirian Cloister of lumberman under an emblem of a black cat.[28]

Duffy declined Havenor's challenge for a city series between the Angels and Brewers in early September.[29] He saw nothing for his first place Western Leaguers to gain in playing their sixth place American Association rivals. Havenor even offered a split pot or winner-take-all to no avail.

Pink Hawley came back to lift the Brewers into fifth place with a September 9th sweep of the St. Paul Saints. The artistic esquire painted a first game, 6-hit shutout before 200 souls and Manager Clingman rescued the "burlesque" of Game Two with the game winning hit in a 13-12 abacus rattler.[30] Quin's Athletic Park could barely contain those 350.

Duffy's Angels maintained their grip on first place until September 11th. Consecutive losses at Denver, a team that was hot on their trail, reversed the leadership.[31] Denver's Jim Delahanty was stranded on a leadoff triple when Charlie Jones (remember him?) went down "under the mighty arm of the fat-

Milwaukee's baseball war of 1902–1903, as seen by *Milwaukee Sentinel* cartoonist Cad Brand.

man from Beertown," Troy, Wisconsin's Doc (Babe) Adkins. Adkins was 5'-10½" and 220 pounds.

That September 10th, 4–3 outcome was derived by Denver's managing catcher Parke Wilson "accidentally" hitting Duffy's good throw to Farmer Vaughn at the plate. That allowed Wilson's pitcher Eyler to score the winning margin. Denver's Whitridge then struck out 10 Angels the next day, engineering Milwaukee's 2nd place tie with Kansas City. The Angels would fly no higher the rest of the way, settling on Cloud Three at 81–56.

Comical lefty Nick Altrock won his 28th and last game for the Brewers on Sunday, September 14th. He needed 11 innings before 3,500 wished him "bon voyage" to Killilea's Bostons. Another southpaw, Pete Nolden of Green Bay, would pick up the mantle in winning his only appearance with the Brewers, a 5–1 job over the 5th place Columbus Senators, whom they tied.[32] That didn't hold and neither did Clingman's managerial position after a 6th place 66–75 end. His last hurrah was a 4–1 exhibition loss to Frank Selee's N.L. Chicago Colts. A meager 500 at Quin's Athletic Park saw the birth of Tinker-to-Evers-to-Chance on that team, later the "Cubs."[33]

Kansas City's Western pennant-winning Cowboys would meet the 4th place A.A. Blues in a post-season 7-game series.[34] President Theodore Roosevelt had an operation to remove an abscess from his knee, but Milwaukee's baseball magnates must've felt as if surgery was performed upon their pocketbooks. In KC, the Westerns lost about $14,000, the Americans $1,500.

Quin and Havenor admitted to losing $5,000 and Gross had no gross left, also $8,000 to the red. This figure was disputed by Duffy, who claimed to be $1,100 ahead as his Angels were the best draw across the league. Of course, he carped about the umpiring at Denver, too, where his catcher [Johnny?] Evers was assaulted by arbiter Moran. He was arrested.[35]

Duffy and his optimism would be back, but the Angels' real "angel," W.T. Van Brunt, was staggered by his league's $30,000 loss. This was substantial when compared to the $23,000 overall profit claimed by Tom Hickey's circuit. Van Brunt relayed his dissatisfaction with Milwaukee's financial arrangement through League president Michael Sexton. Sexton also headed the Three-I League.[36]

Charles Havenor's first step in changing his Brewers' on-field fortunes was to hire popular "Pongo Joe" Cantillon to manage, as of October 11th. The Wisconsinite was the majors' highest paid umpire at $500 a month, but he managed the 1894 Western Association pennant club at Rock Island and also at Dubuque and Columbus. He was thoroughly endorsed by ex-Brewer pitcher Fred Barnes.[37]

Cantillon's colorful moniker came from his 1889 playing days in San Francisco. Baseball writer and nationally renowned humorist Charley Dryden responded to many inquiries about Joe's nationality by fabricating a lie that he was Italian. He said he was really Pongo Pelipe Cantillon, runaway son of a nobleman in the old country. Bay Area Italians cheered their "countryman" on in droves, and he'd respond to their Italian in guttural tones so natural, the young 2nd baseman even kept teammates guessing.[38]

Harry Quin was prepared to take responsibility for the 1903 Brewers, but Havenor ascended to the presidency. The alderman/tailor also sold Clingman to St. Paul and had Cantillon's men train down in Nashville. A stray poodle there escaped becoming the team's mascot.[39]

Henry Killilea was back from Boston and touting New York as an American League market. It was an age of $2,500 touring cars and starving Jews in Russia. President Roosevelt, personally armed, would visit Wisconsin and Merrill Park residents would revive the peculiar sport of *sargol*, an outdoor game like duck-on-the-rock. The Ragaboos cinched a bowling pennant at Terry's alleys.[40]

Hugh Duffy's team was now being called the Creams and they trained at the University of Illinois at Champaign. His New England pipeline had a penchant for Canadian imports such as Bill O'Neill from New Brunswick. Ex-Brewer pitcher Adolphus Vollendorf, the stonecutter from Manitowoc, Wisconsin, signed on. Henry Killilea promised Duffy he'd return 1st baseman Jack O'Brien before the season opened. The Creams were the first Milwaukee professional team to have their group photo in *The Sentinel.* "The Piazza Gown and its Coming Glories" was heralded in a Sunday edition.[41]

Curiously, Van Brunt's own hometown St. Joseph Western League franchise was sold to two Iowa men for $4,000. Branded as an "outlaw league" outside of the National Agreement, Tom Hickey's American Association was being welcomed, albeit slowly, into the mix.[42]

The Creams toyed with Illinois collegians in practice play, while Brewers Roy Hale and Elmer Meredith held the host Atlanta Southern Leaguers to a 4-hit shutout. Atlanta's shortstop, a Milwaukeean named Gruebner, shone on a "pretty" double play. Cantillon's final tune-up was a 14–4 rout on another Southern League outfit at Memphis, while Duffy's three hits helped polish off Central League Terre Haute, 9–6. The hosts retaliated, 20–7. Cantillon's Captain Billy Phyle moved from short to center until another body could be found. Returnees like Jiggs Donahue, Kid Speer, and Sam Dungan were enthused.[43]

Henry Killilea could only sit back and count the coin in Boston as his Pilgrims opened to a doubleheader total of 27,558 while his cross-town National rivals drew only 5,094.

Bald men were convening in Cleveland as the Brewers batted around the Saints in their Athletic Park curtain raiser on Wednesday April 22, 1903.[44] Billy Phyle was back at short and 3-for-5, while catcher Bob Woods went 4-for-4, including a homer. Of an anticipated 5,000, only 1,200 were undaunted by the cold. The Brewers beat former University of Wisconsin pitcher Charlie Chech.

Problem child Clingman opened for Columbus by injunction despite St. Paul protests. Havenor said Columbus would find locked gates at Milwaukee and St. Paul if Clingman tried to play for Columbus in either city.

Pitchers Elmer Meredith and Bill McGill, plus Bob Woods, 3rd baseman Bob Unglaub, and outfielder Jack Dunleavy were the handful of new Brewers to have their photos in the paper. Wood wielded the wood at an early .640 clip.

Duffy's Creams would not open their regular season until Tuesday, April 28th. They faced an uneasy, underpaid team at St. Joseph as 2,000 of its citizens declared Mayor Borden a hoodoo in their 5–1 loss. Ed Kenna's 5-hitter benefited from the ragged Missouri Saints' fielding. Kenna was the "Pitching Poet" of his college sorority.[45]

The 1903 Brewers: 1. Quate Bateman 1BP, 2. Cliff Curtis P, 3. Tom Doughery P, 4. Pongo Joe Cantillon Mgr., 5. Reeve McKay P, 6. George Stone RF/LF, 7. Frank Hemphill OF, 8. Jack O'Brien 2B, 9. Harry Clark 3B, 10. Elmer (Spitball) Stricklett P1B, 11. Kid Speer C, 12. Jack Slattery C. Milwaukee Public Library Historical Photograph Collection.

Cantillon's Brewers kept a half-game first place lead by May 13th. A late arriving fan made Number 113 in the "penetrating chill" at Athletic Park, but he put a hex on Meredith's 6-0 lead in the 8th. Donahue's single past second made Phyle the winning 7-6 score. That same day, the Creams' Len Swormstedt shut out host Omaha, 8-0.[46]

Cantillon's "yellow and black costumed gang" also wore a black and white crepe out of respect and sympathy for Unglaub's departed wife. They also beat the Blues at KC, 8-2, that Sunday, May 17th. At Des Moines, the Creams creamed deaf mute Leitner off the mound in the 4th en route to a 16-2 feast. They remained 3 games behind Colorado Springs for first.[47]

The baseball wars had nothing on the northern parts of Wisconsin, Minnesota, and Michigan who sought to form their own state of "Superior." The Creams may have felt like they were in the middle of Lake Superior. Memorial Day approached and they had yet to play a home game. That 13th win, against eleven losses, must have been unlucky.

The Monday June 1st headline said it all: "DUFFY'S NINE MISSING — Whereabouts of Western Association (sic) Team Is Unknown — IS DELAYED BY TOPEKA FLOODS."[48] Business Manager Porter Higby had no word from them since that Friday. They were thought to be marooned in the "wilds of

Kansas," safe and sound at Manhattan. "N.B.-This is not the place where cocktails come from."

Stranded with them in "the land-or lake — of prohibition and sunflower" was the Peoria team, with whom they were supposed to have played Saturday and Sunday. Those games would have had to have been played in rowboats on the flooding Smoky Hill River not before cheering Peorians.

Silence was all that came to Higby from the 14 men in the deeps of Kansas. He could only hope "the gallant Duffy and his retainers were holding a war council" and would sail "into port on a charted flatboat with the colors nailed to the mast." Local fans hoped to see them by the weekend.

With that club in logistical straits, Havenor again issued a challenge to a series for late June now that the Brewers were in first and the Creams in second. While Duffy's men were washed out, Claude Elliott whitewashed the Columbus Senators on 6 hits, 5-zip, before 4,000 at Athletic Park.[49] Jack Dunleavy added a double and a homer over the left field fence. Elliott's brother, sister, and sweetheart from Pardeeville saw the Brewers' tenth straight win.

Cantillon had to worry about the majors ravaging his 23–8 team: Comiskey's White Sox wanted Dunleavy (.296) and Unglaub (.358). Washington's Tom Loftus wanted Jiggs Donahue (.409). Pongo Joe vowed to keep them all through the season.[50] Duffy finally got a midnight telegram to Higby that their Thursday east-bound Rock Island passenger liner from Denver got no further than Clay Center, 35 miles from Manhattan.[51]

Center fielder Frank Hemphill joined Elliott as the only errorless Brewer to date. Bob Wood was still a rampant .436, with only a couple miscues behind the plate. Farmer Claude tossed his third straight shutout of the young season, 1–0 over the "Rev. Mr. Crabill" and Columbus. The Parson was an actual evangelist in charge of a winter congregation near the Ohio capital.[52]

The telephone operator at Zeandale, Kansas, four miles from Manhattan, was able to relay that no lives were lost as the Creams were among 300 "imprisoned for three days" on the stalled train between Manhattan and Wamego. They were rescued that Sunday and were being lodged at the Kansas Agricultural College at Zeandale. It was still uncertain if the 26 safe players rode the Rock Island train being pushed out west of Manhattan.[53]

There was a strange, frantic convergence to the departing Brewers' 11-game home win streak and anticipation over the Friday arrival of the Creams and their long-delayed opener. Havenor went on a Lac du Flambeaux fishing trip with his secretary (and fellow alderman), Con Corcoran, but had Arden Buell of Berlin, Wisconsin, accompany Pongo Joe and the boys on their eastern swing.[54]

Western League president Mike Sexton still fretted to Higby by wire as to the Creams' whereabouts. Arrangements were made to use Gimbel Bros.' flagpole, with a blue banner to indicate to fans that a game is scheduled on a given day.[55]

George Stone, the Jewish outfielder from Lost Nation, Iowa, was loaned to Duffy by Killilea's Bostons and was already working out at Lloyd Street each morning. Stone would be one of the five men — Jack Thornton, Adolphus Vollendorf, Bill O'Neill and Duffy were the others — to play in Milwaukee for both the Brewers and the Angels/Creams.[56]

Duffy reported that they were royally treated during their adventure, but "Poet Laureate" Kenna said Kansas needed a sewer system, not irrigation. He was a noble rescuer. Summoning volunteers to retrieve a man waist deep on a shoal, they trudged through 4 miles of mud to get a boat to the man. Waters had receded when they reached him. Connections to Omaha only led to a final wreck delay near Chicago.[57]

When the Creams belatedly rolled in on Saturday, Vollendorf was greeted by his wife of three weeks.

Everyone's patience was rewarded. Ideal weather and the anticipation climaxed with 7,000 seeking out the old Lloyd Street Grounds on Sunday, June 7th. During the Creams' 8–2, 6–4 sweep of St. Joseph, Duffy, Kenna, Swormstedt, Cockman, and McVicker were among the recipients of flowers. Cockman banged out 3 hits in Game One, catcher Lucia and Bill O'Neill had a pair apiece in each contest.[58] John McPherson and Kenna chalked up the victories. Thornton had been benched for three games by Umpire Kelley way back in Denver for talking too much. Milwaukeean George McBride played second for St. Joe.

The Brewers would struggle just over .500 on their road trip, though Elliott's continued brilliance in all 3 Columbus games kept St. Paul at bay in the standings.[59] Duffy's Creams gained ground on Colorado Springs, but were stymied by old ex-Milwaukee southpaw Bert Jones' 3-hitter for those visitors. Old Bunk Congalton roamed right for them, too.[60]

Both Milwaukee teams ruled their leagues on July 4th. Three of Cantillon's comrades were tossed in the holiday twinbill split with the Blues at KC, and 1,800 saw Duffy's dependables do likewise with the Peoria Distillers. At Omaha, old Tony Mullane, the ambidextrous, Irish-born "Apollo of the Box," replaced the disappeared Leo Messmer as umpire.[61]

Up in Superior, Wisconsin, Miss Olive Clark, the "clever little danseuse" of the Northwestern Opera Company, solicited local Cardinals manager Lagger about playing in his outfield. She claimed to run a 100-yard dash in 11 3/8 seconds, led her seminary team in batting, and "played some professional ball." No word from him on a tryout.[62]

The Brewers dropped to second in mid-July, losing a double dip to Louisville. Claude Elliott arrived from Pardeeville in time to pitch all of Game One and the final 11 innings of Game Two in relief of Elmer Meredith.[63] Some 1,200 attended. The Brewers were first shutout on 11 hits. At Denver, the winning run scored on Charlie Jones' error, but O'Neill's 2-run homer and Kenna's 9 Ks led the Creams in 11 over the Grizzlies.

So this went, this tit-for-tat. Boy Wonder Alonzo Hedges' one-hit shutout

Cad Brand's jaundiced eye, Sunday, June 7, 1903, *Milwaukee Sentinel*.

for the Brewers happened the same day of Kenna's whitewash at Des Moines on July 22nd. Both clubs fell to second by August 1st. Milwaukee pondered its own municipal flag while its ballclubs pursued their pennants.[64] Former University of Wisconsin student Walter Mueller was a Brewer stopper in Toledo. The Creams regained first with a twin sweep of Denver before 3,000.

Duffy would not see the audacious base-running of his "fast young Canuck," O'Neill, in those games. Another trait would rear its odd head: Just like 1901, he "secretly" disappeared. Rumors floated about Milwaukee's status in the Western League, that it likely wouldn't return the next year, and a dissatisfied Duffy might serve elsewhere.[65]

Only 680 saw Elliott lose a pitching battle royal to Louisville's Tom Walker, but Havenor and Cantillon were trying to keep their Brewers intact. Rooney Viox replaced Captain Phyle at short and Charlie Comiskey would sign Jiggs Donahue by late August.[66] As a Memphis 3rd baseman in the Southern League, Phyle would end up being expelled by the National Board on October 26th. He refused to appear and back up his charges that Southern League games were being thrown.[67]

Success bred demand. Cantillon turned down other managing offers to stay closer to his Chicago business interests, via Milwaukee. Elliott was pegged to move up to Cleveland. The Brewers would slip to third by the end of August and finish there.[68]

John McPherson would brutally lose an August 15th one-hitter at Omaha, due to his 1st inning wildness. The Creams were also referred to as the "Brewers" in the August 24th dispatch from Denver. Still, they forged their hold on first place.[69]

A Rock Island Road train wreck on August 29th again affected the Creams' ability to reach home in time and again meet up with Peoria. St. Louis and Cleveland American Leaguers, including Nap Lajoie with a sprained knee, were also injured in a Wabash railroad wreck near Peru, Indiana, the same day.[70]

Duffy's men would clutch for the pennant with crippled fingers. Shortstop Frank Gatins broke one of his and was done for the year. Captain Cockman had a bruised digit, and with no one else to work behind the plate, Lucia had to work with a badly split one. Gatins was replaced by a Robert Hall from New Haven in the Connecticut League. Hall wasn't the Big & Tall Men's Clothier.[71]

Duffy became more amenable to Havenor's post-season series as well.

Cantillon forfeited the second half of an August 30th double bill at Louisville after refusing to let his men come out. Bob Wood was injured the day before and Pongo Joe argued that the make-up of a postponed Milwaukee game didn't have to be replayed unless by mutual consent. The 9,800 at Eclipse Park had to settle for a single victory.[72]

Wood's injury compounded the straits of Donahue's return home from Indianapolis on crutches. His ankle, badly sprained in a slide home, cost the Brewers their two best hitters. At home, only 900 saw the Creams best Peoria's venerable old "cosmopolite," Billy Hart.[73]

Tom Hickey and Michael Sexton were among the minor league heads to reject a new National Agreement crafted at Buffalo.[74]

"SENATORS AGAIN BEAT CRIPPLES" was the dispatch from Columbus after Larry Schafly had to replace Rooney Viox and his split-throwing thumb. Unglaub went down at the Ohio capital with a sprained ankle. The colony of attrition grew at home, which was stolen by Dunleavy at Columbus.[75]

Vollendorf's sensational form in topping Peoria's Hart at Lloyd Street on September 4th made 5 straight Cream wins. Only 400 would appreciate it. Milwaukee's Western Leaguers remained 5 losses ahead of Colorado Springs, even after Peoria's 5-game revenge in Illinois. Vollendorf took that bookend loss.[76]

Aussie Joe Quinn's threat of "we're laying for you, Duff" turned into a joke at Des Moines on Sunday, September 13th. Vollendorf's 5-hitter and Kenna's 4-hitter were the punchlines to double-header shutouts. Another win at Des Moines was the Creams' last hurrah.[77] Quinn's Undertakers were named for his offseason occupation. May they rest in peace.

Cad Brand, *Milwaukee Sentinel*, June 19, 1904.

The front page of Friday morning's September 18th *Sentinel* told all: "WESTERN LEAGUE ENDS SEASON — President Sexton Cancels All Scheduled Games to Save Expenses-PENNANT TO MILWAUKEE — Cream City At Last Has Baseball Club Finish First in Race." It was called the "first time a Wisconsin city had ever won a pennant in the history of professional baseball," something the 1884 Cream Citys, 1887 Oshkoshs, and even 1891 Brewers would certainly dispute. Forty remaining Western games were snuffed.[78]

Business manager Porter Higby relayed Sexton's decision to a bitter Creams' president and managing center fielder Hugh Duffy. The skipper resented the broken faith of shorted contracts to his 78–44 champions. The likes of 2nd baseman "Curly" Miller and "Silver" Braun were already unappreciated heroes at Lloyd Street. Players denounced Van Brunt's "one man league."[79]

Pongo Joe Cantillon and Jiggs Donahue led the Brewers' personal overtures to Cream members for a series between the two teams. Word that Western Denver magnate D.C. Packard was arranging the transfer of the Milwaukee franchise to Lincoln, Nebraska ballpark owner/manager Glenn Odell seemed to scuttle that idea. "With Duffy and Milwaukee out the cities on the prairie will be in the running."[80]

Hugh Duffy would eventually return to Milwaukee. His bitter departure had the immediate salve of a flattering 3-year hitch to pilot the Phils on his horizon. The Brewers could only size up the remnants of players no longer under reserve, like Denver's Charlie Jones and the Creams' George Stone.[81]

The Milwaukee Creams won the Western League battle, but ultimately lost the Class A level minor league war to the Milwaukee Brewers and the American Association.

Pongo Joe Cantillon's finally healthy Brewers would celebrate that day by pounding the St. Paul Saints, 12–1. Three Bobs, Ganley, Wood, and Unglaub, each chipped in with a pair of hits and Meredith kept the Minnesotans at his mercy on 3 hits. Joining this celebration at Athletic Park were a grand total of 165 diehards.[82]

Milwaukee's Henry Killilea would bask in the arrangement of his Boston Americans facing the National League Pittsburgh Pirates in the first modern World Series.[83] Killilea staked a claim for Unglaub and would ultimately have him by the end of 1904.

Cantillon barnstormed his Brewers through eastern Wisconsin, into Upper Michigan, and back down through northern Illinois. After the St. Paul whipping, his men limped 1–4 to a vastly improved 77–60, 3rd place finish.[84] In October, the American Association compensated the aggrieved Western owners in Kansas City and Milwaukee for territorial encroachment, though those franchises no longer existed. It paved the way for the A.A.'s formal admission into the minors' National Agreement.[85]

Prince Heinrich of Prussia, "not a handsome man," had visited Milwaukee during the year, as did Der Vaterland's Finance Minister, Baron von Rheinhaben. The latter marveled at the city's industry as "marvelous" and "wonderful." Maybe he hadn't seen the baseball industry? The German name Unglaub essentially translates into "unbelievable." The year 1903 was certainly that![86]

Charles Havenor would now have Milwaukee all to his Brewers. He even bought out Quin's interest in Athletic Park by mid-June 1904. Just what did he, business manager Joe Holland, and Pongo Joe Cantillon now have?

Milwaukee was considered a "compact city" compared to its rivals, yet it was not a congested place. For all its industry, it was viewed as a "big country village," with neighborly elbow room to spare. In the context of the American Association, its scheduled rivalries were evolving in its third season.[87]

The two Ohio cities, the Columbus Senators and Toledo Mud Hens, were a natural match-up, as were the Minnesota Twin Cities clubs, the Minneapolis Millers and St. Paul Saints. This left the Indianapolis Indians (no longer the "Hoosiers") in proximity with the Louisville Colonels and the

Kansas City Blues for the Milwaukee Brewers.

This was as the American Association would exist for its first 50 seasons.[88] The world shrunk a little more when the Wright brothers' flying machine succeeded that December in North Carolina.[89]

What Manager Cantillon did have were only five returning players for 1904: pitchers Alonzo Hedges, Walter Mueller, and Elmer Meredith, plus center fielder Frank Hemphill and popular backup catcher George "Kid" Speer. He was no kid anymore. The 1903 A.A. batting champion, Jiggs Donahue (.344) now wore white sox. League strikeout king (226) Claude Elliott turned a Cincinnati Red.[90]

Fred Steele, the half-breed son of a full-blooded Pottawatomie Indian, was expected to step forth from the Missouri Valley as the team's premier pitching ace. The season decided otherwise.[91]

The American Association's new president, J. Edward Grillo, followed the National League's Mr. Pulliam in seeking stricter enforcement of rules concerning balks, hit batsmen, players congregating near home plate to distract a catcher as a teammate potentially scores, and

Manager Pongo Joe Cantillon, 1904. The Janesville, Wisconsin, native was an A.A. fixture at Milwaukee and Minneapolis. Milwaukee Public Library Historical Photograph Collection.

"the really radical new rule ...which permits two coaches."[92] The latter was seen as "problematical" and overall the effort was seen to foster the game's pleasurability.

The current Russo-Japanese War inspired the comment that it was a good thing there weren't too many Russians playing in the American Association, or the "Japanese cast of countenance" of Louisville outfielder Dan Kerwin would be a never-ending source of trouble.[93]

Pongo Joe had a classic dilemma as his ballclub worked its way north from its Springfield, Illinois tune-ups. Would his Opening Day starting pitcher be the Texas cowboy, Reeve McKay, or the half-Indian, Fred Steele? One new arrival at third base left no such doubt.

Harry Clark came to a 15-game trial, finishing up with the '03 White Sox, known there as "Pep." He came to Chicago from Union City, Ohio, via a stop with Dallas in the Texas League. What neither Cantillon nor he knew was that Pep would go on to become "Mr. Brewer" for the next 13 years.[94]

Oh, and Pongo Joe could thank the legacy of the Creams for 2nd baseman Jack O'Brien and that Jewish right fielder, George Stone. Germany Schaefer was a shortstop who would gain more notoriety on major league basepaths as a wacky, backwards-running Detroit Tiger. He would captain Milwaukee in 1904.

The turnover of newcomers wrought the "SONG OF THE SEASON PASS"[95]:

> I am proud of your team, Mr. Magnate
> I am sure that the pennant is ours;
> I'll be there at the opening session
> To greet the brave Brewers with flowers;
> There is not a gazabe in Milwaukee
> More loyal than I — that's no stall
> Loosen up, Mr. Magnate, and give me
> A pass for the season — that's all.
> What is that? You are hounded by hundreds?
> I know how those grafters will talk;
> Turn them down, the cheap blokes, when they brace you.
> And tell them to take a long walk!
> Yes I know that good players cost money-
> I used to play shortstop myself,
> And I certainly raked in the shekels
> Before I was thrown on the shelf.
> And I know you depend on the public
> To help you square up in the fall;
> I don't ask for a share of the profits-
> A pass for the season — that's all
> Now with me it's little bit different,
> And so I just thought I would call
> Make me out, when you find it convenient,
> A pass for the season — that's all!

Henry Killilea was one such magnate, who would no longer have to listen to such pleas. He sold his Boston American League franchise to John S. Taylor, son of Charles H. Taylor, proprietor of *The Boston Globe*.[96]

Milwaukee's infamous climate muddled that home opener and the Indianapolis club was telegrammed to halt in Chicago. Some 2,000 persons didn't take the heed of no flag atop the Pabst Building and showed up at Athletic Park that Sunday, April 24th. The Brewers opened at Indy instead.[97]

4 — *Last Team Standing* 117

Left: Catcher Kid Speer, 1904. The popular backstop joined Larry Twitchell's Western League Brewers in 1896. Milwaukee Public Library Historical Photograph Collection.

Right: Pitcher Al Hedges, who was traded by Cantillon to Springfield Manager Frank Donnelly for a $250 English bull terrier that Pongo Joe named Sue. Cantillon gave club Secretary Joe Holland one of the pups. Hedges was never heard from again, Spring 1904. Milwaukee Public Library Historical Photograph Collection.

Left: Outfielder Frank Hemphill, one of five returnees for 1904. Milwaukee Public Library Historical Collection.

Right: Defiant pose by half-breed Pitcher Fred Steele, 1904. Milwaukee Public Library Historical Collection.

The May Day standings would close with the Brewers sharing second with the Indians.

Thanks to 3-hit hurling by Elmer Meredith at Columbus, O'Brien sent the 9,000 paid into near apoplexy by breaking up John Malarkey's shutout.[98] O'Brien's cut of first base was missed by Umpire Pears on a right field single, opening the door to a 5–3 Brewer win.

Delaware, Ohio's Cliff Curtis came early that month from Cleveland to replace Claude Elliott as Cantillon's ace. Home attendance suffered from awful weather—790 at a chilly, error-riddled 9–3 win over Louisville on May 9th. Curtis was on the short end of Milwaukee's first whitewash, a 3–0 number by Indy on Tuesday, May 19th.[99]

The Brewers sputtered to improve to second by Memorial Day when a 2–1 hard-luck Curtis loss to the Millers was still seen by only 600. The Brewers may have felt like the "LOST MANHOOD" ad sponsored by the Wisconsin Medical Institute, which was in the Alhambra Theater Building, of all places.[100] That was the same day that loop President Grillo would add an eastern collegiate umpire to his staff. The future Hall of Famer was Bill Klem, who "never called one wrong."

Curtis' efforts were finally rewarded when Milwaukee leapfrogged the Saints into first, with another 5–3 showing at Columbus. Hemphill and 1st baseman Quate Bateman each doubled twice. Maybe they were benefiting from Pabst Extract, the "best Tonic" to restore "natural digestive powers"? Cantillon supposedly sent pitcher Elmer Stricklett to a physician to see if his salivary glands were "out of order!"[101]

The National Baseball Commission decided that Milwaukee would not be forced to pay on the old Fultz-Anderson deal of a couple years earlier. The Brewer road show generated more enthusiasm about the circuit than at home.[102] Captain

Less defiant pose by Steele. Milwaukee Public Library Historical Photograph Collection.

Schaefer had to baby-sit the club in mid-June after Cantillon was escorted by Columbus police for his row with Umpire Bauswine. Pongo Joe did his suspension in Chicago and Umpire Pears resigned at that time.

At least he wasn't assassinated like the Russian governor general to Finland, Bobrikoff. That incident on the Helsinki senate entrance had the Russ on an "ofer" streak that included getting whipped by the Japanese at sea.[103]

Cantillon's cotillion of ballplayers floundered about in third, dropping to 4th place by July 4th. Reeve McKay would take their frustrations out, 13–2, at Kansas City. He spread out 9 hits, but it was his own triple that was the longest drive of the game.[104] The 2,500 Blues' loyalists saw every Milwaukee batter but Speer get two or more hits. Bateman led the assault with 4 of the 21.

A cigar was only a cigar, but the 5¢ "Milwaukee Sentinel" was a smoke! The paper puffed about some Brewers having "the Western League habit" of seeing what happened to a ball before legging it out. Clark, Schaefer, and Stone were praised for their refreshing aggressiveness in that regard.[105]

Charlie Jones, the Denver Western League refugee who never did join the Brewers, did put on a July 30th amusement show at Athletic Park for his St. Paul Saints. He won over the 1,400 Milwaukeeans by volunteering to relieve his beleaguered starter, Sessions. The 17–1 onslaught was indeed on when Jones came in from center to walk a couple and gave up a pair of hits. When he finally KO'd Kid Speer on strikes, he went into a cap-tipping bow. Then Jones struck out George Stone "and in glee executed a few steps of the horn pipe." He received his manager Mike Kelley's congrats for retiring the side. Bateman's telegraph pole, "which draws a salary as a bat," squarely launched another of his team-leading homers over the 8th Street car tracks.[106]

Jones still had the last laugh. The Saints remained in first, Milwaukee, third.

Arrangements were already made that George Stone, the Brewers' real story of 1904, would be sold to Boston's Americans in mid-August, but he wouldn't see the Hub until the A.A. finished. Local press thought his legitimate batting wizardry would be squandered on the Boston bench. He could shine, with the right opportunity, for a lesser team.[107]

Stone would have to remain the story because no matter what exploits occurred, like long Tom Dougherty's sixth consecutive win in an August 1st rout of Minneapolis, the Brewers would not budge from third. It was that 10–2 victory, where the Brewers batted around in the fourth that 5,000 Athletic Park faithful gave George Stone his due, especially the bleacher creatures in left.[108]

The left handed–hitting Stone would do something, in the heart of the Dead Ball Era besides, that no other American Association batting champion would ever do: He finished at an astonishing .405, nearly 50 points higher than his nearest rival, teammate Germany Schaefer. Stone would prove it was no fluke by winning the American League batting title with the St. Louis Browns in 1906. He would return to Milwaukee after his major league run.[109]

Schaefer led the A.A. with 159 runs and Cliff Curtis with 210 strikeouts.

Left: A reserve catcher named Buckwalter, 1904. Milwaukee Public Library Historical Collection.
Right: Buckwalter, after learning the "splendid catcher and thrower" would be allowed to "develop in slower company." Milwaukee Public Library Historical Photograph Collection.

Pongo Joe's boys compiled a better finish than 1903: the 89–63, .585, and 8½ games back were all improvements, but still good for the same 3rd place, looking up at St. Paul on top.

The American Association pennant still seemed as elusive to Joe Cantillon's Brewers as Belgium's Princess Velva Marie von Dornberg, youngest daughter of King Leopold. The occasional actress was the subject of international intrigue, but it turned out she was just hiding in a humble cottage, with her Venetian nobleman husband as "Mr. & Mrs. Philip Alton," smack dab in Mil-

Tom Dougherty (left) gabs with a Columbus man, as Kid Speer (catcher) looks on, ca. 1904? at Athletic Park. Milwaukee Public Library Historical Photograph Collection.

waukee! Her father yearned for his favorite's return; she yearned to be a simple shop girl.[110]

The Cantillons were nowhere near as dysfunctional a family as the von Dornbergs. In fact, Pongo Joe took his team to Des Moines in the spring of 1905 to spar with brother Mike's Western Association Underwriters. The two teams maintained a rare working relationship, with the Iowa capital serving as a sort of Brewer farm. Fred Steele was there as was Claude Rossman, who'd be the 1st baseman of Ty Cobb's Detroit Tigers pennant-winners.[111]

The black sheep of the family turned out to be recalcitrant catcher Monte Beville. He seemed hell-bent upon playing on his own terms for Kansas City, until the weight of the National Agreement and KC manager Arthur Irwin made him a Brewer.[112]

Another indication of how history has since repeated itself is new American Association president Joseph O'Brien's putting his headquarters in Milwaukee. Sort of like the commissioner, now. Columbus would have the first concrete and steel ballpark in the circuit, the remodeled Neil Park. It would prove a boon to their attendance.[113]

Quin's 1902 reopening of Athletic Park would remain wooden for the next 50 years. Cantillon's cast of characters opened 1905 at Indianapolis with a 5–4 dividend. Beville was an immediate contributor in every facet, his speed as a catcher being noteworthy. Ex-Cream Canadian Bill O'Neill, another light-foot, and right fielder McChesney both doubleed in the winning margin. Tom Chivington now had the *Sentinel* byline, and he reported 4,500 at the game.[114]

A third of Pongo Joe's batting order was again new, but 6,000 Toledoans saw Billy Clingman and their Mud Hens thrash with Milwaukee to a 12-inning

4 — *Last Team Standing*   123

The 1904 Brewers. *From left:* Captain Germany Schaefer SS, Cliff Curtis P, Jack Slattery C, Quate Bateman P/1B, Lou Manske P, Tom Dougherty P, Elmer Stricklett P, Kid Speer C, Jack O'Brien 2B, Reeve McKay P, Frank Hemphill OF, George Stone OF, Harry Clark 3B. Rabbit Robinson behind "Little Hans" mascot. Milwaukee Public Library Historical Photograph Collection.

tie on April 30th. The Brewers jumped to a 7–1 record and the league lead in this eastern swing.[115]

Future Hall of Fame hurler Jack Chesebro would talk up the attributes of the spitball in the American League, while neglecting to credit ex-Brewer Elmer Stricklett as its inventor. In Hutchinson, Minnesota, a flag-draped woman temperance reformer tried to disrupt a Sunday game. A second battery set up to pitch around either side of her as she stationed herself between the mound and the plate. A good-natured swarm of fans finally forced her away.[116]

The Brewers' fast start stalled by mid-May when an angular, young Kansan named Franz shut out host Milwaukee on a 10-hit "hoodoo" of his "educational curves." The one hour, 40-minute ministration occurred before 1,020 rooters. The 6–6 stretch dropped Milwaukee into second.[117]

Milwaukee's population was growing to 340,000; it was growing like the Brewers' Memorial Day run production at KC. Umpire Gilford called the 8–2 game after the first half of the eighth, so the Brewers could catch a train. Brewer leadoff man shortstop Rabbit Robinson was hitless, but scored two runs and stole a base. Back in first, Milwaukee (25–11) was two games up on Columbus. The census later coughed up only 313,000 souls.[118]

The first illuminated parade of automobiles, some 250 in a line led by Barney Oldfield would occur back in Milwaukee. The University of Wisconsin's baseball coach, a famous football playing Seneca Indian from New York State named Bemus Peirce (sic), did not cast his professional diamond play with the Brewers. He reported after June 1st with St. Paul.[119]

Cartoonist Cad Brand, *Milwaukee Sentinel*, 1905.

The Brewers' race with Columbus flip-flopped as Cantillon went on a hunt for another hurler. Barry McCormick's fluid play at second was a glue and the big Texan, Bateman, would be remarkably valuable with his triple duty between pitching and both the infield and outfield. He again led the team in homers through the year. He filled in for McCormick when Barry's mother-in-law died.[120]

Only half of the July 4th doubleheader at Athletic Park could be performed on a wet field and the Brewers reveled in the home mud. They flattened Kansas City, 7–1, on Long Tom Dougherty's 6-hitter and 3 hits each from Robinson and Bateman before a holiday 3,840.[121]

Opposite Top: The Brewers on the road, 1905. Front Row: Pongo Joe Cantillon Mgr., Rabbit Robinson SS, Harry Clark 3B, Harry McChesney OF, Jack Slattery C. Middle Row: Monte Beville C, Tom Dougherty P, Jack O'Brien 1B/OF, Barry McCormick 2B, Frank Hemphill OF. Back Row: Babe Towne C, Clyde Goodwin P, Quate Bateman? 1B/OF/P, Cliff Curtis P. Bateman didn't press charges, when slashed by C Charlie Dexter at Des Moines on October 2nd. Milwaukee Public Library Historical Photograph Collection.

Opposite Bottom: Jack O'Brien 1B, Barry McCormick 2B, Rabbit Robinson SS, Harry Clark 3B, on the road in 1905. Milwaukee Public Library Historical Photograph Collection.

Milwaukee Public Library Collection.

The team fluttered between first and third like the weather and Cantillon even developed a surplus of pitching arms. Clark Griffith, now managing the A.L. New York Highlanders, attempted to pry suspended Brewer holdout catcher Jack Slattery away. Griff's own injured backstop was a Milwaukee boy, Jack (Red) Kleinow. Havenor saw the offer as extraordinary bad faith.[122]

Only 700 would see a remarkable pitchers' duel of 2-hitters at Athletic park on Wednesday, July 19th. Louisville's Ferguson was steadier than Tom Dougherty, but the Brewer defense, led by the circus outfield catch of "Tip" O'Neill was enough to prevail, 3–2.[123]

Timely Milwaukee batting, led by Harry (Red) McChesney's homer and fine fill-in play at third, won the day at Indianapolis on July 31st. It pulled Cantillon's crew back within 5 games of the first place Columbus Senators.[124]

The Brewers took advantage of the tail end KC Blues and got revenge on Walter Frantz in mid-August. The Blues had been on the road for three weeks and only 320 welcomed them back. Barry McCormick finished a triple shy of the cycle in securing Clyde Goodwin's 8–2 pitching victory.[125]

The same two clubs split a rugged doubleheader in Missouri, just before Labor Day, when a train delay from Milwaukee made for tired and hungry players. Both teams had little more than some sandwiches for breakfast on the return trip. Milwaukee still could not penetrate the fortress of Columbus' 6-game lead.[126]

The Dead Ball Era sounded like anything but in the 14–7 batting bee inflicted by the Minneapolis Millers in the first half of a September 14th twin bill. The Brewers' 5 errors made for only a third of the game's total runs to be earned. The 7-inning track meet, called on account of darkness, spared the 1,130 on hand to a 100-minute bombardment.[127]

The 1905 season ended at home, with the Brewers unable to draw any closer than eight games to the Columbus Senators. The standings weren't on the line, but some of the final game's 521 bucked about the farce between the Saints and the Brewers. Virtually everyone played out of position, except Milwaukee's battery of John Hickey, catcher Babe Towne, and Bateman at first. Hickey went the distance and even whacked a home run himself, but he gave up two dozen hits and suffered the short end of a 10–9 affair. Harry Clark played left in the exhibition, which drew editorial comment.[128]

Pongo Joe's brother, Mike Cantillon, did his elder one better by insuring his Des Moines Underwriters the Western League pennant. Cowboy Reeve McKay's shutout of Pueblo and Louie Manske's 3-hitter swept those Indians at home to seal the deal. Claude Rossman led the loop with his .357 and 229 hits. Old George Hogriever scored 122 runs for them, too.[129]

Charles Havenor and Joe Holland could boast that the 1905 Brewers were still the A.A.'s best road show, drawing 125,000, with home support growing an estimated 30 percent around the loop.[130]

Before breaking for the season, the Brewers were to barnstorm a couple

Outfielders Harry McChesney and Frank Hemphill, and erstwhile catcher Jack Slattery, 1905. Milwaukee Public Library Historical Photograph Collection.

exhibitions down in Chicago and then play a series at Des Moines, with indefinite touring beyond. Havenor, Joe Cantillon, Umpire Haskell, and Peck Sharp were then taking a month's fishing excursion through southern Missouri's Currant River, into the White River, and thence the Mississippi. After barnstorming, Rabbit Robinson and Frank Hemphill were to winter at Havenor's Squirrel Lake lodge in Wisconsin if they'd take it, so far removed "from the centers of baseball gossip."[131]

Incremental progress would stand to reason that, after third and second place finishes, Pongo Joe's Brewers could seize the 1906 flag. Factional warfare amongst the A.A.'s own magnates eased. Former loop president J. Ed Grillo owned the Toledo Mud Hens and old Bill Watkins of Indianapolis wrangled that Louisville's George Tebeau shouldn't be recognized as chairman of the circuit's board of directors. Mike Kelley wasn't even recognized as president of the Minneapolis Millers, at least until he would buy his release from the St. Louis Browns. Joe O'Brien came up with a ball box to protect player abuses of spit and the like on "pink" balls.[132]

Harry Clark, Frank Hemphill, and Tom Dougherty all availed in a Chicago White Sox "Blues-Whites" intrasquad game at Vicksburg, Mississippi, on March 11th. The status quo held that Cantillon would have his men back at Colfax Springs, Iowa, and Des Moines for their initial workouts. Havenor associate Arden L. Buell was now the Brewers' business manager and new catcher Frank Roth of Burlington, Wisconsin, would conduct practice until Pongo Joe arrived from the recuperative waters of Hot Springs, Arkansas.[133]

Chess and checkers players were being honorably mentioned as competitive sportsmen every inch as much as their fellow practitioners of more athletic pursuits in the sports page. Arthur Marcan, the Milwaukeean who played 2nd base for all 5 years of the St. Paul Saints' existence, resigned with president George Lennon and manager Dick Padden's club. Marcan would be traded to Indianapolis during the season.[134]

Harry McChesney attempted to contractually flee Milwaukee but was brought back into line by Secretary Farrell of the National Association of Minor Leagues. A heavier Barry McCormick showed up in Des Moines. Frank Roth and several Des Moines Champs players were robbed in the sleeper coming from Chicago. Roth lost $15 of the total $20 taken, but no trace of the thief was evident. Tip O'Neill had to explain his break-in to a Memphis Y.M.C.A. gym.[135]

Roth would share time behind the plate with Monte Beville, and outfielder Danny Green and pitcher Frank Oberlin were the only other significant additions to Pongo Joe's roster. Harry Clark was still helping the White Sox win a March 31st exhibition at KC when the Brewers doused their Des Moines hosts, 8–5. McCormick capered around the middle sack in "old fine form" for the 500 in the audience.[136]

Joe O'Brien may have had his ball box device, but the American Association's board of directors remained at odds with their fellow magnates over which brand of ball to make official. Havenor was among the board voters authorizing to go with the Reach ball, but T.J. Bryce of Columbus led the Bill Watkins faction that George Tebeau was financially obligated to the Victor people. Three-quarters consistently voted against Victor.

As much as Havenor won a tug-of-war with Tebeau, who claimed Rabbit Robinson's rights, Milwaukee's president had even more animosity for Watkins. The Indy head angled for Havenor's support to replace Tebeau on the arbitration board of the National Association.[137]

Watkins' own behavior at the New York winter meetings spawned the maneuvering that guaranteed O'Brien's retention as A.A. president and sent Tebeau back to the arbitration board. Watkins and associate Ruschaupt of Indianapolis held the controlling stock for Minneapolis and wanted to have Mike Kelley take the Millers' reins. The Havenor-Tebeau-Lennon faction held like the national commission that Kelley had to purchase his release from St. Louis, or he wouldn't be allowed in the A.A. They won.[138]

The Brewers couldn't take advantage of a wild Cy Swaim at Dubuque and were reduced to a conservative approach on muddy basepaths as Cantillon's men fell to the Three-I League club by 2–1. Pongo Joe would plan, with Havenor, improvements to Athletic Park's infield, cutting sod off the corners and leveling the dirt. The time was opportune as the home opener wasn't until May 2nd.

A Janesville pitcher named Akin was not a Brewer signee, but he kept absorbing their exhibition losses, including another 2–1 decision at Western League Omaha in mid-April.[139]

Rabbit Robinson and Frank Hemphill opened the season on major league rosters when the Brewers finally got underway at Toledo on Wednesday, April 18th. These two clubs used the Reach ball, but O'Brien's edict to use the Victor brand at Columbus nearly threatened postponement of that opener versus Kansas City.[140]

The debate must have literally shook the earth at its core, for it was the same day as the historic and horrific San Francisco Earthquake.

Over 7,000 Toledoans saw their Mud Hens land on young Frank "Flossie" Oberlin for a 7–2 tale. Oberlin lost to future Pirates' star Howie Camnitz, but gave all to support his own cause with three singles in four trips.[141]

The frustration of a 5–6 road start boiled over in Louisville when Cantillon was bounced. The newly returned Rabbit Robinson hit a ball near the plate that Umpire Sullivan ruled fair, thus the throw out at first. Cantillon's protest that it was foul put him off the grounds.[142]

"Superb weather" brought 6,000 out to the Athletic Park May 5th premiere, but Oberlin was knocked out in the fifth and the "Hoosiers" romped, 10–5. Pat Hynes was still performing winning outfield work and mopped up in relief, one of a precious few consolations.[143] Games started at 3 p.m. from here on out, no longer at 3:30.

A 6–1 start thrust Cantillon's Brewers back into second, thanks to Danny Green's 8 years of major league experience powering his home run surge. Harry Clark's drop of a Frank Roth throw to third set up a 5–3 home loss to Columbus in mid-May.[144]

This sort of hard luck sank the Brewers into fourth after a Memorial Day loss at KC that guaranteed the Blues third. Despite an early 3-zip lead, Oberlin choked on another defeat, 6–4, in 7 innings.[145]

The Brewers drew slightly more than the 800 who packed the South Side kindergarten hall to applaud Knights of Pythias minstrels singing "If the Man in the Moon Were a Coon."[146]

June 1906 marked the beginning byline of *Sentinel* baseball beat writer Manning Vaughan. His name would remain synonymous with the Brewers for the next quarter century.

Harry McChesney's homer to the Indianapolis scoreboard, with two down and two men on in the ninth, drew the Brewers to within a half-game of the league-leading Toledo Mud Hens by June 15th. Oberlin was a 10–8 beneficiary of Red's heroics.[147]

4 — *Last Team Standing* 131

Columbus wedged themselves between the clubs by Independence Day after the Brewers received a second game forfeit from Kansas City. Blues' manager (and ex-Brewer) Jimmy Burke kicked about Oberlin being hit by a pitch enough that 6,000 fans were denied a legitimate sweep to celebrate.[148]

The Senators grabbed the A.A. lead from Toledo within days, and it would again be Columbus whom the Brewers would chase. Cantillon enlisted a firethrower from Fond du Lac named Leo Sage to win the late portion of a July 18th deuce versus Toledo.[149] Sage resembled his name, showing veteran savvy and poise in the 6–1 finale.

The *Sentinel* editorial page noted that New York had "50,000 slaves to opium, morphine, and cocaine. We always knew here was something wrong with that town." The *Kansas City Journal* seemed to have a like view of Beer City: "Gov. Folk seems to have some genuine heroism in his makeup. He told Milwaukee to her face that she ought to keep the Sunday lid on Milwaukee, mind you."[150]

These places sounded mundane compared to the Russian revolutionaries battling Cossacks at Helsinki's Finnish seaport stronghold.

The Brewers' struggle to beat Mike Kelley's visiting Minneapolis Millers on that same July 31st wasn't as vital to human existence, but "the Yellow Kid," blond catcher Frank Roth, singled home the 11th-inning, 3–2 game winner. It was off St. Paul native son Henry Gehring.[151]

Cantillon's brew crew could not crack the half-dozen game margin kept by Columbus. Henry Killilea resurfaced in the baseball news to defend A.A. Umpire Owens against charges of crookedness by loop president Joe O'Brien. Cantillon testified at a Chicago hearing, but Mike Kelley, whose Millers were behind the charges, failed to show. The opinion was that Owens was being set up for ruin.[152]

The *Sentinel* circulation department now offered free baseball scorecards to boys and everyone who called upon them. They could then keep track of the mid-August twinbill sweep to the Hoosiers from which 1,500 saw the Brewers fall to third place. Hometown Milwaukeean Arthur Marcan rapped 3 hits in the two games and 4 Brewer miscues sabotaged Game Two. Umpire Owens may have survived his investigation, but his eyesight was questioned here.[153]

Another Milwaukeean, Gus Koch, held ownership of the Millers when they did away with the Pongomen twice on Labor Day. "The appearance of Dan Patch" at Minnesota's State Fair dented attendance, but the games were umpired by Flour City legend Perry "Moose" Werden.[154]

Milwaukee just could not make any September inroads on Columbus, despite some sparkling moments like Quate Bateman's 6-hit pitching over KC on the 9th. The 90-minute event with Jimmy Burke's "misfit cripples" was also highlighted by Milwaukeean George McBride's play at short for the visiting "Burkes."[155]

The historical ledger of 1906 will read that, just as the previous season, the Brewers went out on a flat note, a twin loss on September 18th at Kansas City. They "bade adieu to the professional side of Father Chadwick's game" by resorting to non-pitchers Robinson and Clark mopping up for a bludgeoned Tom Dougherty in the closing game.[156]

That ledger would also read that Cantillon's Brewers would finish identically 8 games behind Bill Clymer's Columbus Senators again. Pongo Joe was popular, for having lifted Milwaukee into regular contention. The pennant, however, still fluttered elsewhere. Columbus would play Eastern League Buffalo in the first "Little World Series."[157]

Not all these Brewers could live, eat, and breathe baseball the whole year. Monte Beville was a foreman at a big Georgia furniture factory. Leo Sage would be back to heaving coal into Northwestern railroad engines. Harry McChesney pursued his bricklaying trade at Pittsburgh. Beville's late season City Leaguer caddy Jim Block would chase rabbits for a week "over the hills near Grand Rapids, Wis."[158]

Others went to Ohio and league leading run scorer Danny Green to Chicago, but Rabbit Robinson hibernated at his West Virginia hutch and Quate Bateman went home to Melisa, Texas. Frank Oberlin and Clyde Goodwin finished the season up with Boston and Washington respectively in the American League.

The assumption seemed to be that Pongo Joe Cantillon would be back for 1907, but two factors were surely at work: He had taken his Milwaukee Brewers as far as he could and his fine work made him in demand by the majors. He would take over the reins at Washington for three seasons and fare no better than his predecessor.[159]

His brother, Mike, moved up to guide the Millers.[160]

Havenor and secretary Joe Holland would begin the succession of Irishman skippers by plumbing the Emerald Isle itself. "Dirty Jack" Doyle was born among the shamrocks at Killorglin in 1869. In his 17-year major league career as a 1st baseman, he hit a lifetime .299.

He would inherit the Cantillon legacy, a team returning all but a few hands. The Brewers went back to Hugh Duffy's old University of Illinois spring training base for 1907.

Monte Beville put Doyle in an early catching bind, holding out from his father-in-law's furniture factory, while Frank Roth would be enjoined with the White Sox. Roth's brother, Braggo, would also rise from Burlington, Wisconsin, to be a major league outfielder, in the next decade.[161] The spring baseball fever was being gratified in "homeopathic doses" once Danny Green signed again, and Frank Hemphill intended to train with the team.

Bowling, once taboo for ballplayers as developing underhand throwers and making for the slowest to round into shape, was now questioned as "mere slander." Of course, in this trust-busting time, a farmer asked a financier if he believed in irrigation systems. According to *The Baltimore American*, the financier said, "I certainly do, when it comes to watering stocks." Baltimore's Staley Starch Mfg. Co. considered a million-dollar plant at Milwaukee, but ended up at Decatur, Illinois. They would be well known for later sponsoring a certain professional football team.[162] The Milwaukee Road was laying off section laborers.

Indianapolis did not have to have its American Association "Browns" travel to train. Manager Charlie Carr's men firmed up at a resort at French Lick Springs, an area that would produce a certain famous basketball player some 70 years later. Boston Red Sox playing manager Chick Stahl committed suicide at nearby West Baden.[163]

The minor leagues continued to grow. The Class C Northern-Copper Country League was nicknamed the "Grasshopper" league for being the smallest circuit in the land, but covered an area equal to the National. The four definite, returning clubs stretched from Winnipeg to Michigan's Upper Peninsula.[164]

Jack Doyle had to borrow a backstop from George Huff's Illini until Frank Roth could reach Urbana from Memphis. Dirty Jack believed in treating his young salaried wings like glass in the earliest semi-chill. He was also without the services of outfielder Pat Hynes, who used the well-worn excuse that he was killed in a St. Louis barroom brawl on March 12th.[165]

Doyle maintained the pipeline to Des Moines and Cantillon even sent pitcher Kiddo Wilson from D.C., giving the Irishman some seven arms to contemplate. The Brewers left a little token collection for "Mac," the veteran janitor at the Illini gymnasium who had "been of much assistance to them." Pitching prospect Eddie Cumiskey of Kenosha went to the Madison Wisconsin State League club.[166]

Cliff Curtis was given the barnstorming opportunity to pitch at his "native hearth" against the Wesleyan University team at Delaware, Ohio. The collegians would use a professional battery consisting of their coach, Branch Rickey, catching and an Ohio-Penn League pitcher named Webb.[167]

Former *Sentinel* correspondent Tom Chivington took over the front office at Louisville, and Kansas City, St. Paul, and Indianapolis were all expected to improve. The "Doyleites" were coming back as the A.A.'s best offensive club, but that meant nothing for 1907. Dirty Jack didn't have the temerity to say his men could win the flag, but expectations ran far too high by the press and public. He did think they'd play the same sort of good ball that they gave Cantillon.[168]

Snow was predicted for the April 17th Brewer opener at Columbus, but the game went on before 5,579 anyway. The Senators flaunted their 1907 pennant 112 feet "above the earth." Their Bob Wicker was wild in walking 6 Brewers, but Clyde Goodwin was pounded hard in the 6–4 loss. Right fielder Jude, a Chippewa Indian, was on the scoring end of a Columbus squeeze, and Barry McCormick drove in one Brewer run the same way.[169]

Hometown boy Frank Schneiberg pitched the final road win at Indianapolis, giving Milwaukee a 5–5 mark to rally the home hearth for Sunday's April 28th opener. The second largest crowd ever at Athletic Park to date, 8,000 "almost frapped" cranks shivered to the Brewers' fall to the same Indy Browns. Only Danny Green could score when a passed ball was stopped by Umpire Egan's (future Brewer manager Jack?) chest protector. Cliff Curtis suffered the 4–1 defeat but would shut out the same club on May 5th.[170]

An April 29th snowstorm covered Milwaukee with three inches, whipped about by 35 m.p.h. winds. This was tantamount to how the Brewers' season would go: blown about and buried.

Former Brewer Bob Unglaub was promoted to manage the Boston Red Sox, and Brooklyn had won only one game by May 10th. Corsets could be had at The Emporium on 308 Grand Avenue for 69¢, and tailor-made shirts for between $2,98–$4,98. If his own team didn't cause it, Doyle's bowels could be exercised by a 10¢ box of Cascarets. The lax training deceptions of an earlier incarnate of "Joe Walcott, Negro Fighter, Bad Actor" were documented and the pitching secrets of a "Ted Kennedy" were being peddled by Samuel Sawyer of New York.[171]

"Doyle's Pets" slowly climbed to the first division, .500 respectability by mid-May, though they were haunted by cold weather at home. Still, 6,000 crazy bleacherites howled themselves into a cushion-throwing frenzy, when the Brewers yanked a May 19th match-up out of the fire. Curtis held off Kansas City when called upon in the 10th. Harry Clark's torrid liner passed Blues' manager Jimmy Burke at third and drove home Barry McCormick, who advanced on McChesney and Beville bunts, after singling. The 7–6 rally left Milwaukee still in fourth, but only 2½ games behind Columbus. It was perhaps the apex of the season.[172]

In an ironic twist of history, General Arthur MacArthur returned to his hometown of Milwaukee to stay after being away on military service for 45 years. He was to escort the Japanese Baron Kuroki, a famous Russo-Japanese War vet, as he passed through Milwaukee on a national tour. What MacArthur's son would later do to Kuroki's homeland is something to consider. The Citizen's Business League was promoting that Milwaukee was "a Bright Spot."[173]

Captain Harry Clark got sick on the way home from Kansas City by Memorial Day, but Red McChesney filled in ably at third. Lanky Cliff Curtis turned away the St. Paul Saints and twirler "Offside" Adams on 3 hits in the 2–1 holiday pitchers' duel.[174]

Samuel Gompers' American Federation of Labor bounced the International Brewery Workers Union from its ranks. Maybe they could have settled their differences over a 5¢ box of ZuZu, "the happiest, snappiest ginger snaps ever known in Gingerville."[175]

Joe and Mike Cantillon both still owned the Des Moines club and Minneapolis, but Pongo was now under fire in Washington from Milwaukee fans.

They thought he was flaunting waivers to the detriment of his old club to help his brother. He claimed good terms with Havenor and wasn't motivated by the A.A. blacklist of Mike Kelley. Circumstances merely dictated player movements, he said.[176]

Toledo's Charlie Chech set a loop record by whiffing 14 Brewers at the Glass City on June 14th, but Kiddo Wilson's own twirling forced a 2–1 decision. A sacrifice by George Perring, Toledo's 3rd baseman from Sharon, Wisconsin, set up the winning score.[177]

Doyle added 1st Baseman Buck Connors from Buffalo of the Eastern League to boost his sagging offense on the No. 3 slot. Doyle's Brewers flailed about in sixth place by July. The same could not be said of Miss Gabriella Worsley of Union Grove, Wisconsin, who finished second in a nationwide newspaper "Beauty Quest." Her charms rose from out of 300,000 entrants.[178]

An "immense throng" saw Columbus pitcher Robertaille lose both ends of a twin show at Athletic Park. The 9,800 bugs were delighted by Clyde Goodwin's 2–1 win followed by an 11–2 slaughter, led by Rabbit Robinson's 3-for-5, with 2 doubles and a homer, plus Connors' 4-for-5.

The Brewers held to within a game of .500 from that July 14th game to August 1st when "Sugar Boy" Tom Dougherty handed away 8 walks to the Colonels at Louisville.[179] Frank Roth returned from injury to retaliate against the same team at home 2 weeks later when his homer started a twin split.

The month of August made the Brewers' unravel. After flirting with fourth place, they fell nine games under .500, hobbled throughout with injuries. The fall in the standings went even deeper in mid-month from sixth to seventh. Only the cluster of Indianapolis and Kansas City gave them any wiggle room.[180]

Havenor was then comforted by the National Commission's decision to allow the Detroit Tigers to repurchase Frank Schneiberg. This, even though Tiger manager Hughey Jennings waived any reclamation by August 25th. Joe Cantillon did buy back Clyde Goodwin and Kiddo Wilson, exercising his option, after Milwaukee paid $1,250 for them. They would finish the season with Milwaukee. Havenor appealed the Schneiberg case to a 3-man tribunal after not being allowed to be heard in the first place. The process was losing its credibility.

Milwaukee's aldermen did no better, losing a ball game to Philadelphia's city fathers.[181]

In the major league draft of the minors, Milwaukee fans foresaw Tom Dougherty or Cliff Curtis as likely candidates to go. All were surprised by the St. Louis Browns' selection of Harry Clark. The 3rd baseman who had an admirable work ethic had been picked the autumn before by the Pirates, but he was brought back before 1907 opened.[182]

Schneiberg remained with Milwaukee and threw a September 1st, 8–0 shutout to nail down the end of a double dip and keep the Saints buried in last. Frank even hit twice. St. Paul returned the sweep at home one week later, but remained 13½ games behind.[183]

The proper end to a frustrating and lethargic 1907 came at Kansas City. The Brewers would drop consecutive doubleheaders to the Blues, who still had old "St. Jacob" Beckley holding down first base. Manager Jimmy Burke homered off Curtis in the third of four games swept, lifting his club over .500 and into the first division.[184]

Harry Clark even pitched the distance in the final 14–6 sham. Unlike the action in the Wisconsin State League, where a mob attacked the LaCrosse club at Freeport, Illinois, Jack Doyle's tenure with Milwaukee ended with a whimper.[185]

The listless seventh place finish demanded change. The personnel, who produced for the popular Pongo Joe Cantillon, simply hadn't responded to Doyle. Two cliques developed between "Scrappy Jack's" own and another led by a man "he wished to confer the degree of G.B." The infighting tore Doyle's Brewers, like the half-hearted McChesney, asunder. McChesney's good pal, 2nd baseman Barry McCormick was promoted as a managing balm to whom all could owe their allegiance. Southpaw Louis Manske, a local "graduate of the Bay View prairie," would be the primary addition to the pitching staff.[186]

The 1908 Brewers scrambled for a 1st baseman. Inducements to "that perverse Turk," John Flynn, seemed to include "all (of) Milwaukee's breweries, the ball yard, and the peanut privilege." The Eastern Leaguer would ultimately come, but not to guard the initial sack.

Speedy Newt Randall looked like the best of the majors' young castoffs to lurch onto the American Association. The outfielder began an eight-year stay in Milwaukee. The A.A.'s two-time defending run-scoring champion, Danny Green, would begin the campaign injured and never fully recover a full-time outer garden job. Harry Clark maintained his 3rd base spot with his intensity if certainly not with his bat.[187]

News of Vermont's Nelson P. Cook and his efforts to promote the baseball gospel in Britain made the spring rounds. From scratch, he organized teams out of a half-dozen London-area soccer clubs and started drawing Milwaukee-sized crowds of 2,500-4,000 in 1906.[188]

Frank Schneiberg opposed the Louisville "Night Riders" and Ambrose Puttmann on the slab to open 1908 in Kentucky. McCormick's Brewers came off a Memphis-Nashville spring polish route to face Milwaukeean Tom Chivington's new skipper, the gingery Jimmy Burke from KC. McCormick placed himself sixth in the batting order and resorted to the St. Louis Browns to settle upon his first sacker. Arthur G. Brown reaped Browns' owner Robert L. Hedges a tidy sum, having won his way up the ranks of the 1906 "Wilkesbarre" team in the New York League to Newark and Montreal in the Eastern League.[189]

Brown arrived not a moment too soon, but Ed Schlatter started the opener. "Schny" overcame his bother with the lighter Reach ball to brilliantly smother the Night Riders on a 4-hitter. An overflow crowd overcame a broken-down streetcar system to reach Eclipse Park. The Brewers' 2–1 lead came on first inning Louisville errors.

Future Brewers manager Danny Shay was declared a free agent by the National Commission that same day. The infielder had been released by the New York Giants to Oakland in the Pacific Coast League.

Kurdish brigands massacred 2,000 Armenians along the Persian border at this time. The 3-time defending A.A. champion Columbus Senators jumped out to an 11–3 start. McCormick's Brewers seemed hunky-dory at 7–7 when they came home from the east.[190]

Schneiberg would lift the home lid on May Day as well versus "the Chesty Columbus Champs" and "old Milwaukee idol" Jack Taylor. The Brakeman's best days with the Cubs, four 20-win seasons, were behind him, but a vast outpouring was expected to see an old favorite. The Columbus "Kilkennys" and "McCormick's Gaelic Teutons" were more than enough proof that Manning Vaughan was at the typewriter.

Brewer pitchers shook off the ill effects of their initial cold road trip to a golden gloss at Athletic Park. Long Tom Dougherty struck out 14 Toledo Mud Hens on Wednesday, May 6th. Cliff Curtis topped that in a huge way, with a no-hitter over the Indianapolis Indians on May 9th!

That breathless feat occurred before 5,500 "frenzied bugs who wanted to parade [Curtis] around on their shoulders."[191] Arthur Brown's 17 putouts and Curtis' own 7 assists were evidence of how the Indians couldn't connect for flies. Peaceful Monte Beville did not catch this milestone, but coached at third when he was canned by Umpire Kerin. That improbable scenario "almost doubled the crowd with laughter," but arguing a throw out of Clark at home gave ol' Mont the "chase to the stable."

Harry Clark was winning the fandom over and the Brewers were now in a second place percentage-points cluster of five clubs, one game behind Indy. The conscientious hustle of extended teamwork was contagious amongst McCormick's men.

The *Sunday Sentinel* answered a sporting query that Milwaukee was officially awarded the 1903 Western League flag, though it was never unfurled. Nearly five years after their invention, the Wright brothers' "aeroplane" and its recent 3-mile flight in North Carolina was still being rightly hailed as "the Marvel of the Age."[192]

The Minneapolis Millers' Mike Cantillon was described as not being as talkative in coaching the baselines as brother Joe but had "the same sylph like legs." Mike employed a sterling vet from St. Croix Falls, Wisconsin, onetime White Sox wonder Roy Patterson, to whitewash the Brewers on 4 hits, Friday, May 22nd. Milwaukeean Jimmy Block caught Patterson and "as tradition ordains," struck out twice after being given two big bouquets by some South Side admirers, among the 3,000 there.[193]

The shakedown of the Brewers in the standings began by Memorial Day.

Cad Brand, Sunday, August 16, 1908, *Milwaukee Sentinel.*

Harry McChesney's left field throw over Beville's head allowed the "Reds" Buck Freeman to score the 2–1 lead-settler at Minneapolis. Lou (Big Finn) Fiene's 3-hitter put Milwaukee a game under .500 and in 5th place, essentially tied with the Flour City.[194]

Depending upon your point of view, the zenith or nadir of the Dead Ball Era for all levels of professional play was 1908. McCormick's Brewers offered themselves up as so many sacrificial lambs to Louis "Bull" Durham of Indianapolis. Durham used both ends of a June 14th doubleheader to shut out Milwaukee, 5–0 and 1–0. Incredibly, the right-hander also known as "Judge" or "Whitey" would win five doubleheaders for the season and five of those ten victories hatched goose eggs.[195]

Even more remarkably, Charlie Carr's pennant-winners dealt him to Louisville before season's end. Before Durham racked up his 5th twinbill, Indianapolis teammate (and future Hall of Famer) Rube Marquard threw the A.A.'s 7th no-no in September.[196]

Barry McCormick's Brewers would not be able to claim any such heroes the rest of the season. In fact, in the maximum year of the pitcher, Milwaukee would have one 20-game loser (Manske) and two 19-game losers (Curtis and Schneiberg). Manske also had the dubious distinction of leading the loop with 146 walks.

Milwaukee, the city, may have been "A Bright Spot," but its lone bright spot on the diamond was right-handed Ohioan Larry Pape. He went 13–5 in 20 appearances and threw the best strikeout-walk ratio on the staff.[197]

Offensively, the Brewers dwindled even worse. Blond Frank Roth, who only caught half of the time (.289), and Rabbit Robinson (.281) were the only remote threats in wielding the wood. Manager McCormick was more reflective of his .231 club, done at .236. Robinson led the team in doubles and triples.

McCormick's effort at the helm proved no better than Jack Doyle. Barry, from Maysville, Kentucky, was not a born-Irishman like his predecessor, but neither had the luck of the green.

The 1908 Brewers finished with exactly the same winning percentage (.461) as under Doyle. They won and lost one less game apiece to achieve it, but McCormick's only boast could be a notch up in the standings to finish sixth. They would end 2½ games further behind the champions, however.

The Irish glint in Milwaukee's baseball eye turned even sharper for 1909. The city was fast becoming the game's epicenter for Kentucky Irishmen. One Irishman who didn't hail from down South, but came from the Amish country of Lancaster, Pennsylvania, was Ulysses Simpson Grant McGlynn.

He was best known as "Stoney" and was a policeman at LeMoyne, Pennsylvania, when he sent in his signed Brewer contract for mid-March 1909. He had been a 25-game loser with the St. Louis Cardinals a scant two years before.[198] He informed Milwaukee business manager Joseph Holland that he'd be able to work off what little "superfluous tissue" he had with a week amongst the Brewers' staff at the West Baden springs in Indiana. The resort would be home to the Sprudels Negro baseball club, named after the sparkling water there. McGlynn would be the man to define the Brewers' season.

As that all-important arm limbered into condition, Manush was dealt to Burlington (Iowa) of the Central Association. The outfielder was neither of the Manush brothers to make it to the majors, Heinie being the Hall of Famer. This was George Manush, who had a 1908 test run with the Brewers but finished that year in the Wisconsin-Illinois League.[199]

The West Baden, Indiana, training quarters, a mineral springs resort where the Brewers first went in 1909. Milwaukee Public Library Historical Photograph Collection.

At the West Baden resort, 1st baseman Dan McGann was acting manager. McGann came from Shelbyville, Kentucky, and had been a stellar, switch-hitting glove man for John McGraw's New York Giants. "Cap" wouldn't exert his pitchers early as they drank in the mineral waters and ran the bicycle track.[200] McGann even had his charges umpire the "well-known Badger fight."

Veteran flychaser Kip Selbach was noted as "the only living player on this or any other planet who quit baseball to go into the spring water business. As a rule those players who needed water in their vocation used it as a chaser."[201]

Arthur Marcan's brother, Dick, would perhaps follow in his brother's professional path and manage the Eau Claire team in the Minnesota-Wisconsin League. Dick was the "popular little president" of Milwaukee's City League and led the champion West Parks two seasons back.[202]

The Brewers poised to chase the A.A. bunting, but Milwaukee itself finally adopted a municipal gonfalon: Blue with a white "M" inside a red circle, as fit the "Bright Spot" slogan.[203] The world-famous Ignacy Jan Paderewski gave a piano recital at the Pabst Theater and "The Kentuckian" was being performed on the Bijou stage.

That show was prescient for it was Honest John McCloskey from Louisville, who would manage the Brewers through their final spring training at Champaign, Illinois. Ironically, the city called Champaign was a dry town. Temperance made beer available only from outside sources. Urbana, 32 miles away on the interurban, was equally dry. The Brewers, welcomed at the Beardsley Hotel, took out their denial of alcohol on the Illini, 18–4.[204]

Ed Lewee, the popular Milwaukee "Kid" who bounced around as a Brewer

Cad Brand, Sunday, April 11, 1909, *Milwaukee Sentinel.*

shortstop, also with Buffalo, Kansas City, and the Three-I League finally settled back home as the managing 2nd baseman for the semi-pro Milwaukee White Sox of the Lake Shore League. Their National Park would hold 6,000.[205]

George Nicol was another old Milwaukee Western League outfielder from the 90s who signed to put his dozen years experience to use with the City League Koerners. Joe Cantillon had Milwaukeean George McBride as his Washinton Nationals' shortstop, although he'd be ill for the American League opener.

Professional baseball had now grown to a $2,000,000 enterprise. The level of Class AA minor ball was thought to be up to major league standards of 20 years prior. The Pittsburgh Pirates were building a triple deck palace (Forbes Field) capable of holding an unheard of 25,000.

In that overall assessment of the national pastime, John J. McCloskey did not come off well. His departure from the last place St. Louis Cardinals branded him a knowledgeable if antagonistic motivator. McCloskey's replacement at the Mound City, future Hall of Famer Roger Bresnahan held up waivers on southpaw Charley Wacker before finally relenting. Foxy old Clark Griffith, now piloting the Cincinnati Reds wanted Wacker, too, but thought he would be better seasoned by McCloskey in Milwaukee.[206]

Yet another Hall of Famer, Jimmy Collins, receded from the American League glare at Boston to pose McCloskey's greatest hurdle at the tiller of Minneapolis. The headline, "HERZOG MAY BE MANAGER," had a different

Cad Brand, Sunday, May 16, 1909, *Milwaukee Sentinel*.

meaning for this generation. Charley "Buck" Herzog, versatile New York Giants' star, was offered the Jersey City job. He would manage Cincy in the next decade.

Another Giants' star, Turkey Mike Donlin, appeared with his actress wife Mabel Hite on Milwaukee's Majestic Theater stage that April. Calling their vaudeville act "Stealing Home," Miss Hite demurs from stealing the spotlight from her husband in the sketch, song, and dance routine. His waddling legs made any comeback unlikely for "Highlonesome."[207]

The stage was finally set for "His Despotic Nibs," Gerald Hayes, to yell "Play Ball!" at the Wednesday, April 14th opener at Athletic Park. Little Louie Manske would be caught by newcomer Artie Hostetter for the Brewers.[208]

Joining Dan McGann and "Hoss" as new to the Milwaukee lineup were 10-year major league vet Jack "Shad" Barry in right field and Texan Eddie Collins (not the Hall of Famer) in left. Charlie Moran backed up Hostetter. The new turnstiles clicked to the tune of a chilly 6,000. St. Paul's Saints offered Oneida tribesman Louie Leroy, who was savaged by 7 errors, including two misplays by ex-Milwaukee Cream Jim Cockman. The "clever redskin," a Gresham, Wisconsin farmer, was good in the pinches for five innings, but allowed 15 hits, like Barry McCormick's solo homer. The 9 to 5 job was completed in 2-hours, 5-minutes. Manske walked a handful on 4 hits.

The promise of the opener made the Brewers early 9–2 league leaders, but an intermittent blizzard between peeks of Ol' Sol put a crimp in a May Day rematch with the Saints. One Saint, who was expected in late on an early morning sleeper from Minnesota, was infielder Nig Perrine. He actually was a millionaire heir who played ball for the fun of it. The speculation was that once the money was all spent, he'd get down to the serious business of play.[209]

It took precious little time for Milwaukee fans to know who they had in Stoney McGlynn. He was already appraised as the best Milwaukee pitcher to ever grab a baseball, "but let him lose a couple and he'll be a lobster." The fans knew, not the Sunday sports page. Then again, a mythical spoof of baseball on horseback adorned that Sunday page, too.[210]

Wisconsin's legislature took a much more practical view towards the success of Sunday baseball than the pastoral ankle-biters, who still sought to nip it at Indianapolis. Besides "St. Jacob," the Old Eagle Eye Beckley at KC, had the early inside track on the A.A. batting crown! If the nation's enormous new President Taft could now publicly take in games, why not on Sundays?[211]

"Schny," Frank Schneiberg, unleashed his own annual hit and stunted the flight of the Toledo Mud Hens on 4 knocks of their own in a mid-May, 6–1 tilt. The 4,000 celebrated a 2-game lead on Louisville.[212]

A certain Judge Kenesaw Mountain Landis visited Milwaukee late that May to see someone hung. No, not a condemned criminal, but a portrait of the late U.S. District Court arbiter James G. Jenkins. A Kenosha Armenian joined the jurist in the hereafter when he was butchered by Turks in the lap of his mother.[213]

McGlynn decorated both ends of the holiday doubleheader on May 31st, along the Kaw River.[214] He mopped up Schneiberg's losing effort to Kansas City's "Beckleyites" in the morning, but won his own decision outright, going the distance in the afternoon. The Kaws stole a quartet of sacks off the cannon arm of "Hoss" in Game One, but idled on the basepaths later.

When the club petered out in the first two weeks of June, "Mistah McCloskey" rhetorically tied the can to their 14-year-old black mascot, "Snowball." Instead of skedaddling home to his "mammy" in Kansas City, where he feared a "mighty" poherful switchin,'" Snowball and the indigestion-stricken Stoney McGlynn, "were the swell guys on dat grea' big train" from Indy back to Milwaukee. The mascot who refused to be fired sought refuge at Hugo Walters, where the tavern gang took a shine to his care, until the club returned. "Chicken, dis am a mighty fine bit ob burd," the kid munched on a drumstick, rolling his eyes when asked if he liked it, in a manner that made your mouth water.

The Brewers kept Louisville's Colonels at bay until Indianapolis hurtled to the fore in mid-June. Minneapolis still lagged a couple games under .500 in fifth place. Dan McGann's 3 hits led the killing of Ducky Swann's KC hoodoo over the Brewers on July 4th. Amos Strunk in center and Jimmy Barrett in left now headed the Milwaukee batting order. Barrett had batted second in the Detroit Tigers' order during that first 1901 American League slugfest with Milwaukee.[215]

The crowd of 8,000 could set off fireworks for their 42–33 "Macmen" in first place. But, they had every reason to dread the advance of the Millers, now tied with Indy.

The head-on collision at Minneapolis had the McCloskeyites seeing "Reds" by mid-July. Irv Young, a.k.a. "Cy Young the second" or "Young Cy Young," single-handedly thwarted the Brewers' attempt at regaining the league lead from the Millers. Young shut out McGlynn in a 1–0 duel, decided by his own individual home run.[216] The record weekday Flour City crowd of 7,000 saw him surpass his 4-hitter. Young extinguished every Brewer but his opposite num-

BLOWING OFF THE FOAM.

Perspective of the 1909 race from Minneapolis.

ber, Tom Dougherty, who made a lone single in the ninth. Former Milwaukee Cream Bill "Tip" O'Neill clouted a 3-run shot to settle the 5–0 count.

Dougherty and Schneiberg anchored an August 1st sweep at Toledo, with Long Tom tossing his own 1-hit shutout and Schny riding the wealth of 13 runs on his own 3-hitter. The Brewers were a valuable road show, drawing 7,659 for the sixth place Mud Hens. Policemen needed to be stationed about the right field bleachers after Umpire Bill Guthrie was twice showered with pop bottles.[217] Manager Socks Seybold's admonishment alone did not cease the outburst.

A box score of Milwaukee's Lake Shore League White Sox revealed a few surnames that would ring through the city's future: Laabs, Knipple, Eldred, and Zeidler.[218]

The Brewers were within one game of the Millers when they extended a win streak to 5. The "effete Mons. Hogg," or Buffalo Bill Hogg of the visiting Night Riders was slammed by Shad Barry, Amos Strunk, Newt Randall, and the Milwaukee hit-and-run attack.[219]

"Ironwings" McGlynn extended the streak to 6 on August 10th, with a 4-hit/5-zip bleaching of Louisville on washday. He relieved Curtis the next day only to have misguided catcher Jack Warner's throw to second score Pitcher Jack Thielman with two out in the 11th. The A.A. pecking order still had the "house of Mack" chasing Minneapolis, only to be chased by Louisville.

Brewer and Toledo members were entertained at the New Star Theater that Friday night by Star Show Girl Company attraction Miss Eva Languay and her own "Stealing Home." She was reputed to be a "good ball player" in her own right.[220]

Harry Clark's long triple broke the longtime hoodoo of Columbus Senator Rube Geyer on August 21st and sent Milwaukee into a single percentage point over Minneapolis. McCloskey and McGann were thumbed by Umpire King at KC a couple days later when Dan tried punching him.

The August 26th split with the Millers made the Friday front-page. Ink-stained Kaw wretches peddled around a tale of dissension between McGlynn and Moran, but the latter finished calling Stoney's pitches harmoniously to defeat the Millers in Game One.[221] "Unser Louie" (Our Louie) Manske's balloon was burst by Young Cy's 2-hit, 9–0 blanking in Round Two. The standoff kept the Brewers on top.

The Brewer "clan felt pretty gay" in the Twin Cities after the "Saintiapolis, Pollysota" pilot Mike Kelley served up Charlie Chech for a 2-inning feast on August 31st. The Saints replaced Chech with "Heap Big Injun" Leroy, all to Grant McGlynn's 5–1 favor. A few miles north, "those B-lose from the banks of the muddy Kaw" answered the Minneapolis "Show-Me" from the cellar by dropping "the Finns" twice.[222] St. Paul reveled in their rivals' misery; Milwaukee was abuzz. It was as if the newly discovered North Pole was right there and the Brewers aimed to fly the A.A. pennant from it![223]

The Brewers went into the ensuing September battle 2½ games up on the Millers and 8 up on Louisville. Incredibly, with 4 home dates against Minneapolis and 5 games with the Falls City, it was the night-riding Colonels who persevered for the championship. The frenetic finish of Heinie Peitz's bourbon-totalers matched the 1907 race as the narrowest in A.A. annals.[224]

Stoney McGlynn won the battle. The iron man with the rubber right arm dominated every pitching category, but walks and winning percentage. His 27–21 record and 183 Ks all led the loop, but his 446 innings and 14 shutouts would stand in the American Association for all time.[225]

Looking from Athletic Park's spacious center field, ca. 1905–1914. Milwaukee Public Library Historical Photograph Collection.

It's just that Louisville won the war, the fifth different champ in the first eight years. McCloskey's bridesmaids were Milwaukee's first team to ever win 90 games (exactly). Charles Havenor relished, 6 years after the Western League parsimony, Milwaukee's last team standing.

5
The Lady Is a Champ

Athletic Park entered its second consecutive decade of use as Milwaukee's home of professional baseball. It was bounded by North 7th Street on the first base side, West Chambers along the home plate side of the horseshoe grandstand, North 8th Street on the third base side, and out to West Burleigh Street in center. The field dimensions, 266 feet along the left and right field lines, and 395 feet in center, reflected what could be crammed into a city block. The deep-roofed grandstand, which focused its attention towards home plate, made viewing the vast rectangular outfield from anywhere other than right behind home plate potentially obstructed. Instead of a foul screen just behind home, it ran all the way along each base side to protect box seat spectators within its peculiar contours. Pop flies along the lines were as good as gone for home runs.

In an era of unique ballparks, this citadel to a team called the Brewers had as its most prime seats, those around the bar directly behind home plate. In Milwaukee, as it should be.[1]

It was at this bastion of baseball that John J. McCloskey's managerial career was vindicated by the 1909 American Association pennant chase. It was to his detriment that he would not return many of the same faces. His entire rock-ribbed defense up the middle was gone. Amos Strunk moved up to Connie Mack's Philly A's.[2]

Tom Chivington would do like Harry Quin before him and Bud Selig much later on. He ascended from Louisville ownership to replace Tom Hickey as the A.A. president. The former Milwaukee wordsmith would be chided for discouraging the use of slang in newspaper baseball coverage, but he dandied up his umpires' garb a might with white "blouses."[3]

Those sports pages wondered why ballplayers worked the futile holdout exercise. The *Milwaukee Journal's* sports agates were now grammatically aligned by "Brownie." He would unearth Joe Holland's spoon-fed diet, aggravated by false teeth![4]

Charles Havenor's Milwaukee Brewers were one of three A.A. franchises as yet to win a pennant. In another Champaign spring of 1910, only the usual home white and road gray with black-trimmed uniforms stayed the same. "Soft, balmy air" wafted through their camp, but how the new addiction to moving picture shows affected their batting eyes, well...[5]

Stoney McGlynn's masterful 1909 didn't warrant a roller skating promotion up to the bigs. He preferred pitching to vaudeville, but lured fellow hurler Hippo Hammond on to a Champaign stage for a skit. Stoney was uncomfortable talking under dimmed lights, but loosened up when he could see his audience.[6] At least he wasn't on the rassling circuit, like a name familiar to modern Milwaukee fans — Stanislaw Zbyszko.[7]

McCloskey missed out on Milwaukeean Fred Luderus, who was on the verge being future Hall of Famer Frank Chance's understudy with the Chicago Cubs. The man we'd probably call "J. Mac" now should've kept the Irish glint in his eye out for one Mun Yung Chun, a Chinaman whose bat work lit up the Yale campus.[8] Luderus became a Phillie that July, where he'd play 12 years.

Cincinnati Reds owner August "Garry" Herrmann chaired the National Baseball Commission and was bent on eradicating rowdyism from the sport. This cause was as hopeless as mixing beer and liquor at Cincy games if Canadian Jack Graney's sarcasm or Ty Cobb's spikes had a say.

After skirmishing with the Illini, McCloskey drew 4,000 fans to an April 12th intrasquad game won by his Regulars 5, Yannigans 0, at upgraded Athletic Park. Lefthander Ralph Cutting's 5-hit, 2–1 dismantling of the Saints opened the 1910 sojourn at St. Paul.[9] Rabbit Robinson's barehanded stop, dozen clean chances, and lead Texas Leaguer RBI to pick up Jimmy Barrett cinched another opening southpaw win for cutting and McCloskey. Barrett would later get Mac's job.

The sports world was expanding: Amos Alonzo Stagg pondered an invite for his varsity Chicago Maroons to repeat the Wisconsin Badgers' groundbreaking 1909 baseball tour to Japan's Waseda University. First black heavyweight champ Jack Johnson faced "Great White Hopes" under personal scrutiny, amidst the dawn of controlling sports photo images released to the public.[10]

The Pittsburgh Pirates' misbegotten flag may have already proclaimed them "Champions of 1910," making Cutting's home opener against suspended Dan Shay's KC "Kawletes" seem almost academic. Five straight Minnesota losses and bats as dead as the newly passed Mark Twain made the 4-hit wing of Ducky Swann flap a 3-1, April 21st defeat.[11] Dan McGann's eye met Spike Shannon's forearm and a price-confused 3,000 mostly watched from the bleachers.

The Brewers were both monetarily and performance-troubled in the early go, but Cutting repeated his 2–1 work over the Saints on May Day. From 3 games within .500 by mid-month to Memorial Day's 7th place collapse, their descent was like watching the visible Halley's Comet speed over the horizon.[12] McGlynn skunked the Indians on 3 hits at Indy on June 1st.

Baseball had less bad mischief, but was still superstitious. None of it helped the crippled Brewers, who dealt away Rabbit Robinson. Bird of a feather Ducky Holmes had his Mud Hens sunk Milwaukee deeper into the cellar abyss by mid-June.[13]

A 14–8 burst, capped by a July 4th sweep of the "Farmers" at Kansas City lifted Milwaukee into the first division, albeit with a sub-.500 mark. Wilber Schardt's 16-inning, 6-hitter was followed up by McGlynn's 5-innings called at 6:30 so the Brewers could catch their train.[14]

Honest John McCloskey was a little too honest for everyone's good, throughout their mid-July tribulations. Chased by umpires 11 times, the Brewers went 2–9. He wasn't as abusive as some, just a persistent pest whose value away from the bench was now being questioned.[15]

Maybe he had more time to read Fred Vogt's card-playing byline as the "Skatonkel" (skat uncle?) Rabbit Robinson, sent down by Cincy to Louisville. Rabbit was back to haunt his old team.[16]

The *Journal's* Brownie laid Havenor's troubles as the only A.A. owner without a scout, something McCloskey was good at. Brownie suggested a couple weeks' talent hunt for Mac.[17]

The Columbus Senators' "puzzling saliva artist," Glenn Liebhardt, gave a 2–1 "black eye" to Milwaukee on August 1st, fending off a 5th place challenge.[18] Wisconsinite George Perring at third, old Milwaukee Canadian Bunk Congalton in right, and former N.L. homer king Fred Odwell at first were among the Ohio retreads. "Mistah Odwell" and his soiled spangles were "prezackly" the subject of Manager Bobby Quin's black washwoman. The "Senegambian empress" willingly laundered each Senator home uniform for a dollar apiece. All, except Oddy's. She sought "fouh dolluhs" extra for his duds and "ratheh yo'd send Misteh Odwell's clothes to a cahpet cleaneh."

Even the dominating Minneapolis Millers withstood four of their own walking away from a curbside auto crash. Pongo Joe Cantillon, now managing for brother Mike, only allowed his athletes on streetcars until the flag was clinched or the season ended, whichever came first.[19]

"Jawn" McCloskey's 6th place nightmare wasn't over before his team enraged him at Minneapolis. Team members had the bus driver leave the ballpark without their "august commander." He visited with an old Louisville friend beneath the grandstand, unaware of what transpired. There was no way the outraged skipper would board a streetcar, "with his Roman chest and Grecian-bend legs encased in those scarlet togs with which the Brewers were decorated."[20]

The growling "Jawn" spent $3 to bite the cushions of a taxi. His verbal discharge at the hotel rang through his players' ears well into the next morning. The team that played better, but meaningless ball, 30½ games behind the Millers leviathan, raced off with McCloskey's job.

Havenor promoted reserve flychaser Jimmy Barrett to manage, who in

O WHERE, O WHERE, WILL HE LAND?

Cad Brand, Friday, April 28, 1911, *Milwaukee Sentinel.*

turn was inundated by "all the small boys in town" to become the Brewers' mascot. The third-year Brewer with the middle name Erigena swung a fine .291 left-handed bat for 10 major league seasons.[21] In records since revised, he was once recognized as the 1900 N.L. base-stealing champ for Cincinnati.

The Massachusetts man replaced sloth-like Dan McGann at first, with a big Pennsylvania Welshman named Tom Jones. Little Nemo Neibold, at 5'-6", 157 lbs., was on his way up to a fine big time career, sharing time with Barrett in the outfield. They were joined by George Stone, the record batting champion back to rekindle fond memories. Chappy Charles (born Charles Shuh Achenbach), a 2nd baseman from the 1910 Cincinnati trade for Rabbit Robinson, formed the double play combo with Cornell grad Phil Lewis, acquired from Indy the previous year also.

The major league experience of bonesetter Doc Marshall carried the catching load for another year and Silver Breen remained valuable in utility.

Outfielder Rube DeGroff was a fellow cut-up to Stoney McGlynn, again the anchor of the 1911 pitching staff. Long Tom Dougherty's draft claim by Cincinnati was negligible, so he was back with Ralph Cutting, who was nearly a mistaken target of upper classmen hazing at the University of Illinois training camp.[22]

Bronco Busting Keenan was a good-hearted giant of a wild Westerner, who would've been popular at Athletic Park had he stuck. One who did, Eleva, Wisconsin's John Nicholson, needed to lose a dozen pounds. He would also go by "Rube" or "Nick."

Barrett set a hustling example for his wimpy offense on Opening Day.[23] His 10th inning, pinch-hit triple off the Columbus "human hatpin," Lessard, ignited a rally cashed in by Little Nemo in Brewerland. The newest hero beat out a barehanded stop from deep short by 5 feet to score his game-tying boss. The "6,000 Apaches" went wild when "the Reuben" DeGroff's ramshot over second scored a walking, base-stealing Tom Jones to win. Lessard died of quinsy, August 26th.

The humorous Rube declined the traditional shoulder ride for his heroics, saying he rode "in nothing but automobiles and seagoing hacks."

The excitement was so much back at "Havenor's Eighth Street aerodrome" that 35-year old saloonkeeper Herman Koepp's heart failed from it. He died 3 days after cheering the opener.

When his Brewers' 12–7 gust of steam propelled them into the first division by mid-May, Havenor tendered an offer to Deerfield, Wisconsin prepster George Auby, fresh off hurling consecutive no-nos.[24] Auby's father had the youth earmarked for the U. at Madison. Those Badgers were harsh to their Japanese Waseda University guests. The largest crowd ever at the state capital, 3,000, saw Manager Abendroth's varsity nine win 8–0.

Jimmy Barrett likewise teased local West Division High School southpaw Shorty Lewis with a contract. Lewis had the "stuff," if not the size, to set the Lake Shore League on its ear for the West Parks. Like Auby, he would never be a Brewer.[25]

Barrett was concise about his team's 10 losses in 14 games by June 1st: "They simply out-lucked us and beat us. Our pitchers have also been going badly. There you have the whole story." The year 1911 marked the hiring of Louis Nahin as Brewer secretary and business manager. The man labeled in print as "Bankroll Louie" served nearly 30 years in those capacities.[26] In his first Decoration Day with the club, Nahin was content to count 25,780 paid beans for 3 days at KC.

"Barrett's Broilers," tied for 3rd with Pongo Joe's .500 Millers, scalped the Indians on June 11th at Athletic Park.[27] A gathering of 10,000 "yelled themselves purple" when 20 hits off a trio of Indy hurlers equaled 20 runs. Tom Dougherty and Dan Marion checked them on 4 hits, 1 run. It was a natural gas to be sure, back when 25¢ a month could get you 100,000 cubic feet.

Some bug, gassed full of hops, broke any lull in the rooting by balancing a beer bottle atop his head, while playing "the national anthem of Halsted street" on a "go to me come from me" accordion. Another bleacher creature ended the concert by toppling the bottle off his dome with a perfectly aimed box of crackerjack. Bennie Kean, the "demon waiter at the ball plant," wasn't satisfied to fuel such patrons. He challenged a saloonkeeper's nine to a side bet of "100 iron men."

The Colonels replaced Minneapolis as the Brewers' co-habitants when Barrett was tossed from the second July 4th game at Kansas City. His protestations over George Stone's out at home nearly led to blows with Umpire Weddige. Barrett earned a police escort out, but his men split.[28]

When "auburn-haired marvel" Marty O'Toole used his portside spitballs to not even allow Stone so much as a foul, the Saint set an A.A. record, whiffing 17 Brewers at St. Paul on July 9th.

Recording the sound of a ball smacking a catcher's mitt should've been on the National Association of Talking Machine Jobbers' agenda at Milwaukee. The entertainment device hadn't met Tom Edison's vision as a business tool, but musical talent needed to promote records better.[29]

The Brewers' acquisition of outfielder Ray Schalk from Taylorsville in the Illinois-Missouri League for $1,500 meant the future Hall of Famer's first serious chance to be a "crack backstop." Barrett would debut the native flatlander against the Kaws' Dusty Rhoades that July.[30]

Paths of Brewers past and future crossed in the Class C Wisconsin-Illinois League. Old George Hogriever still cuddled his cudgel at Appleton, while Rockford's Cy Slapnicka didn't lose his first game until July's end en route to a marvelous 26–7. Oh, and a certain future manager named Casey Stengel won the batting title (.352) for the Aurora Blues.[31]

All hell broke loose when Ducky Swann's Maumee Mud Hens pasted Milwaukee, 9–0, on Saturday, July 29th. Barrett was again banned to the "booby-hatch" for defending the banished Phil Lewis' rush of Umpire "Two Bits (plus a nickel)" Bierhalter.[32] A Toledo-supporting suffragette responded to the joshing taunts, in a sea of Brewer fans, by calling for the cops to arrest two men. Five minutes later, she slugged an innocent bystander of a big lug. "It was as peaceful as a large night at a Donegal ball."

That there was as much action in the stands told of Milwaukee's inability to pass .500. "Broiler" run-ins with arbiters continued when Dougherty threw his glove in the face of "Chivington's Bumpire" Gerald Hayes for calling a grooved pitch a ball. Tom snapped like the loss streak. Doc Marshall went with his batterymate in the 9th, and reliever Andy Harrington was bounced at bat in the 11th. John Nicholson finished the Saturday, August 12th win in 13 by 7–4.[33]

This chaos just dogged the Brewers. An Athletic Park benefit played on September 2nd for Art Holskoetter/"Hostetter" probably should've been for

5 — *The Lady Is a Champ* 153

A Close Game In Milwaukee

Penny postcard, or tall cool reality? Self-image is everything. Milwaukee Public Library Historical Photograph Collection.

Barrett's job. Recent former Brewers Quate Bateman and Louie Manske represented "All-Stars" against the "Police." Again, surnames of the Brewers' future were almost spooky: Becker, Griswold, Laabs, and Mauch.[34]

German hops merchant Paul Reinemann of Frankfurt-am-Main traveled through Milwaukee to praise the modern and efficient cleanliness of American breweries as the best in the world. The same could not be said for their namesake baseball club.[35]

Garry Herrmann's ideal for less rowdy ball was beaten to a pulp by Barrett's 1911 Brewers. Plummeted to 7th place by September, a frustrated Dougherty again received the thumb from "the incompetent Jeribald," Jerry Eddinger. A foot injury did not put out the "diamond king" for the year as hoped.[36] Phil Lewis, the college-educated shortstop, would assault him by season's end.

Dougherty couldn't blame Eddinger for his poor pitching in the home finale. He was outdone by the Mud Hens' "Chinese Baptist, Wun Lung (Earl) Yingling."[37] Jimmy Barrett's brand of fire went out with a quiet puff of smoke on Sunday, October 1st. Stoney McGlynn, eager to go hunting, finished off the Saints, 4–3. Old Brewer hero Ginger Beaumont was in center for St. Paul and their "mild-mannered and unpretentious" Barry McCormick was tossed from the keystone. Darkness called Game Two and the season. Vaughan's *Sentinel* byline now had A.J. Shinners.[38]

Infielder Cy Bennett directed the Brewers' post-season barnstorm of Lake Shore League teams, but maybe they'd been better off taking in the International Dairy Show to hear "Warbling Flo from Kokomo." A German criminologist claimed ragtime was producing idiocy and hysteria amongst U.S. people. Obviously he hadn't seen the Brewers play.[39]

Idiocy was that half of the visiting Negro Chicago Union Giants should have played in the majors. They met the West Parks at Athletic Park and the Motl Jewelers on the South Side.

The treadmill Brewers turned to a retread to right their listing vessel. There was no small irony that Charles Havenor called upon onetime archrival Hugh Duffy for this task. Duff came off a better 77–74, 4th place run for the 1911 White Sox. The aging "Angel Child" was now the only man to manage Milwaukee clubs in 3 different leagues (A.L.'01, W.L.'02-'03, A.A. 1912).

Duffy seemed a magnet for water, as flooding drove his new assignment from their Cairo, Illinois, spring quarters. Like Tom Dougherty, Harry Clark dabbed "war paint" mud under his eyes to cut the sun's glare. Colored locals speculated as to who peppered Pep's black eyes. Not "Tar Baby" champ Jack Johnson![40] Duffy found dry refuge from his Cream flashbacks up in Robin Yount's birthplace, Danville.

It was never said whether the pressure of pursuing an A.A. pennant played a part, but on early Wednesday, April 3, 1912, 50-year old Brewers owner Charles S. Havenor died. Succumbing to pneumonia, he never saw a championship flag fly over Athletic Park in his decade there.[41]

Havenor, a Berlin, Wisconsin native, came from tailoring concerns at Waupaca, Wisconsin, and Peoria before arriving in Milwaukee in 1897. Besides the Brewers, he once owned the Des Moines club, and, along with Wisconsin-Illinois League president Charles F. Moll, had an interest in the American Grinder Manufacturing Co. The former alderman also held interests in other manufacturing enterprises, plus considerable property in Milwaukee and Chicago.

Havenor's death made the front page, though it was not the prominent story. His widow, Mrs. Agnes Malloy Havenor retained sole Brewers ownership, but in her grief, E.J. Archambault, Alderman Cornelius "Con" Corcoran, and Charlie Moll handled team affairs. Business manager Louis Nahin was lost in the Cairo flooding for 36 hours, but made his way back for the visitation at Havenor's 10th Street home. The A.A. sent a "beautiful blanket of Easter lilies."

The memorial service was held that Friday afternoon as a special train left Milwaukee for Berlin at 7:40 a.m. The three aforementioned men were joined by Michael Carpenter, Frank Fitzgerald, and sportswriter Manning Vaughan as active pallbearers. Joe Cantillon offered praise and gratitude from Minneapolis.

The Irishman, Corcoran, would represent Milwaukee's Little Italy as part of the Nonpartisan electoral success that repudiated Milwaukee's first dalliance with Socialism's potholes. Some Italian locals hung lemons as tassels for a red flag to celebrate.[42] A "FAN" suggested that the Nonpartisan goat, "Woozy," be presented from *The Journal's* custody to be the Brewer mascot.

The leap year 1912 would cast a peculiar pall on Milwaukee despite the Socialists' ouster. The Allis-Chalmers Co. went into receivership and the "backward" city was one of the few without motor fire apparatus, yet it hosted the Vanderbilt Cup auto race. "The Flying Merkel, the only motorcycle with a spring frame and fork," went for $200-275 at Milwaukee Sycle Sales & Supply Co. It shouldn't have been confused with Watertown, Wisconsin's Fred (Bonehead) Merkle, the infamous New York Giants' 1st baseman. Maybe the ad was right: "The Peevish Child Needs A Laxative." In Milwaukee, he needed more grounds to play baseball, an "inalienable right" championed by *The Journal*.[43]

Mrs. Havenor made front-page news for assuming the Brewers' presidency. The April 8th directors and stockholders' meeting confirmed that and Corcoran's election as vice-president. Secretary Pease replaced Henry Bauman, an original director. Ex-W.—I.L. president Moll became Mrs. Havenor's personal rep and general business manager. She joined the St. Louis Cardinals' Mrs. Helen Britton as the sport's only female owners. Her success led Mrs. Havenor to opine that a woman's intuition and diplomacy made baseball a business field best adaptable for such qualities. With no strong suffrage view, she'd lead her club from her Majestic Building office desk and actively attend all home games. Nixing road travel, she left on-field judgements to Hugh Duffy.[44]

Believed to be Chappy Charles, Brewers 2B from 1910 to 1912. Milwaukee Public Library Historical Photograph Collection.

The hands Duffy played with were mostly strangers. The Brewers' most vocal baseline coach since the days of Pongo Joe, Duffy immediately changed his signals. He feared the Mud Hens stole them, but no matter. His season sank like the *S.S. Titanic* that April 15th with six Wisconsinites on board.[45]

The only flag to fly over Milwaukee, on this Duffy watch, was steeplejack pro Henry Thomas' unfurling of the Stars and Stripes over City Hall to thousands of Nonpartisan cheers.

Duffy compared these slow-starting Brewers with the '01 vintage, when Pete Husting's intervention kept Virg Garvin's bat from being a murder weapon on a black man. Those colored Chicago Union Giants helped open the Kosciuskos' new Lake Shore League park and George Stone led a handful of Brewers in a local semi-pro tryout exhibition versus the Green Bay W.—I.L. club.[46]

Duffy threatened trades and demotions early on, but his purchase of Rockford's Cy Slapnicka made the future ace just the tonic for a poorly conditioned pitching staff. Center fielder Larry Chappelle was the club's only real new regular. Ex-Brewer Rube Waddell, now a Miller, hawked news "EXTRAs" on Toledo streets.[47]

Rainy gusts of 40 m.p.h. delayed the Milwaukee home opener, but maybe the Friday, April 26th game was better left unplayed. Duffy's 5-7 team slithered home from the east, just to let 5,000 see an atrocious 13-1 dismembering by shortstop Ray Chapman and Toledo. The ugly outcome was reported by Brownie in *The Journal Green Sheet* five minutes after the final out.[48] The game was so rotten that the new screen over the center field bleacher runway wasn't about to contain one William Fisher, fined $10 for speeding on Chambers at 25 m.p.h. He was "trying to get away from the park as fast as possible."

Duffy ascribed his team's play to a luckless jinx and George Stone was an early cut. He signed up with Portland by mid-May, but Harry Clark and Ray Schalk battled bad colds. Ladies Day may have been the cure in the won-loss ledger, but Angel Child Duffy ducked through under the stands, condemning umpire Two Bits Bierhalter saying, "You'll burn when you die."

Tom Dougherty was back to getting the ump's rush. Umpire Irwin ran him in the morning of Decoration Day at KC, only to throw a few pitches the next inning. Upon being discovered, Dougherty claimed his 5-minute display confirmed Irwin's blindness. Whining was still the norm.

Though he hadn't played since his Milwaukee Western League days of nearly a decade earlier, Duffy considered donning the spangles as a pinch-hitter. Anything for his last place team.

"BONE DOMED WORK" by the Milwaukee outfield gave July 4th's first game to the visiting Blues. Cy Slapnicka relieved Joe Hovlik for the third straight game. Groundskeeper Will Stocksick came from St. Louis to salvage the playing field. The 7,000 waited on the matinee.[49] Incredibly, July 4, 1912, was the first time that an American flag flew at 24-year old Athletic Park. General Manager Moll made the first time patriotic decorations look like "big league stuff."

The political season of 1912 may well have been hotter than that on the ball diamond. Wisconsin's so-called "Progressive" movement threatened to make an income tax reality, while nationally, President William Howard Taft faced not only Democrat Woodrow Wilson, but upstart "Bull Moose" Republican Theodore Roosevelt. In Stockholm, Sweden, future Brewer Jim Thorpe led the United States domination of the Olympic Games as "The World's Greatest Athlete."[50]

The Brewers weighed making some state league club a farm, and bids on Ray Schalk grew like the "dope" that Hugh Duffy had Eastern League offers to manage the next season. Both Duff and the financially-distressed St. Paul Saints could have used Louisville railroad engineer William T. Madden's luck: He caught a foul ball in his passing locomotive's window.[51]

Word from the Windy City came that ex-Brewer Danny Green was dying of tuberculosis. Schalk was sold to the ChiSox there, and his Louisville replacement, Johnny "Runt" Hughes, authored a 20–20 finish for the Brewers from August 15th on.

Moll and Duffy beat the bushes for young help, but John Nicholson was out under a doctor's care for a week, former State League southpaw Bruce Noel wandered off to Oshkosh and a Duffy suspension, and Joe Hovlik was the victim of Toledo's alleged "doping" of the ball. That "scandalous" practice meant a substance that made spitball throwers sick when they licked their fingers. Throwing the spitter itself though, was in the realm of "fair play."[52]

If the Brewers weren't stimulating entertainment, the grounds at 35th and Clybourn had Buffalo Bill and Pawnee Bill's combined Wild West and Far East Shows two final times. Indianapolis Indians demoted manager shortstop Charlie O'Leary handed Milwaukee an August 16th win with 4 miscues. Their third pilot, his replacement O'Day, had all the spunk of a dullard.[53]

Despite the arrival of 22-game winner Doc Watson (of Oshkosh, Wisconsin) and his "Beedle ball" and Green Bay homer champ Earl Smith to go with Phil Lewis' clutch hitting and Nemo Leibold's shoestring scoops, the Brewers' first division hopes were wrecked in a September 16th double loss at KC.[54] Enmity between Duffy and Mrs. Havenor boiled over in print. Duffy ripped everything, refusing a pay cut and calling his men bush. She cited the $200,000 investment and that he spoke only a half-dozen times with her all season. Players resented the "bush" tag.[55]

On October 14, 1912, Col. Theodore Roosevelt survived an assassination attempt in Milwaukee by New York Bavarian immigrant bartender John Schrank. "TR" did give his speech.[56]

Roosevelt could beat death at close range and lose the election to Wilson with his Rough Rider reputation intact. Hugh Duffy's complaints were made to look foolish by 1913.

Mrs. Agnes Malloy Havenor struck gold when she decided to promote popular pepperbox 3rd baseman Harry Clark, captain and a 9-year Brewer, to manage her baseball club. She ended the 5-year parade of skippers by making Clark the highest-paid manager in the American Association. *The Journal* trumpeted his promotion, which closed 1912, with the Brewers' 2-of-3 season-ending series victory over Minneapolis.

The pennant-dominating Millers had ex-Brewer and major leaguer Bob

Unglaub, ex-Tyger Claude Rossman, and a future Brewer leader, center fielder Jack Lelivelt. Pongo Joe Cantillon's platitudes for his protege weren't idle. Clark would break his death-grip on the league title.⁵⁷ Pep modestly returned home to much rejoicing in Paulding, Ohio.

Kansas City Blues owner George Tebeau figured in the center of two controversies: The suspected arson burning of his Association Park and the Indianapolis signing of manager Mike Kelley, still under contract to St. Paul.⁵⁸

Harry Clark's businesslike continuity and stability welded a group of luckless umpire baiters into a heady team that would execute winning baseball. He would have none of:

> THE RECRUIT⁵⁹
> There once was a baseball recruit
> Who was perfectly certain he'd suit
> But he'd pull every day
> Some fool "bonehead" play
> Now he's farming that's all there is to't.

Mrs. Havenor's Milwaukee Brewers trained at Owensboro, Kentucky, a town noted for its distilleries. Whatever snow was in Milwaukee that March didn't compare to District Attorney Yockey's "coke" crusade. He targeted a few druggists for illegally trafficking the substance, but had yet to question Eva Perry, dubbed "Queen of the Snowbirds."⁶⁰

"Old warhorse" Stoney McGlynn offered some doggerel on Jim Thorpe, Chief Meyers, and John McGraw's Indian tribe of New York Giants before being sold to Salt Lake City.⁶¹ Harry Clark's players swore by their "strict task master," affectionately also called "Nig." He disdained his pitchers' use of the spitter, as a strain on right-handers and virtually unused by lefties. Sugar Boy Tom Dougherty led the Brewers' hallelujah chorus over departed southpaw nuisance Ducky Swann from the A.A.: "We kept him in the league for two years and I for one am glad he has gone. He surely did have a humpbacked, double jointed jinx on us."⁶²

"The elongated strategist," Charles Moll, organized another Milwaukee team, not as a direct challenge to the Brewers, as the old Creams were, but for entry in the Wisconsin-Illinois circuit. Nicknamed the "Mollycoddles," they'd end up in Fond du Lac by mid-summer.⁶³ The outlaw Federal League did not yet claim major status, but delved into Indianapolis and Kansas City. Cubans made their first modern major league appearance, as two won jobs with Cincinnati.⁶⁴

Clark's St. Patrick's Day intrasquad game pitted the victorious "Irishers" (regulars) over the A.P.A.s (rebels). His work ethic by example struck Milwaukee like the fierce tornado that destroyed five hoisting cranes and Gimbel's mammoth department store sign, besides blocking the interurban system. It spawned from a cyclone that killed 200 across Omaha and Iowa.⁶⁵

A doctored *Sentinel* photo led to this Owensboro sidebar: "All the nig-

5 — The Lady Is a Champ

Harry Clark (left foreground) jousts and jests with his 1913 Brewers. Milwaukee Public Library Historical Photograph Collection.

gers in the hotel have had great respect for Johnny Hughes since they saw... the midget holding up Joe Hovlik. They can't understand how such a little fellow can possess such great strength."[66]

A.A. President Tom Chivington was schooling his umpires at Chicago and Milwaukee. Guess the last few years of kicking by the Brewers wasn't education enough?[67]

The Brewers' route to the 1913 pennant was like the Panama Canal, which was finally navigable in the fall after 10 years of construction. Ohio River flooding at Owensboro and rain doused the home opener's delay, making more time for reminiscing. Jimmy Barrett's 38th birthday occurred in the auto business in Detroit. Rumors of Jigg Donahue's death in a Chicago insane asylum were in reality his hospitalization with paresis. Well-known Milwaukee businessman Otto Schomberg and West Side Police sergeant Tony Falch vented the baseball tradition of "Well, in my day..."

Their 1884 Milwaukee spring training at snow-covered Rockford stood in stark contrast to the pampered Pullman sleepers and expensive hotels of 1913. Old *Sentinel* sporting editor Oliver E. Remey's memories of cigar-chomping Charlie Cushman, "Hi Hi" Moritz Seligman, Gen. Charles King, and Harry Quin blended with J.J. Delany's like recall of 1894 and 1902, with Billy Clingman at both, Charlie Havenor, and Nick Altrock's current vaudeville form of baseball.[68]

Pope Pius X was likely to be joining financier J.P. Morgan in the hereafter soon, as well as the Virginian who authored the amendment to abolish slavery, John Brooks Henderson. Those deceased were as cold as the arctic-like April 12th opener at Milwaukee.[69] Cy Slapnicka warmed the fur-bundled 2,500 fans' Saturday with a 2–0 blanking of Topsy Hartsel's Toledo Mud Hens. "Flashy Frenchman" Larry Chappelle made unusually knowledgeable 3½-year old Henry Kerns' day with the first hit and steal, plus a brilliant shoestring catch. The youngest bug would learn how to keep score from his older brother this season.

The front-running Clarkmen were clearly marked men. Mike Kelley's Indy tribe winged three Milwaukee base runners each in the noggin with "coco balls" in a 9-run 8th on April 20th. Maybe Kelley's Indians resented that Charles Milwaukee Sivyer, the first white boy born in the city, observed his 77th birthday that May 4th out in San Diego?[70] Gang activity by Milwaukee's near North Side "Teutonia Indians" resulted in a member's shooting death at a saloon dance.

Harry Clark was no less feisty. He was leniently fined $50 and given a "verbal slap on the wrist" for duking it out with Millers shortstop Daredevil Dave Altizer in early May. Pep's shift of Phil Lewis to second led chattering shortstop Russell "Lena" Blackburne to drive 8,000 "nutty," with his May 19th stab of a Gardner liner to twin sweep Toledo.[71]

Memorial Day meant the breakout of straw hats, but fans could only tip them to their 3rd place Brewers' 13–8 morning win at Kansas City. Dougherty and his fellow cripples were walloped 10–1 in Game Two, but they now trailed Columbus by only five games.[72] Dwindling numbers of Grand Army of the Republic Civil War veterans, including Milwaukee's Sgt. Francis H. Hans, who fired the first shot at Gettysburg, were stilled honored in the city a half-century later.[73]

A "home run slump" in the Dead Ball Era may sound like an oxymoron, but for Newt "Clear the Bases" Randall, it cost little Jimmy Jonas 30 days in the workhouse for vagrancy. Jonas had avoided that fate as Athletic Park's unofficial home run chaser, but once Randall quit eyeing the sphere "like a bull gone wild over a red rug," the jig was up.[74]

Harry Clark's June 1st .230 batting average didn't deter his men from seizing the loop lead by mid-month, with identical 5–3 results, before 11,000 of Columbus' humbled own. John Nicholson relieved Ralph Cutting and Sheboygan Lake Shore product Buster Braun in each game. The W.—I.L. Mollys, with future major leaguers Possum Whitted and shortstop Hap Fel(s)ch, had a better winning percentage than the Brewers and drew 3,000 for a Sunday, June 15th victory.[75] Fond du Lac won out over Aurora, Illinois, to relocate the second place team, chasing Oshkosh.

The *Sentinel* editorial page declared bullfighting doomed in Barcelona now that a baseball team was formed there. Moreover, it elaborated on the attraction of baseball because it is so "tarnal uncertain." It said if every team played to its maximum all the time, it wasn't worth seeing. Ed Remley took up their byline in describing a 4–3 home loss to the Kaws as a "tragedy." Killer heat, that left 5 dead in Milwaukee and thrice that many prostrated was a matter of perspective.[76]

Stoney McGlynn cracked fire in Milwaukee for Jack Herzog's Manitowoc Huskies in their Independence Day bout with the Lake Shore League Kosciuskos. He fared better over the Poles than the Clarkmen did at KC. Bill Powell shut the Brewers in the second of twin losses that left Milwaukee 2½ games behind Columbus.[77]

The Senators' King Cole, a former Cub 20-game winner, took advantage of Milwaukee's sale of Larry Chappelle to gyrate a no-hitter at them. Gutsy Tom Dougherty's 11-hitter hung with Cole until the ninth when the King sealed his 3–1 masterwork with the last run. One of Cole's 3 walks let 3,000 cheer the Brewers' lone run, the same day Brooklyn's new Ebbets Field opened.[78]

Harry Clark spared no effort in seeking an edge for his Brewers. Long-promised John Beall arrived from the Cleveland Naps' outfield. Irv "Young Cy" Young brought his left wing down from Minneapolis, and that same Bill Powell came from the Kaws. Happy "Felch" (Felsch) was on his way from Fond du Lac to be converted to a strong-armed outfielder. That July 16th no-no notwithstanding, Milwaukee now led Columbus by 3½ games.[79]

Southpaw Ralph Cutting etched his own 2-hitter at Toledo, leaving the Mud Hens to lay goose eggs, on Saturday, August 9th. Louisville now chased the Brewers. Milwaukeean shortstop George McBride was torn between two ex-Brewers managing in the American League. Clark Griffith's Washington veteran was wanted by Jimmy McAleer in trade to manage the BoSox. No go.

A near riot at Louisville required post-game police protection for Umpire Murray. His close safe call of Milwaukee's Tom Jones at the plate ignited a 6th inning assembly of the entire home squad around him. Murray ejected Colonels' manager Jack Hayden and catcher Hank Severeid. A "wild eyed bug" rushed the arbiter with a sledgehammer, but several players restrained him until the gendarmes arrived.[80] Murray was under constant jeering and hissing the rest of the game. Police reserves lined the diamond in the 9th, only to be pelted with cushions and bottles. Two ex-Colonels, catcher Johnny Hughes and right fielder Orville Woodruff drove in 4 of Milwaukee's 5 runs to the Colonels' pair.

Mexican rebel Gen. Huerta demanded U.S. recognition, but President Wilson thought otherwise. An ice hockey league of Canadian and American teams was mulled. Germany's silver jubilee kaiser Wilhelm II sailed regattas amongst Norwegian locals in the fiords of his retreat. His Vaterland offered its 1916 Berlin Olympics head trainer job to Milwaukeean Alvin Kraenzlein.[81]

White Sox castoff pitcher Frank Lange's 2-run homer aided his 4–2 repression of the Brewers at KC on August 30th. Future Brewers Jap Barbeau and Bunny Brief wore Kaw blue. A long homestand and Athletic Park booster party

Tom Dougherty (right) runs to third, 1913. Milwaukee Public Library Historical Photograph Collection.

made the Brewers and visiting Indy Monday, September 15th guests to ardent fan and leading lady Marion Barney's Schubert Theater Stock Company performance of "Alias Jimmy Valentine."[82]

John Beall may have wanted an alias after his goat outfield work allowed Columbus to sweep before 11,000 that Sunday. Only a Colonels' split at Minneapolis kept the Millers 2 percentage points back. The tail end Indians knocked Milwaukee off its lofty perch on Tuesday. Frustrated by Clark's plight, "Ishkabibble," is all they could say on Cherry Street.[83]

Out of the woodwork came R.B. Pixley's "Diamond Driftwood"[84]:

"Cheer up! Remember Jonah-
He was riding in a boat
And just because a storm came up
They said he was the goat;
They threw him in the water
He was swallowed by a whale
But he landed high and dry because
His courage did not fail

Cheer up! Remember Job-
He had a lot of boils
And some other sad afflictions
Had him in their toils,
He lived in rags and tatters
Suffered trouble without end,
But he just watched and waited
And affairs began to mend

Cheer up! Remember Noah
He had to build an ark
And forty days it rained on him
And things were very dark
But Noah got his paddle
And rowed around awhile

> He lived for days on water
>   Yet, even he could smile
>
> Cheer up! Remember Abel
>   He was murdered in his bunk
> And Cain took all his bearskins
>   And a lot of other junk;
> But Abel had his innings
>   That a very, very plain
> For the folks who lived in Eden
>   Simply wouldn't speak to Cain
>
> Cheer up! Keep up your courage-
>   The Brewers may have lost,
> But bumper crops are harvested
>   In spite of fate or frost;
> Let's take defeat and bear it,
>   And boost a little more-
> Remember Job and Jonah, bugs,
>   Let's hear the final score.

Whether these Old Testament parables that washed ashore actually turned the tide, we'll never know. Milwaukee hit the road for their final 1913 trip without speedy Larry Gilbert's balky knee and injured Orville Woodruff.

Cy Slapnicka's second game win at Columbus on September 21st, combined with the Millers' double loss at Indianapolis made Joe Cantillon's face as red as his famous vest. Slapnicka's singles made the heroic difference against Donkey Eayrs and Ferry. Pixley's prose was a regular feature of the home stretch in the *Sentinel*, but it's hard to resist this last dose[85]:

> OLE LAMENTS
>
> Ay skol tenking ve har gude time
> Ven Meelwaukee he ban slump,
> But by Yudas, Yo Cantillon
> He ban hitting dis har bump
>
> Ay skol tal my friend, Yon Yonson,
> Yon, ay vin fem dollar yet,
> But he tal you skol vaiting
> Some lok hal to cash that bet
>
> Ay skol tenking ve har gude time
> Vinning pennant four times straight
> But Yon Yonson, he ban saying
> Ole, ve har start too late
>
> Dis har Kelley he ban beat us
> Some lak hal he can play ball
> Ay skol vishing dis har Kelley
> He been staying in St. Paul.

"Ralph Cutting a Few Capers" before a mere 29 Toledoans, while former N.L.er Grover Lowdermilk heaved a one-hitter at the Millers in Louisville, all

Milwaukee's first A.A. pennant-winners, 1913 (as best as can be identified). ***Back Row:*** Hap Felsch OF?, Cy Slapnicka P, Newt Randall OF, Johnny Hughes C, Phil Lewis SS, unknown. *Sitting:* Lena Blackburne IF, Buster Braun P?, Cy Young P?, Tom Jones 1B, Harry Clark Mgr./3B, Tom Dougherty P, unknown, Jap Barbeau? ***On ground:*** Ralph Cutting P, Joe Berg IF?, Joe Hovlik P with goat mascot. Milwaukee Public Library Historical Photograph Collection.

just nudged the Brewers a couple losses to the good. Woody even made it to the Maumee, if needed, and Gilbert was back to "smashing the ball right on the nose." Milwaukee's officialdom readied to celebrate its diamond heroes.

The Brewers stole 8 bases off Toledo backstop Rex DeVogt as Tom Dougherty skunked the Mud Hens, 5–0, on 6 hits. Another Miller loss at Louisville opened a 2-game lead. Joe Berg replaced cold-suffering Phil Lewis at second in the 3-game win streak, but Clark finally smiled.[86]

An effusive and optimistic Mrs. Havenor thanked her men by actually traveling down to Louisville for the final 4-game series. A new electric scoreboard at the Hungarian Cafe allowed fans to follow all association results at 161 Second Street. In the strange twists and turns of baseball, Harry Clark's Brewers staved off the Millers of Joe Cantillon, the man who had previously brought them closest to the top. They clinched at Louisville, who kept them second 4 years ago.[87]

Wisconsin's governor Francis McGovern, a Milwaukeean, joined Mayor Gerhard Bading and the public bandwagon's "royal reception" of hoisted flags, whooping resolutions, and an appreciation of what better advertising Milwaukee could have. "Der Zweck heiligt dar Mittel" (the deed is sanctioned by the cause) came from F. P. Blumenfeld, president of the Merchants and Manufacturers Association. President Raymond T. Carver of the Advertisers' Club advocated a dinner dance with July 4th speeches and other activities all at the Auditorium.[88]

If there had been any larger outpourings of *gemutlichkeit* and good cheer in Milwaukee history to date, none may have been more gratifying than that first, full-blown pennant bash!

Charles Havenor could only look down from above. Thanks to Pep Clark's achievement, Agnes, the widowed owner lady, was a champ!

Players who weathered a merry-go-round of managers now had their most satisfying reward: Tom Jones' last 3 years at 1st base. Phil Lewis and Ralph Cutting (league-leading .700 win percentage) each were here four seasons. Newt Randall had six. Cy Slapnicka was the only other major statistical leader, with 25 wins, for the first Milwaukee club ever to win 100 in a season.

But most of all, for two men who had endured every ordeal together since 1904, Long Tom Dougherty and Harry Clark, baseball fortune finally smiled broadly upon them. And deservedly so. Their entire nucleus would return for a 1914 encore.[89]

Future Brewer pilot catcher Bill Killefer tested the reserve clause for the Federal League. The rebirth of the moustache, worn by a Cleveland trio, was balanced by the death of eccentric ex–Brewer Rube Waddell, at a pulmonary sanatorium in San Antonio. It made perfect sense that he died on April Fools' Day.[90]

The pre-Ruthian heart of the Ty Cobb era, named Wee Willie Keeler was still the best batter. Cincinnati Reds manager Buck Herzog's "pretzel infield" could be appreciated by Teutonic Milwaukee: Heinie Groh at 3rd, future Fed and Brewer skip Marty Berghammer at short, Bert Niehoff at 2nd, and Dick Hoblitzell at first. A Buck Herzog byline was later from Hollywood "Along Amusement Row." German-born Milwaukeean Fritz Mollwitz would make the Cubs, only to be traded to these Rhineland City Reds during the season.[91]

To counter all that Germanity, Harry Clark added reserve shortstop and resident shrimp Jap Barbeau, the 5'-5," 140 lb. Oriental countenance with the French surname. On the way up north from Owensboro, "Cy No. 2" Young threw a 3-hit shutout at the Central League Evansville Evas.

For 1914, the Milwaukee Brewers no longer had the Toledo Mud Hens to pick on. Milwaukee won 19 of the 23 games between them the previous season, but the franchise now operated as Jimmy Sheckard's non-smoking Cleveland Spiders. Only Columbus held a 13–12 edge on the 1913 champion Brewers.[92]

The A. Spiegel Co. offered "Lillian Russell's Own Toilet Preparations" to the fairer sex, but one of their number, former Southerner Mrs. Otto Broecker, lectured at Milwaukee-Downer College on the cultural loss of the slave-time "darkey."[93]

Another tradition tossed to the wind, like bald Tom Jones lost Phil Lewis' college chapeau, was Harry Clark's regulars not wearing the last year's whites in camp. They clinched their pennant on the road, hence the reversal. The champs new threads "bordered on big league stuff": Home whites with black pinstripes for the first time, with caps to match. The gray-blue road mix had a brown "hairstripe" (pinstripes?) and caps to match. Both uniforms had black stockings.[94]

Bankroll Louie Nahin's sensitivity about the amount of balls used in the spring should've been recouped by 24 of the Brewers' first 28 games at home. The opening guest St. Paul Saints joined the home team at the premiere of Cyril Slapnicka's Pennant Buffet on 3rd Street. The restaurant was managed by ex-Brewer Louie Manske. Once Brewer head John J. McCloskey was hired out of Louisville to scout for Cincinnati. He was credited with discovering their Hoblitzell, Wisconsinite Big Ed Konetchy, and further back, future Cooperstown enshrinee Fred Clarke.[95]

Another gainfully re-employed individual was Ralph Cutting's goat as Brewer mascot. He made for its winter care at a nearby farm after it proved so lucky a gift. It grew notorious as Athletic Park's unofficial lawnmower during road trips, its stench over its press box roof home reeked.[96]

Still, reporters joined everyone else in tub-thumping baseball at all levels. Lake Shore League president Klocksin weighed the addition of ex-Brewer Eddie Lewee to join returning Nig Laabs on his umpiring staff. Downtown fans could catch special Terminal Building streetcars for the Tuesday, April 14th Brewer opener. The 8,000 faithful would not see the antsy Harry Clark at third for the first time in 9 years. His bum leg let Joe Berg bat second, behind Barbeau. The scrawny Jap would've led the 1913 champions with his 11 homers.[97]

Irv (Cy) Young's 98-minute, 6-hitter blanked the Saints, 4–0. John Beall accentuated his circuit clout by hitting it to the new pennant home. Future Brewer interim man and St. Paul skip Bill Friel pled few workouts versus lefties. He saluted the champs as Mexico's Huerta did Old Glory. Right-hander Joe Hovlik allowed only a scratch hit to Charley Hemphill the next day.[98]

Clark didn't get to bat until game four in Minneapolis, but had his tonsils removed by May Day. At least he didn't suffer the fractured skull that KC's mustachioed major league vet, Silent John Titus, received from Minneapolis' Bill Burns. The A.A. batting leader should have called Milwaukee's annual Northwestern Mutual Life Insurance confab from his hospital bed.[99]

Milwaukee held a 10-percentage point edge over Indianapolis after a May 30th split at KC's new park, which held 6,000 for the affair. Bill Powell was pinch-hit for in a 7-run 9th, so he wasn't credited with the Game One triumph over his old club. Newt Randall was tossed by Umpire [old pitcher Huyler?] Westervelt. Blues 2nd base/leadoff man Morrie Rath was a future Red.

Veteran leadership, with a now healthy Clark hitting .338 and Tom Dougherty's five undefeated starts, made up for the league leaders' 7th ranking in batting and fielding. A 2–9 Sunday record was exacerbated by Cleveland's double dose of Athletic Park whitewash in mid-June.[100]

Milwaukee's "man-girl" Cora Anderson, known for a decade as Ralph Kerwineo, sought police protection against threats made at a West Side boarding house. He/she was but a mere blip in the news after the Monday, June 29th assassination of Austria-Hungary's Archduke Franz Ferdinand and his wife, the Duchess of Hohenberg. At Sarajevo, Bosnia, this event plunged the imperialized world into war.[101] An explosion at Milwaukee's Kenwood Ave. intake tunnel imperiled 51.

In the face of such heavy-hearted and consequential news, the Brewers did their small part to keep buoying local spirits, at least until July 2nd. Red Killifer, the catcher at the heart of the reserve clause controversy, stole second, third, and home for the Millers as Milwaukee's Buster Braun and backup catcher McGraw snoozed.[102] That gift dumped the Brewers back into second.

Joe Hovlik was again stellar in his opening 4-hit shutout at the July 4th twinbill at KC. The Blues just pounded Cy Young and Tom Dougherty, 14–5, in the late game.[103]

Lethargic Brewer lumber didn't have the P.C.L. Venice Tigers' "Fifty per cent Dick" Bayless at their disposal, but summer sun woke bats like Phil Lewis, Newt Randall, and John Beall.

The Brewers were surviving the Federal League incursion unscathed, but "Cousin Ed" Barrow, former Tigers manager now president of the minor International League, was at the vortex of a National Commission-sanctioned plan to mix I.L. cities Baltimore, Buffalo, Toronto, along with Pittsburgh in the East, with the A.A.'s Indianapolis, Kansas City, Louisville, and Milwaukee. "Square sportsman" Barrow would be executive head of this major league effort to force the collapse and take the name of the Federal League. Beer City now had 418,000 inhabitants.[104]

This preventative to "Fed-jumping" left International League standbys Montreal, Newark Providence, and Rochester intact; they were to be joined by Binghamton, Syracuse, and either Albany and "Wilkes-Barre," or from Richmond, Springfield, or Worcester. If Barrow's proposed loop took the American Association name, A.A. remnants Cleveland, Minneapolis, St. Paul, and Toledo would be reorganized under Tom Chivington as a Western League with Denver, Omaha, and Sioux City.

Surprisingly little ado was made in Milwaukee of these developments. But then again, "Snow fell at Muncie, Ind. with the thermometer at 100 and yet some persons think the St. Louis Browns could not win a pennant." Barrow's idea didn't fly and a Brownie flag was 30 years away.

At this point, all of baseball may have done well to follow the example of the Chicago White Sox' Buck Weaver. With a 3/4-inch dent in his "rubber skull," vainless Buck ignored worry and surgical removal of the depression

Cad Brand, Wednesday, July 16, 1913, *Milwaukee Sentinel.*

from his Philly beaning. The future scandalous Black Sox trotted out a specially made leather head protector to continue playing.[105]

Toledo's ersatz Cleveland Spiders remained a dent in the collective Brewer head. Buster Braun pitched both parts in greasing the skids in Ohio. The Spiders overtook Milwaukee for second place on July 20th and trailed Louisville by only a game.[106] The mobilization of A.A. pennant contenders was not unlike that of the great armies going on in Europe.

Watering the grass at Louisville, after the Falls City went two months without rain, was a sure precursor to Milwaukee and the Colonels being rained out there. Once underway, a Hap Fel(s)ch double and triple led Red Shackleford's 2-hit, 10-zip Game Two of the July 29th double up. The Brewers reclaimed the league lead the next day by destroying Grover Lowdermilk, 17–0.[107] He "was as wild as the famous man from Borneo, at 10 cents a throw," and reliever Hod Leverette walked 5 more. Tom Jones' homer aided the plurality and Fel(s)ch swatted a pair.

Europe's "Worst Conflict in All History" looked mild as Harry Clark emulated the Kaiser's loosening of the dogs of war upon visiting Louisville.[108] Clark settled at the No. 2 spot in his order to pepper a homer, and only the leftfield fence held Fel(s)ch to two triples in the July 30th, 9–0 extravaganza.

Wisconsin dairymen responded to the war with the cooperative sale of cheese, but no base thieves could cheese past the most effective arm of Milwaukee's midget backstop Johnny Hughes. The "Runt" allowed .696 steals per game, as it was kept. [109]

Already frayed by the Federal outlaws, baseball was further agitated by ex-Brewer Dave Fultz's fraternity of ballplayers. The Brewers had a favorable slate against its loop's eastern clubs, but agitation of a railroad strike threatened the A.A. schedule in its western outposts.[110]

Mrs. Havenor remarried to one Al Timme, who assumed the Brewer presidency for the rest of her ownership. He struck the August 9th sale of Happy Fel(s)ch to the Chicago White Sox for $12,000, plus an infielder and outfielder. The Brewers' top sacrifice martyr and A.A. home run leader remained with his hometown nine through 1914.[111]

Fel(s)ch was tickled to be Harry Clark's fifth Brewer to make the bigs. Half-pint Nemo Leibold was a Cleveland Nap, Larry Gilbert, a Boston Brave, and now Fel(s)ch would join Ray Schalk, Larry Chappelle, and Lena Blackburne at Comiskey Park, thanks to Pep's seasoning. A son of the local carpenters' union president, who was also a strong semi-pro player, Hap's youngest brother also carried on the lineage as a City League pitcher. An unhappy end wore Black Sox.

Calculators tilted in the Brewers' unhappy August 8th lambasting at Minneapolis. Cutting and Slapnicka were slapped around, 26–5. The brutality was compounded by Louisville's new southpaw, Dauntless Dave Danforth, who enhanced their 3-game lead by shutting out Cleveland. For the first time in

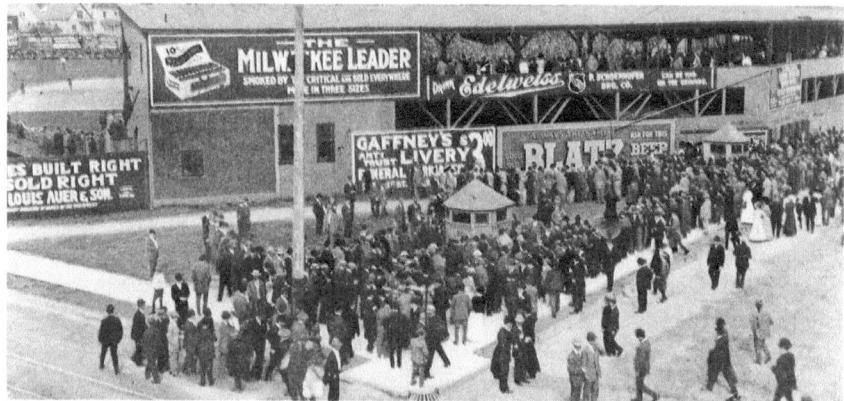

Top: The 1913 pennant winning Brewers were given a great ovation on their return to town after a winning streak on the road. The North Western depot was brilliantly decorated for the occasion. Milwaukee Public Library Historical Photograph Collection.

Bottom: Saturday afternoon overflow, baseball park, Milwaukee. Milwaukee Public Library Historical Photograph Collection.

the 20th Century, the Brewers laid Beaver Dam city leaguers low in a 16–5 stop for a mid-season exhibition. At least they weren't playing "Sis Comstock's Krockers."[112] The Brewers literally made their own pennant bed when, on a return trip from St. Paul, missing chambermaids from their Pullman car forced all 16 players and Al Timme to pitch in with the art of tucking and folding.

"The Human Slaughter House" wasn't about the Minneapolis debacle, but a pictorial expose on the terrible effect of mechanized warfare in Europe. Morgenroth's at 210 West Water Street now also offered an electric scoreboard as "General Clark" led his Brewer troop a game back up on the Colonels. Louisville's 11-game win streak was snapped by Cleveland.[113]

In spite of the grim diet of war news, funny guy Billy Nye was honored by his Wisconsin hometown of River Falls and the comics featured Oscar and

Cad Brand, *Milwaukee Sentinel*, 1913.

Cad Brand, Sunday, August 10, 1913, *Milwaukee Sentinel.*

Adolph "at their gay pranks." The Braves pressed on with their National League miracle in Boston and old Milwaukee favorite Connie Mack was on the verge of his Philadelphia Athletics locking up a 4th A.L. flag in 5 years.[114]

War analogies plastered the Brewers' spate of double-ups. Cy Slapnicka was fined $50 for duking it out with Duke Reilley at an August 30th Indianapolis fracas. Both were suspended by President Chivington for a game.[115] The previous rain day at Indy had Clark's crew poking cardboards for prizes, like reporter Brownie's gold watch or Felsch's automatic revolver, an exercise that led to a flurry of trading.

The September offensive upon Louisville began with Cy Young's 6-hit, 1–0 victory. "Private" Beall's triple and "Drummer Boy" Hughes' squeeze home of him did the rest in the 10th. It was the Colonels' largest Monday crowd of the year — 2,600. Pongo Joe's Millers made a mockery of Young, Slapnicka, and Cutting to outlast the Brewer brigade 15–10 on September 10th. The Colonels loomed 1½ games ahead.[116]

It took another 10 days for the "Clark-o-mobile ... spitting fire, going sixty miles an hour," just to whittle a game off that lead. Fel(s)ch's 10th inning smash, with Randall on at KC on Saturday, September 19th, made it so. The A.A.'s worst fielders rode their power stroke back to the top.

One more week couldn't crowd the war news off the front page in 1914, but Harry Clark and his tired lot of Milwaukee Brewers shelved the "ifs." Cleveland's Spiders — a.k.a. Bearcats — downed Louisville, 5–2. Pep was at home, smoking his corncob pipe a mere half-hour after his team's 11–3 pasting of St. Paul cinched their second straight A.A. flag on Saturday, September 26th. His own three barehanded stops at third and 4-for-4 day said it all.[117] The crowd surrounded the Brewer bench in celebration.

The pitching emphasis shifted from Slapnicka and Cutting to Hovlik and Young, but a quartet of .300 bats (Randall .321, Beall .312 and 10 homers, Felsch .304 and 19 homers were 5 ahead of his nearest rival, and Clark's own .301 and loop-leading 143 walks) spelled a pennant.

The kaiser commended the flower of German youth to God. Harry Clark could only commend his champions to Al Timme.

The joyous week ahead was almost dreaded by a drained group of modest men, who were ballplayers, not after-dinner speakers. A 98–68 title equals a lot of invites. It was good that Harry Clark could relish his off-season in Paulding, Ohio, as a pipe-smoker because the war put 10,000 Cuban cigar makers out of work. That jeopardized the island's winter league sponsors.[118]

The twice champion Brewers represented a Milwaukee that was still America's most German large city. News of the kaiser's atrocities didn't have a direct bearing upon Americans, so loyalty to Der Vaterland was strong. Emanuel L. Philipp, speaking German on the campaign trail was elected governor of Wisconsin. Milwaukeean Otto L. Kuehn gave a 200-mark reward to German Iron Cross winner Gustav Schlaechtle.[119]

Glamour in motion pictures grew in stature and the question, "Do photo players speak in films?" was likely best left unanswered by D.W. Griffith's "The Birth of a Nation." The *Journal* solicited photoplay scenarios from it readers and Miss Margaret Edwards' literal portrayal as The Naked Truth was prohibited in Milwaukee. Treatment for "victims of habit-forming drugs" was advocated.[120] Wisconsin's only first place claim in 1915 would be in the packing of peas.

St. Patrick's Day brought out a bit o' Rockwell Hinkley's limerick in the German-Athens[121]:

HOT OFF THE BAT

They're off today, fighting Brewers
   In camp to train for that third flag
Down at the Springs where waters boil
   Bent on winning that pennant rag

All of the old ones, a few new,
   Except Ralph Cutting, Husky Phil,
Buster Braun, Bill Powell, Hap Felch [sic]
   Can the remainder fill the bill?

Leave it to Harry, leader brave,
   He is the man who did it all;
Twice in succession came he first,
   In the A.A. league of baseball,
One more clouter is all he needs
   To make the team a ripping one;

> 'Fill the shoes of Felch,' we say,
> And the Brewers will cop the 'mon.

It was the last time anyone would write anything this kind about the Brewers for the rest of the decade. Evangelist Billy Sunday, the former ballplayer, probably could not have appealed to divine intervention for what was to come. Milwaukee's own Oak Henning, a powerful 1st baseman from the defunct W.-I.L., did not survive Clark's long term cut. Mexican barkeeps who sold liquor to Pancho Villa's men didn't survive his cut either, only the difference was fatal. The dry movement grew.[122]

The healthful effects of West Baden and Owensboro didn't keep Clark from sitting out his second straight Opening Day. Johnny Hughes barely missed a homer in his first at-bat, but after that triple off the left field screen, he hit another to the center field bleachers in the 4th. Add in a single and he drove in 4 of Milwaukee's winning 6 to visiting Minneapolis' 4. New left fielder Harry LaRoss, via Battle Creek, Michigan, batted 3-for-5. "Big Six" Joe Hovlik went all nine.[123]

Kansas City's George "Big Noise" Tebeau wailed about the shortened A.A. schedule and gave out free tickets to future games whenever his Blues lost and their Federal Packer rivals won. The Blues' first game under future Brewer skip Dan Shay came versus Milwaukee. Another future Brewer leader, Jack Lelivelt, launched his assault on the 1915 A.A. batting title by going 4-for-4. Flame Delhi burned the Brewers on 7 hits in that damp 5–0 April 24th debut.[124]

The Wisconsin Trust Company offered 5 percent gold debentures under the obligation of the Province of Manitoba as Charley Moll brought his Northern League Winnipeg Maroons into Milwaukee to test the Lake Shore League Kosciuskos. Tall Fritz Mollwitz, the German-born local known as "Zip," won praise for his outstanding first base glove work at Cincinnati.[125]

The Brewers staggered 2-7 out of the chute, but bounced back with an 11-4 stretch ended by Indy's 19-3 mid-May blind-siding at Athletic Park. The only pennant was a white flag. The 16-man A.A. roster limit hurt Milwaukee's double dips hard into Memorial Day. Big Dixie Walker's poor control forced Cy Slapnicka into both ends of one pair. Red Shackleford was the appropriate shade to have a scarlet fever attack. Tom Dougherty hadn't reached KC, supposedly due to floods, but just where he lost track of the club was "hard to tell." A foul tip to Frank Brennan's groin (and they did print the word "groin" in 1915, too) left him uncertain. Hughes literally caught the slack.

Such obstacles left Clark's champs holding .500 by their fingernails.[126] A Newt Randall throwing error cost them a long, wild 12–11 ride at Louisville on Saturday, June 12th. Don't judge the veteran right fielder too harshly, though. Phil Lewis' ejection forced Clark over to short and Newt to third. Only Cy Young, the last of four Brewer pitchers, could get anyone out.[127]

Wisconsinite Frank Holt confessed to shooting J. Pierpont Morgan and attempting to bomb the U.S. Capitol in Washington. This was precisely the type of versatility Al Timme needed for his fast-sinking Brewers. At least Harry Clark didn't have Harry Harper's extremes to ponder. Pongo Joe's southpaw had an early no-no in Minneapolis to an A.A. record 20 walks in 9 frames. The constant 5-under-.500 dropped Milwaukee to seventh by mid-July.[128]

One indicator of decline was Clark's plucking of ex-nemesis Lou Fiene off the Millers' scrap heap. The pitcher was reduced to pinch-hit and 1st base reserve duty. The Brewers' long sigh at Columbus on July 31st was due to the last place Senators' long Cy Ferry shutting them out.[129]

Mexican soldiers invaded American soil near Nogales, Arizona, and Germans were putting a serious hurt on the tsar's forces. The Lusitania sinking still divided American opinion. One *Journal* letter writer signed "NAMREG ORP," the opposite of Pro-German.[130]

The Brewers could only admire from afar in KC as Minnesota's Twin Cities rivals contended atop the A.A. St. Paul's Lexington Park set a loop record 18,000–20,000 when the Millers beat the "Calliopes," 8–4. Auto parties came from both Dakotas and one Montana group by rail.[131]

"The German Side of the War" was presented by the *Chicago Tribune* on 5 film reels at Milwaukee's Orpheum Theater on 3rd and Wells. Chances are that drew better than the faltering Brewers' final home stand with the 6th place Cleveland Spiders. The home team badly needed the black-faced "Mangler of Melancholy," Al Jolson, who danced around Milwaukee's Winter Garden.

Harry Clark sat out the closing two Saturday contests on September 11th. Billiken Stutz played third in Pep's place, handling a busy 4 putouts and 7 assists flawlessly. Stutz added a couple singles in Game One of the local twin killing.

"One of the smallest crowds that ever witnessed a closing game here was on hand, but then the fans have soured on the game and are tickled that the season is over."[132]

What a difference a year makes!

The gild was off Harry Clark's lily. He probably felt like following Hall of Fame namesake Fred Clarke into a wealthy retirement of wheat farming, but he could only take his unlucky 13 men on their final road trip. The last at Columbus was dumped when "hardly 300" showed for a Monday twinbill. It cost $15 to open the gate there, so Tuesday wasn't a profitable idea.[133] The Brewers only won season series over the Kaws and cellar-dwelling Columbus.

Milwaukeeans had only the thrills of a fire-delayed state fair to turn to. The 65th annual event had "1915's Greatest Auto Show," sensational auto races, and two daring aviators enacting a 2000-foot "Battle in the Sky."[134] All for 50¢.

On St. Patrick's Day 1916, former president William Howard Taft extolled the virtue of American patriotism, in the face of international crisis at Milwaukee's Auditorium. William Henry Eldridge of Twin Falls, Iowa, solicited *The Milwaukee Sentinel* for a genealogical query of possible Milwaukeean descendants of the Eldred-Eldredge-Eldridge clan. It's likely that another Iowan, who would pitch for the modern Milwaukee Brewers over 75 years later, Cal Eldred, was from that extended family.[135]

That same Irish holiday, Harry Clark was delighted to open a new spring training camp at Pine Bluff, Arkansas. The man most identified with his club, and his own lucky seventh manager in his 13 years with Milwaukee, Pep, no longer had fellow traveler Long Tom Dougherty to call upon. What he had were 30 invitees from which to rebuild his fallen fortunes.[136]

Further south, at the New York Giants' Marlin, Texas, training site, the proud Sac and Fox warrior known as Jim Thorpe fought his inability to hit major league curveballs. Though he didn't possess as strong a baseball-throwing arm or succeed as well at the major league level, Thorpe was very similar to another future superhero in that regard: Bo Jackson. Facing fastballs, a bat in Thorpe's hands was a war club. His name was already legendary on the cinder path and gridiron. He wanted his native name, Wa-Tho-Huk, meaning "Bright Path," to shine on major league basepaths as well. He still had much of his great speed.[137]

As much as politically correct people now may recoil at the racial stereotypes of that day, all ethnic groups were fair game. Look no further than the "Katzenjammer Kids" of the funny pages, Hans und Fritz.[138]

Milwaukeean Dick Marcan remade a semi-pro version of the Wisconsin State League. A half-dozen baseball clubs would play Sundays only. League treasurer Edward Melms secured the twirling arm and red chemise of old Tom Dougherty for his Milwaukee White Sox. The Sunday ball was noteworthy because as much as ballplayers were often thought of as hell-raising scoundrels, many of Harry Clark's men attended church services. Every prayer was needed.[139]

One *Sentinel* wag, J.J. Delany, observed that Albertus Timme, like Mexico's Carranza, was being knocked before he showed his goods. Delany also lamented the Federal League blow-up. Bandito Generale Pancho Villa would've made a willing jump to the outlaws.[140] Noted Brewer rooter (and scribe) Bascom Nolley Timmins wired from Amarillo of his way to the border. He arrived in Milwaukee on a Sunday and crossed the border to Winnipeg by Wednesday. At least poker wasn't banned at Brewers camp. It was just the magnet to draw Manning Vaughan post haste.[141]

Vaughan was in rare form: "Moving pictures of a 4-year-old pickaninny, who was hobnobbing with the players, were taken on Monday. The little ball of chocolate enjoyed being a screen hero almost as much as the players and that is saying a lot. "Vaughan declared that Frank Lloyd (Love Cottage) Wright would despair at the negro shanties on Pine Bluff's outskirts. The worst northern bums would turn their noses up at the lean-tos. "Still the brunette gentlemen occupying them seem to be happy, especially when his lone pig or mule doesn't interrupt his snooze by getting into his cabin or walking over him while

5 — The Lady Is a Champ   177

Athletic Park workout, ca. 1916. Milwaukee Public Library Historical Photograph Collection.

he dozes on his 2 × 4 front porch. It's certainly a gay life, if you don't weaken."[142]

Ex-Brewer Lou Fiene signed as an outfielder/pitcher with the Fairbanks-Morse industrial team at Beloit, Wisconsin. The team was nicknamed the "Fairies." [It's football team would be the first to ever defeat the Green Bay Packers in 1919.][143] It looked like Lou, too, had the makings of a gay life, if he didn't weaken.

The weather at Pine Bluff was the only thing to shine for Milwaukee in 1916. Oh, two Wisconsin lefties, Harry Gervais from Peshtigo and Franklin Krasnicky of Oconto, had tryouts. So did Fond du Lac shortstop Heinie Berger, bought from Winnipeg. None made the cut, but Harry Clark was distracted by the severe illness of his spouse back in Ohio. Timme made the last cuts.

The Edison Shop in Milwaukee peddled unbreakable Diamond Discs to play on Inventor Tom's latest musical instrument. The threat of socialism renewed its dubious head as Daniel Webster Hoan would remain Milwaukee's mayor for the next 24 years. One republican congressional endorsee, Waupaca's John Jardine, shared the name of a University of Wisconsin head football coach of 55 years later. The hunt for Pancho Villa resembled that for a current Arab terrorist.[144]

Another Timme cut was a pitcher named Ursella, believed to be Rube Ursella, who went on to be a triple-threat back in the National Football League. One gridder goes, another comes. Jim Thorpe arrived at Pine Bluff on April 3rd in fine fettle. The Milwaukee Brewers now had the World's Greatest Athlete at their disposal. He ended up being all they had.[145]

The "king of Sweden's pal" bore baggage from Eastern critics who saw Thorpe as a minor league washout. John McGraw's disappointing left-handed batting experiment led to the Indian being optionally released to Milwaukee. Thorpe's presence drew 2,000 to a Pine Bluff match with the Chicago Cub seconds. Big Jim had a couple catches in center, but went hitless in his Brewer debut. Hovlik and Slapnicka shut out the Cub scrubs on 4 hits. "Bright Path" continued under more scrutiny than any Brewer in memory.[146]

Harry Clark wasn't too accurate in assessing Mike Kelley's Saints as the team to chase, but after beating St. Paul in a couple exhibitions, a delusional Timme gushed over his own club. The Brewers were being shut out by the Lexington Ohio State Leaguers at the time.[147]

Other than Phil Lewis at first, Cy Slapnicka on the knoll, and himself at third, Clark had a completely new lineup to face the reborn Mud Hens in the Toledo opener.[148] New native manager Roger Bresnahan, the future Hall of Famer and "Duke of Tralee," gave former BoSox standout Hugh Bedient the ball. Flush with an order of ex-Federal Leaguers, including Wisconsinite George Perring at third, 18,000 welcomed back A.A. baseball. Bresnahan caught Bedient's 4–2 win.

Jack Fluhrer, who'd be sent back to the Cubs by Harry Clark, was presented with a gold watch at the game. Jim Thorpe's regular season Milwaukee bow consisted of 2 singles in 5 trips, a steal and a run, plus 3 putouts. His speed to third, on Jay Kirke's single, set up Lewis' sac fly.

That Opening Day in Milwaukee could generate any enthusiasm at all was a minor miracle.[149] Al Timme's tepid troops marched home bowlegged by their 2–10 burden. Bankroll Louie Nahin hired an "aggregation of German hornblowers to dispense three-pronged notes to the assembled populace." Phil Lewis was already released to Kansas City outright.

Rudy Hulswitt's Columbus "O-high-Oans" supplied the opposition for 5,843 bugs. Jim Thorpe now led off and dumped gooseneck lefty George's delivery into left. Alex "Larry" Chappelle, now an alien enemy, muffed it in his mitt and Thorpe's daring sped him to second. He scored off that, adding another single and a handful of putouts in center. His last two "sterling" catches preserved Cy Slapnicka's 6–3 victory in the 9th. Toddling Jim, Jr. soaked up the crowd noise. Only the Senators' Bratwurst Bratchi really got to Cy.

More telling of the season was the frozen slapstick witnessed by a few and proud 137 on Tuesday, May 16th. The Indianapolis Indians slapped Thorpe and the Brewers around like a red-skinned stepchild, 11–5. Thorpe had no role in the 5 errors, but the club fell to 5–20.[150]

Highlights of this season were at a premium. Thorpe's 2-out, 9th inning single gave the "son of the forest" the game-winning RBI in a 2–1 win over Columbus. That first series won by the Brewers finally came June 13th.[151] Thorpe rode off those heroics to dip his toes into the lecturing waters. Boy Scout executive W.L. Davidson invited him to address 800 scouts at a council campfire on McKinley Beach.

Veteran slabster not so Young Cy Young retired to a fine Kennebec Falls, Maine farm, "financially fixed enough to keep the hounds from the door for the rest of his life." Joe Hovlik cleared waivers and was unlikely to join the Western League Topeka Savages. His Oxford Junction home down Iowa way beckoned. Buster Braun was back in Sheboygan.[152]

MILWAUKEE, SUNDAY MORNING, JULY 30, 1916

How the Heat Affected Cad Brand

Did the *Milwaukee Sentinel* cartoonist envision 1953 this early?

Harry Clark finally threw in the towel, too, on Tuesday, August 15th. Despite Timme's efforts to keep hunting for help, the Brewers languished in dead last, 7 games behind the Senators. His resignation was a surprise, but he didn't take the rumored Columbus offer, either. He wasn't forever done with Milwaukee by any means.[153]

Shortstop Happy Jack Martin, who batted second behind Thorpe much of the season, became Clark's interim successor. Thorpe's two homers and Martin's 8 whirlwind chances made his 4–1 inaugural over Louisville an undefeated one. Thorpe's first shot cleared 8th Street to the north side of Burleigh. No one had a blast of such proportions since Hap Felsch two years earlier. Sailor Stroud's second serving to the fabulous Indian was equally tremendous. Future Brewer skip Red Killifer could only watch wistfully from the edge of left field as the ball cleared the beer ads over the last fence.[154] The 1916 season was Thorpe, all Thorpe, and nothing but Thorpe.

The additions of catcher Pickles Dillhoefer, slugging 1st baseman Clarence "Big Boy" Kraft, left fielder Austin "Slats" McHenry, and favorite Milwaukee son, dapper backstop Eddie Stumpf, just weren't enough. Satan Stutz, a.k.a. "Billiken," but never "Bearcat," now held third.[155]

Two future Brewer managers continued fine playing careers: Jack Lelivelt walloped two homers off Slapnicka in the first game of a September 14th split at KC. Outfielder Casey Stengel was "proving a big help to the Brooklyn team." Ty Cobb owed his success to Nuxtated Iron. Shoeless Joe Jackson, Heinie Zimmerman, Slim Sallee, and Wild Bill Donovan all pimped Coca-Cola, with which Cobb was a major stockholder. Players' commercial endorsements were now common.

G.O.P. presidential nominee Charles Evans Hughes stumped in seven Wisconsin cities.

An earlier incarnate of an actor named Tyrone Power starred in a birth control photoplay, "Where Are My Children?," at Milwaukee's Orpheum Theater. "Rolling Stones," a breezy western comedy, played at the Schubert Theater Stock Co.[156]

Nothing could mask just how God-awful the bad comedy of the Brewery Boys, the first Milwaukee team to ever lose 100 games in any league, was. They finished 18½ games behind 7th place Columbus! Thorpe was the only worthy footnote: .274, 25 doubles, a team-high 14 triples, 10 homers, 85 runs, and league-high 117 strikeouts and 48 steals. The latter figure wasn't an A.A. Brewer standard, but could hold as a modern major league Brewer record.[157]

Nomadic Oklahoma tribesmen Thorpe and pitcher Jim Bluejacket migrated to other hunting grounds. The staff could've used future Brewer manager Allen Sothoron, the Portland Beavers' 30-game winner, in the longer Pacific Coast League schedule. The resurrection from what was far and away the worst Milwaukee team ever would literally be murder.[158]

German U-boat attacks on American shipping drew the U.S.A. closer to war. Milwaukee's own Thea Talbott struck a rather sultry barefoot pose, by the front-page standards of 1917, as *The Milwaukee Journal* praised the silent screen actress' growing resume. Born Thea Schemmer, she appeared in one of McClure Pictures' Seven Deadly Sins series, "Wrath."[159]

Milwaukee baseball fans were ready to vent their wrath on Al Timme if he didn't right the Brewers' misfortunes. Jack Martin remained the shortstop for new manager Dan Shay. Danny Shay was a 41-year old Springfield, Ohioan born Daniel C. Shea. He spent 4 seasons as a light-hitting major league infielder in the early 20th Century.[160]

In three full seasons of managing the Kansas City Blues, Shay's solid 250–230, .520 record revealed nothing in his background to suggest what was going to happen.[161]

John Beall joined Martin and McHenry as the only regular returnees. Slapnicka and promising lefty Bill Sherdell were pitching holdovers when the spring venue moved to Wichita Falls, Texas. Jap Barbeau, back as a utility man, was a deputy for Sheriff McManus in Milwaukee.[162]

McManus needed a prisoner escorted to the state prison at Waupun and Jap got the duty. He buckled on a gun for the train ride, but when Barbeau took off his coat, the gun dropped on a car seat. Only after a kindly passenger signaled his attention at Waupun did he even realize his firearm was gone.

Lil' Jap admitted to Al Timme he was more afraid of the gun than the prisoner.

The Russian Empire convulsed under the tsar's abdication and the ensuing power struggle led by Nikolai Lenin (e)'s Communist Bolsheviki. Everyone crossed their fingers for the Central Powers' autocrats to likewise fall.[163] German Milwaukee now showed true American colors.

Ten years of experimentation made Wisconsin a hemp-growing state, thus giving the Brewers enough rope to hang their season again. Danny Shay's club reflected its local loyalty by being the first A.A. club to take up military drills and marching maneuvers, a coming baseball feature for the next 18 months.[164] They wore the Stars and Stripes on their left sleeves.

Maybe it was a telling "clew" that, while his guys tried to land the one fish in the local Wichita Falls lake, Shay brought a gun with him. His boys had far better luck bagging the plentiful jackrabbits with that.[165] William Joseph Barbeau wasn't a likely hunter.

Shay's assurances of a first division contender were backed up by a 25–8 pillaging of local Lawton, Oklahoma, semi-pros, with an audience including a number of Native Americans. An even more promising sign was the 10–1 trouncing of eventual Texas League champion Dallas.[166]

Statistical calculations showed athletes reached their peak at 26 and big leaguers lasted about 8 years. No one told future Hall of Famer and Connecticut League president Orator Jim O'Rourke, who caught all 9 innings of a 1912 New Haven game in his league, at age 60.

Milwaukee scratched its head at the explosive growth of Detroit and Los Angeles, while much of Germanic Wisconsin was embarrassed by pacifist progressive senator "Fighting Bob" LaFollette's opposition to the April 6th U.S. war proclamation. Also, 9 Wisconsin congressmen objected. Handicapping the dark horse Brewers fell secondary to whether war would allow a full season.[167]

ChiSox manager (and soon-to-be Milwaukee owner) Clarence "Pants" Rowland denied selling outfielder Brick Eldred to the Brewers. A fight was on. Thomas J. Hickey, back presiding over the A.A. he founded, and Connie Mack were both pessimistic for different reasons. Hickey feared the all-consuming war effort's effect upon his circuit. Old Milwaukee manager Mack wondered about the behavior of his A's outfielder, the ex-Brewer Amos Strunk.[168]

Having their fill of Texas sandstorms and monotonous food, the Brewers drilled under ideal skies at Athletic Park, led by army Sgt. Jack Waldley. Camera flashes and flowers greeted Shay and Barbeau as 5,000 enjoyed the Wednesday, April 11th 4–0 shutout thrown by Red Shackleford against St. Paul. Saints leadoff shortstop Marty Berghammer was a future Brewer skip.[169]

A united American "melting pot" saw Honolulu-bred shortstop Vernon Ayau as the first Chinese descendant in Organized Baseball with the Northwest League Seattle Giants. Jimmy Claxton (1916 P.C.L. Oakland) was the only 20th century negro in white ball until Jackie Robinson.

Hizzoner, Milwaukee's socialist mayor Daniel Webster Hoan, throws out the first ball on April 11, 1917, a Wednesday. Milwaukee Public Library Historical Photograph Collection.

The melting pot boiled over badly at Indianapolis on May 3rd. It was only a small newspaper item that Shay sued his former KC Blues employers in Milwaukee civil court for $125 in back pay. The Milwaukee club was named garnishee defendant, as it owed Kansas City that amount. The case was postponed until the Blues' arrival on June 4th.[170]

The Brewers had just been beaten at the Indiana capital, 3–1. Texan George Dickerson walked 5 and gave up 2 runs in 5 innings. Milwaukee was in 5th place, with a conventional 7–8 start. Al Timme was even happy with improved home attendance, despite overall league losses.

In the cafe of the Hotel English at Indianapolis, Danny Shay shot and killed a Negro waiter, Clarence Euell. Shay, charged with 2nd degree murder, refused to talk and Timme sent club attorney L.S. Pease to represent him.[171]

The root of the dispute was a frivolous lack of respect between the two men, manifested in an argument over the placement of sugar bowls. No other diners or players were around when Shay complained to a "colored busboy," Eugene Jones, about the small amount of sugar in his table's bowl. Jones supposedly ignored Shay and had Euell come back to address the problem.

It was the manner that Euell brought two sugar bowls from other tables that triggered the argument. Shay allegedly shot Euell in the abdomen. Euell then grappled Shay to the floor, keeping his foot on Shay's neck and striking his head to the floor several times.

Waiter Herbert Miller intervened when Euell asked him, "[W]hy shouldn't

I treat him that way, he just shot me?" It was the first Miller knew of any shooting.

Shay was taken into police custody and Euell died at the city hospital about an hour later. He'd never get to I.D. Shay directly. Shay acknowledged only that the gun "looked like his" and that Euell had called him a vile name.

Indy manager Jack Hendricks, the Saints' Mike Kelley (wired by Timme), and several other baseball people were at Shay's interrogation. Timme conducted his own investigation, but instructed Secretary Nahin to appoint a player as temporary manager.

Timme already prepared care for his players' dependents should any of his men be called to war. He preferred a 50 percent tax on team profits, rather than a proposed 10 percent war tax on receipts. He saw that as unduly penalizing teams already losing money because of the war.[172]

Manicurist Gertrude Anderson, a young woman with Shay at the time, supported his assertion that he acted in self-defense, thinking he'd be attacked. She claimed a surly Euell came at Shay with a clenched fist. Shay claimed he objected to Euell's vile profanity in the presence of a lady and that the negro advanced at him with clenched fists. Miss Anderson fled at that time.[173]

Cafe cashier Elizabeth Braskett was supposedly a short distance away and seemed to give a watered-down version of the verbal exchange, but she fled to the kitchen after Euell knocked Shay down from the shooting. Shay remained held over, without bail, for a November trial. Columbus manager and future Hall of Famer Joe Tinker raised a baseball defense fund for Shay.[174]

Timme wired scout Billy Doyle at nearby Portsmouth, Ohio, to join up with acting Captain/3rd baseman Zinn Beck and the rest of the Brewers at Louisville. Coincidentally, a Princess Theater 10¢ Triangle photoplay, "The Pinch Hitter" with Charles Ray, ran in Milwaukee.[175] Jim Thorpe now filled that role in Cincinnati, still unable to win a regular major league job.

Team Turmoil couldn't have been any worse off than the United States Brewers Association, fined $10,000 by the Federal Government for trying to influence the 1916 congressional elections. The dogs of Prohibition barked ever closer.[176]

The Brewers — the baseball team — won their first Louisville game without Shay, but the Colonels then shut them out in both ends of a twinbill. A "stormy" May 7th Chicago retrenchment placed Timme amongst magnates against reducing A.A. rosters or cutting players' pay. Tom Hickey united them on defraying Dan Shay's legal defense costs.[177]

Hickey also allowed Timme to name umpire Bill Friel as his interim manager. Under Billy Doyle's care, the Brewers went 1–5. Friel, a utility man on the 1901 A.L. Brewers, was an A.A. fixture: 9 years at Columbus, three of which he managed (273–223, .550), 2 years with St. Paul (131–198, .398), and in his second year of umpiring, worked in Milwaukee, when appointed.[178]

Friel had to be shoehorned into one of last year's uniforms, but if he wore

Springtex underwear, it may have cushioned the 5-hit, 5-1 mowdown that old Mordecai Brown, a "Three-Fingered" future Hall of Famer, applied for Columbus. Friel shifted the order against his old team.[179]

"KERR BLOWS AND BLUES WIN" Little lefty Dick Kerr served a Memorial Day Lelivelt jack to consign the Brewers to last. Friel's woeful 23-40 mark was no loss. Timme coaxed released Cardinals catcher Paddy Livingston from his Cleveland home to rejoin a tail end Brewer club he bolted, only to manage also. Backstop Eddie Stumpf was bumped, only to join owner Louis Fons' Lake Shore Kosciuskos.[180]

Livingston(e) "donned the windpad" and got the Brewers' Irish up. With his well-turned shillelagh of ash as his staff, he led the Brewers out of the morass, going 40-28. They survived a triple play by pennant-winning Indianapolis to win their last game 11-4. A surprising fifth place.

Ex-Brewers Nemo Leibold, Ray Schalk, and Happy Felsch led Pants Rowland's ChiSox to a World Series title. Lou Nahin testified, before the November 21st acquittal of Dan Shay.[181]

The baseball season survived 1917, but Russia did not survive its Red October. The Communist Revolution imposed its 73-year sentence across Eurasia. Even with war, the dormant idea of western A.A. clubs (including Milwaukee) joining a third major league was rehashed. Tom Hickey weathered that threat to his presidency. Al Timme used his other veteran Cardinal pickup, speedy, switch-hitting outfielder Bob Bescher, as an example of his prediction that A.A. salaries would fall to pre-Federal League levels.[182]

Bescher's monthly $1,200 was shared by both the Cardinals and Milwaukee. Though he liked Bescher a lot, Timme didn't think he was worth more than $300 monthly to any A.A. owner. Timme already lost 1st baseman Mal Barry and Andy Anderson to war service.

Livingston should have been "St. Paddy" for his wondrous spark of the Brewers, but Timme saw his threat to remain a $72-a-week Cleveland shipbuilder, as a bargaining ploy. It was not. By November 24th, life with his wife and children won out. Paddy, we hardly knew ye.[183]

The World War had the real say over everything, both for baseball and all of American society. A man named Joseph P. Cotton wasn't the fabric of his life, but the nation's "meat dictator." Produce more, use less, and do it under Daylight Savings Time, the bane of Wisconsin farmers. Young Americans were shoveled into French trenches, including nominal Milwaukeean Col. Douglas MacArthur. Wounded, he received a Distinguished Service Cross "over there." At an opposite end of the spectrum, Milwaukee's socialist Mayor Hoan saw the war only as profiteering.[184]

Much like they ended their first decade, the Milwaukee Brewers hired a succession of Irishmen to manage their baseball club: Dan Shay, Paddy Livingston, and now, from a half dozen candidates, Jack Egan. His presence was de-emphasized at the 1918 West Baden conditioning.[185]

Austin "Slats" McHenry was returned by legendary Cincy pilot Christy Mathewson, but not before a Sherry Magee foul ball broke his nose, hospitalizing him; he would miss a month. Cozy Dolan, the Oshkosh pride and joy who applied for Livingston's job, was a disgruntled Indy Indian. The outfielder finally came in a 3-way trade that sent Bob Bescher to Louisville. Lefty Bill Sherdel(l), now a Cardinal, praised Livingston for making him into a real pitcher. Zinn Beck earned Yankee pinstripes as 3rd base insurance for Mighty Mite manager Miller Huggins.[186]

News of the National Hockey League "Torontos" defeating the Vancouver Pacific Coast champions took up all of a small paragraph in the sports page. Bowling still ruled in Milwaukee.

Jack Egan, long an A.A. umpire, asserted himself once the Brewers camped at Beloit, Wisconsin. They trained at a park built for Fairbanks-Morse employees, lodged at one of the former Greek fraternity houses at Beloit College, and ate at the local Y.M.C.A.[187]

The city of Milwaukee had supplied Camp Custer at Battle Creek, Michigan, with unnaturalized aliens, but the Camp's ballclub had to indefinitely postpone a Soldiers' Athletic Fund benefit with the Brewers. The unpredictable April weather let Egan's men join a Beloit Liberty parade. Ex-scout Billy Doyle, now up with the Phils, didn't have as patriotic a time of it at Miami. Arrested for taking pictures of the government playing field near there, Doyle spent a dozen hours in the hoosegow. He pled in vain to military authorities that he wasn't one of the kaiser's hired henchmen. Ray Cannon, a noted Milwaukee lawyer training with the Phillies, said Doyle's "oratory forsook him entirely," and it took half the baseball community in Florida to vouch for him.[188]

The Prohibition debate now divided individual Wisconsin communities between the wet and dry sides. Beloit was a wet town that voted dry during the Brewers' presence there.[189]

Down in Dallas, Nemo Leibold recalled how Hugh Duffy released Ralph Capron for his showboating steal of home before University of Minnesota friends in a 1912 Minneapolis game. Jim Thorpe doubted that men in baseball flannels could run 100 yards in under 11 seconds.[190]

Jack Egan renewed a tradition of working out winter kinks against the U.W. Badgers. Dr. Wheeling Johnston of Chattanooga tabbed to be the Brewer 1st baseman, held out for 400 "iron men" a month, after coming from the Southern Association Birmingham Barons for Cy Slapnicka. The "doctah, sah," was receiving only $225 and Timme wired him that he wouldn't pay for his transportation to Beloit. All Johnston would do is win an abbreviated .374 batting title.[191]

It was an odd aside, but as Europe's Slavs asserted their national identities, the influence of Iowa Slavs like Slapnicka and Hovlik vanished from the Brewer pitching corps. Douglas Fairbanks held up Charlie Chaplin by the ankles, before a jammed Wall Street to pitch for Liberty Loans. The "Sammies over there" repulsed the evil Huns, who used Russian prisoners as troops.[192]

"BREWERS DEFEAT FAIRIES IN FIRST GAME, 7–4" read the Sunday morning, April 14th banner. There was only so much pride they could take in that accomplishment, considering Egan's "phenomenal success in the International League." If the fair and strict disciplinarian's Opening Day pitching choice was any barometer, well, Reese Williams would end up 4–10.[193]

Egan expected another Jigg Donahue (not the turn of the century 1st baseman) to develop into his biggest star. Blood poisoning from a spiking incident nearly wrecked the .361-hitting Waterloo second sacker's career. After medical treatment in his hometown Boston, Donahue reconditioned his pin over the winter by lugging heavy pipes for a radiator concern. Unlike Doc Johnston, Jiggs was so eager to crack the Brewer lineup that he paid his own way to impress Egan. Sadly, he only hit a minuscule .136 in an unlucky 13 games for Milwaukee.[194]

Ahead of the majors by two years, Tom Hickey banned spitballs and other "freak deliveries." First and second offenses each cost $25, with the second carrying banishment. KC's John Ganzel went a step further, saying he'd fine tamperers $100 on his own. The H.C.L. (high cost of living) was most likely to discourage the practice.

Al Timme accepted auto dealer A.E. Paffauf's huge American flag, and like veteran slugger John Beall, his award-winning drillmaster, joined players in the Third Liberty Loan subscription. Anyone in war service was a Brewer passholder and all excess receipts went to war bonds. When the Saints burst Milwaukee's patriotic Opening Day balloon with 10–1 fireworks, their Joe Riggert may have inspired what became a traditional turn of phrase for Athletic Park.[195] According to Manning Vaughan, Riggert hooked one in the 8th inning "onto Mrs. Herman Hassenpfeffer's lawn on Eighth street, for a home run." It was indeed "May Day! May Day!"

Austin McHenry's May 10th grand slam helped Milwaukee jump to a 10–2 start, and Timme's leading 17–8 "Eganites" kicked in $1,779.15 to Uncle Sam's amusement tax coffers by June 1st. Twilight baseball wasn't working with the Twin Cities war garden set though. When McHenry was sold to the Cards and Johnston to Cleveland, 3rd place Milwaukee's pennant hopes were "given the raus" by mid-June. Before Secretary of War Baker's "Work or Fight" edict, Dickie Kerr won 4 games in 6 days by July 4th, and nearly half (17 of 38) of the Brewers' wins by the August halt. For his 5th place club, Kerr led the league in games and innings pitched, hits allowed, and Ks.[196]

Milwaukee's venerable *Turnmeister*, gymnastics instructor George Brosius, had a son training army troops in the South and a grandson fighting "the Boche" in France. The "S.S. Teutonic" was sinking, but German submarine warfare still probed the New York area.[197]

Brewers' Providence demotees Jiggs Donahue and a young Joe "Zip"

Hauser were unemployed when the Eastern League gave up the ghost on July 20th. Cozy Dolan was the only Brewer beyond draft age when Maj. Gen. Enoch Crowder declared baseball a "non-essential" occupation. After closing up shop with a cheerless home twin loss to St. Paul, Timme made good that every player would get a $50 bond, but Nahin said $100 was possible had they won, placed, or shown. "Every Ready" Kerr kicked, despite a couple double-header bonuses. "Leo the Red" Murphy and he went to work at Beloit and be Fairies. Happy Felsch was now homering for Eddie Stumpf's Lake Shore Kosciuskos after his ChiSox season was also clipped.[198]

The war drove Mrs. Agnes Malloy Havenor Timme to finally sell the Brewers. "Yanks win! Yanks win!" wasn't the crackling sound of a baseball celebration on the radio, for commercial broadcasting had not yet developed. It was the outcome of the Great World War.

Clarence Henry Rowland was a 40-year old man from Platteville, Wisconsin. His baseball alias was "Pants." He amassed a 4-year record of 339–247, .578 and the 1917 World Series title for the Chicago White Sox. Fate freed him a year from the Black Sox scandal when Hugh Brennan and he bought the Milwaukee American Association franchise.[199] Rowland managed.

Nationwide Prohibition of alcohol was appearing more and more to be a certainty. It was never fully explained in print, but Messrs. Rowland and Brennan apparently thought it foolish to keep the "Brewers" nickname. It's also unclear whether it was derived from Rowland's monicker of "Pants," but for 1919 only, the Milwaukee baseball club was the Panthers.[200]

The partners pulled out all the stops in drumming up booster support for their Panthers. A Knights of Columbus banquet was actively promoted in *The Journal* sports pages. Governor Philipp, Mayor Hoan, Gen. Charles King, Henry Killilea, Cubs Veep William L. Veeck (Sr.), and Tom Hickey were among the luminaries to speak. The $1.50 tickets were available from Henry Winkler (Fonzie was already in Milwaukee?!) at John Morgenroth's, the Plankinton Arcade, and the K. of C. cigar stand.[201] Some 500–1,600 heard Big Ed Walsh's intro as pitching coach.

Pants' Panthers were tailored at the cleaned-up municipal Bosse Field at Evansville, Indiana, for 3 weeks beginning April 4th. Mal Barry was expected to receive his honorable discharge from Bordeaux, France, in time to report. Robert Ripley kiddingly ripped on French attempts to learn baseball in his cartoons, but he hadn't seen the Milwaukee Panthers play.[202]

The Jacob Hoffmann Brewing Co. in New York tried to keep government arrest at arm's length for selling 2¾ percent beer by hiring men to guzzle so much of their full strength suds. It proved "they couldn't (hic) get shoushed in (hic) — million years on that (hic) stuff."[203]

On Tuesday, March 25th at 4 a.m., a 27-year old "colored man" named George Bell was shot and killed in a Milwaukee rooming house. All the more newsworthy was that he was 7'-11" tall, 375 pounds, with size 23 shoes, and a habit of eating 4 pounds of steak when hungry. A post mortem exam of the inebriated New York giant revealed his brain weighed one ounce less than average. Shot by a 25-year old colored woman weighing 130 pounds, they traveled with the Chu Chin Chow Company, playing at the Davidson Theater. He was a bit player; she didn't perform.

The sports angle is of course two 1980s namesakes: Biola College's 7'-8" basketballer George Bell and Dominican baseball star Jorge "George" Bell, who had a Milwaukee tiff.[204]

It was telling that the new Panthers offices at 1411 Majestic Building had a temporary Grand 3457 telephone number. Cleveland's Tris Speaker stole home to nip them at Evansville, but 2nd baseman Jimmy Smyth's jaw was representative of the Panthers' regular season. It met with a left hook from the Night Riders' Bob Bescher — the ex-Brewer — at the Louisville opener.[205]

Perhaps Hugh Brennan should have considered hiring the "darky" prognosticator, who "manicured gents' shoes in a downtown tonsorial establishment." The shoe shiner (bootblack?) told Brennan he knew who the three White Sox were to join the Panthers before any announcement was made. Brennan was astonished when the negro correctly wrote down their names. The prognosticator could not reveal it to anyone else, but Brennan would make good on his $5 offer for that correct guess — after the players arrived.

After throngs welcomed home Milwaukee's doughboys, a May 1st ban on brewing was anathema. An "ardent handful of followers" saw "Steamboat" Reese Williams' wet 5th straight win over Toledo on June 7th. Siberia A.E.F. vet Johnny Miljus hurled for the Mud Hens in the rematch. Only the Hens kept the Panthers out of last place until the very end of the season. Rowland went through 3-dozen players, though Smyth, K.K. Kirkham, and Johnny Mostil were credible. Moundsman Tony Faeth kept the faith, but Earl Howard pitched more like Moe, Shemp, or Curly.[206] Sam Levy now had the sorry *Journal* baseball beat, and would for the next 30 years.

That fall, another Curly, Lambeau, formed an epoch in Wisconsin sports history with his gridiron enterprise at Green Bay.[207] As for Pants Rowland's Milwaukee Panthers, well, if you were asked to put those cats out, you had best use chloroform.

6
Borchert's Orchard

If there was ever a right man in the right place at the right time, no one personified Milwaukee and its Brewers of the Roaring 20s better than Otto Borchert. He was born in the city, August 12, 1874, the son of a brewer, Fred Borchert. His firm, F. Borchert & Sons, later became Falk, Borchert, & Jung and then just the Jung brewery. Otto attended the Humboldt School at 4th and Galena Streets. He was 14 years old in 1888 when he went to work for wholesale saddler Benjamin Young. His gift for commerce made him a traveling salesman with Julius Andrae & Sons Co. electrical appliances for more than two decades.[1]

Otto Borchert was probably what we now call a "sports geek." His hunger to get directly involved "in the game," as it were, was first fed by the interest he purchased in the Cream City Athletic Club. They conducted boxing shows at the Auditorium. Of course, his love of the fistic world took him to the legendary Jack Dempsey–Jess Willard heavyweight title fight in Toledo on July 4, 1919. Borchert attended with Henry Killilea and "Uncle Tom" Andrews, who had just been elected president of the newly organized Sports Writers' Association of America. Borchert originally wagered on Willard, but after seeing him work, picked Dempsey. Jack's legend was born.[2]

Borchert headed the syndicate to buy out Pants Rowland's failed Milwaukee Panthers experiment in early 1920. There was no compunction in the face of Prohibition about restoring the treasured "Brewers" name to the baseball club. Otto would buy out his partners, one by one, until he became sole owner of the team. In an age before farm systems, his wheeling and dealing with the majors was unsurpassed.[3]

Otto Borchert seems to have been mischaracterized by some, but he was no doubt a colorful figure, with his ever-present stogie and walking cane. Youngsters would wait for him at the Athletic Park gate, hoping for gratis entry. He did not name the place for himself.

There was not a huge purge of talent for those 1920 Brewers, only the return of Jack Egan. Three Milwaukee sandlot products and two other Wisconsinites would get a look-see at the Evansville camp.

Joe Hauser led the Eastern League in homers for 1919, with 6 at Providence and was in his second hometown audition. Catcher Fred Klevenow and outfielder Steve Covington were just local kids. The other two hailed from Waushara County in the Badger State's Central Sands region. First baseman Earl Chesebro was a standout on Coloma's village nine and Wautoma's Webb Schultz was a "star heaver" at LaCrosse Normal.[4]

Charley Moll was at first president of the Western Canada League and still magnate of the Winnipeg Maroons. The Milwaukeean had recommended big right-hander Ed Miller to Egan, but snatched up Lake Shore League star Wilbur Braby and North Side 3rd baseman Rube Lutzke for himself. The crack Lutzke would join Hauser as native Brewer regulars during the season.[5]

Former Wisconsin-Illinois Leaguer Joe Kernan brought his Saskatoon Quakers from that Western Canada League to train at Oshkosh. Moll's Winnipeggers were likely to play them there. Heading "south" for spring training seemed a matter of perspective.[6]

"Dainty" Dennis Gearin, an 11–2 southpaw, joined Hauser from his own hometown Providence. More known by the corrupted "Dinty," he would pitch in Milwaukee for the next dozen years, a diminutive 5'-4", 148 lb. fan favorite. His club longevity was a feat only old Tom Dougherty could love. Gearin would also see lots of outfield action in his first year. The second go-round for Doug "Buzz" McWeeny established the big Chicago righty as the No. 2 hurler.[7]

Egan wasn't the only man back in a position of authority. Prussian Junkers staged a reactionary coup to try and restore Germany's monarchy, only to be quelled. Humble saddler Friedrich Ebert returned to his democratic Weimar presidency. The Allies fortified the Rhine.[8]

If winning wasn't everything, but the only thing, Egan may have wanted to take in a certain New York comedy playing at Milwaukee's Davidson Theater. There, 5th generation Californian and once Frisco newspaper cartoonist Leo Carrillo performed in "Lombardi, Ltd."[9]

Egan was elated about landing one of baseball's early second-generation players. Prize shortstop Jimmie (Scoops) Cooney, son of Anson's old shortstop Jimmy Cooney on the Chicago Colts, brought a couple years' major league value from the Giants' camp at San Antonio.

Scoops would give Milwaukee 4 very fine seasons before another 5-year run in the bigs. Egan juggled bodies at the corners and in the outfield throughout 1920. He thought he had a left-handed answer in Iowan Art Reinhart. Alex "Alphonse" Gaston's assumption of the catching mantle freed "E-meal" (Hap) Huhn, Panther leadoff man, for first base.[10]

The powerful bat of 9-year major league vet "Sheriff" Del Gainer made a huge impression in Evansville. One clout over the leftfield garden wall there, something no one had done before, made Egan's prediction of Gainer feasting at Athletic Park's shorter fence the "real dope." Jim Thorpe flirted with joining Pongo Joe Cantillon's Millers after being released by the Giants again to Akron.[11]

Baseball in 1920 underwent the fundamental change of introducing a livelier ball and fine tuning of statistics. Tom Hickey's American Association responded to the H.C.L. (high cost of living) by increasing their admission prices from the 30¢ that included a war tax to 50¢, still with that tax. Grandstand seats were raised from 60¢ to 75¢, war tax included. Only reserved seats held static at 85¢. Each club determined its own box seat prices. The Brewers had no reserved seats on weekdays, but 90-centers on Sundays, with $1.10 box seats.

Postwar inflation and just 19 years of operation doubled expenses in the A.A. Hickey cited rosters now increased to 18 players and increased hotel rates. Baseball shoes that once ran $6 now ran $21, and uniforms went from $10 to $25. Even the ball, itself, doubled from $1.25 to $2.50. Add in the rest of the higher park expenses, including ushers, groundskeepers, rent, and the like, and it was a new world, without question.[12]

Former Panther and future Hall of Famer Big Ed Walsh now managed the Bridgeport Americans of the Eastern League. He predicted a pennant for the Park City, but would finish 5th out of 8, at .500. Cyril C. Slapnicka was now in business with former Federal Leaguer Rebel Oakes' oil gushers down in Louisiana.[13]

Otto Borchert was so enthused with his Evansville inspection that he thought the "all star infield" of Gainer at first, returning major league vet Art Butler (born Bouthillier in Massachusetts) at 2nd, Cooney at short, and Paul Smith at 3rd looked like "$1,000,000." As shrewd as Otto became at developing talent, this was the assessment of a neophyte.[14]

Egan's Brewers aroused hope in splitting with the as-yet undiluted Black Sox in final anti-season action. The second game, a 10-inning, 1–0 classic, thrilled the 2,500 who forgot all about the Sunday, April 11th pneumonia-inducing conditions. "Dutch" Hauser singled with 2 gone in the last frame and Gaston's game-winning triple settled the Buzz McWeeny-Earl Howard combo's shutout over Eddie Cicotte and Roy Wilkinson. McWeeny was declared "Irish in spite of his name" by Manning Vaughan. Ex-Brewers Nemo Leibold, Hap Felsch (now spelled correctly), and Ray Schalk went a combined 1-for-8 on Nemo's double.[15]

When it came down to serious business, Mike Kelley's new St. Paul 3rd baseman, Goldie Rapp, snuffed out the aspirations of 6,000. Rapp arrived just in time to start and his glove work held the Brewers to a 10-inning, 3–2 loss on Wednesday, April 12th. Local boy Rube Lutzke nearly matched Rapp's 9 errorless chances, with 7 of his own. The Saints were off to the most monstrous season in A.A. history. Egan could do no better than search for mediocrity.[16]

Catcher Emil Huhn was the first player to have his 9th inning homer count in its entirety when his 2-run clubbing to "the neighborhood of the wooden slippers" lifted Milwaukee, 3–1, over the visiting Pongomen from Minneapolis. It was the Brewers first win in four tries.[17]

Milwaukeean Al Cissa received a great opportunity to play in Peoria, as it were, as a 3rd baseman with the Three-Eye League Tractors. Clarence Rowland was a stockholder and recommended him. Tom Hickey called a summit to confront the industrial league raids upon his A.A. Poles changed the names of formerly Prussian towns and clergy fretted over nudity as the next step on the U.S. stage.[18]

The Brewers climbed into the first division, a game over .500 on May 19th. (This was the day the author's mother was born on Milwaukee's North Side.) Lefty Al Schultz, a Toledo man referred to the Brewers by Roger Bresnahan, hurled a 5-hit, 7-0 pill for Louisville to swallow. The first real baseball weather of the season drew 1,500 to that Tuesday affair.[19]

Milwaukee climbed as high as second in late May, as close as 6 games to the red-hot Saints. July 4th errors by Lutzke and erstwhile center fielder Art Reinhart led to a 5-4 fall at "Kaysee," with Milwaukee clinging to the first division, a game over .500. Northern Ireland was swept up in the hatreds that still plague it and Republican Warren G. Harding advanced towards the U.S. presidency as the Brewers still clung to third in late July. Doug "McWheeney" threw a 5-hit, 1-0 win, salvaged by Artie Bues' single to score Lutzke.[20]

They kept coming. A Columbus shutout by "Lengthy" Ed Miller and a 10-1 trouncing of the Colonels were hallmarks of a 10-game August winning streak. Cooney, Gaston, and Johnny Mostil were "Murderers' Row" for jerky Jake Northrop, the A.A. vet en route to a 20-17 season. The Colonels broke the streak on Saturday, August 22nd, humiliating Milwaukee in a twinbill before a large Athletic Park crowd.[21]

Their streak broken like an Olympic record at Antwerp, September marked the slow unraveling for the Eganites. The very end of the season would be shot like the rioting coal miners in West Virginia and blown up like the explosion between the New York Stock Exchange and J.P. Morgan's bank. From a 68-65 fifth place stand on September 1st, they were relegated to sixth permanently on the failure of a 10-23 (including 4-12) dive.[22]

The Black Sox scandal was now on full display, and the way Milwaukee dropped doubleheaders like hot potatoes, one almost had to wonder. Chet Koeppel of *The Sentinel* reported that one Brewer who took the money and ran was Johnny Mostil. Only he did it in a legitimate fashion: He copped most of the $100 put up by Otto Borchert for the home finale by winning a 100-yard dash, a bases-circling race, and finishing second to Rube Lutzke in a ball put. The latter "nearly heaved the pill from the center field bleachers to the press box." Mostil stole 27 bases for the year.[23]

It was the only proof of any Brewer throwing anything. Despite the horrendous end, and a 78-88 record leaving them 38 games behind the 115-49 Saints, Egan was invited back. Joe Hauser may have been "Zip" or "Dutch," but his 16 triples and 15 homers led the club, and his 79 RBI the first year the stat was tabulated was second on the club to the 84 by Art Butler.[24]

If Jack Egan hoped to keep his job beyond 1921, he needed more stability than the 3-dozen men who walked through 1920's revolving door. His top 4 pitchers — Jake Northrop, Doug McWeeny, Art Reinhart, and Lou North — would all be gone before the end of 1921. He had turnover at second and third — Fred (King) Lear took the keystone and Alex McCarthy, the hot corner. McWeeny went to the ChiSox, North to the Cards.[25]

Joe Hauser was now fixed at first as "Unser Choe." This German expression for "Our Joe" was born of the idea that, being the hometown boy, Athletic Park fans weren't supposed to ride the budding slugger. If he came off a bad day and some did jeer, others told them to knock it off because "Das ist Unser Choe."[26]

One of Unser Choe's "vicious homers" tamed the Southern Association Mobile Bears, a 5–0 exhibition won by Cecil Slaughter and

"To My Dear Friend, Arnold Herbstreith from Rube Lutzke," the ex-Brewer with Cleveland, ca. 1923–1927. Milwaukee Public Library Historical Photograph Collection.

Bob Trentman, that late March. An overweight Kenzie Kay Kirkham, the former Panther, was responsible for 4 of those 5 runs.[27]

The Black Sox were re-indicted that spring also, as Eddie Schaack emerged a savvy young hurler to head the Milwaukee staff. The Chicagoan was referred to the Brewers' Gulfport, Mississippi, camp by "Charles Fredrick Moll, the demon West Depere (winter) farmer." Ol' "Uncle Charley" took on semi-pro Milwaukeean and once Brewer tryout Erwin Scherbarth for his Winnipeg Maroons, in camp at Whitewater, Wisconsin, southwest of Milwaukee.[28]

Just like the Black Sox wouldn't go away, those defeated in the world war wouldn't let sleeping dogs lie. The exiled Kaiser Karl tried to regain the Austro-Hungarian throne by coup. Milwaukee youngsters went coup-coup overthrowing the weatherman to flex their spring vacant lot baseball muscles by April 3rd.

Otto Borchert and Jack Egan finagled with the Giants' "Jawn" McGraw and the Braves' George Stallings for additional pitching and outfield help.

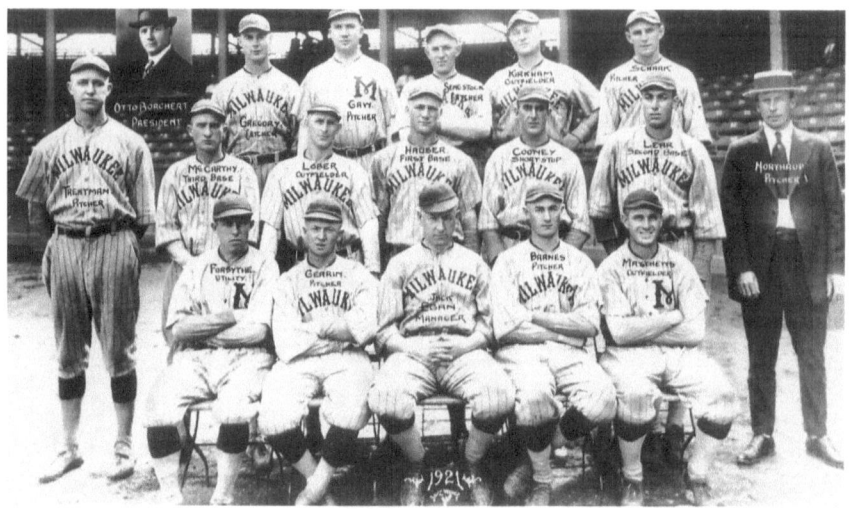

The 1921 Brewers. *Back row:* (inset President Otto Borchert), Gregory C, G. Gaw P, F. Sengstock C, Kenzie Kirkham OF, Eddie Schaack P. *Middle row:* Bob Trentman P, Alec McCarthy 3B, Ty Lober OF, Joe Hauser 1B, Jimmy Cooney SS, King Lear 2B, Jake Northrop P. *Front row:* C. Forsythe UT, Dinty Gearin P, Jack Egan Mgr., Virgil Barnes P, Wid Matthews OF. Milwaukee Public Library Historical Photograph Collection.

Borchert was even tipped off to the Boston potential by eminent baseball statistician Irwin Howe. Oscar Melillo, later known as a popular Brewer 2nd baseman nicknamed "Ski" or "Spinach," got a Gulfport try in the outer garden.

Dainty Dinty Gearin was being called everything from "Dresden Doll" to "Kewpie." Big semi-pro Jimmy Dodge, "possessed of a spitball that is a bird," knocked down better dough from the Lange Red Sox of the Lake Shore League than many major leaguers. He made $1,300 the previous August alone, pitching all around the state, and if his arm withstood it, he made $100-250 a game. He made $800 in 4 straight days and struck out 35 in a doubleheader shutout for Whitewater of Wisconsin's Central State League. The "big frog in a little pond" turned a deaf ear to pro offers.[29] His profitable business at Prairie du Sac on the Wisconsin River being the siren song of home.

"The Kaiserin is dead! Long live the Kaiserin!" The former German empress, Augusta Victoria died in Holland on Monday, April 11th. Her exiled husband was barred from her Berlin funeral, but Milwaukee's "King" Lear celebrated with a pair of exhibition homers over the visiting Chicago White Sox.[30] A restless 6,000 watched in chilly winds as the royal effort fell short, 4–3.

New Brewers secretary Alfred A. Thimmesh, an army veteran, wasn't off on a good foot either. His wife, Pearl Vera, refused to join him since he took the position, so he filed for divorce.

Unser Choe Hauser lifted the spirits of Thimmesh and 5,000 other fans when his 2-run "Herculean smash" powered the Brewers over defending champion St. Paul, 6–1, on the Wednesday, April 13th Opening Day.[31] Jake Northrop was still there for the victory, but it was Hauser's blast, traveling some 50 feet over the "bull" sign, that set off a 7th Street scramble. One proud kid was hell-bent for "election in the direction of Williamsburg." It could have cleared "the biggest ball yard in the land."

The Saints couldn't even play the third game, for snow swamped Athletic Park into so much Alaskan scenery. Brewer management tried to trade the next Miller series to Minneapolis, but that was foiled by Kansas City's owners, who wanted their Opening Day cut at the Flour City.

Egan's men grabbed a very early league game up in St. Paul, but his "cubs," or seconds, lost to Charley Moll's Winnipeg Peggers at Athletic Park, Sunday, April 24th, by a 3–2 count. Bunny Raab "breezed along much like Mano War" before giving up a crucial 7th inning homer. The previous day, former Panther/Brewer Earl Howard pitched a 4–3 gem over visiting Saskatoon for the semi-pro Simmons Bedmakers at Kenosha. Howard fanned 14 for the Beautyrest mattress company.[32]

It's not exactly clear how he pulled it off, but "Sheriff" Del Gainer hit a 2-run home run at St. Paul's Lexington Park and roamed center field for the regular Brewers at the same time he was listed in left for the second string box score versus Winnipeg in Milwaukee. Only he knew.

Fred Lear was again "king for a day" when his April 30th shot "over the wall into the the lawn once mowed by Mr. Herman Hassenpfeffer," built a 7–1 lead on the KaySee Kaws. "Mr. Hassenpfeffer has moved and Pat Cohen and

Cad Brand, a Sunday *Milwaukee Sentinel*, 1921.

family now reside in the palatial duplex." Hauser busted a hit off future Brewer Bunny Brief's shins at first. Joe went on to score on a sac fly from Gearin, who needed Northrop's help in the 9th, to save an 8–6 win and 3rd place tie with KC.[33]

Saturday, May 14th was Clarence Rowland Day at Athletic Park. "Pants" was now at the managerial helm of the lowly Columbus Senators, but it was the double whammy of freckle-faced redhead Willie Smith's first day on the mascot job since last season, and right-handed ChiSox loanee Joe Kiefer that spoiled the outcome. Kiefer's "dazzling fast ball and excellent curve" dominated the Michigan League for Muskegon in 1920 and it did likewise to shut out the Ohioans on 3 hits.[34]

Still, as lowly as the Senators were, Milwaukee trailed them by a half-game, in last.

Memorial Day was shrouded in black after one nearly died and 16 people were hurt in an air stunt crash at State Fair Park. Milwaukee's Billy Mitchell escaped a Washington, D.C. crash.

Baseball rode the Athletic Park airstreams that very pre-holiday Sunday as Jim Cooney's homer solved the 13–12 opener over "roly poly boss" Otto Knabe's KC Blues. A trio of Brewer pitchers survived a 3-homer Blues barrage to save Game Two, 9–8. Milwaukee was out of last.[35]

Babe Ruth again punished lively home runs at a major league record pace when Hauser scored a winning run for the Brewers to surpass St. Paul in mid-June. Bad blood of a few seasons between Saint catcher Nick Allen and "handsome" umpire Jim Murray spilt into near fisticuffs before both teams jumped in. This wasn't the type of boxing Borchert normally promoted.[36]

Milwaukee was still a city that was over ½ foreign-born, and of those, 1/3 were Germans and 1/5 were Poles. Its ballclub, still an Irish-Anglo-German mix, made 3rd place by July 4th. In Milwaukee that holiday, the 10-game win streak of the William Counsell team was snapped by Time Insurance's company team, 5–3. Any relation to current big league infielder Craig Counsell (Milwaukee-bred) is uncertain.[37]

Hauser was on a Brewer homer record pace, but to retaliate for a 10–1 frying, Toledo's big, pigeon-toed "redskin" center fielder and ex-Brewer Jim Thorpe won a "croix de swat" with a line drive shot over the left field fence, "fully 50 feet within the foul line," that would've cleared any park in the country, a 6th inning clout to the edge of the center field seats, as well as a 8th inning response to fans' call for "another — a clean lick over the left field wall."[38] His 9th inning at-bat yielded only a single, but at his old Milwaukee happy hunting grounds, Jim Thorpe's war club pounded out a 17–4 August 14th Mud Hen triumph. He'd finish with .358–9–112 and 34 steals.

Virgil Barnes, the right-handed Kansan "Zeke," who tipped Borchert onto speedy Toronto flyhawk midget Wid Matthews, scattered 4 hits in a 5-zip shutout at Columbus. The Black Sox were condemned as "murderers of sport" when the Brewers closed the July 30th gap to 3 games.[39]

Otto Borchert's Athletic Park also hosted the Lake Shore League collision between Jap Barbeau's visiting Two Rivers club and Eddie Stumpf's Lange Red Sox, abetted by Jimmy Dodge.

The lively ball was the centerpiece of the Brewers' march into September. The Milwaukee Eganites split, 3–12, 14–13, with the traveling Minneapolis Pongomen on August 9th. King Lear's 3-run double on Charley "Sea Lion" Hall kept the 13–4 hit parade marching over St. Paul, the 13th. Maybe Milwaukee's "automatic traffic cop," the stop-n-go light, should've regulated basepaths?[40]

The Brewers survived the first division by September, but the Mud Hens of Milwaukeean 1st baseman/manager Fred Luderus knocked them further under .500. Majors castoffs Hugh Bedient and Doc Ayers, who, according to *The Sentinel's* Chet Koeppel, "started pitching baseball at the close of the Civil War," dealt Milwaukee a 3–1, 2–1 double whammy.[41]

Egan's Brewers were going down like Fatty Arbuckle's silent film career. The fatman faced manslaughter charges in the death of actress Virginia Rappe. Spain slaughtered Morocco's Moor men. A familiar name in Milwaukee banking, John H. Puelicher, was elected first vice-president of the American Banking Association. Egan couldn't bank a first division bonus when Roy Sanders of the pennant-winning Colonels (Colonel Sanders?!) polished them off to end it.[42]

Hauser was Milwaukee's first man to ever hit 20 homers in a year (.316–20–110), but he led the A.A. with 103 strikeouts. The top three flingers all had ERAs over 4.24, but Lear (.358–13–112, 113 BB, 24 SB), Gainer (.340–9–124), and Matthews (.338) made it just plain offensive.[43]

The Milwaukee Brewers were in a 7-year drought, without any serious pennant contention. Otto Borchert entered his third year of ownership in 1922. He would turn to the one man who led Milwaukee to American Association championship glory. He would turn to Harry Clark.

Clark, in turn, wanted to pick up Cleveland's waived Doc Johnston, but susceptibility to the "charley horse" made him an unlikely candidate to replace Zip Hauser at first. Borchert sold Unser Choe's services to Connie Mack and the Philadelphia Athletics for a fine 5-figure sum.[44]

Alabaman Ivy Griffin had the left-handed bat, if not the power, to supplant Hauser. Griffin would play first longer than any Brewer ever — 8 seasons for 3 managers. He brought his consistent average and glove work from Atlanta, traits with which the ex-player Clark identified.

Clark took his new Brewers to Caruthersville, Missouri, just across the Mississippi from Tennessee in the Show-Me State's little southeast panhandle corner. The fixation with river locales always proved a wet impediment to the conditioning progress. The Millers were unable to cross a washed-away bridge at Miston to reach an exhibition tilt. Borchert was in Florida, fishing for more talent and guaranteeing that Milwaukee would have its best team ever.[45]

Recollection of Milwaukee's days as a roller polo hotbed, some 40 years earlier, appeared in *The Sunday Sentinel*. The contemporary fad of young local women posing for their own saucy photos was also displayed. Dry agents raided 50 saloons in Milwaukee city and county.[46]

A curious practice match-up pitted Clark's Brewers against Hugh Duffy's Boston Red Sox. Harry Clark called upon Bob Clark, Eddie Schaack, and Paul Sherman to hold the big leaguers to a 2–0 loss. Nemo Leibold now led off for the BoSox against his old teammate, Harry Clark. Future Brewer manager Frank "Blackie" O'Rourke of Hamilton, Ontario, played short for Duffy. Only returning Milwaukee leadoff center fielder Ty Lober solved Sam Dodge and Alex Ferguson.[47] Harry Clark didn't defeat the man he replaced as Milwaukee's pilot in 1913, but he'd have the last laugh by season's end. Duffy's BoSox would finish last, early in the "Curse of the Bambino" era.

King Lear, a late signee, joined Lober in homering to shock Branch Rickey and Rogers Hornsby's N.L. pennant-contending St. Louis Cardinals, 5–2. The L-&-L tandem teed off on ex-Brewer Dixie Walker, who relieved veteran right-hander Bill Doak. Sherman and Ray Lingrel held St. Louis to 7 hits. Cards shortstop Specs Toporcer, the first position player to wear glasses in the majors, saw none of the Brewer offerings clearly. He went hitless. Missouri was Brewer turf.[48]

Speedy Brewers Lear, Lober, wee Wid Matthews, and newcomers Griffin, outfielder Paul Johnson and catcher Glenn Myatt (all three came in the A's/Hauser deal) could leg it to first in 3½ seconds. Teammates wagered Myatt could "outstep any athlete in Mr. Tom Hickey's loop."[49]

Borchert offered Russell (Lena) Blackburne a return engagement, but the free agent infielder signed with Toledo, only to be dealt to KC during the season. "Swallowtail Otto," described as "one of the hardest working birds at the camp dinner table," tried to train the "colored belle" waitress to deliver his specialty 6-minute eggs before he left.[50]

Oscar Melillo, the auburn-haired Chicago Italian, was back from Charley Moll's Winnipeggers to stay as an outfield reserve. The 6'-4" Bob Clark was the biggest Brewer on a revamped staff, standing in his Milwaukee-made Phoenix hosiery. Lefty Nellie Pott (don't confuse with Nels Potter of 20 years later) from Cincy rose as the stopper, while Lyle Bigbee (brother of Pirate flyhawk, Carson "Skeeter" Bigbee) from Oregon and Texan Turk Riviere shared the load with Lingrel and Gearin.[51]

Regular Carson Bigbee wasn't among the Pirate seconds, who lost to Milwaukee at Caruthersville, 3–2. Pittsburgh did have its "sewing machine battery" of Rip Wheeler and Mike Wilson, not to mention a certain future Hall of Fame fly-chaser named Kiki Cuyler. Wild rumors persisted at Pittsburgh that the Pirates would eat red monkey meat supplied to them from South America by a wealthy fan, George L. Kerr. Ty Lober didn't need it—he already had a touch of malaria.[52]

In a curious historical coincidence, a man named Emmet T. Flood, the Chicago rep of the American Federation of Labor, said his organization would boycott professional baseball as long as Judge Kenesaw Mountain Landis was the newly created commissioner of baseball. Landis was, in Flood's words, a "tool of big business."[53]

Marshall "Babe" Ruth, a 210-pound guard on the Beloit College football squad, went to California on business, where he was discovered as a heavyweight comedian. He contracted with Sunshine Screen Productions.[54]

Harry Clark's return sparked so much hope that the Brewers' pre-Opening Day banquet was limited to 300 capacity. The club opened 1922 on the road, as Eddie Schaack absorbed the 5–4 defeat to Pants Rowland's Columbus Senators. Ivy Griffin christened his A.A. career with a homer and Paul Johnson invited himself to the loop with a triple and 2 singles.[55]

Turk Riviere was threatened with suspension for failure to report at this point. Wid "Bert" Matthews underwent an operation for blood poisoning at a Toledo hotel on Wednesday, April 19th. He was left behind as the Brewers traveled onto Louisville. He was expected to be out for a week. Struck on the leg by a pitched ball in training, it flared up as the players returned to the clubhouse that Wednesday. Wid was back for the home opener.[56]

Denny Gearin was also fined for haggling with Borchert over the $3,500 he wanted for the season and the $500 monthly that he was willing to settle for. He could draw $7,500 on the market. Banished Happy Felsch claimed the White Sox owed him pay, too.[57]

Maybe President Warren G. Harding should have assuaged these two men, like he tried with Europe, that its post-war healing should draw from America's Civil War. He narrowly escaped catastrophe when a vessel he was to ride on the Ohio River collapsed, injuring two dozen of 200.

Former veteran Detroit Tiger catcher Oscar Stanage tried to get Sacramento teammates to grow "49er" beards to boost the California capital's "Days of '49" celebration.[58]

The Brewers opened the Harding "normalcy" era returning home from a .500 trip. WAAK radio (360 meters) broadcasted from Gimbel Brothers department store in its infancy, but baseball was not yet on the agenda. Harry Clark received a floral horseshoe and good luck goat before 7,500 at Athletic Park.[59] Schaack's 7-K pitching turned back native Fred Luderus' Mud Hens, 4–2. The sunshine made it the largest opening crowd ever in Milwaukee, but they weren't close to The Hickey Cup number at St. Paul's loss, 12,000, that Friday, April 28th.

A delirious gathering of 10,000 flooded the field with cushions after Lear's single set up a loony Ernie Koob wild pitch. That handed a 3-run 9th and 11–10 win over Louisville to the Brewers. Lear was again on a tear, going 3-for-5, including a double and a homer.[60]

Jim Thorpe was released by the P.C.L. Portland Beavers in favor young blood. Handicapped by a bum shoulder, Thorpe was bought from Toledo for $5,000 and got $1,000 monthly.[61]

Harry Clark's Brewers held 3rd place at 25-19 by June 1st, but dribbled down to 31-29 by mid-month after dropping a series to the "Pongos" and the Colonels. The Kansas City Blues clubbed four Brewer pitchers (Gearin, Bob Clark, Baldy Rose, and Schaack), 12-8 and 7-2, before a July 4th overflow of 12,000. The Athletic Park ground rules weren't necessary for the Kaws' Bunny Brief, who swatted out a pair in Game Two. At Fennimore, in southwestern Wisconsin, 5,000 saw the Negro Gilkerson Union Giants of Chicago best Lancaster, 7-6. Milwaukee chased third.[62]

Otto (wan?) Knabe's Kaws snapped "elongated" Ray Lingrel's personal 5-game win streak on July 15th by hammering him for 19 hits and a 10-5 setback at KC.[63] Unser Choe Hauser produced effectively for Connie Mack's A's and, sans Joe, the Brewers hit a league second .314.

Lingrel struggled again, allowing Columbus to tie him on July 31st, but Oscar Melillo's hit scored a 10th inning 8-7 victory for 1,200 partisans. The Brewers were now a percentage point behind second place Indianapolis. A 5-game slide dropped them back fourth by mid-August.[64]

For 2¢ in Milwaukee County, 3¢ elsewhere, *The Sentinel* beat writer J.J. Delany reported on the Saturday, August 26th triumph over the Millers' Rube Schauer, who was born Dimitri Ivanovich Dimitrihoff in Odessa, Russia. Homers by Dinty Gearin (playing right) and Lear sent Pongo Joe's crew packing and grabbed second solely from them. St. Paul was a distant 11 games up.[65]

The nation worried over its critically ill first lady, Florence Harding, in September. Milwaukee's homegrown "Bucketfoot," Aloysius Szymanski, known to the baseball world as future Hall of Famer Al Simmons, now roamed right field for the Brewers. He was one of three Clarkmen to connect off the Saints' Sea Lion Charley Hall in the September 9th goose egg he laid at St. Paul.

When 1922 began, *Toledo Bee* sports editor G.R. Pulford saw Milwaukee's weakness behind the plate. By September 9th, Cleveland Indians president E.F. Bernard was in Milwaukee to purchase catcher Glenn Myatt, who at .370, won the A.A. batting title. Borchert thought Myatt and his slapstick, "Betsy Joe," were worth 50 grand. It looked as if fortune finally looked kindly on the Arkansas-born Myatt. Losing his engineer father to a railway accident at age 6, the family moved to Texas and young Glenn hustled to support it.[66] Borchert wouldn't seal the deal, while his 5th place club treaded water.

A charity old-timers game at Boston's Braves Field featured Cy Young, ex-Brewer Bobby Lowe, Honus Wagner, and "the one and only" clown, old Brewer Nick Altrock. They drew 23,000 to see the A.L. win 27-8 over the Nationals.[67]

Exhibitions begin and end a season. Even though the "Clark clan" halted their skid at 5th place and the 85-83 record was the Brewers' first winning finish since 1918, Joe Hauser was paid tribute by 4,000 admirers. His Philadel-

phia Athletics lost, 9–8, at Athletic Park and Unser Choe summoned a pair of singles from his wood. Ironically, it was fellow homegrown Al Simmons' pinch-hit double that advanced Wid Matthews to third and set up Alec McCarthy's game-winning single. Simmons and Hauser would be teammates before too long.[68]

Otto Borchert believed Harry Clark's foundation gave his ballclub a sorely needed winning touch. Oh, the Mackmen got a little March 1923 revenge at Montgomery, Alabama, when an 8th inning Tilly Walker double led the A's 3–2 over Milwaukee. Clark trained his men at Troy, Alabama, and even the Beloit Fairies, with former major league hurlers Hippo Vaughn and Dave Davenport,

Cad Brand, Sunday, April 1, 1923, *Milwaukee Sentinel*.

and ex-Yankee leadoff man Elmer Miller, went to Hot Springs, Arkansas. Ex-Brewer Dick Kerr was laid up with a bad ankle there, training with Kenosha's Simmons Bedmakers.[69]

A tanned and optimistic Borchert came back from Alabam' to find a March blizzard at home. Milwaukeean Rube Lutzke, now up with Cleveland, was being compared to the greatest hot corner men in the pastime's history, like Bill Bradley (not the basketball-dribbling politico). Harry Clark was bold enough to predict a top three finish for his team. Easter in Milwaukee was a chilly April Fool's.[70]

Milwaukee-made heavy equipment dredged the earth from the "farthest north" to Siam to the Andes to the tropics of the Belgian Congo. Even the Panama Canal was dug by Milwaukee. Verily, in an article-cum-Bucyrus-Erie ad, the steam shovel and dredge were truthfully called "the Esperanto of the Romance of Achievement."[71]

Well, mining for pennant gold proved a bit more daunting. The tall tale of Paul Bunyan's legendary home run lumber, related by Hezekiah Butterworth Snodgrass via Pat Cook at Boot Jack in Michigan's Upper Peninsula, had to entertain the home folks until "Play Ball!" was called.[72]

Another Arkansan, Enoch "Ginger" Shinault, replaced Myatt as backstop. Oscar Melillo established himself as the double play pivot over Fred Baldowsky — "Baldy" in the box scores. Harry Clark's reliance on right-hander Dave Keefe, a major league washout, was to his detriment. Before taking their leave of Troy, Alabama, the Brewers fell 10–4, over and out, to Cleveland. Both Rube Lutzke and Glenn Myatt went hitless for the Indians. The exhibition drew 1,000. Native Clevelander Pat McNulty brought his lefty bat from the Tribe to join Al Simmons and old Sherry Magee in the outfield. Tommy Heilberger of Sheboygan backed them up.[73]

The "sun gods" at Athletic Park would have a nice new set of center field bleachers from which to worship Ol' Sol. After years of pounding the old boards, the new stand would withstand 2,000 gold bugs. The infield was resodded after the first home stand.[74]

In New York City, Babe Ruth christened the new Yankee Stadium he helped to build. His homer, in a 4–1 triumph over the Red Sox, set the record mammoth crowd of 74,200 into bedlam.

Ruth may have warranted his own statue, but a movement in Washington, D.C. to erect something alike to the "old colored Mammy of the old South" churned nothing but consternation. Milwaukee's own record Opening Day crowd of 10,582 may have wanted to erect a giant finger at Dave Keefe. Clark's decision to start him backfired; he was chased off the mound by the Minneapolis Millers, 10–2. Pongo Joe Cantillon tapped the thatch of his blond Norse prince, Eric Erickson, to puzzle the Brewers on 5 hits. Toledo's 12,556 led all Thursday, April 19th A.A. openers.[75]

A 4-game win streak at Minneapolis made May Day a break even, 6–6 call. Ex-Brewers Lutzke, Myatt, Wid Matthews, Johnny Mostil, and even Bill Sherdell all lit up The Big Show.

That 1923 marked another companion pro baseball club to the Brewers in Milwaukee. Scant coverage of the "Local Darkies," the Milwaukee Bears entry in the "Colored National Baseball League" at Athletic Park, came in the white majority press. A Saturday, May 5th loss to Rube Foster's Chicago Giants was reported, as pitcher G. Boggs blew a 9th inning 3–3 tie into an 8–5 romp. Milwaukee did turn a couple "fast double plays," and Cuban Cristobal "Torrentte" (Torriente) starred in Chicago's outfield. Foster really set up the Bears to farm his Chicago leftovers.[76]

The Brewers weren't as poor as their pigmented contretemps, but they struggled with a puny offense and middling defense by Mother's Day. The new Nash Motors Stadium at Kenosha was dedicated by a 1st place Nash ballclub in the Middle West Baseball League. The team was a mesh of former major and minor leaguers, like ex-St. Paul 1st baseman Leo Dressen and outfielder Al Wickland, last of Toledo. Industrial semi-pro ball remained a lure.[77]

Otto Borchert wouldn't flinch at tossing any clique mutineers overboard from his injury-riddled team, but the man often branded a goat by fight managers and ballplayers got to ride one. On Monday, May 14th, he underwent the mysterious initiation before the Tripoli Shrine's select few, attaining a "fine crop of blisters crossing the well-known burning sands." He survived that gluttonous punishment well, shaking his intact swallowtail determined to buy a pitcher.[78]

"Sorrel topped backstop" Ginger Shinault picked up where Glenn Myatt left off, going 4-for-4 to lift his good buddies 10–4 over the Colonels. By May 23rd, they were two under .500.

Three Columbus men bought the Boston Red Sox for one million dollars and former Milwaukee/Oshkosh clothier Carl Laemmle returned to Wisconsin a cinematic giant. The short-statured Bavarian immigrant was now president of Universal Film Mfg. Co. His onetime kaiser, the deposed widower Wilhelm II, dottered between remarriage and rewriting the Bible in his Dutch exile.

"The Milwaukee Negro Giants" were exiled to a brief paragraph in their 7–6 Memorial Day loss at St. Louis. Milwaukee drove off two St. Louis pitchers, but the "special" dispatch credits a 2-run Stratton homer as making the winning difference in the 7th inning. Leroy Stratton, a 3rd baseman, was supposed to have played with Milwaukee in 1923, not St. Louis.[79]

Meanwhile the flummoxed second division Brewers should have consulted Dr. Theodore H. Larson's radical "gland transplant" demonstrations in Milwaukee. He supposedly put "youth restoring" goat glands into a 33-year old married woman. It wasn't said whether Harry Clark's mascot supplied the vital organs.[80]

Tom Hickey transplanted a $50 fine from Milwaukee pitcher Nelson Pott's wallet after investigating a June episode against Umpire Boyle. Otto Borchert was bamboozled by the weatherman, calling off a Millers game during Hickey's time in Milwaukee. "Sir Tummas" raved about attendance, which ranked Milwaukee third, as Pongo Joe and Peck Sharpe entertained him at one of Cantillon's old North Side sausage haunts. Hickey suspended Melillo 5 games for a fight with St. Paul's Marty Berghammer, a future Brewer manager.[81]

Denny Gearin stepped forth as the Brewers' ace and King Lear brought back punch to a moribund offense, but "Three-Fingered" Dave Keefe and Jim Lindsey won the July 4th doubleheader at Kansas City. Milwaukee still lagged a half-game behind Indy, for fifth. Ex-Brewer Jap Barbeau could have used a fifth, when he up and quit as manager at Fond du Lac in the semi-pro Wisconsin State League. Umpire Jansen forfeited a game to Kaukauna after Barbeau refused to leave the field. Ex-Brewer Buster Braun still threw winning ball for the W.S.L. Sheboygan Chairs.

The Brewers used a 9-run fourth inning to pass Indianapolis on July 14th. Eddie Schaack threw a 5-hit, 13–2 job over the Indians. The 7th-ranked Brewer bats had six .300 regulars.[82]

In the first two weeks of August, the nation was gripped by President Harding's pneumonia, which he contracted on a far west vacation trip. He suddenly died of an apoplectic stroke on August 3rd.[83]

The first native "Porto Rico" baseball team, since the game's introduction there in 1899, came to New York's Governor's Island to compete for the Second Army Corps championship. Milwaukee's "Negro Nine" made 3 straight wins of St. Louis, taking the first game of double duty. The second game was called after seven, falling to St. Louis' favor. Negro National League standings were never known in *The Sentinel* sports pages.[84] They were also never actually called the "Bears" in that paper either, nor was their contraction after a 14–32, .304 mark listed.[85]

When President Harding died, former Ohio State University star Pat McNulty hit a 2-run homer in the 9th, giving Milwaukee a 5–3 win at Columbus, Harding's old Ohio stomping grounds. The commander-in-chief's funeral train rolled cross-country to silent multitudes. Calvin Coolidge inherited a prosperous, peaceful nation where a round trip train ride from Milwaukee to Kilbourn-the Dells of Wisconsin ran $2.65. The Teapot Dome scandal hadn't tarnished the Cabinet yet. At least Coolidge didn't have to explain the Kewpie Gearin sale to the New York Giants as "self defense."[86]

Gearin nearly jumped to the Kenosha Nash outlaws from which the Brewers would have received nothing. Fred Lear did jump to that club in early August, prompting Brewer attorneys Roger Trump and Henry J. Killilea to contest removal of injunction proceedings from Milwaukee to Kenosha County's Circuit Court. Lear was a Milwaukee resident under a Brewers contract of $600 monthly. He got $4,000 from Nash for the season and made Borchert smile broadly with his testimony that the Brewers' rough infield was his reason to jump. Borchert was indignant at Lear's claim that he wanted nothing better than a 3rd or 4th place team in Milwaukee. Lear's bridges seemed burnt in Milwaukee, but the injunction kept him from playing for Nash, though he still received a weekly paycheck from them.[87] A Minneapolis editor pimped a $10,000 draft price.

To replace Gearin, who won his August 6th N.L. bow over Cincinnati, Borchert paid heed to his new scout, Dan Shay. The ex-Brewer pilot, acquitted in that 1917 murder charge, suggested pitcher Bud Shaney of the Southwestern League Topeka Kaws. He came to Milwaukee with his 2nd baseman Harry Strohm for "Baldy" Fred Baldowsky.[88] In the Texas League, San Antonio's Ike Boone set a consecutive game hit streak record at 34, breaking ex-Brewer Kenzie Kirkham's mark there of 1922.

Lefthander George "Rube" Walberg would not pitch for the Brewers until 1924, but his rise from the Minnesota wheatfields to Connie Mack's A's was already incomparable. Coal miner-types in the majors had nothing on the "young gent." Working the summer of 1921 in the grain fields, he "got the fever." Pitching brilliantly for a Seattle semi-pro team, Portland inked him up. He got "Jawn" McGraw's attention after 1922, but didn't fit well with Giant veterans and Mack had him for keeps.[89] Harry Clark could have used Walberg!

His Brewers were as stagnant as the city's water supply. The health department called for boiling water because chlorine tank pressure at the North Point pumping station was low. Shades of cryptosporidium![90] Then again, the city experimented with turning waste sludge into what became Milorganite fertilizer, the first municipally produced waste substance of its kind.

The Brewers must have rolled their bats in the stuff because they grew 22 hits in a frantic 16–10 win at Toledo on August 8th. Five Clarkmen rapped 3 or more hits apiece, but no homers off a triumvirate of Hen hurlers.[91]

The weird, frustrating year for personnel left Milwaukee losing extraordinary pinch-hitter Lyle Bigbee to a Louisville waiver claim. Clark couldn't get Artie Bues to re-up from Kaukauna, and Borchert dropped his injunction against Lear after believing Mr. Nash's ignorance of his Milwaukee contract. The liberated Lear singled and tripled on the Beloit Fairies that Labor Day.[92]

In a year when a Dolf Luque-Casey Stengel baseball fight rivaled Dempsey-Firpo, a massive earthquake wrecked "Tokio," and the real Aunt Jemima was killed by an auto. One bright spot was Sherwood Buckingham Magee. Sherry's September 5th homer slowed the Kaws' flag cause. Nelson Pott started that 3 days earlier when his 5–0 gem broke the Blues record tying 238 game streak without being shut out.[93] The Brewers fought off Minneapolis for 5th, while an A.A. record 20,000 at KC saw the Blues' September 14th triumph over St. Paul.

At Kenosha, King Lear's single enabled Nash Motors to beat their archrival league-leading Simmons Bedmakers on September 22nd. The Simmons club was offered to play for a $5,000 purse against the rival Racine Horlicks at the Columbia County Fair in Portage.[94]

Al Simmons was back with his hometown Brewers before making his own bed in the City of Brotherly Love. He was a homer shy of the cycle at Toledo on September 31st. Another Wisconsinite in Philly, Three Lakes farmer/banker Cy Williams won his third N.L. homer title. The second man, after Babe Ruth, to ever hit over 40 in a major league season ended up with 41.

Schizoid was the Brewers October 4th double up at Columbus. The Senators took Game One, 21–12, off 4 Milwaukee pitchers, though their own William Gleason went the distance. Eddie Schaack's 14–0 "whole works" gave up a 4-hitter, as many as Simmons and Griffin each.[95]

If 1923 wasn't weird enough for all the aforementioned, it surely was because for the first time in 44 years, 61-year old Bill Kearns of Crown City, Illinois, did not catch in his bare feet. Most of the time he never used a mask or a glove either.[96]

In the off-season, the Teapot Dome oil scandal blew wide open and former President Wilson was laid to rest. Milwaukee's socialist mayor Hoan refused to send condolences, giving the city a "black eye." Nonpartisans recruited old David S. Rose to run as a result.[97] The Milwaukee Badgers were the city's pro basketball infant, sharing their nickname with the city's N.F.L. team.

Harry Clark's Milwaukee antecedent at third, Jimmy Burke, took over the Toledo reins. Though Philly A's fans were sorry to see "Prof. Sparkplug" Wid Matthews sent back to Milwaukee, Otto Borchert sold Al Simmons to them for a handsome coin. Flyhawk Frank McGowan and 2nd sacker Herr Heinie Scheer retired as the "Beau Brummel" of his Bronx billiards room came with Matthews.[98] The 1924 drawing board began at Palmetto, Florida.

"Good hurlers are scarcer than Kukluxers over in the local colored settlement," so Clark brought back the blade of New Orleans, Roy "Dixie" Walker. He would lose like David Rose. Taking lickings from the likes of the Brooklyn Trolley Dodgers and Washington Senators, Clark should have offered the sort of incentive the Burlington Athletic Club made back up in Wisconsin. Everyone hitting a home run on their grounds won a barrel of sauerkraut. No matter how high its price would go up, it helped to have the club president own the local kraut factory.[99]

Al Simmons developed a bum knee for the White Elephants and the Cardinals' Branch Rickey boasted about 3rd base prodigy Lester Bell. Milwaukee was foiled by St. Louis in a Bradentown exhibition by slabsters future skip Allen Sothoron and ex's Lou North and Bill Sherdell. Borchert even canceled a couple tune-ups at Mobile, priming his men for their Toledo opener.[100]

A huge and happy turnout of 14,473 at the Glass City on Tuesday, April 15th, watched their "solemn Jack Scott, giant son of the backwoods of the Carolina hills," outdo Eddie Schaack, 5–3. Umpire Jim Murray, "the cyclops of the diamond," came in for his usual razzberry.[101]

Al Simmons' debut with the Mackmen was equally modest — a single in four trips, as Walter Johnson threw his 101st career shutout for Washington at them.[102]

The diminutive Schaack took the ball over Ray Lingrel for the May Day home opener as well. Frank McGowan arrived from working out with the New Haven Eastern Leaguers in time to go hitless from left field.[103] Among the 10,000 on hand, one Marguerite Stanton provided *The Sentinel* with a comical female perspective of the festivities. Her description of a tired catcher sitting on his heels, waiting for something to happen with a bird cage on his head, aside, Alec McCarthy's dramatic left field drive with one out and two on in the 9th scored Jim Cooney. "Hoot mon!" Brewers won, 2–1.

And all Marguerite could think about was Mr. Borchert in his counting room, counting all his money. Borchert lost so many balls the year before that he had his "silver-tongued announcer," Bozo, offer free passes to anyone returning balls hit into the crowd. Sherry Magee was in charge of the mascot, Snowball, and the club strolled out to a 6–5 start in their "classic" sweater coats. A 5-game slide had Borchert on the hunt for Walberg.

Cooney won himself a pair of Nunn-Bush shoes and a carton of smokes for his Opening Day home run, but a week later, he went to the Cardinals in a trade. Trotting out second division clubs, while pocketing the booty of sold-off potential stars, made Borchert a lightning rod of mounting criticism. Cooney was another dissatisfied operator, who thought his performance earned his sale to the bigs. He dickered with Racine Midwest outlaws, so Otto pulled the trigger on dealing him. The highly regarded bat of Lester Bell was compensation for Cooney's defense and speed at short. Veteran Verne Clemons was desired as defensive backstop backup help.[104]

The modern major league Brewers have never produced a batting champion in their 32-year existence. For all the rap on Borchert's bottom line m.o., he had his second batting champ in three seasons by acquiring Bell.

Countess Heinie, the former Washington Park Zoo elephant, was back in Milwaukee to enthrall the kiddies with the Al G. Barnes Circus. Despite Borchert's prominent attainments, his club looked like a cellar-dwelling white elephant into mid-June.[105]

Borchert now had Walberg from Mack, too, but Ray Lingrel was suspended indefinitely for a KC run-in with Umpire [former pitcher Happy?] Finneran. Tom Hickey abandoned league fines entirely in favor of player suspensions only. The Brewers settled on a true leadoff hitter when Lance Richbourg arrived on the scene. Still, the tail-enders could only draw 1,500 on the post Independence Saturday. Bankroll Louie Nahin could only deny that hurler George (Lefty) Winn hadn't been waived, despite a bloated ERA that let him rarely live up to his name.[106]

The frustrations of the Brewers' flutterances in and out of the cellar were vented directly at Hickey, who personally faced the Borchert protest music, while taking in two at Athletic Park. Colonel shortstop Morrie Shannon was the heart of a ruckus in which he was given new life on a bollixed 3rd strike call in the sixth. Milwaukee led that first game 3-1 at the time, but the Nightriders' cleanup man haunted the Clarks single-handedly to rally a sweep. Shannon had 7 hits.[107]

The public never wavered in their regard for old pepperbox Harry Clark, but he could not summon his club beyond a 7th place tie with Columbus through August. Maybe it was the "happy go lucky" Les Bell, who buoyed them through their hardship? That and a 5-for-11 doubleheader from Lance Richbourg's bat led to a 3-of-4 plundering of Toledo in the dog days of August.[108]

The Rickenbacker Vertical 8 was now sold at Stebbins-Dentz Motor Co. on Van Buren and Martin Streets. Why anyone would ever want to buy a car from someone named "Dentz" is anybody's guess, but the Brewer machine still stalled in last by the turn of September. The clustered standings left them only 3 games out of fourth, however.[109]

Rube Walberg proved to be Milwaukee's most valuable left-winged hick since that goofy Waddell character from the turn of the century. That comparison was made by an old slugger who faced Waddell and now called balls and strikes in the American Association. Buck Freeman was not in an official capacity to enthuse over any player, but thought Walberg fooled hitters as well as Waddell, only with less velocity.[110]

The Brewers used a September 2nd exhibition stop between Kansas City and St. Paul to rope in three recruits. Milwaukee squelched the Mississippi Valley League champion Waterloo Hawks (same nickname as their future N.B.A. franchise), 7-3, then took a "trio of corn shuckers," batting champ Clem Schult and leading flingers Claude Willoughby and Ovid McCracken onto Minnesota. They were now 9 games under .500, but in the first division.[111]

The team crossed the .500 threshold finally in mid-September when Lester Bell piled on a 5-for-8 double day over Kansas City. Catcher Bob McMenemy also rode into the rescue from St. Paul. By the final home 50-50 matinee with the Columbus Senators, the won-over faithful turned to kiss their sisters. They bid "Auf Wiedersehen" to a 1924 club that won as much as it lost.[112] It was the first of two occasions in the Brewers' entire A.A. history that they finished exactly .500.

The first division club's Lester Bell (.365-8-114) led the loop in average, hits, runs, and led the club with 16 triples. Floridian paint brush artist Richbourg chipped in a swift .321, while the top three pitchers went 43-33. Walberg's 175 led the A.A. in strikeouts.[113] Bell's offensive talents were better suited for a 3rd baseman, where he'd shine for the 1926 Cardinal champs.[114]

Baseball's 1924 World Series was plunged into another Black Sox-like scandal when Commissioner Landis traced ex-Brewer-then-Giants coach Cozy Dolan as the instigator. Dolan was implicated by "$75,000 beauty" flyhawk

Jimmy O'Connell in a $500 bribe to Heinie Sand. Three Future Hall of Fame Giants were cleared, but Dolan and O'Connell were ineligible for the Series. Washington celebrated its only World Championship ever and Republican Calvin Coolidge's outright election to the presidency in November. Milwaukee celebrated its even-handed baseball finish by re-electing a socialist mayor who would spread the wealth equally.[115]

One Milwaukee area man unlucky with the Cards was Monches, Wisconsin, outfielder Ralph Shinners. Followed by "Col. Jinx," the injury-prone bounced between the bigs and the A.A. He went down again, with a March 1925 ankle sprain against the P.C.L. Sacramento Senators.[116]

The question mark surrounding the National Pastime's integrity didn't keep Otto Borchert's Buster Brown-cut daughter Florence from making the society page. The Milwaukee-Downer seminary attendee made it for being with her parents at the Brewers' Sanford, Florida, site.[117]

There, the Cincinnati Reds turned Dainty Dinty Gearin's portside arm inside out when a 2nd inning 10-run spree routed the Brewers in a 13–9 exhibition. A new slugger was there, too.

Antonio Bordetzki was born at Remus, Michigan, on July 3, 1892. This Polish powerhouse packed 185 pounds on his six-foot frame. His 3 home run titles and 4 RBI crowns with the Kansas City Blues made his American Association exploits near-Ruthian.

And yet, like the tender-sounding Babe, this newly acquired Milwaukee Brewer went by a baseball sobriquet more suitable to a burlesque dancer at the Empress Theater. Antonio Bordetzki strode mightily to the plate as "Bunny Brief."[118]

Brief removed all doubt as to whom would be Harry Clark's cleanup hitter. From his dead ball start with the West Michigan League Traverse City Resorters in 1910, Bunny racked up Michigan State League home run titles there in 1911-1912, bounced up to the bigs as an outfielder/1st baseman between 1913–1915. In the longer P.C.L. schedule with the Salt Lake City Bees, he hit an unheard of 33 homers and likely faced future Brewer manager Allan Sothoron in 1916.

After a final shot with Pittsburgh, he emerged with the Kansas City Blues. His 1920 manager was now his Brewer 3rd baseman, Alex McCarthy. Another Bunny, Fabrique, was his KC shortstop that year, too. Brief's 1922 total of 42 dingers was the A.A. standard until future Brewer manager Nick Cullop came along for St. Paul in 1930. Brief's 191 RBI from that same outburst were unmatched in A.A. annals and bettered Hack Wilson's 1930 major league record.[119]

In bringing these mountainous credentials to the Brewers, Bunny Brief became a lifelong Milwaukeean after 1925. The adoption of man, fans, and town was mutual. Brief's Brewer feats would surpass Unser Choe Hauser's time in Milwaukee, although Connie Mack called the hometown hero "the most valuable 1st baseman in the American League." Small wonder. Hauser came off a .288–27–115 year, his only fully healthy one in the majors.[120]

If it seems impossible to remain brief about Bunny, "The Tall Tactician" was no less effusive about the Brewers than he was about Unser Choe. It took Mack's Milwaukeeans, Hauser and Al Simmons, to defeat Milwaukee 4–3 at Sanford on Tuesday, March 31st. A Hauser single scored Camera Eye Max Bishop to tie the game, and Simmons' long sacrifice fly made Bing Miller the margin of victory. Earl Smith, who lost a 1–0 no-no with Topeka in 1923 lost this.[121]

Harry Clark still had Sherry Magee around to impart his hitting knowledge. Experts saw Milwaukee as stronger than 1924, but the horse-drawn manicure used by Borchert's Athletic Park caretakers would make a better analogy. The celery capital of Sanford wanted Otto back though.

Brief wagered "two high class straw hat skimmers" that no one could reach the Athletic Park center field bleachers. Alec McCarthy and George Armstrong took him up on it, figuring the Bunny would do it himself.[122]

Such jocularity did not remain between Harry Clark and his one-dimensional fastballer, Dixie Walker. Clark released the indifferent Southerner after a verbal fallout at Fort Meyers.[123] Right-handed Roy Sanders pitched the Tuesday, April 14th opener at his hometown Louisville. Nick Cullop, not the tomato-faced slugger, but the Grand Old portsider of the Kentucky nine,[124] got the better of the native, 3–2. Future pro football Hall of Famer Joe Guyon, the Minnesota Chippewa of Carlisle Indian fame, singled in Cullop's pinch-hitter, Gaffney, for the victory. The Colonels were off for a pennant.

A silent movie playing at Milwaukee's Garden Theater shared a title later used by 1970s blues-rock guitarist Robin Trower. That title, "The Bridge of Sighs," would go a long way to explain Harry Clark's final 1925 season as Brewer manager.[125]

The team just seemed to come up short. An unlucky 13-inning loss at Louisville by another Bell, Herman, was followed by Ray Lingrel's 14-inning defeat at Indianapolis on April 18th. Manning Vaughan, now "Putting 'em on the Pan" for *The Milwaukee Journal*, still believed Clark had a first division club brewing. And in the middle of Prohibition, all Milwaukee's old breweries offered were products like Blatz Malt Extract, Eline (Uihlein) chocolate bars from Schlitz, and Pabst Pale Extra Dry Ginger Ale. A city once also famous for its classical music was now as flat as near beer on both counts.[126]

Two curious streaks bisected at the Tuesday, April 30th opener at Athletic Park. "Barbara Belle," Bunny Brief's big war club, was stifled at an 11-game hit streak, but Oscar Melillo kept an 8-game streak of 2 hits per game, alive.[127] It was the grand slam from center fielder Frank Luce that warmed the 9–3 outcome for the 4,612 cash customers in Alaskan-like air. Before bombarding Columbus, Luce was the Michigan-Ontario ("Mint") League Caliph of Clout.

Vaughan called out Borchert in print for passing on shortstop Tommy Thevenow.[128] Branch Rickey sent Double-T to his own Syracuse farm even after Borchert intimated that he had first dibs on the wayward Card.

Old-timers learned that ex-Brewer Jack (Shad) Barry was now a one-man committee to guide customers to their proper business at a Los Angeles bank. From Hollywood, cowboy Tom Mix rode into Milwaukee to shake hands with *Journal* newsy Wade Dunphy, who outsold his colleagues for the privilege. Otto Borchert was willing to shake hands with anyone willing to take Oscar Melillo for $100,000. Mix also dropped $40 Canadian into a former Spanish-American War cellmate's hands, leaving everyone teary-eyed.[129]

Lil' ol' "Prof." Wid Matthews went from collecting a World Series check on the Washington pine to a 3-year deal as athletic director at Caruthersville, Missouri High School. Matty would teach football, baseball, and track and field at the old Brewer training site in his off-seasons.

Oscar (not-so-Happy) Felsch also made news. He was placed under a year probation on a guilty plea to false swearing in the Joe Jackson case against the White Sox. Felsch, supposedly retired from the game as a roofer, had a perjury charge dismissed. Jackson faced a district court *capias* issued for his arrest for failing to appear on a perjury charge. He played ball in Georgia.[130]

Ray Lingrel was claimed by the Blues and left in Kansas City, where Milwaukee tried to snap a mid-May losing streak. The Brewers raced to St. Paul with President Coolidge, who passed through Milwaukee on a brief June 7th train stop. He didn't wait around to see that Sunday burlesque staged by the Brewers. Newcomer little Al "Heinie" Reitz was pounded off the slab and the Saints' Bruno Haas pillaged his old team for 6 straight hits. It ended 18–3 for St. Paul, but "Bruno likes his base knocks better than a Senegambian loves his watermelon and chicken and he retired from the scene of the combo wearing a large chest and a larger smile."[131]

The Class D Reitz cost Borchert $5,000, but he did stop Carlton Molesworth's Columbus shortstop Fred Nicolai who had reached base 10 straight times. The Brewers slowly dropped as dead as two famous politicos, "Fighting Bob" LaFollette and William Jennings Bryan, that summer. No, Bryan's "Scopes Monkey Trial" didn't settle when catchers evolved to walk upright.[132]

Harry Clark fined shortstop Tom Connolly $100, with a June suspension for insubordination, but replacement Otis Miller paid immediate dividends. He, along with new leadoff center fielder Taylor Douthit, roughed up past Brewers Ray Lingrel and Nels Pott at a July 4th sweep in Kansas City. The holiday 18,000 saw a tamed Blues lineup with ex-Brewer Frank McGowan, future Cubs star Riggs "Hoss" Stephenson, and future Brewers Eddie Pick and Bevo LeBourveau.[133]

Accusations of payroll padding hounded the City of Milwaukee Sewer Department. The Brewers' crawl out of the A.A. sewer, no thanks to hurler

Stubby Mack, so wild that he should've been at the Tennessee monkey trial, was as immense as Gertrude Ederle's English Channel swim.

"One-Eyed" Jim Murray, an A.A. arbiter since 1912, still put up with the abuse to pay off his 5-acre chicken farm outside Minneapolis. The Brewers' broken jinxes of beating St. Paul and doing it in extra innings made life lighter for Otto Borchert. He made peace on the local fistic front by renting Athletic Park for a couple outdoor cards, and the fish were biting at Lake Nagawicka in Waukesha County.[134]

Unlike his first tenure as Brewer manager, Harry Clark didn't throw in the towel during a season of August progress succumbing to a lackluster September. Arkansan Douthit, who starred as a California collegian, was recalled by the Cardinals, which gave a "big LaCrosse Viking" a late preview for the sixth place flounderers.

Oswald Christian Orwoll came from Portland, Oregon, via Luther College in Decorah, Iowa, a poor man's cross between Ernie Nevers and Jim Thorpe. The consummate lefty pitched like Nevers, ran the outfield and basepaths like Thorpe, and was a sound 1st baseman. Old Brewer Eddie Stumpf, from his Merrill, Wisconsin, managing perspective estimated the big blond all-around athlete Wisconsin's greatest semi-pro prospect in the last decade. Stumpf also claimed Ossie refused major league bonus offers of $1,500 to refine his game with Milwaukee.[135]

Orwoll was greeted with a floral horseshoe from Decorah friends when he took over for Douthit on September 23rd. He overcame that traditional good luck curse to double home Brief in his first at-bat versus Minneapolis. Brief's 37 homers, 175 RBI, 105 walks, and 403 total bases were the only championships for Milwaukee. Borchert honored Oscar Melillo at the September 27th curtain call where the Third Ward was expected to march into Athletic Park like columns of Roman legions in praise of their scampering *favorito*.

As much as Borchert might shower him with "an imported case of spaghetti entwined in garlands of garlic," he saw Melillo as a way to rebuild for players, not just a cash windfall.[136]

George F. Downer, who had the curious conflict of interest in coaching the Milwaukee Normal (now University of Wisconsin–Milwaukee) football team, while serving as sports editor of *The Sentinel*, was Borchert's harshest critic. When not lambasting Otto for prematurely selling his stars, Downer set a precedent to be followed in 2002. Calling for a change in ownership, he asked fans to write to his paper with suggestions for how to fix the Brewers.

John "Doc" Lavan left as the KC Blues manager to become that city's epidemiologist. Milwaukee's Col. Billy Mitchell, an army air critic, was relieved from active duty. Harry Clark's Brewer managerial curve went from the wild blue yonder of pennants past now into the sunset.[137]

There seemed no hard and fast formula for piloting pennant success in the American Association. If the old line Mike Kelley or Joe Cantillon-types weren't copping the gonfalon, playing managers like KC's Wilbur Good, the Saints' Nick Allen or Bill Meyer might. Joe McCarthy parlayed his transition from Colonels infielder into Louisville flags and a Hall of Fame career.[138]

To turn all his 7th place wheeling and dealing into something viable, Otto Borchert hired experienced hand Jack Lelivelt, the once outstanding minor league batsmen with the lefty swing. The 1915 A.A. batting champ and 6-year big league reserve hit an eye-popping .416, with 274 hits and 70 doubles during the 1921 Western League Omaha Buffaloes' 170-game schedule.[139] He played under ex-Brewer leaders Jack Egan at KC and Joe Cantillon at the Flour City.

Brewers road secretary Rudy Vizay, the "dancing master," lined up Hot Springs, Arkansas, for spring training. Borchert's boxing background apparently drew defunct middleweight champion Harry Greb and eastern bantamweight Babe Herman (not the ballplayer) to join them.

Bunny Brief never crossed paths with Lelivelt on the Blues, but demonstrated his muscle immediately, socking a couple out for the Regulars over "McCarthy's Shamrocks" in practice.[140] Pongo Joe's host Little Rock Travelers trotted out ex-Brewers George Armstrong, Paul Johnson, and Lena Blackburne, but it was that wild Stubby Mack's 4-hit, 1-zip shutout that opened all eyes. Mack was caught by a young Bill Dickey. Old Dauntless Dave Danforth could thank Brief's fine peg on a dash to third and Ossie Orwoll's "magnificent running catch far back in center field" for keeping him in the game. Danforth was chased by the Southern Leaguers on April 3rd, too.[141]

A dozen squatter families were evicted from their unique Jones Island shanties by the Illinois Steel Co. in Milwaukee, and Athletic Park's new big league dugouts and other remodeling were buried by a late March out-like-a-lion blizzard. The same foot of snow wiped out Brewer exhibition tilts at Terre Haute, Indiana.[142]

Baseball percolated everywhere. Onetime near Brewer Wilbur Braby managed a team of crack Milwaukee amateurs and semi-pros at suburban Menomonee Falls. Glenn Myatt was groomed for Cleveland's right field job by Tris Speaker, so that Luke Sewell caught for shortstop brother Joe's team. Rube Lutzke battled Indy A.A. alum Johnny Hodapp for the Tribe's hot corner.[143]

South Side Milwaukeean Ray Thompson challenged for the Opening Day Brewers catching job, but we have seen Bob McMenemy, and he is us. He replaced debonair Bill Skiff, who became Lil' Orphan Annie before being peddled to the Yanks. Russ Young backed up big Bob.[144]

Manning Vaughan's now foolish-sounding prognostications, along with baseball scores, could be heard on "The Umpire" every Sunday at 7 p.m. on WHAD Radio. It became a tradition to identify Brewer player pictures in Opening Day booster ads to win season passes. The Elks Club welcome home banquet was an institution, due in part to Borchert's membership.[145]

Athletic Park was adorned in icicles, when Borchert and Lelivelt were greeted with floral horseshoes that Wednesday, April 14th. The 6,500 partisans hoped their 1926 natty white-and-blue Brewers were a breath of fresh air. What they got was an arctic chill of a 10–5 whipping by good, gray Louisville. Maybe Vaughan's dreary treadmill prediction was correct?[146]

Little Filipino boxer Sencio Moldez died after a match at Milwaukee's Auditorium. The Colonels then did Milwaukee up like so many punch-drunk thugs with a 10–0 May Day thrashing. Milwaukee's finest grew so tired of watching inept pros that the police formed a handful of their own precinct teams. Among the talent in blue were semi-pro Walter Techel, former Three-I Leaguer Bill Enright, former Army player Arnold Baars, former Brewer Richard Klein, and Charlie Felsch, the notorious Happy's brother.[147]

"Co-operation will MAKE MILWAUKEE MIGHTIER, will you help?" The civic campaign promoting its pillars of goods and services, "substantial progressive institutions and public spirited citizens," must have been brought to bear upon the baseball club representing the city.

If Milwaukee could have the largest appraisal company and mutual life insurance company in the world and lead in the manufacture of everything from silk hosiery and work shoes, to outboard boat motors and large gas engines, steam and water turbines to heavy excavation and rock crushing equipment, to auto parts and streetcar brakes to refrigeration, heavy pumping, cement, and saw mill machinery to heavy lubricating equipment, hydro-electric units, electric controls, wheelbarrows, and even trunks, why in hell couldn't it lead the American Association?[148]

If the beautiful, thrifty, and prosperously diversified city that was the second largest and only municipally-owned harbor on the Great Lakes could thumb its nose at the economic effects of Prohibition, why, oh why couldn't it do likewise to the rest of the A.A. pack?

It was a curious place that could produce a resilient, husky North Sider like Rube Lutzke who hung on in the majors after a rash of health setbacks. It was a place that would never adopt pro football for its own, relying upon the benevolence of a certain Bellicose Belgian up north.

Milwaukee was a place that had given the world Gilda Gray, the Polish Cudahy girl who was the exotically bare-midriffed "Shimmy Queen" of stage and screen. Yet its baseball club was a conundrum. Civic forecasts of a 3 million metro population by 1950 were loopy as Vaughan.[149]

The dichotomy was reflected in the May 23rd breaking of Bunny Brief's 26-game hitting streak at Minneapolis. They could dash all the way to .500 and 6th place. They finally coalesced by Memorial Day. Dandy Dave Danforth won their 10th straight when the "Larrupin' Lels" larruped the Saints, 6–3. The first air mail route to Milwaukee soared and so did the Brewers' season.

The modern George Webb hamburger chain promise of free burgers should the Brewers win 12 straight did not yet exist, but after demoting former bullpen king Grits McCracken to Alec McCarthy's Three-I League Springfield Senators, Milwaukee made the Millers lucky 13! Bunny Brief's 9th inning tie homer to center turned the Sunday, June 6th 11,000 maniacal. McMenemy's 10th inning double "splashed" off the left field fence to set up Lance Richbourg's delivery of him. Norseman Ossie Orwoll overcame a poor mound start to work versatile wonders for Lelivelt.[150]

Columbus had future Brewer skip Nick Cullop now in their outfield, but Ivy Griffin's two homers nailed number 17. A storm of 1,200 bugs fawned all over their new heroes at a Knights of Columbus dinner. Henry J. Killilea praised their "splendid sportsmanship," while an unusually modest Otto Borchert could only look like a sly dog.

Fritz Schulte's 9th inning triple off the Senators' auburn-haired Cuban, Emilio Palmero, made 18 in a row for the rumbling GMC Big Brute truck that was Pepper John's speed boys. The Chicago-born Dutchman gave Borchert reason to strum his muse and mull memoirs of a first pennant. The *Journal* put sportswriter Sam Levy on their WHAD radio station at Marquette University to actually broadcast the sensational Brewers' games live.[151]

Anyone who could afford a Cine-Kodak would've wanted their own motion picture record of their league-leading exploits. And still they weren't done! Some 5,000 had to be turned away from the misty double cannonade over Columbus. This surpassed a White Sox 19-game run of several years before and the Brewers were within the 1916 Giants' wonder streak of 26. Fritz Schulte's hefty "Tillie Teutonia" whaled out 4 hits, including a homer in the 11–4 opener. Gearin was magically effective as Game Two starter Orwoll and each allowed only a hit apiece in the 6-inning 6–3 bookend.[152] The 14,484 was topped only by a 1913 crowd of 14,901.

Only rain and right fielder/manager Casey Stengel's Toledo Mud Hens could slow "Baron Borchert's Brigade" down. Chilly breezes kept the Tuesday, June 14th attendance to 4,000, but lightweight shortstop Lloyd Flippin's 3 safeties made a 9–1 "Mudhen a la mode" for Roy Sanders.

Anyone photographing the event in color should've thanked newly-deceased Miss Florence Warner for it. Her father and she developed the process 20 years earlier in Milwaukee.[153]

It was dandelion time in the Athletic Park neighborhood, "where every good *hausfrau* forsakes the pumpernickel board on these June mornings to brew the wine of the dandelion and store up *katzenjammers* for next winter." Borchert had 20 youths digging those weeds from his outfield. Under his watchful eye, "an innocent bystander" quizzed him on the cost of such labor. The astute financial wizard replied, "Oh, not so much... You see, I let them keep the dandelions."

Such benevolence and beverages flowed freely from a 21-game American Association record win streak, even if the Hens snapped it the next day, 9–6, without Stengel in the lineup.[154]

Old Elmer "Ty" Lober, the "ball player's player," who used to tread the dandelions at 8th and Chambers, abandoned Pongo Joe's Little Rocks in the White Mule Belt for Racine's outlaws.

Were Lelivelt's Brewers really as good as their streak, where Silent Joe Eddelman won 5, and Gearin, Sanders, Orwoll, and Danforth each won 4? Or were they as lucky as Manilla Jackson, a 35-year old well-dressed negress, who found an envelope at 4th and Wells with $1,000?

Harry Clark sent wishes from Paulding, Ohio, that his old club win it all in a walk. Louisville owner Col. Bill Knebelkamp was less gracious, offering Borchert "enough Armour company grease gratis to keep your team slipping." The Baron von Nagawicka's expletives labeled Knebelkamp a "round-headed Dutchman," a "square head," and a "lucky stiff," among other things.[155]

The bombast between the muckety-mucks paled compared to the attention paid by an official Athletic Park record crowd of 15,502 on Sunday, June 20th. Knebelkamp had the ace up his sleeve as his defending champion "Kurnels" high-handed a pair and dropped the Lels into second. An overflow watched 4 hours of ball, with 2,000-3,000 turned away. The Brewers were within 18,000 of their 1925 total by late June.[156]

"DamnedifIknow" became the rallying cry the rest of the way. Everyone from the barber, the grocer, the butcher to the bootlegger was puzzled. The quiet, gentlemanly Lelivelt was "turned in" by umpire Dolly Derr for one meek protest and Borchert glommed "The Undertaker," Claude Jonnard, for right-handed pitching reinforcement from the St. Louis Browns.[157]

Neither 180,000 women at a Chicago outdoor mass nor "abducted" Evangelist Aimee Semple McPherson had enough prayers to dislodge the entrenched Colonels. Louisville had a colorful contingent of its own, with Bruno Betzel, Pinky Pittenger, future majors' record-setter for doubles (and future Brewer) Earl Webb, Cuban Melito Acosta, and Okie Indian Ben Tincup.[158]

History did not bode well for the Brewer record-breakers. Those 1916 Giants finished no better than 4th. Just keeping the talk of the baseball world together was an obstacle. Orwoll denied signing a '24 contract with Texas League Dallas. Second sacker Clyde Beck was recalled by the Cubs, one of four pivot men used during the year. Fred Schulte still led the A.A. at .405, in mid-July, when the Browns came calling for a 1927 deal.[159]

A twin win at KC put Milwaukee 1½ up on July 19th and a Brief homer at Toledo kept the pace. The Colonels snatched infielder Danny Boone from the house cleaning Blues before Milwaukee. Danny Boone was probably a better fit for Kentucky, anyway. The winning Blues swept house because management thought they lacked "color." The Brewers had no such shortage as the league's best road attraction.[160]

Schulte battled Toledo's LeBourveau for the batting lead, but both fell under .400 by August 1st. Bevo contracted pleurisy, but that's no excuse. Roy Sanders' bat, not his arm, kept Indy biting at Brewer ankles and another big

August 17th turnout saw Ownie Bush's Indian hopes rolled, 11–7. The Texas League Beaumont Exporters tied Milwaukee's 1925 Organized Baseball record of turning 193 double plays, and it was only late August.[161]

Dashing Jack's speedy A.A. stolen base leader, Lance Richbourg, couldn't outrun KC's Ginger Shinault and his 4-for-4 revenge to push his old Brewers out of first at Muehlebach Field. Premature talk about facing the unknown Toronto International League champs was booted away at the September 9th St. Paul game before visiting Al Simmons. Remarkably, Indy owner Bill Smith, Jr. came under Milwaukee fans' fire for selling 4-eyed ace Carmen Hill. It was thought his move conceded the flag to Louisville, and the Brewers 12–6 pasting of Ferdie Schupp in Indiana assuaged no one. Schulte was hurt and Orwoll cleared of his Dallas distraction when Louisville took 2-of-3 on Knebelkamp's knoll, fending the Brewers off to 3rd place.[162]

The flaxen-haired Orwoll, winner of 14 baseball, football, and basketball letters at Luther College, was gently chastised by Vaughan in print for risking his southpaw on National Football League gridirons with the Milwaukee Badgers.[163] He emulated Ernie Nevers' course from Browns flinger to Duluth stevadore to Eskimos' fullback, but Orwoll only carried the ball thrice, attempted three passes and caught one in two games as a 6-foot, 165-pound halfback.[164]

Milwaukee's answer to Bo Jackson and Deion Sanders was back for 1927 as was Lelivelt. After 3 years at Tulsa and Omaha success, Jack received a Willys-Knight Great Six Sedan from Milwaukee Willys-Overland branch manager Perry C. Gartley and area dealers.[165]

If Gene Tunney's upset of Jack Dempsey seemed stunning that autumn, it was nothing compared to the shocking delay of the Brewers 1927 home opener.

The very March 2nd that Babe Ruth signed an astronomical 3-year, $210,000 contract, Otto Borchert saw 8 of his men off to Hot Springs. Even Fred "King" Lear was back in the good graces of Judge Landis and Borchert. The fun and frivolity included Rudy Vizay's iron black bowler being bowled under by a medicine ball, while upon Denny Gearin's noggin. "It took a plumber and half the club to pry the wee Mick out of the wreckage."[166] Rudy bought the dandy hat at Chicago's World's Fair. With a stiff upper lip, he said he needed a new one anyhow.

In the age of scantily-clad flappers, women's liberation took another turn as Peggy Williamsen, a basketball guard on the Marquette varsity, wrote a *Journal* women sports column.[167]

From a water-logged trip up to a Nashville "wetter than a third ward cellar" to the grandest opening ever at Toledo, 15,000 saw Stengel's Hens fall 9–2 to Milwaukee on Jonnard's 3-hitter and new infielder Harry Riconda's 4 hits of his own. All was wondrous, save Umpire George Magerkurth's Sunday, April 24th personal beating of Ivy Griffin outside his Indianapolis hotel room. After print demands for it, Magerkurth was released.[168]

Borchert and Lelivelt appealed that Milwaukee finally win the A.A. opener attendance cup, something it had never done, despite being the league's largest city. When the 7–5 team arrived home for its banquet, one black face was in the picture. "Doctah" Buckner or "Doc" was now the trainer for the next 11 years. He was once referred to as George Washington Buckner, but he was known as Harry Buckner by his death. If he was the latter, he may have been a prominent, turn of the century pitcher in Negro baseball.[169]

The merry gathering of 600 fans at that Wednesday, April 27th Elks banquet came to an enthusiastic head when the Brewers' impresario, its colorful poobah, Otto Borchert gave an address full of his usual wit and sarcasm.

Just plain Otto recalled his early business career: "I always made it a point to be loyal to my employees and," slumping into his chair, he tried rising to his feet, mumbling, "give them the best I had." He then tumbled into the arms of Elks exalted ruler Chauncey Yockey and Mud Hens president Richard Meade seated to his right.[170]

The ensuing chaos startled radio listeners, hearing his talk live. The unconscious mason was passed over the crowd as everyone tearily sang "Auld Lang Syne." City health commissioner John P. Koehler, a previous speaker, and two other doctors tried vainly for a half-hour to resuscitate Borchert. but he died 5 minutes after collapse of a cerebral hemorrhage.

The front page headline blared: "OTTO BORCHERT STRICKEN AT DINNER, DIES" Only his closest friends knew of any recent complaints of ill health and it was wondered if he had a premonition of his dramatic exit.

After toastmaster Patrick Bowler's lyrical introduction made platitudes about Borchert's generous loyalty and "harps" and "beatitude," Otto only smiled at the good-natured chaffing to remark. "When they say all those fine things about me, I won't be here to hear them." The memorial altar tribute to deceased brother Elks had been his gift.

Otto Borchert has been mistakenly characterized in some baseball books as a man Milwaukee "loved to hate." The outpouring of adulation at his death refutes that. The multiple social club member, who was happiest as a "$50 a month drummer," parlayed his good ear as a traveling salesman into a $300,000 commission and bonus. That option on the Waterloo Gas Works plant sale to the Deere Plow Co. gave him the means to buy the Brewers.

He passed on an English linen deal that might have made him a millionaire, but he was content to raise his White Rock chickens in the converted skaters' dressing room at Athletic Park and become the envy of every baseball magnate for turning $250,000 in talent to the majors. He was more of a kid magnet, telling those at the ballpark for the umpteenth time that it was their last free game. They were prominent among the hundreds to display their grief at his visitation.

From John W. Radke's funeral chapel at 4304 W. Lloyd St. to the Elks Club memorial service which drew 3,000 people, among them a "Who's Who" of the baseball community and Milwaukee officialdom, the 52-year old Borchert's unwieldy police cortege out to his Northwest Side Valhalla Cemetery burial place hardly smacked of someone unpopular.[171]

His players attended as a team, as did ex-managers Bill Friel and Harry Clark, who applied to Tom Hickey for an umpiring job. Among his actual pallbearers were Fred "Shorty" Mendelson (future overseer of Milwaukee County Stadium) and Louis Nahin. Wisconsin's new governor Fred Zimmerman broke away from South Side youthful recollections of smoking his grandpa's tobacco to attend. Burial commenced Saturday, April 30th.

The Brewers postponed their opening series with Toledo and the Elks canceled a boxing show. Athletic Park groundskeeper Roman Bartz lowered the flag to half-mast until the opening series with Columbus was finished. Widow Ruby Borchert retained permanent ownership of the ballpark, but the ballclub's affairs were handled by Henry Killilea, who'd purchase her interest.[172]

Otto Borchert's shocking departure left Lindsay Hoben thanking Sir Walter Scott[173]:

> THE VACANT CHAIR
>
> Sportsman, rest! Thy game is o'er
> Sleep the sleep that knows no breaking
> Dream of baseball fields no more
> Days of worry, nights of waking
> Watch no more the rolling ball
> From thy lone and lofty seat
> Strike three. Out. The ninth. That's all
> No more vict'ry nor defeat
> Sportsman well thou played thy game,
> Played until the ninth was past;
> No more chaffing, no more blame
> Rest, the game is done at last

Perhaps the biggest tribute to "poor Otto" Borchert, as Manning Vaughan called him, were the 15,282 who renewed the season at Athletic Park. Out of respect, none of the usual hubbub of the first pitch or march to the pennant pole took place. Lelivelt was given a chest of cutlery by admirers, as well as the surprise gift of a $100 wristwatch that Borchert intended. Among the players with black crepe on their sleeves, Harry Strohm made the 8–3 decision over Columbus his own. Strohm sliced the Senators' Pie Biemiller for 3 hits, driving in 4 runs.[174]

If the Brewers were to dedicate their season to their fallen boss man, they were slow to realize it. Old Unser Joe Hauser was back in the A.A., but was no longer Our Joe as he was Kansas City's. He gave his hometown Brewers the blues by a smashing an historic homer, the first over Muehlebach Field's wall in a regulation joust. It was 70 feet inside the foul line and a full 15 feet in the air when it went over the wall into the center of the street.[175]

The first inning smash came off his old roommate Denny Gearin, and was rewarded by Blues' owner George Muehlebach with a $20 gold piece. It took Babe Ruth some 20 shots at that fence before he could break that barrier in batting practice. Kaysee officials estimated it to be a 500-foot blow and Manning Vaughan wrote that it was the longest drive he had yet witnessed in 20 years of baseball. Oh, and Dutch Zwilling's Blues copped the May 15th game, 5–2, too.[176]

Crusty John McGraw belied his public image by aiding old tubercular Mike Donlin.[177] Borchert's frugal ghost seemed psychic about Dave Danforth's decline, having cut his salary only to load up with incentives of $5,000-6,000 before his passing. Lelivelt added fast outfielder George "Pickles" Gerken in June, who'd turn up again with the '31 Brewers. Like Joe Hauser, the Columbus' K.K.K., Kedzie "Kloutem" Kirkham was another former Brewer to dog his old team.

Lel guarded against stolen signals during a mid-June 5-game surge to second. Charles Lindbergh was now all the rage, his Transatlantic flight spawning imitators.[178] Dainty Gearin showered encouragement upon young slab mate Hank Johnson. The Everglades sheik failed under terse Nick Allen at St. Paul, but soaked up the milk of human kindness in the Cream City to be vital to the rotation. Silent Joe Eddelman quietly had 11 wins by July 4th, due to Bunny Brief's bat.

Otto Borchert's "Kohinoor of them all," Fred Schulte, broke his wrist with the St. Louis Browns and even more ex-Brewer Ty Lober took a pitching turn for Two Rivers against the semi-pro Wausau Lumberjacks. Borchert's 1922 signing of bashful Al Simmons, now an A.L. monster, was recalled at $150 a month for 5 months. Otto got $42,500 from the A's for Bucketfoot.[179]

Casey Stengel's league-leading Toledo Mud Hens were plucked before a Sunday, July 10th doubleheader Milwaukee record crowd of 16,178. Claude "Bubber" Jonnard (his big league catching brother, Clarence, actually went by that nickname) made feathers fly with his own homer, among 20 hits in the 18–1 Game One and Ossie Orwoll neatly threw a 4–1 afterpiece.[180]

"The Undertaker" Jonnard danced with no-hit fame at St. Paul on Wednesday, July 27th when lax outfielding by Frank Wilson and Bunny Brief left him with a 2-hit, 2–1 escape.[181] The 22-game winning Jonnard led Brewer barnstormers in post-season play against the Lake Shore Kramers. An All-Milwaukee Barnstormers outfit traveled to face Lober's Two Rivers with Al Simmons, Joe Hauser, Ralph Shinners of Oakland's P.C.L. champs, Rube Lutzke, and Ray Thompson with Brewer Lloyd Flippin, the Browns' Oscar Melillo, pitchers Tony Welzer of the BoSox and Eddie Schaack now with KC. Former Cub Mandy Brooks and catcher Bernie Tesmer also joined.[182]

In the year of Babe Ruth's 60 home runs, Jack Lelivelt's Brewers had to wait for Otto Borchert to die before their potent offense rendered its best 99-win, 2nd place tie with KC of the decade. Stengel's Mud Hens faced the I.L.

6 — Borchert's Orchard

Ex-Brewers Eddie Stumpf (Mgr., *center*) and his brother Benny Stumpf (C, *2nd from back right*), and Eddie Schaack (P, *front left*) are among the familiar names on this Union Oil & Supply Co. club of the 1928 Wisconsin State League. Future *Milwaukee Sentinel* sports editor Lloyd Larson is third from back right and is "Heine Groh" (*2nd front left*) the longtime National Leaguer? Was "Bill" Braby (*2nd from front right*) ex-Brewers Wilbur Braby? Milwaukee Public Library Historical Photograph Collection.

Buffalo Bisons in the 1927 post-season. Any clouds over Athletic Park were puffs of joy from Otto's stogie.[183] Harry Riconda led the A.A. in hits and doubles, Orwoll in win percentage, while hitting .370.

Milwaukee's hotbed of baseball bloodlines expanded in 1928. Al Simmons' brother, Walter, had a Brewer tryout and Joe Hauser's lefty pitching 1st baseman of a kid sibling George inked up with Cedar Rapids of the Mississippi Valley League. The city's Jack Kloza, winner of batting titles in 3 leagues, had a rendezvous with Washington, but would soon be a Brewer.[184]

Pants Rowland, the old Milwaukee Panther, looked to join the A.A. as an umpire after several years of arbiting detail in the American League. Jack Lelivelt redid half his lineup again at Hot Springs. King Lear's red flannel undershirt was gone but not forgotten, but Spence Adams, a Utah cowboy, lassoed the 2nd base job. Otis Miller gave it a second shot at short. Eddie Pick was valuable utility strength as an outfield starter, flanked by Frank Luce and light-hitting leadoff man Herschel Bennett from the Browns. Bennett keyed Lel's Tulsa pennant winners.[185]

Harry Riconda was up with Brooklyn, Orwoll joined Connie Mack, and Hank Johnson pitched in the Yankee rotation. Those two arms were replaced by a pair of St. Louis Browns. Owner Philip DeCatesby Ball now had a direct interest in the Brewers, so his 3rd-year "Old Pard" of Kentucky, Noble Winfield Ballou, and 4th-year Alabama lefty Ernie Wingard came on.[186]

Unlike Milwaukee's last known cowboy, the bourbon-guzzling Virgil Garvin at the turn of the century, the vagabond Adams was a multi-sport star at the University of Utah. Yo-yoing in and out of the majors, with 6 clubs in 6 years, he only laughed, "I guess I can only fool 'em one year at a time." He came with Miller, also down from the Browns.[187]

Lelivelt's Arkansas camp was a laid back allowance of golf, poker, and if found in those prohibitive times, the occasional beer. Hard booze was an absolute no-no, but Jack was like Harry Clark in wanting early risers for a game that was still played only in daylight.[188]

Ivy Griffin's throwing was back on track after he pulled his shoulder in the 1927 "Bushelhead" Magerkurth tete-a-tete. The tall 1st baseman paid for a bulls-eye to the bullish ump's eye. Manning Vaughan longed for the "bally-hoo" of Otto Borchert and pondered the diminished impact of his fellow Irishmen upon an increasingly diverse National Pastime. His Jewish editor Sam Levy received 9,125 letters in 1927, Vaughan, 9,011. The Irishman now in charge of the Brewers, Henry Killilea, thought a duplication of the splendid 1927 pennant chase was possible.[189]

Some 90 miles south, Chicago conducted a gangland-style, ballot-stuffing election of murder and kidnapping mayhem. And Hey! Hey! Gilda Gray was back home at the Davidson Theater with a company of 16 to promote her Tibetan-set photoplay, "The Devil Dancer." The "Queen of Syncopation, Vibration, and Undulation" couldn't have been any more wild and crazy than the Tuesday, April 10th slugfest opener at Columbus.[190]

Win Ballou started against Nemo Leibold's choice, George Lyons, but a half-dozen pitchers between both clubs shook out an 11–10 Brewer blitz in ten. A Harry Strohm single scored Eddie Pick for the permanent lead. Milwaukee overcame 3 errors with 19 hits.[191]

In light of Branch Rickey's developing St. Louis Cardinal chain and the Indianapolis experiment with Three-Eyed Quincy, Illinois, the Brewers again contemplated their own farm club. Old Buster Braun still peppered the pill on a Sheboygan mound when Bunny Brief exercised his bunions at the Friday, April 27th Athletic Park opener.[192] Two home run trots by the North Side Pole around the basepaths and those Columbus Senators thrilled 10,000 fans. Future Brewer Walt "Cuckoo" Christensen was among the Buckeye fly-chasers with no fly to chase.

"Rosie at the bat" aptly fit the noontime women's factory baseball games between the Schulz Box Co. and the National Knitting Co. The right to vote and flapping weren't enough.

Claude Jonnard's 1-hitter against the Kaws capped a 5-game mid-May streak to tie KC again for second. The Blues mixed up-and-comers Joe Kuhel and Joe Cronin at the corners with vets Topper Rigney and Bill Wambsganss up the middle. Wamby had that legendary 1920 World Series unassisted triple play for Cleveland.[193]

Wallpaper went 8¢ a roll, men's broadcloth shirts for $1.69. Young Milwaukeean Pat O'Brien graced the Davidson Theater stage in "Broadway," en route to playing a cinematic Knute Rockne. General Rufus King, Milwaukee's baseball pioneer, was remembered as an early U.W. regent. A Cadillac at the 8th and Wells Jonas dealership went for $1,950, and nearby meat market man Butch Luer recalled the Lloyd Street Brewers of 30 years earlier. The contemporaries were just fine.[194]

Lelivelt's cries for pitching help fell on Connie Mack's deaf ears, so while waiting on the Browns, Den Gearin was back from an International League Rochester shutout after they refused to pay $4,000 for his release.

Few in the Athletic Park stands recognized a suspended Casey Stengel in his civvies because they were too busy watching Bob McMenemy pilfer Toledo signs. Stifling the Mud Hens running attack that August 19th meant an 8–4 Brewer win, 3½ games behind first place Indy.[195] Who but ex-Brewer little Wid Matthews should step up with 2 Indians on at Minneapolis and sock his 12th homer in 9 years! His clout bagged a 10–8 scalp for Indianapolis.

Milwaukeean Edward Wilmer was now president of the Dodge Motor Co. and voting machines were first tested in the city of Milwaukee. If only the Brewers were elected the pennant! Instead, they relied on a 7-game spurt and 10 straight wins over the Kaws that Labor Day at Kansas City. Toledo's 1926 A.A. batting champ, DeWitt "Bevo" LeBourveau was now on fire, as Milwaukee's center fielder batting third. "Slug" Strohm's 4-for-5 opener and newly acquired Guy Sturdy's hook slide of home on an Otis "Tubby" Miller pinch-hit single won the nightcap. That made Ernie Wingard the winningest pitcher in the circuit, with 22 triumphs.[196]

"Slow Music, Professor, Brewers Lose Another." No, Casey Stengel had nothing to do with that headline, but a Joe Eddelman floater parked over the rounded Lexington Park roof at St. Paul, by Hy Davis, did. On September 10th, Milwaukee's pennant hopes went out of sight, also.[197] Gone, just like the shocking passing of 36-year old Yankee spitballer Urban Shocker.

That 1928 was the sort of season when Bob McMenemy could be scared into missing a bag, during a July home run trot, by a 3-foot high 6-year-old patting him on the back and a late September postgame fire, in the stands behind home plate, nearly brought a new ball park, thanks to a dropped cigar or cigarette.

Brewer attendance had the wind knocked out of it, just like a St. Paul line drive did to Win Ballou's stomach. The 3rd place club was ignored by circuit writers for A.A. All-Star selections. To play for the Brewers was to make "21 ski-doo." For 3 years in a row, the player who wore No. 21 went to The Big Show: Schulte in '26, Orwoll in '27, and now Wingard to the A's. Al Simmons' cameo for the Kosciusko Reds drew 4,000 to their South Side ballpark, but Jonnard and Gearin "hurled air-tight ball" in the 4-hit, 3–0 exhibition.[198]

Milwaukee's 81-year old Catholic Archbishop Sebastian G. Messmer (for whom a high school is named) came back from two months at his Swiss hometown to say that they were puzzled by American Prohibition. Swiss alcohol was state-controlled, but had he seen the Brewers' limp to the wire, he may have sought something stronger than sacramental wine![199]

Henry Killilea had thanked fans and the press for their 1928 "liberal support." The old Milwaukee Road attorney, associated with Milwaukee baseball for over 30 years and who had tasted the pinnacle of Boston's 1903 victory in the first World Series, died in the off-season. His 27-year-old daughter, Miss Florence Killilea, became the third woman president of the Milwaukee Brewers in the last 16 years.[200]

Phil Ball's St. Louis Browns came off a winning year, but their perennial ne'er do well nature now trickled down to Milwaukee's "Little Browns North." At Hot Springs, Joe Hauser even homered for the old home team, as did "Old Ironsides" McMenemy and Eddie Pick hit two, too, in a crazed 19–13 batathon over the Little Rock Travelers. Milwaukee, the city later associated with TV's nostalgic "Happy Days," offered hometown pitcher Al Fons a 10-game opportunity. Ayyy… This Fons would only go 1–0 with that chance.[201]

Manning Vaughan was as inaccurate in calling Toledo's pitching staff, with free agent Ernie Wingard's addition, one of the minors' greatest ever, as he was picking Milwaukee for fourth. The stock market, despite economic developments in radio and infant television, already wavered in late March and 10,000 Milwaukeeans lost power on April Fool's, the worst sleet storm in 8 years. Still, things looked "Rosy" for Lelivelt's veteran, A.A. right-hander Bill Ryan.[202]

He didn't stay that way, either, for very long. The futility of Prohibition was such that Jack applied an iron fist in a Lelivelt glove. Virgil Barnes claimed he only broke up a buddy's fight, that he wasn't drunk himself, when Lelivelt dismissed him. Another red flag.

Losing to Pants Rowland's Southern League Nashville Vols was another. Milwaukee's first division chances were as dead as former Panther-Miller-Fairie hurler Tom Phillips was from Bright's disease. The Pennsylvanian had just been reinstated by Judge Landis for outlaw ways.[203]

Hauser's status was also in Landis' hands, but he forced Ivy Griffin to right in the 10–6 opening loss before 8,000 Indianapolis sun bathers. Future pro football Hall of Famer Morris "Red" Badgro led off as Milwaukee's center fielder. Griffin was sold to Louisville for $4,500, only to return before season's end.[204] A familiar baseball name, Jim Perry, owned that Indy tribe.

Griffin was the Colonels' 1st baseman at the Tuesday, May 2nd Athletic Park opener. Wintry blasts drew a scant 3,000, but didn't prevent prior U.W. coed Miss Florence Killilea from throwing the first ball from the grandstand. She wouldn't drop Ladies Day, as was suggested.[205] Louisville's all-Milwaukee battery of German-born Tony Welzer and Ray Thompson anchored a 4–4 tie, called after 13 innings for darkness. Darkness enveloped the rest of the season, really.

Ex-Brewer Al "Bucketfoot" Simmons, now a famous big leaguer, dedicates a Sturtevant, Wisconsin, field in his honor, May 8, 1929. Milwaukee Public Library Historical Photograph Collection.

Florence was red hot with excitement after newcomer Herb "Sonny Boy" Cobb's May 13th 5–0 gem over Toledo's Wingard. "Wasn't that a wonder? I think that was the most thrilling game I ever saw." Stengel's dead-last-to-be Hens wore gray-and-purple flannels, ridiculed as racetrack "carnival costumes."[206]

It was the Brewers who deserved ridicule as their season crashed like the stock market would in October. Jack Lelivelt's high personal standards drove him to resign from the 22–38 seventh place disaster. He could only wish former Federal Leaguer and St. Paul shortstop Marty Berghammer luck. The explicit Bergy's fiery expectations of hustle were no better answer. Florence Killilea pooh-poohed swirling local interests that her ballclub was on the market.[207]

7
Framed in Black

The consequences of the October 1929 stock market crash loomed over the economy and baseball. Some companies, like the world record-setting pipe welders at A.O. Smith in Milwaukee and White Rock Mineral Springs in Waukesha, grew in the face of overall collapse. Al Jolson pitched toasted Lucky Strikes as a lead pipe cinch against gaining weight. In a nation of frayed nerves, that meant a 20 percent net jump for the American Tobacco Co. by March 1930. Even Amelia Earhart promoted Veedol motor oil, proving everyone was out to get theirs before the crash (the stock market's, not Amelia's).[1] Conditions drove people, all the more, to seek liquid solace in illegal speakeasies.

Baseball's response to their threatened attendance was to get juiced, only in a legally agreed way. The ball, itself, already livelier since 1920, had its core even more tightly wrapped. It jumped off the bat, as to be called "rabbit ball." Offensive numbers again went out of sight.[2]

Incredibly, the National League Brooklyn Robins considered selling their left-handed slugger, who would most benefit from this development. Daffy outfielder Babe Herman held out for $25,000 a year when Robin President Frank B. York put him on the block that March.[3] Like Brooklyn, the Milwaukee Brewers also trained that 1930 in Florida at Fort Pierce. *The Milwaukee Sentinel* now had Amos "Red" Thisted on their baseball beat, which he would tread the rest of the Brewers' A.A. days in Milwaukee.

The "Home Brews," as he called them (occasionally "Near Brews"), certainly had to be rebuilt. Florence Killilea and Lou Nahin gave Marty Berghammer every chance to shed the shiftless weight that burdened the end of the 1920s. Berghammer kept even more of a lid on his camp than Jack Lelivelt, giving the O.K. to two-bit poker, but banning crapshooting. Teammates in financial hock to one another were a source of distraction, to say the least.[4]

Things weren't so regimented that a veteran like Rosy Ryan couldn't be on the butt end of a practical joke. Seems a small bullfrog was caught and placed in one of Ryan's personal socks, while he was out on the field. Bill, as Wilfred was also known, erupted into his paranoia of snakes when toes met frog slime.

Popular black trainer Doc Buckner ended up with the "sportive pair of silk socks" that were once Ryan's.[5]

How odd that black men couldn't share the locker room as players, but one was allowed to rub these white Brewers down with the ministrations of his hands and lotions. That sort of socks hijinx was unlikely between the Milwaukee Electric Co. "girls," who chose up sides for indoor baseball. As unlikely as finding life on newly-discovered Pluto.[6]

Amazing as it seemed, in the face of hard times, the tradition of ballplayers holding out went unabated. The Brewers were taken to school by their parent Browns in spring exhibition play, but appeared to solve their unstable 2nd base situation. Ever since Oscar Melillo's graduation to the Browns, Milwaukee tried a patchwork parade, where no one played the position 2 years running. Pete Turgeon was hoped to be an answer via Wichita Falls. Melillo's infield partner Frank O'Rourke was in line as next Brewer skip, unbeknownst to anyone at this point.

Three Wisconsinites were given tryouts on the mound: Oscar Stark, a "mountainous" Watertown right-hander; Oshkosh right-hander Alvin Retzlaff, and Milwaukee's own amateur southpaw, Ralph Blatz. Was he from Amber Private Stock? What better name for a Brewer? Only Stark and Blatz would see any A.A. regular action, the latter was optioned to the Western Association Springfield (Mo.) Midgets by June 1st.[7]

Fort Pierce had its shortcomings and Nahin was as discriminatory as investors in the past panic market. The Brewers broke camp now as Berghammer's team, one that had only infielder Ed Grimes, outfielder "Black Tom" Jenkins, and catcher Russ Young back as regulars. The institution known as Ivy Griffin had his first base shoes filled by another Southerner, a slight North Carolinian named Buck Stanton. A mere 150 lbs. hung on 5'-10" Dan Bloxsom was an unusual power source in the infield. F(Red) Bennett and Cuckoo Christensen, ol' Seacap, were part of the outfield beautification committee. Milwaukeean Anton "Tony" Kubek (Sr.) got his first look.[8]

Another Pole, burly Ed Strelecki, was the club's lone winning moundsman for 1930. The relief work of Strelecki and Gearin faltered, along with starter Rosy Ryan, in the 11–2 opening humbler at Louisville on Tuesday, April 15th. Jenkins had 3 of 5 Milwaukee hits.[9]

The "Bunny Brief Cigars" did much better in the St. Anthony Home bowling league back home. They topped the Smukowski Tog Shops, Keystone Prints, and Mueller Markets.[10]

One sign of how the 1930 season would go was in Nahin's $10,000 purchase of Detroit Tiger catcher Merv Shea. Shea wasn't good enough to play over Russ Young. Rabbits, however, multiplied all over in the late April series at Indianapolis. Shortstop Rabbit Warstler was the leadoff Indian and likewise was Stan "Rabbit" Benton for the Brewers. The Indians met the wrath of potent pinch-hitting native Milwaukeean Elmer Klumpp, too.[11]

Eddie Pick was still a Brewer outfielder and the subject of *The Sentinel's* "Fanogram" contest. The winner received a free season pass and the next 5 got a ticket good for any day after the opener. There were 1,500 entries. Florence Killilea laid low after the rugged 5-9 road start, so she let Mayor Hoan toss out the first ball at newly re-christened Borchert Field on Friday, May 2nd. Louie Nahin and she hoped for more than knotholers to put the home opener over 10,000 attendance, but 9,538 had to do. A rainy windstorm swept through the day before.[12]

Unpredictable southpaw Bob McIntire up and left the squad in a snit over being lifted for a pinch-hitter. Herb Cobb, that pride of Pinetops, N.C., out-dueled Dick Wyhoff and Nemo Leibold's Columbus Senators, 2-1, thanks to Eddie Grimes' 1st inning solo homer and Danny Bloxsom's single and steal to set up Red Bennett's game-clinching RBI single in the sixth.

Bergy's Home Brews then promptly hit the river bottom like a former Scarface Al Capone client. It took Charley Robertson, who'd go on to lose 19 games for the year, to snap an 11-game losing streak on Saturday, May 17th. It was Mike Kelley's Minneapolis Millers, who heard the boisterous "Hoch! Hoch!" of the glass-clinking merry North Side burghers. Robby won his first.[13]

Milwaukee County grew to 715,587, a 32.6 percent increase.[14] The city grew to 568,962, up 24.4 percent.

Sterling defense from Pete Turgeon's flawless 6 putouts and 9 assists, aided Dennis Gearin's big curves and Burly Bill, that Rosy Ryan, thwarted KC in relief for a second straight win over the defending champs on June 1st. The Brewers remained an ugly 1½ games above "mournful" last place Minneapolis.[15]

"Why Girls Go Wrong" was on tap at Milwaukee's Gayety Theater and the "Top of the Morning!" newspaper feature offered a photo test to see if you could listen to "The Masked Baritone" on the radio for 5 seconds without tuning her out. It was Uncle Sam's nice way of identifying morons.[16]

Florence Killilea had to wonder if she was a moronic girl gone wrong as her club straddled that fine line into the basement. Her Home Brews had a penchant for catching league leaders napping, like Robertson's 4-3 fooling at Louisville in mid-June. Still, it was a "disillusioned and disappointing" team that added Brownie southpaw Fred Stiely belatedly to its staff.[17]

Of 35,000 phone-users in Milwaukee who switched from manual to dialing connections at four exchanges, it wasn't estimated how many called out S.O.S. for their baseball club.[18]

Galloping George Gerken even jumped back into the bottom brine, as Milwaukee's Independence Day split with the Blues left them looking bluely up at Columbus and the rest of the loop. Minneapolis righted itself to fifth. Eddie Pick went to KC for Pickles.[19]

The Brewers were much like the Niagara Falls daredevil who died in a barrel of suffocation, only they were going over the falls in bottles, kegs, and

Milwaukee Barnstormers (fall of 1930). 1. Ward Braby ("deceased"), 2. Jim Murray (Umpire), 3. active Brewer Black Tom Jenkins, 4. ex-Brewer Ivy Griffin, 5. active Brewer Dennis "Kewpie" Gearin, 6. World War I vet "Whitey" Berghausen, and 7. ex-major/minor leaguer Ralph Shinners. Milwaukee Public Library Historical Photograph Collection.

cases. A sweep by St. Paul in mid-July permanently left Milwaukee wallowing between last and seventh. Only by the grace of Red Corriden's Indianapolis Indians would they in fact finish the year in seventh, a slight 2½ games ahead of the Tribe. Berghammer's 63–91 finish left Milwaukee only 30½ games behind the pennant champions of future Brewer leader Al Sothoron.[20]

Another future Milwaukee manager and 1st baseman Mickey Heath made his 12th consecutive hit on September 4th for the Pacific Coast League Hollywood Stars.[21]

The American Association hit .307 overall and Bergy's Brewers led in at bats and triples. They had a couple 20 homer, 100 RBI men in Jenkins and Bloxsom. Geoff Jenkins of the current modern Brewers has yet to reach that combo, but Bloxsom's utility duty made his feat impressive. That Berghammer didn't lose his job proved Nahin was better at bean counting than baseball.[22]

Nahin traded places with Florence Killilea to become president of the Brewers; she stayed as vice-president. She also wed Dr. Michael Boley on November 25, 1930. He was a surgeon.[23]

Ed Leewe, the former "Kid" Brewer shortstop from the Connie Mack era, died on March 10, 1931, at the age of 58. Buried that Friday the 13th at Wanderer's Rest on the city's Northwest Side, he was once the envy of local dudes with his white puff tie.[24]

The cornerstone of change on the Brewers came at 1st base. A free-swinging lefty, with a talent to articulate, Texan "Art the Great" Shires rolled into Milwaukee with his self-promotional machine. He wrote in *The Wisconsin*

News of his screen role in "The Champion," rolling on the Alhambra Theater projector. The last of the "leather pushers" was up against the likes of Charlie Chaplin in "City Light," the African adventure "Trader Horn," and Joan Crawford in "Dance Fools Dance."

The Brewers' comic sideshows, Shires and Cuckoo Christensen, were slow arrivals to the Hot Springs camp. Dan Bloxsom, the only returning regular, was penciled in for an outfield slot, but set out to win the hot corner. Shires was detoured by his hardwood activity.[25] The Great scored only one basket for Skinny O'Connor's Milwaukee Badgers, who were trounced at the Berlin, Wisconsin High School gym by the Red Granite Red Ramblers, 34 to 22. This gave Marty Berghammer time to stifle Al Simmons' World Series talk, with reminiscences of his $8.05 share from St. Paul's 1924 post-season versus Baltimore and Seattle.

Ex-Brewers Tom Jenkins, Russ Young, and Texas League home run king Larry Bettancourt battled for berths up with the parent Browns. George Gerken may have been embarrassed by his burst suitcase and scattered clothes at the Hot Springs train platform, but his two homers led the Regulars over the Rookies in the first intrasquad game.[26]

Shires made it by 4 a.m. to play, driving with his wife for 18 straight hours from Chicago. The Cuckoo "flew" in from the West Coast "in an overcoat that looked like a blanket."

Wisconsin-born pitchers again were tested: Gerald Davis, from Wild Rose, relieved "Val" Blatz for the rooks, but Lefty Barrer from Red Granite (near Wild Rose in Waushara County) struck out 4 of the first 6 he faced on behalf of the Regs. Howard Bowers, a 21-year old outfielder from Appleton, wisely said his favorite movie star was Art Shires.

John Kloza and Tony Kubek were Polish Milwaukeeans to finally stick. Kloza's bat already did his mentor Stormy Kramer proud. The Western League Des Moines Demons had an all Milwaukee battery in the works: 18-year old hurler Al Gizelbach and 19-year old catcher Roman Bialk, both from the 1929 Wisconsin Vibrolithics local amateur champs.[27]

Clyde Manion had the type of veteran ambition, like Benny Bengough, to tutor the appropriately-named Jack Crouch behind the plate for Milwaukee. Manion brought 9 years of majors' know-how, Bengough 8, plus two World Series. Bernie "Li Chang" Hungling also came in from Dayton and the Browns. Berghammer's paddists were a strong suit on this edition.[28] Throwing to them was Americus Polli, a.k.a. "Lou" or "Crip," a right-hander rife with high expectations.

Milwaukee's Al Simmons flirted with a six-figure contract from Connie Mack, but signed a reported 3-year, $90,000 deal. Unser Choe Hauser came off a monstrous 1930, where he set an Organized Baseball record, at the time, of 63 home runs with the I.L. Baltimore Orioles.[29]

The House of David baseball aggregation was clipped by the Mud Hens and Red Sox over in Florida, but Hot Springs warm weather drew no better than 50 to see Claude Jonnard and Herb Cobb get wrecked, 17–4, by the Minneapolis Millers. The airplane crash death of Notre Dame football coach Knute Rockne rocked the sports world, but Bergy saw his spirit in his club.[30]

Neil Park in Columbus is where Sam Levy reported on *The Journal* wire that 10,000, besides Milwaukeeans Mr. & Mrs. Nahin, A.C. Villwock, and Sam and Ed Urdan were at the opener.[31] Marty's brother, Mr. & Mrs. Pete Berghammer drove in from Pittsburgh. The wives of Pete Turgeon and Herb Cobb were also on hand. No amount of sideline comedy by former Columbus birdbrain Cuckoo Christensen and his able assistant, Art Shires, made up for the wild and woolly 15–10 ruffling of new "Redbird" feathers. Former Green Bay Packer Pid Purdy, a Nebraskan, played left field for the Redbirds. Jack Kloza celebrated his Milwaukee debut with a 2nd inning homer. Fellow native Tony Kubek bowed in with a homer in Game Three, a 13–6 romp at Columbus.[32] Shires went 4-for-5, launching his march towards the batting title.

Milwaukee's Burghardt Sporting Goods watered the hotbed even further with 1st baseman's mitts for $3.95 and fielder's gloves and shoes for $2.95 each. Boy's Louisville Slugger bats and Junior league balls went for 25¢ and up. Playgrounds expanded amongst nine facilities.[33]

A woman contributor to *The Journal*, identified only as "J.E.M.," called Milwaukee "The Happy Housewife" in comparison to the Twin Cities, where she now lived. Bustling Minneapolis was "The Gay Debutante" and St. Paul, "The Chaperon." Staid Milwaukee had a slightly better baseball club than its lustier Nordic sister right then.[34]

It was the Depression, yet an Ernst Scharpegge-Gus Sonnenberg rassling match at Milwaukee's Auditorium drew 8,000. "Tweest der kopf out Ernst" gave way to "Play Ball!"

"Whataman," the Great Shires, "spilled a few capital I's" at the Elks banquet for 700 supporters, but all the hype for an opening record 13,113 was punctured by a 6–1 Toledo victory. Major league veteran shortstop Jackie Tavener now led off for the Brewers, but the Mud Hens had ex-Brewers Ernie Wingard, Bevo LeBourveau, and Bruno Haas in tow, too.[35]

A Milwaukee outfielder from way back, 66-year old Jimmy McAleer, died at his Youngstown, Ohio, home. The only man to play for Cleveland in 3 different leagues was an A.L. pioneer. Another who passed on, Milwaukee sausage maker Fred Usinger, left an estate of $1,390,000. Some of his meat could have been applied to the "blond knob" of Merton (Bat) Nelson, a Brewer flinger who was among the many unable to tell whether the ball had been "deadened." He took a wicked cue shot from the Colonels' Len Koenecke, an Adams, Wisconsin, man of major league ability. That Sunday, May 10th, team physician Dr. Michael Boley ordered bed rest for Nelson's headache, but the effect of cold weather on his wing was something else.[36]

Another 10,000, of which 7,000 were women, saw Americo Polli close out that Borchert Field homestand, 13–8, over Louisville. By contrast, only a microscopic 500 turned out at "The Gay Debutante" for the Brewers' second May 25th game at Minneapolis.[37]

KC manager Dutch Zwilling copped himself a new straw hat when his Blues swept the Memorial Day dual duel at Borchert Field. A fan cheering Bud Connolly's first game homer sent the boater sailing onto the field. Zwilling got to it before anyone else, and it made a good fit in the dugout. It wasn't on when he coached from the 3rd base box.[38] Boths clubs tied for fourth.

Manning Vaughan reported that Blues' owner George Muehlebach, who built a $500,000 ball yard for 2 pennants and 5 first division finishes in the last decade, now suffered from slipping baseball interest on the Kaw and the sort of ink venom that hastened Otto Borchert's death here.[39]

Baseball man Eddie Stumpf had the encouragement of National Football League president Joe Carr at Columbus to lure an N.F.L. team to Milwaukee. Carr had been an honorary pallbearer at Borchert's funeral and Otto's spunk could have saved the fizzled local money efforts. Stumpf stuck to what he did best, adding 3 Home Brew rookies to hurl for his State League Milwaukee Red Sox against that House of David. The Friday, June 5th show was the first ever under lights at Borchert Field. Hometown Harry Lauper, whiskers and all, combined with two innings from old clean-shaven reliever Grover Cleveland Alexander to hold the MilSox to 6 hits. Some 6,000 saw locals Ralph Shinners, Happy Herbstreith, Ralph Blatz, Larry Kessenich, and Lloyd Larson fall 9–4 to the Daves.[40]

Old Aleck wouldn't grow the facial spinach made famous by the Benton Harbor, Michigan, cultists, but Cuckoo Christensen stole the show, coaching 3rd for the Sox in bogus whiskers. A rabbit's foot, given to the Cuck via a Senegambian friend of Doctah Buckner's, did his bat no good, and in fact he broke his leg on June 12th. His home life with the former Wisconsin Hotel soda fountain girl Sadie Potratz and 3 kids were chronicled during his debility. His "Seacap" nickname came in St. Paul because his California mother used to send him to school in a sailor suit. Cuckoo volunteered to coach the MilSox/Daves July 3rd rematch from his wheelchair.[41]

Jocularity was the byword, as Scrappy Jack Doyle, the old Brewer skip scouting St. Paul for the Cubs, thought Al Simmons deserved to be the A.L. president instead of Will Harridge. The Saints' owner Bob Connery upheld Borchert's wheeler-dealer mantle, much like Mussolini cozied up to the pope, only Connery had a "$100,000 infield." That wonderful summer, college girls played ball at Milwaukee-Downer seminary and an estimated 75,000 turned out for a Sunday of amateur games all around Milwaukee in early June.[42]

It all took a sad turn when a downplayed paragraph appeared on the lower front page. Mrs. Michael H. Boley, the former Florence Killilea and vice-president of the Brewers was sick with pneumonia she contracted during a blood transfusion. The June 10th development revealed she was treated for a blood infection during her 2-week stay at Milwaukee General Hospital. The 29-year old woman died of a heart attack 5 days later after undergoing 3 blood transfusions.[43]

The Riverside High School and University of Wisconsin graduate was a member of Sigma Kappa sorority and also still a Brewer board member. A resident at 2527 N. Stowell Ave., she absorbed her father's passions for the University of Michigan, the railroad, and baseball as a very young girl. An avid horseback rider, she laid in state at S.F. Peacock & Son, 1028 N. Van Buren.

Her private funeral received only respectful attention. Judge John C. Karel, who officiated her marriage only 6 months earlier, was there. Louis Nahin again was a pallbearer, as was her only brother, Harry Killilea. And again, the baseball, legal, and medical communities were heavily represented at the Capuchin fathers' services. Lifelong family friend Attorney Edward Yockey presided over her Calvary Cemetery gravesite at the family plot.[44]

Miller Park can now be seen from that plot. Her Brewers' 5-game win streak was broken at Toledo, the day after her death.

Herbert Hoover could only tell the nation that the Depression was loosening its grip as former President Coolidge and he belatedly dedicated the Harding Memorial in Ohio after 8 years. Prince August Wilhelm von Hohenzollern called Adolf Hitler a godsend to Germany.[45]

Brewer outfielder Alex "Dutch" Metzler, a speedy Fresnoan, recovered from a broken 17-game hitting streak at Toledo to give Earl Caldwell his 3rd straight win. Berghammer would not give in to scouts who sought Clyde Manion.[46]

Onetime Brewer Jim Thorpe now donned a chieftain's war bonnet for Hollywood and the team itself after its first ever starlight game at Indianapolis on Friday, June 19th, lost before 700 in the Indiana capital, in stifling heat the next day. Jack Kloza had 14 homers already.[47]

Former Brewer hurler Al Fons shot a 73 at Tuckaway Country Club and "several thousand" Milwaukee admirers of Al Simmons traveled to Chicago, where his A's met the White Sox. The boosters presented the former Brewer with a silver bat. Milwaukee dropped 4 road games.[48]

Road secretary Rudy Vizay went back to wearing his iron bowler and *voila!* Jack Knott threw calcimine and Dinty Gearin nailed a double dip at Louisville. Cuckoo Christensen could only hear WTMJ's Radio's Russ Winnie give the results at his home. Americus Polli, the Vermont right-hander, was busted at the Falls City for back rent from his 1930 Colonel days. The landlord lost the case.[49]

Crimeless Milwaukee, on the other hand, again drew the national spotlight. Homicides in the ersatz beer capital averaged 11 a year for the last seven in an era when gangland crime crept out into middle American places Kansas City and New Orleans. The city of Milwaukee's population in 2000 was very similar to 1931, yet the homicide rate is over 10 times as great.[50]

Brewers pennant fever rose with the 90° heat. Fred Stiely came back to pitch them into 1st place by Sunday, June 28th. Sparked by Bud Connolly's switch to third, four of the top seven batting lead qualifiers were Brewers. Memories of 1909 echoed.[51]

The season looked like a young John Wayne's movie career: nothing but bright lights ahead. Lightfoot Rudy doffed his magic hat, but no sooner than their 35-31 put them over, they faltered like Gilda Gray's divorced broken heart. They should've undergone the psychograph, or "head reading machine." The searing heat, which killed over 40 in Wisconsin and 230 across the nation between June 29-30th burnt Brewer hopes along with it. Any rumors of a cool 4 percent beer comeback were squelched by President Hoover.[52]

When "wee Dinty blew," so did the Brewers, from first. Their lead stood all of 3 days. They didn't just fall to third, the wilt became more alarming as June 30th topped 100°. Showers broke the inferno and 8,124 (including Cuckoo) saw a June 7th split with Indy. They could've used their flinger of 14 years earlier. Frank Shellenback tore up the Pacific Coast League.[53]

At least Phil Ball, who now owned the Brewers, didn't call Art Shires up to his St. Louis Browns, but his Texas League Wichita Falls Spudders sent outfielder Ted Gullic up to Milwaukee. Help from the future fixture was too little, too late. A limping Cuckoo made himself available for pinch-hit duty, but ended up umping a game with Louisville's Babe Ganzel, due to Umpire Clayton's illness there. The infield help Ball and Brownie manager Bill Killefer (a future Brewer boss) came up with was 3rd baseman Frank O'Rourke, who unceremoniously replaced Marty Berghammer as manager. "Blackie's" .304 bat couldn't inflate the 5th place bottom line, but the team was now his. Nahin remained president, Shires the bat champ and Jonnard the K king.[54]

Wisconsinite Len Koenecke sold for $75,000 from Indianapolis to the New York Giants. The International League seemed a haven for old Brewers. Al Simmons' boyhood pal, Ralph Shinners, hit .297 and 14 homers for Jimmy Cooney's Buffalo Bisons. Wid Matthews wielded a .290 willow for Pants Rowland's Reading Keystones and Baltimore's Joe Hauser hit 31 home runs.[55]

The shadow hanging over the Brewers, since Otto Borchert's dramatic death, crept further on Thursday, April 7, 1932. Five days after refusing medical attention for an accident during the Brewers' spring pass from Hot Springs up through Memphis, 44-year old Manning Vaughan died at St. Louis Barnes Hospital. With his wife and 9-year old daughter along, recovery from what turned out to actually be a fractured skull seemed likely.

The dean of Milwaukee sportswriters was promoted as *The Sentinel's* 19-year old sports editor when Tom Chivington resigned to take over the Louisville Colonels. The erudite South Division student already wrote high school sports for that paper while still in school. His brother, Irving, also wrote baseball for the *Chicago Tribune*. As racist as his era, the classic storyteller switched to *The Journal* in 1924, "Putting 'em on the Pan" as one of the Midwest's foremost baseball writers. A resident at 854 E. Lake Forest Ave. in upper-crust Whitefish Bay, his visitation was at Peacock's facility, like Florence Killilea Boley. Interred at Valhalla's mausoleum, the cemetery where Borchert was buried, the penultimate Irishman wasn't even Catholic. He was buried under Episcopalian rites.[56]

Among his pallbearers were Elmer Netzow, Art Schinner, and his *Journal* editor who'd take over as the Brewers beat writer for the next 21 years, Jewish Sam Levy.

For the fourth time in 5 years, someone prominently associated with the Brewers (Borchert, Henry Killilea, Mrs. Boley, and now, Vaughan) died relatively young.

At *The Sentinel*, James B. McGlynn began a 15-year run as sports editor. His byline was "Stoney McGlynn," not to be confused with the Ulysses Simpson Grant McGlynn who threw iron man ball for Milwaukee 20 years earlier. That Stoney was a night watchman at a Manitowoc aluminum products company.[57] Old Tom Dougherty did factory service at Milwaukee's Ford plant.

Frank "Blackie" O'Rourke, the Canadian promoted from the Browns' infield to guide the Brewers. Baseball Hall of Fame Library, Cooperstown, NY.

Modern baseball promotes the hiring of minorities. Frank O'Rourke was born in Hamilton, Ontario, Canada, making him the first non–American born to manage the Brewers in some 25 years since Irish Jack Doyle. O'Rourke's nickname, despite his flashing smile, was "Blackie." How that washed with Doc Buckner, we'll never know, but it's worth some brownie points.

O'Rourke ran counter to the Teutonic tint of middle America that his fellow A.A. pilots represented: Nemo Leibold, Bibb Falk, Dutch Zwilling, Lefty Leifield, and Bruno Betzel. These guys might have been at home in Milwaukee's Strand or Pabst Theaters, watching German films like *Der Liebesexpress* (love express). Hitler's Nazis were still branded a "revolutionary sect," not a political party in Der Vaterland. Milwaukee's socialists still did well at the polls.[58]

At Hot Springs, at least O'Rourke lost no one to stabbing, the way Red Sox pitcher Ed Morris died from a fight at a fish fry in his honor at their Florida camp. Ineligible U.W. pitcher Bobby Poser snubbed the Brewers because of his disdain for the Browns' chain. He took his sinker to a brief glance with Minneapolis, but at least he didn't end up with the financially troubled Mud Hens, now in receivership to Cleveland Indians' owner shipper George A. Tomlinson. To confuse matters, 1st baseman John Brewer was optioned by KC to the San Antonio Indians.[59]

Art Shires, taking his greatness to the Boston Braves, admitted to liking a "good glass of beer" while lecturing on abstinence in Massachusetts. Only 40 were arrested in Helsinki, Finland, to celebrate its dry repeal. Ex-Brewer Harry Strohm whet his managerial appetite at Little Rock.[60] O'Rourke had a new 3rd baseman in Horace "Pip" Koehler, an old 1st baseman in Buck Stanton, and two important additions, Ash Hillin and Garland Braxton, on the mound. Jackie Tavener, the "Mighty Atom," had 3 doubles, a homer, and 4 RBI to royally crush Montreal on 30 hits, 22-6, at Hot Springs. The right arm of Hillin endured 8 innings on the hill.[61]

Blackie O'Rourke hoped to kidnap the A.A. flag, the way the Lindbergh baby now engrossed the country. He was a better prophet than the late Mr. Vaughan. A cold wave at Toledo delayed the 1932 opener. Once under way, Milwaukee swung into action like Johnny Weissmueller's "Tarzan," bringing a 5-5 fourth place stand home to Borchert Field.

Right-hander Jack Knott, who never said "forget me," combined with crouching Jack Crouch to make the Thursday, April 28th opening battery. Some 10,000 were expected, but 8,602 actually showed for the 3-hit, 4-0 blanking of Indianapolis. Buck Stanton had a triumphant return in Brewer togs, with a perfect day at bat, two steals, and he drove in the winning run.[62]

Crouch was hit in the head by a pre-game warm-up ball, but played through the fourth and would be out for "several days."

Japan, the other half of the future Axis that would imperil the world, was convulsed by the murder of its premier Syoshi Inukai in mid-May, but their professional baseball now engaged in its second season. The Brewers, not yet as hot as the 88° temps in the city, gave a 7,300 crowd "57 varieties of baseball" in three 5-run rallies to overwhelm KC, 15-7, in a nightcap split.[63]

Henry Ford, who recently saw his first "fast game" of hockey, took out large ads espousing self-help in hard times. The Brewer helped themselves stay between 3rd and 4th place through June. O'Rourke sat on the Borchert Field dugout steps, taking *The Sentinel's* "new scientific Personality test" before an exhibition with the New York Yankees.[64]

Franklin Delano Roosevelt received his Democratic Party's nomination on a 4th ballot just before Independence Day—first step towards his burgeoning "New Deal" alphabet soup. O'Rourke misspelled victory with his own error to literally open the holiday opener with the Blues. Cuckoo Christensen and Pip Koehler combined for a 3-run, 9th inning rally, with 2 out, to save the 9–5 flip side. Still Milwaukee remained a couple games behind 4th place KC.[65]

Chicago Cub shortstop Billy Jurges was wounded by jilted Miss Violet Popovich, 3 days later in the Windy City. It was a rare instance that flying bullets down there didn't involve gangland retaliation. Incredibly, she was released on bail, intent upon visiting him.[66]

Ted Gullic's .378 league-leading batting average was one number that couldn't be fudged like the city of Milwaukee's supposed Depression-era surplus. To the swift goes the race and with the Los Angeles Olympics looming, black Ralph Metcalfe of Milwaukee's Marquette University distinguished his race by dominating the U.S.A. sprint trials. Once Brewer Jim Thorpe was given Vice-President Charles Curtis' pass to those Coliseum games, 20 years after his Stockholm feats. Carrying 30 pounds over his baseball trim, he had fallen upon ditch-digging hard times.[67]

He never dove into the ocean for steamship tourists' nickels like Cuban boxer Kid Chocolate, but if the Brewers had a nickel for every advance in their race, they'd dove under .500. Crip Polli couldn't halt the reverse in his August 11th 2–1 duel with Toledo's Roxie Lawson either.

Frank O'Rourke kept his team from being relegated to a sports page afterthought with a remarkable 31–15 drive the rest of the way. If kids clipped out the "Lucky Buck" from the "Skippy" page of the *Sunday Sentinel* comics they were admitted free to Borchert Field.[68]

Things got worse before they got better. "Bedraggled" from a 9–21 extended August road trip, Larry Kessenich even lost an August 17th exhibition to the Class D Mississippi Valley League Islanders under the Douglas Park floodlights at Rock Island, Illinois.[69]

As sure as Zasu Pitts was a great dramatic actress, the St. Louis Browns sent slugging outfielder George "Showboat" Fisher up the Mississippi to bat cleanup for the Brewers. The Iowan's 44 hits in 36 games was a .361 pace that smashed the pill like German scientists did to the atom.

On the screen of the Gayety Theater was Gilda Gray's "He Was Her Man." On the theater stage, her unsupported father from Cudahy, Max Michalski, did a little clog dance in a one-act comic appearance, "I Am Her Old Man." Despite raising her 19-year old son, Max bore no — what was it called?— animosity — towards his famous daughter.[70]

The Home Brews clog-danced to finish third, their best record of the Hoover presidency. Ted Gullic (.354–27–123) and Alex Metzler (.322–14–106), along with 17-game winners Fred Stiely and Jack Knott made it so. *The Sentinel* endorsed Hoover for re-election, despite his 3-year Depression slump. Of the two, O'Rourke got to keep his job.[71]

A certain well-known Sultan of Swat makes a Borchert Field barnstorming visit in the early 1930s. Milwaukee Public Library Historical Photograph Collection.

Once the "New Deal" took root was "3.2 Beer Stark Genug? Ja!" In the old days, Pabst Blue Ribbon was 2.9, Schlitz 3.1, Cream City Pilsener 3.3, and Blatz Muenchner 3.5 in percentage of alcohol volume. Anheuser-Busch's Budweiser may well have been "the King of Beers" at 3.8

The statue of King Gambrinus (a.k.a. the Duke of Brabant, inventor of lager beer) atop the Pabst stock house would no longer hoist an empty vessel. Tankmakers and wooden box makers were flooded with orders from breweries. The United States House of Representatives stood pat, with its stronger 3.2 bill. The Senate nit-picked for 3.05. Anticipation grew. The Senate caved.

The illegal trade of the speakeasies dreaded the adjustment, but after weeks of legislative tinkering, Blatz became the first Milwaukee brewer to start bottling in late March. Rationing of supply to pent up demand was expected. "Dreimal Hoch!!" (Three Cheers!), indeed.[72]

Joe Beer was already graduated from the University of Detroit football team, but there was just one catch. It was one with an all too familiar ring to modern Milwaukee: The City Health Commissioner advised "Boil All Water."

Bacteria buildup, polluted by rain flooded sewers, bred the ancestors of cryptosporidium.

Caps popped off those bottles at the turn of midnight, Friday, April 7, 1933. In America's once and again Beer City, 100,000 Milwaukeeans cheered the rolling out of the proverbial barrels. One 25-year old man, Arthur Stelter, was killed between trucks, as he watched the unloading at Pabst. That aside, BEER in all its creamy amber glory was back!

Prohibition fell the way of scrip currency, and finally the Milwaukee Brewers baseball club had the legitimacy of their name restored.[73]

In the midst of all the mirth and merriment, manager Frank O'Rourke was nothing if not brutally honest. In a time when the term "superstar" was first used for ice hockey greats Bill Cook and Eddie Shore, O'Rourke had nothing of the kind. He publicly acknowledged his squad was weaker than in 1932. Enthusiasm out of Hot Springs was such that E. Garland Braxton, the rebel southpaw from Snow Camp, N.C., contemplated retirement. He ended up the winningest Brewer. Retiring from baseball, when about a quarter of the nation's workforce was unemployed, was like heresy. It may have explained the arrival of honeymooners Mr. & Mrs. Larry Bettencourt.[74]

The onetime Brewer was back, only consummating his marriage from their Oakland home. Brewer eyebrows were raised, not only by the Marlene Dietrich pants that Mrs. B. wore in the hotel lobby, but by the shotgun she carried. The Cuck, Walter Christensen, beat her man out for a regular outfield job.

Maybe she already knew that without Ted Gullic and Jack Knott, the team's pennant chances were shot to hell. O'Rourke sent future St. Paul star Aloysius "Ollie" (Pajamas) Bejma, the Polish-German infielder from South Bend, Indiana, back down to the Texas League San Antonio Missions. Bejma would become the favorite player of later Charlie Brown "Peanuts" cartoonist Charles Schulz in the Minnesota capital.[75]

The "demon pants presser from the South Side," Tony Kubek, also seemed ticketed for the Alamo city, but Blackie shook him of his tendency to place his hits to the right.

"We Made More Money On Old Nero" was the hue and cry of Brewer boss Louis M. Nahin. He claimed the club profited better selling near beer and would not sell bottled beer unless the $2.60 case price was cut a dime. In 1931, they made 15¢ for a bottle at the ballpark. For 1932, it was only a dime. At the $2.50 or $2.60 case price, they would only make 55¢ out of it, at 15¢ a bottle. They could make $1.20 off the old near stuff. In an ironic threat, no Milwaukee-made beer would be sold at Borchert Field unless the price was cut, or else a state brewery would get dibs on the club's business.[76]

It would be that sort of year. The team would've been better off hiding incognito behind whiskers like Babe Ruth's Florida masquerade against the House of David. In Kentucky, a trial charged Bible-waving cultists with human sacrifices. It was not said if these actions advanced a runner to the next base.[77]

On April 12th, the Brewers' "18-carat" defense forced a 3-3 tie in 14 innings. When Indians' second sacker Frank Sigafoos tried to ignite a double steal in the 12th, Milwaukee catcher Russ Young threw to pitcher Crip Polli instead of going to second. Polli snapped a relay to Pip Koehler at third, who nailed Siggy to quell the Indianapolis uprising.[78]

Polli got the starting nod for the home opener against Louisville on Thursday, April 27th. To combat the Brewers' shaky pitching, trainer Docktah Buckner dressed Americus up for a *Journal* cameraman, with a huge feather in Polli's cockeyed cap. He now had his "witching eye."

Its effectiveness should've scared the 4,500 on hand to see Polli deal a 5-hit, 3-0 shutout. One of 3 hits allowed by the Colonels' John "Moose" Marcum was a Bud Connolly homer. Polli then had 11 chances in 9 innings on May 10th. The 10th frame foiled credit for a record.[79]

Former Brewer "Art the Great" Shires was soberly traded down by the St. Louis Cardinals to their Columbus Redbird farm for 2nd baseman Burgess Whitehead. "Whataman" had just been bought from the Boston Braves. Four others went down with him, but it was hell to be great.[80]

An even earlier Brewer 1st baseman, old Unser Choe Hauser, wasn't just back in the American Association, yet again, but was off to a season for the ages. Using the friendly confines of the Minneapolis Millers' bandbox of a Nicollet Park to maximum advantage, Milwaukee's native son would eclipse his own Organized Baseball record with 69 home runs. That most excellent mark would stand 20 seasons and win him a visit from woman superhero Babe Didrikson.[81] The Brewers' Garland Braxton was his favorite victim, with a half dozen. Three came at Borchert, 11 against Milwaukee overall.

Ol' Zip wasn't the only slugger around by any means. The Sunday doubleheader that finished the initial series at Borchert Field was rained out. However, Blackie O'Rourke, not known for swinging a heavy bat, had no problem with landing his left fist on Wade "Red" Killefer's jaw. The Brewer manager, who took the scientific Personality Test just the prior year, also took umbrage with his Indianapolis rival. O'Rourke made good on a promise to punch the Indy pilot, but wasn't offended by Killefer calling him a "crybaby" in a Kansas City newspaper. No, Red made Blackie see red by calling Cuckoo Christensen a "halfwit."[82]

O'Rourke's right hand was wrapped in bandages from a spike wound and broken thumb he suffered the previous Friday in tagging a Louisville runner out at second. He got his shot in on Killefer, while Red was under his clubhouse showerhead. The punch knocked Killefer over a trunk and his Indy players rushed in to end any fight.

"I'd be a fine mug to hit you while you can only use one hand," said Killefer, as he was restrained by his Tribe. O'Rourke wasn't about to let that stop him, but all he could see was Red for a few hours afterwards. Blackie raged on that if Killefer made good on his promise to dust off Brewer batters, the next time they met, "there will be some more fun."

O'Rourke berated that sort of Red herring from Killefer's tactics in his P.C.L. days. Indians' owner Norman Perry downplayed the *Kansas City Star* interview with Ernest Mehl, saying Killefer was just trying to "generate fan interest." O'Rourke would have none of it. He wouldn't be party to what he saw as a "cheap publicity stunt."

Blackie's embroglio with Red recalled earlier Brewer fisticuffs between Harry Clark and the Millers' Dare Devil Dave Altizer, Phil Lewis' tangle with Louisville 2nd baseman Polly McLarry, and Oscar Melillo's fiery slide into Marty Berghammer when "Chewing Gum Bergy" was St. Paul's keystone cop. Oscar didn't get the worst of Marty's punch either.

O'Rourke's pugilistic reputation took on the sort of "King Kong" proportions then flickering across the nation's movie screens, but what example did it set for the Dover A.C. girls, one of Milwaukee's better Muni Major AA League teams? Why couldn't there be the sort of orderly control like the Nazis imposed upon all of Germany's athletics? Some 80,000 turned out for the mid May opening of Milwaukee's sandlot year. The Verifines had ex-Brewer tryout Earl Ches(e)bro from Coloma, Wisconsin, and former Brewer 3rd baseman Rube Lutzke.[83]

The addition of 2nd baseman Ollie Marquardt did little to keep Milwaukee from tumbling through the American Association like a lopsided kittenball. No amount of legal beer could wash away the stench of 7th place by August. Their season was as detached as the two-piece bathing suits now seen on the beaches of France. They would finish 20 games under .500.

To make the nosedive worse, St. Louis Browns owner (and by turn, Brewer honcho) Philip DeCatesby Ball was injured in a St. Louis auto accident. His auto was struck on August 17th by a woman driver and thrown against a telephone pole. He refused medical treatment.[84]

Fortunately for the Brewers, Allen Sothoron hadn't made enough of an impression on Ball that in one of the owner's worst moves, he replaced Al with Rogers Hornsby. Sothoron, who had survived appendicitis during his 1930 Louisville pennant run and the loss of his 29-year old wife, replaced the deposed O'Rourke. On the West Coast, ex-Brewer skip Jack Lelivelt could only laugh with his Los Angeles Angels all the way to the P.C.L. pennant.[85]

Phil Ball died that October 1933. Business associate Louis B. Von Weise, personal friend Walter Fritsch, and G.M. Carle McEvoy, men without baseball savvy, were the executors of Ball's estate. The ownership void, the Brewers' fourth upheaval in 7 years wasn't fixed until Saturday, April 28, 1934.

The regular season was already underway when attorney Henry Bendinger led a local effort, with Eugene Tiefenthaler, sales manager of the Worden-Allen Co. They were the principal stockholders, but former assistant district attorney Walter Hofer, business manager Louis Nahin (who kept that job), and Al Sothoron each also had part interests in the organization.[86]

The Depression reflected the deflated value of a Class AA minor league baseball team. The group put $5,000 up front and would settle 50 percent of

The 1934 Brewers. *Bottom row, left to right:* Elton (Jim) Walkup, pitcher; Ray Walentowski, pitcher; Ira Hutchinson, pitcher; Lee (Rubber Arm) Stine, pitcher; Earl (Spider) Webb, right fielder; George (Tony) Rensa, catcher; Eddie Marshall, shortstop, and "Doctah" George Washington Buckner, trainer. *Center row, left to right:* Eddie Hope, utility infielder; E. Garland (Joe) Braxton, pitcher; Jack (The Giant Killer) Kloza, left fielder; Billy (The Kid) Sullivan, third baseman; Tony (Push 'Em Up) Kubek, utility outfielder; Ted Gullic, center fielder; Russ Young, catcher; Allan (Fidge) Sothoron, manager. *Top row:* Rolland (Lena) Stiles, pitcher; Americo (Crip) Polli, pitcher; Rudy Laskowski, utility infielder; Forrest Pressnell, pitcher; Lin Storti, second baseman; Ernie Wingard, first baseman. Milwaukee Public Library Collection.

the $100,000 price before paying the remainder to the Ball estate (read: Browns) in installments.

Sothoron, who was to get a percentage of the gross receipts, had his contract rewritten from 3 years to 5. Al Wilmot represented Mrs. Idabel Borchert, who still owned the ballpark. They agreed to some rental concessions to help bring the ballclub back to local ownership. The Brewers' lease with her had 19 years remaining.

Ronald McIntyre, the *Sentinel* sports editor, A.A. President Tom Hickey, and the players themselves all rejoiced that the Home Brews would now, in fact, be home owned. Only four players weren't under absolute obligation to Milwaukee. Billy Sullivan, Jr., the 3rd baseman whose White Sox catching father was a Wisconsinite, was ChiSox property himself. Elton (Jimmy) Walkup belonged to the Browns, but spent the majority of the season in Milwaukee. Ted Gullic was turned over from the Browns outright as part of the deal.[87]

Bendinger, Tiefenthaler, and Hofer cheered on at radio side as their new Brewers rallied over the Apostles in an 11-inning, 6–5 duel up in St. Paul. Milwaukee was 4–5 in fifth.

The balding, 39-year old Bendinger was a product of Milwaukee's public schools, serving in various supervisory capacities for the Wisconsin Telephone Co. He had graduated from the law school that was now part of Marquette University. Admitted to the bar in 1911, he belonged to multiple professional associations, the Tripoli Country Club (where he golfed consistently in the low 80s) and Milwaukee Athletic Club. The new Brewers president was a married father of two daughters (why did all these Brewer owners seem to have just daughters anyway?) and still a partner in the law firm of Bendinger and Hayes. The avid fisherman was one of the city's best ping-pong players. He had helped to promote 6-day bicycle races in Milwaukee.

Tiefenthaler, slated to be vice-president, was a 49-year old grad from West Division High and though his sports interests revolved around hockey, the native was one of Otto Borchert's original 1920 Brewer investors. He later sold his 1/7 interest to Borchert.

Marquette Law School graduate Hofer served as an assistant to District Attorney George Bowman for several years before retiring to private practice. After separate efforts by Chauncey Yockey and Rudolf Hokanson fell through since the December past, the trio went from being among the 30,000 to pay their way into Borchert Field for all of 1933 to owning the Brewers.[88]

For the second straight year, Wisconsin's Democrat governor, Al Schmedeman, threw out the first ball. The first few home games already drew 12,000, when the Browns deal became announced. Trying to find Brewer fans had been like the southern Wisconsin manhunt for George (Baby Face) Nelson, but that was about to change.

The Sunday, April 29th game at Borchert Field drew 7,188, close to the Opening Day's 8,000. Roger Peckinpaugh's Kansas City Blues saw fit to spoil all the fresh outlook and *gemutlichkeit* by bowling the Brewers over, 13–3. Jimmy Walkup, Forrest "Tot" Pressnell, and Clarence Fieber absorbed the impact of 4 flat-footed errors in the debacle.[89] Despite the major league experience of Glenn (Buckshot) Wright, who could now only underhand the ball across the diamond from short, and future major leaguers Mel Almada (a Mexican pioneer) and Mike Kreevich, the Blues would prove a lowly lot. Still, the new stockholders weren't disheartened after one bad day.

Out of Hot Springs, Sothoron laid a foundation that would be vindicated two years hence. It smacked of Little Italy, as veteran utility man George Detore came from Louisville and Polli was caught by George "Tony" Rensa, a.k.a. "Pug." He was backed up by George Susce, the "Good Kid." Switch-hitting Californian Lin(do) Storti brought huge power from the Browns to the infield.

Offense galore, in a 15–3, 15–1 mid-May slaughter of the Colonels showed potential. Eddie Marshall, a $5,000 shortstop with an I.L.-best 19 errors in 684 chances, came from Albany.[90]

Like beer itself, Happy Felsch was indeed here again. The ostracized Black Sox was now a 42-year old batting champ with the Dairies of Milwaukee's municipal AAA league. Another former Brewer outfielder, Frank (Powerhouse) Luce, cracked triples before 10,000 Pulaski Park fans playing for the Matuschkas in that circuit.[91]

First Lady Eleanor Roosevelt now turned the $3,000 weekly from doing commercial radio broadcasts with Floyd Gibbons over to a Quaker charity, "The Friends Service Committee." She also wrote a daily column advocating a "bloodless revolution" of women's role in society.[92]

Ernie Wingard, now more a 1st baseman than pitcher, took his lean, lanky Alabam' shuffle around the basepaths for a circuit clout, with a pair of Brewers on in the 9th, to single-handedly terrorize the Indy Tribe that just dealt him away. The 5–4 victory at Indianapolis that Wednesday, May 15th, was the first night tilt of the season, as well.[93]

Sothoron's hit parade didn't just wake up the robins nesting at the once quiet confines of Borchert Field, it allowed him to release a couple A.A. veterans: shortstop Paul (Pee Wee) Wanninger and 1st baseman Dud(ley) Branum. "Fidge," as Sothoron was sometimes known, still had outfielders Earl Webb and Ted Gullic. Webb, who still holds the major league doubles record, with 67 for the 1931 BoSox, had 4 hits and Gullic a 4th-inning homer in the Saturday, May 19th football-sounding 17–14 slugfest to bag a flock of Columbus Red Birds.[94] The Ohio club had two future Brewer managers in its order: Nick (Tomato Face) Cullop in right and Minor "Mickey" Heath at first. The exercise looked more like

Allen Sothoron, the manager who revived Milwaukee's flagging Depression-era fortune. Copyright unknown [via Baseball Hall of Fame Library].

the "Vliet Street Bullet Stoppers were playing the Mosinee Tigers for the county fair championship" in the appraisal of *The Sentinel's* Red Thisted.

Be that as it was, the Brewers were still a sixth place club, 2 under .500, yet. Maybe 6-year-old Ernie Wingard, Jr., known amongst the teammates as Sonny, deserved an early, early call up?[95]

Free from the Browns' agenda, Milwaukee went on to post its best season since 1928. They had to survive Louisville's Jack Tising, who whiffed 15 of them on August 6th, but Sothoron's Brewers boasted its second batting champion in four years (Webb, .368), the hits leader in Billy Sullivan (222), an RBI king in local boy Jack Kloza (148), and a 20-game winner in Garland Braxton. At second, Lin Storti (.330–35–145) was a monster.[96] Home ownership meant 3rd place.

Professional baseball was clearly revived in Milwaukee. In the Depression, the game's popularity still multiplied like the newly born Dionne quintuplets. Chicago's Lane Tech High School had 1,100 candidates for its baseball team, all trying to be the next Phil Cavaretta to reach the Cubs from there. It would have done the late Otto Borchert's heart good to know that a Billy Borchert was the only Wisconsinite left in a Windy City amateur boxing tournament.[97]

The success of the Brewers could not be mandated by F.D.R.'s National Recovery Act, but in the era of this particular N.R.A., Sothoron was gunning for a pennant. He recovered from 17-game winning Oklahoma right-hander Lee Stine's promotion to the bigs by adding the Class C Middle Atlantic League's top ace, Wayne LeMaster. With the Charleston (W.V.) Senators there, he led that loop with 17 wins and 168 Ks. Luke (Hot Potato) Hamlin was a less effective right-hander down from the Detroit Tigers, but southpaw Clyde (Mad) Hatter was a Kentuckian, with 4 years of A.A. duty at Louisville. He would win the 1935 ERA title for Sothoron.

One Wisconsinite, who didn't make the cut, was 18-year old Norwalk right-hander Roland Schell. "Very robust," at 6'-5" and 226 pounds, Schell dominated the Southwestern Minnesota League for Laura Ingalls Wilder's little town on the prairie, Walnut Grove. In racking up a 13–1 ledger there, Schell once struck out 22 in one game on 2 hits. Another time, he fanned 18, but lost on just 3 bingles as cartoonist Robert Ripley would put it, believe it or not.[98]

It was the same for fellow Wisconsinites Harris Kahl from Prairie Farm, Pulaski's Allen Johnson, southpaw Marshall Schoepke, who played with Eagle River, 23-year old right-hander Leonard Kletinski, who pitched independent ball at Stevens Point, and even Milwaukeean Ray Wallen (Walentowski). None of those state boys should've been discouraged, though. Even Mississippi's Claude Passeau, who led the Central League in whiffs for Grand Rapids and would go onto a winning 13-year major league career, didn't make it past ex-pitcher Sothoron either.

Clevelander Frank Doljack, a 5-year Detroit Tiger, kept Jack Kloza and

Tony Kubek out of the starting outfield, but the hot corner was handled like a pepper game — by committee. Returnees George Detore and Eddie Hope took a back seat to George Trapp.

Speaking of committees, a harebrained Wisconsin assemblyman named Michalski saw taxation on boxing, wrestling, and even ping-pong parlors as a way to grow state coffers. He wanted to slap a $25 license fee on pro athletes like the Brewers, mostly non-residents, to play in Milwaukee. Sothoron might face a $50 manager's fee and Bendinger $200 as a promoter. No wonder it was the Depression![99] Michalski ended up looking like Ripley's "One Man Nation" — the last member of the ancient Yukaghir tribe who inhabited a vast stretch of northern Siberia. Ripley also recounted the 19th Century rebel leader of the Caucasus, Shamyl, who refused a million, but accepted a thousand rubles for the ransomed uncle of the tsar. Guess Shamyl never hung out with Otto Borchert...[100]

One hard-hitting youngster exceeded the expectations of Sothoron and Nahin. Milwaukee sandlot sensation Chet Laabs was of Pomeranian German-Polish extract, a classic Milwaukeean if there ever was one, but he was rough-edged as an infielder. It was decided that utility work at the Double-A level would do Laabs' bat no good whatsoever, so he was farmed to the Fort Wayne Chiefs of the Class B Three-I League. He would win the Triple Crown, there.[101]

Laabs made the all-time amateur local team chosen for *The Sentinel's* Stoney McGlynn by a Milwaukee sandlot stalwart named Stoney Steinke. The rambunctious "little fella" began catching with the Milwaukee Advertisers in 1912, but "didn't state what they advertised nor what the team's record was." The Athletic Park squatter faced the best stuff Slapnicka, Hovlik, Cutting, and Dougherty had to offer during the Brewers' pennant prime of his youth. Of 4 different local clubs he masterminded, he considered his 1921 West Side Arcades, 2 games shy of a national tourney, his best.[102] Steinke's all-time local amateurs made an instructive list:

• Pitchers Tony Welzer and Al Klawitter, catchers Ray Thompson and Bernie Tesmer. All four played in Class Double-A professional organizations.
• 1st Base — Wallie Neustedter (Joe Hauser was a pitching outfielder in his amateur days)
• 2nd Base — Happy Herbstreith and Chet Laabs, the latter a huge bat better suited to another position
• 3rd Base — Rube Lutzke, the ex-Brewer also with the KC Blues and Cleveland Indians
• Shortstop — Jack Wambach and a prize outfield consisting of: Al Simmons, Happy Felsch, Jack Kloza, Mandy Brooks, and Tony Kubek. Felsch had also been cited by Tom Dougherty as the greatest talent he ever played with. The retiring Steinke would resist the urge to jump back in the game.

Al Simmons wore Pale Hose, to welcome hometown visitors to Chicago's Comiskey Park, ca. 1933–1935. Milwaukee Public Library Historical Photograph Collection.

Marty Berghammer was now a coach with the St. Paul Saints and his preseason jawboning with the Brewers at Hot Springs was sure to pave the way for a heated return to Milwaukee.[103]

Three things would underline the 1935 Brewer campaign that began with an 8–7 conquest at Kansas City's Muehlebach Field. There would be Eddie Marshall's hitting steak and Americo Polli's ho-hitter, but mostly, it was the inability to get off center. Ernie Wingard was a one-man rescue of a shaky Polli in the sixth and his 10th inning lead sac fly sent 8,500 home sad.[104]

Henry Bendinger, known to be a sandwich-fetcher for his proteges in camp, had a never-say-die sort of team.

"Gay Styles to Dominate Gotham Easter Parade" was the April 20th headline, but 2 days later in Milwaukee, George Detore's home uniform was purloined. The "eye-averting" white-and-red outfit that had his name stitched in its collar was on display in the window of A.G. Spalding & Bros. on 709 N. Water St. A trio of burglars made off with another $35 worth of gloves and other baseball accessories.[105]

Public relief crises set off a hunger march in Illinois and a jobs bill in Wisconsin when the Brewers finally swamped the Mud Hens in the home opener on May 10th. They came home a 3rd place, 10–8 club, but a paid attendance of only 533 saw the 11–2 attack. Joe Doljack was the only effective Hen hurler, allowing only a single to brother Frank.[106]

They should've given the man a contract: Right-hander George Kojis

Pre-dating the All-American Girls League by 8 years, sisters Anne (catching) and Margaret Head practice at Milwaukee's 18th St. School playground in July 1935. The girls lived at 816A N. 20th St. Milwaukee Public Library Historical Photograph Collection.

threw a May 19th perfecto for Beaver Gas & Oils in a 15–0 rout over Devision (sic) 998 at Washington Park. The Kojis name would later be made famous by basketball forward Don Kojis, who starred at Marquette University and went onto a good N.B.A. career.[107]

The Brewers floundered about into June, losing 8 of 11 and drawing only 1,500 for a Saturday game. Eddie Marshall's hitting grew like Luke Hamlin's personal losing drought. Marshall's unprecedented American Association record was halted at 43 games when the Apostles' Monty Stratton held him to only one ball out of the infield on Saturday, June 15th. Marshall hit .323 (66 for 202) in that span. Stratton went on to have a James Stewart movie made about his one-legged major league comeback from a hunting accident. The Texas "Gander" also nipped a 4-game Brewer win streak in the 7–4 interlude, stretching his won streak to 5.[108]

That Marshall hit only .239 for the entire season was more indicative of how the Brewers short-circuited. It was much like how one Floyd Verette won his July 1st beer-guzzling contest in front of 10,000 at Cedarburg's Hilgen Spring Park. He downed a half-gallon in 34 seconds, only to literally piss it away. That's how the few Brewer highlights, like Polli's September 7th no-no over St. Paul, went. A 6th place finish helped get Marshall a bitter one-way ticket to Kansas City.[109]

If Al Sothoron was to fatten his percentage of the gross, they would have to set much higher sights at their 1936 spring training at Lake Wales, Florida. They made the World Champion Detroit Tigers their first exhibition opponent. The possibility of slugging prospect Rudy York coming over from the Motor City was still gummed up when Milwaukee went toe-to-toe with the champs. Outdone by the Tigers 18–14 after losing a 12–5 lead, Chet Laabs' homer on that March 18th previewed how Milwaukee could bash with the best.[110]

The old Carlisle Indian-cum-Louisville Colonel, Joe Guyon, was now one of Sothoron's coaches and Laabs was made into an outfielder. Injured Ted Gullic came off leading the A.A. in doubles, but ended up sharing garden time with Chet Morgan. Bernard "Frenchy" Uhalt brought his left-handed bat and speed from Bakersfield and the White Sox to give this lineup an ideal leadoff man.

The middle infield settled with Chet "Wimpy" Wilburn coming from KC in the Marshall deal to replace Eddie at short. Eddie Hope graduated from a utility role to 2nd base and Lin Storti shifted his big bat to third. Cuban Salvador Ramos was hot corner insurance and though he never caught in the regular season, he was taught some of the tricks of that trade by George Detore and backup Bill Brenzel.

Right-hander Joe Heving brought 4 years of majors experience and was the top arm at Indy in 1932. The final ingredient was without a doubt Rudy York at first. The Badger Music Publishing Co. even printed the lyrics of

Michael Neyses and music by Oscar Baker for "Our Team's Leading the Hit Parade," a paean to these 1936 Brewers.[111]

A mock print argument between Umpire "Badblud" and "Butch" became a *Journal* feature throughout the season. Harold (White Pants) Schiefelbein, long a Milwaukee sandlot arbiter, won an American Association job after a Florida tryout. He had umpired under the name "O'Brien" in the Three-I League in 1935 and was assigned to St. Paul's opener at Columbus.[112]

The opener 6–1 loss at Louisville on Monday, April 13th offered little inkling for the procession to come. Wayne LeMaster, the product from across the Ohio River, gave 10,550 Colonels rooters a taste of revenge over his old team. Only Chet Laabs' solo shot prevented a shutout in the 7th. Ray Thompson caught LeMaster's gem against his hometown nine.[113]

George Detore caught more than Joe Braxton in that game. He got an earful from some Louisville crank in the 4th inning when his Italian ancestry was abused. George took exception and along with Tot Pressnell challenged the customer to come down from the stands and fight. The gendarmes did prevent any fisticuffs from arising.

Some 9,270 Milwaukeeans welcomed their fast-starting newcomers home on May Day. The 7–4 results were much better as Laabs and Storti drove for the circuit off the Colonels' Ed Holley.[114] Luke Hamlin required some "nice Heving" from Kentucky Joe in the 4th to preserve victory. LeMaster, a wicked-hitting hurler for Milwaukee in '35, actually pinch-hit for Holley.

New governor Philip LaFollette was content to watch mayor Dan Hoan uncork a wild first pitch over the Colonels' Canadian, Goody Rosen.

Milwaukee took 10 of 13 from the eastern clubs, forging a 2nd place, 16–9 mark by mid May. They drove the rest of the A.A. into submission, just like Mussolini did to Haile Selassie in Ethiopia, when they broke away from the pack by Memorial Day.[115]

They were a half-game up on the home Blues when Brewer officials were disappointed by a holiday gathering of 11,883. They expected more than 15,000 for the bargain bill at Muehlebach Park. Garland Braxton's relief of Clyde Hatter, with a 2–1 KC lead in the 7th, set up a 14-inning 8–2 runaway. Chet Laabs' homer tied it in the 9th. University of Wisconsin grad Milt Bocek did a fine job for the Blues in right, but Brewer bats delivered Tot Pressnell's 7th straight win out the gate. York (.341-12-41), Laabs (.339-14-42), and Storti (.281-12-33) were huge early.[116]

Sothoron's charges expanded the gap over St. Paul to 3½ games by July 4th. The season attendance already surpassed 100,000 by then, so another sweep had York and Laabs hovering near 80 RBI already and Storti had 20 homers. That 46–33 looked mighty ...well, mighty.[117]

Al Sothoron was wary of such prosperity. He would have preferred to see a second place team keep pressing the chase than one that risked choking on its own defense of the top. He worried over their lack of hitting throughout a

13–10 July homestand. The Brewers had occupied first since June 4th and led the Saints by 5 full games until that homestand. Now Sothoron had his wish. Despite a twin sweep over Indy, they chased St. Paul by 2 games now.[118]

Eddie Hope's erratic fielding was a cause for concern and umpires Bill Guthrie and Cotton Kearney were ribbed for their courage in finally donning their gray summer garb. Kearney's odd way of signaling a runner safe, with his right thumb, had Milwaukee out to challenge a call.[119]

Fabian Gaffke, another product of the Milwaukee hotbed who would reach the majors, ranked fifth in A.A. batting for Minneapolis, with a .352 average from the right side.[120]

A temporary spring injury changed Tot Pressnell's delivery for the better. A tip from aged Phillies' coach Hans Lobert altered his 3/4 overhand serve to a less painful sidearm approach. George Detore was his biggest booster and like Joe Heving, the Tot was transformed from a mild-mannered soul into one "big parcel of confidence."[121]

The Milwaukee Brewers were on track to win the first-ever Governors' Cup, which would be awarded to the winners of the new Frank Shaughnessy, 4-team playoff format. The pennant-winners would face the 3rd place team and the 2nd and 4th place clubs would each meet in a best-of-7 series. Those winners would then meet for the Governors' Cup and the playoff champion would then meet the International League playoff champion in a "Little World Series."

George Trautman succeeded A.A. founder Tom Hickey as circuit president and was the man to award the 4-foot silver cup on an ebony base. The trophy was surmounted by a gold replica of winged "victory" and a silver globe with a relief outline of the league's six states. That was supported by baseball player figures of gold.[122]

If that all sounds impressive, well, the playoff was anything but golden to the so-called "purists." Anything but a straight-up pennant, based upon league standings, was something less than a real title. *The Journal* sports editor, R.G. Lynch, saw Milwaukee winning by default.

The Brewers of 1936 would allay all doubts as to whom the best team was in their league. Chet Laabs won universal praise as a slugger with major league potential, but he would've fit right in with the modern major league Brewers. He was on an unofficial record pace for striking out.

The Berlin Olympics, where Jesse Owens would thumb his nose at Nazi notions of Aryan supremacy, fast approached. Heinie Bendinger mulled over a post-season trip to Cuba for his Brewers from his rooftop private box. The largest Borchert Field Ladies Day crowd (7,000 out of 12,000) saw Heving's 18th win over the Kels, Thursday, August 20th. Laabs was honored by the local Catholic Order of Foresters on Friday, August 21st. On his first trip to the plate for the critical first game of that St. Paul series, he was presented with a pot of cash amidst rampant rumors that he'd say "I do" in the off-season. On

1936 pitching stars Tot Pressnell, Luke Hamlin, and Joe Heving. Uncredited illustration from George W. Hilton article, "Milwaukee's Charter Membership in the American League." Clipping File, Art & Music Department. Milwaukee Public Library.

the night in his honor, "Little Dynamite" blasted not one, but two home runs, the first of which was a grand slam![123] In order for 13,500 of Laabs' closest pals to consummate the celebration, Luke Hamlin had to bail out Clyde Hatter. The 9th inning rally by the Saints was stayed, 10–8, and joy ensued.

Errors made for mayhem in each of the double losses at St. Paul on August 31st. The second game just beat the 6 o'clock curfew and the Brewers, as uneasy as at mid-season, snuck into Minneapolis by twilight. Al Sothoron resembled a "professional pallbearer" after the beating even though his team was still 7 games up. Umpire Bill Guthrie's recommended solution to the nervous skipper was strong drink, "so they can become unlax for de rest of the season." After all, Wisconsin's summer drought had definitely ended.[124]

By early September, any civic reception for Milwaukee's likely pennant-winners was cast in doubt when Bankroll Louie Nahin reported that any exhibition with a local amateur all-star team may violate the A.A. constitution. Would George Trautman make an exception?

This quandary required an emergency meeting of the civic committee under the auspices of acting mayor Harry J. Devine. Alderman John E. Koerner was named to head the welcome wagon for the team's arrival via the Milwaukee Road at 9:20 a.m., Tuesday, September 1st. A band was furnished by the Milwaukee Brewers Association. Fire sirens and factory whistles were to sound off.[125]

The ballplayers would ride aboard fire apparatus in a parade, east on W. Michigan St. to N. Water, then north to Wisconsin Ave. and west back to the Court of Honor. Trautman was to award the pennant that night as part of a wrestling show at Borchert Field.

It was suggested that the Brewers remain in Kansas City an extra day and celebrate Wednesday when the playoffs would begin. No stone was unturned when it had been 22 years between pennants! Several hundred Brewer rooters from Rice Lake, Wisconsin, went into Minnesota to see their newly crowned champs. A telegram, with over 2,000 fans' signatures, was also received when the pennant was officially clinched on Friday, September 4th, with a sweep of the Millers.[126]

It may have been premature, but George Detore offered insight into Buffalo and its Bisons, who clinched the International League pennant. He had played there and foresaw the left field wall as a haven for Brewer sluggers Laabs, York, and Gullic. Storti could tee off, too, if the Bisons employed a lefty.[127]

Provided they could dispose of their A.A. brethren, Al Sothoron's 90–64 Brewers would likely face Ray Schalk's Bisons. The onetime Brewer backstop and future Hall of Famer guided the pride of western New York to a spring grapefruit league split with Milwaukee.

Milwaukee's longtime Socialist mayor Dan Hoan sips a soda in this candid Borchert Field shot. Milwaukee Public Library Historical Photograph Collection.

It sounded like another day at the office, each score being 9 to 5 and all. As much as the team whooped it up in the showers, there was a weary relief. The team was eager to win it for their popular skipper and he was proud that they had not backed their way into a championship. Ex-Brewer Rosy Ryan was the main Miller victim.

Clyde Hatter sealed the second win at Minneapolis and wanted the souvenir ball clutched by Wimpy Wilburn for the final out. It remained in Doc Buckner's trunk until that presentation could be made.

Of Ted Gullic's 3 homers in that doubleheader, his last sent the 2,615 Miller fans to the exits. For Minneapolis, fellow Milwaukeeans Joe Hauser and Fabe Gaffke each factored in. Unser Choe had a wild throwing error on a Game One Wilburn bunt, but hit a 2-run poke in Game Two. Gaffke had an RBI in each contest.

Lou Nahin also looked forward to Buffalo. The Bisons drew 300,000 for the season and 87,000 for 5 straight night games. Buffalo was just a great baseball town. Heinie Bendinger could only relish how far he had come from a sandlot catcher, who used to check bikes at the Lloyd Street Grounds for Charley Moll for free. He might cringe in losing at *schafskopf* (sheepshead) cards to the Irish, but Heinie had a pennant in 3 years! His favorite dish, "sooner-buckles," tasted even better now.

"Hail to the Champs!" rang through Milwaukee when page one coverage of that finely-planned parade finally took place on Tuesday, September 6th. The passageway at the railroad depot was roped off to about 6,000. Some 40,000 cheered the entire route. Kids were in abundance from the Knothole Gang to team mascot, Ray Jaskulski of 2231 S. 15th St. He wore a huge "24" on his uniform back and had the envy of every kid as he boarded a fire truck.[128]

For all the bigwigs there, so were Jack Kloza's nieces, Roseanne and Jacqueline, and Chet Laabs' nephew, Jerry. Chester Collins Morgan (Chich, Jr.) got to ride in dad's lap and ring a fire bell. Even old Tom Dougherty, who pitched for Milwaukee's last flag-bearers, was there.

A sweating, smiling trainer Doc Buckner clambered onto a fire truck, working his rabbit's foot overtime. George Detore had "miseries in his stomach," Wimpy Wilburn had a hip injury, and Morgan was just out with an eye infection. With Doc's lotions, all would be ready for KC.

And ready they were. The club already lined up pitcher Ralph Winegarner and outfielder Tom Henrich for the next season, while they inflicted a 4-game sweep upon the Blues.[129]

Rudy York's 8th inning triple won the opener, 4–1, before 8,460, and got the early lead for the Junior Chamber of Commerce MVP Cup. Tot Pressnell handcuffed the Blues, 4–2, with 9,109 looking on. KC manager Dutch Zwilling was ridiculed for not walking catcher Bill Brenzel to get at Eddie Hope. Brenzel's "lusty" double broke open a tie game. Game One winner Luke Hamlin relieved Joe Heving in the 8th, but homers by Laabs and York, off John Niggeling, made Game Three, 7–4. Dale Alexander drove in all 4 Blues runs, without any extra-base hits.

Wimpy Wilburn laid it on thick to the Blues' negro trainer, who paid a social visit to Doc Buckner, saying, "You can put the uniforms in mothballs after tomorrow's game, we'll make it four straight." An angry Eddie Marshall was unable to show up Al Sothoron for peddling him to the Blues. The KC dressing room wound up as quiet as the Marx Brothers "A Day at the Races" set in memory of deceased impresario Irving Thalberg, who resurrected their careers.[130]

Clyde Hatter's 3-hit shutout polished off this series at Kansas City. The postseason games were broadcast back to Milwaukee on two radio stations: W9XBY (1530 kilocycles) and a telegraph report was relayed over WISN. Local politicians were now out of the woodwork to replace "ramshackle" Borchert Field with a stadium that could be built as a Works Progress Administration (W.P.A.) project. The Feds would provide all the labor, the city all the materials. Just who would initiate the project was debated.[131]

"With a Heil Nazi, Nazi and a Hot Ja! Ja!" 100,000 storm troopers convened upon Nuremberg when the Brewers took after the Indianapolis Indians on Tuesday, September 17th. Luke Hamlin's 5-hit calcimining and Chet Laabs' 6th inning homer made 2–0 possible. It was the second straight post-season shutout for Milwaukee. The "best batter in the minors," Ox Eckhardt, went down before 5,684 as Hamlin's 7th strikeout victim. Onetime Boston Brave slugger Wally Berger, "a tough hombre in the clutch," rolled out to Eddie Hope for the final out.[132]

The Buffalo Bisons had eliminated the Newark Bears and were now 2 up on the Baltimore Orioles. The Brewers did likewise to Indy when Brenzel saved a homer to beat his old boss, Wade "Red" Killefer. It was only Brenzel's second homer of the year, but anchored the 10–3 blowout. Ted Gullic's 9th inning belt won Game Three, 7–6, as he was mobbed "for mayor on the people's ticket." Clyde Hatter's 11 strikeouts didn't hurt either. Gullic was hugged and kissed by the gals, punched on the back and mauled by the guys. And that was in a London-like pea soup of fog.

Luke Hamlin rode a 5-run hitting spree in the 7th straight out of Indy and into the Little World Series. His third straight playoff win made Hamlin "a big leaguer" in Sothoron's eyes.[133]

The Brewers were then allowed to play the local sandlot semi-pro All-Stars while awaiting the Bisons. Future Brewer and DiMaggio hit streak-stopper 3rd baseman Kenny Keltner was among the Stars, but after they threw a 14–11 scare into the Brewers on Tuesday, September 22nd, Sothoron signed up pint-sized leadoff shortstop Stanley Galaszewski to a future tryout. The All-Stars had 6–0 lead after 4, and Wimpy Wilburn and sandlot 2nd sacker Jimmy Adlam each had 3 RBI. Lefty Al Eckert had enough Organized Ball savvy to fool the champs in the first 2 stanzas.[134]

That diversion and a banquet of 700 at the Pfister Hotel aside, Milwaukee worked over the visiting Bisons. The provincial nature of the minors made them an unknown quantity to Brewer backers.

The Borchert Field denizens, some 10,000 strong, waited for the dynamite in the Brewer bats to explode and with 3 runs in the 5th and another 4 scores in the 8th, it did.[135] Six of Milwaukee's 11 hits went for extra bases — a Gullic homer, 4 triples, and a 2-bagger. The final was Milwaukee 7, Buffalo 5.

The explosion of "soft ball" was also being recognized across the land, with 2 million players, 60-thousand teams, and a thousand lighted parks. Baseball great George Sisler headed a Midwestern "major" league and one semi-pro pitcher made $50,000 for tossing 200 games.[136]

Four Brewer home runs were more hardball than the Bisons could stand in Game Two. Ted Gullic's blast tied it in the 11th and Lin Storti's broke up the deadlock, 6–5. The two heroes chanted, "They can't beat us!" to the delight 10,529 frantic fans. Gullic and Storti were cronies going back to their rookie days.[137]

Sothoron was more impressed with this team than his 1930 Colonels, and

Slugging first baseman Rudy York took his monstrous power from Milwaukee's 1936 pennant winners to the Motor City. Milwaukee Public Library Historical Photograph Collection.

Harry Clark compared them to his pennant-winners of 1913-1914. Detore growled, "I could have bitten those passed balls in half!" after handling Pressnell's knucklers all year, only to let a couple get away in a most important game. After the first two Borchert Field games, which drew a combined 21,101, the $16,923.15 in receipts had 60 percent, or $9,256.30, going to the players' pool, with each club receiving $1,928.40. And the merits of a Social Security act were being hotly debated at the time.[138]

A Detore homer bested the Bisons at Buffalo, 3-1, as 15,212 overflowed into center field. Luke Hamlin was aided by another Laabs' circuit clout off of Carl Fischer, but it was suspected that Ray Schalk was stealing Milwaukee's signals on a 3rd inning hit-and-run play.[139] The Bisons were held to only 4 hits by Joe Heving in Game Four, but Buffalo managed their only break-through, 2-1. Heving's blunder was a home run to Buck Crouse, who had been in the majors "back when peg top pants were all the rage."[140]

Milwaukee could finally give its first Little World Series Champions a rousing welcome Friday, October 2nd after the Brewers pounded the southpaw Fischer and three other Bison hurlers, 8-3. Chet Laabs cracked 2 more homers and Wimpy Wilburn added another to give Milwaukee a total of 10 in the 5 games. It also gave Tot Pressnell his third win over the Bisons.

Sothoron told the crowd assembled at the Northwestern station at 12:15 p.m. to greet their conquering heroes, saying, "This is the greatest minor league club I've ever seen! I wish I could have them all back next year." With most of the players' wives there, Lou Nahin disbursed a championship reward of a $648 check to each man for their winning work. "Hail the Champions!"[141]

The classic clash between two similar Great Lakes industrial cities, both famous for their wintry weather and German and Polish inhabitants, may have been short-lived but doubly gratifying. The wait of nearly twice as long from the Brewers' first two pennants to its next put Al Sothoron in a very select pantheon of flag-waving Milwaukee managers. Unlike Harry Clark, he had the added jewel of playoff titles to boast about, but he also had a far more heinous task to construct a repeat.

Of the Brewers' power quartet, Gullic and Storti had proven their might only at the Double-A level. The Detroit Tigers knew Rudy York and Chet Laabs had major league muscle and pounced upon their services. Even George Detore and Chet Wilburn needed replacing.

The pitching rotation was ravaged even more. Mad Hatter also went up with Detroit, Hot Potato Hamlin to Brooklyn and Joe Heving to Cleveland. Sothoron's wish was a pipe dream.[142] The quality of his 1937 staff was exposed early on at the Biloxi, Mississippi, training. Pulaski, Wisconsin, portsider Allen Johnson kept his outfield on the run when those powerful Cleveland Indians rammed over 8 runs in the ninth for a March 31st, 11–4 nosedive.[143]

One of the more intriguing men to emerge out of that game was Bill Zuber. He had been brought up from New Orleans by the Indians' Steve O'Neill after a hard-working winter to plow farm fields and handle 100-pound sacks of livestock feed. Zuber, who was nicknamed "Goober," came from Middle Amana, part of the famous Amana Colonies in eastern Iowa.[144]

His unusual upbringing and heavy German accent made him an affable verbal jouster amongst his teammates and great copy in the Milwaukee press. Zuber learned English only 4 years before Cleveland optioned him to the Brewers on April 23rd. The flame-thrower learned baseball after the all-German Amana Society lightened up its rules on such recreation.

His sweetheart remained in Homestead, Iowa, and his refreshing naivete would make the *landsmann* welcome amongst the good burghers of Beertown. Al Sothoron could only drool over his untamed fast ball. Zuber was appreciative of Sothoron's encouragement after enduring so much comment on his wildness while pitching his way up the ranks of Cedar Rapids, Zanesville, Fargo-Moorhead, and New Orleans. He was discovered by Cleveland scout and old Brewer flinger Cy Slapnicka who lived in Cedar Rapids.

Any hopes Milwaukee had of having future Yankee star Tommy Henrich in their outfield blew up when the commissioner, Judge Landis, ruled Henrich a free agent. He signed on to become "Old Reliable" in the Bronx.[145]

The Brewers association with Cleveland also went beyond getting a good look at Bob Feller's sensational heat in the spring. Cleveland native Happy Al Milnar and George Blaeholder brought their arms and Canadian Jeff Heath, of Ft. Williams (now half of Thunder Bay), Ontario, brought his bristling bat from the northern shore of Lake Superior. Another Heath, personable Minor "Mickey," now played first.[146]

These players would represent a Milwaukee that ranked second in the nation for fire safety, but was a little too safe and stagnant as debate on a "soldier's memorial stadium" crept on. At least the ongoing Spanish Civil War ended more decisively.[147]

Writers around the A.A. consigned Milwaukee to a predicted seventh place, but that did not deter between 8,700-9,000 from welcoming their defending champs on Saturday, April 17th. Al Milnar held the St. Paul Saints to 9 hits in 19 innings in arctic conditions at Borchert's "Kodiak island" Field.[148] It grew so cold that "fans were letting only half-full bottles slip out of their fingers." The season would not end up as dire as forecasted. Thanks to a 16-4 start and a 23-game home-winning streak snapped May 30th before only 1,500 by Kansas City.[149]

Brewer shortstop Otto Bluege, brother of major league 3rd baseman Ossie Bluege, even walked 5 times in succession during the May 10th game, an A.A. record.[150]

Rookie Milwaukeean Fabian Gaffke had a better time of it before 6,500 at Worcester, Massachusetts. He led his new Boston Red Sox with a triple, a home run, and 3 RBI to vanquish the Holy Cross Crusaders, 5-0, but wound up with Minneapolis.[151]

The Brewers' own hometown boy, 3rd baseman Ken Keltner, was given his own 'Night' at Borchert Field on Wednesday, September 8th. The team had just not had the horses to do better than teeter on the brink of a 4th place playoff spot. Kansas City's Ted Kleinhans, a Deer Park, Wisconsin, lefty from St. Croix County in the northwestern part of the state, just shut them out.

Keltner's Bay View followers presented the Boys Tech grad (like Laabs) with a Chrysler car and his teammates gave him a golf bag. Between 9,000-10,000 were thrilled by Kenny's ignorance of the honor night jinx as he rapped a homer in each game of the double bill over Minneapolis.[152] Wilhelm Heinrich Zuber helped his own "gilt-edged" 5-hitter with an RBI single in the opener and Forrest Pressnell's shutout in the nightcap clinched the postseason berth. The Brooklyn-born Tot was the only starter left from '36.

Keltner's night continued in jubilation at George Devine's Eagles Ballroom, but it was also announced that the 3rd baseman was sold to Cleveland for 6 players and $25,000.

There was a twisted irony in the national headlines that a man named Hugo Black, an F.D.R. nominee to the U.S. Supreme Court, should come into the public crosshairs for his alleged ties to the Ku Klux Klan. It was a year when a trotter named "Greyhound" would win and a bride-to-be was named Batchelor.[153]

In Milwaukee, the Borchert Field welcome mat was rolled out for a couple games in the championship series of the American Negro League. One of the earlier games was called in Chicago, curiously enough, on account of "darkness," but the Kansas City Monarchs and Chicago American Giants brought excitement with them. A "big rumpus" ended the first game on September 13th when the Monarchs scored the 8-7 lead run. Chicago protested vehemently to the ironically-named umpire, Virgil Bluitt, and he was ultimately overruled via telephone by league president Maj. R.R. Jackson in Chicago.[154]

The Brewers playoffs weren't quite as colorful and drew disappointing crowds in the 3,000 range. A Frenchy Uhalt homer won the first game against Toledo, but a Babe Herman clout evened the series. Sothoron's surprise start of "Swedish sphinx" Allen Johnson won Game Three, and Ted Gullic and Lin Storti each supported Bill Zuber with a homer and a triple in a 15–6 spree. Ralph Winegarner was then victimized in an 11-inning, 11–10 setback. Milwaukee eliminated the Hens on Sunday, September 19th with a sick Sothoron confined to his hotel room.[155] Mickey Heath acted well, 12–3.

The Brewers would have to go through more feathers, if they wanted to see a second consecutive Little World Series. The Columbus Red Birds had another idea, as future Cardinals star Mort Cooper bested a wild Zuber in Game One. The Flock upended Pressnell in Game Two, then Ralph Winegarner struck out 7 to shut Columbus out. Future Brewer Max Macon's 2–0 whitewash over Herr Zuber had Milwaukee on the ropes, but Mickey Heath's Game 5 homer delayed the inevitable. Gullic's homer gave a 4-run lead, but that was it. Winegarner was hammered and Columbus advanced out of a 10–4 game six, over and out.[156]

And Ken Keltner went to Cleveland with a $500 bonus from Henry Bendinger.

Allen Sothoron's sojourn with the Brewers was further decimated by the defection of Frenchy Uhalt to the Pacific Coast League. After seeing his old *amico*, George Detore, win the P.C.L. batting title with San Diego in '37, the Frenchman decided to return to his sunny California roots.[157]

To offset the losses of Pressnell and Milnar, Sothoron hired 9-year major league vet Whitlow Wyatt to be his ace. The old "Georgia cotton grower" was up to the task and would win the A.A. pitching Triple Crown for 1938. His velocity wasn't all his speed. He could outrun anyone in camp, too.[158]

The catching corps was remade but was still something of a platoon operation. Just a pair of regular Joes, Becker and Just, replaced the also doubly-initialed Bill Brenzel and Hank Helf. The left side of the infield saw Cleveland hopefuls Oscar Grimes at third and Tommy Irwin at short to replace Keltner and Blondy Ryan, respectively. Mega-talented Jeff Heath held out at Cleveland.[159]

For all the reshuffling, the Brewers ended up with essentially a rerun of 1937. Ex-Brewers continued to move up the baseball evolutionary food chain. Wausau greeted Bunny Brief with a banquet of 800 for him to pilot their Northern League Lumberjacks. Brief had been a gym attendant for the Milwaukee Public Schools Extension Department. He received a farewell "loving cup" made out of a tomato can. Lou Nahin arranged for Wausau to serve as sort of a Brewer farm and Milwaukee's assistant treasurer, Rudy Schaffer, also spoke up there.[160]

Dainty Denny Gearin also wanted in on this sort of action and pled with Nahin over the phone for a baseball job. Ol' Bankroll Lou lined him up to manage Cy Summers' team in the municipal amateur league, where it was believed he would most help young pitchers.

A boxer named Tony Bruno was Milwaukee's Third Ward "cock of the walk," while the Brewers held heat-shortened workouts in Hot Springs. Lin Storti and "Winey," Ralph Winegarner, did the holdout act. Winegarner would do an Orwollian turn of versatility, proving valuable as a pinch-hitter and at the corners of the infield, in addition to his mound labors.

It was also the first look in camp at a large-footed lefty from Wausau's American Legion team, Johnny Schmitz was tabbed "Beartracks." Right-hander Louis Ahlf from Milwaukee had a "schoolboy complexion." The outfield added two vets in prodigal son Fred Schulte and Roy Johnson, one of two Oklahoma Indian brothers (the other being Bob, also a future Brewer) to enjoy life in the American League.[161] Schulte claimed he never legally changed his name from Schult, but Otto Borchert outargued him about tacking that extra "e" on his early paychecks. So Fred's kids became "Schultes" in school.[162]

Harry "Doc" Buckner was ordered home due to ill health. Brewer coach Red Smith, the old tubby backstop who also assisted Curly Lambeau's Green Bay Packers on the gridiron, immediately phoned Ticonderoga, N.Y., to have Myron "Mush" Esler ride into Hot Springs by rail. Thirty-six hours later, Red's fellow Kaukaunan didn't know what he would be paid, but he was a riot as a mimic. The good "Docktah," possibly a former standout turn-of-the-century Negro pitcher, did pass away.[163]

The widow of Otto Borchert held up her ballpark lease as a possible obstacle to any new stadium construction. Any violation of the remaining 15 years could forfeit the franchise back to the Borchert family. Press and official sentiment was that the park be condemned in its crowded residential neighborhood. A veteran's memorial county stadium proposal at the west end of the Soldier's Home grounds gained traction through the County Board's Building & Grounds Committee.[164]

In that political milieu, the Brewers went from being greeted home on the Riverside Theater stage to thrashing the Columbus Red Birds, 9–2, in the home opener. Whit Wyatt not only held the Flock to 4 hits, but doubled in 3 runs himself. "Heil, Whitlow!" The 9,265 paid also had the added treat of seeing football's Slingin' Sammy Baugh open at short for Columbus. He went 0-for-4, with an error.

The first night doubleheader ever at Borchert Field took place on Wednesday, June 15, 1938. The ballpark's configuration already made viewing difficult — as old Mike Kelley once said, a person would have to go to Borchert Field twice just to see one game, once from the leftfield side and the other to see what happened in right field.[165] Well, the 100-foot telephone poles that held the lights because the fragile grandstand roof couldn't, were inside the sight lines to exacerbate the problem. That first June 15th game started at 8 p.m., but no inning would start after 11:30. Roy Johnson's outfield speed was an asset, but since he was unaccustomed to starlight ball, his average suffered.

Three Brewers, Wyatt, Grimes, and Becker, were among the American

Association All-Stars to play the league-leading host Indianapolis Indians on July 14th. Ray Schalk now managed the Indians and the All-Stars were guided by the previous year's pennant-winning manager, Columbus' Burt Shotton. A certain "one-dimensional " outfielder from Minneapolis, named Ted Williams, was at Shotton's beckon call. The lanky San Diego kid could hit, like for the triple crown...[166]

An "automatic pitcher" was developed by St. Louis banker Byron Moser, but "it cannot throw a curve." The August military mobilization in Europe was to do that for the world. Of course, Nazi preparedness to march had no bearing on the "Schnickelfritz Band" playing at Milwaukee's Riverside Theater stage nor on the German Kino Radio Theater at 2459 W. Fond du Lac Ave., offering "Unser bliche Melodien" (immortal melodies) featuring the music of waltz king Johann Strauss.[167]

All hell was on the verge of breaking loose again in Europe and all the 3rd place Brewers could do was fight the St. Paul Saints to a 7-game loss in the first round of the A.A. playoffs. It was Al Sothoron's late show-up for a post-season game that ingloriously cost the ex-spitballer his job. At age 46, the Ohioan who delivered 4 winning seasons out of his 5 in Milwaukee would die on June 17, 1939, at St. Louis. It was how he died that was most telling: Acute hepatitis caused by chronic alcoholism. The decade ended much like it started for the Brewers, on a dark sad note.[168]

For 1939, the managerial mantle was turned over to the team's well-liked home run leader, Mickey Heath. He vainly tried to instill hope into a ballclub that was even more depleted of talent. There were no postseason hopes to worry about, but goober-growing Buck Morrow and Tex Carleton kept the top of the rotation competitive. Outside of Ted Gullic, the order was ordinary. The new manager's own stick work wilted under the demands of the job. His homers fell by half.

Whatever spirit Heath could drill into his team at Ocala, Florida, it was clear that this was the weakest Brewer outfit yet under Bendinger's ownership. The season would make as much sense as the April 10th Bavarian "edelweissfest" that drew 2,000 participants to *Bohemian* Hall. Who needed Hitler marching into Czechoslovakia's Sudetenland?[169]

Milwaukee mustered but 4 hits in the opening loss at Louisville. Roy Johnson's 7th inning homer was one of those hits, but 10,000 got to revel in the 3–2 win by their "new deal" Colonels. The Borchert Field faithful ushered in baseball's misguided "Centennial" year on April 27th. The 10,594 saw Lone Ranger Tex Carleton lasso the Indianapolis Indians, 4–2, to reliever George Blaeholder's "Tonto." The fans became acquainted with utility mancum-new-catcher Ramos "Chico" Hernandez and the "Mad Russian," outfielder Lou Novikoff. Both were thought to become popular attractions in the A.A., but Novikoff's intro lasted a mere 11 games. He was described as a powerful cross between Hack Wilson and pro rassler Stanislaus Zbyszko.[170]

An unidentified Brewer hurler from March 26, 1939. Milwaukee Public Library Historical Photograph Collection.

Despite a small win streak, May Day, the first Ladies Day of the year, drew only 1,300, of which only 528 were paid. It was a sign of things to come that a younger Vivian Vance played Milwaukee's Davidson Theater in "Kiss the Boys Goodbye." Brewer secretary Rudy Schaffer's May 9th wedding at Mother of Good Counsel Church in Wauwatosa was about all the team had to celebrate for 1939. Even the Firemen versus Police Fund game drew 2,400 on June 17th, and former major leaguer Fritz Mollwitz was now a *polizist* in suburban Shorewood. Billy Orr, an old reserve infielder with the 1910–1913 Philly A's, was now an engineer for Shell Oil, visiting Bunny Brief at Shorewood. Orr reported that former Brewer and his A's teammate Amos Strunk did right well for himself in the insurance business in the City of Brotherly Love.[171]

Another old Brewer from back then, *bon vivant* Eddie Stumpf, was now on the baseball stump at Tarboro, N.C., in the Plain States League. By slapping his young beer parlor swains with fines enough, he could have the Tarboro social playing field wide open for himself. Stumpf was in a partnership with Buck Morrow to own this team, and Mrs. Buck was slated to become president over G.M. Eddie. A Brewer farm was in the making.[172]

Stanley Stencel was a Milwaukee youth offering a ray of hope with the Class D Hopkinsville (Ky.) Hoppers in the Kitty League. His lefty bat led the loop in hits and RBI for catching manager Harry Griswold, the University of Wisconsin alum.[173]

The Brewers didn't need their own alum, visiting baseball clown old Nick Altrock, nor the Negro baseball antics of the Ethiopian Clowns and Chicago American Giants, who drew about 2,500 to Borchert Field and featured a homer by "Wahoo."[174]

No, by September 4th, the "peculiar odor from the near North Side wasn't from the glue factory or one of Hitler's promises ... just boots, bobbles, and mental blunders between the lines" that drew 621 people. Lou Novikoff's nickname aside, it became a mad, mad, mad world.[175]

8
Pennants 3, World War II

If Mickey Heath wasn't quite prepared to run up the white flag for his 1939 Milwaukee Brewers, he would do so by 1940. Just as Hitler's blitzkrieg now had much of central Europe in abeyance, the rest of the American Association steamrollered over Milwaukee.

America was not yet directly involved in the international conflict, but for those Milwaukeeans wary of a constant drumbeat of an expanding war, Molitor's High Life Nite Club was one source of refuge. On 2763 N. 3rd St., Molitor's served chicken, steak, chops, and barbecued ribs. Amateur shows were every Wednesday night, as Kay Crandall and His Orchestra were the house band. Cab Calloway's jivers played the Riverside.[1]

Despite the lingering effects of the Depression and the uncertainty of the war, sentiment grew that President Franklin Delano Roosevelt should seek an unprecedented third term. Milwaukee's socialist mayor of 24 years, Dan Hoan, was swamped by a singing, young Carl Zeidler.[2]

Well, Mickey Heath's terms ran by the baseball season. And in Ocala, Florida, he had even less to work with than before. Alan Hale of WISN Radio conducted special interviews from the spring training site at 1120 on your dial. Hal Walker also hosted that station's "Dugout Doings." Hale, who was elected presented of the A.A. chapter of baseball broadcasters by July, had plenty of new faces to visit with. Other than Ted Gullic, the entire starting lineup was new. George Blaeholder, promoted from reliever to ace, joined Buck Morrow and Ken Jungels back on the mound.[3]

Thanks to the winter snowshoe war, where the Soviet Union invaded little neighboring Finland, the Helsinki newspaper *Uusi Suomi* declared that the Olympic Games could not be held "here or elsewhere" for 1940. *Pesapallo*, the Finnish baseball, was pretty well whacked, too.[4]

Johnny "Bear Tracks" Schmitz didn't need snowshoes to pitch his way back to the Three-I League Madison Blues. His "unnatural motion" saw to that. The little Stanley Galaszewski, who had been signed in that 1936 Brewer exhibition against local sandlot all-stars, was now trying to win a job as Stan

"Galle." His bobble hands at short just didn't yet make the grade. Left fielder Hal Peck, from nearby Big Bend just southwest of Milwaukee, had a left-handed wrist action at bat that Heath thought made him a real "comer."[5]

Ted Gullic and "colorful as a rainbow" new 3rd baseman Charlie English, a 4-year vet of limited major league exposure and a year at KC, were both "incurable anglers." They could barely be dragged from their last casts in Florida. Gullic was from Koshkonong, Missouri. No one ever said if he ever fished Lake Koshkonong, southwest of Milwaukee. The only thing outfielder Paul Dunlap, 2nd baseman Barney Walls, and Lou Nahin caught when camp broke were colds.[6]

They opened at a Columbus diamond that was inundated with heavy rainfall. Walls was well enough to swat a 325-foot blast over the wall, with Eddie Morgan aboard in the Thursday, April 18th curtain raiser. Milwaukee humbled the Red Birds, 5–2, and Frank Makosky easily could have had a shutout in a "frost bitten and dreary afternoon" that lured 2,371. However, there were 3 ducats sold, which went unused.[7]

Nahin helped Bud Connolly and Red Smith finalize the Madison Blues roster and the Milwaukee Municipal Recreation Department's director of athletics, Harold (Zip) Morgan, announced that ex-Brewers Bunny Brief and Jack Kloza would conduct baseball classes throughout the city. Kloza was assigned the Pumping Station Field, Merrill Park, Hawthorne Field, and Auer Avenue Park, up on the North Side. Bunny would hop around the South Side—Burnham Field, Lewis Field, Lincoln Field, and Kinnickinnic Field.[8]

Interest in the unknown Brewers actually brought a couple hundred people to their first Borchert Field workout before May Day. Fans wanted to see how $30,000 was spent upon their rebuilding. "Robust Robert" Kline, a veteran pitcher who came from Buffalo for Roy Johnson, tested out a knee brace donated by Dr. Clarence Wiley Spears to his young protege, Brewer trainer Mush Esler. Brewer players like Kline, who saw both teams, debated whether the '36 Brewers or '38 Newark Bears were better. Jimmy DeShong, who would lose 15 games on the slab, "had more life than an alfalfa grower on Broadway." His gift of repartee kept everyone on their toes and the fans yukking it up at his antics.[9]

Tex Carleton had won his first 3 games up with Brooklyn, and the swastika now flew over Norway when energetic "Boy Mayor" Zeidler told 800 at the Elks that "a boost for the team is a boost for Milwaukee." Hizzoner shared the noisy cheers with Wisconsin governor "Julius the Just" Heil, a German-born Milwaukee industrialist and relentless dairy promoter.[10]

Of all the Opening Day newspaper booster ads, best of show was Lee Specialty's "Best of Luck from Matilda the Metal Duck, makes sprinkling a pleasure. A decorative and useful bird for any lawn or garden." The May 2nd opener was postponed when Makosky, Dunlap, and Paul Sullivan clowned with a snowman batter in their coats. Esler wore little more than a football

Ted Gullic's 11 seasons in Milwaukee threads made him "Mr. Brewer," through thick and thin. Copyright unknown (via Baseball Hall of Fame Library).

helmet, complaining not of the cold, but of the humidity. But for 4 pinch-hit at-bats, Mickey Heath pretty much laid his 37-year old swing to rest. He offered a free "Baseball School" to boys and girls on Gimbel's department store 3rd floor.[11]

It was Makosky who found the Mud Hens to be "decorative and useful birds" when he blanked them on 2 hits that Saturday, May 4th. Some 10,000 were expected, but only 5,814 saw Hal Peck's 2-run triple seal the 3–0 outcome. It was Makosky's third win, second shutout.[12]

The *Sentinel's* Lloyd Larson reported on how former major league slugging standout Cy Williams built cabins for that newspaper's Sports Show. The natural athlete and carpenter finisher now swung lumber from his Island Lake home near Three Lakes, Wisconsin.[13]

The spring weather that had turned A.A. diamonds into so many lakes forced a pile-up of doubleheaders. Eddie Morgan had some punch with Cleveland back in the '30s, but was dealt to St. Paul for another outfielder, Ted Abernathy. The search for sock went on ...[14]

Hal Peck, the farm boy a couple years removed from the milk truck, made one of the greatest catches in the "long history of the ancient amphitheater at Eighth and Chambers streets." The Brewers were still in 3rd place and chasing Minneapolis on May 17th when Peck crashed headfirst into a plank with one paw at the west end of the center field bleachers.[15] He fell flat on his back, but held on, stunned. His 8th inning rallying double helped defeat those very Millers, 6–5.

Columnist Stoney McGlynn wondered whether Charlie English would follow the path of future Brewer manager and champion Cincinnati Reds ace Bucky Walters. Buck started out at 3rd before his conversion to the mound. English tested twisters to go with a high, hard one and snapping curve.[16]

The 31–35 Brewers still held 3rd place by Independence Day. An Adelaide Yount was to play a leading role in a late-July comedy staged at Port Washington, north of Milwaukee. "What a Life" might have summed up the Brewers' plummet to last by then. Well, the polo season was in full gallop, anyway... And Ted Gullic played All-Star at Kansas City. And there was the $5,000 Milwaukee Open golf tournament coming to North Hills Country Club.[17]

Ray Schalk took over for Mickey Heath and though the old "Cracker" came into a club without dissension, he too was unable to stop the hemorrhaging. Baseball's chain store system came in for criticism, but the Brewers simply failed in every facet of the game. All Henry Bendinger did was catch for Mayor Zeidler at a Stars of Yesterday function at Borchert Field. Lyman Linde, a 19-year old right-hander, threw a no-no for Beaver Dam of the Rock Valley League. This potential backyard answer fanned 9 and walked only one, Lone Rock batter from the Scenic Wisconsin circuit. Lymie reached the Cleveland Indians by 1947, but never via the Brewers.[18]

The August 18th Old-Timers reunion at Borchert Field was maybe the only highlight left to a dismal season. Players from the turn-of-the-century, like Pete Husting and Ginger Beaumont, shared the same field with recent graybeards Ray Thompson and Jack Kloza. It was a hit, without a doubt. George Perring's appearances for reunions here and in Cleveland were just the proof to his son back in Beloit that his career hadn't been the bunk of bedtime stories.[19]

Word came that Lou Novikoff was purchased by the Cubs for the next spring after winning the P.C.L. Triple Crown (.363–41–171) in 177 games. Despite their wretched fall, the Brewers ranked fourth in A.A. attendance, with over 182,000. Baseball's roving clown, Al Schacht, was expected to add to that number. He claimed to have been born on the site of Yankee Stadium.[20]

Speculation on the interim Schalk's replacement centered upon Foster (Babe) Ganzel, tutored by the late Al Sothoron and winner of the 1938 A.A. pennant at St. Paul. A major league outfielder in the late 1920s, Babe was a nephew of former A.A. player and manager John Ganzel and a son of 19th century major leaguer Charlie Ganzel, a Waterford, Wisconsin, native. Babe's consecutive 5th place placements with the Saints left his plans uncertain.[21]

The Nazi blitz of London raged on and pro football tried again in Milwaukee in the form of the American League Chiefs. Women who longed "for hands men like to hold" were urged to do their dishes with "Klek" beads of soap. After George Blaeholder's shutout wrapped up a twin split with St. Paul, the Brewers sought to just wash their hands of 1940. A full 35 games behind the Yankee farm at KC, the Brewers' 58–90 was Milwaukee's worst record since the 1919 Panthers and their first basement finish since then, too. The press was for promoting up Madison talent.[22]

When the Ganzel preference washed out, Bendinger's home grown touch escaped him further with the hiring of flinty Reindeer Bill Killefer. The onetime major league catcher, who challenged the reserve clause in the Federal League showdown, brought 9 years of a no-nonsense, subpar .457 Big Show managerial mark with him. Only one of his 3 winning Cubbie teams of the early '20s was first division stuff. The Brewers would be his only A.A. attempt.[23]

Killefer's brother, Wade the "Red," was well-known to Milwaukee fans for his handful of seasons as the Chief of the Indianapolis Indians and even more from the punch he received from ex-brewmaster Frank O'Rourke. Red had again set up his tepee with the Indiana red men.

Heinie Bendinger kept his Brewers training in Ocala, mostly to satisfy his own fishing indulgences. Joining Bear Tracks Johnny Schmitz in the traditional Badger-born parade of arms for Brewer tryouts were Menasha's Dave Koslo(wski) and Milwaukee's Jerry Crowley.

The re-elected President Roosevelt had a military draft in effect that spring, although only 41 players (in 1941) from 300 clubs were accepted into service at that point. Milwaukee's John J. Pershing, of 636 N. 14th St., was a World War I namesake amongst the February 28th draftees.[24]

The Journal's Sam Levy took that spring passing of Two Bits Bierhalter to remember one of the A.A.'s most colorful umpires. The bizarre little Bierhalter flaunted the old taboo about not fraternizing with the players, especially off the field. The arbiter was christened William, but his nickname derived from the name of a horse he once bet upon. Two Bits retired as a trainer for the Boston Red Sox, but he loved umpiring at first base in Milwaukee. The bleacher creatures on that side were mostly a source of wisecracking fun to him, but once, when they rated one of his calls with a rain of empty beer bottles, he implored the "wild Dutchmen" to throw a full one once in a while. One just missed his dome shortly thereafter.[25] His German name meant "beer keeper."

Eddie Stumpf was back in Wisconsin as G.M. of the Class D State League Janesville Cubs, a Chicago farm. That small town support across Wisconsin, where pro football thrived in Green Bay, as well as pro basketball in Oshkosh and Sheboygan, while Milwaukee failed to build a new stadium or arena was examined by *The Journal's* R.G. Lynch. Had "dry rot" set in upon an otherwise fine city? Athletic Park/Borchert Field was now 53 years old.[26]

The story of 1941 wasn't Bill Killefer, who would rather have had less-talented hustlers than nonchalant underachievers. It wasn't Ted Gullic's move to 1st base, or even the ability of Stan Galle, Stan Stencel, Koslo, and Schmitz to make the team. It wasn't the violent strike at Allis-Chalmers or that the sport of curling was nearly a century old in the city. Not even the .370 batting title by "the Mad Russian" tops the list.

Oh, Galle's 3rd base work, where he stopped line drives with his chest, evoked memories of Harry Clark. And the Killefers chucked their brotherly love out the window when their clubs faced one another. Their gag tussle for the cameras featured Green Bay Blujay G.M. Red Smith as peacemaker. Red Killefer was now 56, Bill 53.

True, Dave Koslo was atypical of the eccentric lefthander mold. The "handsome Pole" garnered attention at *The Sentinel's* state tournament at Borchert Field in 1938. He threw 1-hitters for his Menasha Fox River Valley club at Wausau and Stockbridge, then shutout Sunset to boot. He went 18-8 for Paducah in 1940, his first year in Organized Ball. He also ranked second with 210 strikeouts there after a sub-.500 start with Hopkinsville the year before. Dave no longer had his brother Herb catching him like back in Menasha, and he lost 10 days at Ocala to a bum ankle. His family and some of the Fox River Valley cheered his May 2nd debut where he was scouted by old Clarence Rowland for the Cubs.[27] Blaeholder and Koslo were the only effective starters.

President Henriette Constantine, treasurer Ethel Barber, and business manager Jeannette Constantine led their lovely young ladies, the Brewer Boosters, in a May 1st dance at the Badger Room of the Wisconsin Hotel. The players attended the public affair. At the Elks dinner, tribute was paid to Louis Nahin, the Brewer business manager of 30 years, who died that February.[28] George McBride introduced other old diamond favorites like Beloit's Bob Roth, who caught for Milwaukee three decades earlier, and Ginger Beaumont, now at Honey Creek, Wisconsin.

Catcher Ray Hayworth, who saw Detroit's pennant fever up close and personally in 1934-1935, said the Motor City had nothing on the enthusiastic 500 for a 3-9 Milwaukee club that night.

Rain retarded that home opener on May Day and the crowd, as well. Fewer than 5,000 saw Wade Killefer's Indians spank Bill Killefer's Brewers 3-0 when it was called in the 8th. The home team lost a loyal listener in 93-year old William Courtney Hinsdale in Wauwatosa. The games were now broadcast on WEMP and the blind, old gentleman died shortly after hearing the home opener.[29] Mr. Hinsdale had followed baseball since the earliest immortals like Cap Anson and knew the batting averages of many players. Radio was his access to the game in the blindness of his last 10 years. He was employed with American Express for 55 years.

Even this venerable gentleman wasn't the story of 1941. Nor was Tony Faeth, the former Brewer hurler of 15 years earlier who, now a liquor salesman, commuted between his St. Paul home base and Milwaukee.[30] Nor was old hurler Stoney McGlynn, dead at Manitowoc in August.

Enough with the teasing already. This was done only because the Milwaukee Brewers were about to be transferred into the hands of a man for whom the lure, the hype was like the very air the rest of us breathe. Henry Bendinger was operating the Brewers without any further subsidy from Chicago Cubs owner Philip K. Wrigley. With that, rumors already started early in the year that the Brewers were financially at peril.

Bill Veeck, the promotional genius who engineered the Brewers' wartime success. Baseball Hall of Fame Library, Cooperstown, NY.

Bendinger, the man who saved the Brewers with local ownership through the Depression, now went to Chicago to peddle his holdings directly to Wrigley. Despite the recommendation of 28-year old Bill Veeck that he do so, Wrigley wouldn't bite. He was staunchly against the idea of farm clubs, which may explain something about the Cubs' plight all these years.[31]

Young Mr. Veeck's father, William, had served the Cubs as their president until his death. Bill worked his way around every aspect of the club's operations. He had the knowledge and he had the energy of promotional ideas bubbling over. What he did not have was money.

On a blustering bluff, he connected with A.A. president George Trautman in Chicago. Trautman had been en route from his Columbus office to see how the Milwaukee situation could be remedied. Veeck claimed he would buy the club.

Veeck wanted his good friend, Charlie Grimm, in on this venture. "Jolly Cholly" had a 7-year run of managerial success for the Cubs, never finishing lower than third and he had the 1935 National League pennant to his credit. The wonderfully outgoing Grimm belied his surname and worked on Cub broadcasts before Veeck coaxed him back into coaching with them. Veeck offered 25 percent ownership to manage the Brewers.

The only thing grim about Grimm was his fiscal status. He was as broke as Veeck.[32]

What ensued was one of the great financial adventures ever, something that Veeck himself acknowledged would give a bad name to a Ponzi scheme. The opportunity to work with a genuine Milwaukee brewer, Herbert Uihlein (like "eeh-line") of Schlitz, blew up when Mrs. Uihlein's cursory glance of the proposed balance sheet called their bluff.

So much for Schlitz broadcasting rights and an exclusive beer concession at Borchert Field. Trautman, who directed Veeck to Uihlein, was about ready to hand the bankrupt franchise to the young man, regardless.

Bendinger owed the City National Bank in Milwaukee $83,000 and was pressed for another $25,000 in debt. That's the amount Trautman hoped Veeck would cover. Heinie's creditors certainly had no interest in owning a baseball club.

This perspective of an otherwise well-recounted tale hasn't been emphasized, but it was old Clarence "Pants" Rowland, whose Milwaukee Panthers failed in 1919, who sort of saved the day. Rowland was now the vice-president of the Cubs. It was his broker son, Clarence, Jr., who couldn't recommend a loan to his company, but led Veeck to colleague Arthur Vyse.

It was via Vyse, who had a "small chunk" of a wealthy father-in-law's money to invest, that Veeck got the Brewers. Only Vyse was under the impression that Veeck and Grimm already had investors who put up the 25 grand. Veeck's con was that Vyse would get a 100 percent return on his investment for every complete calendar year that they kept his money.

Veeck traveled between Milwaukee and Chicago "on the elevated" instead of by railroad as a means of squeezing money. Grimm and he then arrived to claim their bankrupt franchise by a mode worthy of new owners—the train. On a cold, drizzly June 21st, the two drank up $10 of the $11 between them, toasting their "glorious future." The other dollar Veeck framed. Most businesses framed their first dollar. He framed their last.

Thus was born the legend of the future Hall of Famer, who would author *Veeck, as in Wreck* and *The Hustler's Handbook*. To Milwaukee, he became beloved as just "Sport Shirt Bill."

The rest of the 1941 season was probably one big blur to the 46 some odd bodies to which Charlie played the Grimm Reaper, laying waste to the insufficient talent. He hadn't actively played in 5 years, but inserted himself once as a pinch-hitter, only to triple to the right center field fence.[33]

Ted Gullic, who had become "Mr. Brewer" in the eyes of the fans, Hal Peck and George Blaeholder were the only ones to win the Borchert Field edition of *Survivor*. Milwaukee could no longer tell the players, even with a scorecard. Another 55–98 dead last end will do that.

It was easier for 50,000 people to turn out and just watch two boxers, middleweights Tony Zale and Billy Pryor, go at it in Juneau Park as part of the Midsummer Festival. Veeck and Grimm were about to embark on the most famous phase of Milwaukee's minor league history, where every baseball game was a midsummer festival.[34]

Even though Dave Koslo was sold to the New York Giants for cash and two players to be named before 1942, Veeck and Grimm had another couple key acquisitions lined up in September. With assurances from White Sox farm director Bill Webb and ex-Brewer-manager-turned-Cubs-scout Jack Doyle, the $10,000 sent to the Texas League Dallas Rebels was for future stars.

At Dallas, Alabaman Grey Clarke was a 28-year old 3rd baseman in Organized Baseball since 1933. His .361 was the best little batting average in Texas.

Heinz Becker played the outfield down there, but had all the earmarks of a 1st baseman. Both men swung lethal bats.[35]

In Heinz Becker, Milwaukee received a player ideally suited to his environs. He was born at Berlin, Germany, on August 26, 1917, when Der Vaterland was over a year away from defeat in the First World War. Becker came to the U.S.A. by way of South America at age 2. He wasn't Unser Choe, or even Bill Zuber, but he was welcome in the city of *gemutlichkeit*.[36]

Adolf Hitler unleashed his massive Operation Barbarossa upon the Soviet Union in that summer of 1941. Maybe it was just a quirk of baseball fate, but German-born Heinz Becker never shared a Milwaukee Brewer roster spot with Lou Novikoff, "the Mad Russian." Novikoff made 1942 his one fully productive major league season with the Cubs.[37]

As much as December 7, 1941, would "live in infamy" by catapulting the United States of America to front and center of the World War II stage, it marked the start of the most unusual prosperity in Milwaukee Brewers history.

It seemed the more the war effort soaked up every human and material resource like a sponge, the more the Brewers' standing atop the American Association was fortified.

To get to that point, Veeck and Grimm turned Borchert Field from a weather-beaten sow's ear into, if not a silk purse, a freshly laundered $50,000 sport shirt. Veeck was able to sell City Bank president Irving Weinhold on that additional loan, without the usual necessity of collateral. What civic pride in a ballclub won't do...[38]

It was classic Veeck that so much attention has been paid to the peripheral hype of his shenanigans, that the substance of the teams he assembled is often overlooked. The only fireworks inside rickety wooden Borchert Field were confined to the baseball action between the foul lines.

Veeck continued to separate the spring wheat from the chaff at Ocala. In the Brewers' St. Patrick's Day 1942 intrasquad game down there, George Blaeholder's "High Lifes" faced Ted Gullic's "16-Ouncers." Cub prospect Handy Andy Pafko, the "Pruschka" from Boyceville, Wisconsin, got a look in Gullic's right field.[39]

Coach Red Smith saw enough of local Florida State University catcher Willard Tietz to sign him up for his Class D Wisconsin State League Green Bay Bluejays. Grimm was more adept at preparing his men for battle than the overlapping bureaucracies of the New Deal were in giving military draftees mock wooden guns to train.[40]

Veeck and Grimm didn't stop with the Texas League batting champ in Grey Clarke. They added the wooden gun of that Al circuit's RBI leader, the Houston Buffaloes' outfielder Bill Norman. When Blaeholder's regulars made the Gullics' 3–2 lead "melt like hips in a steam cabinet," little did they know that the man at the bottom of the regs' order, shortstop Eddie Stanky, was a batting champ waiting to bust out. The "Brat's" patient eye would lead the A.A. in walks and runs.

While the Yanks, our servicemen, not the Bronx baseballists, defiantly bombed the Japanese in the Phillippines, Milwaukee opened its 1942 campaign on Thursday, April 16th. Thanks to folks like Walter Felber who dusted the seats, peanut salesman Tony Beitzinger, John Kusch vending beer, scorecard hawker Curley Jenkins, Mrs. Rodger Beyersdorf and Mrs. George Zeller dispensing beer and hot dogs, one Fred (Shorty) Mendelson now sold tickets to the greatest show in Double-A.[41]

And as the appropriately named Henry Tolle checked you in at the turnstile, lovely Dorothy Effenberger could offer you a soft seat cushion for a dime. All to watch 9-year major league right-hander Roxie Lawson take the mound for Milwaukee and fulfill as F.D.R. put it, baseball's "vital contribution to the nation's morale."

Lawson had a real American, Charlie "Greek" George, catching for him, too. Roxie had allowed only 1 run in 18 exhibition innings and "Muggsy" Stanky was now promoted to leadoff. General Mills (a Minneapolis company, oddly) and Lever Bros. sponsored all home and away games on WISN Radio, then 1150 on the dial. (It's now 1130.)

Likeable Mickey Heath rebounded from being a distraught manager to doing radio play-by-play; he was joined by Dutch Underhill. Heath was a recipient of the rotating loving cup, with a replaceable nameplate, handed out by business manager Rudy Schaffer. He was Veeck's right hand.[42]

Jazz drummer Gene Krupa and His Orchestra played at the Riverside, but not even the legend of the chopsticks could have drummed up the Brewers' highest level of anticipation since 1936. The hype brought out an Opening Day record of 15,599 and won Milwaukee its first Attendance Cup.

Even though rain washed away Lawson's ineffective 2–0 deficit by the 2nd inning, A.A. president George Trautman remained convinced the cup belonged in Milwaukee, but it was a rainout. Veeck's first full season of tickling the good burghers' "love for light laughter and hearty food" was on when he awarded the city his own cup, the one with the replaceable nameplate.[43]

Veeck was a man of the people, hanging out with the ticket-buyers throughout the stands. The merriment grew as Jolly Cholly Grimm, "baseball's only left-handed banjo player," led a rag-tag band of Rudy Schaffer on a homemade bull fiddle, Mickey Heath on washboard drums, and "Sport Shirt Bill" himself on the jazzbo (sliding tin whistle). One pitcher, who was "terrible" on the mound, was kept on the roster as an excellent violinist. It wasn't said whether Heath's musical accompaniment led to his elevation as a vice-president.[44]

The near-circus atmosphere of good times and promotional gags may have lured Milwaukeeans to old Borchert Field, but both Veeck and Grimm were shrewd enough to know that it was a real winner that would keep them coming back.

To that end, they did not disappoint.

Whether it was the May Day display of wondrous fielding, like Hal Peck's leaping one-handed stabs of two certain triples or Stanky "playing hob" with sure Toledo base hits, or Bill Norman's 4 RBI to back up a 10th straight home win on May 2nd, barbed quipster Veeck could give Columbus Red Bird president Al Bannister (not the 1970s-1980s shortstop) the typewritten bird.

The Birds may have stopped the streak at an even dozen on Wednesday, May 6th, not that the first home defeat wasn't without a fight to the bitter end. They scored two and had the bases filled, but Lou Klein's 2-run homer made the difference. A surprising 400 were all a week of cold and rain would allow. A worrisome Veeck could not con Mother Nature.[45]

Still, that 14–5 start made the 8–2 exhibition lesson taught by the visiting New York Yankees on Wednesday, May 20th less painful. Joe Gordon and Red Rolfe homers led the 11-hit assault upon Russ Mears in 5 frames. Baseball's very best brought out 10,250.[46]

Brewer pitching began to turn back its opposition, the way U.S. bombers repulsed the Japanese probe of the Alaskan coastline. The hurlers weren't as heroic as Dr. John Grindlay of 2853 N. Marietta Ave. who won a Purple Heart in the Burma Campaign, but Walt Lanfranconi's 64-minute shutout in June and Ed Hanyzewski's 1-hitter in mid-July kept the home front happy.

Grimm's fairy tale Brewers drew within one game of first place Kansas City on August 1st even though they had dropped 6 of 9 at that stage. That trend led to a 4th place dip in mid-month. The offense turned like the revolting Moslems in India.[47]

No amount of squab-holding, lobster-poking door prize winners could contain the Brewers' final thrust at the Blues in early September.

Milwaukee pressed KC like a zoot suit with reet pleats when Hanyzewski was credited with both wins on Sunday, September 6th, 7–2 and 5–4. Eddie threw shutout ball for 8 1/3 innings in Game One and relieved Johnny Berly to capture the second. Johnny Hudson's heavy hitting drove in first encounter runs off a double and a triple. Stanky's slam that was "5 feet fair" was ruled foul by umpire Jim Boyer, prompting a torrent of pop bottles and cushions. "The Brat" (not *brat*, as in bratwurst) ended up walking afterwards, but it was Ted Gullic's own stroll on 5 Rinaldo Ardizoia pitches that forced in the winning Game Two margin.

This set up a finale to decide the pennant, only a costly 7th inning bobble by Stanky undid Hy Vandenburg's duel with Herb Karpel. The Blues clinched the flag, 9–2, and Karpel ran up an incredible 11–1 record. Stanky's magnificence as the .342 batting king was dimmed. Still, they must've stoked on Gurda's tip of Gross Coal and Oil, a Milwaukee concern at Wisconsin and Water since 1883 because their 27½ game turnaround tied for sixth-best in league annals.[48]

Their chance at redemption came against the Toledo Mud Hens in the first round of the playoffs. Game One was a confounding affair. Late season addition Hershel Martin compensated for a pair of outfield miscues with 3 RBI, and Ted Gullic and Grey Clarke homered. Despite 4 runs in the bottom of the ninth, 2,362 saw Emil Kush lose, 6–5

Martin redeemed himself further by winning Game Two, 4–3, with a bottom of the ninth, 2-run shot and an important 8th inning run-saving catch. The series was tied at Toledo when 7,000 rabid onlookers saw Moose Marcum allow 3 of Milwaukee's 8 hits to Eddie Stanky.

The Brewers divided their $2,000, 2nd place finish reward into 23 full shares and 4 quarter shares. Everyone but John Berly, Russ Mears, Hershel Martin, and Groundskeeper Eddie Kretlow got $83.33 each. Those four were given $20 apiece.

Chet Laabs was off hitting his 27th homer for the St. Louis Browns when Toledo bested Walt Lanfranconi, 8–6. Vallie Eaves, the wayward, imbibing Oklahoma Indian started the Brewer parade of 4 pitchers. The Mud Hens kept it up, like the ongoing siege of Stalingrad, taking two of the last three, just as they had done with the first three.[49]

Future Yankee Hershel Martin was a favorite of Brewer fans, including a young Bud Selig. Copyright unknown (via Baseball Hall of Fame Library).

The Brewers may have been turned out, but they certainly turned a corner. Stanky, who was bought for $2,500, was now sold to the Cubs for $40,000. And he took his fiery habit of brandishing firearms at needling roommates, like Greek George, with him.[50]

The ensuing 3 seasons were the pennant-winning zenith for the Milwaukee Brewers, but even after the 1942 bouncing by 4th place Toledo, writers like *The Sentinel's* Stoney McGlynn still saw the post-season playoffs as an anticlimactic sham. If he thought that after his local narrow runners-up were eliminated, just wait...

The war exacted a logistical toll upon the 1943 spring training. Travel restrictions took the Brewers no further than nearby Waukesha, where Grimm's ideas of forming a Polar Bear Club to swim the icy Fox River in March were nixed by Veeck and Schaffer. The value of the Hot Stove League took on new meaning.[51]

Ex-Brewer Jeff Heath "resigned" from baseball after returning a third unsigned contract to work in a Seattle shipyard. Onetime Milwaukee ace Tot

Pressnell said he was through, too, and would keep his sales job with an oil company in Findlay, Ohio.[52]

If Lou Novikoff was "the Mad Russian," he probably wasn't as mad as Victor Starffin. The Russian-born pitching superhero of Japanese baseball was now under scrutiny in Japan as a possible Soviet spy. Nippon had set aside its baseball fever as "too American."[53]

If there was such a thing as being "too American," the Native red man Vallie Eaves may have qualified. The right-hander, for whom Bill Veeck hunted every Toledo nightspot, was lushing in a hotel bar a mere couple blocks away. The unreliable one, who needed a superhuman monitoring job by Brewer trainer Bob Feron, was now Mike Kelley's problem up in Minneapolis.[54] The Brewers were the Brewers not the guzzlers, and Kelley was skillful with that sort. Real brewers and bottlers donated their scrap to the war effort. None was more off the scrap heap than Vallie Eaves.

As a former 1st baseman, Charlie Grimm relished watching young Merv Connors gobble up everything his way at Waukesha's Frame Park. Heinz Becker, who finished second in the A.A. batting race, was definitely Milwaukee's main man at the initial bag and had made great defensive strides himself. His weak throwing arm was a drawback, but Connors, the '42 Texas League home run king with the Ft. Worth Cats, had a future. New 2nd baseman Don Johnson was equally slick afield. Tony York played short with Connors down in Lone Star land.[55]

To bolster that final step over the top, Milwaukee bade farewell to popular veteran Ted Gullic. He was sent to the P.C.L. Portland Beavers in exchange for outfielder Ted Norbert, that loop's batting (.378) and homer (28) champ. If it looked like the Brewers were cornering the market on minor league swing kings, well, they were.[56]

Greek George rigged up an elastic band to give his damaged wing some badly needed whiplash behind the plate. And Veeck being Veeck, well... He traded Charlie "Greek" George to the Southern Association Nashville Vols — for a set of golf clubs.[57] Sport Shirt Bill made use of his Lewis Institute training as an engineer to construct a 60-foot chicken wire fence for Borchert Field's short right field. Powered by a hydraulic motor, he would keep the fence moved up if the visiting team had left-handed power. When the Brewers were at bat, it remained reeled back to the foul line.

Veeck went from employing the fence on a series-by-series basis to moving it between innings. He tried it once until the A.A. legislated against such antics. No edge was too great, but as fun as his creativity was to the home folks, the league took an increasingly dim view. At Columbus in '42 though, the lights were so dim and their pitchers threw so hard that Veeck outfitted his players with lighted miner helmets to make a point. The coaches lit the way to the field and 2nd baseman Packy Rogers took meter readings in his spare time around the keystone.[58]

The only thing the Red Bird front office saw was red.

The zany hijinx belied the fact that there was a war going on. Professional ballplayers did not need ration coupons for their game spikes as they were considered "work shoes." Amateurs and semi-pros couldn't claim that benefit.[59]

The Brewers replaced Vallie Eaves as their "designated native" with Hawaiian Henry "Prince" Oana. The Prince saw spring action, despite a charley horse, against the Heil industrial team at Waukesha, but would be the team's least effective hurler. He would reach the bigs though.

It's a good thing our soldiers were better at soldiering than at baseball because the Brewers beat a team of them, too. Kimberly, Wisconsin's John Van Cuyk, last of the Wisconsin State League Appleton Papermakers, pitched for the servicemen, and Andy Skurski hit a home run out of Waukesha's Frame Park into the Fox River. The Brewers won the battle, 6–3. Fortunately, the soldiers would help win the war.[60]

Union coal miners threatened the supply lines to those serving on every front with strike talk. F.D.R. responded by seizing the mines as a vital war industry. If there were any doubts about their ability to receive a flow of materiel, servicemen were in concurrence on one issue: They wanted professional baseball to continue.[61]

The Brewers suffered from an interruption of firepower in the frozen May Day opener up in Minneapolis. Prince Oana had to abdicate from the mound before a frostbit 3,500. Only Ted Norbert, the man with the least amount of spring training, had any punch with 4 hits in the 6–3 loss. Ironically, it was Vallie Eaves who closed out his old mates.[62]

Merv Connors collected $100 for his homer at the Friday, May 7th home opener at Borchert Field. Connors received his money from club veep Armin McGregor. McGregor won the money from one Yab Rice, who gave up on a bet that the Brewers wouldn't play 20 games for the season. Still, the hometown heroes were beaten 5–2 by tail end Minneapolis.[63]

Even though Milwaukee drew the largest A.A. home opening crowd— 12,036—Indianapolis won the cup because its 10,553 was a higher percentage of the city's population.

That next day, Saturday, May 8th, Veeck's Brewers received national publicity due to a wartime train delay. The St. Paul Saints couldn't make it on time for the morning game Veeck had specially scheduled for night shift defense workers. More than 2,000 stuck it out, many of whom were women war workers in slacks. To keep them entertained, breakfast fare of free milk, doughnuts, and coffee was distributed by ushers in gaudy nightshirts and nightcaps. A similarly attired 6-piece band kept the good-natured gathering docile. Workers from some 20 plants were assigned places for their companies in the stands.[64]

The morning game was scheduled for 10:30, but the Saints couldn't take the field until noon. Veeck wanted to run the promotion again on June 5th

At the annual Old Time Baseball Players Association reunion picnic at Borchert Field on July 18, 1942. From 152 ex-Brewers there, these five first basemen re-enacted their stretch *(left to right):* Tom Casey, Bill Knipple, Ray Saveland, Cis Comstock, and Fred Luderus. Milwaukee Public Library Historical Photograph Collection.

when the Louisville Colonels would be in. He honored rain checks from this first attempt.

In the afternoon game that was actually played, the fans got more than their money's worth. Bill Norman belted 3 consecutive homers and scored 5 times off an additional 2 singles. His 5-for-5 day led a record-setting 50 total bases performance by the Brewers. They annihilated the Saints for 24 hits, including 4 other home runs, 5 doubles, and 10 more singles. Four pitchers were martyred, 20–0, like St. Paul himself. The 8-run first inning outburst included homers by a young Bud Selig's favorite, Hershel Martin and catcher Hank Helf. Milwaukee was already up 12–0 after just three.

Winston Churchill wasn't satisfied with just having his countrymen withstand the Nazi aerial blitz. He now told the U.S. Congress that "Nippon must lie in ashes to win the peace" and his nation would fight the Japanese to its "last breath." Britain even allowed shivering Jamaicans from its West Indies possessions to come up and help Wisconsin farmers.[65]

Louisville 2nd baseman Stan Sperry, an Evansville, Wisconsin, man, had high praise for the Brewers, especially the pitching of Oana, Wes Livengood, and the once and again Earl Caldwell. That, after Sperry's Colonels just notched a couple wins over 5th place Milwaukee in May.

By August, Jolly Cholly's gang fulfilled everyone's expectations by taking 1st place. The military draft was wreaking havoc upon the contractual side of baseball. President W.G. Bramham of the National Association of Minor Leagues ruled that Milwaukee didn't have to pay Fort Worth $5,000 for Hank Oana (where he hurled a no-no in '42), but that the Cats of the disbanded Texas League would have to pay the Brewers a like 5 grand for Merv Connors.

Both cases were determined by the players' military draft status. The Brewers bought Connors' contract earlier in the year, with the proviso that his draft status not change within 15 days after the season began. Upon investigation it had and Milwaukee wasn't advised of it. Connors simply said he was "never asked." He had already been dealt to the Southern Association Memphis Chick(asaw)s for $2,500 in June. Bramham ruled that the Brewers return that amount, but would get $5,000 from defunct Fort Worth. Connors became a free agent.[66]

As promising as Connors seemed, the Brewers didn't need him. Not with Heinz Becker at first. Heinz was most happy in Milwaukee. He threatened to go home to Dallas if the Cubs tried to recall him up. He had some unhappy weeks in the Windy City before and didn't have the German societies there, who'd pay tribute to him with a night, like Beertown. Becker was an oddity — a powerfully built 1st baseman-type who could hit, only without home run power.[67]

Jolly Cholly Grimm would turn 45 on August 28th. He had joked with Veeck that all he wanted for his birthday was a "left handed pitcher." With the team in first, Veeck certainly wanted to give him something more than that worn-out cup.

Sport Shirt Bill zeroed in on a Norfolk Tars lefty in the Class B Piedmont League named Julio Acosta. A pitcher at his level was going for $5,000, but Veeck offered $7,500 and an additional five grand, just to keep everything hush-hush.

When Grimm was presented with a $1,000 war bond at the Borchert Field party, he choked up to the point of tears, admitting that he owed "it all to his dear wife Lillian" who was at his side. Evidently, he did, because "he turned it over to her on the spot." It was when the 15-foot tall birthday cake was rolled out that Grimm was blown away. Its magnitude alone was astounding enough. When Julio Acosta stepped out of it, all 8,255 overlooked the dancing girls who first broke through. And the banjo. And the rocking chair from the players. And the old-timers' electric clock.

At Veeck's comically dour insistence, Grimm started the Cuban. It was not a story book ending, as 7 of the 15 hits Acosta allowed came in the last 4 innings. Indianapolis tied the Brewers in the 9th, only to win on Carl Fairly's homer in the extra frame. Still at 70–52, Milwaukee kept 3 games up on the Indians.[68]

The September 15th that the Brewers pushed the Millers near the "Rathskeller," one John Schrank, the 67-year old Bavarian immigrant who had attempted to assassinate Theodore Roosevelt in Milwaukee in 1912, died in the Central State Hospital at Waupun.⁶⁹ Minneapolis had been shut out in 4 games of a 5-game Borchert Field series that 1943.

Five days later, the Milwaukee Brewers gave 8,935 every good reason to enumerate the thrills: The doubleheader win over Kansas City made 8 in a row, 20 of their last 23, and sewed the silver lining up around their first pennant since 1936!⁷⁰

Hershel Martin was hit on the chin by a batting practice ball pitched by local semi-pro Bobby Anderson. Martin was not as his center field station in the first game of that final twinbill, but came out between games in uniform to receive a traveling bag as the Most Popular Brewer in a season-long poll of fans. Martin's chin and Ted Norbert's shoulder were ready for the opening playoff with the 3rd place Columbus Redbirds.⁷¹

The 90–61 Brewers set a club attendance record, excluding exhibitions, of 332,597. That exceeded the 275,191 set in 1936, the last pennant year.

The pennant would have to be the highlight, because the Red Birds brought Milwaukee back down to earth. Columbus was the first first division team the Brewers had faced since August 29th, and it showed. The opener strategy of relieving ace Jittery Joe Berry with Wes Livengood led to a 5-run 7th for Columbus and the 11–1 rout maintained Ted Wilks' dominance over Milwaukee. Martin's 9th inning error led a fan to yell, "Take down that pennant!" The general opinion out the exits was, "Hell, you can't win 'em all!"

No, in fact, the Brewers would only win one in the best of five thanks to a Martin grandslam in Game Two. Otherwise, Preacher Roe fanned 10 Brewers in a 6–1 Red Bird rampage and southpaw George Dockins' 11 K, 3-hitter ended the season on a 7–0 goose egg.⁷²

No American Association playoff championship. No Little World Series. After that Friday, September 24th elimination, Charlie Grimm could only sigh, "Boys, we're mighty lucky to be alive!" At 3:45 Saturday morning, the Brewers' rail car barely missed being wrecked near Logansport, Indiana. The axle broke as some players dozed and others played cards. The team had to board another car, but they were further delayed by engine trouble. They arrived in Chicago an hour late before dispersing home from Milwaukee with their final paychecks.⁷³

Veeck would go some time without seeing his baseball cohorts, like "Willie Card" Norman. Veeck had converted the boozehound into a fellow beer drinker. For all his wacky, shoestring sense of baseball showmanship, Bill Veeck left to join the Marines after the season. Having a nearly 30-year old minor league baseball owner in basic training with the 'Devil Dogs' spoke more about American egalitarianism than anything Veeck's publicity machine could embellish.

He trusted the affairs of his Brewers with his good friend and partner, Charlie Grimm. And well he should. What Bill Veeck didn't count upon, stationed eventually in the action of the faraway South Pacific, was Phil Wrigley.

The Chicago Cubs owner played a most peculiar role, directly and peripherally, in allowing Milwaukee to make baseball history in 1944.

America was now knee-deep in the blood and guts of waging World War II upon two fronts. Organized Baseball, in a somewhat *contracted* form, proceeded with official Washington and general national encouragement. The caliber of major league play, with retreads and 4-F youngsters, was certainly downgraded. The trickle-down effect of the manpower depletion reverberated through the minors proportionately.[74]

To address part of this situation, Philip Wrigley was the force behind what became known as the All-American Girls Professional Baseball League. Though of small scale, in its original 1943 incarnation, it encompassed four Midwestern factory towns not in Organized Baseball: the South Bend Blue Sox in Indiana, the Rockford Peaches in Illinois, and two Wisconsin teams, the Kenosha Comets and the Racine Belles, who won the first title.[75]

The modest success of beskirted girls in cleats, slapping leather without mussing their make-up and keeping their hairdos intact, led to a 1944 expansion to two larger cities: Minneapolis and Milwaukee. Besides the prescribed maintenance of femininity from the league's hierarchy, small adjustments were made in the actual game after that first year.

The ball itself had been reduced from a circumference of 12 inches to 11½, the distance between basepaths expanded from 65 to 68 feet. The pitching distance for 1944 remained 40 feet and the delivery was still underhand. To best grasp the 12-year history of this league is to understand the 54-year evolution of men's 19th century baseball being compressed into those dozen years, That, and the obvious physical and gender difference.[76]

Charlie Grimm himself said of Dottie Schroeder, the blonde, pig-tailed shortstop from Sadorus, Illinois, who played in all 12 years of the loop: "If that girl were a man, she'd be worth $50,000 to me." He would make that comment when he was back managing the Chicago Cubs. And therein lies the rub.[77]

Before we dismiss the Girls League as some odd historical footnote, a number of Milwaukeeans, ex-Brewers, and even brothers of ex-Brewers took a turn at managing in the circuit. Jack Kloza was known as "Nap" when he was associated with the Rockford Peaches; dapper Eddie Stumpf was one of the original pilots of 1943 with that same Rockford club; Ralph Shinners, the man from Monches, guided the Kenosha Comets; Carson "Skeeter" Bigbee was a brother of old Brewer lefty Lyle Bigbee and led the Springfield Sallies; and the real Bubber Jonnard, brother of former Brewer hurler Claude (who was also given that Tennessee monicker in Milwaukee), was a onetime big league backstop who took on the Minneapolis Millerettes' assignment.[78] Judge Edward J. Ruetz presided over the Kenosha Comets' $25,000 stock subscription.[79] Was he related to Babe Ruetz of 1920s Racine pro football?

But that is to digress from Phil Wrigley and Charlie Grimm. Jolly Cholly wasn't so grim in again training his guys at Waukesha that he didn't emulate the Ben Gay ad cartoon character "Peter Pain"—"Jumping on chests is my pet exercise!" He did sweat the early whereabouts of his No. 2 pitcher Charlie Gassaway and one Bill Swift (not the modern namesake). Grimm was pleased with the poise and assortment of stuff that Jack Farmer, a Mobile semi-pro, offered. So much so, that despite Farmer's lack of velocity, Charlie still called him a "cutey" in print.[80]

The Japanese claimed a base in India (where the author's father was stationed) and the Soviets reached the Czech border when the Brewers seized upon a half-dozen Badger errors to wallop the University of Wisconsin, 14–4, at Waukesha's Frame Field. Yeoman like Jimmy Pruett emerged as the frontline catcher, but there was concern that Cuban Julio Acosta, like all other Cubans and Puerto Ricans in baseball, may have had to return to his homeland island by mid-June. A rule out of Washington said that if all such non-residents didn't go home, they would have to register for Selective Service.[81]

"Guadalcanal Diary" was on local movie screens and Mickey Heath did Miller Beer "Sports Highlights" on WISN Radio, but the Brewers were not being broadcasted. Chain programming and the Brewers' mismatched schedule of morning, afternoon, and evening games were blamed. A 15-year old *Sentinel* paperboy, with the good baseball name Robert Rawlings, named Bill Norman as his favorite Brewer.[82]

The idea of "D-Day" and when it would come was already in the wind when the always optimistic Jolly Cholly beamed at George McBride's home opener banquet. His pride was justified when he gave 39-year old righty Earl (Teach) Caldwell the ball. Caldwell was in his 18th year of pro ball as he subdued the St. Paul Saints, 5–2, with his sidearm curves.[83] This was better than what acting mayor John L. Bohn did in dropping the first ball 10 feet short on that Wednesday, April 19th.

Bohn won outright election that year, but his presence was another sad reminder of the war: Young mayor Carl Zeidler went off to it and lost his life when the ship he was on was presumably torpedoed by a German submarine. The city lost its biggest sports booster.[84]

Frank Secory thrilled the jam-packed 13,619 at that Borchert Field opener, with several running catches in the outfield. They overcame 3 Brewer errors in the 1st inning.

The fortunes of Phil Wrigley's Chicago Cubs and Bill Veeck's Milwaukee Brewers began 1944 in diametrically opposite directions. Cubs' G.M. Jim Gallagher, an ex-sportswriter like the late William Veeck, was at odds with his owner over his desire to build a farm system and lacked the respect of field manager Jimmie Wilson, a noted ex-catcher.[85]

In that untenable atmosphere, Jimmie Wilson resigned by May 2nd after the Cubs lost their first 13 unlucky games. Wrigley and Gallagher knew who had once made the Cubs winners. That man's Milwaukee Brewers galloped off to a 10–2 start. That man was Charlie Grimm. The Cubs made an offer Grimm couldn't refuse.

Grimm, in turn, put out an S.O.S. to the Old Professor, Casey Stengel. Milwaukeeans were well-acquainted with ol' Case from his Toledo days in particular, but since his move up to the National League in 1934, Stengel didn't win.[86]

This was not yet the Stengel of ready-made pennants with the Yanks or his later lovable mishaps with the Mets. This was a manager, who in 3 seasons with the Brooklyn Dodgers and 6 with the Boston Bees/Braves, had only one .500 record to show.

This was the Stengel that Bill Veeck knew and measured from his remote climes in the South Pacific. Outside of his personal fondness for Grimm, Veeck would have a peculiar track record in assessing managerial ability. When he was later with Cleveland, he wanted to oust young shortstop Lou Boudreau as pilot—a man who delivered a World Series title to him.[87]

Casey Stengel, unwanted by Veeck, led Milwaukee to its best record ever, anyway. Copyright unknown (via Baseball Hall of Fame Library).

Veeck was not only furious about the selection of Stengel, but he was also upset that from his vast distance, he had no say as to who would run "his team." He went so far as to denigrate Stengel, professionally and personally, in a letter to a Milwaukee paper.[88]

Stengel was no left-handed banjo player, but his affability made him an immediate hit with the fans. Whatever Veeck didn't see in the future Hall of Famer's aura as a leader was quickly dispelled. Upon assuming the job on May 5th, Stengel kept his new troops playing at another 10–1 clip, leaving them atop the A.A. at 20–3 by mid-month.[89]

On May 23rd, Stengel's "Battling Brews" hit the jackpot on Casey's old Toledo team. Milwaukee established a new American Association record on that Tuesday. Many would later claim to have been there, but the actual attendance was huge enough, 13,517. What the Brewers did was storm over the Mud Hens by the equivalent of 4 touchdowns and 4 extra points, 28–0! This mauling at Maumee Bay was brought by 27 Milwaukee hits, 4 Toledo errors and 8 Mud Hen walks.[90] Heinz Becker and Hal Peck each went 4-for-6 as Harold drove in 5 runs. Peck homered, along with 3rd baseman Bill Nagel, Hershel Martin, and two by 2nd baseman Tom Nelson. Becker, Nagel, Martin, and shortstop Dick Culler each drove in 3 runs, Jimmy Pruett four. Culler, Martin, and Nagel each scored 4 runs. Only Willis Norman had a lone triple, but Milwaukee even left 8 on!

Milwaukeeans John Ermi and Elmer Regner were in Toledo and took credit as "whammy artistes."

Even this sensation would not win Veeck over to Stengel. Veeck only wrote to his front office staff and refused any direct communication with his manager.[91]

It was in the heat of that moment that over 100 American and Canadian girls were going through the training grind at Posen, Illinois. They were placed amongst the six clubs of the All-American Girls Baseball League by the discerning eyes of league president Ken Sells and vice-president/chief scout Jim Hamilton.[92]

The Sentinel even had its own correspondent, Milly W. Keene, follow the developments of the unnamed Milwaukee club, operated by general manager Eddie Stumpf and managed on the diamond by future Hall of Famer Max (Scoops) Carey, the old Pittsburgh Pirates flychaser. Carey's playing abilities as a bunting base-stealer made him a good fit for this style of ball.

Favorable newspaper coverage and promotion greeted the new venture in Milwaukee. All the attached hoopla of a Borchert Field opener — marching WACs, WAVEs, SPARs, and women marines — the whole four bases, as it were, greeted the girls on Saturday, May 27th.

A modest 800 saw their new female heroines fall in 10 innings, 5–4, to the South Bend Blue Sox. A 6th inning home run by Milwaukee's Tiby Eisen tied matters at 2-all. Olga Grant's right field bobble off a Dottie Schroeder hit put South Bend up by two in the 9th. Grant's bases-loaded single helped to tie it again after nine, but Bonnie Baker drove in the Blue Sox winner.[93]

Olga Grant was one of 3 Canadians on the roster, chaperoned by Dorothy Hunter, herself from Winnipeg. Watertown, Wisconsin's Doris Tetzlaff was one of the league's finer fielders at 3rd base and she was backed up by Vivian Anderson of 2417 N. 68th St. in Milwaukee. Vivian was one of the older members, all of a grizzled 23.

When the Milwaukee girls hatched, the Brewers were already 24–10 and advertising special group discounts for the first time by calling Concord 3180.

The female team was not a direct, combative advisory to the Brewers like the old Western League Creams of over 40 years earlier, but more of a parallel auxiliary. This was especially true in its level of play, which was also topping its circuit. Max Carey found a winning combination for this compact *galball* hybrid of fastpitch softball and Dead Ball Era baseball.

It should have been a style contrast to satisfy all baseball followers in Milwaukee, but with Casey Stengel's Brewers blasting away with both offensive barrels, the base-to-base path of galball would be a tough row to hoe. The "Chicks" nickname didn't really take hold until about mid-season, which didn't help in creating any image. That name was supposedly derived from a Broadway show, "Mother Carey's Chicks," after "Brewettes" never caught on.[94] On the basepaths, Carey's girls were never caught onto either, stealing 37 bases in one 3-game stretch. The team finished its first half split season in 3rd place, 30–26, 4½ games behind Kenosha.[95]

She wasn't a ballplayer, but Milwaukee's June Shielman was a June 11th finalist on the "General Electric Hour of Charm Auditions," a 9 p.m. program broadcast on WTMJ Radio.[96]

The Brewers didn't just clobber the pill either. Tommy Nelson had a streak of 170 consecutive errorless chances at second broken at that time. Both of Milwaukee's baseball teams continued to storm their standings as if every game was D-Day on the Normandy beaches. War bond-buying Milwaukeeans gave "shekels to shackle Schickelgruber," even as 109,621 of the city's children were under a polio quarantine. "Storm" was also the operative word when high winds ripped off part of the Borchert Field first base side grandstand roof during the 7th inning of the June 15th game against Columbus. The blackout sent panicky fans onto the playing field, and 35 people were injured. The structurally weak grandstand remained as sun seats, the roof beyond repair.[97]

As defending pennant champs and current league leaders, the Brewers hosted the A.A. All-Stars, much to their own chagrin. Milwaukee was 10½ games up on Louisville when 3 All-Star pitchers combined to allow only 5 hits to the potent Brewer order. The 18–0 revenge by the rest of the league's best was a shortcoming witnessed by 12,004 at Borchert Field. It was one of a few shortcomings to be seen, for the Stengelmen poured it on at a 33–21 from that July 27th on.[98]

The Chicks followed their big brothers' lead, pecking away to a 40–19 second half crown. Sylvia "Roni" Wronski, all 5'-2", 140 pounds of Milwaukeean twirler, bolstered an already imposing pitching rotation of two 22-year old Detroiters, Connie "Iron Woman" Wisniewski and Josephine Kabick. Another right-hander, Annabelle "Tommy" Thompson, came from Edmonton, Alberta, to flesh out the main trio. Kabick's 26 wins and Wiz's 23 led all.[99]

The Milwaukee girls compiled the best overall record for both halves of the season at 70–45 (.609), some 6½ games better than South Bend. Galball was not an offensive show, but the Chicks' Arizona assassin, Merle "Pat" Keagle, split time between short and the outfield to win the home run title with 7 and lead the loop in total bases.

Vicki Panos, another Edmonton product, brought her fleet feet from South Bend during the season to finish sixth in league batting (.263, right behind Keagle's .264), as well as second in stolen bases (141) and runs (84).

Casey Stengel had the sort of powerful lineup at the minor league level that he'd grow accustomed to with the Yankees. His boys led the A.A. in hits, runs, RBI, homers (135) and a .307 batting average. The 1944 Milwaukee Brewers won their pennant by 7 full games over Toledo. The 102–51, .667 record is the best by any Milwaukee pro baseball team ever.[100]

Ironically, it was the only season under Veeck's ownership that the club didn't have the league batting champion. Earl Caldwell, however, did tie for a league-high with 19 pitching victories (versus 7 losses) and a .792 win percentage. Outfielder Hal Peck did lead the league with 200 hits exactly and 140 runs exactly. He finished .345–13–83, with 18 steals.

Pick your heroes: 1st baseman Heinz Becker (.346–10–115), 2nd baseman Tommy Nelson (.303–20–97), 3rd baseman Bill Nagel's war club did .303–23–117 damage, Dick Culler hit .303 with a team-high 19 steals at short, and George (don't call me 'Jar Jar') Binks (.374–10–66) joined an awesome Hershel Martin (.358–8–56, in 58 games) in less than full-time duty.

Charlie Gassaway (17–8, .680, 2.75) and Charlie Sproull (16–7, .696, 2.50) also made Stengel, who modestly said, "I had the horses," look like a damned genius.[101]

Where the muscular Brewers and pecking Chicks parted company further was in their ironic post-season results. The Home Brews would again come up flat in their 6-game opening round loss to the 3rd place Louisville Colonels. Milwaukee led the best American Association attendance year since 1939 with their 235,840 and received $4,388 for their 1st place finish. Second place Toledo got $1,755.

Don Hendrickson, traded to the Brewers by Kansas City during the season, opened the series with a 5–0 blanking of Louisville before 2,396. Because of lack of fan support and the Brewers' playoffs, the Chicks had to play their entire Scholarship Series against the first half champion Comets down in Kenosha. The Comets copped the opener for Helen Nicol when singling Phyllis (Sugar) Koehn scored after an infield out and one of 6 Milwaukee errors for the 4–3 insurance run. Of the 1,500 at Lakefront Park, some 150 came down from Milwaukee.[102]

The Brewer front office had a laugh at a misbegotten rumor that their Fred Mendelson was somehow going to buy Mike Kelley's Minneapolis Millers. He had only $17 in his pocket during a recent trip up there. "Shorty" was now being called "Moneybags," but he was no Bill Veeck! It was probably the only humor left at that time of the year.[103]

The distraction of Veeck's determination to oust Stengel probably affected the club in that Louisville series, which they lost 4 games to 2. In the likelihood of Casey's departure, *The Sentinel's* Red Thisted lobbied for Rosy Bill Ryan, the onetime Brewer moundsman, who just came off a credible Millers piloting effort.[104]

The same Don Hendrickson wilted in the Tuesday, September 19th elimination of the Brewers, 7–5, in which the Colonels took 3 straight games at home. The *Sentinel's* Stoney McGlynn, a print voice of encouragement all season, showered rhetorical orchids upon Max Carey's Chicks, who came from behind twice in their series at Kenosha. The girls promised their manager that they would take the last two games on hostile grounds. Connie Wisniewski was queen, winning her series record third and fourth victories, including a 3-hit shutout to win the playoff championship before 3,166 in Kenosha.[105]

Max Carey, who made Ripley's "Believe It or Not" as the only player to reach base 9 times in a 16-inning game, now sealed baseball history for Milwaukee. In the 12-year run of the A.A.G.P.B.L., Milwaukee was the only city to ever have both men's and women's pro baseball teams win the pennants of their leagues for their city in the same year. And each club was managed by a future Hall of Famer. It was the most unique season ever.[106]

Unfortunately for galball, the Minneapolis Millerettes drew so badly in their bigger city that they turned into a terminal road show. Milwaukee should have enjoyed its pink-laced pennant and playoff heroines all together, but the hard-edged establishment of its high minors tradition made Milwaukee more interested in Casey Stengel's replacement.

The Millerettes folded entirely and the Fort Wayne Daisies were created in their stead. The Chicks moved to Grand Rapids, Michigan, where they would peep along the rest of the Girls League merry way until 1954. The genteel enthusiasm towards the female players just seemed better suited to smaller, mid-sized cities than beer-swilling Milwaukee.[107]

Industrial strength Milwaukee now had consecutive A.A. pennants to defend for the first time in 30 years, even if the Brewers couldn't advance to the Junior World Series. Some fans organized to "Bring Back Stengel," but his chilly treatment by Veeck from afar led Casey to declare that he would not return "under any circumstances."[108]

The Milwaukee Journal sports editor, R.G. Lynch, browbeat Veeck in print for abusing whom everyone else saw as a "swell guy." Vice-president Mickey Heath would only acknowledge that a search was underway for a new headman and that it was Bill Veeck who would name him.

Veeck ultimately wrote to Stengel, who lived in California in the off-season. Sport Shirt Marine Bill was now in the Corona naval hospital, with a leg badly damaged in the war. He invited Stengel for a visit, and Lynch's advice proved correct.[109]

The two hit it off, as Lynch wrote, "two good guys always will." Veeck then telegrammed Lynch for his opinion about bringing Stengel back to manage. Stengel, who helped Charlie Grimm go back to turn the Cubs into a 4th place finisher poised for the 1945 flag, would have the last word. Casey signed to manage his hometown KC for 1945. Joining the Yankee affiliate set the stage for his fabulous New York run, only after another pennant triumph with the P.C.L. Oakland Acorns.[110]

When Bill Veeck turned to Nick "Tomato Face" Cullop, he chose wisely.

Hal Peck, the Wisconsin man who was Veeck's favorite good luck charm, minus a couple toes. Copyright unknown (via Baseball Hall of Fame Library).

The former slugging outfielder just wrapped up 25 years as a player, pinch-hitting for his Columbus Red Birds at the last. He just came off a 170–134, .559 pair of seasons at the perch of the Flock. It was under him that Columbus knocked Milwaukee out of the 1943 playoffs.

Cullop was an affable baseball man in the down-to-earth way with which Milwaukeeans could relate. His better known nickname of "Tomato Face" came from the sunburnt, pugilistic look his demeanor could take, when provoked. The Milwaukee press was as more likely to refer to him as "the old Hipper Dipper."[111]

Veeck saw the war dissect his pennant-winning roster the same way Hal Peck accidentally shot off a couple of his toes in a rat-hunting expedition at his Genesee Depot chicken coop. Veeck considered Peck his favorite player and good luck charm. Offers still abounded for a 3-toed outfielder, who had a planter's wart amputated.[112]

Peck went through Veeck's fiscal carousel before going to the Brooklyn Dodgers and Chicago Cubs in transactions that netted Veeck $30,500. But it was on Sport Shirt Bill's party line, at his West Bend farm northwest of Milwaukee, that he sold Peck to Connie Mack's A's once and for all.[113]

A neighborly fan horned in on the conversation when Veeck was ready to part with his favorite native son for twenty grand and a couple players. "Oh, Will, he's worth more than that." The aged Mack could not discern the remark from a bad connection or interference. With that, Veeck upped the ante to $30,000 and Mack had his new Athletic after the '44 playoffs.

F.D.R. did not live long into his historic fourth term as president. The hellacious war had turned in such favor of the Allies that the Nazis were now pinched from west and east. Japan was being beaten back also, only more stubbornly. One former Brewer, Aubrey (Yo-Yo) Epps, a catching outfielder from late 1941, received a marine citation for service in the invasion of Saipan in the Mariana Islands. Sadly Lt. Stanley Klores, once a Brewer camper from West Allis and later baseball coach at Northwestern University, was reported by the Navy Department as changed from missing in action to dead. He had been on the U.S.

Destroyer Cooper in the Phillippines. Ken Keltner reported to the Great Lakes Naval Station in Illinois.[114]

The toll was genuine. Bill Veeck needed to look no further than at his own leg. And yet, the wheeling and dealing he continued from his naval hospital bed was as legendary as anything that was Veeck. It was left to Mickey Heath and Rudy Schaffer to wage their own war with the Mexican League. Catcher Salvador (Chico) Hernandez was bought from the Cubs in 1943, but refused to sign and hit .305 for Rogers Hornsby's Veracruz club south of the border. Pfc. Veeck had the Cuban reinstated in the off-season, but when time came for 1945 spring training in Waukesha, Chico wasn't the man. He went back to Veracruz, where he hit .341, with some pop.[115]

An aged Connie Mack was taken for an upped ante on Hal Peck, thanks to Bill Veeck's West Bend party line. Milwaukee Public Library Historical Photograph Collection.

The "green light" to keep baseball going didn't aid Cullop in dealing with Bill Norman's resentment at being listed as a "player-coach." Willis expected to win a regular outfield job. Tommy Nelson was sold to the Boston Braves, along with Dick Culler. Frank Secory and Heinz Becker were now Cubs. George Binks would back up Joe Kuhel at first, in the nation's capital. Bill Nagel wore White Sox and Hersh Martin, Yankee pinstripes. If the cupboard looked bare, Veeck and Cullop didn't give in.[116]

Nick Cullop was the least famous of the three managers to lead Milwaukee to back-to-back-to-back pennants in the '40s. Yet, it is his 1945 effort, with a completely different starting lineup, that may be the most remarkable. Eugene Nance, the 3rd baseman who would be his top run producer, was an early holdout.[117]

Anything that seemed to be set up, would get knocked over like so many pins in the Kulwicki 800 Average Bowling League. Still, Cullop had a trio of valuable arms to return to: Owen Scheetz, Don Hendrickson, Floyd Speer, and Julio Acosta, who kept in fine shape during his Havana winter. Second sacker Joe Rullo awaited 4F clearance.[118]

Groundskeepers Ed Kretlow and Ed Polzin groomed the battlefield at Waukesha's Frame Park just so Cullop's new Brewers could beat a detail representing the Soldiers' Home, 7–5. All 5 runs were allowed by Jack Farmer before 397 people, on April Fool's Day. Bob Casey, the 47-year old Soldiers' Home backstop was a better prospect than some of the youngsters.[119]

Elks Exalted Ruler and Toastmaster Howard Ott welcomed A.A. honcho George Trautman, Minneapolis Millers president Mike Kelley, and chief specialist Bob Feller to speak at the home opener banquet.[120]

Rudy Schaffer and Mickey Heath also returned from Middletown, Ohio, where arrangements were made for a possible Brewer farm in the Ohio State League. Former Brewer favorite Ivy Griffin was tabbed to manage there.[121]

Former Brewers were active in the Pacific Coast League, too. Lou Novikoff was back from his fear of the ivy at Chicago's Wrigley Field to play at Phil Wrigley's field in L.A. again. The "Mad Russian" opened the season with a couple triples for the Angels, but the San Francisco Seals won, 6–5. Ted Norbert socked a couple homers to lead the Seattle Rainiers to a 10–2 win over the San Diego Padres. Norbert would go on to win another home run crown in that circuit and old out-of-sorts Vallie Eaves of the Padres would be the strikeout king.[122]

One quality Heath liked about Cullop was that he didn't put himself above his players when it came to accommodations or transport. But he could brood ugly in defeat, even in exhibitions, to the point of a lost appetite.[123]

Veeck was recovering from leg operations out in Corona, but promised his skipper, the old Hipper Dipper, in a pep talk over the phone that more help was being sought. The Wednesday, April 18th opener at Minneapolis was postponed, due to cold. *The Journal's* Sam Levy, a baseball scribe since 1909, joined a couple other graybeards, George A. Brown and Halsey Hall of Minneapolis, to kick around an All-Time American Association team. Two Brewers, Long Tom Hughes and the deceased Stoney McGlynn (not *The Sentinel* writer, in his last year there) made it, as did catcher Ray Schalk, Unser Choe Hauser, the 1st base *schafskopf* expert (unanimously), Ted Gullic, Bevo LeBourveau, and Nick Cullop made the outfield.[124]

One-armed Pete Gray made his major league debut with the St. Louis Browns and 20 Negroes picketed around Yankee Stadium, imploring that blacks be allowed in the bigs. "If We Can Pay, Why Can't We Play?" and "If We Can Stop Bullets, Why Not Balls?" were among the signs.

Adolf Hitler celebrated his 56th and last birthday just before the Brewers finally got underway on Friday, April 20th. The smallest opening crowd in Minneapolis history — 1,598 — saw a bad "Class X exhibition" of the "rankest base running to be seen anywhere west of Brooklyn."[125] Be that as it was, Joe (The Barber) Rullo launched his life as a Brewer on a 3-for-5, 3 RBI initiation. He led a 17-hit attack in a 10–5 victory.

Cullop had a knack to spin a good baseball yarn and tales of his parents watching him play were recounted by *The Journal's* R.G. Lynch: After seeing her son slide in for a double and slide home with the winning run, Nick quizzed Mama Cullop on his performance. "Well, I guess it was all right, but you're just as clumsy as ever, Nick; you fell down twice!"[126]

His luck with his father was no better. Nick was a pitcher early in his career and Papa Cullop was due to watch him on the mound. He got no one out and was staked to an immediate 4–0 deficit and sent to the showers. In street clothes, Nick went out to join his father by his reserved seat. When noting that he had arrived late in the second inning, only to see someone else pitching, Nick could only say, "Shucks, Dad, you've got to get here in the first inning if you want to see me pitch."

Cullop's Brewers gave the home opener away when raw shortstop Florian "Zollie" Zielinski was responsible for 4 of a half-dozen Brewer errors. He heard the groans of 8,109 "frozen customers" when the Minneapolis Polar Bears took advantage of Milwaukee's Eskimos, 7–4, on Thursday, April 26th. None of the Miller runs were earned.[127] Milwaukee was off to a 4th place start at 9–7.

Adolf Hitler was dead 5 days later. U.S. Senator Happy Chandler from Kentucky was unanimously elected to a 7-year term as baseball commissioner at $50,000 per year.[128]

For a team that turned out to be as good as the Brewers were, the turnover rate of 34 players was unusual. Elmer Weingartner stepped in at short by July 4th when Milwaukee swept Casey Stengel's KC Blues after climbing into 1st place.[129] The Brewers saved up some of their vaunted power that was corked all season to the pleasure of 5,577. Weingartner's winning ways with his bat carried over to a smoother functioning infield. Arky Biggs shouldered most of the play at short, but he was a valuable bat without the strain of defense.

Former Brewer Jeff Heath's dugout sign at Cleveland wasn't too popular with the paying populace, but spoke volumes: "Don't boo our players — They're harder to get than customers."[130] Harvey Kuenn, Jr., was among those playing in Milwaukee's Stars of Yesterday tourney under the "Keltners" banner. He would win the local amateur Triple-A batting title.

A Negro American League game was played on Monday night, July 16th, at Borchert Field. The Memphis Red Sox utilized 4 Chicago American Giant errors and a 2-run poke out of the park by catcher Casey Jones to win, 14–3. Fred Bankhead, one of 5 Bankhead brothers in the Negro Leagues from Empire, Alabama, handled 10 unerring chances at second for Memphis.[131]

On the day President Harry S. Truman ordered the fury of split atoms in a bomb unleashed upon Hiroshima, Japan, the Brewers split a doubleheader at Columbus. Charley Root, the man who gave up Babe Ruth's alleged "called" home run in the 1932 World Series, managed the Flock. Floyd Speer started the first game for Milwaukee, who used a 4-run, 9th inning rally to win, 7–4. Speer also finished the second game, unable to match the ageless Root, himself, in a 10–9, 10th inning loss. The world changed that August 6th, thanks in part to 30 U.W. physicists.[132]

Knowing an effective weapon when they saw the A-bomb's effect, Russia decided to pile on by finally declaring war upon Japan. When the second bomb devastated Nagasaki on August 9th, Milwaukee again split one of many doubleheaders crammed into the schedule.[133] Only this time, Julio Acosta bested Jack Miller 1–0 at Toledo in Game One and Al LaMacchia returned the compliment over Floyd Speer, 3–0, in 7 innings. The Brewers were still in 2nd place, 3 losses behind the Indianapolis Indians at 70–47.

In the 10-day period between August 20th and September 1st, Milwaukee made a 5½ game turnaround on Indy. In Milwaukee, that latter day of official Japanese surrender was celebrated at the Heil plant with a strike of 1,600 workers. The issue was of a "general" nature. The city's Common Council finally voted for a plan to obtain a site for an arena.[134]

The Brewers were now in 1st place, but Julio Acosta failed in his attempt to "bamboozle" the Minneapolis Kels' array of left-handed clubbers for the second time in 3 nights. The Indians' loss at Columbus kept Milwaukee 3½ games ahead of Indianapolis.[135]

A paid newspaper ad stressed the Christian church's role in the "new world order." Nominal Milwaukeean Douglas MacArthur assumed command as the military governor of a defeated Japanese empire.[136]

Earlier in the summer, Cullop threatened utility man John Price's snake collection with a bat. In the last game of the regular season, the second half of a Sunday, September 9th twin spin, Cullop had the snake charmer play one inning at every position. Price was the first Brewer to perform that feat since Ralph Winegarner on the last day of the 1938 season.[137]

Price made the most fun out of the 8th inning when he donned the catcher's "tools of ignorance." With an official rule book tucked in his hip pocket, Price caught a few Floyd Speer tosses then launched into a mock "argument" with umpire Pat Padden, who was in on the gag. Price pulled out the rule book to prove his point. Before he pulled his mask back down, Price pinned a "blind" sign on Padden's back. The ump acted as if he knew nothing.

Padden and fellow umpire Charley Moore (who shared the name of a future major league Brewer) each received a presentation of $25 from the fans between games. In thanking the patronage, Moore said, "In my many years as an umpire, this is the first time I've received anything but abuse from the fans." The final split with the Saints and their 2nd baseman, future Milwaukee Brave Red Schoendienst, made 9,057 a happy lot.

Nick Cullop's Brewers finished 93–61, a 2½ game lead over Indianapolis. *The Journal's* R.G. Lynch warned the city's fandom not to take these pennants for granted as this third straight one made for the A.A.'s first dynasty in 30 years.[138] Final home attendance was 250,821.

Milwaukee had its fourth batting champ of the '40s in outfielder Lew Flick, the circuit's RBI leader in Gene Nance and durable Owen Scheetz topped the pitching charts at 19 wins. What Cullop also had going into that first playoff round was a nicked-up team. Nance played through a couple weeks with a toe injury and center fielder Larry Rosenthal pulled a muscle in his left leg. Cullop's own son, Nick, Jr., "retired" from the Minneapolis prep gridiron to avoid any injury for baseball.[139] From a $12,000 players' pool, the 1st place Brewers collected $5 Gs. The $185 apiece would be all they got.

Mayor John Bohn expressed the city's appreciation in a letter to Veeck, who was out of Milwaukee's St. Joseph Hospital, after yet another operation on his leg, and back at West Bend. Bohn called for rewarding the Brewers' pennant success with a new ballpark.[140]

The playoff series with Louisville was carried on WEMP, but it was the diamond equivalent of a captured Tojo trying to commit suicide. These series never drew well, crowds in the 3,000 range, analogous to what the modern minor league hockey Milwaukee Admirals have experienced.

Even a Bill Veeck, welcomed back to Borchert Field on crutches, made for a ready source of agitation. He badgered the Colonels' road secretary, Fred Grimm (apparently no relation to Charlie), about travel for the next season's schedule. If not for Julio Acosta, who protected an 11th inning win at Milwaukee and beat the Colonels at Louisville, Cullop could only chide his injury-riddled charges. Veeck and Shorty Mendelson drove hurt 1st baseman Otto Denning all night down to Louisville. Pitcher Wendell "Bill" Davis had filled in at first.[141]

Game Six made for a remarkable scene beyond Chick Genovese's 10th frame game wining hit with 2 out for Louisville. Umpire Milt Steengraffe had already been the target of Acosta's ire the previous night. A sour 1st base decision in the 9th of this game brought a rush of Cullop and his men. Veeck, a war vet with crutches, yelled from his seat behind the visitors' dugout. A Colonel fan barely missed him with a pop bottle. Brewer trainer Bob Feron hurdled the wire railing and collared the culprit. Veeck picked up his crutches and headed for the fan, but police led the man away.[142]

This raucous scenario was Bill Veeck's last stand as Milwaukee Brewers owner. He later called his "fine careless rapture in Milwaukee" the best time of his life. But, to save his failing marriage and heal his damaged leg, he decided to sell his beloved ballclub to buy a guest ranch in Arizona.[143]

While watching the Cubs in their last World Series down in Chicago, Veeck came across Rogers Hornsby, who had once tried to buy the Brewers. Bill let the Rajah know that the team was again for sale. Hornsby himself would pass but sent a serious buyer Veeck's way.

Chicago attorney Oscar Salenger appeared at Veeck's room the next night. When Veeck said he wanted to come away with $250,000 after taxes, Salenger told him to draw up the paperwork to sign. In a flash, Veeck parted with the lightness and laughter he loved in Milwaukee.

Dilapidated "Borchert's Orchard," in all its peculiar glory, from 7th and Chambers at the bottom corner. Milwaukee Public Library Historical Photograph Collection.

And the wildest and most wildly successful era in the minor league history of the Milwaukee Brewers went with him.

Oscar Salenger was an astute man, who other than working out with the team in game flannels, kept a lower profile in seeking the best for his new ballclub. He still had Rudy Schaffer to run the team as president and wisely kept Nick Cullop on as pilot.

The post-war world had little time to celebrate peace. The reconstruction of Europe and Asia posed an enormous undertaking and thanks to Josef Stalin's aggressive Soviet Union, the "red menace" of the Cold War loomed.

For the baseball world, and Milwaukee in particular, it meant a flood of returning talent and a rapid expansion of the minor leagues. What it all meant to Nick Cullop was that his 1945 pennant-winners, who led the American Association in hits, RBI, and .292 batting average, would be completely disrupted again.[144]

Every club in the A.A. underwent so much overhaul, from the top of the standings to the bottom, but for the 45 bodies to wear Brewer flannels in 1946, the magic wouldn't reoccur.

As much as the Federal government maintained a tight rein on certain segments of the economy, travel restrictions were finally lifted. Salenger could send the Brewers to Mineral Wells, Texas, for a spring training change. The only returning position player that Cullop could count on was hot corner man Gene Nance, and that, only after the ChiSox optioned him back.[145] Some past Brewer hurlers, like Walt Lanfranconi, Wes Livengood, and 29-year old Hy Vandenburg all toed the slab, but the front of the rotation was cradled in the arms of Ewald Pyle and Lee "Buck" Ross.

Ivy Griffin sent base-stealing shortstop Homer Chapman for the Tomato Face seal of approval, but "Home" was at least a year away from advancement. Chapman was a Veeck discovery, but it was another shortstop, whom Veeck pined for in his Hal Peck dealings with Branch Rickey, who won the job. The aptly named Charlie Brewster would hit an exact .300 for Cullop.[146]

The old Hipper Dipper even had the peripatetic Eddie Stumpf and Harry Griswold, along with Ivy Griffin assisting his conduct of the rookie drills. Another shortstop was a Texan named Johnny Russian. His name may have sounded like some Cold War rockabilly star of a Hollywood movie title, but he actually was of Russian descent. Griswold even pinch-hit in a 14–12 loss to the Fort Worth Cats at Wichita Falls.[147]

The first two Negroes in Organized Ball, one being a certain Jackie Robinson, found their spring training with the Montreal Royals to be very inhospitable. Jacksonville canceled an exhibition, where the two black men were to face the Jersey City Giants. *The Milwaukee Journal's* R.G. Lynch was among those writing that Organized Baseball better back these men up and not tolerate such hostile treatment. He cited how football stars Fritz Pollard and Paul Robeson had played for the N.F.L. Milwaukee Badgers in the 1920s without so much ado. Lynch nobly asserted that "sports should demand of a man only that he be a good competitor and a good sportsman." Of course, he wrote that in the same newspaper that used to publish "Nigger Hair" tobacco ads only a few decades earlier.[148]

Basketball's first supposed 7-footer, Bob Kurland, was poised to lead his Oklahoma Aggies to a second straight N.C.A.A. title when the April Fool's Day temperature in Milwaukee reached a balmy 75. Some 400,000 coal miners did go on strike and the Brewers accumulated lumps of coal in exhibition losses to the Texas League Dallas Rebels.[149] Ghost of Brewer past Hank Oana, the Hawaiian "Prince," made base hits "scarcer than Republican votes in a Texas election." One game drew 3,987. The Brewers played their way north by way of Oklahoma City and Tulsa.

Milwaukee couldn't beat Chicago at a State Fair Coliseum roller derby either, but another sort of derby was won by Mexico's wealthy Pasqual brothers: They signed prize American League home run king Vern Stephens to a 5-year deal and he promptly won a game at Veracruz before 20,000 with a 9th inning single.[150]

The first television broadcasting chain was in its infancy in the East, and Milwaukee's Henry S. Reuss was in charge of price controls for America's military government in occupied Germany. Bill Veeck came up from his Tucson ranch to take in the Brewers' opener on Wednesday, April 17th.

The defending A.A. pennant-fliers were welcomed back by 14,109 fans but the 1945 5-0 mastery of the St. Paul Saints by Owen Scheetz could not be maintained. The Apostles chased him in the 6th and Lew Flick, still with the team, left the bases loaded in the 9th. The final 6-3 loss was Mr. and Mrs. Oscar Salenger's baptism into professional baseball.[151]

The umpire for that game, Bobby Hicks, had fought in Guadalcanal. He was one of 35 in his squadron ordered to take out a rolling artillery gun hidden in a cave. His captain was beside him when struck and killed by a shell fragment. His closest buddy, whose wife was expecting a baby, died also. Welcome back to the mundane arguments of baseball![152]

Sam Levy continued the tradition: Saints second sacker Ed Basinski led off the 4th, parking "the season's first home run on Frau Hassenpfeffer's stoop."

R.G. Lynch began a tradition of presenting "Dr. Jekyll" and "Mr.Hyde" versions of all the good and bad about Opening Day. It was either bright, sunny skies and "the Brewers will show them," or cold peanuts that tasted like last year's leftovers and warm beer with "too much rigmarole."

May Day traditions often called for socialist-inspired labor demonstrations, but Allis-Chalmers in Milwaukee was under the "anarchy" of a strike. Wisconsin's governor Walter S. Goodland had to call out the National Guard. Six Wisconsin breweries were sold as the government ordered a 30 percent cut in grain use.[153]

Bunny Brief, the old Brewer, was back teaching kids at Lapham Park about strikes of a baseball sort, complete with movies. Another couple ex-Brewers, Heinz Becker and Emil Kush, helped Charlie Grimm's Chicago Cubs put the hurt on Brooklyn. Jim Delsing of Rudolph, in central Wisconsin, just returned from the service unprepared to help out the Brewer outfield. Delsing played no ball in the army and requested to be sent to the Northern League Eau Claire Bears in order to regain his game. He ultimately hit .318 for Milwaukee en route to a fine majors run.[154]

One Manny Fernandez, who split time with better-hitting Marv Felderman behind the plate, was the lone Hispanic Brewer in this edition. He would not be the man to singe Oscar Salenger for the Mexican League, however. Veteran White Sox 3rd baseman Floyd Baker, who was to be Nick Cullop's shortstop, refused to report to Milwaukee. According to Salenger, he was to receive his same A.L.-level contract, including its bonus clause. Baker finally relented.[155] For the former White Sox batboy and Comiskey Park box seatholder, Salenger, this had to be disconcerting. He counted once Brewer Johnny Mostil among his ChiSox boyhood favorites.

One American reliever, who did go south of the border, Giants veteran Ace Adams, was astonished by Mexico's zeal for "El Beisbol." Picture firemen with hoses ready to keep 35,000 whooping and whistling squatters under wraps in a park that holds 23,000. They even took over the players' benches![156]

Milwaukeeans weren't quite that fanatical, especially with the Cullopmen

The view from behind home at Borchert Field, ca. late 1940s. Milwaukee Public Library Historical Photograph Collection.

creeping out ever so slowly from the basement. The Brewers got to see Toledo's one-armed outfielder, Pete Gray. With the war over, Gray's major league moment in the sun had set. Improved play brought Milwaukee to within a couple games of .500 by June 1st.[157]

This was due in part to the stout defense up the middle, with Brewster now set at short and Baker at second. Dave Philley, the fleet Texan outfielder, was clearly the best offensive threat. He led Milwaukee in batting, extra-base hits across the board, RBI, and steals. The Lone Star switch-hitter was the Brewers' lone all-star representative.[158]

It didn't take Bill Veeck long to saddle up back in baseball. By the 4th of July, when the Brewers were twice wiping away the Blues, Bill celebrated the removal of his leg cast by assuming the presidency of the Cleveland Indians. You can't keep a wild man down.[159]

John (Wall-Eye) Dickshot was now off to a hot start in the Brewer hinterlands. Waukegan's Johnny Dickshot was Philley's opposite. Dickshot came off the best of his half-dozen major league campaigns and Philley was on his way to an 18-year major league career, particularly as one of the game's great pinch-hitters. Indian Bob Johnson, the long-time Philly A's slugger, was now a Brewer like his brother Roy once was.[160]

And so it was for the club with the cartoon beer-barreled mascot named "Owgust." They obviously lacked the power of their pennant-winning predecessors, but they weren't awful. They were just the best of the second division. Reminders of the way they were came from the likes of Columbus Red Birds keystone keeper Tommy (Hollywood) Nelson. He homered in each game of a July 15th double up before 5,966 of his old supporters.[161]

Nick Cullop came in for some second-guessing in that first game when he refused to pinch-hit for lightweight, switch-hitting 1st baseman Joe Mack. They had the tying run on base and only one out with a more threatening

Marv Felderman on the bench. Mack failed to get the ball out of the infield in 9 trips to the plate, including that one. It was that type of year.

The City of Milwaukee may not have had a baseball club that could add to the folderol, but its 100th year of incorporation was indulged in the "Centurama" celebration at the lakefront. Personalities like Eddie Cantor, Donald O'Connor, singer Jessica Dragonette and harmonicist Larry Adler were part of the festivities.[162]

Little Nemo Leibold, who broke in with the Brewers 3 decades before, had his Colonels on course for the A.A. pennant when he was suspended for the rest of the year. That July 17th, he was originally suspended for 5 days and fined $100 for his Milwaukee run-in with umpires Milt Steengraffe and Frosty Peters. The latter claimed the wizened little Leibold struck him. Both arbiters resigned, saying Nemo's suspension was insufficient. National Association president W.G. Bramham overrode first-year A.A. proxy Roy Hamey in extending the ban for the rest of the way. Leibold complained of not being allowed a hearing before Bramham.[163]

Without their banished skipper, Louisville lost the Junior World Series to the Montreal Royals of Jackie Robinson. Catcher Fred (the Whale) Walters took Leibold's place.[164]

Despite the spirit of pitcher Buck Ross, who deferred on an operation to help the Brewers stretch drive, Cullop's men ended up at 70–78, 19½ games out. Not even the "Monarchs of Monkeyshines," featuring Teddy Fabian, the "Crown Prince of Comedy," at the LaConga nightclub on 2537 N. 3rd St. could have given Nick Cullop real solace in his only losing year with Milwaukee.

He already hummed the old ballad, "There'll Be Some Changes Made," before 1946 ended. He could see only a handful of players being brought back. The exodus wasn't quite as gargantuan as the German expulsion from Poland, but Cullop's Brewers would never miss the post-season again. Oscar Salenger was so disappointed, he sold his interest to Lou Perini's Boston Braves.

Talk continued to grow that the Story quarry site in the Menomonee River Valley could be the future home of a 25,000-seat sports stadium. The city pursued an indoor sports arena, but the County Board's Parks and Land Commission evaluated transit access to the 40-acre site. The proposed stadium could add a 40,000-60,000 expansion.[165]

The project that had drifted aimlessly for 9 years finally came together on February 24, 1947. Wisconsin's U.S. Senator Alexander Wiley pushed a bill through Congress that added 120 acres from the adjacent Soldiers' Home grounds to the quarry site. That parcel would be sold to the county for parking after the County Board voted that day to proceed with building the stadium. It took President Truman another 2½ years to sign the bill, and the new addition actually made a better ultimate site. But it was finally moving forward.

The Milwaukee Brewers had had casual working arrangements with major league clubs over the years, the White Sox in the 1910s, Borchert's sales to Connie Mack's A's in the '20s, and the Wrigley subsidies from the Cubs in the late '30s. Only when the St. Louis Browns' Phil Ball owned the Brewers at the turn of the '30s was there a direct farm relationship.

Lou Perini and Braves general manager John Quinn installed Jake Flowers to be president of the Milwaukee ballclub. D'Arcy Raymond Flowers was a 10-year N.L. infielder during the late 1920s-early '30s. The entire atmosphere changed. No longer would year-end fire sales by independent operators like Borchert or Veeck be the norm. Players were instructed in playing the game the way the Braves wanted.[166]

This also posed a new challenge for Milwaukee, now as has always pervaded the minors, whether late season parent club call-ups could ruin a Triple-A franchise's pennant chances.

Minor league baseball restructured after the war. What had been the uppermost level of Double-A became Triple-A, as it remains to this day. On December 4, 1946, William G. Bramham retired after 14 years of overseeing all the minors. George Trautman, who left the A.A. keys to Roy Hamey in order to become the Detroit Tigers' executive vice-president, succeeded Bramham. Bramham died on July 8, 1947, at age 73 in Durham, N.C.[167]

Milwaukee's good old Unser Choe Hauser now managed the Wisconsin State League Sheboygan Indians in Class D. The old Brewer and minor league home run titan would guide that club to 4 pennants in 8 years, 1946–1953. Other Milwaukee and ex-Brewer hands were in that circuit also, like Joe Skurski at Wausau, Jimmy Adlam, Fond du Lac's still active homer champ, and Harry Griswold at Green Bay.[168]

It was a different world in spring training at Cocoa, Florida. Now, instead of relying on an independent scramble for talent, Nick Cullop could make his needs specifically laid out to the parent Braves.

The Boston Braves were long perennial National League also-rans, with even future Brewer manager Bob Coleman leading them to 6th place in 1944 and 1945. John Quinn's ascension to the G.M. post over his own father, and the subsequent hiring of St. Louis Cardinal pennant pilot Billy Southworth changed everything.[169]

The Braves supplied the likes of former L.S.U. All-American halfback Alvin "Blackie" Dark to get full-time seasoning at short. Cullop wanted him to beat out Damon Phillips, whose shaky glove led him to third. Outfielder Tom Neill would be an important lefty-swinging RBI bat, sent down by Boston at Cullop's request.[170]

Cullop's original 3rd base designee, Gene Patton, could not overcome complications of the rheumatic fever he first contracted in the army. Patton, who was born at Coatesville, Pennsylvania on the September 26, 1926, night that Gene Tunney took the heavyweight boxing belt from Jack Dempsey, was touted as a big league talent by Jake Flowers. He'd never see the majors.[171]

Tom Neill was the reigning Southern Association batting and RBI king. The Brewers purchased fellow S.A. alum, Tennessee-bred Carden Gillenwater from Indianapolis. "Gilly" had a productive 1945 as a Brave and would be the cleanup man "until a harder clubber comes along."[172] One didn't, and didn't need to. He would be the 1947 A.A. home run leader, albeit with only 23.

Billy Southworth laughed at Cullop's pleas for help after the Brewers needed only 5 days of practice to beat the Braves! A 5-run rally in the 8th overcame 4 Brewer miscues. Al "Skippy" Roberge, the stocky Massachusetts Frenchman whose slowness afoot kept him from the Braves' own wigwam, proved his utility value right away when his 6th inning homer was the first Brewer run of 1947. It was his 2-run single in the 10th though that scalped the parents, 8–7. Roberge may have been in the Brewers' Gallic tradition of Frenchy Uhalt and Bevo LeBourveau, but he was also the poster child for what would be their dead last standing in steals.[173]

Of course, 1947 marked Branch Rickey's bold step of promoting Jackie Robinson to the Brooklyn Dodgers' big league stage. That, in spite of the recalcitrance of some southern players in his own locker room. R.G. Lynch wrote in *The Journal* of how Julio Acosta might still have been a Brewer if he had been given the sort of protections that Rickey surrounded Robinson with.[174]

Acosta was a white Hispanic Cuban without any known trace of Negro blood. Yet, none of his Brewer teammates would room with him, calling him "showboat," "nigger," and a "shine ballplayer." Julie was driven to tears more than once, having only the trainer as his road roomie. If Acosta, with his "mercurial temperament," had a hint of the safeguards offered to Robinson such "ruinous treatment" may not have denied his ability to win more. Bill Veeck, the man who brought Acosta to Milwaukee, flirted with buying the Phillies and switching them all with Negro Leaguers, too.[175]

The Minneapolis Millers played the Thursday, April 17th opener at Borchert Field. Both clubs joined in a letter to an ailing Babe Ruth: "You are still the greatest home run hitter to all of us. It's our fondest hope and fervent prayer that the Great Umpire will keep you in the lineup for many, many years to come."[176]

Opening Day in the new Braves era wasn't without one catch. Jake Flowers opened the Brewers' new uniform packages to find they were, in fact, Braves clothing. That he had the Indian heads removed from the sleeves and Braves name substituted in such short order was a tribute to ingenuity and industry. What would John Quinn or visiting A.A. head Frank Lane think?[177]

Traditionally cold weather held attendance to 8,500–9,000, and the Brewers led 1–0 after 2 innings. Light snowfall threatened an early end to the game. They tried again the next day, Friday, April 18th, and 11,337 saw their retooled heroes fall, 11–8. Gillenwater and Roberge were batting stars in a game where Mrs. Nick Cullop saw her hubby go through five pitchers' arms.[178]

The team lacked clout at a couple positions. Joe Mack just wasn't an answer at 1st base and the team went through a handful of catchers, including Shawano, Wisconsin's Ken Raddant. Weak-hitting Bob Brady played the most until fracturing his leg in July. Feisty Danny Murtaugh, later known as the skipper of the Pittsburgh Pirates, established himself at second.

The pitching would not glitter either, though lefty Glenn Elliott, Iowan Al (Pard) Epperly, and prickly Vern Bickford all came up winners. Buck Ross' off-season arm surgery did him in. Maybe this club needed the sort of "beer time" guzzling clause that 6,000 union brewery workers won in their new contract nationwide. In Milwaukee, Atlas Prager Beer ("Got It? Get It!") went for $2.90 a case.[179]

By mid-May, the prodigal Heinz Becker agreed to terms and was again Milwaukee's favorite German import. Max Macon, a man who once preened as a left-handed Dizzy Dean, was now a utility man, filling the 1st base gap until Becker's arrival.[180]

Oscar Salenger was among the 1,474 watching the Thursday night, May 15th spanking of the Columbus Red Birds. Again, it was Skippy Roberge leading the way, with a single, 2 doubles, and a triple. Alvin Dark, John Dickshot, and Gene Nance each added 3 hits to the total of 18 off 4 Red Bird wings. The offense crafted its 18-1 rout in 2 hours, 16 minutes. Salenger offered to re-buy the team, but Lou Perini, seated next to him, could only smile. The win vaulted Milwaukee from sixth to third in a congested race.[181]

Nick Cullop's commute from his Pewaukee Lake home was made easier by Becker's return. Heinz may not have been a Tetsuharu Kawakami, the Yomiuri Giants' "Lord of All Batters" in Japan, but he was light years better than what Milwaukee had. Becker ended up giving the Brewers their fifth batting champion (.363) of the decade, with no duplicates.[182]

Alvin Dark and Tom Neill led the further fattening of Brewer batting averages with another 18-5 blowout in the second half of a Father's Day doubleheader. Columbus was again the sacrificial Red Bird to entertain 6,730. They did it on 26 hits, too.[183]

A 9-5 road trip into Independence Day kept Milwaukee in third, but it was Kansas City Blues pitcher Carl DeRose who stole the attention. He recently hurled a perfecto versus Minneapolis, so his home fans rewarded him with a check of $2,005.52. Each teammate who participated in that June 26th game was given a $25 check. DeRose was given a trophy by the A.A. chapter of baseball writers and a $1 bill signed with congrats from Gen. Dwight D. Eisenhower.[184]

There was no chance that Milwaukee's new arena, now with its land by the Auditorium acquired, would be done in time for Wisconsin's 1948 Centennial. Mayor Bohn invited Gen. MacArthur to settle down in Milwaukee for his retirement.[185]

Milwaukee's man about baseball, Eddie Stumpf, now with Bill Veeck's Cleveland organization, was a passenger in a freak San Diego car accident. His

56-year old driver died at the wheel of a heart attack and Stumpf steered the vehicle towards the curb. But it still went through a plate glass window. Another scout also escaped injury, but the three were sizing up naval prospects.[186]

They could've had auto racer Tony Bettenhausen at the wheel and fared no better. He also just suffered a spectacular spill, rolling over his midget car at Milwaukee's State Fair Park. He wasn't injured either, but was later the namesake of an annual memorial race there.[187]

Skippy Roberge battled teammate Heinz Becker for the A.A. batting lead much of the year, only he did it from a variety of positions. The Brewers as a whole straddled a few games over .500 and hung in 3rd place, despite ineffective pitching and a hitting slump that led to a 4-game losing streak by August 1st. That .500 home stand drew 82,335 for 13 games (or 6,333 per) and put the season total over 217,000 already.[188]

Ol' Will Norman, who was called "Willie Cardinal" when Eddie Stanky was his Brewer roommate, hardly had the temperament of a leader as a player. However, the man who was a raging, fine-imposing failure for St. Louis' Toronto farm in 1945, now had his Wilkes-Barre Barons in second place of the Eastern League.[189]

The Brewers' Al Epperly was one pitcher in the A.A. who held a jinx over KC's pennant-bound Blues. The right-hander was the first Milwaukee slabster to reach a dozen wins when he topped Calvin Coolidge Julius Caesar Tuskahoma McLish, 7–1. Brewer bats were finally off the snide again by mid-August. In that same game, Carden Gillenwater missed equaling a record in his second at-bat foul out in the 2nd inning. Gilly had reached base 11 consecutive times, falling 2 shy of the record held by onetime Blue Frenchy Bordagaray.[190]

F.M. Younger, the radio-sounding backstop who caught on in late June, fell prone to a broken finger and was through for the season.[191]

Nick Cullop's Brewers held consistent to a 3rd place, 79–75 finish, 14½ games behind the Blues, whom they'd face in the first round of the playoffs. The match-up pitted the two worst records at those positions in league playoff history, but Milwaukee was oblivious. The post-season march began on September 9th as bespectacled Glenn Elliott remained undefeated at KC, despite serving up 4 homers in a 9–8 win. Yankee prospect Hank Bauer showed off for Larry MacPhail, bashing 2 over the distant left field barrier. Attendance was 11,245.

The Brewers beat the Kaws again in a completely opposite game. Vern Bickford disappointed 9,689 rooters with 2-hit, 2–1 craftwork. Danny Murtaugh flared up into words with Ed Stewart after tagging him out at second. The umps had to shoo everyone back to their dugouts. The Kaws then mauled the Brewers at Borchert Field, 14–2. It was Frank Hiller's 4th straight win over Milwaukee and the hopes of 9,315 were doused by "prodigious" Blas Monaco and Steve Souchock blasts. John Quinn and Oscar Salenger took in the game.

Kansas City evened the series when manager Bill Meyers' gamble on starting Cuddles Marshall paid off, 5–2. The handsome right-hander went instead of Tommy Byrne and withstood 9 walks with the support of 3 double plays. The Brewers drew 7,054 while the Green Bay Packers drew 17,895 at State Fair Park. Lefty Glenn Elliott methodically made good, 5–3, over a Tommy Byrne who was "wilder than a dockwalloper on a spree." The smallest gathering of the series, 4,180, watched Milwaukee cash in 5 Byrne walks for 4 runs. Al Dark's bases-loaded double did severe damage.

Dark's home run and 4 sparkling DPs did in the Blues before 12,158 at KC. Bickford again handcuffed the Kaws, 4–2, and Gillenwater had his first hit in 15 at-bats. The Brewers advanced to face the Louisville Colonels who disposed of Minneapolis in 7 games.[192]

In a measure of "$40,000 beauties" at shortstop, Alvin Dark clearly had the better of the Colonels' Billy Goodman. Goodman's 6th inning error paved the way to Milwaukee's 5–2 opening win. Dark was a one-man show to the sorrow of 12,194. Four straight singles off Jim Wilson, 2 RBI in a big 5th inning rally, and glove work like "Mr. Shortstop" made Goodman look like a "10¢ stone dub." Cullop's crew then demoralized 5 Colonel pitchers with 20 hits in a 12–5 rout. Second place Louisville still drew 10,309 and the Brewers had to replace Carden Gillenwater with rookie Ray Fletcher in the 7th. Gilly went out with a pulled muscle in his left leg. Fletcher was called up from Evansville two weeks earlier.

The crippling continued as the Colonels surged with a 6–4 comeback. Trepidation grew when Murtaugh injured his shoulder, and Roberge moved from right to cover second. Pete Whisenant, 17-year old call-up from Northern League Eau Claire, went out to patrol right field. Lou Perini disposed of rumors that he would replace Nick Cullop with Al Lopez.

An old-fashioned pep talk by longtime Colonel leader Nemo Leibold revitalized his team into a 2-all series tie. So-so Columbus acquisition Jack Griffore tamed the Brewers, 4–1. Even the *landsmann,* league batting champ Heinz Becker, whiffed twice. The 40° chilled them to 4 hits.

Class B call-up Ray Fletcher found everything in the 10th inning of Game Five to be the same as it was in the Three-I League. "Shucks, this is just another ball game." His slashing double to right beat Louisville for reliever Jimmy Wallace, 4,213 customers, and a joyous Nick Cullop.

Alvin Dark's 3 errors and Skippy Roberge's pair of miscues bobbled away Game Six, 11–1, a product of 6 unearned runs. Jim Gleeson and Class B leadoff man Ken Chapman combined for 5 of 15 hits and 6 RBI off Ewald Pyle, Jim Davis, and Wallace. The 3,150 could only sigh.

Thursday night, September 25th, Unser Heinz Becker, der Dallas "Schlager" (slugger), stroked 3 hugely profitable home runs to his teammates' chorus of "On to Syracuse!" His 7th inning belt propelled Milwaukee into the Little World Series against the equally 3rd place International League Chiefs.

The 5–4 decider over the right field fence was a Ruthian/Reggie Jax performance that netted about $1,000 for each of his eligible playoff champions.[193]

Herr Becker's blows countered a like trio of Louisville blasts that ended Glenn Elliott's night. Vern Bickford's brilliant relief work set the stage for 3,360 to sound like 10,000 at the end.

In the unintelligible "gabble" of clubhouse bedlam, players took turns whittling off trainer Bob (Doc) Feron's 4-year moustache. He nervously made good on allowing it to come off if the guys made it to the Little World Series.

Nick Cullop's knowledge of the Syracuse Chiefs dated from his 1943 Columbus Red Bird LWS joust with them. He only feared the outstanding .339/50 homer power of Hank Sauer. Three former Brewers were also on their roster: South Side Milwaukeean catcher Joe Just, the son-in-law of Milwaukee police chief John Polcyn, Al "Dutch" Mele from 1936, and the 1940 shortstop Claude Corbitt. They played for Henry J. Bendinger, now manager of *The Milwaukee Journal* classified ad department.[194]

The series opened with a pair of Brewer losses at Syracuse, 7–6 and 7–1. Glenn Elliott walked in the winning run before 9,222 frozen rooters in Game One and the first 5 Chiefs reached base off Vern Bickford in front of another 10,654. The Brewers were now a disappointed team, irked that their per man share for winning the A.A. playoffs was a piddling $162. The club itself raked in $25,000.

Brewer players felt as if they fell behind on personal family bills the longer the post-season went. And Harry Truman asked every American to save a bushel of grain to help the hungry overseas on top of it.

The home team took its frustrations out upon the Chiefs. Bickford was redeemed in the 10th of Game Three by Damon Phillips, a former Syracuse favorite. He drove in the first 3 runs for Elliott, who squandered them in the 9th. Roberge got on by way of a booted grounder to start their 10th. Gillenwater sacrificed him over and Phillips' single moved Skip to third. Brewer catcher Walter Linden scored the skipping Roberge as the grounding clincher to Frank Drews. The 7,834 endured 35° temps for their reward.

Phillips and Becker rescued Epperly's cold bum arm to square up the series. "Demon Damon" and der Schlager shone both at bat and in the field, seizing upon 5 Chief errors. Danny Murtaugh was back as the double play pivot man to the cheers of 7,929. Tom Neill's 9th inning homer over the 7th St. boards won Game Five, a 6–5 heart-stopper to halt the premature exiters. Crafty Howie Fox trapped the Brewers in his pitching den, 3–2, to force a Game Seven. That Friday night, October 3rd crowd of 11,675, the season's largest, would have to wait once more.

Cullop's larrupers satisfied the 11-year thirst of 10,131 and handed Elliott a 9–1 torture of Syracuse. Rookie Linden stole the spotlight with 3 singles and insured that Shorty Mendelson would write out winning checks of $482.82

A late '40s or early '50s view from the third base side at Borchert Field. Note the light poles in front of the grandstand. Milwaukee Public Library Historical Photograph Collection.

for each man. Rookie Ray Fletcher wasn't voted any share, but the club saw to it that he was rewarded for his important hits.[195]

Pakistan parceled its share of India and Israel its share of Palestine. The world was far from its new "United Nations," but Milwaukee had its Little World Series champions! Now if the local sportswriters only hadn't protested to the Braves about Jake Flowers' "abusive language" at a post-series party. The Brewers' president received the cold shoulder from the local press after giving priority to attending the major league Dodgers-Yankees World Series in New York. The insinuation that his club's achievement was just so much small potatoes gave everyone a bad taste.[196]

The Braves hamstrung Cullop's ability to duplicate anything by promoting Bickford and Dark to join ex-Brewers Eddie Stanky and Jeff Heath as important contributors towards the Hub City's first N.L. flag in 34 years for 1948. Stanky would go from being one of the walkingest batsmen ever to a fine managerial career. Dark was an even better player who piloted 3 major flags.[197] Winning Brewers baseball made Milwaukee a breeding ground for future managers, but the current man, Nick Cullop, did well enough for 1947 as the first Milwaukee skipper to win *The Sporting News* Minor League Manager of the Year since Al Sothoron in 1936. It was Cullop's second such honor, having won it with Columbus in 1943. Curiously, the bigs never called for him.[198]

Al Lopez, once rumored to be Cullop's replacement, took over the Indianapolis Indians instead. Also matching wits with the old Hipper Dipper during the course of 1948 would be St. Paul's future Dodger Hall of Fame leader, Walter Alston, former Brewer George Detore at Toledo, Frank Shellenback who'd start out at Minneapolis, and Owen Scheetz, replacing Nemo Leibold at Louisville. It was just baseball's unbroken circle...[199]

Another former Brewer retired to the Great Clubhouse in the Sky. DeWitt Wiley "Bevo" LeBourveau, the .399-batting outfielder of 1928, died in his sleep at his Nevada City, California, home. He was only 51 years old.[200]

Old Tomato Face had three-quarters of his infield and 2 of his 3 main pitchers back in 1948. Skippy Roberge now had the keystone all to himself and Damon "Dee" Phillips shifted to short, where Cullop originally envisioned him. Californian Froilan "Nanny" Fernandez was sent down after 3 utility years with the Braves. Lefty-swinging Marv "Twitch" Rickert brought 3 years of Cubdom with him to fill the outfield slots with Nanny. Carden Gillenwater was dealt up to Washington after a hot regular season start. Al Epperly was called up to the Braves to end '47, but was back.

Down in spring training, the University of Texas Longhorns humbled the Brewer rookies 9–6 at Austin on Monday, March 15th. The Brewers got 13 hits off of star football Q.B. Bobby Layne and future Brewer Murray Wall. Braves farm director Harry Jenkins promised mound help. Pitcher Dave Sheehan pondered matrimony and whether two could live as cheaply as one on anything less than a Class A salary. He hurled 2 no-nos for the Class B Evansville Bees in Three-I League competition for Bob Coleman. He lost 20 lbs. to sickness in the Appalachian League.[201]

Milwaukee was on the verge of having another socialist mayor as the brother of the late Carl Zeidler, Frank, defeated the non-partisan Henry Reuss. Zeidler would serve 3 terms for a dozen years after which Reuss would lose again, only to become a longtime Democrat congressman.[202]

The city's Gettelman Brewery now sponsored wrestling on television when serious-minded Glenn "The Mouse" Elliott plucked the Columbus Red Birds, 12–2, in the Friday, April 16th opener at the Ohio capital. The largest opening crowd there ever, 14,128, saw Elliott's "lively fastball and crackling curves" disarm their heroes. Gillenwater, Becker, and rookie Bill Sinton each had 3 hits to jump on 3 Bird pitchers, and Phillips' 2-run knock over left led off the 2nd as 1948's first. A shortstop named Johnny Logan saw his first Brewer action.[203]

Before the game, Columbus admirers presented Cullop with a live hog. By Milwaukee's home opener, he suffered from abdominal pains. Cullop that is, the hog's fate was unknown.

The Brewers came home to a new mayor who intervened in the local beer strike. Wages were at issue, and though music and *gemütlichkeit* were on the picket line, there was no beer.[204]

Dee Phillips' grand slam not only made 13,705 happy about thwarting Toledo 7–5, but likely cured what ailed Cullop, too. The Wednesday, April 28th win for fat Cy Buker, the Greenwood, Wisconsin, "fireman" who relieved Elliott, lifted Milwaukee to a 7–7, 4th place stand.[205] Buker, who turned 83 at the time of this writing, would be honored by his hometown as its longtime high school baseball coach.

In a sign of changing times, Kansas City fans honored 18-year old Negro Jackie Douthard, who died after an April 23rd boxing match with Bert Lytell in Milwaukee.[206]

Television may have been changing baseball, but the fledgling medium still didn't cramp the second guessers. Only now, the announcer may be labeled a bum instead of an umpire after a botched call. John, a Milwaukee bartender who used to play in the minors, summed it up: "It ain't exactly like being at the ballpark, but it's a lot better than radio."[207]

A major trade sent veteran lefty Ewald Pyle and right fielder Sinton to Louisville for young right hander Don Grate and veteran switch-hitting outfielder Jim Gleeson. "Gee Gee's" 5 years in the Big Show at the turn of the '40s solidified an already strong Brewer order. Grate was a basketball and baseball star at Ohio State University, who was signed by Herb Pennock to the Phillies in 1945. Pennock, the "Knight of Kennett Square," Pa., pitched his way to the Hall of Fame.[208]

The Cullopmen extended a 5-game win streak, nicking the Kaws in both ends of the Memorial Day doubleheader in Missouri. Catcher Paul Burris stabilized the staff and his "Big Bertha" drove in 4 on 2 timely singles in the opener. KC's generous Jack Robinson (no, not *him*) served up 5 runs in the 9th inning of the 10–6 game. Columbus acquiree Les Studener mesmerized the Kaws with no hits for 5 of the 7-inning windup, despite walking 8 men.[209]

Milwaukee beat up Kansas City again in the Independence Day weekend twinbills. The Brews went through 13 pitchers, the Blues 14. Cy Buker was credited with the Monday opening victory, despite pitching only 2/3 of an inning, but Nanny Fernandez whipped out the grand salami. Twitchy Rickert drove in 8 runs in the second game. Roberge added a homer amongst his 8 hits in 2 days. Blues right fielder/Yanks prospect Hank Bauer reached base 8 straight times.[210]

In a footnote appearance, Joe Bauman had one hitless at-bat for Milwaukee. Bauman would go on to set professional records of 72 home runs and 224 RBI for the 1954 Class C Longhorn League Roswell (N.M.) Rockets.[211] Barry Bonds eclipsed the homer mark in 2001.

The Brewers took the league lead on July 21st, shellacking the Indianapolis Indians for a fourth straight time. Indy had been atop the standings since May 21st and 12,380 reveled in the 13–3 upbraiding. Ed Wright won his third straight, while Jim Bagby, Jr. had to turn tail in the 4th. *The Journal* box score roared "Custer Avenged!"[212] Custer's Last Stand was perhaps the concession stand in this case. Concessions manager Jack Schwid said it was his busiest night in his 7 years, maybe in the history of the park. Sold were 19,454 bottles of beer (and several groups brought in cases also); 11,345 bottles of soft drinks; 6,380 hot dogs; 2,700 bags of peanuts; and 2,400 bars of ice cream for $7,500 worth of business.

Jubilation was short-lived as an 11-game dump into August forced a confounded Cullop to raise hob with his players. He even reprimanded Heinz Becker for being tossed in inning No. 1 of a game over a called 3rd strike. Nick wanted to rest Gleeson, but the ejection forced Rickert to first and Gee-Gee off the pine.[213]

A bristling Tomato Face couldn't tolerate some players giggling after that 11th loss. Eau Claire mentor Andy Cohen telegrammed a buffaloed Cullop: "After every rain some sunshine must follow. Hang in there." The bottom crapped out at an even dozen. The cure was Louisville's Bill Zuber, the Amana plowjock and ex-Brewer. Astonishingly, Milwaukee survived in 2nd place.[214]

Those standings did not essentially change to the finish line. Cullop could boast an improved 89–65 with a lineup where every starter but Burris reached double-digit homers. "Mousey" 3rd baseman Gene Markland (20), Rickert (27), and Fernandez (23) all passed that barrier, with Nanny's 183 hits leading the loop. Elliott was the first Brewer ERA titlist (3.76) in a decade.[215]

Still, when it came to the first round of the playoffs, Harold Anderson's Columbus Red Birds, the team they humiliated on Opening Day, a team that finished 8 games behind them in 4th place, a team with home run king Mike Natisin, a pitcher named Harvey "The Kitten" Haddix, and a backup backstop named Joe Garagiola, prevailed in 7 games. And the parent Boston Braves would lose the World Series to Bill Veeck's Cleveland Indians besides.[216]

At least the $10,000 awarded to ex-Syracuse outfielder Dutch Mele in an exploding beer bottle accident wasn't from a Milwaukee brewer.[217]

Despite the losing streak and early playoff exit, there was no doubt that Nick Cullop, popular with his boys, would be back to lead the Brewers. The year 1949 was the most gargantuan in minor league history. A total of 59 leagues operated in 438 cities, but the fact that Schuster's in Milwaukee advertised 23-square inch Hallicrafter TVs marked down to $139.50, plus a $6.95 aerial, well… Baseball's wave crested and WTMJ-TV was Milwaukee's only station.[218]

An ex-player, Moose Solters who once refused a Bill Veeck Brewers' contract, couldn't enjoy the new form of entertainment. The 40-year old was almost totally blind, the effect of a 1941 pre-game accident, where a thrown ball struck his left temple, fracturing his skull.[219]

The Milwaukee Brewers went from fourth in American Association attendance in 1947 to second in 1948. And yet, competition for the sports dollar grew. Milwaukee now had a Chicago Black Hawks ice hockey farm team at State Fair Park Coliseum, and the Milwaukee Bright Spots were an independent semi-pro outfit, playing basketball at the Auditorium.[220]

Former Brewer flyhawk Frank Secory now umpired in the Texas League when Cullop weeded out another squad of 40 at the Austin camp. Old '36 catcher George Detore was now on board as a coach and once Brewer outfielder Ralph Shinners became the traveling secretary. Becker was a Brewer no more.

Dutch now had more time for his occasional professional soccer appearances. The Skippy Roberge Era was indeed over. Former Brewers dotted the managerial landscape in this maximum expansion of the minors. Hershel Martin guided the Class C Albuquerque Dukes towards the West Texas-New Mexico League flag. Ted Gullic would bring the Class D Bartlesville Pirates within one game of doing likewise in the Kansas-Oklahoma-Missouri (K-O-M) League. Martin was still the defending batting and doubles leader of his circuit.[221]

Dee Phillips, Jim Gleeson, and Paul Burris were positional survivors for Milwaukee. Nashotah, Wisconsin, farmer Gene Edwards from the Braves' Eastern League Hartford Chiefs farm and a young Delmar Crandall were reviewed as second string nackstops, but Phillies acquisition Al (Moose) Lakeman topped that depth chart.

Tall Vermonter Ernie Johnson tested his arm for the first time in this camp. Another righthander, Dick Donovan, was up from Evansville. A mix of vets were shaken and stirred as well: Buffalo pitcher Henry Perry became the No. 1 starter, Nick Etten was a good wartime Yankee 1st baseman, and Howard (Howitzer) Moss reigned as the I.L. homer king from Baltimore.

Flychaser Alvin Aucoin and second sacker Roy Hartsfield, like long collegiate pitcher Dick Manville, were on their way up with Johnny Logan. Just so they didn't drive up in a Hudson, "the only car you can step down into."[222]

This pitcher was identified by Milwaukee photograph collector Bob Koehler as Sid Schacht from the 1951 season. The Brewer uniforms now looked like the parent Braves. Milwaukee Public Library Historical Photograph Collection.

In a spring where commissioner Happy Chandler could call now-established Jackie Robinson on the carpet for fighting with rookie teammate hurler Chris Van Cuyk from Kimberly, Wisconsin, young Harvey Kuenn, Jr. was rumored to take his wicked bat and all-around athleticism to rejoin a few Milwaukee Lutheran High School champion teammates at Valparaiso University.[223]

An old scribe like Sam Levy lamented about modern players being too proud to bunt. Even the old Brewer batting champ, "Art the Great" Shires, willingly bunted for Marty Berghammer. Future Brewer pilot Bucky Walters debated with his own coach, Johnny Neun, at the Cincinnati Reds' Tampa camp. Walters wanted to practice "one of the most thrilling plays in baseball," while Neun said, "The hell with bunting, just hit the ball!"[224]

This spring of '49, the Brewers whitewashed Bibb Falk's Southwest Conference champion Texas Longhorns in consecutive games. When Milwaukee opened the regular season at Toledo on Wednesday, April 20th, war broke out on China's Yangtze River front. It was the start of Mao Zedong's drive to turn the yellow giant red.[225]

The Mud Hens' Milwaukee-bred 2nd baseman, Bobby Mavis, debuted to 6,288 boosters who saw a vastly different Maumee Bay Brood than what the Brewers bowled over in the spring. So different, Milwaukee lost, 10–6. Bill Barnacle didn't cling beneath anything in the bay, but was at home in the outer regions of Swayne Field. Any hopes of reclaiming Marv Rickert were dashed when 3 major league clubs refused to clear waivers on him from the Braves.[226]

The traditional Elks welcome home was still considered the best of its kind, major league or minor. Sam Levy's *Journal* sports editor, R.G. Lynch, rated Borchert Field's peanuts as not quite up to the previous year's standard. Levy reminisced with long-ago editor Oliver E. Remey on the 1894 opener of 55 years earlier. Baseball was the only sport where that was possible.[227]

Hank Perry did the losing old-timers far better, cooping up those same Mud Hens, 9–1. Dee Phillips' 2-run shot "gave Frau Hasenpfeffer her first souvenir of the season." "Silver" Gleeson was just golden with his 3-run golf swing to the center field bleachers. Paul Burris' 4-for-4 made the Brood brood.[228]

After that opener, all games but Sundays and holidays were under the lights. May 15th brought a patriotic swell of pride on Citizenship Day: Concern about the intent and extent of Communist aggression gripped a war-wary U.S.A.

Perry was more concerned about cutting the Apostles' lead to 4 games, so he struck out 10 of them, begrudging 2 of their 6 hits in the final 6 frames. The 7–0 discourse wrung the halo around St. Paul's collective neck.[229]

"It's Dipsy Doodle! It's Gay! It's Fun Laff…Laff…Laff…and Forget Your Cares…Cause It Happens Every Spring." The Ray Milland-Jean Peters-Paul Douglas movie started at the Fox Wisconsin Theater on June 1st for "37¢ plus tax."[230]

In a frightful scene, all too reminiscent of the 1999 disaster at Miller Park, a giant crane toppled at the site of Milwaukee's new Arena. Loaded with 1½ tons of concrete, it tipped over on its side. Thankfully no one was hurt, but the 105-foot boom slammed across the concrete tiers.[231]

In a Wisconsin State League doubleheader, the Appleton Papermakers' Joe Bianclana lowered the boom on the Green Bay Bluejays with 3 home runs. Milwaukee's Jim Prendergast kept his league leaders' 6-game win streak alive, allowing Indy 3rd baseman Nanny Fernandez's 1st stanza, 2-run jack to have the only impact on an 8–3 triumph. Milwaukee slipped to 3rd by mid-month, kept there by the Saints' Del Hines' 2–0 job over Ray Martin before a 10,000 "sellout."[232]

Kansas City was almost a July 4th refuge, compared to the record 96° in Milwaukee. The Brewers made no better use of Howie Moss' pair of pokes and Tim Triner's relief than to split.[233]

The man who might be called "J.Rob" nowadays, Jackie Robinson, won editorial praise for refuting pro-communist opera singer Paul Robeson before the House Un-American Activities Committee in Washington. Calling Robeson's view "silly," Jackie was hailed as a "good American, a good athlete, and a good representative of his people."[234]

The Brewers had no such representatives on their roster as yet, but with the Howitzer firing at full bore, they jolted Walter Alston's Saints in a Twin City twin killing in late July. Moss again followed the script with an overtime blast to settle the first game, 3–2. Norman Roy ("Wah?") pitched before his future in-laws from Abraham, Massachusetts, teasing the visitors with only 4 hits. Future Milwaukee Brave Jim Pendleton, a "Negro speedster," pinch ran for St. Paul. The Yalie Eli, Richard Manville, rode a "Boola-Boola" of a wild start in Game Two, walking 5 in the first 3 innings. Save for a Danny Ozark 8th inning swat, Dick settled down, with hunt-and-peck help.[235]

One Oscar Salenger sat in the Borchert Field press box, still singing the praises of Milwaukee as the best minor league city in baseball. The doublebreasted barrister, residing in Beverly Hills, was "now as much a part of Hollywood as its sweater girls." For all his 1946 mistakes, he wouldn't trade his Brewers experience "for all the gold in Fort Knox." He had eyes for the P.C.L. Hollywood Stars or Los Angeles Angels, "But give me Milwaukee — this is the best!"[236]

Oscar's old Brewers were at a season-high 15 games over .500 during his visit. When Braves G.M. John Quinn made it clear that Milwaukee faced the classic "youth movement" for 1950, the heart seemed ripped from Nick Cullop's final .500, 3rd place finishers. They stunned the bewildered 1st place Saints in 7 games before succumbing to the Indy Tribe in six.[237]

The new A.A. President, Bruce Dudley, awarded the rookie of the year award to Brewer 2nd baseman Roy Hartsfield. The future Toronto Blue Jay manager led the circuit with 203 hits. The most decorated decade in Brewers history went down fighting.[238]

9
From Curtain Call to Wrecking Ball

At the midway point of the 20th century, only ten cities had major league baseball. Milwaukee moved up one notch in those 50 years to become the nation's 13th largest city proper.[1] The concept of "suburbs" and "metropolitan markets" was embryonic. The majors extended no further south or west than St. Louis.

Of the dozen cities larger than Milwaukee, these were also without the National Pastime at a major league level: Los Angeles, Baltimore, and San Francisco. The "open" status of the Pacific Coast League, above and beyond the Triple-A classification, attempted to address some of that disparity. The frequency and ease of air travel would eventually make the long-term difference.[2]

Canada's two largest cities, Montreal and Toronto, were also of a size and baseball tradition to warrant major league attention. Five cities had a team in both the National and American Leagues: New York, Chicago, Philadelphia, St. Louis, and Boston. And of course, the Brooklyn Dodgers were in New York.

The early 1950s would shake major league baseball from its half-century slumber of tolerating weak sisters in Philly, St. Louis, and the Hub. It seemed incongruous that Lou Perini's National League Boston Braves, who had actually put a better product out on the field now, could still barely draw much better than their Triple-A American Association farm, the Milwaukee Brewers. Both teams suffered from dilapidated facilities.[3]

Milwaukee's Brewers now represented the unabashed Beer Capital of the World that had more than doubled its population since its entry into the American Association. The city was without doubt the 900-pound Samson the gorilla in the confines of that smaller midwestern cage.

The franchise endured two world wars, the Great Depression, and peripheral baseball distractions: The Western League Creams, Negro League Bears,

The days of the hand-operated scoreboard at Borchert Field were numbered. Milwaukee Public Library Historical Photograph Collection.

and Girls League Chicks. It was always Brewers *über alles*, the city's only professional sports constant.

Coming off its most tumultuous but most successful decade of three pennants, a Junior World Series championship, and 7 playoff appearances, the Brewers underwent a "youth movement."

Braves owner Lou Perini and general manager John Quinn swept away a popular, winning manager in Nick Cullop and about half his personnel for 1950. Whether they felt they were simply confronting their own developmental needs or disabling Milwaukee, it took the heat off the parent club's inadequacies, will never be certain.

What was sure was that the Brewers would suffer their worst performance since 1941. The curious scapegoat for this "youth movement" would be a consummate company man, one Bob Coleman. The 59-year old Indianan had been a reserve catcher with the Pittsburgh Pirates in 1913-1914 and Cleveland Indians in 1916. He even caught 9 games for Pongo Joe Cantillon's 1918 Minneapolis Millers.[4]

Coleman's one previous try at piloting in the A.A. was his 67–84, .444 record with the 1934 St. Paul Saints. They finished 19 games behind their rival Millers then. He was ineffective when the Braves promoted him to be their wartime leader. From the time he took over into the 1943 season until he was demoted during 1945, his 128–165 could not budge a poor team stuck in a 6th pace rut.[5]

On the other hand, he knew how to win at the Class B level, his... Three-I League Evansville Bees were improving every year: a fifth place 70–55 in 1947, third place 67–54 in 1948, and the 1949 pennant at 74–51. That 3-year run of .568 ball deserved a promotion.[6]

Whatever gift Bob Coleman possessed for coaxing more out of lower level talent, it just didn't mesh when they all advanced the baseball ladder. He still had winning veterans to draw upon like Howitzer Moss and Al Lakeman, Glenn Elliott and '49 playoff star Raymond Martin. Walter Linden had been a clutch post-season performer. Utility infielder Mark Christman was in the sunset of a career that made him a fine 3rd baseman on the 1944 pennant-winning St. Louis Browns.[7]

Youth would be served, however, and spitfire Johnny (Yatcha) Logan, "the little Russian" at short, was already a Milwaukee favorite. After his major league days with the Milwaukee Braves, Logan ran for Milwaukee county sheriff a few times and in a scouting capacity with the modern Brewers, has always remained popular in the city.

Bob Coleman made Shawano, Wisconsin's Billy Reed his 2nd baseman. A Jackson, Tennessee, 1st baseman named Dallas Womack evoked memories of a less "willowy" Ossie Orwoll from a quarter-century before. Womack wouldn't survive the spring cut at Austin, but Reed's ticket was his .333 Eastern League batting title from Hartford.[8]

Utility man Jack Weisenburger swung the sort of hot spring bat that would have to win him a job after the briefest of 1949 pinch-hitting duty. Outfielder Bob Addis, one of the American Association's top echelon bats and triples hitters, was imported from the St. Paul Saints. Bob Montag dominated every major category of the Class B New England League for pennant-winning Pawtucket except RBI. Teammate and future fellow Brewer George Crowe denied him there, but after recovering from a line drive to the head in a Braves' B squad game at Atlanta, Montag had a Brewer outfield job locked. Bob Jaderlund went from spring rookie prize to valuable fourth outfielder.[9]

Catcher Manley Fossen, from Wisconsin's River Falls Teachers College, joined Gene Edwards after a train arrival mix-up, to challenge Percy Hough and Frank Baldwin for reserve backstop duty.

The gala events to mark the opening of Milwaukee's new sports arena were threatened by a strike of the building trades until a 2-year peace was reached with the unions. It could have been all academic, as explained by Cornell University's Dr. Hans A. Bethe. One hydrogen bomb could kill all in Milwaukee County. The scare made Wisconsin a leader in civil defense.[10]

Milwaukee's socialist mayor Frank Zeidler, a man who openly invited black southerners to come up and work in his city's industries, had a "Commission on Human Rights." He solicited the cooperation of the American Bowling Congress to drop the "for white males only" clause from its constitution by going directly to local bowlers.[11]

This significant slice of social change finally caught up with the Brewers in 1950. No Negroes were in the Austin camp or Opening Day lineup — Bob Coleman was still too busy sifting out the likes of pitcher Bob Buehl, alcoholic-sounding outfielder Jack Daniels, and Sobieski, Wisconsin, 1st baseman Hank Ertman.

Brewer President Jake Flowers fretted over the possible loss of Austin as a practice haven only because owner Ed Knebel of the Austin Pioneers was likely to become selfish enough to want the park all to his Class B Big State League club. His skipper, the ex-Brewer Hawaiian Hank "Prince" Oana, tutored 20-game winner George Estock to the top of Milwaukee's rotation.[12]

Not to be confused with American League slugger Gus Zernial, a Milwaukee boy named Gus Zernia tried to win the Houston Buffs 1st base job, but a catch by the Brewers' Bob Jaderlund ended his string of reaching base 11 straight times (8 hits, 3 walks). Worse yet, Zernia's red-hot .423 was still surpassed by rival Frank Kellert's .490 clip.

The Brewers were beating the bushers, like the Texas League Tulsa Oilers, 18–8. Tulsa had some future finds, too, like shortstop Roy McMillan, center fielder Wally Post, and right fielder Bob Nieman, who homered. Pitcher Ken Polivka was pinch hit for by a man named Knoblauch. Evansville's Bob Gordon held the Brewers helpless for 5 innings, but Milwaukee prevailed 7–2, on the way home.[13]

Mickey Heath still called Brewer games on WEMP Radio when old catcher Tommy (Cracker) Heath brought his pennant-favorite Minneapolis Millers in for Milwaukee's Borchert Field opener on Tuesday, April 18th. Bob Coleman even had the counsel of former big league 1st sacker and Toronto Maple Leaf manager Del Bissonette to aid his young team, but the prognosticators still saw the Brewers for fifth or sixth. It was a festive inaugural with mayor Frank Zeidler throwing the first ball, a wide breaking curve, to a mugging "catcher" named Jack Dempsey.[14] *The Sentinel's* Red Thisted claimed it was an all-time official record attendance, that 13,856, but Bill Veeck surely had grounds to dispute that. (How about the 15,559 for the '42 opener?)

For the second straight year, the second man in the Minneapolis batting order was the only Negro starter in the American Association. Veteran 3rd baseman Ray Dandridge of the Negro Leagues and Mexico brought cat-like defense and a brilliant bat to the scene. He wouldn't just go on to the 1950 MVP Award in the A.A., he would be enshrined at Cooperstown.[15]

Dandridge scored an unearned run off a Johnny Logan error in this particular game. Ray Martin's 5th inning collapse laid credit for the 8–5 loss at his feet, but neither little Don Liddle, who gave up a John Kropf homer, nor George Estock could cope. Al Lakeman's masterful blast was the foremost highlight before driving rains washed away a chance at a Brewer rally by the bottom of the sixth.

Another Negro League veteran, Dave "Impo" Barnhill, an "aspirin tablet" hurling right-hander, was expected to work the third game for the Millers.

A May Day mock communist takeover in Mosinee, Wisconsin, went awry when 49-year old mayor Ralph Kronwetter was stricken with a heart attack and lapsed into a "grave coma." Venerable Connie Mack, now 87, ignored doctor's orders and was back managing the A's after stomach trouble caused by fatigue. His jubilee looked more golden after he credited his wife's cooking for his rebound and his club won 5 straight. Rain and cold hampered by 20 percent the majors' gate.[16]

Jake Flowers and KC Business manager Parke Carroll favored a return to the old 3-trip schedule instead of 4 when that issue came up in the fall. A Joan Crawford flick called *The Damned Don't Cry* ran in early May at Milwaukee's Warner Theater. Bob Coleman thought his hustling Brewers still had what it took, but it could have been the title of their season. Narrow, heartbreaking losses added up.[17]

William Bendix wasn't satisfied to just give a paltry portrayal of Babe Ruth on celluloid. Now he was in *Kill the Umpire,* too, playing on Ascension Day at the Fox. *The Sentinel's* Ray Grody wrote about "Plenty of 'Jack' for Jackie"—Jackie Robinson's cinematic life story and endorsements netted $135,000 for the social pioneer.[18]

The Brewers were even in 2nd place when Louisville blanked Glenn Elliott's chance for a 4th straight win, 6–0, before 2,092 paid at home. Errors by Jack Weisenburger, Al Lakeman, and Pete Whisenant compounded the Mouse's own 5 walks. Willard Nixon struck out 11 Brewers and young Jim Piersall tripled for the visitors.[19]

A "robot kidney" devised by Allis-Chalmers won 2nd prize at a medical session and signs of booming economy were reflected in the hand-woven "Rohchas," antiqued brown calfskin Freeman shoes available for $14.50 at Stumpf's on 164 W. Wisconsin Ave. Western allies tried to woo Berlin's Soviet zone youth with jazz, Commie jokes, and a give-away quiz program. "Tail Gunner Joe" McCarthy, the U.S. Senator from Wisconsin, targeted Reds in the upper echelons of the federal government. The Cold War turned hot in Korea.[20]

As the Brewers tumbled to 7th place, facing the likes of notable pitchers such as the Millers' Hoyt Wilhelm, the Saints' Clem Labine, or the Blues' "Whitey," Ed Ford, Milwaukee's County Park Commission submitted a plan to the entire county board for a $2,640,000 double deck stadium with a partial grandstand roof and a 26,000 seat capacity. An additional $800,000 was needed for work on the surrounding site that became County Stadium.[21]

Southpaw Chet Nichols mastered the Kaysees for 17 scoreless innings in a couple late June appearances. The last place Blues had notables like Fenton Mole, basher Bob Cerv, and a young pitcher named Lew Burdette. The Braves' chief scout, Jack Zeller, proved less stringent about the youth movement, with 26-year-old ex–Texas Longhorn Murray Wall's signature to a contract.[22]

The young Brewers' inability to control their own fate was further amplified by a nighthawk that pecked at a Borchert Field fly ball on Thursday, June 29th. That fine-feathered assist fell in for a trick double to set up a 4–3 margin for the Millers. Milwaukee pedestrians on *terra firma* were a safer lot, according to the Automobile Association of America's 2nd place ranking of the city amongst those with a half-to-a million people.[23]

Oshkosh, Wisconsin, southpaw Bill Hoeft, a 17-year old bonus sensation who whiffed 18 for the Ohio-Indiana League Richmond Tigers on July 24th, threw safety to the wind, along with firecrackers at passing motorists. With fellow outfielder Keith Jones, they made the mistake of tossing one at a detective sergeant's car in Richmond, leading to $20 fines apiece.[24]

The overwhelming force of the communists in Korea was reflected in the July 26th letter from Pfc. Walter Horning to his parents in West Allis: "Of the 167 in my company, only 83 have returned. I was not wounded, but I lost a lot of weight." His folks were Mr. and Mrs. Paul Horning. Californian ex-Brewer catcher Del Crandall got a 1-A draft rating, but wasn't yet called for a physical.[25]

Shortstop Johnny Logan was the Brewers' "Iron Man" for a second consecutive year, and without fanfare, the club's first two African-American players contributed at the corners. Both powerfully-built 32-year olds from the Negro Leagues, 1st baseman Len Pearson carried a 10-game hit streak into mid-August and 3rd baseman James Buster "Buzz" Clarkson from the Philadelphia Stars made folly of the youth movement. The notion of the "Milwaukee Brown Brewers," who whipped a local Trojans club at Sparta, Wisconsin, 12–7, on August 14th, now seemed passe.[26]

No-hitters were in the air as ex-Brewer Vern Bickford threw one against Brooklyn at Braves Field and southpaw Jean Cione likewise tossed 12 innings for the Girls League Kenosha Comets versus the old Milwaukee franchise, the Grand Rapids Chicks.[27]

Bob Coleman's Brewers were stalemated like the Korean War into 6th place. They had yet another batting champion in outfielder Bob Addis (.323) and hit the second-most homers as a team, but their poor record made them the second-worst drawing team in the A.A. Toledo led that dishonor as the 609 who attended the August 15th Brewer game there could attest.[28]

At least Nick Cullop didn't let his release from the Brewers stand in the way of guiding the I.L. Baltimore Orioles to a fine 3rd place finish. Maybe the fallacy of the Brewer youth movement should have paid heed to the Lenten guidepost offered by, of all people, the late Babe Ruth?! Recalling his incorrigible youth, the honest self-appraisal, written not long before his 1948 death, said kids may fail religious training, but it won't fail them if only it was offered.[29]

The 1951 Brewers trained, if not religiously, at least at Austin, Texas. Billy Reed, the multi-sport Shawano, Wisconsin, star re-signed at 2nd base, coming off a .313 year, his first in the A.A. The man he would report to came off a 74–78, 5th place season with the Texas League Dallas Eagles. Bob Coleman was reassigned back to Evansville where he led a runner-up club to the Three-I loop's best attendance. The new man Reed reported to was a popular old face — Charlie Grimm![30]

Grimm would take another look at the right-handed "Big Abner" from Wild Rose, Wisconsin, Paul Erickson, who hurled the deciding 1945 pennant game for him with the Cubs. The flipper just wasn't what it was anymore. Lou Perini voted for commissioner Happy Chandler's unhappy ouster.[31]

Perini's Braves delivered 3 pitchers to business manager Red Smith and Grimm: Art Fowler, Austin resident Charley Gorin, and most importantly, Ernie Johnson. Murray Wall was not yet sent down by Boston, but righthander Maynard Thiel, from the Waupaca County village of Marion, Wisconsin, who went by his middle name of Bert, "might do us a lot of good." Jolly Cholly was proven right.[32]

Len Pearson's knee buckled during winter play and was heavily taped. He was demoted to Hartford, where he hit .272 after beginning the regular season with Milwaukee. Buzz Clarkson also played winter ball in Puerto Rico. Despite being slow to sign and report, he was ready to claim the shortstop job. The popular Buzz was later recalled by a young Eddie Mathews as the heaviest shortstop he ever saw.[33]

With Pearson out of the 1st base picture, outfielder Bob Montag kept the bag warm for big George Crowe, another Negro, who was a "redoubtable slugger from Hartford." The 28-year old ironically from Whiteland, Indiana, was a bespectacled lefty, who didn't just hit his way from the Negro Leagues through the minors. True, he led the Eastern League with .353 and in hits, runs, and doubles, with 24 homers and 106 RBI. The 6'-2", 210-pounder excelled on the hardwood also. In the 1948 World Professional Basketball Tournament championship at Chicago Stadium, the New York Rens forward scored 12 points in a loss against Hall of Famer Jim Pollard and the Minneapolis Lakers of George Mikan fame. Crowe would arguably be not just the Brewers' MVP but the league's.[34]

That honor fell to a veteran who was first brought in as a stopgap backstop until the Braves decided who among Walt Linden, Paul Burris, or Ebba St. Claire would be sent down. Al Unser had 4 years of major league exposure and came now from Nick Cullop's I.L. Baltimore Orioles. He may not have been related to his future famous New Mexico auto-racing namesake, but the Illinois man was the father of 1970s-80s outfielder Del Unser.[35]

Another to hit high notes for the '51 Brewers' "symphony in swat" was 28-year old center fielder Jim Basso, the most valuable player of the Big State League. He was *Basso Profundo* indeed, hitting .353–33–143, with 40 doubles for the Temple Eagles down Texas way. Stability and the curve were always the bane to Basso's advancement, but Grimm batted him third.[36]

The Sentinel sports editor, Lloyd Larson, teased readers with the idea that not the Boston Braves but the St. Louis Cardinals might move to become the new stadium's tenants. "Stan Musial in a Milwaukee uniform! Won't that be scary?" He went through a litany of other improbable items before reminding readers of the calendar. April Fool![37]

9— *From Curtain Call to Wrecking Ball* 319

In a move that socially split the country unlike World War II and would echo through the Vietnam era, President Truman's order to defer collegians from the military draft affected 1 million youths in 1951. Television prices didn't decline, though production fell by 2½ million sets. "Stairway to Heaven" was one of Robert Montgomery's anthology presentations on WTMJ-TV's "Your Lucky Strike Theatre." Two people who weren't using that stairway were the convicted atomic spy couple, Julius and Ethel Rosenberg. They rode the electric chair straight to hell, due to the treasonous result of 50,000 American casualties in Korea laid upon them by Judge Irwin R. Kaufman.[38]

The Brewer "Brown Bombers," Crowe and Pearson, went atomic on the Texas League Shreveport Sports with 3 RBI each before bidding adieu permanently to Austin. Before 891 "apathetic witnesses" on a chilly April 15th Sabbath at Evansville, Milwaukee was downed by 7–6, by Bob Coleman's farmhands.[39]

Charlie Gorin lost the Wednesday, April 18th opener in front of 6,713 Indianapolitans. John McCall won the 7–4 decision on 3 hits. Lloyd Larson noted Milwaukee's obvious vital interest in the smallest St. Louis Browns opening crowd in 18 years—5,660. Along with the 6,081 at Braves Field in Boston and 8,285 for the Athletics at Philadelphia, real speculation grew about major league candidates to fill Milwaukee's new stadium.[40]

Old Borchert Field held 11,001 patrons, including Waupun police chief Teddy Tetzlaff who took in his 29th straight opener. Hugo (Sluggy) Walter, "Mr. Baseball of Milwaukee," the 10th and Chambers tavernkeep, was there for his 49th consecutive time. The first Thorpe to roam a Milwaukee outfield since Jim did 35 years earlier, promoted Atlanta Cracker Bob, cracked 2 home runs to the center field bleachers. It took Virgil Jester's bases-loaded relief to quell a 9th inning Louisville rally at an 8–7 final decision on May Day. Mrs. Grimm was happy to be back in Milwaukee enjoying the frolic alongside Mrs. Red Smith. The Smiths were presented with a cocktail set by the Baseball Writers' chapter of Milwaukee before the game.[41]

All three of the 1st place Brewers' losses had been to southpaws at that point. Oshkosh's Billy Hoeft won his second game for the Toledo Mud Hens as they chased Kimberly, Wisconsin's John Van Cuyk off the mound for the St. Paul Saints in the 4th inning of an all-Wisconsin duel.[42]

It was a right-hander, Ernie Nevel of Kansas City, who dropped the Brewers into 2nd by May 19th when he outdid Bob Hall. Lloyd Larson waxed upon the Boston Red Sox Old-Timers Day at Fenway Park, celebrating their golden anniversary. Deaf mute Dummy Hoy, the 89-year old Oshkosh alum of 1886, was joined by Milwaukee's 70-year old "kid" of the lot, George McBride, who looked 10 years younger. McBride recalled returning from the Dakotas to be "drafted" from the stands by the 1901 Brewers. Four other members of that team, whom McBride hadn't seen in 40 years or more, manager Hugh Duffy, Bill Friel, Wid Conroy, and Billy Maloney, were all there, as were Clark Griffith and Connie Mack.[43]

A staple of Milwaukee radio, "The Heinie Show," was presented on 1250 WMAW by Gundersen Motors. Art Fowler grabbed his Brewers by the heinie and lifted them back into first with a glistening 5-hit, 1–0 shutout of those Blues and southpaw Bob Wiesler. Johnny Logan's bases-loaded single scored Crowe, but a fine play by shortstop Bob Thomson kept Basso from crossing the plate. This was not the Bobby Thomson, the famed "Staten Island Scot" of the Giants.[44]

The pre-Father's Day chuckle was "How long did it take your wife to learn how to drive? Well, let's see... It'll be 10 years this coming April." The last place Indy Indians drove Charley Gorin's 4-game win streak to the record books by falling upon him for 4 runs in the 3rd inning. Lefty Royce Lint, the Tribe's thin man, helped his 7–2 cause with a brace of singles. Milwaukee stayed a game up in first on KC and box scores still didn't provide the sort of pitching breakdown with which we're now accustomed.[45]

Ironically, Gen. Matthew B. Ridgway, the man Harry Truman replaced Douglas MacArthur with, did what Mac advocated as truce talks were bandied about in Korea. The July 4th outcome between the Brewers at Kansas City was an equal standoff. Murray Wall's 7-hitter blanked the Blues in Game One, but Bert Thiel was victimized by a Bob Cerv double and Kite Thomas single in the 10th frame of the 4–3 nightcap.[46]

The year 1951 happened to be when both Mickey Mantle with the Blues and Willie Mays with the Millers were shooting stars, Triple-A being merely a brief wayside to the majors.[47]

The parent Braves went through Buddy Kerr, Sibby Sisti, and Gene Mauch at short and exercised their option on Logan, sending Mauch and right-hander Sid Schacht down in return. Logan had a Milwaukee string of 47 error-less games, an A.A. record. The Brewers took a break for exhibitions with the Northern League Eau Claire Bears, where young Bill Wolf of West Bend pitched against them.[48] Yes, Bill Wolf of the Bears.

Lou Perini continued to deny published reports that a group of Milwaukee businessmen would buy his beleaguered Braves and move them to Wisconsin. Fred Miller, who had a $25 million expansion of his brewery in the works, also backed Ben Kerner's efforts to transfer the Tri-Cities Blackhawks National Basketball Association franchise to the Milwaukee Arena by autumn 1951. Miller failed in his attempt to buy the St. Louis Browns, but also denied any dealings with Perini. Meanwhile, none other than Bill Veeck, who sold his stock in the Oklahoma City Indians, took over the Browns. He would immortalize midget Eddie Gaedel shortly thereafter.[49] The *Boston Traveler* also cited a "highly regarded source" said that the Braves would move to Milwaukee by 1953. Perini said he believed Milwaukee deserved a big league team, but that baseball should expand to two 12-team leagues, growing to the West Coast with the country.

Eddie Stumpf, now business manager for the Cleveland Indians' far-flung farm system, passed through his old hometown on the way back from conducting two huge baseball schools in "Canuckland," Canada. Enthusiasm to the north, among prospects without flash or fancy bonuses, who weren't subject to draft calls, was reflected in radio magnate Jack Kent Cooke's purchase of the International League Toronto Maple Leafs.[50]

Charlie Grimm relived his 1943 Milwaukee pennant days, only now his Brewers had to fight St. Paul to do it into August. Charley Gorin walked 12 Millers but ground them down to 3 hits in a late July win. Gene Mauch's ability to get hit by pitches proved invaluable. The heat applied by the Blues dissipated when the Yankees called up Bob Cerv and Bob Wiesler, but opted Jackie Jensen down and sent Cliff Mapes to the Browns for 10 grand.[51]

In this supposed "Golden Age of Baseball," the game suffered an overall 9 percent attendance dip. The Oshkosh Giants wore black armbands to mourn the loss of their fans as they drew about 1/9 of their 1949 Wisconsin State League record. Democrat Congressman Celler of New York chaired a committee investigating Organized Baseball. He cited Milwaukee and Minneapolis as examples of why there should be 4 major leagues, reaching all four corners of the nation. Others saw his attack on the game's monopoly as his own grandstand lobby to be commissioner.[52]

Pitcher Dick Donovan was the target of good-natured ribs for his Herculean smash over the 440-foot barricade at Columbus on August 2nd. Al Unser insisted it could have gone through the boards, if not over them, and Bob Montag thought he should have been satisfied going for a short fence, instead of showing off. Donovan just wound up and swung, looking for a 3–1 count fastball, and "there it went."[53]

As early as August 4th, Mayor Zeidler already arranged a parade to welcome the Brewers back from their long and highly successful road trip. Hizzoner urged citizens to meet the league leaders at the Milwaukee Road station at 9:30 that Monday morn. The parade was led by a band that marched west on Michigan Ave. to 8th St., north to Wisconsin Ave. back east to N. Water St., where the players' convertibles would arrive at City Hall to be greeted by Zeidler himself.[54]

Lloyd Larson saw history repeating 1936 when the 144,000 attendance was nearly doubled in the last 22 games. The 1951 amount stood at 157,258 with 21 games left. The final tally, 245,066, did lead the A.A. George Trautman testified before Congress on how the saturation of broadcasting threatened to destroy the operation of smaller leagues. The well-worn threat of baseball losing its anti-trust protection was again writhing about.[55]

In the "What are the odds?" category, the first casualty in the Green Bay Packers football training camp was a 5'-11" 210-pound guard named Paul "Buddy" Burris. He was born January 20, 1923, and played his college ball at Oklahoma. The Brewer catcher named Paul Burris stood at 6-feet and 190-pounds and was born July 21, 1923, at Hickory, N.C. The football one tripped

"Jolly Cholly" Grimm, the prodigal left-handed banjo player returned to bridge the Brewers to the Milwaukee Braves. Baseball Hall of Fame Library.

and fell on a ladder, requiring stitches to close a severe cut in his armpit as the baseball one drew a walk in a victory over the Mud Hens. It was the blistering Brewers' 17th win in their last 19 games, with 11 of those won on the road. Buzz Clarkson had an 11-game skein snapped, with only a walk in 5 trips.[56]

Though he cleared waivers to be eligible for the A.A. playoffs, Eddie Mathews was happy to rejoin Atlanta on a 24-hour recall. Playing everyday to develop, he slugged 32 home runs for the Crackers the previous summer. Milwaukee's .982 topped A.A. fielding.[57]

The Colonels snapped the Brewer win streak at 8 a couple games later. Bert (Bobo) Thiel only gave up one run in that loss, but on WEMP Radio Appreciation Night, with former Green Bay Bluejay Earl Gillespie and Tommy Shanahan at the mikes, Thiel shut out Toledo. Only 2 Hens reached on a walk and an error. It was the only no-hitter in the A.A. for 1951. His walk was to Milwaukeean Bobby Mavis, but Bob Thorpe's leaning catch of a 6th inning long high Bill Barnacle fly and a pair of fancy snares by Paul Burris on foul pop-ups were the toughest defensive chances. The stocky little Thiel helped his 12th triumph against 8 defeats with 2 singles in a 12-hit attack. George Crowe's 19th homer contributed to the 5–0 classic. Thiel admitted that he knew he had a no-no all along, but didn't notice any particular tenseness until the last inning. The crowd of over 10,000 took over, cheering his every pitch and even the easy outs. Thiel had a 7-inning no-hitter for Hartford the previous summer, but this was the Brewers' first full 9-inning gem since Dinty Gearin in 1926. Thiel's no-hitter that Friday August 17th kept the Brewers 9 games up on St. Paul.[58]

Milwaukee clinched the pennant, its first since 1945, when Al Unser's Saturday, September 1st single nudged the Millers, 8–7, in a see-saw battle. Speedy Puerto Rican Luis Olmo beat out an easy roller through Ray Dandridge's legs, with 2 out in the 9th, and advanced on walks to Paul Burris and Buzz Clarkson, who pinch-hit for Virgil Jester. Unser, on his way to the league MVP award, pinch-hit for Billy Klaus and lined the first Adrian Zabala pitch to right, scoring Olmo to win. It was Unser's 19th year in Organized Ball.[59]

Grimm celebrated the pennant by snuffing rumors of his return to the majors with another Brewer pact for 1952. He had won 3 National League pennants outright with the Cubs and set up Gabby Hartnett to win the 1938 flag, much like this was his second outright Milwaukee pennant, and he bequeathed the '44 squad to Casey Stengel. Every "manjack" on his team swore by Grimm. The clincher was the 8th win in another 9-game streak.[60]

The post-season A.A. all-star selections were dominated by 7 Brewers: the MVP Unser, the outstanding rookie Crowe, Reed, Klaus, Basso, Wall, and Ernie Johnson.

Eddie Mathews was recalled to back up Klaus at third when the first playoff series versus Kansas City began at Borchert Field. Canadian George "Twinkletoes" Selkirk, the old Yankee flyhawk, led his team into Milwaukee's grinder. The champs voted 26 full shares that amounted to $273 each and several half-shares as Ernie Johnson and Virgil Jester combined to hold a 10-7 Game One victory. A vicious, 65 m.p.h. windstorm ripped into Milwaukee to postpone the Wednesday, September 12th Game Two, but the next night, George Crowe's 3-run homer in the 6th off Ernie Nevel sent an 8-2 lead over the left wall. The final read 8–5.

Madison, Wisconsin, sports columnist Roundy Coughlin groused about baseball's post-season going on too long and a familiar name to Milwaukee rassling fans for another 3 decades, erstwhile Green Bay Packer Verne Gagne threw the Mighty Atlas at Milwaukee's Auditorium. Four slave states, Poland, Hungary, Romania, and Bulgaria, were to "join" the U.S.S.R.[61]

Dick Donovan threw the Blues a 3–0 shutout at KC on September 15th before 2,685. Buzz Clarkson overcame a slippery infield to start a pair of DP's as part of his 9 assists. Milwaukeean catcher Bob Scherbarth was recalled, with 3 others, by the Boston Red Sox after Louisville's elimination by St. Paul. Jim Basso's grand slam led the 11–3 ouster of the Blues, another win for Ernie Johnson, father of modern TBS basketball host Ernie Johnson. [The Johnsons resided in the far West Side Milwaukee neighborhood of the author's maternal uncle and aunt.][62]

Veteran umpire Bill Klem died in Miami at age 77. In his last Spring 1944 appearance behind the plate, he claimed afterwards to be blind in one eye. Ford Frick was lauded by Lloyd Larson as baseball's new commissioner, and Boston Braves farm director Harry Jenkins regretfully resigned after 2 seasons on the job. The World War II flier accepted a position with a shoe firm in Australia, but left a legacy with 8 of 10 farm clubs finishing in the first division. The Racine, Wisconsin, Umpires Association held a benefit game for ex-Brewer and fellow arbiter Eddie Hope, confined to a Racine hospital with a serious illness.[63]

Milwaukee's first one-stop shopping center, Southgate, opened on Thursday, September 20th, and confirmation of the N.B.A. Tri-Cities Blackhawks move from Moline, Illinois, to Milwaukee was all but a done deal in commissioner Maurice Podoloff's eyes. Fresh Korean-led troops stopped an Allied drive as weary U.N. soldiers failed in 11 attacks. The United States first coast-to-coast live telecasts over a microwave network took place.[64]

The Six Fat Dutchmen, "2,000 pounds of solid fat," featuring a "Bard of the Bass Horn," played for a $1 admission at the Nightingale Ballroom on Highway 55, 8 miles northwest of Milwaukee. In the International League, the Montreal Royals (a nickname sort of redundant for a place named 'Mount Royal?') of Walter Alston disposed of the Syracuse Chiefs, 18–9, to advance to the Little World Series. Milwaukee led St. Paul, 2 games to none.[65]

Murray Wall handcuffed the Saints after allowing 3 of their 7 hits in the 3rd, to triumph 8–1. Only 2 Saints reached second and a 5-run splurge in the 9th did in the heavenly hosts. Sid Schacht then lost a slick 3-hit, 5–0 lead after six, only to have a 2-run Eric Tipton homer tie it in the 8th. Virgil Jester gave up a Danny Ozark homer for 7–5 setback, Sid's second playoff loss. On Monday, September 24th, Ernie Johnson then defrocked the Saints once and for all.[66]

It was only the fourth time in the history of the Shaughnessy playoff format that both pennant-winners advanced all the way to the Little World Series. Walter Alston's pitching staff had great credentials: Two former Colonels, Hamp Coleman and Bob Alexander, who threw a no-no at the 1950 Brewers, were joined by lefty Tom LaSord(a), Negro Leaguer vet Dan Bankhead, and to open against Wall, Kimberly, Wisconsin's Christ Van Cuyk, brother of St. Paul's John.[67]

Grimm had another chance at redemption, never winning any of the World Series at either level he managed. Rain and cold at Montreal postponed the first game by two nights. Ernie Johnson reconsidered winter ball in Puerto Rico, thinking the season would end sooner.

Whether the Brewers could enter Milwaukee's new County Stadium as early as 1952 depended upon the weather. The materials rolled in at the end of September by the tons. Lou Perini still insisted that Milwaukee's path to the majors laid in expansion, not relocation. He saw 4 West Coast clubs joining one major league, but Milwaukee, Houston, Baltimore, and Montreal in the other. Perini agreed with Oscar Salenger that a committee should determine the market value of a draft price, instead of a flat fee, to eliminate "promiscuous drafting."[68]

The Brewers evened the series at Montreal at a game apiece when doubling Luis Olmo tied it at 3 on Earl (Rootin Tootin) Wooten's pinch single with 2 outs in the 9th. Olmo hit off cagey old right-hander Bill Voiselle who was hastily yanked by Alston. After a cat-and-mouse of "Edwin" Mathews announced to pinch-hit for Unser, Alston went to Van Cuyk, who faced Paul

Burris anyway. Wooten did his damage off Van Cuyk as did Gene Mauch whose smash to right center drove Wooten home to win. The Royals drew 7,785 despite wintry blasts.

Earl Gillespie not only did Brewer baseball for WEMP but U.W. Badgers basketball and Marquette University football, plus wrote his own two evening sportscasts. Sunday, September 31st, he had to report that Bert Thiel was within one out of an 11-inning victory at Montreal, then George (Shotgun) Shuba slugged his second 2-run homer of the game. Al Gionfriddo's pinch-hit double for starter Tom LaSord(a) tied it 3-all for the 12,937 on hand. The 5-3 final gave the Royals a 2-1 edge going back to Milwaukee. The Beer City's founder, Solomon Juneau, was born in, of all places, Montreal.[69]

The Soviets exploded their second atom bomb test and not coincidentally the sci-fi epic movie *The Day The Earth Stood Still* still played at Milwaukee's Fox Palace. Bustin' Buster Clarkson exploded for a 3-run homer to scatter the bleacherites among the shirt-sleeved largest and most enthusiastic crowd of the year, 11,595, on Wednesday, October 3rd. Clarkson's early smart defense and 5th inning line drive trumped the Royals, 4–2, to tie the series off of Chris Van Cuyk. Coverage in the morning paper made page 3 of the sports section.

Bobby Thomson's "Short Heard 'Round The World" made the earth stand still as "the Giants won the pennant! The Giants won the pennant!" that same day. Ex-Brewer Dave Koslo of Menasha, Wisconsin, won that memorable National League playoff.[70]

Ernie Johnson sidearmed the Royals on a 4-hitter, blanking Montreal 6–0 for 9,188 paid patrons. On Thursday, October 4th, a "tempestuous battle" saw Charlie Grimm's gallant A.A. champs regain an 8-run deficit, with the door opened by Jim (Junior) Gilliam's muff of a George Crowe fly. Tempers flared when Dick Hoover threw too close to Gionfriddo's noggin in the 5th. Al Unser's homer tied the slugfest at 10-all in the 6th, and Luis Olmo's 3-run triple off LaSorda won for reliever Virgil Jester in the 7th. Hundreds of the 6,020 stormed the ancient parapets to carry the sturdy Denverite off the mound to a riotous clubhouse. Cholly Grimm finally won it all! The Royals each received $593.60, a full cut of $880.35 went to 26 Brewers.[71]

It was a 6-game battle royal between two of the minors' best cities. Montreal's season attendance would have easily led the American Association and finished second to Seattle, with the longer P.C.L. season. Only Class A Western League Denver drew more than Montreal in a 154-game schedule. Yet 50 years later, Montreal is considered dead, as a baseball city. In 1951, the Dodger farm gave all, but it was Milwaukee that stood on top![72]

Luis Olmo managed a half-dozen of his fellow Brewer champions on his Caguas, Puerto Rico winter club: Murray Wall, Bert Thiel, George Crowe, Billy Klaus, Buzz Clarkson, and Charlie Gorin. Al Unser, Bob Thorpe, Jim Basso, and Gene Mauch went to Havana for the Cuban Winter League. Charlie Grimm rode cloud nine to his Missouri farm home.[73]

Ten days after the Brewers claimed their 1951 Little World Series championship, bids were opened by Milwaukee County treasurer Clarence M. Sommers for the second $2.2 million bond issue towards the County Stadium. Bill Veeck signed Rogers Hornsby of the P.C.L. pennant-winning Seattle Rainiers to manage his St. Louis Browns. It was recalled how Veeck talked Oscar Salenger out of hiring Hornsby to pilot the Brewers in '46, even though it was Hornsby who introduced Veeck to Salenger, so he could sell the Brewers to him. Salenger felt a moral obligation to pay Hornsby a substantial amount not to manage the club and upped Nick Cullop's contract at the time. Veeck was remembered as "a funny guy."[74]

Equally curious was that 60-year old retiring Milwaukee County sheriff's deputy John Schrank shared the same name as the late man who tried to assassinate Theodore Roosevelt in Milwaukee 40 years earlier. In 1950, this Schrank justifiably killed an escaped prisoner.[75]

Milwaukee actually had the N.B.A. Hawks, albeit a last place failure at the gate, before wooing the return of major league baseball in that spring of 1952. "Robert Hall Rocks The Town!" The big and tall men's clothing store turned that phrase with gabardine slacks going for $3 and gabardine jackets for $5. Gen. MacArthur asked Wisconsinites not to vote for him in the G.O.P. presidential primary, but would serve if asked by the convention. 'Pinky' Black tickled the ivories at the East Town cocktail lounge on 775 N. Jackson St. in Milwaukee.[76]

In what was to be the final year of the franchise, unbeknownst to anyone but maybe Lou Perini, Charlie Grimm's Milwaukee Brewers opened their mid-March spring training camp at Kissimmee, Florida. The legacy of former Brewer employees managing throughout the minors was indeed large[77]:

Manager	Class	League	Team
Joe Becker (started '52)	Triple-A	International League	Toronto Maple Leafs
Danny Murtaugh	Double-A	Southern Association	New Orleans Pelicans
Jimmy Gleeson	A	Eastern League	Binghamton Triplets
Del Bissonette	A	Eastern League	Hartford Chiefs
Ralph Winegarner	A	Western League	Wichita Indians
Les Bell	A	Western League	Lincoln Athletics
Harry Strohm	A	Western League	Des Moines Bruins
Charlie Gassaway	A	Western Int'l League	Tri-City (Wash.) Braves
Tony York	B	Big State League	Texarkana Bears
Ted Gullic	B	Big State League	Waco Pirates
Max Macon	B	Florida Int'l League	Miami Sun Sox
Owen Scheetz	B	Piedmont League	Roanoke Ro-Sox
Bob Coleman (pennant)	B	Three-I League	Evansville Bees
Mark Christman	C	Longhorn League	San Angelo Colts
Nick Cullop (started '52)	C	Northern League	Fargo-Moorhead Twins
Harry Griswold	C	Western Association	Ft. Smith (Ark.) Indians
George Detore	D	Appalachian League	Bristol (Tenn.) Twins

Manager	Class	League	Team
Wes Livengood	D	Coastal Plain League	Goldsboro (N.C.) Jets
Charlie Brewster (pennant)	D	Florida State League	DeLand Red Hats
Greek George (started '52)	D	Georgia-Florida League	Tifton (Ga.) Blue Sox
Hershel Martin (" ")	D	Kansas-Oklahoma-Missouri League	Bartlesville Pirates
"Julian" Acosta	D	Mississippi-Ohio Valley League	Decatur (Ill.) Commies
Joe "Rulio" (Rullo?)	D	PONY League	Corning Athletics
Joe Hauser	D	Wisconsin State League	Sheboygan Indians

Milwaukeean Jimmy Adlam also started the year with the Wisconsin State League Fond du Lac Panthers. Old Clarence "Pants" Rowland, the Wisconsinite who owned and managed Milwaukee as the 1919 Panthers, began his 9th season as president of the Pacific Coast League.

If Grimm thought his Brewers were set at most positions, the truth was that another 3 dozen bodies would be juggled and that only 5 would play over 100 games: Wisconsinite Hank Ertman at first, Gene Mauch and Billy Klaus in the infield, and swift newcomers colored Bill Bruton from Alabama and Puerto Rican Negro Luis Marquez in the outfield. Giant (6'-8") basketball player Gene Conley, Ed Blake, and Bill Allen were important pitching additions.

Bruton, Marquez, and strikeout artist little Don Liddle emerged as quality. The Jim Bassos were expecting. Al Unser held out stubbornly, only to split time with Dewey Williams. Al Dumouchelle was a 150-pound Canadian right-hander up from Evansville where he was compared to former Cardinal relief star Blix Donnelly. Like big Howard Anderson, the promoted Atlanta Cracker right-hander, his impact would be negligible.[78]

Anderson did check the parent Braves with "one point in three frames," but Pete Whisenant's 2-run homer in the 9th decided the 14–12 exercise for Boston. Braves manager Tommy Holmes, their former outfield star, had a 6-way battle for his club's 3rd base job and promoted George Crowe gave veteran 1st baseman Earl Torgeson a run for his money. The Fox Lake, Illinois, native Klaus began 1952 as Holmes' shortstop, with Roy Hartsfield as his double play partner.

Mayor Zeidler took time out as a defense witness for Alderman Albert J. Krause, who denied receiving a bribe from auto dealer Walter J. Sawyer, to throw out the first ball from the stands at the final Borchert Field opener. At a minimum, it was figured the defending champion Brewers would move into the new County Stadium. The Minneapolis Millers spoiled any sense of event for 11,190 sun-bathed fans by crushing Milwaukee, 11–5. Ertman hit a 3-run home run and Buzz Clarkson hit the longest ball of the day in the 8th, but Miller catcher Ray Katt's 6th inning blow saddled young Anderson with the defeat. This was one slow Katt though as he was thrown out at second on another ball hit off the right field screen.[79]

Four names familiar as future Milwaukee Braves dotted the Brewer batting order: Bruton led off in center, Chuck Tanner batted behind him in left, 2nd baseman Jack Dittmer hit third, and Johnny Logan hit eighth at short. Liddle, who went on to average 10 Ks per 9 innings for the season, started on the mound. Clarkson was back at 3rd, joining right fielder Basso and Unser as the only returning full-timers. Logan's boot on his first chance equaled his 1951 total, so maybe the pressure was off early.

Teddy Tetzlaff was now said to be at his 34th straight opener, but notably absent behind the Brewer dugout in the 3rd base stands was Leo Morris, who fought off an attack of pneumonia in Columbia Hospital. Lou Chapman, *Sentinel* columnist, wrote of a little round man whose torrent of memories at this last Borchert Orchard opener made him realize he was getting old. The ballpark had been a symbol of his youth when he carved out his own knothole in the right field fence...the delicious red-hots for a dime, the ice-cold nickel "sody," the puffs of smoke and smell of burning tobacco from the grown-ups. The parade of players, ghost-like from the days of King Lear in flapping red sleeves, swarthy Black Tom Jenkins and his need to shave 2 or 3 times a day, Ossie Orwoll... Dinty Gearin... Danny Bloxsom... Lin Storti... Chet Laabs... Ted Gullic... Hal Peck... Hershel Martin... Heinz Becker.

The kaleidescope of a ballpark that died with his youth was interrupted by the sound of his own son's voice. It was through him that nothing really died or nobody actually grew old.

A different Ernie Johnson, a 64-year old scout who sent the likes of Ted Williams, Dom DiMaggio, Johnny Pesky, and Bobby Doerr among others to the Red Sox, died May Day at Monrovia, California. The born-Chicagoan was a standout shortstop, the first to command a $300 a month salary from P.C.L. Los Angeles in 1912-1913 and had 10 fine years with the ChiSox and Yanks. He was the father of Cubs' second sacker Don Johnson.[80]

Milwaukee Lutheran High School graduate Harvey Kuenn now captained the University of Wisconsin Badgers as their shortstop and chased the Big Ten batting title. He'd soon have 8 major league clubs offering him $50,000. Wisconsin Rapids Indians catcher Erminio Gaido and Appleton Papermakers outfielder Dick Schneider were the 1952 Wisconsin State League's only active Milwaukeeans.[81] (Kuenn would manage the 1982 American League champion Brewers.)

Virgil Jester's pitching was no joke in the early go, as he sought his 8th win by mid-May. Cold weather caused 3 postponements in 6 days. Brewers G.M. Red Smith tried to deal veteran shortstop Buddy Kerr to another Triple-A club so he'd have a better chance to play his way back up to the bigs. He was only a year and a couple months away from being a 10-year major leaguer. The weight of Tommy Holmes' heavy hand on the struggling Braves led to Smith's amazement that he couldn't fraternize with the Boston players on Chicago's Wrigley Field. Not even to just say "Hello." The pressure on the

11–15, 7th place parent club was lifted when John Quinn promoted light-hearted Jolly Cholly Grimm from Milwaukee to Boston on June 1st. Grimm was up for the rest of 1952, and for all of 1953, he signed on.[82]

Grimm was chastised by Lloyd Larson in print for abandoning Milwaukee, which Grimm said was his "kind of town," one he chose to make his last stop on the managerial merry-go-round. That he could only act as a company man when he was needed led Larson to criticize the company, i.e., the Braves and its yo-yo of talent and the manager. Three men, Billy Southworth, Frankie Frisch, and Bucky Walters, were in line for Grimm's job, but Red Smith assumed on-field duties himself for the interim.

Southworth, fired by Boston in mid-1951, still scouted for them from his Sunbury, Ohio, home and had little interest in changing his freedom as a legman. Future Hall of Famer Frisch led the Cards and Buccos before replacing Grimm on the Cubs. Walters managed at Cincinnati, but was now a Braves coach. Grimm was effusive about helping the Brewers from his new position. Milwaukee public opinion was split over his sudden departure. Larson foresaw Grimm returning to Beertown as manager of the Braves.[83]

Red Smith's steady hand elevated the Brewers from one percentage point ahead of the Blues to a 6–0 stretch under him that put KC 2½ games behind. His tenure opened with a twin sweep of Columbus, where Dick Hoover won his second straight match-up against basketball star Ralph Beard. The 5'-10" "giant" couldn't throw "hard enough to break a pane of glass," but his "nothing ball" bothered the Brewers until Billy Klaus' 2-run double in the 5th and 2-run homer in the 7th iced Game One. Murray Wall hurled a 4-hit shutout to win the backside.[84]

Logan was then called back up by Grimm, with Conley and Clarkson (for cleanup duty) sent back to Milwaukee. Warren Spahn won Grimm's second game with Boston. Red Smith named Bucky Walters to take over on Saturday June 7th. The former infielder-turned-pitcher's 81–126 mark at Cincinnati hardly looked like a good endorsement, but if he didn't work out, the Brewers could try the gimmick that the Corning Athletics had. Every ticket-buyer to the Sunday night, June 8th game received the valuable door prize of one potato. The largest family attending received a whole peck.[85] (And we don't mean Hal, either...)

Walters knew most of the Brews in spring training and saw no reason to tinker with the winning formula he inherited. By turn, the team saw no reason to lose his first game. Future manager Mauch, for one, was glad a stiff disciplinarian like Frisch wasn't on the bench. George Estock threw a 1-hitter at the Colonels, and Hank Ertman's solo shot was all they needed for an 8th consecutive win dating back to Grimm's last game. Walters rewarded Estock with a free plane trip to Wilmington, Delaware, where his wife just gave birth to a 9-pound second son that Saturday forenoon.[86]

The American Association was about the one league Bucky Walters hadn't

Former Reds ace and Braves coach Bucky Walters was the last of the Borchert Field brewmasters. Baseball Hall of Fame Library, Cooperstown, NY.

seen in his vagabond career, but the Indianapolis Indians snapped the streak the next day. The Reds, the club where Brewer coach Joe Just caught some of Walters' major league pitching days, optioned 22-year old outfielder Wally Post to Milwaukee in exchange for veteran Willard Marshall from the Braves. Dwight Eisenhower exercised his options about running for president.[87]

Milwaukee fans, 11,894 of them, got their first look at Walters when Clarkson stole 3 bases to lead a 4-3 conquering of Phil Cavaretta's red-hot Chicago Cubs on Monday, June 9th. It was a role reversal of what Chicago's John Clarkson did to Milwaukee back in the 1880s. Everyone took to Walters a lot better than Bill Veeck took to Rogers Hornsby, whose rift over the waiver acquisition of Stubby Overmire made their parting as friends a minor miracle. Harvey Kuenn, the Big Ten's "best in 20 years," took $55,000 from the Detroit Tigers.[88]

Howard Anderson was sent back to Atlanta on a 24-hour option and the Crackers returned "midget" Al (Dim Dom) Dumouchelle, who was promptly sent to Hartford outright. Ah, life in the Braves' chain...Milwaukee didn't go as far as the Interstate League Harrisburg Senators, who signed curvaceous 24-year old stenographer Eleanor Engle as a "gag." The folding Fond du Lac Panthers, averaging 500 people a game, could have used her. She could have bought a baseball uniform for as little as $3.90, half-price at Heller's on 72nd and W. Greenfield in Milwaukee.[89]

Maybe the Brewers could have used Miss Engle's services after Walters and Whisenant were ejected in the Independence Day dual loss at Kansas City. The Blues retook the A.A. lead by a percentage point. Umpire Mike Briscoe's balls and strikes drove the placid Walters to beyond misery. Whisenant had to be restrained by teammates from committing assault. Marquez and Hartsfield were also fined, but coach Joe Just, also ejected, wasn't.[90]

Entertainers Bob Hope and Bing Crosby staged a 14½-hour telethon to raise money for the U.S. Olympic team to go to Helsinki, where the Finnish version of baseball, *pesapallo,* would be a demonstration sport. Many pledged but few paid. Gene Conley raised the bar on the Blues by driving in the decisive run in his 5–2 victory over the power-laden Yank farmhands.[91]

Near Manitowoc, old Stoney McGlynn's resting place, members of the Milwaukee Monarchs grabbed bats and chased manager Jimmy Carter through 5 miles of woods and thickets after being gypped for $2 when each expected $20. Carter had $200 from Kellnersville management. With real *esprit de corps,* members raised $50 bail for his disorderly conduct charge so he would not have to spend the night in jail. If he had ran all the way up into Florence County, he might have crossed paths with a timely game warden named Richard Nixon.[92]

Herb Score, the Indianapolis Indians' $60,000 "Bonus baby," wasn't very game when the Brewers roughed up his left-handed slants in his July 11th Organized Ball debut. A 3-run 4th and a 7-run 5th had the young man in search of a fifth after the 12–0 initiation.[93]

On the 1970s TV sitcom "M*A*S*H," the fictional Korean War corporal Max Klinger pledges his allegiance to his hometown Toledo Mud Hens. Well, by June 1952, the boa-wearing Section-8 character would've been left featherless, for owner Danny Menendez took Klinger's beloved Brood and flew the coop for Charleston, West Virginia. It was the American Association's first franchise shift since that same Toledo franchise tried Cleveland in the 1910s. The new "Senators" home became the first time the Brewers ever traveled by air. Ball-bashing Babe Barna made the Milwaukee aviational tourists unwelcome that Sunday, July 13th night when his 3-run homer off reliefer Dick Hoover wiped out a 4–2 lead in the 11th and left 5,691 witnesses pop-eyed.[94]

Shorty Mendelson, the longtime Brewer secretary who was affectionately honored in his promotion to oversee the new stadium, said the Miller beer scoreboard advertising rental was a greater package than the Chicago White Sox received from Chesterfield cigarettes.[95]

Bucky Walters, Charleston manager Rollie Hemsley, Earl Gillespie (who played under Red Smith at Green Bay), and *The Sentinel's* Red Thisted judged the Stars of Yesterday preliminary at Borchert Field, Thursday, August 21st. Conducted by the School Board's Department of Municipal Recreation, Bunny Brief's "National League" all-stars faced Jack Kloza's "American Leaguers." It may have been no coincidence that a flying saucer scare spooked Washington, D.C. into August, but Kloza had batting third, a center fielder named Bob Uecker. Kloza's cleanup kid was shortstop Tony Kubek, who advanced with Kloza's own catcher son, John, to the Hearst National All-Star Classic in New York City.[96]

Other city products moved up the Organized Baseball ladder: Paul Schramka of Messmer High made it to the Cubs' L.A. farm before entering the service, Bob (Red) Wilson was the most valuable backstop in the ChiSox chain, joined by another West Allis star at Seattle, Nick Krsnich. Rocky Krsnich already made it to the bigs and Mike Krsnich, who came off a monster RBI run in the 1951 Mississippi-Ohio Valley League, would eventually get there, too. Harvey Kuenn made it up to the Tigers before season's end. The White Sox drew 9,575 in a late July exhibition win over the Brewers at Borchert.[97]

Representing this still abundant reservoir of diamond talent, the Brewers galloped off like Bob Uihlein's new Milwaukee Polo Club and zeroed in on the A.A. flag the way the mysterious, new guided missiles made aerial warfare over Korea a 9-1 kill advantage for the Americans. Buzz Clarkson's mouth supposedly watered when he won 6 frozen chickens from "the IGA" for hitting the first homer during their promotion.[98]

Milwaukee fought off Kansas City through August and Red Smith even rescheduled the Saturday, August 16th night game with the Blues so as not to conflict with the Green Bay Packers' Shrine Charity clash with New York Giants at Marquette Stadium. The crucial daytime contest drew only 2,368, but Smith's goodwill inspired Ed Blake to out-duel Eddie Erautt, 3-2, and put Milwaukee a half-game back up. Clarkson doubled to set up his lead run off Hank Ertman's bouncer to a hesitant Don Bollweg.[99]

The Brewers also beat Charlie Grimm's visiting Braves, 3-1, in a Monday, August 18th exhibition preliminary, then beat the Blues, 5-1, afterwards. A blood drive for the Armed Forces in Korea was sponsored by the Jewish War Veterans.[100] The Braves finished 1952 in 7th place.

The Milwaukee Junior Chamber of Commerce formed a sports booster club through the 9th grade level where members were admitted with a card at a reduced 10¢ price at Borchert. The Teutonia Avenue Advancement Association and Milwaukee Theatre hosted the Brewers to a special screening of Ronald Reagan's portrayal of the alcoholic epileptic Grover Cleveland Alexander in "That Winning Season." That Association also made Tuesday, August 26th "Farewell to Borchert Field Night." Lou Perini still insisted that, though Milwaukee was a cinch for big league baseball, it may have had to wait for expansion, not a franchise shift.[101]

The reigning franchise waited for no one, building their lead to 10 games with an 8-4 triumph over a St. Paul club that had basketball star Bill Sharman in its outfield. Five days later, 681 customers shivered through a blown 6-run lead that led to a 12-11 Saints victory. Figures conflict, possibly between the inclusion of exhibitions or not, but the Brewers drew between 195,000 and 225,000, leaving some to wonder whether concerns about parking and traffic at the new facility were warranted. The winning pitcher for St. Paul in that woolly affair was Don Otten. It was not said if he was the same 7-foot Don Otten who played center for the N.B.A. Milwaukee Hawks.[102]

Three days later, Clarkson hit 2 homers and Conley one as the Brewers retaliated to nip the Saints by the identical 12-11 score to open the first round playoffs. Milwaukee was only the sixth A.A. team to win over 100 games in a

9— *From Curtain Call to Wrecking Ball* 333

From left: Martin Weber head of the amateur Land O'Lakes League, ex-big leaguer George McBride, honoree Al Simmons, former sports writer Art Schinner, Sam Levy of *The Journal,* Mack Kehoe, p.r. director of Miller brewery, and Milt McGuire, President of the Milwaukee Common Council. In 1953, "Bucketfoot" was the only homegrown ex-Brewer ever elected to the Baseball Hall of Fame. Milwaukee Public Library Historical Photograph Collection.

154-game schedule. Mauch went 4-for-5 with 3 runs, Montag homered, and like Bruton and Crowe (back since mid-August) had 2 RBI in Game Two. Clarkson and Crowe hit solo shots among the 6 hits off Earl Mossor as he walked 9 in a 3–2 loss, leaving the Saints behind a 3-zip eight ball. St. Paul was only 4–18 versus Milwaukee in the regular season, so the 4-game sweep was inevitable. Attendance ranged between 3–4,000 per game.[103]

As the Brewers awaited the outcome of the Kansas City-Minneapolis series, an "unbending" Gene Raymond Conley got bat instruction from mom Kay and dad Big Gene, while 2-year old Leanne Mauch learned the rudiments of golf from Mr. and Mrs. Gene. Red Smith signed 22-year old Pete Dellios, who hurled 2 no-hitters for the Waukesha Dales in the Land O'Lakes League going 8–3 with an ERA under one. The Carroll College grad was expected at Kissimmee for the Brewers the next spring. The Blues polished off the Millers in 5 games by September 14th.[104]

The opener with Kansas City was a convoluted affair that took 2-hours,

The 1952 American Association Pennant-Winning Champion Milwaukee Brewers (Final Borchert Field edition). *Top row:* OF Wally Post, INF Buzz Clarkson, OF Pete Whisenant, P Muray Wall, 2B Billy Reed, P Bert Thiel. *Middle row:* GM Red Smith, P Don Liddle, C Dewey Williams, OF Bill Bruton, P George Estock, P Bill Allen, P Gene Conley, OF Luis Marquez, P Dick Donovan, P Eddie Blake, Trainer Bob Feron. *Front row:* C Al Unser, P Dick Hoover, 1B Hank Ertman, Mgr. Bucky Walters, Coach Joe Just, INF Billy Klaus, OF Bob Montag, INF Gene Mauch. *Bat boys:* Billy Walters and Johnny Reiter. Baseball Hall of Fame Library, Cooperstown, NY.

36-minutes on the field, but it wasn't until 3 a.m., Tuesday, September 16th that A.A. President Bruce Dudley officially confirmed the Blues' 4–3 win. Umpire John Mullen's failure to automatically eject the Blues' coaching catcher Mickey Owen when he rushed the plate in the first placed the game under a protest cloud that the Brewers lost both ways gracefully.[105]

The A.A.'s top fielding pennant-winners were plagued by rashes of errors in this series. They had 4 in a 10–8 victory where Pete Whisenant drove in 6 runs on a pair of homers. Another 4 miscues cost Don Liddle, 10–4 over and out, when 5,687 sat through a frigid afternoon. Like G.O.P. vice-presidential nominee Sen. Richard Nixon on the eve of his famous "Checkers" speech, the Brewers stared down their fate in Game Seven for the A.A. playoff championship.[106]

On the Sunday afternoon of September 21, 1952 [The sixth wedding anniversary of the authors' parents, coincidentally], the ancient rafters of venerable Borchert Field trembled from the stomping of 6,427 partisans. The Blues built up an 8–2 advantage in the first 5 rounds on 3 home runs. Bill Renna was nearly the first to ever clear the center field bleachers off Eddie Blake who was unsuccessfully relieved by Gene Conley in the 4th.

9 — *From Curtain Call to Wrecking Ball* 335

On the road to becoming a road. What the wrecking ball did to the Borchert Field grandstand. Milwaukee Public Library Historical Photograph Collection.

Eddie Erautt was chased to the showers and the Brewers continued their comeback upon Dave Jolly. Don Liddle and Dick Donovan kept KC under wraps the rest of the way. The first 3 Milwaukee runs in the 9th came on Kansas City errors. The tying run was on base when Billy Klaus hit a routine fly to Renna to end an era. The 8–7 struggle was truly a "dazzling windup"[107]:

Kanasas City	AB	R	H	C	*Milwaukee*	AB	R	H	C(hances)
Kermit Wahl, SS	3	1	1	1	Bill Bruton, CF	5	0	0	1
Don Bollweg, 1B	4	1	1	9	Gene Mauch, 2B	4	1	1	3
Bob Cerv, RF	5	2	2	0	George Crowe, 1B	5	1	1	11
Bill (Moose) Skowron, LF	5	2	2	0	Luis Marquez, LF	5	1	3	4
Bill Renna, CF	5	1	2	6	Billy Klaus, SS	5	0	1	6
Vic Power, 3B	5	0	3	4	Buzz Clarkson, 3B	3	1	1	3
Kal Segrist, 2B	5	0	0	4	Bob Montag, RF	3	1	1	2
Mickey Owen, C	4	1	1	7	Dewey Williams, C	4	1	1	5
Eddie Erautt, P	3	0	1	4	Eddie Blake, P	1	0	1	1
Dave Jolly, P	0	0	0	1	Gene Conley, P	0	0	0	0
Totals	39	8	13	36	Don Liddle, P	1	0	0	0
e-popped up for Liddle in 7th					e-Hank Ertman	1	0	0	0
					Dick Donovan, P	0	0	0	2
f-singled for Donovan in 9th					f-Billy Reed	1	1	1	0
					Totals	38 (1)	11		38

Kansas City 0 0 1 3 4 0 0 0 — 8
Milwaukee   0 0 1 1 0 0 0 0 5 — 7

E-Cerv, Segrist, Klaus RBI — Wahl, Renna 3, Bollweg 2, Skowron 2, Blake, Montag, Marquez 2, 2B — Erautt, Power, Blake, Crowe HR — Renna, Bollweg, Skowron S-Erautt DP — Marquez and Mauch Left — Kansas City 8,

Milwaukee 7. BB — Erautt 1, Jolly 1, Conley 1, Liddle 1, Donovan 1. SO — Erautt 7, Blake 1, Liddle 2. HO — Erautt 9 in 8 1/3, Jolly 2 in 2/3; Blake 6 in 3 (pitched to 4 in 4th); Conley 2 in 1 1/3; Liddle 3 in 2 2/3; Donovan 2 in 2 HBP by Erautt (Clarkson). W-Erautt L-Blake A-6,427

Appropriately, the closeout came against their long designated geographic rivals. The next day, Lou Perini already changed his tune about shifting his financially wrecked Braves to Milwaukee, and Lloyd Larson floated the Brewers' possible A.A. move to Toledo. During the Milwaukee Chicks' 1944 banner Girls League year, Dr. Julius Ehrlich conducted 4 Milwaukee Sinfonietta "pops" concerts at Borchert Field. Perhaps they should have been brought back to play Ravel's "Pavannae for a Dead Princess" for an encore when the 64-year old grandstand gates were padlocked. For Milwaukee baseball fans, the Locust St. exit off the Interstate-43 to run over the old ballpark would just become Memory Lane.[108]

Appendix A
Notes from a Conversation with Bud Selig

On Tuesday, April 24, 2001, Baseball Commissioner Allan H. (Bud) Selig graciously consented to a half-hour of his time to be interviewed for this book. The man most responsible for preserving major league baseball in Milwaukee and Wisconsin was actually born in the city on July 30, 1934, nearly 6 months after future friend Henry Aaron entered the world in Mobile, Alabama, and 6 months before his longtime announcer buddy Bob Uecker was hatched(?) in Beertown.

Selig's lifelong devotion as a genuine fan of the game was fueled early on by his mother. Her intense interest in baseball had the little Bud attending Brewers' games at Borchert Field by age 3 or 4. He acknowledged that his father was little more than an erstwhile fan until Bud's direct involvement with returning Milwaukee to the big leagues. That ascent to majority stockholder of the bankrupted and transferred Seattle Pilots to Milwaukee at the end of spring training in March 1970, much less to his current position, is something the young fan at Borchert Field never envisioned.

Although he could not recall being a part of any "Knothole Gang" at Borchert Field, his most vivid memories were of piling into their neighbor's car to go to the ballpark. On occasion, they rode the streetcar from their West Side neighborhood, one of the city's traditional Jewish enclaves, or rarer still, they took the bus.

What may not be generally known to people outside the city and state is that one of Bud Selig's boyhood chums was Herb Kohl, the once grocery magnate now United States senator who owns the Milwaukee Bucks N.B.A. basketball franchise. Like Kohl's immigrant Jewish father fostered a single grocery into a chain of supermarkets and department stores, Bud Selig returned from the University of Wisconsin in the early 1950s, where Kohl was his roommate, to work in his family's Knippel-Selig auto dealership on 70th and W. National Ave.

As early as his mother's exposure brought him to the game, Bud Selig's admittedly vague memories were not of awe at the sight of Borchert Field, nor could he understandably recall the first game he ever attended. The ballpark was already 50 years old when he first passed through its turnstiles as a toddler, but for Selig, Borchert Field was a "quaint" haven for "fond memories" of the "good baseball" played in the American Association.

He guesstimated that between 1941 and 1950 or the September 1952 he left for U.W., he probably saw about 40 Brewer games a season. There was only a vague recollection of Casey Stengel's stint as Brewer skipper, but he admitted that Nick Cullop's nickname of "Tomato Face" was a fit description. It was the wartime prime of the Brewers' 3 straight pennants, yet he could not remember any homage to those accomplishments in the form of displayed pennants, banners, or the like.

He was certain that he never personally attended any of the 1944 Milwaukee Chicks Girls League games, and really doubted whether his mother, as devout a baseball fan as she was, ever did either. Longtime Brewer outfielder Ted Gullic was among specific players in his memory bank, as well as shortstop Alvin Dark and 1st baseman Heinz Becker. He associated the "Mad Russian," Lou Novikoff, more as the Cubs' right fielder than a Brewer.

Bud Selig was at the 1943 game where southpaw reliever Julio Acosta popped out of flummoxed Brewer manager Charlie Grimm's birthday cake. He was less certain it if may have been his own birthday also, but for the record, Grimm turned 45 on August 28th, nearly a month after young Bud turned 9. The youngster did collect some player autographs.

Selig's older brother was, in fact, employed as a vendor at Borchert Field. He believed he was even old enough to sell beer and was actually working that Thursday, July 15, 1944, game where a wildly windy thundersquall ripped off a 100-foot grandstand roof section along the first base side. Debris was dropped upon several homes along N. 7th St.

From his young fan's perspective, there wasn't any bitter rivalry between the Brewers and any other American Association teams, but two of his favorite opposing players were Kansas City outfielders Hank Bauer and Cliff Mapes. That they were Yankee prospects was all the better, for it surprised the author to learn that Bud Selig grew up a Yankees fan. Far and away, his favorite Brewer was outfielder Hershel Martin, the clutch slugger once voted Most Popular Brewer by the fandom. Martin played at Newark and Kansas City on the way to becoming — you guessed it — a Yankee!

He thought the Brewers may have played an exhibition down at Wrigley Field in Chicago and that as media went, Mickey Heath may have given ticker reports on WTMJ Radio (it was WISN). About 1948, he believed WTMJ even televised a few Brewer games. He remembered Earl Gillespie doing Brewer games before gaining even wider fame with the Milwaukee Braves.

Jackie Robinson's entry into the majors made the arrival of black players like Buzz Clarkson to the Brewers pretty much a non-issue in the young Selig's

Appendix A: Conversation with Bud Selig

eyes. Other than the Acosta cake gag, he was too young to remember Bill Veeck's other sideshow antics in Milwaukee or really connect him with buying the Cleveland Indians.

Much like some of us would not lament the passing of the spartan socialist decor at the giant tin can that was Milwaukee County Stadium, the teenage Selig had no sentiment towards the dilapidated Borchert Field. It needed to go, as he put it. He also said the expectation was still that the minor league Brewers would move into that new stadium and the coming of the Braves, while he was off to college, was still something of a shock.

The focus of our interview was on his formative days as a self-professed "just a great fan" of the game. In bequeathing the executive leadership of the modern National League Brewers to his daughter, Wendy Selig-Prieb, Bud Selig had no idea that the old Brewers won their first pennant for a woman owner. It was hoped that our interview would be a reminiscing respite from all of the issues that have made Bud Selig a lightning rod, both as head of the Brewers and now over all of Major League Baseball. His input here is very deeply appreciated.

Because of the long, rich tradition of the minor league Milwaukee Brewers, no consideration was ever given to nicknaming the relocated Seattle Pilots anything else. The political hurdles to constructing Miller Park may have made the process seem like forever, but maybe this book will remind everyone of how long and how much Milwaukee has always loved baseball. It's why Miller Park, as Bud Selig put it, "is the place to be, without a doubt."

Appendix B
Milwaukee Baseball Statistics

Year	Team	League	Record	Place	Manager
1878	Grays	National	15-45, .250	6th(last)	Jack Chapman
1884	Cream Citys	Northwestern	41-30, .577	1st	James McKee
					Tom Loftus
	(major)	Union Assn.	8-4, .667	2nd	Tom Luftus
1885	Cream Citys	Western	(league folded)		Tom Loftus
1886	Milwaukees	Northwestern	35-42, .455	5th(of 6)	Ted Sullivan
1887	Milwaukees	Northwestern	78-43, .644	2nd	Jim Hart
1888	Brewers(?)	Western Assn.	(unreliable)	5th	Jim Hart
1889	Milwaukees	Western Assn.	59-63, .484	5th	Ezra Sutton,
					Capt. Geo. Shoch
1890	Brewers	Western Assn.	78-41, .649	2nd	Charlie Cushman
1891	Brewers	Western Assn.	59-37, .615	1st	Charlie Cushman
	(major)	American Assn.	21-15, .583	3rd	Charlie Cushman
1892	Brewers	Western	17-9 .654	2nd	Charlie Cushman
1894	Brewers	Western	50-74, .403	8th	Charlie Cushman
1895	Brewers	Western	57-67, .460	6th	Larry Twitchell
1896	Brewers	Western	62-78, .443	6th	Larry Twitchell,
					Bob Glenalvin
1897	Brewers	Western	85-51, .626	4th	Connie Mack
1898	Brewers	Western	82-57, .590	3rd	Connie Mack
1899	Brewers	Western	55-68, .447	6th	Connie Mack
1900	Brewers	American	79-59, .572	2nd	Connie Mack
1901	Brewers	American (major)	48-89, .350	8th	Hugh Duffy
1902	Brewers	American Assn.	66-75, .468	6th	Billy Clingman
	Angels	Western	81-56, .591	3rd	Hugh Duffy
1903	Brewers	American Assn.	77-60, .562	3rd	Pongo Joe Cantillon
	Creams	Western	83-43, .659	1st (folds)	Hugh Duffy
1904	Brewers	American Assn.	89-63, .585	3rd	Pongo Joe Cantillon
1905	Brewers	American Assn.	91-59, .607	2nd	Pongo Joe Cantillon
1906	Brewers	American Assn.	85-67, .559	2nd	Pongo Joe Cantillon
1907	Brewers	American Assn.	72-84, .460	7th	Dirty Jack Doyle

Appendix B: Milwaukee Baseball Statistics 341

Year	Team	League	Record	Place	Manager
1908	Brewers	American Assn.	71-83, .461	6th	Barry McCormick
1909	Brewers	American Assn.	90-77, .539	2nd	John J. McCloskey
1910	Brewers	American Assn.	76-91, .455	6th	John J. McCloskey
1911	Brewers	American Assn.	79-87, .476	5th	Jimmy Barrett
1912	Brewers	American Assn.	78-85, .479	5th	Hugh Duffy
1913	Brewers	American Assn.	100-67,.599	1st	Harry "Pep" Clark
1914	Brewers	American Assn.	98-68, .590	1st	Harry "Pep" Clark
1915	Brewers	American Assn.	67-81, .453	6th	Harry "Pep" Clark
1916	Brewers	American Assn.	54-110,.329	8th	Harry Clark, Happy Jack Martin
1917	Brewers	American Assn.	71-81, .467	5th	Dan Shay, Billy Doyle, Bill Friel, & Paddy Livingston
1918	Brewers	American Assn.	38-35, .521	5th	Jack Egan
1919	Panthers	American Assn.	58-93, .384	8th	Clarence "Pants" Rowland
1920	Brewers	American Assn.	78-88, .470	6th	Jack Egan
1921	Brewers	American Assn.	81-86, .485	5th	Jack Egan
1922	Brewers	American Assn.	85-83, .506	5th	Harry "Pep" Clark
1923	Brewers	American Assn.	75-91, .452	5th	Harry "Pep" Clark
	Bears	Negro National	14-32, .304	(folded)	Pete Hill
1924	Brewers	American Assn.	83-83, .500	4th	Harry "Pep" Clark
1925	Brewers	American Assn.	74-94, .440	7th	Harry "Pep" Clark
1926	Brewers	American Assn.	93-71, .567	3rd	Jack Lelivelt
1927	Brewers	American Assn.	99-69, .589	2nd(T)	Jack Lelivelt
1928	Brewers	American Assn.	90-78, .536	3rd	Jack Lelivelt
1929	Brewers	American Assn.	69-98, .413	7th	Jack Lelivelt, Marty Berghammer
1930	Brewers	American Assn.	63-91, .409	7th	Marty Berghammer
1931	Brewers	American Assn.	83-85, .494	5th	M. Berghammer, Frank O'Rourke
1932	Brewers	American Assn.	88-78, .530	3rd	Frank "Blackie" O'Rourke
1933	Brewers	American Assn.	67-87, .435	7th	Frank "Blackie" O'Rourke
1934	Brewers	American Assn.	82-70, .539	3rd	Al Sothoron
1935	Brewers	American Assn.	75-79, .487	6th	Al Sothoron
1936	Brewers	American Assn.	90-64, .584	1st	Al Sothoron
1937	Brewers	American Assn.	80-73, .523	4th	Al Sothoron
1938	Brewers	American Assn.	81-70, .536	3rd	Al Sothoron
1939	Brewers	American Assn.	70-83, .458	6th	Mickey Heath
1940	Brewers	American Assn.	58-90, .392	8th	Mickey Heath, Ray Schalk
1941	Brewers	American Assn.	55-98, .359	8th	Bill Killefer, Charlie Grimm
1942	Brewers	American Assn.	81-69, .540	2nd	Charlie Grimm
1943	Brewers	American Assn.	90-61, .596	1st	Charlie Grimm
1944	Brewers	American Assn.	102-51, .667	1st	Charlie Grimm, Casey Stengel

Appendix B: Milwaukee Baseball Statistics

Year	Team	League	Record	Place	Manager
	Chicks	All-Amer. Girls	70-45, .609	1st(overall)	Max (Scoops) Carey
1945	Brewers	American Assn.	93-61, .604	1st	Nick Cullop
1946	Brewers	American Assn.	70-78, .473	5th	Nick Cullop
1947	Brewers	American Assn.	79-75, .513	3rd	Nick Cullop
1948	Brewers	American Assn.	89-65, .579	2nd	Nick Cullop
1949	Brewers	American Assn.	76-76, .500	3rd	Nick Cullop
1950	Brewers	American Assn.	68-85, .444	6th	Bob Coleman
1951	Brewers	American Assn.	94-57, .623	1st	Charlie Grimm
1952	Brewers	American Assn.	101-53, .656	1st	Charlie Grimm, Red Smith, & Bucky Walters
	all-time A.A. total		4,022-3,886, .509		

American Association Playoffs / Little World Series

1936 defeated Kansas City 4 games-0, defeated Indianapolis, 4 games-1/defeated Buffalo, 4 games-1
1937 defeated Toledo 4 games-2, lost to Columbus 4 games-2
1938 lost to St. Paul 4 games-3
1942 lost to Toledo 4 games-2
1943 lost to Columbus 3 games-1
1944 lost to Louisville 4 games-2
1945 lost to Louisville 4 games-2
1947 defeated Kansas City 4 games-2, defeated Louisville 4 games-3/defeated Syracuse, 4 games-3
1948 lost to Columbus 4 games-3
1949 defeated St. Paul 4 games-3, lost to Indianapolis 4 games-2
1951 defeated Kansas City 4 games-1, defeated St. Paul 4 games-2/ defeated Montreal, 4 games-2
1952 defeated St. Paul 4 games-0, lost to Kansas City 4 games-3

Brewers as A.A. Statistical Leaders (league records in bold)

Batting

1905 George Stone	.405		1941 Lou Novikoff	.370
1918 Doc Johnston	.374		1942 Eddie Stanky	.342
1922 Glenn Myatt	.370		1943 Grey Clarke	.346
1924 Lester Bell	.365		1945 Lew Flick	.374
1931 Art Shires	.385		1947 Heinz Becker	.363
1934 Earl Webb	.368		1950 Bob Addis	.323

Homers

1906 Ed Green	8		1926 Bunny Brief	26
1914 Happy Felsch	14		1943 Ted Norbert	25
1925 Bunny Brief	37		1947 Carden Gillenwater	23

RBI

1925 Bunny Brief	175		1945 Gene Nance	106
1934 Jack Kloza	148		1951 George Crowe	117
1943 Ted Norbert	117			

Appendix B: Milwaukee Baseball Statistics 343

Stolen Bases

1916 Jim Thorpe	48	1926 Lance Richbourg	48	
1923 Jimmy Cooney	60	1936 Frenchy Uhalt	36(T)	

Pitching Wins

1909 Stoney McGlynn	27	1938 Whitlow Wyatt	23
1913 Cy Slapnicka	25	1944 Earl Caldwell	19(T)
1918 Dickie Kerr	17	1945 Owen Scheetz	19
1928 Ernie Wingard	24	1946 Ewald Pyle	15(T)

Win Percentage

1927 Ossie Orwoll	.739	1951 Ernie Johnson	.789
1938 Whitlow Wyatt	.767	1952 Don Liddle	.810
1944 Earl Caldwell	.792		

Earned Run Average

1935 Clyde Hatter	2.88	1951 Ernie Johnson	2.62
1938 Whitlow Wyatt	2.37	1952 Don Liddle	2.70

Strikeouts

1903 Claude Elliott	226	1928 Claude Jonnard	150
1904 Cliff Curtis	210	1931 Claude Jonnard	130
1909 Stoney McGlynn	183	1936 Clyde Hatter	190
1918 Dickie Kerr	99	1938 Whitlow Wyatt	208
1924 Rube Walberg	175	1952 Don Liddle	159

Lifetime Records

Harry Clark,	1834 Games	Bunny Brief,	276 homers
Bevo LeBourveau,	.360 avg.	Bunny Brief	1,451+RBI
Bunny Brief,	1,342 runs	Bunny Brief,	2,196 hits
Bunny Brief,	458 doubles		

Most Valuable Player

1936 Rudy York, 1b (unofficial)
1951 Al Unser, C

The Sporting News Minor League Manager of Year

1936 Al Sothoron   1951 Charlie Grimm
1947 Nick Cullop

Game Record

Aug. 17, 1926 Bob Lamotte, SS; 11 assists

Season Records

1904 George Stone, .405 BA
1907 Frank Schneiberg, 22 HBP
1909 Stoney McGlynn, 14 shutouts and 446 innings
1914 Johnny Hughes, C 680 chances accepted

Appendix B: Milwaukee Baseball Statistics

Season Records
1928 Lance Richbourg, 28 triples
1935 Eddie Marshall, 43-game hit streak

Consecutive Errorless Game Streaks
1937 Lin Storti, 49 at 3rd
1947 Danny Murtaugh, 42 at 2nd
1951 Johnny Logan, 46 at short

Brews A.A. No-Hitters
May 9, 1908 Cliff Curtis v. Indianapolis
August 30, 1910 Wilbur Schardt v. Indianapolis
August 20, 1912 Joe Hovlik v. Louisville
August 21, 1926 Dinty Gearin V. Columbus
September 7, 1935 Americo Polli v. St. Paul
August 17, 1951 Bert Thiel v. Toledo

Notes

1— From the Mists

1. Bob Buege *The Milwaukee Braves: A Baseball Eulogy.* Milwaukee: Douglas American Sports Publications, 1988, pp. 179, 182.
2. Philip W. Goetz, ed. *Encyclopaedia Britannica, Volume 7, Micropaedia Ready Reference.* Chicago: Encyclopaedia Britannica, Inc., 1991, p. 89.
3. Brian Podoll. "Milwaukee's Turners: 125 Years of Prominence" in *Milwaukee Magazine,* December 1979, p. 78.
4. Ellen Langill, and Dave Jensen *Milwaukee 150: The Greater Milwaukee Story.* Milwaukee: Milwaukee Publishing Group, 1996, pp. 19, 43. Hereinafter cited as Langill, *Milwaukee 150.*
5. Ron McCulloch. *How Baseball Began.* Los Angeles: Warwick, 1995, pp. 9-20.
6. Bill O'Neal. *The American Association: A Baseball History 1902–1991.* Austin: Eakin Press, 1991, p. 281. Hereinafter cited as O'Neal, *A.A.*
7. Langill, *Milwaukee 150.*
8. Curtis B. Miller, S-B., Marquette University thesis, "Rufus King and the Problems of His Era" (Pasadena, CA: April 1963), Milwaukee Public Library Humanities Collection. Hereinafter cited as Miller thesis.
9. Harry H. Anderson, "The Ancient Origins of Baseball in Milwaukee," *Milwaukee History* (Milwaukee County Historical Society, summer 1983), pp. 42-57. Hereinafter cited as Anderson, *History.*
10. William J. Ryczek, *When Johnny Came Sliding Home: The Post–Civil War Baseball Boom, 1865-1870* (Jefferson, NC: McFarland, 1998). Hereinafter cited as Ryczek, *Post–Civil War.*
11. Anderson, *History.*
12. *Milwaukee Sentinel.*
13. City Directory, Milwaukee Public Library Humanities Collection.
14. Anderson, *History.*
15. Anderson, *History.*
16. *Milwaukee Sentinel.*
17. *Ibid.*
18. Ryczek, *Post–Civil War.*
19. *Milwaukee Sentinel.*
20. *Ibid.*
21. *Ibid.*
22. Miller thesis.
23. *Ibid.*
24. Ryczek, *Post–Civil War.*
25. Anderson, *History.*
26. *Milwaukee Sentinel.*
27. *Ibid.*
28. Anderson, *History.*
29. Ryczek, *Post Civil War.*
30. *The Milwaukee Sentinel* newspaper.
31. *Ibid.*
32. Miller thesis.
33. *Ibid.*
34. Printed for private distribution, *Rufus King (1817–1891) in the Development of Cincinnati During the Last Fifty Years* (Cincinnati: Robert Clarke & Co., 1891), p. 113.
35. Jonathan Fraser Light, *The Cultural Encyclopedia of Baseball* (Jefferson, NC: McFarland & Co., 1997), p. 673.
36. Stephen D. Guschov, *The Red Stockings of Cincinnati: Base Ball's First All Professional Team* (Jefferson, NC: McFarland & Co., 1998), pp. 145 & 72. Hereinafter referred to as Guschov, *Red Stockings.*
37. Ryczek, *Post–Civil War.*
38. *Milwaukee Sentinel.*
39. *Ibid.*
40. Guschov, *Red Stockings.*
41. Anderson, *History.*
42. Harvey Frommer, *Primitive Baseball: The First Quarter Century of the National Pastime* (New York: Atheneum, 1988), pp. 19-28.
43. Miller thesis.
44. *Ibid.*
45. *Milwaukee Sentinel.*
46. Anderson, *History.*
47. Rick Wolff, ed. dir. *The Baseball Encyclopedia,* 9th ed. (New York: Macmillan, 1993). Hereinafter cited as *Baseball Encyclopedia.*
48. Anderson, *History.*
49. *Ibid.*
50. *Ibid.*
51. *Ibid.*
52. *Baseball Encyclopedia.*
53. *Ibid.*
54. Donald Dewey and Nicholas Acocella, *The Encyclopedia of Major League Baseball Teams* (New York: HarperCollins, 1993), p. 301. Hereinafter cited as *Encyclopedia Teams.*

2 — Northwestern

1. Langill *Milwaukee 150*, p. 34.
2. Author's collection.
3. *Milwaukee Sentinel.*
4. *Baseball Encyclopedia.*
5. *Milwaukee Sentinel.*
6. *Ibid.*
7. *Ibid.*
8. *Ibid.*
9. *Baseball Encyclopedia.*
10. *Milwaukee Sentinel.*
11. *Ibid.*
12. Anderson, *History.*
13. *State of Wisconsin 1987-1988 Blue Book* (Madison: Wisconsin Legislative Reference Bureau), p. 53.
14. Anderson, *History.*
15. *Ibid.*
16. *Spalding's Official Baseball Guide 1885* (Chicago: A.G. Spalding & Bros.), p.68.
17. *Encyclopedia Teams.*
18. *Baseball Encyclopedia.*
19. *Ibid.*
20. *Ibid.*
21. *Ibid.*
22. Anderson, *History.*
23. *Encyclopedia Teams.*
24. *Milwaukee Sentinel.*
25. *Ibid.*
26. *Ibid.*
27. *Baseball Encyclopedia.*
28. *Milwaukee Sentinel.*
29. *Ibid.*
30. *Baseball Encyclopedia.*
31. *Milwaukee Sentinel.*
32. *Ibid.*
33. *Ibid.*
34. *Ibid.*
35. *Ibid.*
36. *Ibid.*
37. *Ibid.*
38. *Ibid.*
39. *Ibid.*
40. *Ibid.*
41. *Ibid.*
42. *Ibid.*
43. *Ibid.*
44. *Ibid.*
45. *Ibid.*
46. *Ibid.*
47. *Ibid.*
48. *Ibid.*
49. *Ibid.*
50. *Ibid.*
51. *Ibid.*
52. *Ibid.*
53. *Baseball Encyclopedia.*
54. *Milwaukee Sentinel.*
55. *Ibid.*
56. *Ibid.*
57. *Ibid.*
58. *Baseball Encyclopedia.*
59. *Milwaukee Sentinel.*
60. *Ibid.*
61. *Ibid.*
62. *Ibid.*
63. *Ibid.*
64. *Ibid.*
65. *Ibid.*
66. *Ibid.*
67. *Ibid.*
68. *Ibid.*
69. *Ibid.*
70. *Ibid.*
71. *Ibid.*
72. *Ibid.*
73. *Ibid.*
74. *Ibid.*
75. *Ibid.*
76. *Ibid.*
77. *Ibid.*
78. *Ibid.*
79. *Ibid.*
80. *Ibid.*
81. *Ibid.*
82. *Ibid.*
83. *Ibid.*
84. *Ibid.*
85. *Ibid.*
86. *Ibid.*
87. *Ibid.*
88. *Ibid.*
89. *Ibid.*
90. *Ibid.*
91. *Baseball Encyclopedia.*
92. *Milwaukee Sentinel.*
93. *Ibid.*
94. *Ibid.*
95. *Ibid.*
96. *Ibid.*
97. *Ibid.*
98. *Ibid.*
99. *Ibid.*
100. *Ibid.*
101. *Ibid.*
102. *Ibid.*
103. *Ibid.*
104. *Ibid.*
105. *Ibid.*
106. *Ibid.*
107. *Ibid.*
108. *Ibid.*
109. *Ibid.*
110. *Baseball Encyclopedia.*
111. *Ibid.*
112. *Milwaukee Sentinel.*
113. *Ibid.*
114. *Ibid.*
115. *Ibid.*
116. *Ibid.*
117. *Ibid.*
118. *Baseball Encyclopedia.*
119. *Milwaukee Sentinel.*
120. *Ibid.*
121. *Ibid.*
122. *Ibid.*
123. *Ibid.*
124. *Ibid.*
125. *Ibid.*
126. *Ibid.*
127. *Ibid.*
128. *Ibid.*
129. *Ibid.*
130. *Ibid.*
131. *Ibid.*
132. Harold Seymour, *Baseball: The Early Years* (New York: Oxford University Press, 1960), p. 221. Hereinafter cited as Seymour, *Early.*
133. *Milwaukee Sentinel.*
134. *Ibid.*
135. *Ibid.*
136. *Ibid.*
137. *Ibid.*
138. *Ibid.*
139. *Ibid.*
140. *Ibid.*
141. Alex Sachare, editor, *The Official NBA Basketball Encyclopedia* (New York: Villard, 1994), p. 705.
142. Anderson, *History.*
143. *Milwaukee Sentinel.*
144. *Ibid.*
145. *Ibid.*
146. *Ibid.*
147. *Ibid.*
148. *Ibid.*
149. *Ibid.*
150. *Ibid.*
151. *Ibid.*
152. *Ibid.*
153. *Ibid.*
154. *Ibid.*
155. *Ibid.*
156. *Ibid.*
157. *Ibid.*
158. *Ibid.*
159. *Ibid.*
160. *Ibid.*
161. *Baseball Encyclopedia.*
162. *Encyclopedia Teams.*
163. *Ibid.*
164. *Milwaukee Sentinel.*
165. *Baseball Encyclopedia.*
166. *Encyclopedia Teams.*
167. *Ibid.*
168. *Ibid.*
169. *Milwaukee Sentinel.*
170. *Ibid.*
171. *Ibid.*

172. *Ibid.*
173. *Ibid.*
174. *Ibid.*
175. *Ibid.*
176. *Baseball Encyclopedia.*
177. *Ibid.*
178. *Milwaukee Sentinel.*
179. *Ibid.*
180. *Ibid.*
181. *Ibid.*
182. *Ibid.*
183. *Ibid.*

3 — That Mack

1. Seymour, *Early.*
2. *Milwaukee Sentinel.*
3. *Ibid.*
4. Dennis McCann, *The Wisconsin Story: 150 Stories, 150 Years* (Milwaukee Journal Sentinel, 1998), p. 133.
5. Peter Filichia, *Professional Baseball Franchises from the Abbeville Athletics to the Zanesville Indians* (New York: Facts on File, 1993), pp. 145–6.
6. *Milwaukee Sentinel.*
7. *Ibid.*
8. *Baseball Encyclopedia.*
9. *Milwaukee Sentinel.*
10. *Ibid.*
11. *Ibid.*
12. *Ibid.*
13. *Ibid.*
14. *Ibid.*
15. *Ibid.*
16. *Ibid.*
17. *Ibid.*
18. *Ibid.*
19. *Ibid.*
20. *Ibid.*
21. *Ibid.*
22. *Ibid.*
23. *Ibid.*
24. *Ibid.*
25. *Ibid.*
26. *Ibid.*
27. *Ibid.*
28. *Ibid.*
29. *Ibid.*
30. *Ibid.*
31. *Ibid.*
32. *Ibid.*
33. *Ibid.*
34. *Ibid.*
35. *Ibid.*
36. *Ibid.*
37. *Ibid.*
38. *Ibid.*
39. *Ibid.*
40. *Ibid.*
41. *Ibid.*
42. *Ibid.*
43. *Ibid.*
44. *Ibid.*
45. *Ibid.*
46. *Ibid.*
47. *Ibid.*
48. *Ibid.*
49. *Baseball Encyclopedia.*
50. Chuck Hershberger, *The Sports Hall of Oblivion* (Where, MI: Self-published, 1985), pp. 3-7. Hereinafter cited as Hershberger, *Hall.*
51. Hershberger, *Hall.*
52. *Milwaukee Sentinel.*
53. *Ibid.*
54. James A. Riley, *The Biographical Encyclopedia of the Negro Baseball Leagues* (New York: Carroll & Graf, 1994), pp. 595-596, 434-436, 872-873, 330. Hereinafter cited as Riley, *Negro.*
55. *Milwaukee Sentinel.*
56. *Ibid.*
57. *Ibid.*
58. *Ibid.*
59. *Ibid.*
60. *Ibid.*
61. Hershberger, *Hall.*
62. Michael Benson, *Ballparks of North America: A Comprehensive Historical Reference to Baseball Grounds, Yards, and Stadiums, 1845–Present* (Jefferson, NC: McFarland, 1989), pp. 230-3. Hereinafter cited as Benson, *Ballparks.*
63. *Ibid.*
64. *Milwaukee Sentinel.*
65. *Ibid.*
66. *Ibid.*
67. *Ibid.*
68. *Ibid.*
69. *Ibid.*
70. *Ibid.*
71. *Ibid.*
72. *Ibid.*
73. *Ibid.*
74. *Ibid.*
75. *Ibid.*
76. *Ibid.*
77. *Ibid.*
78. *Ibid.*
79. *Ibid.*
80. *Ibid.*
81. *Ibid.*
82. *Ibid.*
83. *Ibid.*
84. *Ibid.*
85. *Ibid.*
86. *Ibid.*
87. *Ibid.*
88. *Ibid.*
89. *Ibid.*
90. *Ibid.*
91. *Ibid.*
92. *Ibid.*
93. *Ibid.*
94. *Ibid.*
95. *Ibid.*
96. *Ibid.*
97. *Ibid.*
98. *Ibid.*
99. *Ibid.*
100. *Ibid.*
101. *Ibid.*
102. *Ibid.*
103. *Ibid.*
104. *Ibid.*
105. *Ibid.*
106. *Ibid.*
107. *Ibid.*
108. *Ibid.*
109. *Ibid.*
110. *Ibid.*
111. *Ibid.*
112. *Ibid.*
113. *Ibid.*
114. *Ibid.*
115. *Ibid.*
116. *Ibid.*
117. *Ibid.*
118. Walter (Chick) Wegner, "The Old Order Changeth," *Once a Year* (Milwaukee Press Club magazine, 1951), reprinted as "Borchert Field Is Gone, But It Had a Grand Opening That Day in 1888," April 14, 1953, *Milwaukee Sentinel.* Clipping File, Art & Music Department, Milwaukee Public Library. Hereinafter cited as Wegner, "Borchert."
119. *Milwaukee Sentinel.*
120. *Ibid.*
121. *Ibid.*
122. *Ibid.*
123. *Ibid.*
124. *Ibid.*
125. *Ibid.*
126. *Ibid.*
127. *Ibid.*
128. *Ibid.*
129. *Ibid.*
130. *Ibid.*
131. *Ibid.*
132. *Ibid.*
133. *Ibid.*
134. *Ibid.*
135. *Ibid.*

136. *Ibid.*
137. *Ibid.*
138. *Ibid.*
139. *Ibid.*
140. *Ibid.*
141. *Ibid.*
142. *Ibid.*
143. *Ibid.*
144. *Ibid.*
145. *Ibid.*
146. *Ibid.*
147. *Baseball Encyclopedia.*
148. *Milwaukee Sentinel.*
149. *Ibid.*
150. *Ibid.*
151. *Ibid.*
152. *Ibid.*
153. *Ibid.*
154. *Ibid.*
155. *Ibid.*
156. *Ibid.*
157. *Ibid.*
158. *Ibid.*
159. *Ibid.*
160. *Ibid.*
161. *Ibid.*
162. Seymour, *Early.*
163. *Baseball Encyclopedia.*
164. *Milwaukee Sentinel.*
165. *Ibid.*
166. *Ibid.*
167. *Ibid.*
168. *Ibid.*
169. *Ibid.*
170. *Ibid.*
171. *Ibid.*
172. *Ibid.*
173. *Ibid.*
174. *Ibid.*
175. *Ibid.*
176. *Ibid.*
177. *Ibid.*
178. *Ibid.*
179. *Ibid.*
180. *Ibid.*
181. *Ibid.*
182. *Ibid.*
183. *Ibid.*
184. *Ibid.*
185. *Ibid.*
186. *Ibid.*
187. *Ibid.*
188. *Ibid.*
189. *Ibid.*

4 — Last Team

1. *Milwaukee Sentinel.*
2. *Ibid.*
3. *Ibid.*
4. *Ibid.*
5. *Ibid.*
6. *Ibid.*
7. *Ibid.*
8. *Ibid.*
9. *Ibid.*
10. *Ibid.*
11. Seymour, *Early.*
12. *Milwaukee Sentinel.*
13. *Ibid.*
14. *Ibid.*
15. *Ibid.*
16. *Ibid.*
17. *Ibid.*
18. *Ibid.*
19. *Ibid.*
20. *Ibid.*
21. *Ibid.*
22. *Ibid.*
23. *Ibid.*
24. *Ibid.*
25. *Ibid.*
26. *Ibid.*
27. *Ibid.*
28. *Ibid.*
29. *Ibid.*
30. *Ibid.*
31. *Ibid.*
32. *Ibid.*
33. *Ibid.*
34. *Ibid.*
35. *Ibid.*
36. *Ibid.*
37. *Ibid.*
38. Stew Thornley, *On to Nicollet: The Fame and Glory of the Minneapolis Millers* (Minneapolis: Nodin Press, 1988), pp. 27 & 25. Hereinafter cited as Thornley, *Nicollet.*
39. *Milwaukee Sentinel.*
40. *Ibid.*
41. *Ibid.*
42. *Ibid.*
43. *Ibid.*
44. *Ibid.*
45. *Ibid.*
46. *Ibid.*
47. *Ibid.*
48. *Ibid.*
49. *Ibid.*
50. *Ibid.*
51. *Ibid.*
52. *Ibid.*
53. *Ibid.*
54. *Ibid.*
55. *Ibid.*
56. *Ibid.*
57. *Ibid.*
58. *Ibid.*
59. *Ibid.*
60. *Ibid.*
61. *Ibid.*
62. *Ibid.*
63. *Ibid.*
64. *Ibid.*
65. *Ibid.*
66. *Ibid.*
67. Lloyd Johnson and Miles Wolff, editors, *The Encyclopedia of Minor League Baseball* (Durham, NC: Baseball America, 1993). Hereinafter cited as *Minor Encyclopedia.*
68. *Milwaukee Sentinel.*
69. *Ibid.*
70. *Ibid.*
71. *Ibid.*
72. *Ibid.*
73. *Ibid.*
74. *Ibid.*
75. *Ibid.*
76. *Ibid.*
77. *Ibid.*
78. *Ibid.*
79. *Ibid.*
80. *Ibid.*
81. *Ibid.*
82. *Ibid.*
83. *Ibid.*
84. *Ibid.*
85. Marshall D. Wright, *The American Association: Year-by-Year Statistics for the Baseball Minor League 1902–1952* (Jefferson, NC: McFarland, 1997). Hereinafter cited as Wright, *A.A.*
86. *Milwaukee Sentinel.*
87. *Ibid.*
88. Wright, *A.A.*
89. *Milwaukee Sentinel.*
90. Wright, *A.A.*
91. *Milwaukee Sentinel.*
92. *Ibid.*
93. *Ibid.*
94. *Ibid.*
95. *Ibid.*
96. *Encyclopedia Teams.*
97. *Milwaukee Sentinel.*
98. *Ibid.*
99. *Ibid.*
100. *Ibid.*
101. *Ibid.*
102. *Ibid.*
103. *Ibid.*
104. *Ibid.*
105. *Ibid.*
106. *Ibid.*
107. *Ibid.*
108. *Ibid.*
109. *Ibid.*
110. *Ibid.*
111. *Ibid.*
112. *Ibid.*
113. *Ibid.*

Notes—Chapter 5   349

114. Ibid.
115. Ibid.
116. Ibid.
117. Ibid.
118. Ibid.
119. Ibid.
120. Ibid.
121. Ibid.
122. Ibid.
123. Ibid.
124. Ibid.
125. Ibid.
126. Ibid.
127. Ibid.
128. Ibid.
129. Minor Encyclopedia.
130. Milwaukee Sentinel.
131. Ibid.
132. Ibid.
133. Ibid.
134. Ibid.
135. Ibid.
136. Ibid.
137. Ibid.
138. Ibid.
139. Ibid.
140. Ibid.
141. Ibid.
142. Ibid.
143. Ibid.
144. Ibid.
145. Ibid.
146. Ibid.
147. Ibid.
148. Ibid.
149. Ibid.
150. Ibid.
151. Ibid.
152. Ibid.
153. Ibid.
154. Ibid.
155. Ibid.
156. Ibid.
157. Wright, A.A.
158. Milwaukee Sentinel.
159. Baseball Encyclopedia.
160. Thornley, Nicollet.
161. Milwaukee Sentinel.
162. Ibid.
163. Ibid.
164. Ibid.
165. Minor Encyclopedia.
166. Milwaukee Sentinel.
167. Ibid.
168. Ibid.
169. Ibid.
170. Ibid.
171. Ibid.
172. Ibid.
173. Ibid.
174. Ibid.
175. Ibid.

176. Ibid.
177. Ibid.
178. Ibid.
179. Ibid.
180. Ibid.
181. Ibid.
182. Ibid.
183. Ibid.
184. Ibid.
185. Ibid.
186. Ibid.
187. Ibid.
188. Ibid.
189. Ibid.
190. Ibid.
191. Ibid.
192. Ibid.
193. Ibid.
194. Ibid.
195. Ibid.
196. Minor Encyclopedia.
197. Wright, A.A.
198. Baseball Encyclopedia.
199. Milwaukee Sentinel.
200. Ibid.
201. Ibid.
202. Ibid.
203. Ibid.
204. Ibid.
205. Ibid.
206. Ibid.
207. Ibid.
208. Ibid.
209. Ibid.
210. Ibid.
211. Ibid.
212. Ibid.
213. Ibid.
214. Ibid.
215. Ibid.
216. Ibid.
217. Ibid.
218. Ibid.
219. Ibid.
220. Ibid.
221. Ibid.
222. Ibid.
223. Ibid.
224. Ibid.

5—The Lady Is

1. Benson, Ballparks.
2. Baseball Encyclopedia.
3. Milwaukee Journal.
4. Ibid.
5. Ibid.
6. Ibid.
7. Ibid.
8. Ibid.
9. Ibid.
10. Ibid.

11. Ibid.
12. Ibid.
13. Ibid.
14. Ibid.
15. Ibid.
16. Ibid.
17. Ibid.
18. Ibid.
19. Ibid.
20. Ibid.
21. Baseball Encyclopedia.
22. Milwaukee Sentinel.
23. Ibid.
24. Ibid.
25. Ibid.
26. Ibid.
27. Ibid.
28. Ibid.
29. Ibid.
30. Ibid.
31. Minor Encyclopedia.
32. Milwaukee Sentinel.
33. Ibid.
34. Ibid.
35. Ibid.
36. Ibid.
37. Ibid.
38. Ibid.
39. Ibid.
40. Milwaukee Journal.
41. Ibid.
42. Ibid.
43. Ibid.
44. Ibid.
45. Ibid.
46. Ibid.
47. Ibid.
48. Ibid.
49. Ibid.
50. Ibid.
51. Ibid.
52. Ibid.
53. Ibid.
54. Ibid.
55. Ibid.
56. Ibid.
57. Ibid.
58. Ibid.
59. Milwaukee Sentinel.
60. Ibid.
61. Ibid.
62. Ibid.
63. Ibid.
64. Ibid.
65. Ibid.
66. Ibid.
67. Ibid.
68. Ibid.
69. Ibid.
70. Ibid.
71. Ibid.
72. Ibid.

73. *Ibid.*
74. *Ibid.*
75. *Ibid.*
76. *Ibid.*
77. *Ibid.*
78. *Ibid.*
79. *Ibid.*
80. *Ibid.*
81. *Ibid.*
82. *Ibid.*
83. *Ibid.*
84. *Ibid.*
85. *Ibid.*
86. *Ibid.*
87. *Ibid.*
88. *Ibid.*
89. Wright, *A.A.*
90. *Milwaukee Journal.*
91. *Ibid.*
92. *Ibid.*
93. *Ibid.*
94. *Ibid.*
95. *Ibid.*
96. *Ibid.*
97. *Ibid.*
98. *Ibid.*
99. *Ibid.*
100. *Ibid.*
101. *Ibid.*
102. *Ibid.*
103. *Ibid.*
104. *Ibid.*
105. *Ibid.*
106. *Ibid.*
107. *Ibid.*
108. *Ibid.*
109. *Ibid.*
110. *Ibid.*
111. *Ibid.*
112. *Ibid.*
113. *Ibid.*
114. *Ibid.*
115. *Ibid.*
116. *Ibid.*
117. *Ibid.*
118. *Ibid.*
119. *Ibid.*
120. *Ibid.*
121. *Ibid.*
122. *Ibid.*
123. *Ibid.*
124. *Ibid.*
125. *Ibid.*
126. *Ibid.*
127. *Ibid.*
128. *Ibid.*
129. *Ibid.*
130. *Ibid.*
131. *Ibid.*
132. *Ibid.*
133. *Ibid.*
134. *Ibid.*
135. *Milwaukee Sentinel.*
136. *Ibid.*
137. *Ibid.*
138. *Ibid.*
139. *Ibid.*
140. *Ibid.*
141. *Ibid.*
142. *Ibid.*
143. *Ibid.*
144. *Ibid.*
145. *Ibid.*
146. *Ibid.*
147. *Ibid.*
148. *Ibid.*
149. *Ibid.*
150. *Ibid.*
151. *Ibid.*
152. *Ibid.*
153. *Ibid.*
154. *Ibid.*
155. *Ibid.*
156. *Ibid.*
157. Wright, *A.A.*
158. *Milwaukee Journal.*
159. *Ibid.*
160. *Baseball Encyclopedia.*
161. Wright, *A.A.*
162. *Milwaukee Journal.*
163. *Ibid.*
164. *Ibid.*
165. *Ibid.*
166. *Ibid.*
167. *Ibid.*
168. *Ibid.*
169. *Ibid.*
170. *Ibid.*
171. *Ibid.*
172. *Ibid.*
173. *Ibid.*
174. *Ibid.*
175. *Ibid.*
176. *Ibid.*
177. *Ibid.*
178. Wright, *A.A.*
179. *Milwaukee Journal.*
180. *Ibid.*
181. *Ibid.*
182. *Ibid.*
183. *Ibid.*
184. *Milwaukee Sentinel.*
185. *Ibid.*
186. *Ibid.*
187. *Ibid.*
188. *Ibid.*
189. *Ibid.*
190. *Ibid.*
191. *Ibid.*
192. *Ibid.*
193. *Ibid.*
194. *Ibid.*
195. *Ibid.*
196. Wright, *A.A.*
197. *Milwaukee Sentinel.*
198. *Ibid.*
199. *Milwaukee Journal.*
200. *Ibid.*
201. *Ibid.*
202. *Ibid.*
203. *Ibid.*
204. *Ibid.*
205. *Ibid.*
206. *Ibid.*
207. Eric Goska, *Packer Legends in Facts: 75th Anniversary Edition* (Milwaukee: Tech-Data, 1993).

6 — *Borchert's*

1. *Milwaukee Journal.*
2. *Ibid.*
3. *Ibid.*
4. *Milwaukee Sentinel.*
5. *Ibid.*
6. *Ibid.*
7. *Ibid.*
8. *Ibid.*
9. *Ibid.*
10. *Ibid.*
11. *Ibid.*
12. *Ibid.*
13. *Ibid.*
14. *Ibid.*
15. *Ibid.*
16. *Ibid.*
17. *Ibid.*
18. *Ibid.*
19. *Ibid.*
20. *Ibid.*
21. *Ibid.*
22. *Ibid.*
23. *Ibid.*
24. Wright, *A.A.*
25. *Milwaukee Sentinel.*
26. Stew Thornley, "Joe Hauser, Home Run King," *Society for American Baseball Research Minor League History Journal Vol. I* (Cleveland: SABR, 1992), pp. 7–10.
27. *Milwaukee Sentinel.*
28. *Ibid.*
29. *Ibid.*
30. *Ibid.*
31. *Ibid.*
32. *Ibid.*
33. *Ibid.*
34. *Ibid.*
35. *Ibid.*
36. *Ibid.*
37. *Ibid.*
38. *Ibid.*
39. *Ibid.*
40. *Ibid.*

Notes—Chapter 7   351

41. Ibid.
42. Ibid.
43. Wright, A.A.
44. Milwaukee Sentinel.
45. Ibid.
46. Ibid.
47. Ibid.
48. Ibid.
49. Ibid.
50. Ibid.
51. Ibid.
52. Ibid.
53. Ibid.
54. Ibid.
55. Ibid.
56. Ibid.
57. Ibid.
58. Ibid.
59. Ibid.
60. Ibid.
61. Ibid.
62. Ibid.
63. Ibid.
64. Ibid.
65. Ibid.
66. Ibid.
67. Ibid.
68. Ibid.
69. Ibid.
70. Ibid.
71. Ibid.
72. Ibid.
73. Ibid.
74. Ibid.
75. Ibid.
76. Ibid.
77. Ibid.
78. Ibid.
79. Ibid.
80. Ibid.
81. Ibid.
82. Ibid.
83. Ibid.
84. Ibid.
85. Riley, Negro.
86. Milwaukee Sentinel.
87. Ibid.
88. Ibid.
89. Ibid.
90. Ibid.
91. Ibid.
92. Ibid.
93. Ibid.
94. Ibid.
95. Ibid.
96. Ibid.
97. Ibid.
98. Ibid.
99. Ibid.
100. Ibid.
101. Ibid.
102. Ibid.

103. Ibid.
104. Ibid.
105. Ibid.
106. Ibid.
107. Ibid.
108. Ibid.
109. Ibid.
110. Ibid.
111. Ibid.
112. Ibid.
113. Wright, A.A.
114. Baseball Encyclopedia.
115. Milwaukee Sentinel.
116. Milwaukee Journal.
117. Ibid.
118. Baseball Encyclopedia.
119. Minor Encyclopedia.
120. Milwaukee Journal.
121. Ibid.
122. Ibid.
123. Ibid.
124. Ibid.
125. Ibid.
126. Ibid.
127. Ibid.
128. Ibid.
129. Ibid.
130. Ibid.
131. Ibid.
132. Ibid.
133. Ibid.
134. Ibid.
135. Ibid.
136. Ibid.
137. Ibid.
138. Ibid.
139. Minor Encyclopedia.
140. Milwaukee Journal.
141. Ibid.
142. Ibid.
143. Ibid.
144. Ibid.
145. Ibid.
146. Ibid.
147. Ibid.
148. Ibid.
149. Ibid.
150. Ibid.
151. Ibid.
152. Ibid.
153. Ibid.
154. Ibid.
155. Ibid.
156. Ibid.
157. Ibid.
158. Ibid.
159. Ibid.
160. Ibid.
161. Ibid.
162. Ibid.
163. Ibid.
164. Ibid.

165. Ibid.
166. Ibid.
167. Ibid.
168. Ibid.
169. Ibid.
170. Ibid.
171. Ibid.
172. Ibid.
173. Ibid.
174. Ibid.
175. Ibid.
176. Ibid.
177. Ibid.
178. Ibid.
179. Ibid.
180. Ibid.
181. Ibid.
182. Ibid.
183. Ibid.
184. Ibid.
185. Ibid.
186. Ibid.
187. Ibid.
188. Ibid.
189. Ibid.
190. Ibid.
191. Ibid.
192. Ibid.
193. Ibid.
194. Ibid.
195. Ibid.
196. Ibid.
197. Ibid.
198. Ibid.
199. Ibid.
200. Ibid.
201. Ibid.
202. Ibid.
203. Ibid.
204. Ibid.
205. Ibid.
206. Ibid.
207. Ibid.

7—Framed in

1. Milwaukee Sentinel.
2. Wright, A.A.
3. Milwaukee Sentinel.
4. Ibid.
5. Ibid.
6. Ibid.
7. Ibid.
8. Ibid.
9. Ibid.
10. Ibid.
11. Ibid.
12. Ibid.
13. Ibid.
14. Ibid.
15. Ibid.
16. Ibid.

17. *Ibid.*
18. *Ibid.*
19. *Ibid.*
20. *Ibid.*
21. *Minor Encyclopedia.*
22. Wright, *A.A.*
23. *Milwaukee Journal.*
24. *Ibid.*
25. *Ibid.*
26. *Ibid.*
27. *Ibid.*
28. *Ibid.*
29. *Ibid.*
30. *Ibid.*
31. *Ibid.*
32. *Ibid.*
33. *Ibid.*
34. *Ibid.*
35. *Ibid.*
36. *Ibid.*
37. *Ibid.*
38. *Ibid.*
39. *Ibid.*
40. *Ibid.*
41. *Ibid.*
42. *Ibid.*
43. *Ibid.*
44. *Ibid.*
45. *Ibid.*
46. *Ibid.*
47. *Ibid.*
48. *Ibid.*
49. *Ibid.*
50. *Ibid.*
51. *Ibid.*
52. *Ibid.*
53. *Ibid.*
54. *Ibid.*
55. *Ibid.*
56. *Milwaukee Sentinel.*
57. *Ibid.*
58. *Ibid.*
59. *Ibid.*
60. *Ibid.*
61. *Ibid.*
62. *Ibid.*
63. *Ibid.*
64. *Ibid.*
65. *Ibid.*
66. *Ibid.*
67. *Ibid.*
68. *Ibid.*
69. *Ibid.*
70. *Ibid.*
71. *Ibid.*
72. *Milwaukee Journal.*
73. *Ibid.*
74. *Ibid.*
75. *Ibid.*
76. *Ibid.*
77. *Ibid.*
78. *Ibid.*
79. *Ibid.*
80. *Ibid.*
81. *Ibid.*
82. *Ibid.*
83. *Ibid.*
84. *Ibid.*
85. *Ibid.*
86. *Milwaukee Sentinel.*
87. *Ibid.*
88. *Ibid.*
89. *Ibid.*
90. *Ibid.*
91. *Ibid.*
92. *Ibid.*
93. *Ibid.*
94. *Ibid.*
95. *Ibid.*
96. Wright, *A.A.*
97. *Milwaukee Sentinel.*
98. *Ibid.*
99. *Ibid.*
100. *Ibid.*
101. *Ibid.*
102. *Ibid.*
103. *Ibid.*
104. *Ibid.*
105. *Ibid.*
106. *Ibid.*
107. *Ibid.*
108. *Ibid.*
109. *Ibid.*
110. *Milwaukee Journal.*
111. Clipping File, Art & Music Department, Milwaukee Public Library.
112. *Milwaukee Journal.*
113. *Ibid.*
114. *Ibid.*
115. *Ibid.*
116. *Ibid.*
117. *Ibid.*
118. *Ibid.*
119. *Ibid.*
120. *Ibid.*
121. *Ibid.*
122. *Ibid.*
123. *Ibid.*
124. *Ibid.*
125. *Ibid.*
126. *Ibid.*
127. *Ibid.*
128. *Ibid.*
129. *Ibid.*
130. *Ibid.*
131. *Ibid.*
132. *Ibid.*
133. *Ibid.*
134. *Ibid.*
135. *Ibid.*
136. *Ibid.*
137. *Ibid.*
138. *Ibid.*
139. *Ibid.*
140. *Ibid.*
141. *Ibid.*
142. *Milwaukee Sentinel.*
143. *Ibid.*
144. Cliff Trumpold, *Now Pitching: Bill Zuber from Amana* (Middle Amana, IA: Lakeside Press, 1992), pp. 44–48, 51, 138.
145. *Milwaukee Sentinel.*
146. *Ibid.*
147. *Ibid.*
148. *Ibid.*
149. *Ibid.*
150. *Ibid.*
151. *Ibid.*
152. *Ibid.*
153. *Ibid.*
154. *Ibid.*
155. *Ibid.*
156. *Ibid.*
157. *Milwaukee Journal.*
158. *Ibid.*
159. *Ibid.*
160. *Ibid.*
161. *Ibid.*
162. *Ibid.*
163. *Ibid.*
164. *Ibid.*
165. Wegner, "Borchert."
166. Wright, *A.A.*
167. *Milwaukee Journal.*
168. Russell Wolinsky, National Baseball Hall of Fame and Museum, death certificate in Al Sothoron file at Cooperstown, NY; phone interview, March 2002.
169. *Milwaukee Sentinel.*
170. *Ibid.*
171. *Ibid.*
172. *Ibid.*
173. *Ibid.*
174. *Ibid.*
175. *Ibid.*

8 — *Pennants 3*

1. *Milwaukee Sentinel.*
2. *Ibid.*
3. *Ibid.*
4. *Ibid.*
5. *Ibid.*
6. *Ibid.*
7. *Ibid.*
8. *Ibid.*
9. *Ibid.*
10. *Ibid.*
11. *Ibid.*
12. *Ibid.*
13. *Ibid.*

14. Ibid.
15. Ibid.
16. Ibid.
17. Ibid.
18. Ibid.
19. Ibid.
20. Ibid.
21. Ibid.
22. Ibid.
23. Baseball Encyclopedia.
24. Milwaukee Journal.
25. Ibid.
26. Ibid.
27. Ibid.
28. Ibid.
29. Ibid.
30. Ibid.
31. Bill Veeck with Ed Linn, Veeck—as in Wreck (New York: G.P. Putnam's Sons, 1962), pp. 46-80. Hereinafter cited as Veeck, Wreck.
32. Ibid.
33. Minor Encyclopedia.
34. Milwaukee Journal.
35. Ibid.
36. Ibid.
37. Baseball Encyclopedia.
38. Veeck, Wreck.
39. Milwaukee Sentinel.
40. Ibid.
41. Ibid.
42. Veeck, Wreck.
43. Milwaukee Sentinel.
44. Veeck, Wreck.
45. Milwaukee Sentinel.
46. Ibid.
47. Ibid.
48. Ibid.
49. Ibid.
50. Veeck, Wreck.
51. Milwaukee Journal.
52. Ibid.
53. Ibid.
54. Ibid.
55. Ibid.
56. Ibid.
57. Joel Cohen, Odd Moments in Baseball (New York: Scholastic, 2000).
58. Veeck, Wreck.
59. Milwaukee Journal.
60. Ibid.
61. Ibid.
62. Ibid.
63. Ibid.
64. Ibid.
65. Ibid.
66. Ibid.
67. Ibid.
68. Ibid.
69. Ibid.

70. Ibid.
71. Ibid.
72. Ibid.
73. Ibid.
74. Wright, A.A.
75. Susan E. Johnson, When Women Played Hardball (Seattle: Seal Press, 1994). Hereinafter cited as Johnson, Women.
76. Johnson, Women.
77. Ibid.
78. W.C. Madden, The All-American Girls Professional Baseball League Record Book (Jefferson, NC: McFarland, 2000). Hereinafter cited as Madden, AAGPBL.
79. Milwaukee Sentinel.
80. Ibid.
81. Ibid.
82. Ibid.
83. Ibid.
84. Ibid.
85. Encyclopedia Teams.
86. Robert Tanzilo, "Stengel Brewed Up a Title—Brewers' job was wrecked by Veeck," Milwaukee Sentinel, Monday, July 5, 1993. Hereinafter cited as Tanzilo, "Stengel."
87. Milwaukee Journal.
88. Tanzilo, "Stengel."
89. Milwaukee Sentinel.
90. Ibid.
91. Tanzilo, "Stengel."
92. Milwaukee Sentinel.
93. Ibid.
94. Ibid.
95. Ibid.
96. Ibid.
97. Ibid.
98. Ibid.
99. Madden, AAGPBL.
100. Wright, A.A.
101. O'Neal, A.A.
102. Milwaukee Sentinel.
103. Ibid.
104. Ibid.
105. Ibid.
106. Ibid.
107. Johnson, Women.
108. Tanzilo, "Stengel."
109. Ibid.
110. Ibid.
111. Milwaukee Journal.
112. Veeck, Wreck.
113. Ibid.
114. Milwaukee Journal.
115. Ibid.
116. Ibid.
117. Ibid.
118. Ibid.

119. Ibid.
120. Ibid.
121. Ibid.
122. Minor Encyclopedia.
123. Milwaukee Journal.
124. Ibid.
125. Ibid.
126. Ibid.
127. Ibid.
128. Ibid.
129. Ibid.
130. Ibid.
131. Ibid.
132. Ibid.
133. Ibid.
134. Ibid.
135. Ibid.
136. Ibid.
137. Ibid.
138. Ibid.
139. Ibid.
140. Ibid.
141. Ibid.
142. Ibid.
143. Veeck, Wreck.
144. Wright, A.A.
145. Milwaukee Journal.
146. Ibid.
147. Ibid.
148. Ibid.
149. Ibid.
150. Ibid.
151. Ibid.
152. Ibid.
153. Ibid.
154. Ibid.
155. Ibid.
156. Ibid.
157. Ibid.
158. Ibid.
159. Ibid.
160. Ibid.
161. Ibid.
162. Ibid.
163. Ibid.
164. Ibid.
165. Ibid.
166. Ibid.
167. Minor Encyclopedia.
168. Ibid.
169. Encyclopedia Teams.
170. Milwaukee Journal.
171. Ibid.
172. Ibid.
173. Ibid.
174. Ibid.
175. Veeck, Wreck.
176. Milwaukee Journal.
177. Ibid.
178. Ibid.
179. Ibid.
180. Ibid.

181. *Ibid.*
182. *Ibid.*
183. *Ibid.*
184. *Ibid.*
185. *Ibid.*
186. *Ibid.*
187. *Ibid.*
188. *Ibid.*
189. *Ibid.*
190. *Ibid.*
191. *Ibid.*
192. *Ibid.*
193. *Ibid.*
194. *Ibid.*
195. *Ibid.*
196. *Ibid.*
197. *Baseball Encyclopedia.*
198. O'Neal, *A.A.*
199. *Milwaukee Journal.*
200. *Minor Encyclopedia.*
201. *Milwaukee Journal.*
202. *Ibid.*
203. *Ibid.*
204. *Ibid.*
205. *Ibid.*
206. *Ibid.*
207. *Ibid.*
208. *Ibid.*
209. *Ibid.*
210. *Ibid.*
211. *Minor Encyclopedia.*
212. *Milwaukee Journal.*
213. *Ibid.*
214. *Ibid.*
215. *Ibid.*
216. *Ibid.*
217. *Minor Encyclopedia.*
218. *Milwaukee Sentinel.*
219. *Ibid.*
220. *Ibid.*
221. *Minor Encyclopedia.*
222. *Milwaukee Journal.*
223. *Ibid.*
224. *Ibid.*
225. *Ibid.*
226. *Ibid.*
227. *Ibid.*
228. *Ibid.*
229. *Ibid.*
230. *Ibid.*
231. *Ibid.*
232. *Ibid.*
233. *Ibid.*
234. *Ibid.*
235. *Ibid.*
236. *Ibid.*
237. *Ibid.*
238. *Ibid.*

9 — *From Curtain*

1. William A. McGeveran, Jr., ed. dir. *The World Almanac and Book of Facts 2002* (New York: World Almanac, 2002), p. 382.
2. *Minor Encyclopedia.*
3. *Encyclopedia Teams.*
4. Wright, *A.A.*
5. *Baseball Encyclopedia.*
6. *Minor Encyclopedia.*
7. *Milwaukee Sentinel.*
8. *Ibid.*
9. *Ibid.*
10. *Ibid.*
11. *Ibid.*
12. *Ibid.*
13. *Ibid.*
14. *Ibid.*
15. Thornley, *Nicollet.*
16. *Milwaukee Sentinel.*
17. *Ibid.*
18. *Ibid.*
19. *Ibid.*
20. *Ibid.*
21. *Ibid.*
22. *Ibid.*
23. *Ibid.*
24. *Ibid.*
25. *Ibid.*
26. *Ibid.*
27. *Ibid.*
28. *Ibid.*
29. *Ibid.*
30. *Ibid.*
31. *Ibid.*
32. *Ibid.*
33. Eddie Mathews and Bob Buege, *Eddie Mathews and the National Pastime* (Milwaukee: Douglas American Sports Publications, 1994), p. 50.
34. Robert W. Peterson, *Cages to Jump Shots: Pro Basketball's Early Years* (New York: Oxford University Press, 1990), p. 209.
35. *Milwaukee Sentinel.*
36. *Ibid.*
37. *Ibid.*
38. *Ibid.*
39. *Ibid.*
40. *Ibid.*
41. *Ibid.*
42. *Ibid.*
43. *Ibid.*
44. *Ibid.*
45. *Ibid.*
46. *Ibid.*
47. Wright, *A.A.*
48. *Milwaukee Sentinel.*
49. *Ibid.*
50. *Ibid.*
51. *Ibid.*
52. *Ibid.*
53. *Ibid.*
54. *Ibid.*
55. *Ibid.*
56. *Ibid.*
57. *Ibid.*
58. *Ibid.*
59. *Ibid.*
60. *Ibid.*
61. *Ibid.*
62. *Ibid.*
63. *Ibid.*
64. *Ibid.*
65. *Ibid.*
66. *Ibid.*
67. *Ibid.*
68. *Ibid.*
69. *Ibid.*
70. *Ibid.*
71. *Ibid.*
72. *Minor Encyclopedia.*
73. *Milwaukee Sentinel.*
74. *Ibid.*
75. *Ibid.*
76. *Ibid.*
77. *Minor Encyclopedia.*
78. *Milwaukee Sentinel.*
79. *Ibid.*
80. *Ibid.*
81. *Ibid.*
82. *Ibid.*
83. *Ibid.*
84. *Ibid.*
85. *Ibid.*
86. *Ibid.*
87. *Ibid.*
88. *Ibid.*
89. *Ibid.*
90. *Ibid.*
91. *Ibid.*
92. *Ibid.*
93. *Ibid.*
94. *Ibid.*
95. *Ibid.*
96. *Ibid.*
97. *Ibid.*
98. *Ibid.*
99. *Ibid.*
100. *Ibid.*
101. *Ibid.*
102. *Ibid.*
103. *Ibid.*
104. *Ibid.*
105. *Ibid.*
106. *Ibid.*
107. *Ibid.*
108. Clipping File, Art & Music Department, Milwaukee Public Library.

Bibliography

Benson, Michael. *Ballparks of North America: A Comprehensive Historical Reference to Baseball Grounds, Yards and Stadiums, 1845–Present.* Jefferson, NC: McFarland, 1989.
Buege, Bob. *The Milwaukee Braves: A Baseball Eulogy.* Milwaukee: Douglas American Sports Publications, 1988.
Cohen, Joel. *Odd Moments in Baseball.* New York: Scholastic, 2000.
Dewey, Donald, and Acocella, Nicholas. *Encyclopedia of Major League Baseball Teams.* New York: HarperCollins, 1993.
Filichia, Peter. *Professional Baseball Franchises from the Abbeville Athletics to the Zanesville Indians.* New York: Facts on File, 1993.
Frommer, Harvey. *Primitive Baseball: The First Quarter Century of the National Pastime.* New York: Atheneum, 1988.
Guschov, Stephen D. *The Red Stockings of Cincinnati: Base Ball's First All Professional Team.* Jefferson, NC: McFarland, 1998.
Hershberger, Chuck. *The Sports Hall of Oblivion.* Where, MI: Self-published, 1985.
Hoffmann, Gregg. *Down in the Valley: The History of Milwaukee County Stadium—The People, the Promise, the Passion.* Milwaukee: Milwaukee Brewers Baseball Club and Milwaukee Journal Sentinel, 2000.
Johnson, Lloyd, and Miles Wolff. *The Encyclopedia of Minor League Baseball.* Durham, NC: Baseball America, 1993.
Johnson, Susan E. *When Women Played Hardball.* Seattle: Seal Press, 1994.
Levy, Alan H. *Rube Waddell: The Zany, Brilliant Life of a Strikeout Artist.* Jefferson, NC: McFarland, 2000.
Light, Jonathan Fraser. *The Cultural Encyclopedia of Baseball.* Jefferson, NC: McFarland, 1997.
Madden, W.C. *The All-American Girls Professional Baseball League Record Book.* Jefferson, NC: McFarland, 2000.
_____. *The Women of the All-American Girls Professional Baseball League: A Biographical Dictionary.* Jefferson, NC: McFarland, 1997.
_____, and Patrick J. Stewart. *The Western League: A Baseball History, 1885 through 1998.* Jefferson, NC: McFarland, 2001.
Mathews, Eddie, and Buege, Bob. *Eddie Mathews and the National Pastime.* Milwaukee: Douglas American Sports Publications, 1994.
Nemec, David. *The Beer and Whisky League.* New York: Lyons & Burford, 1994.
Obojski, Robert. *Bush Leagues.* New York: Macmillan, 1975.
O'Neal, Bill. *The American Association: A History, 1902–1991.* Austin, TX: Eakin Press, 1991.
Riley, James A. *The Biographical Encyclopedia of the Negro Baseball Leagues.* New York: Carroll & Graf, 1994.

Ryczek, William J. *When Johnny Came Sliding Home: The Post–Civil War Baseball Boom, 1865–1870.* Jefferson, NC: McFarland, 1998.
Seymour, Harold. *Baseball: The Early Years.* New York: Oxford University Press, 1960.
____. *Baseball: The Golden Age.* New York: Oxford University Press, 1971.
Thornley, Stew. *On to Nicollet: The Fame and Glory of the Minneapolis Millers.* Minneapolis: Nodin Press, 1988.
Trumpold, Cliff. *Now Pitching: Bill Zuber from Amana.* Middle Amana, IA: Lakeside Press, 1992.
Veeck, Bill with Ed Linn. *Veeck — as in Wreck.* New York: G.P. Putnam's Sons, 1962.
Wright, Marshall D. *The American Association: Year-by-Year Statistics of the Baseball Minor League, 1902–1952.* Jefferson, NC: McFarland, 1997.
____. *The International League: Year-by-Year Statistics, 1884–1953.* Jefferson, NC: McFarland & Co., 1998.
____. *The National Association of Base Ball Players, 1857–1870.* Jefferson, NC: McFarland, 2000.

Articles

Anderson, Harry H. "The Ancient Origins of Baseball in Milwaukee," *Milwaukee History.* Milwaukee: Milwaukee County Historical Society, Summer 1983.
Coenen, Greg. "Milwaukee Baseball: Before the Turn of the Century," *All-Star Souvenir Magazine 1975.* Milwaukee: Milwaukee Brewers Baseball Club, 1975.

Special References to Individual Brewer Players

Levine, Peter. (Batting champion George Stone and catcher Broadway Alec Smith, pp. 101–102) *Ellis Island to Ebbets Field: Sports and the American Jewish Experience.* New York: Oxford University Press, 1992.
Schoor, Gene, with Henry Gilfond. (Jim Thorpe's time in Milwaukee, pp. 130, 135) *The Jim Thorpe Story: America's Greatest Athlete.* New York: Julian Messner, 1951.
Slater, Robert. (Biography of George Stone, pp. 213–214) *Great Jews in Sports.* Middle Village, NY: Jonathan David Publishers, 1983.

Yearbooks and Guides

The old minor league Milwaukee Brewers yearbook collection and clipping file in the Art & Music Department, Milwaukee Public Library.
The Spalding Official Baseball Guides 1884–1885. Chicago & New York: A.G. Spalding & Bros.

Non-Baseball Books

Langill, Ellen, and Jensen, Dave. *Milwaukee 150: The Greater Milwaukee Story.* Milwaukee: Milwaukee Publishing Group, 1996.
McCann, Dennis. *The Wisconsin Story: 150 Stories, 150 Years.* Milwaukee: Milwaukee Journal Sentinel, 1998.

Index

Aaron, Hank 6, 12
Abbaticchio, Ed 94–95
Abendroth, Manager (U.W.) 151
Abernathy, Ted 266
Acosta, Julio 279, 282, 289, 292–293 300, 327
Acosta, Melito 216
Adams, Ace 296
Adams, "Offside" 134
Adams, Spence 221–222
Addis, Bob 314, 317
Adkins, Doc (Babe) 105
Adlam, Jimmy 255, 298, 327
Ahlf, Louis 260
Akin, pitcher 130
Alamada, Mel 243
Albany (I.L.) 244
Alberts, Gus 50, 52–53, 56–57, 62, 64
Albuquerque Dukes (W.T.-N.M.L.) 309
Alexander (pitcher) 51
Alexander, Bob 324
Alexander, Dale 254
Alexander, Grover Cleveland 232, 332
Alexander, Nin 39
Alhambra Theater (Milwaukee) 80, 119, 230
All-American Girls Professional Baseball League 248, 281, 284, 287, 313, 317, 336
All-Milwaukee Barnstormers 220, 229
All-Stars (Milwaukee) 255
Allen, Bill 327, 334
Allen C(hester) B. 7–9, 12
Allen, Nick 196, 213, 220
Allen, R., Jr. 16, 21–22
Alloway, pitcher 103
Alsted, H. P. 43
Alston, Walter 305, 311, 324
Altizer, Dare Devil Dave 160, 241

Altrock, Nick 103, 105, 159, 200, 263
American Association (major) 30, 34, 39, 41, 45–46, 48–49, 52, 54–56, 59–62, 65, 82
American Association (minor) 91–92, 94–97, 101–104, 106–107, 114–115, 120–122, 128–129, 133, 135–137, 139–141, 143–145, 147, 149, 152, 154, 157–159, 166–167, 173–175, 181, 183, 185, 191–192, 197, 199, 202, 208–209, 211–216, 218, 221, 229, 235–236, 240–242, 244–245, 249–253, 257–261, 264, 266–268, 270, 273, 276–280, 283, 285–287, 290, 292–294, 296, 298, 300–301, 304–308, 311–315, 317, 320–323, 325, 329–332, 334
American Eagles (team) 38
American Federation of Labor 199
American Football League 267
American League 25; founding in Milwaukee 90–92, 97, 101, 106, 112, 116, 123, 127, 132–141, 143, 154, 161, 200, 210, 221, 231–232, 260, 295–296, 312, 315, 328, 331
American Negro League 258
Anderson, Andy 184
Anderson, Bobby 280
Anderson, Gertrude 183
Anderson, Harold 308
Anderson, Harry H. 10
Anderson, Howard 327, 330
Anderson, John 92, 94–96, 99, 119
Anderson, Varney 44

Anderson, Vivian 284
Andrews, "Uncle Tom" 189
Anson, Cap 41, 55–56, 62, 64, 72, 75, 190, 269
A.O. Smith welders (Milwaukee) 226
Appalachian League 306, 326
Appleton (W.-I.L.) 152; Papermakers (W.S.L.) 277, 311, 328
Archambault, E.J. 154
Ardizoia, Rinaldo 274
Ardner, Joe (Old Hoss) 49
Armstrong, George 210, 213
Arundel Tug 40, 47
Association Park (Kansas City) 158
Athletic Park (Milwaukee) 46–48, 52, 56, 58, 62, 68, 91, 102–104, 106–109, 114, 116, 120, 122, 124, 127, 129, 134–135, 137, 142, 146–148, 151–152, 154, 156, 160–161, 166–167, 174, 177, 181, 186, 189–190, 192–193, 195–197, 199–203, 208, 210, 212–216, 218–219, 222–224, 246, 268
Atlanta (S.L.) 107, 197; Crackers 319, 322, 327, 330
Atlas Prager Beer 301
Attendance Cup 273
Auby, George 151
Aucoin, Alvin 309
Auer, Louis 31
Auer Avenue Park (Milwaukee) 265
Aurora Blues (W.-I.L.) 152
Austin, Henry 21
Austin Pioneers (B.S.L.) 315
autos, first in Milwaukee 92
Ayau, Vernon 181
Ayers, Doc 197

357

Baars, Arnold 214
Bach, Eddie 87
Bader's bowling alley (Milwaukee) 68
Badger Music Publishing Co. 249
Badgro, Morris "Red" 224
Bading, Mayor Gerhard 164
Bagby, Jim, Jr. 307
baggataway (lacrosse) 3
Bagnall, Benjamin 8
Baker (Secretary of War) 186
Baker, Bonnie 284
Baker, Floyd 296–297
Baker, George 45
Baker, Kirtley 68–70, 72
Baker, Oscar 250
Baldowsky "Baldy," Fred 202, 205
Baldwin, Charles Busted "Lady" 33, 35, 38
Baldwin, Clarence "Kid" 33, 35–36
Baldwin, Frank 314
Baldwin, Mark "Fido" 33
Ball, Neil 77
Ball, Philip De Catesby 221, 224, 234, 241, 242, 299
Ball Players Protective Association 93
Ballou, Win 221–223
Baltimore American 132
Baltimore Monumentals (U.A.) 33, 35
Baltimore Orioles (major A.A. to N.L.) 60, 84
Baltimore Orioles (A.L.) 75, 96, 99
Baltimore Orioles (I.L.) 230, 234, 255, 309, 317–318
Bankhead, Dan 324
Bankhead, Fred 291
Bannister, Al 274
Barbeau, Jap 161, 164–166, 180–181, 197, 204
Barber, Ethel 269
Barclay, (William) H. 7–9
Barna, Babe 331
Barnacle, Bill 310, 322
Barnes, Fred 76, 78, 80, 88, 91, 106
Barnes, John 67
Barnes, Virgil 194, 224
Barnes Hospital (St. Louis) 234
Barney, Marion 162
Barnhill, Dave "Impo" 315
Barnickel gym (Milwaukee) 102
Barnie, Bald Billy 68
Barrer, Lefty 230
Barrett, Jimmy 143, 148–153, 159
Barrow, Ed 167

Barry, Jack "Shad" 142, 145, 211
Barry, Mal 184, 187
Bartlesville Pirates (K-O-M L) 309
Bartz, Roman 219
Basinski, Ed 296
"basket ball" 78, 91
Basso, Jim 318, 320, 323, 325, 327–328
Bateman, Quate 108, 119–120, 123–125, 131–132, 153
Bauer, Hank 302, 307
Baugh, Sammy 260
Bauman, Henry 155
Bauman, Joe 307
Bauswine (umpire) 119
Bay City (Nw.L.) 31
Bay View (Milwaukee) 39, 42
Bay Views club 40
Bayless, Dick 167
Beall, John 161–162, 166–167, 172–173, 180, 186
Beard, Ralph 329
Beardsley Hotel (Champaign, Ill.) 140
Beaumont, Clarence "Ginger" 82–84, 153, 267, 269
Beaumont Exporters (T.L.) 217
Beaver Dam: R.V.L. 267; Wisc. club 70
Beaver Gas & Oils (Milwaukee club) 249
Beck, Clyde 216
Beck, William 8–10
Beck, Zinn 183–185
Becker (player) 153
Becker, Heinz 272, 276, 279, 283–284, 286, 289, 296, 301–304, 306, 308–309, 328
Becker, Joe 259–260, 326
Beckley, Jake 47, 136, 143
Bedient, Hugh 178, 197
Beer, Joe 238
"Beer City," Milwaukee's reputation 65, 238–239, 312
Behel, Steve 35, 40
Beitzinger, Tony 273
Bejma, Ollie 239
Bell, George 187–188
Bell, Herman 210
Bell, Lester 206–208, 326
Bellan, Esteban "Steve" 20–21
Beloit, Wis. (spring training site) 185–186
Beloit Fairies (industrial team) 177, 186–187, 201, 205, 224
Bendinger, Henry 241, 243, 246–247, 251, 253–254, 259, 261, 267–271, 304

Bengough, Benny 230
Bennett, Charlie 25–28, 98
Bennett, Cy 153
Bennett, F(red) 227–228
Bennett, Herschel 221
Bennett Field (Detroit) 98
Benton, Stan "Rabbit" 227
Berg, Joe 164, 166
Berger, Heinie 177
Berger, John 62
Berger, Wally 255
Berghammer, Marty 165, 181, 204, 225–231, 233–234, 241, 247, 310
Berghammer, Mr. & Mrs. Pete 231
Berghausen, Whitey 229
Berly, Johnny 274–275
Bernard, E.F. 200
Berry, Jittery Joe 280
Bescher, Bob 184–185, 188
Bettencourt, Larry 230, 239
Bettenhausen, Tony 302
Betzel, Bruno 216, 235
Beville, Monte 122, 124–125, 129, 132, 134, 137–138
Bevis (pitcher) 72
Beyersdorf, Mrs. Rodger 273
Bialk, Roman 230
Bianclana, Joe 311
Bickford, Vern 301–305, 317
bicycling boom 63, 66
Biemiller, Pie 219
Bierbauer, Lou 93
Bierhalter, "Two Bits" (umpire) 152, 156, 268
Big State League 315, 318, 326
Bigbee, Carson "Skeeter" 198, 281
Bigbee, Lyle 198, 205, 281
Biggs, Arky 291
Binghamton Triplets (E.L.) 326
Binks, George 286, 289
Birdsall, Dave 20–22
Birmingham Barons (S.A.) 185
Bishop, Max 210
Bissonette, Del 315, 326
Black Sox scandal 167, 187, 191–193, 196, 208, 244
Blackburne, Russell "Lena" 160, 164, 169, 198, 213
Blaeholder, George 257, 261, 264, 267, 269, 271–272
Blake, Ed 327, 332, 334–336
Blatz, Ralph 227, 230, 232
Blatz Bock Beer 86
Blatz Malt Extract 210
Block, Jim 132, 137
Bloomington club 47
Bloxsom, Dan 227–230, 328

Bluege, Ossie 258
Bluege, Otto 258
Bluejacket, Jim 179–180
Bluitt, Virgil (umpire) 258
Blumenfeld, F. P. 164
Boardman, M.A. 22
Bocek, Milt 250
Boggs, G. 203
Boggs, Wade 20
Bohn, John L. (mayor) 282, 293, 301
Bolan, Patrick 70
Boley, Dr. Michael 229, 231–232
Bollweg, Don 332, 335
Bonds, Barry 307
Bone, George 100
Boone, Danny 216
Boone, Ike 205
Borchers, George 73
Borchert, Florence 209
Borchert, Otto 189, 191–194, 197–201, 203–207, 209–222, 232, 234–235, 245–246, 260, 299
Borchert, Mrs. Ruby (Idabel) 219, 242–243, 260
Borchert Field (Milwaukee) 228, 232, 236–240, 243–244, 251–252, 254, 256, 258, 260–261, 263, 265, 267–273, 276–280, 282, 284–285, 291, 293–294, 297, 300, 302, 305, 310–311, 315–316, 319, 323, 327–328, 330–332, 334–336
Bordagaray, Frenchy 302
Bordetzki, Antonio 209
Bosse Field (Evansville) 187
Boston (A.L.) 96, 99, 103, 106–107, 114, 116, 120, 132–134, 141, 198, 202–203, 220, 224, 231, 236, 244, 258, 268, 319, 323, 328
Boston Beaneaters (N.L.) 49, 96
Boston Braves (N.L.) 169, 172, 193, 236, 240, 255, 283, 289, 298–300, 305–306, 308–309, 311–313, 316, 318, 320, 323, 327–330, 332, 336
Boston Globe 100, 116
Boston Red Caps (N.L.) 26
Boston Red Stockings (N.L.) 50, 62
Boston Reds (major A.A.) 59–60
Boston Traveler 320
Bosworth, F. J. 6, 8–9
Botkin, A.C. 17–18
Boudreau, Lou 283
Bowers, Howard 230

Bowler, Patrick 218
Boyer, Jim (umpire) 274
Boyle (umpire) 204
Braby, Ward 229
Braby, Wilbur 190, 213, 221
Bradley of Sioux City 52
Bradley, Bill 202
Brady, Bob 301
Brady, James 57
Brainard, "Count" Asa 23
Bramham, W.G. 279, 298–299
Brand, Cad 98, 105, 111, 113, 124, 138, 141, 142, 150, 161, 168, 170–172, 179, 195, 201
Branum, Dud 244
Braskett, Elizabeth 183
Bratchi, Bratwurst 178
Braun, Buster 160, 164, 167, 169, 173, 178, 204, 222
Braun, Silver 113
Braves Field (Boston) 200, 317, 319
Braxton, Garland 236, 239–240, 242, 245, 250
Breen, Silver 150
Brennan, Frank 174
Brennan, Hugh 187–188
Brennan (umpire) 48
Brenzel, Bill 249, 254–255, 259
Bresnahan, Roger 141, 178, 192
Brewer, John 236
Brewer Boosters 269
"Brewers": first air trip 331; first mention as 46, 54; permanently 65
brewing industry 46, 238, 296, 301
Brewster, Charlie 295, 297, 327
Bridgeport Americans (E.L.) 191
Brief, Bunny 161, 196, 200, 209–210, 212, 214, 220, 222, 227, 259, 262, 296, 331
"Bright Spot" civic campaign 134, 139–140
Briscoe, Mike (umpire) 330
Bristol (Tenn.) Twins 326
Britton, Mrs. Helen 155
Brooklyn (N.L.) 83–84, 95–96, 102, 134, 180, 206, 221, 226, 257, 265, 283, 288, 296, 300, 305, 312, 317, 325
Brooklyn Atlantics' game at Milwaukee 14–17, 19–20, 22, 25–26, 59
Brooklyn Bridegrooms (N.L.) 68, 82
Brooklyn Excelsiors 5, 11

Brooks, Mandy 220, 246
Brosius, George 17, 186
Brotherhood War 53
Broughton, Cal 31–33, 41, 43–45, 47, 49–50, 53
Brouthers, Big Dan 60
Brown, Arthur G. 136–137
Brown, George A. 290
Brown, Mordecai "Three-Fingered" 184
Brown, John, execution 5
"Brownie" (sports editor) 147, 149, 156, 172
Brush, John T. 65, 78, 90
Bruton, Bill 327–328, 333–335
Bruyette, Ed 100
Bryan, W.C. 47–48
Bryce, T. J. 129
Buckenberger, Al 41, 74
Buckley, George? 57
Buckner, "Docktah" (George Washington or Harry) 218, 227, 232, 235, 240, 242, 253–254, 260
Buckwalter (catcher) 121
"Buehl," Bob 314
Buell, Arden 109, 129
Bues, Artie 192, 205
Buffalo: (A.L.) 93–94, 96; (E.L.) 82, 102, 132, 141; (N.L.) 31; (P.L.) 74, 89; (W.L.) 85–86, 89–90
Buffalo Bill's Wild West Show 157
Buffalo Bisons: (I.L.) 221, 234, 253, 255–256, 265, 309
Buffalo Courier 89
Buffalo Express 91
Buffinton, Charlie 60
Buker, Cy 306–307
Burdette, Lew 316
Burdick, Bill 52
Burg, Pete 103
Burghardt Sporting Goods (Milwaukee) 231
Burke, Eddie 56
Burke, Jimmy 92, 96, 99, 131, 134, 136, 206
Burkett, Jesse 56
Burlington (C.A.) 139
Burnham Field (Milwaukee) 265
Burns, Bill 166
Burns, Dick 34, 38
Burns, Tom 102
Burrell, Henry 61–62
Burris, Paul 307–310, 318, 321–325
Busch, Adolphus 65
Bush, George C. 77, 80
Bush, Ownie (Donie) 217
"Bushville" 3

Butler, Art 191–192
Byrne, Tommy 303

Caldwell, Earl 233, 278, 282, 286
Calvary Cemetery (Milwaukee) 233
Camnitz, Howie 130
Camp Reno grounds (Milwaukee) 13–14, 19
Campion, W.J. 56–58
Canadian (or Ontario) League 34
Canavan, Jimmy 59–60
Cannon, Ray 185
Cantillon, Mike 122, 127, 132, 134–135, 149
Cantillon, Pongo Joe 39, 72, 78, 93, 105–108, 112–117, 119–122, 124–137, 141, 149, 151, 154–155, 158, 163–164, 172, 175, 190–191, 200, 202, 204, 212–213, 216, 313
Capital City Base Ball Club (Madison) 16–19
Capron, Ralph 185
Carbine, John 25
Carey, George "Scoops" 67–68
Carey, Max 284–287
Carleton, Tex 261–265
Carley, William 97
Carney, Jack 59
Carney, Pat 76
Carpenter, Michael 154
Carr, Charlie 133, 139
Carr, Joe 232
Carroll, Fred 51
Carroll, Parke 316
Carter, Jimmy 331
Cartwright, Alexander 4
Cartwright, Jumbo Ed 49
Caruthers, Parisian Bob 73, 75
Carver, Raymond T. 164
Casey, Bob 290
Casey, Tom 278
Cassidy (player) 76
Castro, Fidel 20
Cavaretta, Phil 245, 330
Caylor, O.P. "Ollie" 35
Cedar Rapids (M.V.L.) 221
Celler, Congressman 321
Central Association 139
Central League 165, 245
"Centurama" (Milwaukee) 298
Cerv, Bob 316, 320–321, 335
Chadwick, Henry 71, 132
Chance, Frank 106, 148
Chandler (player) 8
Chandler, Happy 291, 310, 318

Chandler, Harry 25
Chapman, Homer 295
Chapman, Jack 14, 26–27
Chapman, Ken 303
Chapman, Lou 328
Chapman, Ray 156
Chappelle, Alex "Larry" 156, 160–161, 169, 178
Charles, Chappy 150, 155
Charleston (W.V.) Senators: (M.A.L.) 245; (minor A.A.) 331
Chech, Charlie 107, 135, 145
Chesebro, Earl 190, 241
Chesebro, Jack 123
Chicago (U.A.) 35
Chicago American Giants (Negro) 258, 263, 291
Chicago Base Ball Club 12
Chicago Black Hawks (N.H.L.) 308
Chicago Colored Unions club 99
Chicago Colts (N.L.) 55, 64, 106, 190
Chicago Cubs 106, 137, 148, 161, 177–178, 187, 216, 220, 232, 237, 245, 267–272, 279, 281–283, 287–289, 293, 296, 299, 306, 318, 323, 328–331
Chicago Maroons (University team) 87, 148; (W.A.) 46–48
Chicago Orphans (N.L.) 78, 84, 94, 97, 100
Chicago Tribune 175, 234
Chicago Union Giants (Negro) 154, 156
Chicago West Ends 25
Chicago White Sox 89, 109, 115–116, 128–129, 132, 137, 154, 157, 161, 167, 169, 181, 184, 187–188, 193–194, 199, 211, 215, 233, 242, 249, 271, 289, 295–296, 299, 328, 331–332
Chicago White Stockings: (A.L.) 90, 92–100; (N.L.) 25–26, 30, 41–42, 47, 60
Chicago Whitings 41
Chivington, Tom 122, 133, 136, 147, 152, 159, 167, 172, 234
Christensen, Cuckoo 222, 227, 230–234, 237, 239–240
Christiansen, Ike 97
Christman, Mark 314, 326
Cicotte, Eddie 191
Cincinnati Commercial-Tribune 76
Cincinnati Outlaw Reds (U.A.) 34

Cincinnati Red Stockings 18, 22–25, 31, 71; (major A.A.) 35, 52, 59, 71; (N.L.) 26–27
Cincinnati Reds 65–66, 78, 90, 115, 141, 148–151, 158, 165–166, 174, 183, 185, 198, 205, 209, 266, 310, 329–330
Cione, Jean 317
Cissa, Al 192
City National Bank (Milwaukee) 271–272
Civil War effect on game 12–13
Clark (player) 21
Clark (senator, Montana) 95
Clark, Big Bill 91–93
Clark, Bob 198
Clark, Charles W. 96, 102
Clark, Dad 58
Clark, Harry "Pep" 108, 116, 120, 123–130, 134–137, 145, 154, 156–162, 164–166, 168–179, 197–203, 205–206, 208–212, 216, 219, 222, 241, 256, 268
Clark, Miss Olive 110
Clarke, F. 7–9
Clarke, Fred 166, 175
Clarke, Grey 271–272, 275
Clarkson, Buzz 317–318, 322–323, 325, 327–330, 332–336
Clarkson, John 42, 330
Clausen, Fred "Fritz" 57, 61
Claxton, Jimmy 181
Clayton (umpire) 234
Cleaver, Herman 63
Clemons, Verne 207
Cleveland (A.L.) 76–77, 93, 95–96, 98–99, 102, 112, 119, 161, 169, 186, 188, 197, 200, 202, 213, 222, 236, 257–259, 266–267, 283, 291, 297, 301, 308, 313, 320
Cleveland, Elmer 44, 52
Cleveland Forest City club 34, 37
Cleveland Spiders (N.L.) 66, 90; (minor A.A.) 165, 167, 169–170, 172, 175, 331
Clingman, Billy 62, 66, 102–107, 122, 159
Clinton, Bill 32
Clymer, Bill 132
Coastal Plain League 327
Coate, Capt. 7–9
Cobb, Herb "Sonny Boy" 225, 228, 231
Cobb, Ty 122, 148, 165, 180
Cockman, Jim 103, 110, 122, 142

Index

Cohen, Andy 308
Cole, King 161
Coleman, Bob 299, 306, 313–317, 319, 326
Coleman, Hamp 324
Collins, (Texan) Eddie 142
Collins, Jimmy 141
Colorado League 34
Colorado Springs Gazette 85
Colorado Springs Millionaires (W.L.) 100, 103, 108, 110, 113
Colored Columbia Giants 92, 95
"Colored National Baseball League" 203–204
Columbia Hospital (Milwaukee) 328
Columbian Exposition (Chicago) 65
Columbus (major A.A.) 60, 62
Columbus (W.L.) 61–63, 72–73, 80, 83, 85, 89–90, 106
Columbus Senators: minor A.A. 106, 109–110, 113–114, 118–124, 127, 130–135, 137, 141, 145, 149, 160–163, 165, 175, 178–181, 183–184, 192, 196–197, 199–200, 206, 208, 210–211, 215, 219–220, 222, 228; Redbirds 231, 240, 244, 250, 259–261, 265, 274, 276–277, 280, 285, 288, 291–292, 297, 301, 303–306, 308, 321, 329
Comiskey, Charlie 34, 69, 71, 76, 79, 90, 92, 94–95, 97, 109, 112
Comiskey Park (Chicago) 169, 247, 296
Comstock, Cis 170, 278
Congalton, Bunk 89–90, 110, 149
Conley, Gene 327, 329, 331–336
Connecticut League 112, 181
Connery, Bob 232
Connolly, Bud 211, 232, 234, 240, 265
Connolly, Tom (umpire) 99
Connors, Buck 135
Connors, Joe 98
Connors, Merv 276–277, 279
Conroy, Wid 92, 96, 100, 319
Constantine, Henriette 269
Constantine, Jeannette 269
Cook, Harry 103
Cook, Nelson P. 136
Cooke, Jack Kent 321
Cooney, Jimmy, Jr. (Scoops) 190–192, 194, 196, 207, 234
Cooney, Jimmy, Sr. 190
Cooper, Mort 259
Cooperstown, N.Y. 37, 49
Corbitt, Claude 304
Corcoran, Con 109, 154–155
Corriden, Red 229
Corning (N.Y.) Athletics 329
Cottrill, J(edd) P.C. 7, 9
Coughlin, Roundy 323
Counsell, Craig 196
Counsell, William 196
County Clare, Ireland 37
County Stadium (Milwaukee) 316, 324, 326–327
Covington, Steve 190
"Crabill, Rev. Mr." (pitcher) 109
Crandall, Delmar 309, 317
Crane, Fred 15–16
Craver, Bill 26
Cream City Athletic Club 189
Cream City Base Ball Club 13–19, 21–26
"Cream City" brick 3–4
Cream City Grounds 14, 19
Creighton, James 5, 11
cricket 4, 12
Cronin, Joe 222
Cronin, John 89
Cross Lutheran Church (Milwaukee) 77
Crossley, W.C. 49–50
Crothers, Dug 45
Crouch, Jack 230, 236
Crouse, Buck 256
Crowder, Maj. Gen. Enoch 187
Crowe, George 314, 318–320, 322–323, 325, 327, 333
Crowell, Billy 52
Crowley, Jerry 268
Cruise, J. C. 9
Cuba, baseball in 37
Cuban Winter League 325
Cubans in modern baseball 158
Culler, Dick 284, 286, 289
Cullop, Nick (pitcher) 210
Cullop, Nick "Tomato Face" 209, 215, 244, 287, 289–308, 311, 313, 317–318, 326
Cullop, Nick, Jr. 293
Cumiskey, Eddie 133
Cummings, Candy 11
Curtis, Charles 237
Curtis, Cliff 108, 119–120, 123–125, 133–137, 139, 145
Curtis, Jim 54
Cushman, Charlie 53–59, 61–63, 65–67, 78, 159

Cushman, Ed 32–34, 45, 48–49, 56, 61
Cusick (pitcher) 38–39, 47
Cusick (umpire) 48
Cuthbert, Ned 19
Cutting, Ralph 148, 151, 160–161, 163–166, 169, 172–173, 246
Cuyler, Kiki 198

Dahlen, Bad Bill 60, 64
Daily, One-Arm 39–40
Dairies muni club: Dallas (T.L.) 116, 180, 216–217; Eagles 317; Milwaukee 244; Rebels 271, 295
Dallas (T.L.) 116, 180, 216–217; Eagles 317; Rebels 271, 295
Dalrymple, Abner 25–28, 53–54, 56–58, 60–61, 64, 66
Daly, Tom 75–76, 79, 82–84
Damman, Wee Willie 73
Dandridge, Ray 315, 322–323
Danforth, Dave 169, 213–214, 216, 220
Daniels, Jack 314
Dark, Alvin "Blackie" 299, 301, 303, 305
Davenport (W.A.) 49
Davenport, Dave 201
Davidson, W.L. 178
Davidson Theater (Milwaukee) 188, 190, 222–223, 262
Davies, George Washington 51, 56–58
Davis, Gerald 230
Davis, Hy 223
Davis, Jim 303
Davis, Wendell "Bill" 293
Dayton club 92
Dean, Dizzy 301
Decker, George 78
DeGroff, Rube 151
Deifert, H. 41
Delahanty, Jim 104
Delahanty, Tom 75–76
Delaney (scorer) 16
Delany, J.J. 159, 176, 200
Delhi, Flame 174
Dellios, Pete 333
Delsing, Jim 296
Dempsey-Tunney fight 217, 299
Dempsey-Willard fight 189
Denning, Otto 293
Dennison Hotel (Cincinnati) 66
Denver: (W.A.) 58, 64; (W.L.) 50–51, 53–56, 100–102, 104–106, 110–114, 325

362　Index

Depression 63, 231, 233, 237, 241, 244–246, 264, 270, 312
Derr, Dolly (umpire) 216
DeShong, Jimmy 265
Des Moines: (Nw.L.) 43–45; (W.A.) 46–49, 51–54, 56; (W.L.) 100–101, 103, 108, 111, 113, 122, 124, 127–129, 133–134, 154, 230, 326
Detore, George 243, 246–247, 249–251, 253–254, 256–257, 259, 305, 308, 326
Detroit Creams (W.L.) 65, 67
Detroit Tigers: (A.L.) 25, 94–95, 97–99, 102, 116, 122, 135, 143, 158, 167, 199, 227, 245, 249, 256–257, 269, 299, 330, 332; (W.L.) 69–70, 73, 77–78, 80, 83, 89–90
Detroit Wolverines (N.L.) 31, 34, 38, 42, 67
Devine, Harry J. 252
Devine's Eagles Ballroom, George 258
Devision 998 club 249
Devlin, Jim 26
DeVogt, Rex 164
Dexter, Charlie 124
Dickerson, George 182
Dickey, Bill 213
Dickshot, Johnny 297, 301
Didrikson, Babe 240
Diggins, Dave 94
Diller (umpire) 61
Dillhoefer, Pickles 179
Dillon, Pop 98
DiMaggio, Dom 328
DiMaggio, Joe 255
Dittmer, Jack 328
Doak, Bill 198
Dockins, George 280
Dodge, Jimmy 194, 197
Dodge, Sam 198
Dodsworth, (Wm. H.) 21–22
Doerr, Bobby 328
Doheny, Ed 94
Dolan, Cozy 185, 187, 208–209
Doljack, Frank 245, 247
Doljack, Joe 247
Donahue, Jiggs 107–109, 112–113, 115, 159, 186
Donlin, Mike 142, 220
Donnelly, Blix 327
Donnelly, Frank 117
Donovan, Dick 309, 321, 323, 334–336
Donovan, Wild Bill 180
Doubleday, Abner 4, 13
Dougherty (infielder) 39

Dougherty, Tom 108, 120, 122–128, 132, 135, 137, 144, 151–154, 156, 158, 160–161, 164–167, 174, 176, 190, 235, 246, 254
Douglas Park (Rock Island) 237
Douthard, Jackie 307
Douthit, Taylor 211–212
Dowd, Buttermilk Tommy 93
Dowling, Pete 91–92, 96, 98, 102
Downer, George F. 212
Doyle, Billy 183, 185
Doyle, Jack 132–136, 139, 232, 235, 271
Drescher (umpire) 52
Dressen, Leo 203
Drews, Frank 304
Dryden, Charley 106
Dubuque club 106, 129
Dudley, Bruce 311, 334
Duffy, Hugh 60, 96–114, 132, 154–157, 185, 198, 319
Duluth (Nw.L.) 40, 44–46, 58
Duluth Eskimos (N.F.L.) 217
DuMouchelle, Al 327, 330
Dungan, Sam 56–58, 77, 80, 90, 93, 103, 107
Dunlap, Paul 265
Dunleavy, Jack 107, 109, 113
Durham, Louis (Bull) 138–139
Duryea, Cyclone Jim 46
Dwyer, Frank 47, 59–60

Earl, Howard "Slim Jim" 58, 60–61
Earle, Billy 52–53, 58
Eastern League 32, 34, 82, 101, 132, 135–136, 157, 187, 190–191, 207, 302, 309, 314, 318, 326
[Eastern] New England League 34
Eau Claire Bears (No.L.) 296, 303, 308, 320
Eau Claire clubs 39–40, 42–43, 45–46, 144
Eaves, Vallie 275–277, 290
Eayrs, Donkey 163
Ebbets, Charles 82
Ebbets Field (Brooklyn) 161
Eckert, Al 255
Eckfords club 25
Eckhardt, Ox 255
Eclipse Park (Louisville) 46, 112, 137
Eddelman, Silent Joe 216, 220, 223
Eddinger, Jerry (umpire) 153

Edison, Thomas 64, 152, 177
Edwards, Gene 309, 314
Effenberger, Dorothy 273
Egan, Jack 134, 184–186, 189–197, 213
Ehrlich, Dr. Julius 336
Eisen, Tiby 284
Eisenhower, Dwight D. 301, 330
Eldred (player) 145
Eldred, Brick 181
Eldred, Cal 176
Eldridge, William Henry 175–176
Eline chocolate bars 210
Elks Club banquets 213, 218, 231, 265, 269, 290, 310
Ellick, Joe 28
Elliott, Claude 70, 78, 99, 103, 109–112, 115, 119
Elliott, Glenn 301–304, 306, 308, 314, 316
Ellis, George E. 69
Ely, Mrs. 80
Elysian Fields (Hoboken, N.J.) 4–5
Emmons, Norman J. 9
Empress Theater (Milwaukee) 209
Endeavor Base Ball Club of New York 21
Engel (club secretary) 70
Engle, Eleanor 330
English, Charlie 265–266
Enright, Bill 214
Enright, Buck 102
Epperly, Al "Pard" 301–302, 304, 306
Epps, Aubrey (Yo-Yo) 288
Erautt, Eddie 332, 335–336
Erickson, Eric 202
Erickson, Paul 318
Ermi, John 284
Ertman, Hank 314, 327, 329, 332, 334–335
Esler, Myron "Mush" 260, 265
Estock, George 315, 329, 334
Ethiopian Clowns (Negro club) 263
Etten, Nick 309
Evansville 31; Bees (3-I.L.) 303, 306, 309, 313, 315, 317, 319, 326–327; Evas (C.L.) 165
Evers (catcher) 106
Evers, Johnny 106
evolution of play 11
Ewing, Buck 38
Exposition Park (Kansas City) 66
Eyler (pitcher) 105

Index

Fabian, Teddy 298
Fabrique, Bunny 209
Faeth, Tony 188, 269
Fairly, Carl 279
Falch, Anton "Tony" 34, 159
Falk, Bibb 235, 310
Fargo-Moorhead Twins (No.L.) 326
Farmer, Jack 282
Farrell (secretary) 129
Federal League 165, 167, 169, 174, 178, 184, 191, 225, 268
Felber, Walter 273
Felderman, Marv 296, 298
Feller, Bob 257, 290
Felsch, Charlie 214
Fel(s)ch, Happy 160–161, 164, 169, 171–174, 179, 184, 187, 191, 199, 211, 244, 246
Fenway Park (Boston) 319
Ferguson (pitcher) 198
Ferguson, Alex 198
Ferguson, Bob "Death to Flying Things" 14–17, 20, 59–60
Fernandez, Froilan "Nanny" 306–308, 311
Fernandez, Manny 296
Feron, Bob 276, 293, 304, 334
Ferry, Cy 163, 175
Ferson, Alex 61–62
Fieber, Clarence 243
Fiene, Lou 138, 175, 177
Finneran (umpire) 207
Finnish nationalism and baseball 87, 120, 131, 264, 331
Fischer, Carl 256
Fisher, Chauncey 90
Fisher, Cherokee 25
Fisher, George "Showboat" 237
Fisher, William 156
Fitch (player) 8
Fitzgerald, Frank 154
Fletcher, Ray 303, 305
Flick, Lew 293, 296
Flippin, Lloyd 215, 220
Flood, Curt 5
Flood, Emmet T. 199
flood in Kansas 108–110
Florida International League 326
Florida State League 327
Flowers, Jake 299–300, 305, 315–316
Fluhrer, Jack 178
Flynn, John 136
Folk (Missouri governor) 131
Fond du Lac: Panthers 327, 330; (W.-I.L.) 158, 160–161; (W.S.L.) 204, 299

Fons, Al 224, 233
Fons, Louis 184
Forbes Field (Pittsburgh) 141
Force Davy "Tom Thumb" 44, 48, 50
Ford, Ed "Whitey" 316
Forest City (Cleveland club) 18
Forest City (Rockford team) 14, 19, 24
Forster, Tom 34–35, 41, 44–46
Forsythe, C. 194
Fort Smith (Ark.) Indians (W.A.) 326
Fort Wayne: Chiefs (3-I.L.) 246; Daisies (A.A.G.P.B.L.) 287; (Nw.L.) 31–32; (W.L.) 63
Fort Worth Cats (T.L.) 276, 279, 295
Foster, Andrew "Rube" 203
Fowler, Art 318, 320
Fowler, [John "Bud"] 37
Fox, Howie 304
Fox River (Waukesha, Wisc.) 275, 277
Fox Wisconsin Theater (Milwaukee) 310, 316, 325
Franklin, Manager 82, 85
Fran(t)z, Walter 123, 127
Freeman, Buck 138, 208
Freeman, Julie 50
Freeport (Ill., W.S.L.) 136
French Lick Springs, Ind. (spring training site) 133
Frick, Ford 323
Fricken, Hen 103
Friel, Bill 97, 166, 183–184, 219, 319
Friese, August W. 49, 64, 101–103
Frisch, Frankie 329
Fritsch, Walter 241
Fuller (1st baseman) 48
Fultz, Dave 92, 95, 119, 169

Gaedel, Eddie 320
Gaffke, Fabian 251, 253, 258
Gaffney (pinch-hitter) 210
Gaffney (umpire) 58
Gagne, Verne 323
Gaido, Erminio 328
Gainer, "Sheriff" Del 190–191, 195, 197
Galaszewski, "Galle" Stan 255, 264–265, 268
Gallagher, Jim 282
Gammons, Peter 87
Ganley, Bob 114
Ganzel, Babe 234, 267
Ganzel, Charlie 267
Ganzel, John 186
Garagiola, Joe 308

Garden Theater (Milwaukee) 210
Gardner (batter) 160
Gardner, Howard C. 8–9
Gartley, Perry C. 217
Garvin, Virgil (Ned) 97–99, 156, 222
Gassaway, Charlie 282, 286, 326
Gastfield, Ed 43
Gaston, Alex 190–192
"Gathering Place at the Waters" 3
Gatins, Frank 103, 112
Gaw, G. 194
Gayety Theater (Milwaukee) 228, 237
Gear, Dale 82, 104
Gearin, Dinty 190, 194, 196, 198–200, 204–205, 209, 215–216, 220, 223, 227, 229, 233–234, 259, 322, 328
Gehring, Henry 131
Genovese, Chick 293
George (pitcher) 178
George, Charlie "Greek" 273, 275–276, 327
Georgetown University team 87, 98
Georgia-Florida League 327
Gerken, George "Pickles" 220, 228, 230
German immigrants 3, 196
Gervais, Harry 177
Gettelman brewery (Milwaukee) 306
Gettman, Jake 94
Geyer, Rube 145
Gilbert, Billy 97, 100
Gilbert, Larry 163–164, 169
Gilford (umpire) 123
Giljohann, Rudolf 101G
Gilkerson Union Giants of Chicago (Negro club) 200
Gillenwater, Carden 300, 302–304, 306
Gillespie, Earl 322, 325, 331
Gillette, H. E. 59–61
Gilliam, Jim "Junior" 325
Gimbel's department store (Milwaukee) 158, 199, 265
Gionfriddo, Al 325
Gizelbach, Al 230
Glasscock, Pebbly Jack 72
Gleason, William 206
Gleason, Jim 303, 307–310, 326
Glenalvin, Bob 72–73, 75, 89
"goldball" (Wisconsin state championship) 18–19
Golden, Mike 28
Goldie, (John) 21

364   Index

Good, Wilbur 213
Goodenough, Bill 67
Goodman, Billy 303
Goodwin, Clyde 124–127, 132–133, 135
Gordon, Bob 315
Gordon, Joe 274
Gorin, Charlie 318–321, 325
Gorman, Stooping Jack 35–36
Gould, Charlie 23
Governors' Cup (minor A.A.) 251
Graham, Henry 30
Granberry, G.L. 8
Grand Avenue Grounds (St. Louis) 100
Grand Rapids: Chicks (A.A.G.P.B.L.) 287, 317; (C.L.) 245; (Nw.L.) 31–32; (W.L.) 65, 67, 70, 73, 75, 78, 90
Graney, Jack 148
Grant, Charlie 75–76
Grant, Olga 284
Grate, Don 307
Gray (3rd base) 88, 90
Gray, Gilda 214, 222, 234, 237
Gray, Pete 290, 297
Great Northern Hotel (Chicago) 69
Greb, Harry 213
Green, Danny 129–130, 132, 134, 136, 157
Green Bay: Bluejays (W.S.L.) 269, 272, 299, 311, 322, 331; (W.-I.L.) 156–157
Green Bay Packers (N.F.L.) 231, 260, 268, 303, 321, 323, 332
Gregory (catcher) 194
Griffin, Ivy 197–199, 206, 215, 217, 222, 224, 227, 229, 290, 295
Griffith, Clark 47–52, 54–56, 97, 127, 141, 161, 319
Griffore, Jack 303
Grillo, J. Edward 115, 119, 128
Grim, John 56
Grimes, Ed 227–228
Grimes, Oscar 259–260
Grimm, Charlie "Jolly Cholly" 270–276, 278–283, 287, 293, 296, 317–319, 321, 323, 325–327, 329, 332
Grimm, Fred 293
Grimm, Lillian 279, 319
Grindlay, Dr. John 274
Griswold (player) 153
Griswold, Harry 263, 295, 299, 326

Grody, Ray 316
Groh, Heinie 165, 221
Gross, Fred 85, 96–97, 99, 101–102, 106
Gruebner (shortstop) 107
Gullic, Ted 234, 237, 239, 242, 244, 249, 253, 255, 257, 261, 264–268, 271–272, 274–276, 290, 309, 326, 328
Guschov, Stephen D. 18
Guthrie, Bill (umpire) 144, 251–252
Guyon, Joe 210, 249

Haas, Bruno 211, 231
Haddix, Harvey 308
Hahn, Noodles 80
Hale, Alan 264
Hale, Roy 107
Hall, Bob 319
Hall, Charley "Sea Lion" 197, 200
Hall, George 26
Hall, Halsey 290
Halley's Comet 148
Hallman, Bill 84, 87–88, 94, 96
Hallstrom, Charlie 41
Hamburg, Charlie 61–62
Hamey, Roy 298–299
Hamilton, Jim 284
Hamlin, Luke (Hot Potato) 245, 249–250, 254–257
Hammond, Hippo 148
Hans, Sgt. Francis H. 160
Hansell (manager) 73
Hansen, L.A. 41
Hanyzewski, Ed 274
Harley, Dick 94
Harper (pitcher) 37
Harper, Harry 175
Harridge, Will 232
Harrington, Andy 157
Harrington, Billy 52, 61
Harrisburg (Pa.) Senators (Is.L.) 330
Harrison, Benjamin 61
Hart, Billy 88, 90, 112–113
Hart, Jim 41–43, 45–49, 55–56, 62, 64, 84, 92, 94
Hartford Chiefs (E.L.) 309, 314, 318, 322, 326, 330
Hartman, Fred (Dutch) 70, 72–73, 93
Hartnett, Gabby 323
Hartsel, Topsy 160
Hartsfield, Roy 309, 311, 327, 330
Haskell (umpire) 128
"Hassenpfeffer, Mr. & Mrs. Herman" 186, 195, 296, 310
Hastings, Charlie 66, 69

Hathaway, John L. 6–11, 27
Hatter, Clyde (Mad) 245, 250–251, 253–255, 257
Hauser, George 221
Hauser Joe "Unser Choe" 186–187, 190–198, 200–201, 209–210, 219–221, 224, 230, 234, 240, 246, 253, 272, 290, 299, 327
Havenor (Timme), Mrs. Agnes Malloy 154–155, 157–158, 164–165, 169, 187
Havenor, Charles S. 91, 95–96, 102, 104, 106, 109, 112–114, 127–130, 132, 134, 146–147, 149, 151, 154, 159, 165
Hawes, Bill 49–50
Hawley, Emerson "Pink" 97–98, 100, 104
Hawthorne Field (Milwaukee) 265
Hayden, Jack 161
Hayes, Gerald 142, 152
Hayne, Marcus P. 85
Hayworth, Ray 269
Head, Anne 248
Head, Margaret 248
Hearst National All-Star Classic 331
Heath, Jeff 257, 259, 275, 291, 305
Heath, Mickey 229, 244, 257, 259, 261, 264–267, 273, 282, 287, 289–290, 315
Heath, Tommy "Cracker" 315
Hedges, Alonzo 110, 115, 117
Hedges, Robert L. 136
Heil, Gov. Julius 265
Heil industrial team 277
Heilberger, Tommy 202
Heimerl, Ed 87
Helf, Hank 259, 278
Heller's Sporting Goods (Milwaukee) 330
Hemphill, Charley 166
Hemphill, Frank 108–109, 115, 118–119, 123–125, 128, 130, 132
Hempsted, H.N. 8
Hemsley, Rollie 331
Hendricks, Jack 183
Hendrickson, Don 286, 289
Hengle, Moxie 62
Henning, Oak 174
Henrich, Tommy 254, 257
Henry (centerfielder) 62–63
Herbstreith, Arnold "Happy" 193, 232, 246
Herman, Babe 226, 259
Herman, Babe (boxer) 213
Hernandez, Ramos "Chico" 261

Index 365

Hernandez, Salvador (Chico) 289
Herr, Joe 50–51
Herrmann, August "Garry" 148, 153
Herzog, Buck 141, 142, 165
Herzog, Jack 161
Heving, Joe 249–252, 254, 256–257
Hewitt, Chauncey P. 8
Hickey, John 127
Hickey, Thomas J. 75, 100–102, 106–107, 112, 147, 181, 183–184, 186–187, 191–192, 198, 203–204, 207, 219, 242, 251
Hickey Cup 199
Hicks, Bobby 296
Higby, Porter 108–109, 113
high cost of living 191
Hilgen Spring Park (Cedarburg, Wis.) 249
Hill, Carmen 217
Hill, F. H(oratio) 7
Hill, F. J. 7
Hiller, Frank 302
Hillin, Ash 236
Hines, Del 311
Hines, Paul 28
Hinkley, Rockwell 173
Hinsdale, William Courtney 269
Hite, Mabel 142
Hitler, Adolf 233, 236, 264, 272, 290–291
Hoan, Daniel Webster (mayor) 177, 182, 184, 187, 228, 250, 253, 264
Hoben, Lindsay 219
Hoblitzell, Dick 165–166
Hodapp, Johnny 213
Hoeft, Bill 317, 319
Hofer, Walter 241, 243
Hogg, Buffalo Bill 145
Hogriever, George 94–95, 100, 127, 152
Hokanson, Rudolf 243
Holbert, Bill 27–28
Holland, Joe 114, 117, 127, 132, 139, 147
Holley, Ed 250
Holly, Edward 90
Hollywood Stars (P.C.L.) 229, 311
Holmes (catcher) 38
Holmes, Ducky 149
Holmes, Tommy 327–328
Hooker, Ed 93
Hooley (player) 15–16
Hoover (umpire) 54
Hoover, Dick 325, 329, 331, 334
Hope, Eddie 242, 246, 249, 251, 254–255, 323

Hopkinsville Hoppers (Kitty L.) 263, 269
Horning, Mr. & Mrs. Paul 317
Horning, Walter 317
Hornsby, Rogers 198, 241, 289, 293, 326, 330
Hostetter, Artie 142–143, 152
Hotel English (Indianapolis) 182
Hough, Percy 314
House of David club 230, 232, 239
Houston Buffaloes (T.L.) 272
Hovlik, Joe 156–157, 159, 164, 166, 173–174, 178, 185, 246
Howard, Earl 188, 191, 195
Howe, Irwin 194
Howe, Shorty 67
Hoy, William "Dummy" 39, 43, 92, 319
Hudson, Johnny 274
Huff, George 133
Huggins, Miller 185
Hughes, Charles Evan 180
Hughes, Johnny "Runt" 157, 159, 161, 164, 169, 172, 174
Hughes, Long Tom 290
Huhn, Emil "Hap" 190–191
Hulbert, William 24
Hulswitt, Rudy 178
Hungarian Café (Milwaukee) 164
Hungling, Bernie 230
Hunter, Dorothy 284
Husting, Bert "Pete" 87, 90–91, 93–94, 96, 98, 100, 103, 156, 267
Hutchinson, Ira 242
Hutchinson, "Willie Bill" 72
Hynes, Pat 130, 133

Illinois-Missouri League 152
Indianapolis (F.L.) 158
Indianapolis Blues (N.L.) 26–28
Indianapolis Hoosiers: (A.L.) first mention as "Indians" 93, 94, 96–97; (N.L.) 47, 50; (W.L.) 34, 37, 61–63, 65–66, 68, 70, 73, 75, 77–78, 82–83, 90
Indianapolis Hoosiers/Indians (minor A.A.) 103, 112, 114, 116, 118–119, 122, 128–130, 133–135, 137–139, 141, 143, 148, 150–151, 157–158, 160, 162–163, 166–167, 172, 178, 182–183, 185, 200, 204, 210, 213, 217, 222–224, 229,

233–234, 236, 240–241, 244, 249, 254–255, 261, 268–269, 277, 279, 292, 300, 305, 307, 311, 319–320, 330–331
International Association 53
International League 167, 186, 217, 220, 223, 230, 234, 244, 251, 253, 303, 309, 317–318, 321, 324, 326
Interstate 43 (Milwaukee freeway) 336
Inter-State League 47, 97, 99, 330
Iron Brigade 12
Irwin (umpire) 156
Irwin, Arthur 122
Irwin, Tommy 259
Isbell, Frank 89, 92–93
Iversen, John C. 31–32, 36, 59–61, 83

Jackson, Bo 176, 217
Jackson, Maj. R. R. 258
Jackson, Reggie 3, 304
Jackson, Shoeless Joe 180, 211
Jaderlund, Bob 314–315
Janesville Base Ball Club (Wis.) 11, 17
Janesville Cubs (W.S.L.) 268
Janesville Mutuals 25
Jansen (umpire) 204
Janssen (police chief) 58
Jardine, John 177
Jaskulski, Ray (mascot) 254
Jefferson (Wis.) club 87
Jenkins, "Black Tom" 227, 229–230, 328
Jenkins, Curly 273
Jenkins, Geoff 229
Jenkins, Harry 306, 323
Jennings, Hughey 135
Jensen, Jackie 321
Jersey City 142; Giants (I.L.) 295
Jester, Virgil 319, 323–325, 328
Johnson, Allen 245, 257, 259
Johnson, Ban 65, 67, 69, 72–75, 78, 83, 87, 90–91, 95–97, 100
Johnson, Don 276, 328
Johnson, Ernie 309, 318, 323–325, 328
Johnson, Grant "Home Run" 75–76
Johnson, Hank 220–221
Johnson, Indian Bob 260, 297
Johnson, Jack 148, 154
Johnson, Paul 198–199, 213

Johnson, Roy 260–261, 265, 297
Johnson, Walter 206
Johnston, Doc 185–186, 197
Jolly, Dave 335–336
Jolson, Al 175
Jonas, Jimmy 160
Jones, Bert 76, 79, 110
Jones, Bumpus 89
Jones, Casey 291
Jones, Charlie 102, 104, 110, 114, 119
Jones, Davy (Kangaroo) 99
Jones, Eugene 182
Jones, Keith 317
Jones, Tom 150–151, 161, 164–165, 169
Jonnard, Clarence "Bubber" 220, 281
Jonnard, Claude 216–217, 220, 222–223, 231, 234, 281
Jordan, Michael 96
Joss, Addie 102
Jude (rightfielder) 133
Juneau, Solomon 5, 325
Juneau Park (Milwaukee) 271
Juneautown (Milwaukee) 4
Jungels, Ken 264
Junior World Series 287, 298, 313
Jurges, Billy 237
Just, Joe 259, 304, 330, 334

Kabick, Josephine 285
Kahl, Harris 245
Kaine, John L. 26–28
Kalamazoo (Nw.L) 41
Kansas City: (A.L. 1900) 93, 96; (F.L.) 158, 174; (major A.A.) 46; (U.A.) 34, 37; (W.A.) 46–49, 54–55, 58; (W.L.) 34, 37, 62–63, 65–66, 69–70, 72, 75, 80, 82, 84–86, 90, 101, 103–106
Kansas City Blues (minor A.A.) 102–104, 106, 108, 110, 115, 120, 122, 124, 127, 129–132, 134–136, 141, 143, 145, 148–152, 156–158, 160–161, 166, 174–175, 178, 180, 182, 184, 186, 192, 195–196, 198, 200, 204–205, 207–209, 211–213, 216–217, 219–220, 222–223, 228, 232, 236–237, 243, 247, 249–250, 252, 254, 258, 265, 267, 274, 280, 286–287, 291, 297, 301–303, 307, 311, 316, 319–321, 323, 329–336
Kansas City Journal 131

Kansas City Monarchs (A.N.L.) 258
Kansas City Star 241
Kansas City World 73
Karel, Judge John C. 233
Karpel, Herb 274
Katoll, John 92, 100
Katt, Ray 327
Kaufman, Andy 23
Kaukauna (Wis.) 100; (W.S.L.) 204–205
Kawakami, Tetsuharu 301
Keagle, Merle "Pat" 285
Kean, Bennie 152
Kearney, Cotton (umpire) 251
Keefe, Dave 202, 204
Keeler, Wee Willie 165
Keenan, Bronco Busting 151
Keene, Milly W. 284
Kehoe, Mack 333
Kellert, Frank 315
Kelley (umpire) 110
Kelley, Mike 120, 128–129, 131, 135, 145, 158, 160, 163, 178, 183, 191, 212, 228, 251, 260, 276, 286, 290
Kellnersville (Wis.) club 331
Kelly, King 59
Keltner, Ken 255, 258–259, 289
"Keltners" team 291
Kenna, Ed 107, 110–111, 113
Kenosha Comets (A.A.G.P.B.L.) 281, 285–287, 317
Keokuk Keokuks (W.L.) 37
Kerin (umpire) 137
Kerner, Ben 320
Kerns, Henry 160
Kerr, Buddy 320, 328
Kerr, Dickie 184, 186, 202
Kerwin, Dan 115
Kessenich, Larry 232, 237
Ketcham, Fred 93
Keystone of Philadelphia (U.A.) 32
Kiefer, Joe 196
Kilbourn (Wisconsin Dells) Independents club 30
Kilbourntown (Milwaukee) 4
Killefer, Bill 165, 167, 179, 234, 268–269
Killefer, Wade "Red" 240–241, 255, 268–269
Killen, Frank 59
Killilea (Boley), Florence 224–226, 228–229, 232–233, 235
Killilea, Harry 233
Killilea, Henry 67, 69–70, 74, 76, 78, 90, 92, 95–96,

99–100, 103, 106, 107, 110, 114, 116, 131, 187, 189, 204, 215, 222, 224, 235
Killilea, Matt 80, 85–86, 95–96, 99
King (umpire) 145
King, Gen. Charles 159, 187
King, Rufus 4–9, 11–13, 17–18, 24, 26–27, 29, 223
Kinnickinnic Field (Milwaukee) 265
Kinnickinnic River (Milwaukee) 3
Kirby (infielder) 51
Kirby House (Milwaukee) 22
Kirke, Jay 178
Kirkham, K.K. 188, 193–194, 205, 220
Kitty League 203
Klaus, Billy 323, 325, 327, 329, 334
Klawitter, Al 246
Klein, Lou 274
Klein, Richard 214
Kleinhans, Ted 258
Kleinow, Jack (Red) 127
Klem, Bill 119, 323
Kletinski, Leonard 245
Klevenow, Fred 190
Kline, "Robust Robert" 265
Kling, Johnny 72
Klinger, Max 331
Klocksin, (Clarence) 166
Klopf, Gus 67–69
Klores, Lt. Stanley 288
Kloza, Jack 221, 230–231, 233, 242, 245–246, 254, 265, 267, 281, 331
Kloza, John 331
Klumpp, Elmer 227
Klusman, Billy 50
Knabe, Otto 195–196, 200
Knebel, Ed 315
Knebelkamp, Col. Bill 216–217
Knights of Columbus banquet 187, 215
Knipple, Bill 144, 278
Knoblauch (pinch-hitter) 315
Knott, Jack 233, 236–237, 239
Knouff, Ed 51
Koch, Gus 95–96, 131
Koehler, Horace "Pip" 236–237, 240
Koehler, John P. 218
Koehn, Phyllis "Sugar" 286
Koenecke, Len 231, 234
Koepp, Herman 151
Koeppel, Chet 192, 197
Koerner, Ald. John E. 252
Koerners (City League club) 141

Kojis, Don 249
Kojis, George 247
K-O-M League 327
Konetchy, Big Ed 166
Koob, Ernie 199
Korean War 316–317, 319–320, 331–332
Kosciuskos: L.S.L. club 156, 161, 174, 184, 187; Reds 223
Koslo(wski), Dave 268–269, 271, 325
Koslo(wski), Herb 269
Kraenzlein, Alvin 161
Kraft, Clarence "Big Boy" 179
Kramer, Stormy 230
Kramers (L.S.L. club) 220
"Krankheit" (cranks, fans) 24
Krasnicky, Franklin 177
Krauthoff, E.A. 59
Krauthoff, L.C. 56
Kreevich, Mike 243
Kretlow, Eddie 275, 290
Krieg, Bill 54, 61, 63
Krock, Gus 40, 42–43
Kropf, John 315
Krsnich, Mike 332
Krsnich, Nick 332
Krsnich, Rocky 332
Kubek, Tony, Jr. 331
Kubek, Tony, Sr. 227, 230–231, 239, 242, 246
Kuehne, Willie 76
Kuenn, Harvey, Jr. 291, 310, 328, 330, 332
Kuhel, Joe 222, 289
Kulwicki 800 Average Bowling League 289
Kusch, John 273
Kush, Emil 275, 296

Laabs (player) 144, 153
Laabs, Chet 246, 249–258, 275, 328
Laabs, Nig 166
Laacke & Joys (Joy Bros.) 77, 78
Labine, Clem 316
labor strife in Milwaukee 37, 39
LaConga nightclub (Milwaukee) 298
lacrosse (sport) 3, 34
La Crosse, Wis. 3; baseball clubs: (Nw.L.) 45–46, 52; (W.S.L.) 136
LaFleur (catcher) 70
Lajoie, Nap 112
Lake, Fred 62
Lake Michigan 3, 80
Lake Shore League (Wis.) 141, 145, 151, 153, 156,
160–161, 166, 174, 184, 187, 190, 194, 197, 220
Lakefront Park (Kenosha) 286
Lakeman, Al "Moose" 309, 314–316
Lally, Bud 76
LaMacchia, Al 292
Lambeau, Curly 188, 260
Land O'Lakes League (Wis.) 333
Landis, Kenesaw Mountain 143, 199, 208, 217, 224, 257
Lane, Frank 300
Lanfranconi, Walt 274–275, 295
Lange, Frank 161
Lange Red Sox (L.S.L.) 194, 197
Langsdorf, A.J. 64
Langsford, Bob 66
Languay, Eva 145
Lapham Park (Milwaukee) 296
Larkin, Martin, Jr. 15–16, 19, 21, 22
LaRoss, Harry 174
Larson, Lloyd 221, 232, 266, 318–319, 321, 323, 329, 336
Lash, Mr. 21
Laskowski, Rudy 242
LaSord(a), Tom 324–325
Latham, Arlie 41
Lathrop, J.B. 9
Lauper, Harry 232
Laurels (Milwaukee amateur club) 64
Lavan, John "Doc" 212
Lawson, Roxie 237, 273
Layne, Bobby 306
League Alliance 26
Lear, Fred (King) 193–200, 204–205, 217, 221, 328
LeBourveau, Bevo 211, 216, 223, 231, 290, 300, 306
Lederer, Phil 42, 65
Ledyard, J.(W.) 7–9, 11
Lee Specialty Co. (Milwaukee) 265
Leewe (or Lewee), Ed "Kid" 75–76, 78, 84, 87, 102, 140, 166, 229
Leibold, Nemo 150–151, 157, 169, 184–185, 191, 198, 222, 228, 235, 298, 303, 306
Leifield, Lefty 235
Leitner (deaf pitcher) 108
Lelivelt, Jack 158, 174, 179, 184, 213–226, 241
LeMaster, Wayne 245, 250
Lennon, George 129

Leroy, Louie 142, 145
Lessard (pitcher) 151
Leverette, Hod 169
Levy, Sam 188, 215, 222, 231, 235, 268, 290, 296, 310, 333
Lewis, Phil 150, 152–153, 157, 160, 164–165, 167, 173–174, 178, 241
Lewis, Shorty 151
Lewis Field (Milwaukee) 265
Lexington (O.S.L.) 178
Lexington Park (St. Paul) 175, 195, 223
Liberty ballclub of Chicago 25
Liddle, Don 315, 327–328, 334–336
Liebhardt, Glenn 149
Lincoln: Athletics 326; (W.L.) 55, 58
Lincoln, Abraham 5, 12, 18
Lincoln Field (Milwaukee) 265
Lindbergh, Charles 220
Linde, Lyman 267
Linden, Walter 304, 314, 318
Lindsey, Jim 204
Lingrel, Ray 198, 200, 207, 210–211
Lint, Royce 320
Lippert (rightfielder) 76
"Little Hans" (mascot) 123
Little Rock Travelers 213, 216, 224, 236
Little World Series 132, 251, 255–256, 259, 280, 303–305, 324, 326
Livengood, Wes 278, 280, 295, 327
Livingston, Paddy 184–185
Lloyd Street Ball Park (Milwaukee) 68, 75, 77–78, 97, 103, 110–111, 113, 223, 253
Lober, Elmer "Ty" 194, 198, 216, 220
Lobert, Hans 251
Loftus, Tom 32, 34, 36, 39, 46, 80, 90, 109
Logan, Johnny 306, 309, 314–315, 320, 328–329
Lone Rock (Wis. S.W.L. club) 267
Long (relief pitcher) 47
Long, Denny 69
Long, Jim 69
Longhorn League 307, 326
Lopes, Davey 19
Lopez, Al 303, 305
Los Angeles Angels (P.C.L.) 241, 290, 311, 328, 331
Los Angeles Dodgers 6

368 Index

Louisville Colonels (major) 41, 46, 50, 59–63, 68, 91
Louisville Colonels (minor A.A.) 101–102, 110, 112, 114, 119, 127–128, 130, 133, 135–137, 139, 141, 143, 145–147, 149–150, 157, 161–164, 167, 169, 172, 174, 179, 183, 188, 192, 197, 199–200, 203, 205, 208, 210, 212, 216–217, 224, 227–228, 231–234, 240–241, 243, 245, 249–250, 255, 261, 278, 285–286, 293, 298, 303–304, 306–308, 316, 322–324, 329
Louisville gambling scandal 26
Lowdermilk, Grover 163, 169
Lowe, Bobby 49–50 52, 200
Luby, Pat 66–67
Lucas (manager) 42
Lucas, Henry 32–33, 60
Luce, Frank 210, 221, 244
Lucia (catcher) 110, 112
Luderus, Fred 148, 197, 199, 278
Luer, Butch 223
Luque, Dolf 205
Lutzke, Rube 190–193, 202–203, 213–214, 220, 241, 246
Lynch, R.G. 251, 268, 287, 291–292, 295–296, 300, 310
Lyons, George 222
Lytell, Bert 307

MacArthur, Gen. Arthur 100, 134
MacArthur, Douglas 184, 292, 301, 320, 326
MacDonald, Dan 15–16
Mack, Connie 17, 74–78, 80–87, 89–97, 99–103, 147, 172, 181, 197, 200–201, 205, 207, 209–210, 221, 223, 229, 288–289, 299, 315, 319
Mack, Joe 297–298, 300
Mack, Stubby 212–213
Macon, Max 259, 301, 326
MacPhail, Larry 302
Macullar, Jimmy 51
Madden, William T. 157
Madison: Blues (3-I.L.) 264–265, 267; (W.S.L.) 133
Magee, Sherry 185, 202–205, 207, 210
Magerkurth, George (umpire) 217, 222
Majestic Theater Building (Milwaukee) 142, 155, 188

Makosky, Frank 265–266
Malarkey, John 118
Maloney, Bill 97–99, 319
Manion, Clyde 230, 233
Manistees (Mich. club) 90
Manitowoc (L.S.L.) 161
Mannasau (umpire) 80, 94
Manning, Jimmy 49, 69, 84, 99
Manske, Louie 123, 127, 136, 138, 142, 145, 153, 166
Mantle, Mickey 3, 14, 320
Manush, George 38
Manush, Heinie 38
Manville, Dick 309, 311
Mapes, Cliff 321
Maple Leafs (Milwaukee amateur club) 38
Maple Leaves of Guelph, Ontario 41
Marcan, Arthur 129, 131, 140
Marcan, Dick 140, 176
Marcum, John "Moose" 240, 275
Marion, Dan 151
Marquard, Rube 139
Marquardt, Ollie 241
Marquette University (Milwaukee) 5, 27, 215, 217, 237, 243, 249, 325; (stadium) 332
Marquez, Luis 327, 330, 334–335
Marshall, Cuddles 303
Marshall, Doc 150, 152
Marshall, Eddie 242, 244, 247, 249, 254
Marshall, Willard 330
Martin, (Al) 21
Martin, Happy Jack 179–180
Martin, Hershel 275, 278, 280, 284, 286, 289, 309, 327–328
Martin, Ray 311, 314–315
Marylebone All-Cricket Club 4
Maskrey, Leech 41–43, 45–46, 51
Mathews, Eddie 318, 322–324
Mathewson, Christy 185
Matthews (ballclub) 75
Matthews, Wid 194, 196–199, 201, 203, 206, 211, 223, 234
Matuschkas (Milwaukee muni club) 244
Mauch (player) 153
Mauch, Gene 320–321, 325, 327, 329, 333–335
Maul, Smiling Al 62
Mavis, Bobby 310, 322
May, A.C. 9

Mays, Willie 320
McAleer, Jimmy 47–48, 161, 231
McBride, George 100, 103, 110, 141, 161, 269, 282, 319, 333
McCall, John 319
McCarthy, Alex 193–194, 201, 207, 209–210, 215
McCarthy, Joe 212
McCarty, John 46
McCauley, Al 68, 70
McChesney, Harry (Red) 122, 124–130, 132, 134, 136, 138
McCloskey, John J. 140–141, 143, 145–149, 166
McCormick, Barry 124–127, 129, 133–134, 136–139, 142, 153
McCracken, Ovid "Grits" 208, 215
McDermott, Sandy (umpire) 72
McDonald, Charles 83, 91
McEvoy, Carle 241
McFarland & Company, Inc. (publisher) 18
McFarland, Herm 92
McFayden, Archie 15–16, 19, 21–22
McGann, Dan 140, 142–143, 145, 148, 150
McGarr, Chippy 61
McGill, Bill 107
McGinnis, Jumbo 45
McGlynn, James B. "Stoney" 235, 246, 266, 275, 287
McGlynn, U.S. Grant "Stoney" 139, 142–143, 145, 148–149, 151, 153, 158, 161, 235, 269, 290, 331
McGovern, Gov. Francis 164
McGowan, Frank 206–207, 211
McGraw (catcher) 167
McGraw, John J. 75, 140, 158, 177, 193, 205, 220
McGregor, Armin 277
McGuire, Milt 333
McGuire, R.O. 91
McHale, Bob 73
McHenry, Austin "Slats" 179–180, 185–186
McIntire, Bob 228
McIntyre, Ronald 242
McIver (umpire) 40
McKay, Reeve 108, 116, 120, 123, 127
McKee, James F. 30–32
McKibben, Byron 102
McKinley, William 62, 77, 100

McLarry, Polly 241
McLish, Cal 302
McMakin, Sam 104
McManus, Sheriff 180
McMenemy, Bob 208, 213, 215, 223–224
McMillan, Roy 315
McNabb, Edgar 54
McNeely (pitcher) 82
McNulty, Pat 202, 204
McPherson, John 110, 112
McSorley, Trick 35–36
McVey, Cal 23
McVey, George 50
McVicker (player) 110
McWeeny, Doug "Buzz" 190–193
Meade, Richard 218
Mears, Russ 274–275
Mehl, Ernest 241
Mele, Al "Dutch" 304, 308
Melillo, Oscar 194, 198, 200, 202, 204, 210–212, 220, 227, 241
Melms, Edward 176
Memphis Red Sox (N.A.L.) 291
Memphis: (S.A.) Chick(asaw)s; 279 (S.L.) 107, 112
Menasha (F.R.V.L.) 269
Mendelson, Fred "Shorty" 219, 273, 286, 293, 304, 331
Menendez, Danny 331
Menges, Ed 46
Menomonee River (Milwaukee) 3–4, 298
Meredith, Elmer 107–108, 110, 114–115, 118
Merkle, Fred 155
Merrill Park (Milwaukee) 265
Messmer, Leo 110
Messmer, Sebastian G. (archbishop) 223
Metcalfe, Ralph 237
Metropolis Hotel (Kansas City) 66
Metzler, Alex 233, 237
Mexican League 289, 296, 315
Meyer, Bill 213
Meyers, Bill 303
Meyers, Chief 158
Miami Sun Sox (F.I.L.) 326
Michalski (assemblyman) 246
Michalski, Max 237
Michigan League 196, 209
Michigan-Ontario ("Mint") League 210
Middle Atlantic League 245
Middle West Baseball League 203

Middlestown (O.S.L.) 290
Mikan, George 308
Miljus, Johnny 188
Miller (beer) 96, 282, 331, 333
Miller, Bing 210
Miller, Curly 113
Miller, Doggy 76
Miller, Ed 190, 192
Miller, Elmer 202
Miller, Fred 320
Miller, Herbert 182–183
Miller, Jack 292
Miller, Otis 211, 221–223
Miller Park (Milwaukee) 10, 22, 233, 311
Mills (catcher) 46, 52–53
Milnar, Happy Al 257–258
Milwaukee: comparison to Twin Cities 231; ethnic composition 196; growth of 93, 123, 214, 228, 312; homicide rate 233; as an insurance center 86; productivity 202, 214, 226; standing as a milling city 61; water quality 44, 238–239
Milwaukee Admirals hockey 293
Milwaukee Advertisers (ballclub) 246
Milwaukee Angels (W.L.) 102–106
Milwaukee Arena 311, 320
Milwaukee Athletic Club 78, 91, 243
Milwaukee Badgers 206, 217, 230, 295
Milwaukee Base Ball Club 8, 10–12
Milwaukee Baseball Grounds 26
Milwaukee Bears (Negro club) 203–204, 312
Milwaukee Braves (N.L.) 3, 6, 311, 314, 328
Milwaukee Brewers (modern) 6, 19, 24, 33, 176, 328
Milwaukee Brewers Association 252
Milwaukee Bright Spots pro basketball 308
Milwaukee Brown Brewers 317
Milwaukee Chicks (A.A.G.P.B.L.) 281, 284–287, 313, 317, 336
Milwaukee Chiefs (A.F.L.) 267
Milwaukee County: Board Buildings & Grounds Committee 260; Park

Commission 316; Parks & Land Commission 298
Milwaukee Cream Citys (W.L.) 35–37
Milwaukee Creams (W.L.) 105, 107–114, 116, 122, 137, 142, 144, 154, 158, 284, 312
Milwaukee Curling Club 3
Milwaukee General Hospital 233
"Milwaukee Giants" 86–87
Milwaukee Grays (N.L.) 26–29, 54
Milwaukee Gun Club 3
Milwaukee Hawks (N.B.A.) 326, 332
Milwaukee Journal 147, 149, 154–157, 173, 175, 180, 187–188, 210, 215, 217, 231, 234–235, 240, 250–251, 268, 287, 290–292, 295, 300, 304, 307, 310, 333
Milwaukee Journal Sentinel 5
Milwaukee Junior Chamber of Commerce 254, 332
Milwaukee Mollycoddles or Mollys (W.-I.L.) 158, 160
Milwaukee Monarchs 331
Milwaukee Municipal Recreation Department 265
Milwaukee Panthers (1919) 187–191, 193, 195, 221, 224, 267
Milwaukee Park (Lloyd Street) 78
Milwaukee Polo Club 332
Milwaukee Red Sox (W.S.L.) 232
Milwaukee River 3, 44
Milwaukee Sentinel 5–6, 8–10, 12, 14–19, 23–24, 26, 28, 31, 35, 37–38, 40, 43, 46–47, 49, 54, 57, 60–63, 67–69, 72–73, 78–79, 81–84, 86, 88–89, 91–92, 95, 98, 101–102, 105, 107, 110, 113, 122–124, 130–131, 133, 137–138, 141, 142, 150, 153, 158–160, 168, 171–172, 175–176, 179, 192, 195, 197, 198, 200–201, 204, 207, 212, 221, 226, 228, 234–237, 242, 245–246, 266, 269, 275, 282, 284, 286–287, 290, 315–316, 318, 328, 331
Milwaukee Sinfonietta 336
Milwaukee Theatre 332
Milwaukee Turnverein 3, 17, 104
Milwaukee White Sox:

370　Index

(L.S.L.) 141, 145; (W.S.L.) 176
Milwaukee Yacht Club 3
Minneapolis (A.L.) 93-96; first mention as "Millers" 55, 58-59, 64; (Nw.L.) 31, 39, 45; (W.A.) 46-49, 51, 53; (W.L.) 63, 65, 67, 69-70, 72, 74-76, 82, 85, 87, 91
Minneapolis Lakers basketball team 318
Minneapolis Millerettes (A.A.G.P.B.L.) 281, 287
Minneapolis Millers (minor A.A.) 102-103, 114, 119-124, 127-129, 131-132, 137-138, 141, 143-145, 149-152, 156-157, 160-164, 166-167, 172, 174-175, 190-191, 195-197, 200, 202, 204-205, 212, 214, 223-224, 228, 231-232, 236, 240-241, 251-253, 258, 261, 266, 276-277, 279-280, 286, 290-292, 300-301, 303, 306, 313, 315-316, 320-322, 327, 333
Minneapolis Times 81
Minnesota-Wisconsin League 140
Mississippi Valley League 208, 221, 237
Mitchell, Billy 196, 212
Mix, Tom 211
Mobile Bears (S.A.) 193
Moldez, Sencio 214
Mole, Fenton 316
Molesworth, Carlton 211
Molitor's High Life Nite Club (Milwaukee) 264
Moll, Charles F. 154-158, 171, 174, 190, 193, 195, 198, 253
Mollwitz, Fritz 165, 174, 262
Monaco, Blas 302
Montag, Bob 314, 318, 321, 333-335
Montreal: (E.L.) 136; (I.L.) 107, 236; Royals 295, 298, 324-325
Moore, Charley 292
Moran (umpire) 106
Moran, Charlie 142, 145
Morgan, Chet 249, 254
Morgan, Eddie 265-266
Morgan, Harold "Zip" 265
Morgenroth's (Milwaukee) 170, 187
Morris, Ed 236
Morris, Leo 328
Morrissey, John 31

Morrissey, Tom 31, 41, 43-44, 48, 50, 56, 58
Morrow, Buck 261, 263-264
Morton, Sam 44, 47, 49, 51
Moser, Byron 261
Moss, Howie 309, 311, 314
Mossor, Earl 333
Mostil, Johnny 188, 192, 203, 296
Mother of Good Counsel Church (Wauwatosa, Wis.) 262
Motl Jewelers ballclub 154
M.-O.V. League 327, 332
Muehlebach, George 220, 232
Muehlebach Field (Kansas City) 217, 219, 247, 250
Mueller, Walter 111, 115
Mullane, Tony 72, 110
Mullen, John (umpire) 334
Muni Major AA League (Milwaukee) 241
Municipal AAA League (Milwaukee) 244
Municipal Recreation, School Department of Milwaukee 259, 331
Murnane, Tim 100
Murphy, Con 45
Murphy, "Leo the Red" 187
Murphy, Tom 70
Murray, Jim (umpire) 161, 196, 206, 212, 229
Murtaugh, Danny 301-304, 326
Musial, Stan 318
Muskegon: (Mich.L.) 196; (Nw.L.) 31
Mutual of New York club 19, 25

Nagel, Bill 284, 286, 289
Nagle, Tommy 40
Nahin, "Bankroll Louie" 151, 154, 166, 178, 183-184, 187, 207, 219, 226-229, 231, 233-234, 239, 241, 246, 251, 253, 256, 259, 265, 269
Nance, Gene 289, 293, 295, 301
Nash Motors ballclub (M.W.B.L.) 203-205
Nash Motors Stadium (Kenosha) 203
Nashville Vols (S.L.) 224, 276
National Agreement 35, 97, 107, 112; arbitration committee 114, 122
National Association (first major league) 24-26, 50
National Association of Base Ball Clubs 12-13

National Association of Minor Leagues 279, 298
National Baseball Commission 119, 129, 135, 148, 167
National Basketball Association 4, 249, 320, 324, 332
National Board of Arbitration 54, 112
National Club of Washington 14; (U.A.) 33, 52
National Football League 177, 217, 232, 295
National League 24-28, 30-31, 38, 41, 47, 50-51, 53-56, 60, 62-63, 65-68, 72-75, 77-78, 90-91, 93, 96-101, 106-107, 115, 133, 163, 172, 198, 200, 205-206, 221, 270, 283, 299, 305, 312, 323, 325, 331
National Military Asylum at Wood (V.A. Hospital, Milwaukee) 23
"National rules" baseball 4, 8
Natisin, Mike 308
N.B.A. *see* National Basketball Association
Nebraska Indians 30
Negro American League 291
Negro Leagues 312, 315, 317-318, 324
Neil Park (Columbus) 122, 231
Neill, Tom 299-301, 304
Nelson, Merton (Bat) 231
Nelson, Tommy 284-286, 289, 297
Netzow, Elmer 235
Neun, Johnny 310
Neustedter, Wallie 246
Nevel, Ernie 319, 323
Nevers, Ernie 212
New England League 100, 314
New Haven clubs 81, 100, 112, 181, 207
New Orleans: Pelicans 326; (S.A.) 257
New Star Theater (Milwaukee) 145
New York Giants: football 332; (N.L.) 97, 137, 140, 142, 155, 158, 176, 190, 193, 204-205, 208, 215-216, 234, 271, 296, 320, 325
New York Highlanders (A.L.) 127
New York Knickerbocker Base Ball Club 4-5, 11
New York League 136
New York Metropolitans (major A.A.) 40

New York Mets 283
New York Nine 4
New York Rens (basketball team) 318
"New York rules" 11
New York State League 34
New York Yankees 3, 185, 202, 221, 223, 236, 257, 267, 274–275, 283, 286–287, 289, 305, 309, 321, 328, 331
Newark: Bears 255, 265; (E.L.) 136; (I.L.) 167
Newhall House (Milwaukee) 8
Neyses, Michael 250
Niagaras club of Buffalo 14
"Nicholl" (player) 80
Nichols, A.N. 19
Nichols, Al 26
Nichols, Charles "Kid" 18, 48, 104
Nichols, Chet 316
Nichols, James 18
Nichols, John 18
Nicholson, John 151–152, 157, 160
Nicol, George 69–70, 72, 75–76, 78, 80–82, 88, 141
Nicol, Helen 286
Nicolai, Fred 211
Nicollet Park (Minneapolis) 240
Niehoff, Bert 165
Niemann, Bob 315
Niggeling, John 254
Niles, Billy 70
Nixon, Richard 331, 334
Nixon, Willard 316
Noel, Bruce 157
Nolden, Pete 106
Nonnemacher, Kid 72
Norbert, Ted 276–277, 280, 290
Norfolk Tars (Pdmt. L.) 279
Norman, Bill 272, 274, 278, 280, 282, 284, 289, 302
Norris, Charles S. 15–16, 19, 21–22
Norstrand, F. W. 52
North, Lou 193, 206
North Pole discovery 145
Northern-Copper Country League 133
Northern League 174, 259, 296, 303, 320, 326
Northrop, Jake 192–196
Northwest League 181
Northwestern League 30–33, 37–39, 41–44, 46
Northwestern Motor Institute (Milwaukee) 30
Northwestern Mutual Life

Insurance Co. (Milwaukee) 30, 166
Northwestern University (Evanston, Ill.) 30, 288
Norton, Pete 30
Novikoff, Lou 261, 263, 267–268, 272, 276, 290
Nye, Bill 37, 170

Oakes, Rebel 191
Oakland: Acorns 287; (P.C.L.) 137, 181, 220
Oana, Henry "Prince" 277, 279, 295, 315
Oberlin, Frank 129–132
O'Brien, Jack 107–108, 116, 118, 123–125
O'Brien, Joe 95–96, 122, 124, 128–131
O'Brien, Pat 223
O'Brien, Willie 62
O'Connell, Jimmy 209
O'Connor, Skinny 230
O'Day (manager) 157
Odell, Glenn 114
O'Doul, Lefty 23
Odwell, Fred 149
Ogden, David B. 9
O'Hagan, Hal 82
Ohio-Indiana League 317
Ohio-Penn League 133
Ohio State League 178, 290
Oklahoma City Indians 320
"Old Northwest," origin of 30
Old-Timers reunions: Boston 319; Milwaukee 267, 278
Oldfield, Barney 123
O'Leary, Charlie 157
Olmo, Luis 322–325
Olympic Games 157, 161, 192, 237, 251, 264, 331
Omaha: (Nw.L.) 34–35, 37–38, 46, 113; (W.A.) 49, 51–53, 54–56, 58; (W.L.) 62–63, 69, 78, 82, 101, 103, 105, 108, 110, 112, 130
Omaha Buffaloes (W.L.) 213, 217, 221
O'Neill, Bill (Tip) 107, 110, 112, 122, 127, 129, 144
O'Neill, Buck 12
O'Neill, Steve 257
O'Rourke, Frank "Blackie" 198, 227, 234–237, 239–241
O'Rourke, Orator Jim 181
O'Rourke, Voiceless Tim 72
Orpheum Theater (Milwaukee) 175, 180
Orr, Billy 262–263
Orwoll, Ossie 212–213, 215–

217, 220–221, 223, 260, 314, 328
Oshkosh: Giants (W.S.L.) 321; (Nw.L) 37, 39, 41–42, 44–46, 113, 319; pro basketball 268; (W.-I.L.) 157, 160
O'Toole, Marty 152
Ott, Howard 290
Otten, Don 332
Otto Bros. City League Champs (Milwaukee) 74
Overmire, Stubby 330
Owen, Mickey 334–335
Owens (umpire) 131
Owensboro, Ky. (training site) 158–159, 165, 174
"Owgust" (cartoon mascot) 297
Ozark, Danny 311, 324

Pabor, Charley "The Old Woman in the Red Cap" 20–22, 33
Pabst, Frederick 65–66
Pabst Extract 119
Pabst Pale Extra Dry Ginger Ale 210
Pabst Theater Building 116, 140, 235
Pacific Coast League 137, 180–181, 199, 209, 220, 229, 234, 240–241, 259, 267, 276, 287, 290, 311–312, 325, 328
Packard, D.C. 113
Padden, Dick 129
Padden, Pat (umpire) 292
Paderewski, Ignacy Jan 140
Paducah club 269
Paffauf, A.E. 186
Pafko, Andy 272
Page Fence Giants (Negro club) 75
Palmero, Emilio 215
Pan-American Exposition (Buffalo) 100
Panos, Vicki 285
Pape, Larry 139
Pappalau, John 79
Pasqual brothers 295
Passeau, Claude 245
Paul Bunyan baseball tale 202
Pawtucket (N.E.L.) 314
Peacock Funeral Home (Milwaukee) 233, 235
Pearce, Dickey 14–15
Pears: as player 104, as umpire 118–119
Pearson, Len 317–319
Pease, L.S.: as attorney 182; as secretary 155
Peck, George W. 37

Peck, Hal 265–266, 271, 274, 283–284, 286, 288–289, 295, 328–329
Peckinpaugh, Roger 243
Peirce, Bemus 123
Peitz, Heinie 145
Penau, Edward 59
Pendleton, Jim 311
Pennock, Herb 307
Peoria (Nw.L.) 31–32
Peoria Distillers (W.L.) 101, 109–110, 112
Peoria Tractors (3-I.L.) 192
Pepper (pitcher) 69
Perini, Lou 298–299, 301, 303, 312, 318, 320, 324, 326, 332, 336
Perrine, Nig 142
Perring, George 135, 149, 178, 267
Perry, Henry "Hank" 309–310
Perry, Jim (owner) 224
Perry, Norman 241
Pershing, John J. 268
Pesky, Johnny 328
Peters, Frosty (umpire) 298
Peters, Johnny 28
Pettit, Bob 54, 56
Pfister Hotel (Milwaukee) 80, 255
Phelan, Dick 35
Phelp, Zack 54
Philadelphia Athletics 14, 19, 25; (A.L.) 76, 96, 99, 103, 147, 172, 197–198, 200–201, 205, 233, 262, 288, 297, 299, 319; (major A.A.) 59
Philadelphia Phillies 56, 77, 91, 96, 114, 148, 185, 251, 300, 307, 309
Philipp, Gov. Emanuel L. 173, 187
Philley, Dave 297
Phillips, Damon (Dee) 299, 304, 306, 309–310
Phillips, Tom 224
Phyle, Billy 107–108, 112
Piatt, Wiley 100
Pick, Eddie 211, 221–222, 224, 228
Pickett, John 49–50, 72
Piedmont League 279, 326
Piersall, Jim 316
Pike, Lip 14
Pine Bluff, Ark. (training site) 176–177
pitcher's mound distance change 66
Pittenger, Pinky 216
Pittsburgh: (major A.A.) 34–35; (U.A.) 35

Pittsburgh Pirates 62, 74–75, 84, 93–95, 114, 130, 135, 141, 148, 198, 209, 284, 301, 313, 329
Pixley, R.B. 162–163
Plain States League 263
Plankinton, John 13
Plankinton Arcade (Milwaukee) 187
Plankinton House (Milwaukee) 23, 31, 35
Players League 54, 65, 74
Podoloff, Maurice 324
Polcyn, John 304
Pollard, Fritz 295
Pollard, Jim 318
Polli, Americo "Lou" or "Crip" 230–231, 233, 237, 240, 242–243, 247, 249
polo 267
Polonia, Luis 3
Polzin, Ed 290
PONY League 327
Poorman, Tom 50, 56
Popovich, Miss Violet 237
Portage (Wis. club) 70
Porter, Henry 33
Porth, George 58
Poser, Bobby 236
Portland 156; (P.C.L.) Beavers 180, 199, 276
Post, Wally 315, 330, 334
Potawatomi tribe 3
Potratz, Sadie 232
Pott, Nelson 198, 203, 205, 211
Potter, Nels 198
Powell, Bill 166, 173
Power, Tyrone 180
Power, Vic 335
Powers, Patrick T. 97
Pratt, Al 15–16
Prendergast, Jim 311
Pressnell, Forrest (Tot) 242–243, 250–252, 254, 256, 258–259, 275–276
Price, Jim 292
Prohibition 183, 185, 187, 210, 214, 222, 224, 238–239
Prospect Avenue grounds (Milwaukee) 13–14
Providence Grays (N.L.) 26, 28
Providence: (E.L.) 186, 190; (I.L.) 167
Pruett, Jimmy 282, 284
Pryor, Billy 271
Pueblo Indians (W.L.) 127
Puelicher, John H. 197
Pulaski Park (Milwaukee) 244
Pulford, G.R. 200

Pulliam, Mr. (N.L. president) 115
Pumping Station Field (Milwaukee) 265
Purdy, Pid 231
Puttmann, Ambrose 136
Pyle, Ewald 295, 303, 307

Quin, Bobby 149
Quin, Harry D. 31, 37, 40, 42–44, 49–50, 54–55, 78, 86, 91–92, 95, 102–104, 106, 114, 122, 147, 159
Quincy: (Nw.L.) 31–33, 36; (3-I.L.) 222
Quinn, John 299–300, 302, 311, 313, 329
Quinn, Uncle Joe 104, 113
Quins (City League club) 73

Raab, Bunny 195
"rabbit ball" 226
Racine Belles (A.A.G.P.B.L.) 281
Racine College club 37–38
Racine Horlicks (M.W.B.L.) 206–207, 216
Raddant, Ken 301
Radke's Funeral Chapel (Milwaukee) 218
Raih, John 75, 79–80
Railway Unions club (Cleveland) 19
Rambone, Paul 309
Ramos, Salvador 249
Ramsey (alderman) 71
Ramsey, Toad 46
Randall, Newt 136, 145, 160, 164–167, 172–174
Rapp, Goldie 191
Rath, Morrie 166
Rawlings, Robert 282
Reach, Al 14, 20, 96
Reach ball (brand controversy) 129–130, 136
Reading Keystones (I.L.) 234
Reagan, Ronald 332
Reccius, (ball-playing brother) 41
Redlington, George 16, 19, 21–22
Reed, Billy 314, 317, 323, 334
Regner, Emil 284
Reidy, Bill 78–79, 82, 84, 90–91, 95–96, 99
Reilly, Duke 172
Reinemann, Paul 153
Reinhart, Art 190, 192–193
Reiter, Johnny 334
Reitz, Al "Heinie" 211
Remey, Oliver E. 159, 310
Remley, Ed 160
Renna, Bill 334–335

Index 373

Rensa, George (Tony) 242–243
Renwick (pitcher) 54–56
Republican House (Milwaukee) 70, 76, 85
Rettger, George 68, 70, 76, 78, 81–82, 84, 87, 90–91, 94–95
Retzlaff, Alvin 227
Reuss, Henry S. 295, 306
Rhoades, Dusty 152
Rice, Yab 277
Richbourg, Lance 207–208, 215, 217
Richmond, Ind. (training site) 91, 97
Richmond Tigers (O.-I.L.) 317
Rickert, Marv 306–308, 310
Rickey, Branch 133, 198, 206, 211, 222, 295, 300
Riconda, Harry 217, 221
Riggert, Joe 186
Rigney, Topper 222
Ripley, Robert 245–246, 287
Ripon (Wis. club) 17
Riverside Theater (Milwaukee) 260–261, 264, 273
Riviere, Turk 198–199
Roanoke Ro-Sox (Pdmt. L.) 326
Roat, Fred 62
Roberge, Al "Skippy" 300–304, 306–307, 309
Robertaille (pitcher) 135
Robertson, Charley 228
Robeson, Paul 295, 311
Robinson, Jack 307
Robinson, Jackie 12, 181, 295, 298, 300, 310–311, 316
Robinson, Rabbit 123–125, 128–130, 132, 135, 139, 148–150
Robinson, Yank 34–35
Rochester, N.Y. club 38, 49–50; (I.L.) 167, 223
Rock Island club 106; Islanders (M.V.L.) 237
Rockford: (3-I.L.) 99; (W.-I.L.) 152, 156
Rockford Peaches (A.A.G.P.B.L.) 281
Rockne, Knute 231
Rockwell, Geo. 9
Roe, Preacher 280
Rogers, Col. John J. 97
Rogers, William P. 28–29
Rolfe, Red 274
roller polo 34, 37, 198
Roosevelt, Franklin Delano 236, 245, 264, 268, 273, 277, 288

Roosevelt, Theodore 106, 156–157, 279, 326
Root, Charley 291
Rose, Baldy 200
Rose, David S. (mayor) 91–92, 206
Rosen, Goody 250
Rosenthal, Larry 293
Ross, Lee "Buck" 295, 298, 301
Rossman, Claude 122, 127, 158
Roswell Rockets (L.L.) 307
Roth, Braggo 132
Roth, Frank 129–133, 135, 139, 269
rounders 4
Roussey (shortstop) 45
Rowe, Dave 51, 53, 55–56, 62
Rowland, Clarence "Pants" 181, 184, 187–189, 192, 195, 196, 199, 221, 224, 234, 269, 271, 327
Rowland, Clarence, Jr. 271
Roy, Norman 311
Ruest (pitcher) 95
Ruetz, Babe 281
Ruetz, Judge Edward J. 281
Rullo, Joe 289–290, 327
Ruschaupt of Indianapolis 129
Russian, Johnny 295
Ruth, George "Babe" 23, 196, 202, 206, 209, 217, 220, 238–239, 291, 300, 304, 316–317
Ruth, Marshall "Babe" 199
Ryan, Blondy 259
Ryan, "Rosy" Bill 224, 226–228, 253, 286
Ryczek, William J. 18

Sacramento Senators (P.C.L.) 209
sacrifice rule 66
Sage, Leo 131–132
Saginaw (Nw.L.) 31–32, 35
St. Charles Hotel (Milwaukee) 76
St. Claire, Ebba 318
St. Joseph club 37–40; (W.L.) 50–53, 82, 84, 101–102, 107, 110
St. Joseph Hospital (Milwaukee) 293
St. Louis (Negro club) 203–204
St. Louis Brown Stockings (major A.A.) 34, 36, 41, 47–48, 50, 56, 59–62, 73
St. Louis Browns (A.L.) 100, 120, 128–129, 135–136, 167, 216–217, 220–224,

227–228, 230, 234–237, 241–243, 245, 275, 290, 299, 314, 319–321, 326
St. Louis Cardinals 80, 100–102, 139, 141, 155, 184–186, 193, 198, 206–207, 209, 211, 222, 240, 259, 299, 318, 327, 329
St. Louis Globe-Democrat 36
St. Louis Maroons (U.A.) 33
St. Louis Whites (W.A.) 46–47
St. Paul: first mention as "Saints" 68, 70, 71–73, 77, 79, 82, 84, 87, 89–90; (Nw.L.) 31–32, 40, 42, 44–45; (W.A.) 46–49; (W.L.) 50–53, 62
St. Paul Globe 82
St. Paul Pioneer-Press 90
St. Paul Saints (minor A.A.) 102, 104, 106–107, 110, 114, 119–124, 127, 129, 133–135, 141, 142, 145, 148, 150, 152–153, 157–158, 166–167, 173, 175, 178, 181, 183, 186–187, 191–192, 195–196, 199–200, 203–204, 208–209, 211–213, 217, 220, 223, 225, 229–230, 232, 243, 247, 249–252, 258, 261, 267, 277–278, 282, 292, 296, 305, 310–311, 313–314, 316, 319, 322–324, 332–333
Salenger, Oscar 293–294, 296, 298, 301–302, 311, 324, 326
Sallee, Slim 180
Salt Lake City club 158; (P.C.L.) Bees 209
San Angelo Colts (T.L.) 326
San Antonio: Indians 236; Missions 239; (T.L.) 205
San Diego: Padres 290; (P.C.L.) 259
San Francisco club 25; (P.C.L.) Seals 290
San Francisco earthquake 130
Sand, Heinie 209
Sanders, Deion 217
Sanders, Roy 197, 210, 215–216
Sands, H. 7
sargol (sport) 107
Saskatoon Quakers (W.C.L.) 190, 195
Sauer, Hank 304
Saveland, Ray 267
Sawyer, E.P. 45–46
Say, Lew 40
Schaack, Eddie 193–194,

198–199, 204, 206–207, 220–221
Schacht, Al 267
Schacht, Sid 320, 324
Schaefer, Germany 116, 119–121, 123
Schaffer, Rudy 259, 262, 273, 275, 289–290, 294
Schafly, Larry 113
Schalk, Ray 152, 156–157, 169, 184, 191, 253, 256, 261, 267, 290
Schardt, Wilber 149
Scharpegge, Ernst 231
Schauer, Rube 200
Scheer, Heinie 206
Scheetz, Owen 289, 293, 296, 306, 326
Scheftels, "Cheer Up" 80
Schell, Roland 245
Scherbarth, Bob 323
Scherbarth, Erwin 193
Schiefelbein, Harold (White Pants) 250
Schinner, Art 235, 333
Schlatter, Ed 136
Schlitz brewery 78, 210, 270
Schmedeman, Gov. Al 243
Schmitz, Johnny "Bear Tracks" 260, 264, 268
Schneiberg, Frank 134–137, 139, 143–144
Schneider, Dick 328
Schoendienst, Red 292
Schoeneck, Jumbo 35
Schoepke, Marshall 245
Scholarship Series (A.A.G.P.B.L.) 286
Schomberg, Otto 159
Schott, Reinhold 63
Schramka, Paul 331
Schrank, John 157, 279, 326
Schriver, Pop 56
Schroeder, Dottie 281, 284
Schubert Theater Stock Company (Milwaukee) 162, 180
Schult, Clem 208
Schulte, Fred "Fritz" 215–217, 220, 223, 260
Schultz, Al 192
Schultz, Webb 190
Schulz, Charles 239
Schupp, Ferdie 217
Schuster's department store (Milwaukee) 308
Schwid, Jack 307
Scenic Wisconsin League 267
Score, Herb 331
Scotch immigrants 3, 19
Scott, Ed 98
Scott, Jack 206
Scott, Sir Walter 219

Seattle Giants: (NW.L.) 181; (P.C.L.) 230; Rainiers 290, 325–326, 332
Secory, Frank 282, 289, 308
Segrist, Kal 335
Seibel (pitcher) 48
Selbach, Kip 140
Selee, Frank 49, 106
Selig, Bud 147, 275, 278
Seligman, Moritz "Hi Hi" 80, 159
Selkirk, George 323
Sells, Ken 284
Sengstock, F. 194
Sentinels ballclub 99–100, 103
Sessions (pitcher) 120
Severeid, Hank 161
Seward, William 12, 18
Sewell, Joe 213
Sewell, Luke 213
Sexton, Jas. 9
Sexton, L. 7–8
Sexton, Michael 106, 109, 112–113
Sexton, Tom (Pete) 35, 38
Seybold, Socks 94, 144
Shackleford, Red 169, 174, 181
Shanahan, Tommy 322
Shaney, Bud 205
Shannon, Morrie 208
Shannon, Spike 148
Sharman, Bill 332
Sharpe (2nd baseman) 70
Sharp(e), Peck 97, 204
Shaw, Al 102
Shay, Danny 136, 148, 174, 180–184, 205
Shea, Marv 227
Sheboygan club 75; Indians 299; (L.S.L.) 160, 222; pro basketball 268; (W.S.L.) Chairs 204
Sheckard, Jimmy 165
Sheehan, Dave 306
Shellenback, Frank 234, 305
Shelly, (Ed) 21
Shenkel (pitcher) 43, 46–48, 50
Sherdell, Bill 180, 185, 203, 206
Sheridan (umpire) 67, 82, 94
Sherman, Paul 198
Shibe, Ben 96
Shinault, Enoch "Ginger" 202–203, 217
Shinners, A.J. 153
Shinners, Ralph 209, 220, 229, 232, 234, 281, 308
Shires, "Art the Great" 229–231, 234, 236, 240, 310
Shoch, George 51–53, 56–58, 60, 68, 78, 80–81, 86, 88

Shocker, Urban 223
Shotton, Burt 261
Shreveport Sports (T.L.) 319
Shuba, George "Shotgun" 325
Siever, Ed 99
Sigafoos, Frank 240
Silch, Ed (Baldy) 151–152
Simmons, Al "Bucketfoot" 200–202, 206–207, 210, 217, 220–221, 223, 225, 230, 233–234, 246–247, 333
Simmons, Walter 221
Simmons Bedmakers (Kenosha M.W.B.L.) 195, 202, 205
Sinton, Bill 306–307
Sioux City: (W.A.) 47–49, 51, 53, 58; (W.L.) 65–68
"Sis Comstock's Krockers" club 170
Sisler, George 255
Sisti, Sibby 320
Sivyer, Charles Milwaukee 160
Skiff, Bill 213
Skopec, John (Buckshot) 99
Skowron, Bill "Moose" 335
Skurski, Andy 277
Skurski, Joe 299
Slapnicka, Cy 152, 156, 160, 163–166, 169, 172–174, 178–180, 185, 191, 246, 257
Slattery, Jack 108, 123–128
Slaughter, Cecil 193
Smith (pitcher) 43
Smith, Bill, Jr. 217
Smith, Broadway Aleck 82–83
Smith, Charlie 16
Smith, Clarence 15–16, 19, 21–22
Smith, Earl 157
Smith, Earl (pitcher) 210
Smith, F.A. 22
Smith, Fred 56
Smith, George 21
Smith, Harry 94
Smith, Paul 191
Smith, Red 260, 265, 269, 272, 318–319, 328–329, 331–334
Smith, Willie (mascot) 196
Smyth, Jimmy 188
"Snowball" (mascot) 143, 207
Socialists 37, 39, 236
softball 255
Soldiers' Home (Milwaukee) 260, 290, 298
Solters, Moose 308
Somers, Charles 96

Index 375

Sommers, Clarence M. 326
Sonnenberg, Gus 231
Sothoron, Allen 180, 206, 209, 229, 241–246, 249–257, 259–261, 267, 305
Souchock, Steve 302
South Bend Blue Sox (A.A.G.P.B.L.) 281, 284–285
Southern Association 185, 193, 276, 279, 300, 326
Southern League 63, 107, 112, 213, 224
Southern New England League 34
Southwestern League 205
Southwestern Minnesota League 245
Southworth, Billy 299–300, 329
Sowders, Bill 39, 44, 49
Spahn, Warren 329
Spalding, Al 10, 14, 20, 25, 30, 41, 44, 55, 76, 247
Spalding's Official Baseball Guide 37
Sparks, Tully 91, 96–97, 100
Speaker, Tris 188, 213
Spears, Dr. Clarence Wiley 265
Speer, Floyd 289, 291–292
Speer, George "Kid" 71–72, 75–76, 78, 82, 87–89, 102, 107–108, 115, 117, 120, 122–123
Sperry, Stan 278
The Sporting News 305
Spring Street Hill grounds (Milwaukee) 5, 11–12
Springfield, Ill. Club 92, 117; (3I.-L.) 215; training site 115, 117
Springfield, Mo. (W.A.) Midgets 227
Springfield Sallies (A.A.G.P.B.L.) 281
Sproull, Charlie 286
Stafford, Bob 70, 73, 84, 88, 90
Stagg, Amos Alonzo 86–87, 148
Stahl, Chick 133
Staley, Harry 47
Stallings, George 193
Stanage, Oscar 199
Stanky, Eddie 272–275, 305
Stanton, Buck 227, 236
Stanton, Marguerite 207
Starffin, Victor 276
Stark, Oscar 227
Stars of Yesterday tourney (Milwaukee) 267, 291, 331
Start, "Old Reliable" Joe 14–16

State Fair Grounds (Milwaukee) 5, 9, 12–13, 302–303, 308
Steele, C. 7–9
Steele, Fred 115–116, 118–119, 122
Steengraffe, Milt (umpire) 293, 298
Steinbrenner, George 3, 10
Steinel, W.F. 102
Steinke, Stoney 246
Stelter, Arthur 239
Stencel, Stanley 263, 268
Stengel, Casey 152, 180, 205, 215, 217, 220, 223, 225, 283–287, 291, 323
Stephens (pitcher) 48
Stephens, George 67, 70
Stephens, Vern 295
Stevens, G.C. 9
Stewart, Ed 302
Stewart, James 249
Stiely, Fred 228, 234, 237
Stiles, Lena 242
Stillwater (Nw.L.) 31–32, 37
Stine, Lee 242, 245
Stivetts, Jack 59
stock market crash 225–226
Stocksick, Will 156
Stone, George 108–109, 114, 116, 120, 123, 150, 152, 156
stool ball 4
Storti, Lin 242–243, 245, 249–250, 253, 255, 257, 259–260, 328
Story quarry site (Milwaukee) 298
Stout, Ralph 62
Strand Theater (Milwaukee) 235
Stratton, Leroy 203
Stratton, Monty 249
Strauss, Joe "The Socker" 41–46, 48, 53, 58
Strelecki, Ed 227
Stricklett, Elmer (Spitball) 108, 119, 123
Strobel, Charles 97
Strohm, Harry 205, 219, 222–223, 236, 326
Stroud, Sailor 179
Struck, John Quincy Adams 47
Strunk, Amos 143, 145, 147, 181, 263
Studener, Les 307
Stumpf, Benny 221
Stumpf, Eddie 179, 184, 187, 197, 212, 221, 232, 268, 281, 284, 295, 301–302, 320
Sturdy, Guy 223
Stutz, Billiken 175; "Satan" 179

Sugden, Joe 92
Sullivan (umpire) 130
Sullivan, Billy, Jr. 242, 245
Sullivan, Pat 38–41, 56
Sullivan, Paul 265
Sullivan, Ted 37–41, 56
Summers, Cy 259
Summers, Kilgoyle 90
Sunday, Billy 174
Susce, George 243
Sutton, "Uncle Ezra" 50–53, 58
Swaim, Cy 87, 89, 129
Swann, Ducky 143, 148, 152, 158
Swayne Field (Toledo) 310
Sweet (player) 15–16
Swift, Bill 282
Swormstedt, Len "Cy" 104, 108, 110, 245, 286
Sylvester, Lou 45
Syracuse club 211; (I.L.) Chiefs 303–304, 308, 324

Tabor, Job 21
Taft, William Howard 175
Talbott, Thea 180
Tanner, Chuck 328
Tarboro (P.S.L.) 263
Tavener, Jackie 231, 236
Taylor, Charles H. 116
Taylor, Jack (Brakeman) 79–82, 84, 137
Taylor, John S. 116
Taylor, Wally 70–71, 73
Taylorville (I.-M.L.) 152
Tebeau, George 80, 101, 128–129, 158, 174
Tebeau, Patsy 47
Techel, Walter 214
Temple Cup (N.L.) 77
Temple Eagles (B.S.L.) 318
10th Street Grounds 34
Terminal Building (Milwaukee) 166
Terre Haute: (C.L.) 107; (Nw.L.) 31–32; (W.L.) Hottentots 69–70
Terry, Adonis 78, 81, 83–84, 91, 96, 107, 124
Tesmer, Bernie 220, 246
Tetzlaff, Doris 284
Tetzlaff, Teddy 319, 328
Texarkana Bears (B.S.L.) 326
Texas League 116, 180, 205, 216–217, 230, 234, 239, 271–272, 276, 279, 295, 308, 315, 317, 319
Thanhouser-Hatch Stage Company (Milwaukee) 87
Thevenow, Tommy 211
Thiel, Maynard "Bert" 318, 320, 322, 325, 334
Thielman, Jack 145

Index

Thimmesh, Alfred A. 194–195
Thisted, Amos "Red" 226, 315, 331
Thomas, Kite 320
Thompson, Annabelle "Tommy" 285
Thompson, Ray 213, 220, 224, 246, 250, 267
Thomson, Bob 320
Thomson, Bobby 325
Thornberg (player) 37
Thornton, John "Jack" 54, 104, 110
Thorpe, Bob 319, 322, 325
Thorpe (player) 19
Thorpe, Jim 156–158, 176–180, 183, 185, 190, 196, 199–200, 212, 233, 237, 264, 313
Thorpe, Jim, Jr. 178
Three-I League 99, 106, 130, 141, 192, 215, 222, 246, 250, 303, 306, 317, 326
Tiefenthaler, Eugene 241, 243
Tietz, Willard 272
Time Insurance team 196
Timme, Al 167–170, 173, 175–187
Timmons, Bascom Nolley 176
Tincup, Ben 216
Tinker, Joe 106, 183
Tinker-to-Evers-to-CHANCE 106
Tipton, Eric 324
Tising, Jack 245
Titanic, S.S. 155
Titus, Silent John 166
Toledo: (Inst.L.) 97; (major A.A.) Maumees 56; (Nw.L.) 34, 37; (W.L.) 63, 65, 67, 69
Toledo Bee 200
Toledo Blue Stockings (major A.A.) 30, 35
Toledo Mud Hens (minor A.A.) 102, 114, 122, 128, 130–131, 135–137, 143–145, 149–150, 152–153, 155, 157, 160–161, 163–165, 167, 178, 188, 196, 198–200, 202–203, 205–206, 208, 215–217, 220, 223–225, 230–231, 233, 236–237, 247, 259, 266, 274–275, 283–284, 286, 292, 296, 305–306, 310, 317, 319, 322, 331, 336
Tolle, Henry 273
Tomlinson, George A. 236
Topeka Kaws (Sw.L.) 205
Topeka Savages (W.L.) 178

Toporcer, Specs 198
Torgeson, Earl 327
Toronto: Blue Jays 311; (I.A.) 53, 56; (I.L.) 217, 302; Maple Leafs 315, 321, 326
Torriente, Cristobal 203
town ball 4, 11
Towne, Babe 124–127
Trautman, George 251–252, 270–271, 273, 290, 299, 321
Traverse City Resorters (W.M.L.) 209
Treadway, M. 16
Trentman, Bob 193–194
Tri-Cities Blackhawks (N.B.A.) 320, 324
Tri-City (Wash.) Braves (W.I.L.) 326
Triner, Tim 311
Trojans (Sparta, Wis. club) 317
Trower, Robin 210
Truman, Harry S 298, 304, 319
Trump, Roger 204
Tulsa: (T.L.) Oilers 315; (W.L.) 217, 221
Turgeon, Pete 227–228, 231
Turner, Ted 10
Twain, Mark 148
Twitchell, Larry 58, 61–63, 67–74
Two Rivers (L.S.L.) 197, 220

Uecker, Bob 331
Uhalt, Bernard "Frenchy" 249, 259, 300
Uihlein, Bob 332
Uihlein, Mr. & Mrs. Herbert 270
Underhill, Dutch 273
Unglaub, Bob 107–109, 113–114, 134, 157–158
uniforms, Milwaukee 66, 76, 92, 166, 309
Union Association 32–35, 39–40, 60, 62
Unions of Lansingbergh club (Troy, N.Y.) 19
Unions of Morrisania club (Bronx, N.Y.) game in Milwaukee 17–22, 24, 33
University of Illinois (training site) 90, 107, 132–133, 140, 147–148, 151
University of Texas Longhorns 306, 310, 316
University of Wisconsin Badgers 76, 80–81, 86–87, 91, 107, 111, 123, 148, 151, 185, 236, 250, 263, 282, 328; basketball 325

Unser, Al 318, 321, 325, 327–328, 334
Unser, Del 318
Urdan, Ed 231
Urdan, Sam 231
Ursella, (Rube?) 177
Usinger, Fred 231

Valhalla Cemetery (Milwaukee) 219, 235
Van Brunt, W.T. 101–102, 106–107, 113
Van Cuyk, Chris 310, 324–325
Van Cuyk, John 277, 319, 324
Vandenburg, Hy 274, 295
Vanderbeck, Detroit president 70
Van Haltren, George 23, 42
Van Schaick (ex-congressman) 58
Vaughan, Irving 234
Vaughan, Manning 130, 137, 153, 176, 186, 191, 210–211, 213–214, 217, 219–220, 222, 224, 232, 236
Vaughn, Farmer 59, 105
Vaughn, Hippo 201
Veeck, Bill 54, 75, 270–277, 279–280, 282–284, 286–290, 293, 295, 297, 299–301, 308, 315, 320, 326, 330
Veeck, William L., Sr. 187, 270, 282
Venice Tigers (P.C.L.) 167
Veracruz (Mex. L.) 289, 295
Verette, Floyd 249
Verifines club (Milwaukee) 241
verse on baseball 31, 85, 89, 116, 158, 162–163, 173, 219
Vickery, Tom 56–58, 62
Victor ball (brand controversy) 129–130
Vietnam era 319
Viila, Pancho 174, 176–177
Villwock, A.C. 231
Viox, Jim "Rooney" 89–90, 112–113
Vizay, Rudy 213, 217, 233–234
Vogt, Fred ("Skatonkel") 149
Voiselle, Bill 324
Vollendorf, Adolphus 78–79, 81, 107, 110, 113
Von der Ahe, Chris 36, 47, 50, 56, 59–60, 99
Von Wiese, Louis B. 241

WAAK Radio (Milwaukee) 199
Wacker, Charley 141

Index

Waco Pirates (B.S.L.) 326
Waddell, Rube 93–95, 156, 165, 208
Wagner, Honus 200
Wahl, Kermit 335
Walberg, George "Rube" 205, 207–208
Waldley, Sgt. Jack 181
Waldron, Irv 75, 78, 84, 87–88, 90, 94, 96
Walentowksi, Ray 242, 245
Walker, Fleet 12, 35
Walker, Hal 264
Walker, Roy "Dixie" 174, 198, 206, 210
Walker, Tilly 201
Walker, Tom 112
Walker's Point (Milwaukee) 4
Walkup, Elton "Jim" 242–243
Wall, Murray 306, 316, 318, 320, 330–331, 334
Wallace, Jimmy 303
Walls, Barney 265
Walnut Grove (S.M.L.) 245
Walsh, Big Ed 187, 191
Walter, Hugo "Sluggy" 143, 319
Walters, Billy 334
Walters, Bucky 266, 310, 330–331, 334
Walters, Fred "The Whale" 298
Wambach, Jack 246
Wambsganss, Bill 222
Wanderer's Cricket Ground (Chicago) 92
Wanderer's Rest Cemetery (Milwaukee) 229
Ward, Monte 23, 61
Ward, Piggy 61–62
Warner, Florence 215
Warner, Jack 145
Warner Theater (Milwaukee) 316
Warstler, Rabbit 227
Waseda University team (Japan) 148, 151
Washington (major A.A. to N.L.) 51, 59–60, 62, 74, 78, 87
Washington Nationals (A.L.) 96, 99–100, 102, 109, 132, 134, 141, 206–207, 211, 221
Washington Olympics (N.A.) 30
Washington Park (Milwaukee) 249
Waterloo 186; (M.V.L.) Hawks 208
Watkins, Bill 34, 94, 97, 128–129

Watson, Doc 157
Waukesha Dales (L.O'L.L.) 333
Waukesha Frame Park (spring training site) 275–277, 282, 289–290
Waupun (Wis. club) 82–83
Wausau (Wis. club) 70; Lumberjacks 220, 259; (W.S.L.) 299
Weaver, Buck (George) 167
Weaver, Buck (William) 69–70, 73, 75–76, 81–82, 90
Webb (pitcher) 133
Webb, Bill 271
Webb, Earl 216, 242, 244–245
Webb, George 214
Weber, Martin 333
Weddige (umpire) 152
Weingartner, Elmer 291
Weinhold, Irving 272
Weisenburger, Jack 314, 316
Welch (2nd baseman) 53
Wells, E.C. 15–16, 21–22
Welzer, Tony 220, 224, 246
WEMP Radio (Milwaukee) 269, 293, 315, 322, 325
Werden, Perry "Moose" 131
Wesleyan University team (Ohio) 133
West, Henry H. 13
West Baden, Ind. (spring training site) 133, 139–140, 174, 184
West Baden Sprudels (Negro club) 139
West End Club (Milwaukee) 25–26
West Hotel (Minneapolis) 59
West Michigan League 209
West Parks (Milwaukee City League team) 140, 151, 154
West Side Arcades club 246
West Texas-New Mexico League 309
Western Association 46, 48–49, 50–52, 56, 58–60, 62, 75, 78, 82, 106, 122, 227, 326
Western Canada League 190
Western International League 326
Western League 34–35, 37, 50, 56, 61, 65–70, 72, 74–75, 77–78, 82, 84–86, 90, 92, 94, 100–104, 106–109, 112–114, 120, 127, 130, 137, 141, 146, 154, 156, 178, 213, 230, 284, 312, 325–326
Westervelt, (Huyler?) (umpire) 166

WHAD Radio (Milwaukee) 213, 215
Wheeler, George 91
Wheeler, Rip 198
When Johnny Came Sliding Home (book) 18
Whisenant, Pete 303, 316, 327, 330, 334
White, Deacon 26, 74
Whitehead, Burgess 240
Whiten, Mark 3
Whitewater (W.C.S.L.) 194
Whitfield, Jim 101
Whitney, Arthur "Pinky" 35
Whitridge (pitcher) 105
Whitted, Possum 160
Wichita Falls Spudders (T.L.) 227, 234
Wichita Indians (W.L.) 326
Wicker, Bob 133
Wickland, Al 203
Widner, Wild Bill 62
Wiesler, Bob 320–321
Wilburn, Chet "Wimpy" 249, 253–257
Wiley, U.S. Sen. Alexander 298
Wilhelm, Hoyt 316
Wilkesbarre (N.Y.L.) 136
Wilkes-Barre Barons (E.L.) 302
Wilkinson, Roy 191
Wilks, Ted 280
Williams, Cy 206, 266
Williams, Dewey 327, 334–335
Williams, Jimmy 61–62
Williams, "Pooh-Bah" 41
Williams, Reese 186, 188
Williams, Ted 261, 328
Williamsen, Peggy 217
Willoughby, Claude 208
Wilmer, Edward 223
Wilmington Quicksteps (U.A.) 32
Wilmot, Al 242
Wilmot, Walt 44, 76, 82, 96, 103
Wilson (pitcher) 49
Wilson, Bob (Red) 331
Wilson, Frank 220
Wilson, George 75
Wilson, Hack 209, 261
Wilson, Jim 303
Wilson, Jimmie 282
Wilson, Kiddo 133, 135
Wilson, Mike 198
Wilson, Parke 105
Winegarner, Ralph 254, 259–260, 292, 326
Wingard, Ernie 221, 223–225, 231, 242–244, 247
Wingard, Ernie, Jr. 245
Winkleman, George 48

Winkler, Henry 187
Winn, George (Lefty) 207
Winnie, Russ 233
Winnipeg Maroons: (No.L.) 174, 177; Peggers 195, 198; (W.C.L.) 190, 193
Winter Garden (Milwaukee) 175
Wisconsin Hotel (Milwaukee) 232, 269
Wisconsin-Illinois League 139, 152, 154–158, 160, 174, 190
Wisconsin News 229–230
Wisconsin Rapids Indians (W.S.L.) 328
Wisconsin State League 97, 100, 102, 133, 136, 157, 176, 204, 232, 268, 272, 277, 299, 311, 321, 327–328
Wisconsin Vibrolithics club 230
WISN Radio (Milwaukee) 254, 264, 273, 282
Wisniewski, Connie "Iron Woman" 285, 287
WMAW Radio (Milwaukee) 320
W9XBY Radio (Milwaukee) 254
Wolf, Bill 320
Womack, Dallas 314
women's baseball 222, 226, 232, 241
Wood, J.H. 15–16, 19, 21–22
Wood, Smoky Joe 23
Woodruff, Orville 161, 163–164
Wood(s), Bob 107, 109, 112, 114

Wooten, Earl 324
"Woozy" (goat mascot) 154, 164, 166
World Pro Basketball Tournament 318
World Series 3, 6, 89, 114, 184, 187, 208–209, 211, 222, 224, 230, 283, 291, 293, 305, 308, 324
World War I 167, 169–173, 175, 180–181, 183–187, 272, 312
World War II 13, 264, 272, 274, 285, 287–293, 312, 319, 323
Worsley, Gabriella 135
Wright, Ed 307
Wright, Frank Lloyd 176
Wright, George 20–23
Wright, Glenn (Buckshot) 243
Wright, Harry 22–23, 71
Wright, Joe 75–76
Wright Street Grounds (Milwaukee) 31, 38, 41–43, 45–46
Wrigley, Philip K. 269–270, 280–282, 299
Wrigley Field: (Chicago) 290; (Los Angeles) 328
Wronski, Sylvia "Roni" 285
WTMJ Radio (Milwaukee) 233, 285; TV 308, 319
Wyatt, Whitlow 259–260
Wyhoff, Dick 228

Yankee Stadium (Bronx) 17, 202, 290
Yingling, Earl 153
Yockey, Edward 233

Yockey, Chauncey 158, 218, 243
Yomiuri Giants (Japan) 301
York, Frank B. 226
York, Rudy 249–250, 253–254, 256–257
Young, Cy 95, 200
Young, Irv "Young Cy" 143–144, 161, 164–168, 172–174, 178
Young, Nick 54, 91
Young, Robert 91
Young, Russ 213, 227, 230, 240, 242
Young Picketts team 38
Younger, F.M. 302
Yount, Adelaide 267
Yount, Robin 154

Zabala, Adrian 323
Zale, Tony 271
Zbyszko, Stanislaus 148, 261
Zeidler (player) 145
Zeidler, Carl (mayor) 264–265, 267, 282, 306
Zeidler, Frank (mayor) 306, 314–315, 321, 327
Zeller, Mrs. George 273
Zeller, Jack 316
Zernial, Gus 315
Ziegler, George F., Jr. 31
Zielinski, Florian "Zollie" 291
Zimmer, Chief 93–94
Zimmerman, Fred (governor) 219
Zimmerman, Heinie 180
Zuber, Bill 257–259, 272, 308
Zuber, Joseph E. 66
Zwilling, Dutch 220, 232, 235, 254

www.ingramcontent.com/pod-product-compliance
Lightning Source LLC
Chambersburg PA
CBHW051205300426
44116CB00006B/444